THE POST-MODERN READER

Charles Vandenhove, Hotel Torrentius Renovation, ground floor, Liège, 1981-82, decoration by Olivier Debré

EDITED BY
CHARLES JENCKS

THE POST-MODERN READER

Stanley Tigerman, *The Sinking of the Titanic*, collage, 1978

ACADEMY EDITIONS · LONDON / ST MARTIN'S PRESS · NEW YORK

Acknowledgements

I would like to thank the many writers and publishers who so willingly gave permission for the reproduction of the essays in this book, and to my publisher and staff at Academy Editions for all their work on this project

Photographic Credits

All photographs are by the editor; other images are courtesy of the following: cover, Frank Gehry, photo Charles Jencks; frontispiece, Charles Vandenhove; title, Stanley Tigerman; p 20 Mario Botta; p 25 above left, Tate Gallery, London, photo John Webb; below left, Martin Charles; below right, Minoru Yamasaki; p 30, above left, Jan Digerud; p 32, photo Yasuhiro Ishimoto; p 171, Dino de Laurentiis Communications, Beverly Hills; p 223, Metro Pictures, New York; p 240, Robert Venturi and Denise Scott Brown; p 241 left, Hans Hollein; right, photo Norman McGrath; p 249, Chorley and Cranford, Wallington, Surrey; p 317, Mary Boone Gallery, New York; p 349, CERN, Geneva

Cover: Frank Gehry with Claes Oldenburg and Coosje van Bruggen, Chiat/Day Building, Venice, California, 1991

CONTENTS

Charles Jencks
PREFACE
POST-MODERNISM – THE THIRD FORCE

Unlikely as it may seem from its name, post-modernism is here to stay. In spite of having recently been declared dead and yesterday's style, in spite of the transience and evasion inherent in the prefix 'post', it will last well into the next century. Perhaps, since the post-modern paradigm highlights time and evolution, I should qualify this.

The post-modern movement will be here as long as the forces to which it responds also continue: modernity and the other modernisms, and pre-modern or traditional culture. These very general *epistemes* have a structural relationship to each other, they bring each other into being and oscillate in fortune like competing species. Modernity, as a condition, grew out of the Renaissance until, in the nineteenth century, it gave birth to cultural modernism. Since then it has been a two-term dialectic between the 'Ancients and Moderns', a struggle which has occasionally been fruitful and in which both sides have enjoyed legitimising their position by exaggerating the faults of their opponent. Like the politics of a two-party system, each side had a vested interest in limiting choice so that wayward free-thinkers were safely channelled into one groove or the other.

No longer is this limitation desirable, or possible. Pluralism, in the First World at least, is now the precondition of politics, especially cultural politics. Indeed there are more positions than the three suggested by my title and argument. But these three do constitute a structural system, the fundamental poles around which others tend to cluster and position themselves. Why? There are historical and epistemological reasons. It is quite natural and logical for people to judge the present in terms of the past, since it is only from the past that they can gauge the relative value of what is happening. By contrast, it is equally valid to judge the present by how far it allows some future, desirable state. Past and future are irreducible axes for judgment and action and have had their defenders and polemicists since the French Revolution. Traditionalism and Futurism are thus not simply 'isms' which come and go like weekly magazines, but permanent categories of thought and existence around which people rally. To these two poles must be added a third – post-modernism – a position which, one might guess, continues aspects of the other two without being a compromise between them. Post-modernists look to the past and future equally and position themselves in the present, seeing time as a broken continuum in need of acknowledgement. They may not always try to heal the rifts in culture, but they do recognise the contradictory pressures at work today and aim to derive an art and politics from them. Hence their typical style – radical eclecticism – hence their characteristic tone – the double voiced discourse which accepts and criticises at the same time. It is this double-coding which makes post-modernism relatively new and not a simple compromise, since both Traditionalism and Futurism are honoured *and* subverted, embraced *and* limited.

There are several anthologies on post-modernism, but none of them is focused on these crucial aspects. Rather, they treat what might be called the 'late-modern condition', that is the condition of consumer society under late capitalism, and the proliferation of simulacra. Pastiche, nostalgia and the secondary reality of signs referring to other signs in an endless play of signifiers is how they see the cultural logic of late capitalism, a kind of hyper-reality which is often characterised as phoney or ersatz. While there is some truth in their analysis of the current signifying condition, it overlooks the eternal nature of sign behaviour.

[A brief summary of the post-modern project, and this anthology, might be: the attempt to go beyond the materialist paradigm which characterises modernism; an intense concern for pluralism and a desire to cut across the different taste cultures that now fracture society; an obligation to bring back selected traditional values, but in a new key that fully recognises the ruptures caused by modernity; an acknowledgment of difference and otherness, the keynote of the feminist movement; indeed the re-emergence of the feminine into all discourse; the re-enchantment of nature, which stems from new developments in science and AN Whitehead's philosophy of organicism; and the commitment to an ecological and ecumenical world view that now characterises post-modern theology.]

All this may sound exhausting, like the platform of an ambitious political party. Indeed one might speak of a rainbow coalition now developing within the post-modern movement. This anthology is unique because, unlike other ones, it does not rehearse the problems of consumer society and a degenerating *condition*, but concentrates on a positive *movement*.

As the table of contents reveals it includes contributions from many areas: culture theory, literature, art, architecture and film as well as economics, politics, sociology, geography, feminism, science and religion. No other collection is quite so wide in scope, nor brings together such a diverse array of specialists. I have tried to make sense of this heterogeneity, and the arguments, in the first essay 'The Post-Modern Agenda' without discussing every contribution. But the readings transcend summary, in any case, because of their calculated differences. They include some of the seminal texts by Daniel Bell and Jean-François Lyotard on the post-industrial society, as well as the most recent reformulations by David Harvey, David Ray Griffin and Hans Küng, among others, on the developing paradigm. As with all growing traditions the commonality is a constellation of overlapping ideas and moods, a similar colouration of material and set of attitudes. Thankfully this heterogeneity will continue and the tradition will go on being contested.

A word of warning: this anthology is big, complex, sometimes argumentative and contradictory like the paradigm itself. Some short essays can be digested at a single sitting, but others have to be returned to again and again as if they were complete books. Indeed, many of them are condensed or abstracted from a bigger argument and for that reason alone need to be read carefully and slowly. Such patient reading will uncover the recurrence of disputed issues – most notably that between Habermas and Lyotard – or more broadly the opposition between totalising and differentiating discourses, the modern and post-modern agendas. Also it will reveal another fracture which is characterised differently – that between 'late' and 'post' modernism, or 'deconstructive' and 'constructive' post-modernism or 'resisting' and 'affirmative' post-modernism. Quite obviously these variations suggest the truth that post-modernism is here to be both embraced and criticised – and not to be suffered as one more totalising discourse. After all, this is the first partial epoch that has the gall to declare its partiality and as such it should be understood and enjoyed.

LIST OF CONTRIBUTORS

TITO ARECCHI Holds the Chair of Physics at the University of Florence, and is author of *Simboli e Realtà*.

JOHN BARTH Alumni Centennial Professor of English and Creative Writing at Johns Hopkins University. He has written several novels, including *Giles Goat-Boy* (1966), *The Sot-Weed Factor* (1967) and *LETTERS* (1979).

JEAN BAUDRILLARD Taught Sociology at the University of Nanterre. His books include *Le Système des objets, La Société de consommation, Oublier Foucault, Simulacres et simulation, Cool Memories* and *America*.

DANIEL BELL Professor of Sociology at Harvard University. Books include *The End of Ideology, The Coming of Post-Industrial Society* (1973) and *Cultural Contradictions of Capitalism* (1976).

CHARLES BIRCH Challis Professor of Biology Emeritus, University of Sydney. He is author of *Nature and God*.

DAVID BOHM Professor Emeritus of Theoretical Physics at Birkbeck College, University of London. He is the author of *Causality and Chance in Modern Physics* and *Wholeness and the Implicate Order*.

JIM COLLINS Assistant Professor, Department of Communications and Theatre, University of Notre Dame, USA. He is the author of *Uncommon Cultures* (1989).

NORMAN K DENZIN Professor of Sociology at the University of Illinois, Urbana-Champaign. His latest books include *On Understanding Emotion* and *The Alcoholic Self*.

UMBERTO ECO Professor of Semiotics at the University of Bologna. World famous specialist in semiotics. Novelist and author of many works on language, literature and art and an authority on James Joyce.

EDWARD GOLDSMITH Publisher and joint editor of *The Ecologist*, which he founded in 1969. Has written, co-authored or co-edited *Can Britain Survive?* (1971), *The Stable Society* (1978), *Green Britain or Industrial Wasteland?* (1986) and *The Great U-turn* (1988).

DAVID RAY GRIFFIN Professor of Philosophy of Religion at the School of Theology at Claremont College, California and founding president of the Centre for a Postmodern World in Santa Barbara, California. He has also edited the SUNY series in Constructive Postmodern Thought.

JÜRGEN HABERMAS Associated with the Max Planck Institute in Starnberg, Germany. He has written *Knowledge and Human Interests, Theory and Practice, Legitimation Crisis* and *Communication and the Evolution of Society*.

DAVID HARVEY Professor of Geography at Oxford University. His books include *Social Justice and the City, The Urban Experience* and *The Condition of Postmodernity*.

IHAB HASSAN Vilas Research Professor of English and Comparative Literature at the Wisconsin University, Milwaukee. He is author of numerous articles and books including *The Dismemberment of Orpheus* and *The Postmodern Turn*.

ANDREAS HUYSSEN Professor of German at Columbia University. Editor of *New German Critique*. Author of books on Romanticism and the *Sturm und Drang*, and author of *After the Great Divide* (1986).

LINDA HUTCHEON Professor of English and Comparative Literature, University of Toronto. Publications include *A Poetics of Postmodernism: History, Theory, Fiction* (1988) and *Narcissistic Narrative: The Metafictional Paradox* (1984).

CHARLES JENCKS Visiting Professor of Architecture at UCLA. He has written several books on post-modernism in architecture including *The Language of Post-Modern Architecture* and *Post-Modern Classicism*.

HEINRICH KLOTZ Until recently Director of the German Architecture Museum, Frankfurt. Author of several books on Modern and Post-modern architecture. Joint editor of *New York Architecture* (1989).

HANS KÜNG Director of the Institute for Ecumenical Research, University of Tubingen. Expert on world religions and their impact on society. Books include *Reforming the Church Today* and *Global Responsibility* (1990).

DAVID LODGE Professor of Modern English Literature, University of Birmingham. In addition to a number of books of criticism he has written many novels including *How Far Can You Go?* (1980) and *Small World* (1984).

JEAN-FRANÇOIS LYOTARD Professor of Philosophy at the University of Paris at Vincennes. He is known for his studies of aesthetics and among his books are *Discours, figure, Economie libidinale* and *The Postmodern Condition: A Report on Knowledge*.

ROBIN MURRAY Fellow of the Institute of Development Studies at Sussex University, and author of a forthcoming book on post-Fordism.

CRAIG OWENS was a critic and Senior Editor at *Art in America*.

PAOLO PORTOGHESI Professor of Architecture at the University of Rome, he was the co-ordinator of the Architectural Section of the 1981 Venice Biennale, and has recently been appointed as President of the Biennale.

MARGARET ROSE Life Member of Clare Hall, Cambridge, and author of *Parody/Meta-Fiction* (1979) and *The Post-Modern and the Post-Industrial. A Critical Analysis* (1991). She is now completing *Parody: Ancient, Modern, and Post-Modern*.

EDWARD W SOJA Professor of Urban and Regional Planning at the Graduate School of Architecture and Urban Planning, UCLA. Author of *Postmodern Geographies* and other writings on the city, urban restructuring and spatial theory.

SUSAN RUBIN SULEIMAN Professor of Romance and Comparative Literatures, Harvard University. Works include *Subversive Intent: Gender, Politics and the Avant-Garde*.

CHAPTER ONE

NEW CULTURE THEORY

James Stirling and Michael Wilford, Neue Staatsgalerie, Stuttgart, 1977-84

Charles Jencks

THE POST-MODERN AGENDA

In the last ten years post-modernism has become more than a social condition and cultural movement, it has become a world view. But its exact nature is strongly contested and this has helped widen the debate to a world audience. The argument has crystallised into two philosophies – what I and many others call Neo- and Post-Modernism – both of which share the notion that the modern world is coming to an end, and that something new must replace it. They differ over whether the previous world view should be taken to an extreme and made radical, or synthesised with other approaches at a higher level.

This fundamental disagreement can be positive, even if it leads to misunderstanding. Like a fertile Rorschach test 'post-modernism' accepts the projection of new meanings and it organises these various interpretations along coherent lines. While some find in this partial plasticity a symbol of The Synthetic Age, others find it a cause for hope, the flexibility needed for a tradition which must still grow if it is to become a mature world view adequate to our complex reality. Indeed all fruitful philosophies of life have the ability to mean more than their initiators intend, and in this sense must become misunderstood – albeit in directed ways. Perhaps, to mix the metaphor, they act as teleological Rorschachs, projections which follow a purposeful growth.

This happened to the concept 'post-modern', which was used for the first time surprisingly as long ago as the 1870s. The initial usage by an English salon painter may have been inconsequential (the desire to go beyond the very Modern French), but it indicates an important and growing feeling: the disquieting idea that many recent 'isms' were quickly becoming 'wasms'. Since then that strange feeling of posteriority has become pervasive, accompanying the rise of countless 'posts', and it underlies the all-encompassing post-modern.

Its root meaning, to be beyond or after the modern, remains common to diverse usages, but, as we will see, some authors use the phrase perversely to mean a cultural movement that *precedes* the modern; and others, such as Umberto Eco, see it as a metahistorical category that cuts across periods of cultural history, just as 'Mannerism' recurs every so often. However diverse the usage, by the 1980s it had become the locus of debate, a place where the values and meanings of contemporary life were contested and affirmed. One of the reasons it became potent was its suggestive ambiguity, the way it specified the departure point, but left open the final destination. There were hints of a direction, but by leaving open the exact goal, the ship of post-modernism could take on a variegated crew and develop its own agenda as it went along. Not a few people are now suspicious of the attendant confusion, or bored with the fashion of the term. Yet I cannot think of an adequate substitute for summarising the possibilities of our condition, and a conference of distinguished thinkers specifically devoted to the subject has also failed to come up with anything better, especially one which enjoys widespread acceptance.

We are stuck with the label and concept *faut de mieux,* for reasons which are his-torical and logical. The modern period, from the 1450s to the 1950s, from the Renais-sance when the West became ascendant to the point where it was incorporated within a larger global culture, is on the wane and something 'post' this period must logically replace it. The feeling of such a shift has recurred so often – in 1875, 1914, 1945, 1960 (each date has its defenders) – that a period 'out of the Modern' needs to be defined.

To be sure, the three forces of the modern movement – modernisation, the condition of modernity, and cultural Modernism – have not ended. Indeed they are often the goals of the Second and Third Worlds. And, in the First World a Late and Neo version of Modernism is intermittently in the ascendant, for short moments. But the uncontested dominance of the modern world view has definitely ended. Like it or not, the West has become a plurality of competing subcultures where no one ideology and *episteme* dominates for long. There is no cultural consensus, even if the actual dissensus and fragmentation into many subcultures has been exaggerated.

Pluralism, One Focus of the Concept
This pluralism is the leading 'ism' of post-modernity, and a condition which most critics agree underlies the period. From Ihab Hassan to Jean-François Lyotard, from David Lodge to David Harvey, from philosophy to literature to architecture, from the EC to Japan, there is, at least, agreement on this point.[1] Post-modernism means the end of a single world view and, by extension, 'a war on totality', a resistance to single explanations, a respect for difference and a celebration of the regional, local and particular. Yet in its suffix 'modern', it still carries the burden of a process which is international and in some senses universal. In this sense it has a permanent tension and is always hybrid, mixed, ambiguous, or what I have called 'doubly-coded'.

[Post-*Modernism* means the continuation of Modernism *and* its transcendence, a double activity that acknowledges our complex relationship to the preceding paradigm and world view.] As John Barth, Linda Hutcheon and Andreas Huyssen point out, this cultural movement is not, like traditional culture, anti-modern.[2] It accepts modernisa-tion, or industrialisation, just as it does so many of the insights of Newton, Marx and Darwin; but it refuses to give progressive technology and these prophets of the modern world view their previously pre-eminent place. Their explanations of the universe, society and nature still have relevance, but a limited one.[Hence Post-Modernism as a cultural movement, or agenda, does not seek to turn the clock back, is not a Luddite reaction, but rather a restructuring of modernist assumptions with something larger, fuller, more true. Just as the post-industrial society did not mean the end of industriali-sation, or the Post-Fordist sector of the economy did not mean that large Fordist corporations had collapsed, so most of the other 'posts' are sublations, not destroyers, of their predecessors.]

Briefly put, the theories of the modern paradigm have not been overturned so much as transformed into parts of a larger framework *where they still keep their identity.* Newtonian sciences of simplicity are now seen to be special cases of the more elaborate sciences of complexity; Marxist materialism is seen as most relevant to an early phase of industrial development; and Darwinian competition, natural selection, is understood to operate within the larger spectrum of a symbiotic view of nature, one that is much more cooperative and holistic than believed in the nineteenth century.

But the post-modern trends and shifts – the end of communism in the East, or the rise of the ecological world view in the West, or the steady growth of post-Newtonian sciences – do not mean the triumph of a single alternative: socialised-capitalism, the

Gaian hypothesis, quantum physics, fuzzy logic or chaos theory. It does not mean the triumph of *any* total explanation; which is why it is so frustrating to comprehend. Used to thinking about these large issues in binary terms, we find it aggravatingly difficult to conceptualise them in fuzzy logical terms (of 'more or less'). But new conceptual models for thinking about this *relative* relativism have been formed: the continuum, net, rhizome and pattern recognition (and I have supplied a diagram at the end of this article so the pattern can be grasped).

So much of the debate on post-modernism is misrepresented by oppositional terms, with many of the protagonists, such as Ihab Hassan and David Harvey, juxtaposing lists of what is supposedly modern against the post-modern ('purpose versus play, centring versus dispersal, signified versus signifier' etc).[3] Inevitably we will construct these two-term tables, and produce lists of identifiable attributes, because each movement and condition is different. But the shift from one to the next is not a reversal, not an opposition; rather it is a hybridisation, a complexification of modern elements with other ones, that is a double-coding.

Why is this so important? Principally because an essential goal of the post-modern movement – the *movement* as opposed to the social *condition* – is to further pluralism, to overcome the elitism inherent in the previous paradigm. Modernists, it is true, claimed to be democratic and creatively open, and so they were in the nineteenth and early twentieth century, especially in opposition to a traditionalism and the *ancien regime*. But then they became part of the establishment and intolerant in their own way. Cultural Modernism became an orthodoxy within late-capitalist society (after 1945? as some claim), its doctrines started to dominate western academies and such institutions as the Museum of Modern Art, and it took on the elitist forms and values of its predecessor. This is most clearly expressed in the central business districts of western cities. By the 1960s, they started to be frozen into the icy anonymity of modernism, a good indication that the ideology and organisation of those working within was also likely to be 'modern'. Of course a civilisation cannot be read directly from its cultural expression, but in this case we know there was a good fit between the forms of bureaucratic power, the ideology of rationalisation, and the architectural style.

Jester

When, in the late sixties, the irrepressible Yippie Abbie Hoffmann was on trial within a Mies van der Rohe building in Chicago, and started jumping around the courtroom like the counter-culture jester he was, Judge Hoffmann said, interpreting the repressive architecture, 'Get back in your place – where Mies van der Rohe designed you to stand.' Playing on the ambiguity of their similar last names, Abbie kept calling the judge 'Daddy', and this humorous polyvalence gave him a degree of licentious manoeuvre and dialogical freedom; but the univalence of Mies's architecture allowed him no freedom of movement, or interpretation, at all. There was one and only one right place to be, a perfect instrumentalisation of life that theorists of the modern world (from Jeremy Bentham to Max Weber) would well understand – control. The black, quasi-Fascist buildings of Mies's late period are a perfect embodiment of the three great 'isms' of modernity – reductivism, determinism and mechanism. Here in this dream of universal progress there is no room for dissent, subculture and history. Modern totalisation is complete.

Thus the agenda of post-modern architects – and by extension post-modern writers, urbanists and artists – is to challenge monolithic elitism, to bridge the gaps that divide high and low cultures, elite and mass, specialist and non-professional, or most generally put – one discourse and interpretive community from another. There is no overcoming these gaps it is true: to believe so would be to return to the idea of an integrated culture, whether traditional or modern, that is another form of universalising control. Rather, the different ways of life can be confronted, enjoyed, juxtaposed, represented and dramatised, so that different cultures acknowledge each other's legitimacy. The motives are equally political and aesthetic. Double-coding, to put it abstractly, is a strategy of affirming and denying the existing power structures at the same time, inscribing and challenging differing tastes and opposite forms of discourse. This double-voiced discourse has its own peculiar laws and beauties and it constitutes the fundamental agenda of the post-modern movement.

However, the post-modern *condition,* to which it relates, has as many negative as positive tendencies, and they come as a package. The increase in communication (and the information glut and advertisement), the growth of knowledge (and the consumer society), the rise of leisure (and of Disneyland simulacra), the flowering of Post-Fordism (and the insecurity of workers), the emergence of a new world order (and the *Pax Americana),* the EC, GATT and global economy (and the Third World debt and IMF riots) – for every positive post-modern trend there is a corresponding negative consequence. In this sense we have not outgrown the world of 1800 with its tragic choices and ambivalent trade-offs. No wonder many people have seen in Goethe's *Faust* the archetypal modern figure, the progressive developer who must sacrifice people and places in order to improve them. The parallel with today is perplexing.[4]

This is why I believe the Marxist critics, such as Fredric Jameson and David Harvey, are a little hasty in calling our condition post-modern when, if the periodisation is going to be made in their terms, it might be more consistently termed *Late*-Modern (to correspond with their characterisation of the economic base as Late-Capitalist). Further confusion arises from equating the post-modern condition with the various post-modern movements, as if there were a total world system and culture (where *is* the pluralism?). Yet there are links between civilisation and culture and because it has now become customary to call the former post-modernity, (or the post-modern condition) I will follow this usage.

However, the reader should be wary; this may lead to confusions between a general condition and the cultural movement, and the implication that there are facile determinisms between culture and civilisation. It will, however, highlight a truth that some positive and negative connections *do* exist and that, as Andreas Huyssen has said, we are well past that point when post-modernism can be accepted or rejected as a totality 'What will no longer do is either to eulogise or to ridicule postmodernism *en bloc*. The postmodern must be salvaged from its champions and from its detractors.'[5]

While furthering pluralism is a fundamental goal of the movement, it does not exhaust the agenda of this growing world view. The new *weltanschauung* or *episteme* (something more than an ideology and paradigm) is overcoming the modern world picture. The Hegelian notion of sublation captures part of the double process involved, of destroying *and* preserving that which has gone before, in a new synthesis on a higher level. Thus for instance reductivism, the key methodology of modern science, is not rejected by post-modern scientists such as James Lovelock and Ilya Prigogine, but subsumed within a larger duality: reductivism/holism, or what Arthur Koestler has shown to be the ubiquitous holonic order. The Janus-faced activity of matter and life reveals that there are no true wholes or parts anywhere in nature, but just contrary-acting 'holons' which act as wholes over their subassemblies, and as parts of larger organisations. We must also be aware, a point stressed by many writers, that a complete

ABOVE: Mies van der Rohe, Federal Center, Chicago, 1964-65. The architecture of control. *BELOW:* Robert Venturi & Denise Scott Brown, Sainsbury Wing, National Gallery, London, 1985-91. Double-coding: classicism confronts Mies, vernacular confronts Pop.

sublation, or Hegelian dialectic which resolves contraries, is not always the result or goal of post-modernism: parts, sub-assemblies, sub-cultures often keep their unassimilated identity within the new whole. Hence the conflicted nature of the pluralism, the radical eclecticism of the post-modern style.

World View

Although they are too large and important to deal with here, one cannot discuss the post-modern agenda without at least mentioning some of its key movements. Together, under a very large and ecumenical umbrella, are many (though not all) of the current liberationist movements: feminism and post-feminism are essential to it, as Craig Owens has shown.[6] The green and ecological movements have contributed important values and ideas, especially the notions of inter-connectedness and holism, and they particularly connect up with liberation theology, ecumenicism and other post-modern religious trends, as Harvey Cox, Hans Küng and David Ray Griffin have been arguing – all from different perspectives.[7] Indeed such new spiritual approaches as the 'creation theology' of Matthew Fox is a good example of such cross-connections. Crossing disciplines itself is a motive force of the wide movement, an idea and practice which was formulated first by critics such as Leslie Fiedler and novelists such as Thomas Pynchon and John Barth. Virtually all post-modern writers mix genres, hence the hybrid subject matter and heterogeneous audience, once again bringing us back to the core idea of contested, or heteroglottic, pluralism.

Like the political platform of a complex party, post-modernism gathers together a rainbow coalition of changing interests and these include scientists, inventors and those with no political axe to grind. James Lovelock, the inventor and chemist who formulated the Gaia hypothesis, shares a view of nature as a self-organising system with the Nobel laureate Ilya Prigogine. And his important *Order Out of Chaos* (1979) relates to both catastrophe theory (René Thom) and the many chaos sciences which have defined a Post-Newtonian paradigm.[8] These sciences of complexity entail non-linear equations, and can deal with the high degree of feedback which characterises all life. Hence the slide from modern to post-modern science can be seen as a shift in study: from fairly inanimate matter (planets and physical objects) to living systems (social groups as well as individuals).

Democracy is the most complex and developed of political forms, the one that demands the greatest information flow to sustain itself and the one that shows most self-organisation. There has been a progressive democratisation of countries and empires since the mid-1970s: Portugal, Spain, the Philippines, Taiwan, South Korea, even Chile and South Africa to a certain extent, and then the Communist world – except for the Chinese. One might say, without exaggerating, that the most significant post-modern movement of all is electronic democracy, information-age pluralism, and the emergent self-organisational movements of the last fifteen years, whether these are national, ethnic, regional or transnational. Increasing information flow drives emergent democracies such as Poland and Czechoslovakia just as higher energy flows drove modern nations in the nineteenth century. Many of these fledgling democracies will slide back and many, like Romania, will remain in an authoritarian/democratic state of limbo; but the world trend is undeniable.

Thus we are looking at a pervasive shift both in world view and civilisation, a shift that is not complete, as they never are. Pre-modern (traditional) and modern systems will continue to exist and mutually define themselves with respect to post-modernism, and I would see all three as continuing indefinitely into the future. The reasons are structural and semiotic: the first *episteme* is focused on the past, the second on the future and the third is positioned across the divide like the hybrid and centrist animal that it is. But this changeable creature is here to stay because it fulfils a unique cross-fertilising role. The four aspects of its world view I have mentioned – pluralism, feminism, sciences of complexity, and the recent self-organising democratic movements – are all deep and sustaining shifts in culture.

Polemical distinctions

Having stressed the breadth of the term, I should make some distinctions. The phrase post-modern has been spelled in ways that differ slightly, like the changing aliases of a criminal desperately wanting to be caught. Sometimes, in historiography and when referring to an epoch, it is styled post-Modern (especially when referring to a period starting in 1875, or 1914, or 1960, my favourite date); often in literary criticism it is streamlined as postmodern (which may indicate a deconstructive, or what I would call neo-modern intent); in architecture and as a cultural event it is usually Post-Modern (to indicate a doubly-coded movement).

But I have to admit there are important writers, such as Jean-François Lyotard, who would disagree. His *La Condition postmoderne,* 1979, positions the word more aggressively as an ultra avant-gardism. The 'post' in the phrase thus signifies for him, and his followers, the overcoming of modernist stereotypes, the continual revolution of the new, the presentation of the unpresentable – in short the sublime and the uncommunicable. He thus asserts, with a little logic and perversity, that – 'A work can become modern only if it is first postmodern. Postmodernism thus understood is not modernism at its end but in the nascent state, and this state is constant'.[9] In effect Lyotard's paradox amounts to a play on words, the fact that Picasso and Braque were 'Post-Cézanne' just before they became 'modern', and that all subsequent modernists overthrew those immediately before them. This is of course true, as true as the opposite generalisation that they continued some aspects of their predecessors: but neither point bears on the more important issue of a post-modern period and *weltanschauung.* Furthermore, Lyotard's usage denies the fundamental fact of post-modern movements: they seek plural codings, and over-codings, precisely the multiple communication his aesthetic of the sublime rejects.

In fact Lyotard's argument in *The Postmodern Condition* (translated 1984) stems from visits he made to the United States in the late 1970s and his readings of Ihab Hassan. At that time Hassan, stressing its decreation and deconstructive aspects, saw the movement as what I would call a Late- or Neo-Modernism, the exaggerated and incessantly revolutionary form of Modernism. This reductive tradition obviously has its *raison d'être,* since there are moments when abstraction and a simplified, even alienating, form-language might be used. Peter Eisenman has made a case for it in a 'museum for the twenty-first century' in Columbus, Ohio, and this deconstructive tendency will continue as long as technology changes quickly, and a randomising fashion rules consumer society: ie from now on. But Post-Modernism is something different, based on further connotations of the prefix 'post' which stress that it comes 'after' not before Modernism and that it has a fundamentally hybridising intent: to reweave the recent modern past *and* local culture. The way this tradition has grown fitfully out of Modernism shows some amusing similarities with previous movements.

The Creative Paranoia of Labels and the Seven Stages

It has been argued by EH Gombrich and other historians that artistic terms often grow from fear and loathing, from the abusive epithets critics invent in order to stop the newest form of heresy. Thus 'Baroque' and 'Rococo' were, before they became descriptive categories, derogatory labels meant to stop the 'illogical' and excessively decorated forms to which they originally referred ('Baroque' meant a 'misshapen pearl', 'Rococo' meant 'shell like'). 'Impressionism' was thought deficient because it gave only hazy, subjective impressions; 'Gothic' meant 'not yet classic' and was created by the barbarian Goths who sacked Rome, and 'Mannerism' meant overly mannered. Ironically, these negative epithets did not always work as intended. Indeed, reworking the old adage, 'some paranoiacs have real enemies', we might say 'through attacks, some paranoid critics create the very enemy movements they fear'.

A quick summary of the term post-modern and its seven main 'stages' reveals both this creative paranoia and the growing conceptual maturity. I put 'stages' in quotes because they not only overlap, but they sometimes refer to different conceptual levels, or distinguishable aspects, of the condition and movement. The complexity of the situation can best be grasped in schematic form, and the following schema I have worked out with Margaret Rose, whose critical review of the concept appeared in 1991.

1 Prehistory, 1870s to 1950s. The term post-Modern was used by John Watkins Chapman, Rudolf Pannwitz, Federico de Onis and Joseph Hudnut in divergent ways to indicate an over-coming of the Modern. Arnold Toynbee conceived it as the latest phase of a proletariat world civilisation – since 1875.

2 Postmodern seen as Modern in decline, 1950s to 1970s. The notion of regression or failure of nerve or perversion of Modernism was assumed by C Wright Mills, Irving Howe, Harold Levine and Nikolaus Pevsner. But Leslie Fiedler and Ihab Hassan, in opposite ways, began to invert this usage.

3 Post-Modern as the counter-culture of the 1960s. A retrospective usage by Andreas Huyssen (1984) and others.

4 Post-Modern as pluralist politics and eclectic style, 1970s and early 1980s. Charles Jencks, John Barth, Umberto Eco and Craig Owens define post-modernism as multiple coding and a respect for minorities, difference, otherness etc. My own writings on *The Post-Modern Movement in Architecture, 1975-80* are the first to identify a movement and a radical eclecticism, but this quickly evolves into –

5 Post-Modern Classicism, a public language, 1979 to the present. The doubly-coded movement in art and architecture which is first evident at the Venice Biennale, 1980, is described as a concern for historical memory by Paolo Portoghesi and others.

6 Critical Reactions to the condition of Postmodernity, 1980 to the present. Jürgen Habermas, Jean Baudrillard, Fredric Jameson, Terry Eagleton, Hal Foster and Marxists criticise, lament and occasionally celebrate the conditions of the consumer culture and the information age, seen as inventive, manipulative, horrific and sometimes neo-conservative.

7 Critical summaries of the Post-Modern paradigm, 1988 to the present. Brian McHale, David Harvey, Ed Soja, Wolfgang Welsch, Jim Collins, Steven Connor, Linda Hutcheon and Margaret Rose give wide, critical overviews of the concept and *episteme* – concentrating on literature, philosophy and architecture where it is most developed. David Ray Griffin distinguishes a constructive from deconstructive post-modernism in theology and elsewhere.

Before looking at the positive usages of the term one might pause to underline the heterogeneity of these seven stages, or meanings, since so often the phrase is used without self-consciousness, as if everyone were referring to the same thing. As for the negative and ambivalent usages, Arnold Toynbee's *A Study of History*, published in abridged form in 1947 and later, typifies the mixture. The modern western and Christian era was giving way to the rise of internationalism, the rule of the proletariat and what he hoped might be a fusion of different religions, a post-Christianity. This positive pluralism remained a defining aspect of all subsequent post-modernisms, but the syncretic faith has, in spite of later attempts at ecumenicism, failed to gel. Toynbee's sense of the 'post-Modern' also represents a near apocalyptic usage signifying 'breakdown and disintegration' for us 'the first children of a post-Christian world'. It took thirty-seven years for this argument to be inverted by Harvey Cox who, in 1984, pointed to the emergence of a 'postmodern theology' – a liberation movement based on the activities of local Christian communities in places like Latin America.[10] But this anticipates a later shift in meaning.

In general, by the early 1960s, 'postmodern' had only been used with any consistency concerning fiction and it was considered as a regression from High Modernism, a compromise with mass culture and midcult. Irving Howe and Harold Levine formulated this negative assessment and, since mass culture was increasing in strength, it led to a certain paranoia; intellectuals and the avant-garde saw their positions under threat. The top-down view of cultural politics, the elitism which modernists took over from traditionalists, was hardly ever stated, but it was the usual premise behind debate. Of course not all intellectuals, modernists and avant-gardists held this elitist position. But enough of them did to create a loose consensus that the citadel of high culture must be defended from the onslaughts of mass culture. The metaphor of the gap between the 'two cultures' (the literary and scientific) was extended in all directions – highbrow, lowbrow, midcult, mass cult – until the cultural site resembled a battlefield criss-crossed with trenches. Thus the scene was set for a new strategy, and it created the first positive phase of post-modernism.[11]

1960s Postmodernism: Pop Art, Counter Culture and Adhocism

Pop Art was started, significantly, by a small group of English intellectuals and artists who consumed American mass culture both unselfconsciously and as an acquired taste. They met as an avant-garde elite, the Independent Group, in the 1950s and lectured on the way the new media – TV, films, advertisements and mass-produced machinery – shaped consciousness. Marshall McLuhan came to some of these meetings, at which anthropology and semiology were discussed, and these disciplines showed the way all culture is a tissue of signs or a form of information exchange. Members of the Group collected mass media ephemera, displayed them in juxtaposition on tackboards and explained the rationale behind these compositions, in this way quite naturally developing an art form of collage. Lawrence Alloway, founder and protector of the concept of Pop Art, describes how it developed from meetings between young working class and urban professionals who made up this London advance guard:

The Independent Group missed a year and then was reconvened in winter 1954-5 by John McHale and myself on the theme of popular culture. This topic was arrived at as a result of a snowballing conversation in London which involved (the artist) Paolozzi, (the architects) the Smithsons, (the photographer) Henderson, (the critic) Reyner Banham, (the painter) Hamilton, (the theorist) McHale and myself. We discovered that we had in common a vernacular culture that persisted beyond any special interest skills in art, architecture, design or art criticism that any of us might possess. The area of contact was mass-produced urban culture: movies, advertisement, science fiction, Pop music. We felt none of the dislike of commercial culture standard among most intellectuals, but accepted it as a fact, discussed it in detail, and consumed it enthusiastically . . .[12]

Richard Hamilton and others produced several Pop collages illustrating this new enthusiasm and they were always, significantly, tied with modernist modes such as abstraction and complex irony. One should emphasise that they were neither populist nor clichéd, as their detractors made out, however much they might use mass cult imagery. Nor admittedly were they very profound syntheses of high and low art, the present and the past. Rather they were *ad hoc* amalgamations of a wide spectrum of tastes – a mixture which the contemporary modernists found distasteful.

Five years later Pop Art grew independently in America where it was more brash and immediate, but equally mixed in method and intention. Robert Rauschenberg was the most original of these adhocists, aggregating a violent heterogeneity of material into his 'combines'; for instance, an angora goat and a car tyre alongside Abstract Expressionist patches and mass media signs formed the word *Monogram*. This mixture immediately led to a new mixed audience. The young and old, scruffy and establishment, who came to see his work in 1959 more or less mirrored the disparities inherent in these combines. Like *Monogram* the variegated audience may not have added up to anything as a whole – certainly not an integrated taste culture – yet this fragmented pluralism has remained both a fundamental fact and aesthetic of post-modernism ever since. By 1965 it had already matured into a shared style and was applied with great skill by hundreds of Pop Artists – the number reflecting the democratisation of the new art scene.

James Rosenquist's *F111* is characteristic of this phase. Its scale is that of the billboards he had once worked on – ten feet high and eighty-six feet long. Its bright, acid, enticing images were taken directly from the mass media but then montaged. Its meaning? Ambiguous, but with the F111 fighter – by then an *obsolete* aeroplane in the Vietnam War – it was an obvious protest against the use to which taxes were put, as was the A-bomb exploding in the painting under an umbrella (tax shelter). On one level the point of the work was the impossibility of its whole meaning, underlined by the impossibility of viewing it as a single entity. Even reading it from left to right, as implied, is difficult because the subject, slick image, scale and colour keep oscillating like a TV set which has gone into terminal multiple exposure. Inevitably its provocative ambiguity and media style agitated critics. Hilton Kramer attacked it as 'slick, cheerful, overblown, irredeemably superficial . . . [it] leaves the spectator feeling as if he ought to be sucking a popsicle'.[13] Here is the paranoid response which the artist must have expected when he aimed his dayglo canvas at the well exposed modernist nerve ends.

The fact that Rosenquist will not make a single political point out of this Vietnam protest, for that is its implicit meaning, accurately reflects his culture's mixed feeling about the war. The painting is more a heroic celebration of this ambiguous feeling than a resolution or reasoned synthesis of arguments, as it might have been if painted by Nicolas Poussin or Jacques Louis David.[14] It is not as beautiful and organically related as these historical genre paintings, because it tries to make a virtue of schizophrenia, but it is more plausible for its time than an integrated Neo-Classical version would have been.

The dramatisation of social and urban reality underlay postmodernism in its first phase in the 1960s. It could be found in such disparate undercurrents as the work of the Advocacy Planners, the defence of local interest groups, the writings of Robert Venturi on Main Street and Route 66, the anti-war movement, the overstated speculations of McLuhan on the new media, the counter culture and Susan Sontag's *Notes on Camp*; and even to an extent the youth movement and student uprisings in 1962 at Berkeley and May 1968 in Paris. A characteristic *ad hoc* architecture to emerge from this period was Lucien Kroll's buildings for the students in Belgium – full of ornament, humour, metaphor and looking in their vital jumble altogether like a constructed version of May 1968. All these different movements and demonstrations were anti-establishment in

Mario Botta, Office Building, Lugano, Switzerland, 1981-85, Violent juxtapositions
within a classical grammar of structural elements.

their celebration of specific political and social realities. They were undoubtedly one-sided and in some ways as infantile as their critics claimed; but as particular strategies they were more responsive to social realities than the reigning modernist culture. Even early defenders of modernism, such as Lewis Mumford, were as quick as the younger postmodernists to point out 'The case against "Modern Architecture"' and by 1960 he had already launched an attack on Mies van der Rohe and 'the apotheosis of the compulsive, bureaucratic spirit'.[15]

If America was the leader of the Free World in the 1960s and if its orthodoxy was a form of modernism tied to liberal capitalism, then the time was ripe for writers and artists to declare a counter-culture. This explains Leslie Fiedler's incantation of the prefix to support all the mini-movements against the centre. The counter-cultures, he proclaimed in 1965, were 'post-humanist, post-male, post-white, post-heroic . . . post-Jewish'.[16] He did not, however, have a fully articulated concept of postmodernism nor a view of the movement as a whole. This had to await the 1970s when, ironically, most of its tendencies had withered or changed course; notably dead or collapsing were the anti-war and student movements, Pop Art and the McLuhanite celebration of TV.

1970s Post-Modernism: Plural Politics, Eclectic Style
It was not until 1971 and Ihab Hassan's essay 'POSTmodernISM: a Paracritical Bibliography' that the movement was *actually* christened and a pedigree provided although even then the term, like its inconsistent capitalisation, was not clearly defined. Nevertheless, from this and Hassan's later writings a clear enough picture emerged of a *literary* movement which focused mainly on the *Late*-modernism of William Burroughs, Jean Genet and Samuel Beckett, the music of John Cage and the 1960s futurism of McLuhan and Buckminster Fuller. 'Post-Modernism,' he wrote, 'is essentially subversive in form and anarchic in its cultural spirit. It dramatises its lack of faith in art even as it produces new works of art intended to hasten both cultural and artistic dissolution.'[17]. The emphasis was thus on ultra-avantgardism, and some literary critics, and not a few artists, accepted it uncritically as the historial truth. In his 1978 definitions Hassan lists the kind of modes POSTmodernISM involves: Paraphysics/Dadaism, Antiform (disjunctive, open), Play, Chance, Anarchy, Exhaustion/Silence, Process/Performance, Happening, Participation, Decreation/Deconstruction . . . Antinarrative, the Holy Ghost, Desire, Polymorphous/Androgynous, Schizophrenia, etc.[18] Strangely, except for the notion of participation, this list represents the antithesis of what was going on in post-modern architecture at the time. Even as an analysis of literature these definitions were one-sided and were inverted in the 1980s by writers such as John Barth and Umberto Eco.

In a most cogent essay on the subject, 'The Literature of Replenishment, Postmodernist Fiction', 1980, Barth writes: 'In my view, if it has no other and larger possibilities than those noted by, for example, Professors Alter, Graff and Hassan, then postmodernist writing is indeed a kind of pallid, last-ditch decadence, of no more than minor symptomatic interest.'[19] Barth outlines a very different programme for postmodernism – similar to the architectural one – that accepts the Modern Movement as a necessary stage of the first half of our century, but as something which now has to become more democratic, and retain its appeal on rereading.

> A worthy programme for postmodernist fiction, I believe, is the synthesis or transcension of these antitheses, which may be summed up as premodernist and modernist modes of writing. My ideal postmodernist author neither merely repudiates nor merely imitates either his twentieth-century modernist parents or his nineteenth-century pre-modernist grandparents. He has the first half of our

century under his belt, but not on his back . . . he nevertheless aspires to a fiction more democratic in its appeal than such late-Modernist marvels (by my definition and in my judgment) as Beckett's *Stories and Texts for Nothing* or Nabokov's *Pale Fire.*[20]

As examples of successful syntheses Barth recommends Italo Calvino's *Cosmicomics* (1965) and, even more, Gabriel García Marquez's *One Hundred Years of Solitude* (1967) '. . . as impressive a novel as has been written so far in the second half of our century and one of the splendid specimens of that splendid genre from any century'. It is interesting to contrast Barth's list of postmodernists with Hassan's – writers such as Englishman John Fowles, the expatriate Argentine Julio Cortazar – and see that he distinguishes them from 'late-Modernists' such as John Hawkes, 'comparative pre-Modernists' such as Saul Bellow and Norman Mailer, and 'consistently traditionalist' writers such as John Cheever and John Updike. Here we find the important conceptual distinctions between major traditions with each one correctly understood – 'traditional', 'post-', 'late-', and 'pre-modern'. These terms mutually illuminate and define each other, and are distinctions which I had proposed quite independently for architecture. Their importance cannot be overstated because they allow the autonomy and legitimacy of different approaches. This pluralism, necessarily founded on conceptual clarity, is the defining aspect of postmodernism in the 1970s. Before we examine it in the other arts, we should note two aspects that Umberto Eco adds to Barth's discussion of postmodernist literature: the new use of history and irony.

Eco, in his *Postscript to the Name of the Rose* (1983) gives a witty characterisation of the way the avant-garde proceeds forward by a series of self-cancelling steps until it reaches the all white canvas, the glass and steel curtain wall, the literature of silence and, in music 'the passage from atonality to noise to absolute silence (in this sense the early Cage is modern)'. Eco continues with this fine parody:

> But the moment comes when the avant-garde (the modern) can go no further, because it has produced a metalanguage that speaks of its impossible texts (conceptual art). The postmodern reply to the modern consists of recognising the past, since it cannot really be destroyed, because its destruction leads to silence, must be revisited: but with irony, not innocently.[21]

And here, if I may emphasise the point because it is the most amusing illustration of why postmodernists must use irony when dealing with the past, Eco comes to a classic formulation:

> I think of the postmodern attitude as that of a man who loves a very cultivated woman and knows he cannot say to her ' I love you madly', because he knows that she knows (and that she knows that he knows) that these words have already been written by Barbara Cartland. Still, there is a solution. He can say 'As Barbara Cartland would put it, I love you madly'. At this point, having avoided false innocence, having said clearly that it is no longer possible to speak innocently, he will nevertheless have said what he wanted to say to the woman: that he loves her in an age of lost innocence. If the woman goes along with this, she will have received a declaration of love all the same. Neither of the two speakers will feel innocent, both will have accepted the challenge of the past, of the already said, which cannot be eliminated; both will consciously and with pleasure play the game of irony. . . . But both will have succeeded, once again, in speaking of love.[22]

Such knowing can get rather tiring, but self-consciousness is a natural consequence of living in a post-Freudian age – one that has created several well-paid professions from linguistic and sexual analysis. There is no going back in time, as Barth would say, no way of eradicating Nietzsche, Einstein, Lévi-Strauss and our view of the expanding universe. But thankfully we *can* move beyond these discoveries and are not limited to any particular world view which may derive from them.

This open pluralism, both political and cultural, was one of the great accomplishments of the 1970s, at least in America where it replaced the modernist notion of an elite avant-garde set against mass culture. The women's movement typifies certain key changes in this respect. Starting in the early 1960s with the writings of Betty Friedan and soon turning into an active political forum, by the early 1970s it had become a large middle-class movement which could point to several legislative victories among its successes – including abortion and employment rights – and a generally changed attitude in society. Feminism, with its unremitting critique of hidden assumptions, aimed its attack on elitism *per se*. Thus one of its main antagonists was modernism and the previously hidden male dominance of its programme.

The women's movement arrived relatively late on the art scene in the early 1970s, when it challenged the major New York museums to put on mixed shows, set up several galleries devoted solely to female artists (AIR in 1972, Sotto 20 and Women's Interart Gallery in 1975) and staged polemical exhibitions and demonstrations to propagate their aims.[23] Much of the art produced had an implicit didactic basis like eighteenth-century historical painting, and an explicit sexual bias.

A polemical and amusing example was Dotty Attie's erotic narrative such as *A Dream of Love*, 1973, which consists of 144 small drawings arranged in a grid, an idea which derives from the Pop Artists' use of the tackboard. In this work Attie appropriates images from Gainsborough and Ingres, from cigarette ads and pornography, to build up a checkerboard of sexual fantasy that reads partly like a novel, partly like a classical painting. Each one of the images tends to become the word of a sentence, repeated with variations of scale and meaning. A headless nude, a stabbed man, a boot crushing a face, signs of sexual fetishisms and repulsion follow each other from left to right, up and down or anyway we want to read them. Their totality does not, once again, add up to a single message beyond the representation of erotic fantasy and repression. What makes this work typical of feminist and post-modern art in the 1970s is its pluralism of technique and reference.

Such mixing of categories and genres became common. In this era of eclecticism the past was consulted (and plundered), lovingly revived (and ridiculed). Often it was hard to tell whether the artist or architect was making a serious attempt at critically contrasting traditions, or was simply confused. Modernism and popular culture were combined in the synthetic music of Terry Riley and Philip Glass, the buildings of Charles Moore and Hans Hollein and in the New German Cinema, especially in the films of Rainer Werner Fassbinder. Jeremy Dixon's low cost housing in London is characteristic of the architecture that is eclectic because it must appeal to plural taste-cultures. At St Mark's Road, for instance, he mixed an Edwardian typology with vernacular and modernist elements. It even includes anthropomorphism – each house suggests a face – and classical symmetries.

The common element in such eclecticism was its assault on the notion of a stable category such as high art, good taste, classicism or modernism. As Craig Owens has argued: 'otherness' and eclecticism were two strategies used against elitism by both the women's movement and post-modern culture generally.[24] Thus Pop Art theory of the 1950s which had shown culture to be a continuum had, by the 1970s, created an eclecticism which represented this continuum. They both related to many other post-modern movements – such as Neo-Realism – which also acknowledged a plural counter-culture.

The Post-Modern Movement in Architecture

While Post-Modernism remained a diffuse series of trends within the arts it quite quickly crystalised into an architectural movement during the mid-1970s. One reason for this, suggested by Andreas Huyssen, is that architecture more than any other form succumbed to the alienating effects of modernisation.[25] The modern movement in architecture promoted industrialisation and correspondingly demoted local communities and the existing urban fabric, as it did virtually everything that stood in the way of the bulldozer. There was a tragic, indeed fatal, connection between modern architecture and modernisation which was more or less directly opposed by the modern movement in the other arts. TS Eliot's *The Waste Land* portrays the characteristic attitude to these other modernisms. But this split on the question of industrialisation is understandable. Architects, to protect their livelihood, must adopt an upbeat attitude towards development, towards the new technology and increased efficiency. There is no such thing as a Dadaist or Existentialist architecture because the profession, or an individual within it, could not bear the contradiction of building a better world for a nihilistic world view. Imagine Marcel Duchamp or Jean-Paul Sartre as the heroic subject of Ann Rand's *The Fountainhead*, and you can appreciate the profound difference in perspective between modern architecture and all other forms of modernism.

The tragic association of modern architecture with modernisation became very obvious in the late 1950s. The first critique of this situation from within the movement came from the Team Ten architects such as Aldo Van Eyck, which quickly resulted in a type of revisionism. This philosophy and practice substituted the notion of place for abstract space, promoting a high-density low-rise building and an abstract form of regionalism, championed today by Kenneth Frampton under the banner of 'critical regionalism'. Mario Botta and the Ticino architects in Switzerland characterise this departure at its best with abstract classical constructions, although whether they are 'regional' can be doubted. But the critique was not very radical (it was after all an in-house revolution) and stopped far short of Jane Jacob's withering attack of 1961, *The Death and Life of Great American Cities*. The rise of post-modern architecture and urbanism really dates from this attack which, along with the succession of urban and social critiques it spawned, resulted in the widespread demolition of modernist housing estates.

Again the other modernisms did not suffer such violent and clear refutations, did not have their Pruitt-Igoes to watch on TV, lifting off the ground in a slow-motion of dust, dynamite and fractured abstraction. This explosion of 1972, copied countless times throughout the world as a radical way of dealing with such housing estates, soon came to symbolise the mythical death of modern architecture. That was how I used it when starting to lecture on the subject in 1974. The notion of a sudden demise, coupled with slides of the explosion, had an enormously liberating impact. For the next two years, in lectures around the world, I used this rhetorical formula – Death of Modernism/Rise of Post-Modernism – aware that it was a symbolic fabrication (I invented a false date) and yet was pleasantly surprised to find that nearly everyone (especially the press) accepted it as truth. If I pointed out that many modern architects were still at work and that my arguments were symbolic, or ironic, caricatures, these disclaimers were ignored. The public response was extremely strong in every country I visited, especially communist ones where modern architecture, being state supported, was the only option. This public reaction should be stressed especially now that so many people discuss the issue as if it were a matter of style, or revisiting the past. The Post-Modern Movement was then, and remains today, a wider social protest against modernisation, against the

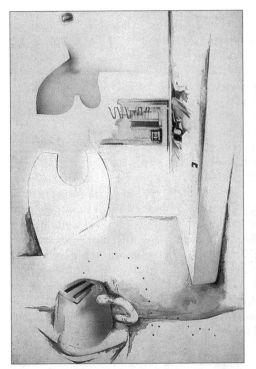

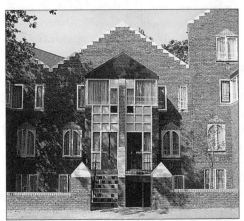

ABOVE LEFT: Richard Hamilton, *$he*, 1958-61, oil, cellulose, collage on panel, 122 x 81 cm. Pop Artists combined abstraction and heteroglot imagery. *ABOVE RIGHT*: Lucien Kroll and Atelier, Dormitory and Medical Faculty Buildings, University of Louvain, Belgium, 1969-74. Adhocism – the expression of May 1968 and the counter-culture. *BELOW LEFT*: Jeremy Dixon, St Mark's Road Housing, London, 1976-80, Edwardian row-housing, De Stijl ornament and classical composition – eclecticism based on context and use. *BELOW RIGHT*: The blowing up of Pruitt-Igoe, St Louis, 1972 (designed by Minoru Yamasaki).

destruction of local culture by the combined forces of rationalisation, bureaucracy, large-scale development, and, it is true, the modern International Style. But style was only one of eleven causes I cited as responsible for its death in *The Language of Post-Modern Architecture*, 1977. The other ten concerned the actual production *system* that architects found themselves saddled with. This system had two major flaws: the scale of its projects and the speed with which they were executed; a billion dollar chunk of the environment could be designed by one man and built within a couple of years.

A consensus amounting to a movement started to gel in 1975 when several architects such as Robert Stern and Michael Graves began working along similar lines to European architects such as Aldo Rossi, Robert Krier and James Stirling. Although they differed somewhat, and might question my labelling them post-modern, they all sought to transcend modernism while hearkening back to a wider architectural language. Not long after, Hans Hollein and Arata Isozaki produced their eclectic buildings and Philip Johnson designed the AT&T Corporate Headquarters. The 'new wave' became a flood, in which I well remember getting wet. On 31 March 1978, at precisely 7.46 am, several architectural students from Yale University burst into my hotel room and thrust a copy of the *New York Times* in my face. On the front page was a photograph of Johnson's new foray into post-modernism and, inside, an article by Paul Goldberger proclaiming it to be the 'first monument' of the movement. The students enquired (from one perspective it looks funereal), 'Is post-modernism dead?' The logic of their question was compelling. If modernism failed because it got too big and corporate, then this design for the world's biggest corporation must be the movement's kiss of death. Success had once again taken its toll, as it had for the last two hundred years. The nineteenth century was littered with the corpses of changing styles which could survive every persecution, except the loving embrace of a commercial society.

I almost agreed with this diagnosis, one which has been made repeatedly; at times with photo-collages of Michael Graves's Portland Building being blown up, at others under the rubric 'Post-Post-Modern' and even more frequently with the simple epitaph 'The Death of P-M'.[26] The linguistic life and death of movements, noted by Vasari in the Renaissance and reaching a high pitch in the 1920s, had now become an integral part of cultural politics. Tony Vidler, a Princeton professor of architecture, took aim at my writings (and head) and, using graphics which showed my cranium disintegrating in slow motion freeze frames like Pruitt-Igoe, took a certain pleasure in the hit job.[27] Perhaps I deserved such summary treatment after announcing the death of modern architecture, but the obituaries were premature. The movement had not so much died as a result of the media 'success' (its image promptly appeared on the covers of the London *Times*, *Time* magazine, the *Observer* colour section etc) as become visibly older. It moved straight into middle age and won the acceptance of the establishment as had its brother, late-modernism, and aged parent, modernism. All three exist partly to deal with very real social forces and partly in response to each other; in other words, they dialectically define each other and their relation to other, external forces. As long as one exists, it is likely the other two will carry on, as will aspects of traditional culture.

By 1980, there were several events which confirmed the movement's widespread acceptance. Most important was the Venice Biennale section on architecture, organised by Paolo Portoghesi. Entitled 'The Presence of the Past', it highlighted the element of historicism within post-modernism – the most conspicuous trend within the movement. The virtue of the exhibit lay in its celebration of architecture as a representational art and its recognition of the new consensus within the post-modern classical style. The public's response to this display was over two thousand visitors per day – a large number for an architectural exhibition. Because of its success it was demounted and reassembled the following year in both Paris and San Francisco. This popular response should be stressed since it vindicated the post-modernists' notion that architecture is a public art which must be comprehensible and challenging.

The other significant event which occurred at this time was the competition for the Portland Public Service Building, a contest Michael Graves won with an eclectic facade that could have come from the Venice Biennale, if it had not been designed beforehand. Partly urbanist with its green arcades, it was also partly modernist – its black glass wall signifying the public space within. The Rationalist Style was acknowledged as well in the little square windows (prompted also by the energy crisis) while its proportions and garlands hinted at Egyptian and Baroque influences. Calling it eclectic is an understatement, but its virtue lay not only in these diverse references (which related to nineteenth-century arcaded building in Portland), but also in the way they were pulled together into what Robert Venturi called 'the difficult whole'. Here was a building which, with its undeniable faults, was inclusive on a visual and urban level.[28] It related to the adjacent city hall as well as the surrounding modernist slabs, it incorporated veiled references to the human body and face, and reintegrated sculpture and polychromy as essential parts of its mixed language.

In other spheres post-modernism was also coming into focus partly as a result of clearer definitions within the architectural movement. Artists reflected on their goals and the way they were part of a growing tradition; while post-modernist writers and philosophers started to define a corpus of key texts and concepts. Characteristic of this gathering tradition were several exhibitions on the new classical art, and a large overview of post-modernism at the Hirshorn Museum in Washington DC (1984-85), called rather bluntly 'Content'.[29] The argument behind the show was that a new concern with content, or 'the will to meaning', united the pluralistic trends of the recent past, trends which stemmed from the conceptual art of the early 1970s. This argument was convincing even if, in making it, the organisers failed to distinguish late- from post-modern works and included too much (even abstract art has content of a sort). In the academic sphere there was an outburst of conferences and specialist journals devoted to post-modernism with one jamboree in Japan attended by 10,004 concerned participants.[30] The movement finally became mainstream in the architectural world, with large corporate practices such as Skidmore, Owings and Merrill switching styles and Kohn Pedersen Fox streamlining the Gravesian synthesis. I had written *Post-Modern Classicism* in 1980 and by 1985 it had become one of the world's leading approaches with a short history and set of monuments.

Post-Modern Classicism – a Public Language, 1979-

What I wrote in the 1980 monograph on the subject of architecture is still largely true today.

> Today Post-Modern Classicism is . . . reviving the classical languages to call up an idealism and a return to a public order, but it is doing so notably without a shared metaphysics or a belief in a single cosmic symbolism. . . . Some architects wish to adopt a full language of architecture that will make discourse with the past richer, and will use the full spectrum of rhetorical means – including polychromy, writing, nature and ornament. Others wish an urban comprehensibility; some want to build like the Ancients, in stone and real oak; others wish to jump quickly on the bandwagon.
>
> But perhaps this variety of motivation is of less importance than the fact that a

loosely shared approach has emerged, for some commonality and consensus must develop in order for architects to communicate with an audience and create significant innovations. The maturity of any movement depends on it forging a style which combines both constancy and change, a duality more easily expressed than achieved. What are the examples that make Post-Modern Classicism such a consensus? James Stirling's Museum in Stuttgart, Michael Graves's Fargo-Moorehead project, Ricardo Bofill's Arcades du Lac (a 'Versailles for the people'). Philip Johnson's AT&T, Charles Moore's Piazza d'Italia, and almost all of the recent work of Robert Stern, Arata Isozaki, Robert Venturi and Hans Hollein. In short, nearly every major post-modern architect has adopted parts of a classical vocabulary'.[31]

Even as I was writing these lines other major architects were shifting towards the approach – Aldo Rossi, Mario Botta, Robert Krier and Tom Beeby – and were soon followed by their many disciples. Once the shift had been made and defined it became, like the International Style of fifty years previously, a self-conscious mode to be improved through imitation.

However, two objections could be made: this new synthesis was neither really classical, nor commendable. The first objection was voiced by Nicholas Penny, among others, in the *Times Literary Supplement*.[32] Penny argued that a true classicism must have ideal proportions, monumentality, solemnity and grandeur – aspects which do indeed characterise some of its canonic revivals. However, as I pointed out, there *is* monumentality, solemnity and grandeur in the work of Ricardo Bofill, Philip Johnson and Aldo Rossi. Ideal proportions are indeed missing, except for a few schemes by Leon Krier and others, but the reason for this is partly explained by my initial statement that the synthesis is 'without a shared metaphysics or a belief in a single cosmic symbolism'. Whereas Alberti and Palladio believed in the harmony of the spheres and that the world's order can be captured by simple ratios and musical harmonies, post-modernists coming after Einstein and the Big Bang theory of the universe could not believe in such a simple picture. Harmonies inevitably play a part within this new approach, but do not make up the whole picture. Thus when a post-modern artist or architect uses simple ratios and composed figures he will fracture this beauty in some respects, or place it in tension with counter forms. One will continually find in art and architecture the oxymoron of 'disharmonious harmony', 'dissonant beauty', 'syncopated proportions' – that is, simple ratios which are set up and then consciously fragmented or violated.

In effect we are dealing with *Free-Style Classicism* as distinct from the *Canonic Classicism* of Vitruvius, Palladio and, today, Quinlan Terry. Canonic Classicism, conventionally defined, means 'Graeco-Roman' and 'of the first rank'. The latter notion stems from its original use by the Roman writer Aulus Gellius, who contrasted the scriptor classicus with the scriptor proletarius – authors of the upper, tax-paying class versus proletarian writers. When classicism became a tradition, and later an architectural language, it retained these intrinsic connotations, always referring to a restricted pedigree, or a set of 'classic authors'. In asserting a wider tradition, Free-Style Classicism expands this definition so it more closely approximates the historical truth: invented by the Egyptians, the style was used in many 'anti-classical' periods such as the Mannerist epoch, and by vulgarians on proletariat building tasks such as the Roman thermae and colosseum. It is this freer, sometimes vulgar, usage which is relevant today when architects like Bofill and Stirling build for the masses using non-canonic materials such as glass and steel. And this commitment to both industrial reality and classicism forces us, like all revolutions, to reassess basic terms.

If we expand the notion of classicism to include the continuum of western architecture – Egyptian, Graeco-Roman, Romanesque, Gothic, Renaissance, Mannerist, Baroque, Rococo, Neoclassical – we do so because, in spite of great differences in articulations, they share many aspects including a related grammar. Gothic architecture at Chartres, for instance used simple harmonic ratios, composite capitals, classical mouldings and a transformation of the Roman basilican plan. Some of the Gothic architects, we now know, even used Vitruvius's writings as a departure point. The same is true of the Baroque period which, for a long time, was censored as anti-classical. With hindsight, theories of transformational grammar and Wittgenstein's notion of 'language games', we can appreciate more clearly the similarities between all these styles. Within Free-Style Classicisms there are a series of overlapping concerns, 'family resemblances' which all of them share, in spite of the fact that none of them are identical. To decide whether an architect is a post-modern classicist would amount to noting these family resemblances, to decide whether he belonged to the wider tradition.

But this brings us to the other objection: what if the architecture is not of 'the first rank'? Here we encounter aesthetic judgments which relate to our understanding of overlapping traditions. To an eye and mind trained in canonic Classicism, the Free-Style variety is going to look ungrammatical, impure and sometimes malevolent.[33] How could it be otherwise, when old canons are broken and supplanted? We should remember Le Corbusier's famous reminder, written three times lest we forget, of 'Eyes Which Do not See – the beauty of I) Liners II) Aeroplanes, III) Automobiles'. Now that these beauties have been celebrated too frequently in architecture, they have lost their charm. But the point holds true and can be generalised to 'The Mind's Eye Takes Time to See' or 'Tastes Will Only Change Slowly'. One cannot expect, nor is it desirable, that a new language of architecture be appreciated by everyone in the first years of its use. As it becomes more widely used, as experiments and not a few mistakes are made, we learn to recognise the limitations of a particular language, what can be said in it and said well. Architects, critics and public are involved in discovering these qualities and bringing them to consciousness in the form of articulated values and rules. When this process is working well we can speak of limited progress towards a goal: for instance, the way Stirling and Wilford's Museum in Stuttgart realises the goal of contextualism, pluralism and symbolic ornament in a way superior to previous work in this tradition. Its central rotunda establishes the public realm in a beautiful outdoor room; a fresh version of a classical shape where the sky above creates the illusion of the 'domeless dome'. This building sets new standards and, along with Michael Graves's Humana Building, is one of the high points of post-modernism. This does not mean the building is without faults, nor that it will be appreciated by those whose tastes have been formed by modernism or canonic classicism. The norm in our pluralistic age is a conflict of taste-cultures, a fragmentation which many deplore; but it has deep historical roots that go back to the nineteenth century with the growth of professionalism, the avant-garde, the middle-class and a host of other, more or less discontinuous, taste-cultures.[34]

A major goal of post-modernists in the 1960s and 1970s was to cut across this spectrum of tastes by using tactics of eclecticism. Today it tries to pull this variety together within a more public language; a Free-Style Classicism inclusive of both current realities (technology in architecture and everyday content in art) and plural tastes. The most sophisticated post-modern architect is, from this perspective, Arata Isozaki, who has consistently developed four *different* approaches since the mid-1970s. Not only will he adopt a variety of 'styles for the job' – with breath-taking openness – but mix them when appropriate; or even design in a purist mode (modern or Japanese traditional) when the context calls for it. Few other architects attain such thoughtful

ABOVE LEFT: Jan Digerud, Skogbrand Insurance, Oslo, Norway, 1985-86. Concrete, steel, glass, Baroque massing, broken pediments, Rationalist windows = Free Style Classicism. *ABOVE RIGHT:* James Stirling and Michael Wilford, Neue Staats-galerie, Stuttgart, Germany, 1977-84. The most convincing post-modernism combines public and contextual meanings with ironic and current signs of the moment. *BELOW:* Ricardo Bofill and Taller de Arcquitectura, Les Arcades du Lac, St Quentin-en-Yvelines, France, 1974-81. A transformation of eighteenth-century grammar by twentieth-century technology, and a palace into mass housing.

pluralism. His most relevant post-modern buildings, like the Mito Art Tower, collage classicism against a high-tech alternative, challenging one taste-culture and paradigm with another. Beauty here consists in a dramatised field of difference, the tensions which create meaning and acknowledge heterogeneity. Canonic Classicism cannot do this any more than can High Modernism. For the language must be sufficiently rich and flexible to deal with the complexities of urban life in an industrial and post-industrial society. This entails a hybrid language. The point is post-modern classicism has its peculiar standards which involve mixing languages, a quality which is much harder to attain than the reductivist purity of modernists and classicists. It is easy to play the game of architecture, as Mies van der Rohe showed, if you disregard place, function, history and the variety of tastes, while the rigours of an inclusive approach demand 'an obligation towards the difficult whole', as Robert Venturi has said. But the rewards can be all the greater, for architect and society.

The Post-Modern Paradigm: Tragic Optimism

As mentioned above, during the 1980s the sixth and seventh formulations of this tradition occurred almost simultaneously. We are still in this last 'stage' of development and it overlaps with previous ones, thus making the notion of discrete stages somewhat problematic (although the different points of view can be clearly distinguished). In any case, the sixth formulation which occurred in the early 1980s was a critical reaction to the information world and consumer culture while the seventh, starting in the late 1980s, was a synthesising overview of the emerging paradigm. It is my impression that over a hundred serious books appeared in the decade showing, if nothing else, that the post-modern was more than a fashion in architecture. It touched every field, it permeated cultural analysis as a whole, it had emerged as a 'condition' to be celebrated or suffered, a world view and set of paradigms, and like anything so all-encompassing it had positive, negative and ambiguous aspects – all three.

Jean Baudrillard, for instance, leaving his Marxist criticism of production behind, adopted a Post-Marxist criticism of the signifying systems of consumption – which he found 'obscene'. However from his various writings on the 'ecstasy of communication', and the endless play of 'simulacra' which in our information world have supposedly replaced primary reality, one is never sure whether he abhors or delights in the obscenity. The question would be of academic interest had not so many academics followed him in hot pursuit of what they call 'excremental culture' (Arthur Kroker, David Cook, *The Postmodern Scene, Excremental Culture and Hyper-Aesthetics*, 1986). And had consumer culture not approached this condition in reality.

The truth (a word at which these deconstructionists sniff) is that the post-modern scene *is* implicated in this reality; the information world has invaded all aspects of life. Media such as television, film, fax and radio, the electronic media, now mediate a large part of our present reality and in this sense simulacra and processed reality have taken over from the previous system of mediation. But, as is apparent, I am sceptical of Baudrillard and others who claim this is new, or distinctive to the scene and therefore constitutes the essence of post-modernism. Symbolism, substitutes and simulacra started *with* language and thus must be well over half a million years old, so anyone who is horrified at our greatest industry of ersatz, the cosmetic profession and its cognate modes, ought to look again at everyday life in Egypt or Rome. 'Excremental culture' is eternal, even if it is particularly amplified today by sound-bytes. Even Kroker and Cook see the longevity of their *episteme*:

It is our general thesis that the postmodern scene in fact, begins in the fourth

Arata Isozaki, Art Tower Mito, Mito, Ibaragi, Japan, 1986-90. Oppositions of culture, technology and nature: a collage of classical forms (theatre, concert hall, gallery) faces a 100-metre titanium tower, while three oaks and a cascade dramatise the cross-axis.

century with the Augustinian subversion of embodied power, and that everything since the Augustinian refusal has been *nothing but* a fantastic and grisly implosion of experience as Western culture itself runs under the signs of passive and suicidal nihilism. Or was it not perhaps, even before this, in the Lucretian theory of the physical world that Serres calls the *simulacrum* (my italics).[35]

Such 'nothing-buttery' is mad, apocalyptic overstatement, just as is Baudrillard's later view, coming from his fixation on media-hype, that the Gulf War could not (or indeed did not) happen. It is true that much of this War was fought out through the media, that it was the Second TV War (after Vietnam), that 'smart bombs' were its form of obscenity, and that nihilism is an important strain of consumer culture. But, I would argue, it is not the most important or distinctive part and that if one stares into the TV void for too long, one is likely to become the simulacrum of a French intellectual and unable to imagine, or sustain, an alternative to nihilism.

Such points became apparent in the 1980s as the two traditions, which shared their common departure from modernism, started to understand their differences; what I have called neo- (or sometimes late) and post-modernism. David Ray Griffin, in his introduction to *God and Religion in the Postmodern World*, 1989, prefers to distinguish between two kinds of *post*-modernism because by then, in America (thanks to the writings of Lyotard, Derrida and Baudrillard) the term had been consistently applied to both. Griffin characterises the strain coming from pragmatism and Derrida as –

deconstructive or *eliminative* postmodernism. It overcomes the modern world view through its anti-worldview: it deconstructs or eliminates the ingredients necessary for a worldview, such as God, self, purpose, meaning, a real world, and truth as correspondence. While motivated in some cases by the ethical concern to forestall totalitarian systems, this type of postmodern thought ends in relativism, even nihilism. It also could be called *ultramodernism*, in that its eliminations result from carrying modern premises to their logical conclusions.

The postmodernism of the SUNY series in Constructive Postmodern thought he is editing can, by contrast, be called *revisionary*. It seeks to overcome the modern worldview not by eliminating the possibility of worldviews as such, but by constructing a postmodern worldview through a revision of modern premises and traditional concepts.[36]

At about the time of writing this, he and a team of others including myself were working on a television series concerning the post-modern world view. I mention this fact not only to acknowledge the Baudrillardian ironies, but to show that there was a fundamental consensus at the time and it was coming from different areas. Architects had for ten years acknowledged the split between late and post-modernism, writers such as John Barth had seen it from their discipline and now scientists and theologians were confirming it from their perspectives. This general point was understood by many of the critics and systematisers who wrote in the seventh 'stage' of the movement, and it forms an underlying schema of perhaps the most scholarly study, Margaret Rose's *The Post-Modern and The Post-Industrial*, 1991.[37] By the late 1980s, after twenty years of reflection and self-reflection, the agenda of post-modernism reached a certain clarification in this book, those of David Ray Griffin, Hans Küng and Jim Collins (particularly the latter's *Uncommon Cultures, Popular Culture and Post-Modernism*, 1989).

My object here is not to analyse this phase, but to conclude by summarising some of its positive points, and the post-modern agenda. I list these below not as a binary opposition to the modern programme and condition, but as an ambiguous slide and shift from one paradigm to another. In nearly every case the post-modern is a complexification, hybridisation and sublation of the modern – not its antithesis. The trends and hybrid slides are the following:

MODERN hybridised to POST-MODERN

in *politics*

1	nation-states	regions/supranational bodies
2	totalitarian	democratic
3	consensus	contested consensus
4	class friction	new agenda issues, green

in *economics*

5	Fordism	Post-Fordism (networking)
6	monopoly capital	regulated socialised capitalism
7	centralised	decentralised world economy

in *society* (First World)

8	high growth	steady state
9	industrial	post-industrial
10	class-structured	many clustered
11	proletariat	cognitariat

in *culture*

12	purism	double-coding
13	elitism	elite/mass dialogue
14	objectivism	values in nature

in *aesthetics*

15	simple harmonies	disharmonious harmony
16	Newtonian represented	Big Bang represented
17	top-down integrated	conflicted semiosis
18	ahistorical	time-binding

in *philosophy*

19	monism	pluralism
20	materialism	semiotic view
21	utopian	heterotopian

in *media*

22	world of print	electronic/reproductive
23	fast changing	instant/world changing

in *science*

24	mechanistic	self-organising
25	linear	non-linear
26	deterministic	creative, open
27	Newton mechanics	Quantum/Chaos

in *religion*

28	atheism	panentheism
29	'God is dead'	creation-centred spirituality
30	patriarchical	post-patriarchical
31	disenchantment	re-enchantment

in *world view*

32	mechanical	ecological
33	reductive	holistic/holonic/interconnected
34	separated	interrelated semi-autonomous
35	hierarchical	heterarchical
36	accidental universe	anthropic principle

| 37 | anthropocentric | cosmological orientation |
| 38 | absurdity of 'man' | tragic optimism |

The most important thing to grasp about this list is the underlying pattern, not the individual items. Like many other lists of the post-modern paradigm, on which this relies, there is a great redundancy in the concepts, and it is the whole system that counts. Furthermore, since I have not explained or mentioned more than ten of the terms (and I am devoting another, entire book to them) the reader has no other choice than pattern-recognition. What pattern emerges?

According to the anthropic principle (item 36) we inhabit a universe full of violence and unpredictability, but one so finely-tuned that it allows us to observe and fathom it; in effect one which has been trying for twelve to fifteen billion years to produce strange and wonderful things that can think, feel and react to it. The circularity, or tautology, involved here is built into the assumptions of science (they cannot contradict the fact of their own existence). Our mere presence entails consequences among which is the idea that a host of very sensitive conditions had to be just right to produce *homo sapiens*. Time and size, the age, speed of expansion and mass of the universe had to be very delicately poised to get us here, and this in turn means that something very like us was predestined (if not exactly predetermined) by the universe. Nature or God had a predisposition to produce us. If the strong force of the atom were just slightly stronger there would be an explosive consumption of all protons, if the nuclear force were slightly weaker, there would be no chain reaction in the sun, and if the ratios of the four fundamental forces were slightly different, we would not be here to know anything about these extraordinary gifts, these un-asked for perfect balances. As Paul Davies and John Gribbon point out:

> These apparent 'coincidences', and many more like them, have convinced some scientists that the structure of the universe we perceive is remarkably sensitive to even the most minute changes in the fundamental parameters of nature. It is as though the elaborate order of the cosmos were a result of highly delicate fine-tuning. In particular, the existence of life, and hence intelligent observers, is especially sensitive to the high-precision 'adjustment' of our physical circumstances.[38]

The fact that the universe shows this kind of non-teleological teleology (a predisposition to produce something like us, if not exactly us) and the fact that it exhibits extraordinary creativity and real novelty, is unbelievable – most of all to a modernist brought up on a steady diet of mechanism, determinism, and materialism. The fact that the universe is fundamentally alive, spontaneously self-ordering at all levels – from the very small to the very big – is a shock to those who thought it was based on a matter that was boring, determined and fundamentally dead.

This surprise to the modernists is behind the shift from an anthropocentric to a cosmological perspective (item 37), it's behind Matthew Fox's 'creation spirituality' and the whole mystic tradition, it's behind the awe of a scientist such as Einstein amazed at the fundamental constants. Of course it is the base of all spirituality. Matthew Fox continuously translates the unlikely discoveries of post-modern science into striking propositions; he thematises cosmology from a Christian perspective and thus goes back to the basic impulse behind the Bible:

> The Fire [of the Big Bang] filled the universe, and the universe expanded for seven hundred and fifty thousand years. For [all these years] the universe was on fire. We now know that if this expansion had taken place at a rate one millionth of a millionth of a second slower or faster, you and I could not be here today. Mother

earth would not have evolved as a hospitable place for us to be. Phew! – we 'lucked out' as you might say. This is what Julian of Norwich, the great creation mystic, wrote in the fifteenth century, 'We were loved from before the beginning.' We have been loved from before the beginning.[39]

The lesson Fox draws from many such recent discoveries is that the universe is a fairly benign place, with a countless set of 'gifts'. These show Christians have had some priorities wrong: they should acknowledge not just original sin, which has been bearing down and repressing consciousness for sixteen centuries, but 'original blessing'.[40] Although there are indeed accidents, suffering, real evil and constant warfare (creativity can be as much negative as positive) we can clarify from our existence here the answer to a perennially important question. It is one that Einstein posed: is the universe a fundamentally good place, should we be optimistic? The answer, of course, hangs in the balance and depends on how we treat the earth and ourselves, as well as the other endangered species.

Beyond this, as a result of discoveries in quantum mechanics and elsewhere (items 27 and 32), it is apparent that what Newtonian science (the underpinning of modernity) conceived as matter ('solid, massy, hard, impenetrable, movable particles' in Newton's words) is more alive than dead. Internal self-organisation must be balanced with external determinism. Every quantum experiment forces 'matter' to make choices, forces an electron to choose its position or momentum, and these operations show – if one uses such words – a bit of mind stuff and free will in all matter. Perhaps at this level 'mind' is as arbitrary as 'matter' – what do they mean? Whatever the answer, quantum physics and the post-modern sciences of complexity show that partial self-determinism, the crucial aspect behind free will, is an inherent property at all levels in the universe.

In addition, there are very materialist implications: the quantum era is the point when electronics has become the biggest industry in history. But more important it is the epoch when software, or whatever we call those programmes and desires inside our brain, is found to be much more significant than hardware. No longer in the post-industrial society (item 9) is matter, the 'solid, massy and hard' stuff, the most important, no longer is the economy fundamentally extractive, like mining, and based on physical objects, like jewellery; no longer are things just limited to one person, and have to be fought over in a zero-sum game (things are either yours or mine); no longer is the basic economic datum, like fossil fuel, consumed in use. Ideas and information, which weigh nothing and occupy no space, are not subject to finite ownership. Like experience itself – eros – they particularly enjoy being communicated and shared. They are not consumed in use, but double in power by use – a positive-sum game if ever there were one.

Since the post-modern age is *the* information era, since knowledge is power and since it is the quality and organisation of information that matter, it is crucially important that free communication be safeguarded and a good education provided for everyone. Otherwise, it is quite certain, we will create more vicious divides within society and between cultures, and deepen the shame of a post-industrial society – the permanent underclass. Such moral points are not out of place, in conclusion, since every post-modern discourse emphasises the interconnectedness of things (item 33). It is true this holism can be taken too far and become reductive itself. Thus to a New Age proclamation 'everything is connected', the post-modern response is 'Yes, but . . . some things are more connected than others'. As Arthur Koestler and others have argued, everything is both connected and semi-autonomous, a Janus-like property he calls 'holonic'. With this proviso, the basic point of interconnection remains, and it is the leitmotif of post-modern literature, philosophy, architecture and religion. This has radical implications for contemporary life for it puts us at home in a universe where values, beauty and morality play a role. They may not always prevail, and one cannot deny the mass extinctions which history reveals. The geological evidence as well as the killing fields of the twentieth century are clear on that: evil and tragedy punctuate evolution. But opposed to the modern world view, that denied the presence of anything more than dead matter, we can afford the solace and optimism of the new world view which shows what really matters is mind, and spirit.

NOTES

1 For pluralism as a leitmotif of post-modernism see my own writings, particularly *The Language of Post-Modern Architecture*, Academy, London 1991, 6th edition, and those of Christian Norberg-Schulz on architecture; for literature, Matei Calinescu, *Five Faces of Modernity*, Duke University Press, Durham, 1987 (and citations), and for the general paradigm, Wolfgang Welsch, *Unsere postmoderne Modern*, Acta Humaniora, VCH, Weinheim, 1988, pp 4-7 (where pluralism is seen as the unifying theme of post-modernism). Also Ihab Hassan, *The Postmodern Turn: Essays in Postmodern Theory and Culture*, Ohio University State Press, Columbus, 1987 (as these essays show, Hassan moves consistently towards pluralism over the period 1971-87); Jean-François Lyotard, *The Postmodern Condition: A Report on Knowledge*, Manchester University Press, 1984 (French 1979); David Lodge, *The Modes of Modern Writing*, Edward Arnold, London, 1977, pp 220-46, but more importantly his *After Bakhtin*, Routledge, London, 1990 (the discussions of dialogic and also Kundera); David Harvey, *The Condition of Postmodernity*, Blackwell, Oxford, 1989; Masao Miyoshi and HD Harootunian, ed *Postmodernism and Japan*, Duke University Press, London, 1989.

2 For John Barth see note 19; Linda Hutcheon, *The Poetics of Postmodernism, History, Theory, Fiction*, Routledge, London, 1988, p 4 f; Andreas Huyssen, *After the Great Divide, Modernism, Mass Culture, Postmodernism*, Indiana University Press, Bloomington, 1986, pp 141-221.

3 Ihab Hassan's list (for reference see note 1) is quoted in Harvey, *Condition of Postmodernity*, p 43, and then reconstructed, pp 340-41. The binary oppositions should be compared to the hybridisations of my last diagram here.

4 Faust has since the Renaissance typified the modernist, or progressivist, who will sell his soul and much else for progress. Since the German myth, Marlowe and especially Goethe, the archetypal problem has been seen, but it is particularly poignant that two Jewish writers, from the same neighbourhood in the Bronx that was destroyed by the arch-modernist Robert Moses, should understand the myth so well: the developer and Le Corbusier are our Fausts. See the most important book on Modernism of the 1980s, Marshall Berman, *All That is Solid Melts Into Air, The Experience of Modernity*, Simon and Schuster, New York, 1982, pp 37-86 (and 327, where the meeting with Herman Kahn is described). Also Herman Kahn and Anthony J Weiner, *The Year 2000*, Macmillan, New York, 1967, pp 409-13.

5 Huyssen, *After the Great Divide*, Chapter 10, 'Mapping the Postmodern' remains one of the best discussions to date.

6 Craig Owens, 'The Discourse of Others: Feminists and Postmodernism', *The Anti-Aesthetic, Essays on Postmodern Culture*, ed Hal Foster, Bay Press, Port Townsend, Wash, 1983, pp 57-82; also *Feminism/Postmodernism*, ed Linda J Nicholson, Routledge, New York, and Susan Rubin Suleiman, 'Feminism and Postmodernism', *Zeitgeist in Babel, The Postmodernist Controversy*, ed Ingeborg Hoesterey, Indiana University Press, Bloomington, 1991, pp 111-31.

7 For Harvey Cox see note 10, for David Ray Griffin see note 36. Hans Küng first takes up the postmodern debate in *Theology for the Third Millennium, An Ecumenical View*, Doubleday, New York, 1988, pp 1-12, 257-285, and then *Global Responsibility, In Search of a New World Ethic*, Crossroad, New York, 1991, pp 1-25. Küng in this last text comes very close to the position on post-modernism which I, Griffin, Rose and others hold.

8 Ilya Prigogine and Isabelle Stengers, *Order Out Of Chaos, Man's New Dialogue with Nature*, Bantam, New York, 1984 (French 1979); James Gleick, *Chaos, Making a New Science*, Viking, New York, 1987; Heinz R Pagels, *The Dreams of Reason, The Computer and the Sciences of Complexity*, Bantam, New York, 1988; also the last five books of Paul Davies.

9 Jean-François Lyotard, 'What is Postmodernism?' appendix in *Postmodern Condition*, p 79. The essay was first published in French in 1982, the book in 1979. My own response to this, *What is Post-Modernism?* Academy, London, St Martin's Press, New York, 1986, shows how the confusions of Postmodern with ultra- or Late-modern stem from Ihab Hassan's writings of the early 1970s.

10 Harvey Cox, *Religion in the Secular City: Toward a Postmodern Theology*, Simon and Schuster, New York, 1984.

11 Andreas Huyssen was the first to periodise post-modernism in this way, and I am indebted to his arguments here, with which I mostly agree; he does not, however, mention the third or 'classical' phase, nor dichotomise Late- from Post-Modern. See his 'Mapping the Postmodern', *New German Critique* 33, Autumn 1984, pp 5-52.

12 Quoted from Lucy Lippard, *Pop Art*, Thames and Hudson, London, 1966, p 32.

13 This review in the *New York Times* is quoted from Judith Goldman, *James Rosenquist*, Penguin Books, New York, 1985, p 44.

14 In fact the *F 111* was shown in a small exhibit along with a Poussin and David in 'History Painting – Various Aspects', Metropolitan Museum, 1968. This exhibit provoked Kramer's response. See note 9 for the source.

15 Lewis Mumford, 'The Case Against "Modern Architecture"' (1960), reprinted in *The Highway and the City*, Secker and Warburg, London, 1964, p 156.

16 Leslie Fiedler, 'The New Mutants' (1965), published in *The Collected Essays of Leslie Fiedler*, Vol 11, Stein and Day, New York, 1970.

17 Ihab Hassan, 'POSTmodernISM: a Paracritical Bibliography', *New Literary History* 3, 1, Autumn 1971, pp 5-30, reprinted in *Paracriticisms: Seven Speculations of the Times*, University of Illinois Press, Urbana, 1975, chap 2.

18 Ibid, note 4, p 123.

19 John Barth, 'The Literature of Replenishment, Postmodernist Fiction', *The Atlantic*, January 1980, pp 65-71.

20 Ibid, p 70.

21 Umberto Eco, *Postscript to the Name of the Rose*, Harcourt Brace Jovanovich, New York and London, 1984, p 67 (first published in Italian in 1983).

22 Ibid, pp 67-68.

23 The women's movement in art is summarised by Corinne Robins in *The Pluralist Era, American Art 1968-1981*, Harper and Row, New York, pp 49-75.

24 Craig Owens, 'The Discourse of Others', *Anti-Aesthetic*, ed Foster. Most of these essays are really concerned with Late-Modernism or the Schismatic Postmodernism that Hassan proffers. See note 2 for my critique.

25 Huyssen, 'Mapping the Postmodern', note 7, pp 13-16.

26 EM Farrelly, 'The New Spirit', *Architectural Review*, August 1986 announces, as if for the first time, the 'death of Post-Modernism'; these obituaries started appearing in American magazines circa 1979.

27 See Anthony Vidler, 'Vidler on Jencks', or 'Cooking Up the Classics', *Skyline*, New York, October 1981, pp 18-21 and my reply the following month. Vidler later apologised to me for the tone and drawings in this piece. From about this time a new vicious tone starts to appear in architectural polemics, as adversaries start treating each other with contempt, and the warfare moves to Britain with the so-called 'Great Debate – Modernism versus the Rest' at the RIBA in November 1982. See my 'Post-Modern Architecture: the True Inheritor of Modernism', *Transactions* 3, RIBA Publications, London, 1983, pp 26-41, which summarises some of the diatribe, more of which appears in the same journal. Much of this polemic results from the pluralism, or 'loss of authority', which characterises the Postmodern age, and is obviously one of the costs paid for this variety.

28 The attacks on Graves's Portland Building resulted in the top pavilions and the side garlands being stripped and simplified. For this controversy see my *Kings of Infinite Space*, Academy, London, and St Martin's Press, New York, 1983, pp 86-97, plus the relevant issues of *Progressive Architecture*, which carried the controversy for several months from 1982-83.

29 'Content, A Contemporary Focus 1974-1984' ran at the Hirshorn Museum in Washington DC from 4 October 1984-6 January, 1985 and has a catalogue written by Howard Fox, Miranda McClintic and Phyllis Rosenzweig. Two small exhibits on the new classicism in art were: 'The Classic Tradition in Recent Painting and Sculpture', The Aldrich Museum, Ridgefield, Conn, 19 May-September 1985, and 'Beyond Antiquity: Classical References in Contemporary Art' at the DeCordova and Dana Museum and Park, Lincoln, Mass, 15 June-8 September 1985 (catalogues for both). Graham Beal organised 'Second Sight', San Francisco Museum of Modern Art, 21 September-16 November, 1986 and, as the title suggests, the exhibit had a historicist bias.

30 The Inter-Design Conference on 'Modern Culture, Post-Modern Culture and What Will Come Next' was held in Sapporo, Japan, 17-20 October 1984, and had over 10,000 participants; two other conferences I attended which also had wide agendas were at Northwestern University in October 1985 and Hanover,

Germany, later that month. Three conferences with published papers are: *The Idea of the Post-Modern – Who is Teaching It?* Henry Art Gallery, University of Washington, 1981, with contributions by Lawrence Alloway and Donald Kuspit among others; 'Postmodernism in Philosophy and the Arts' held in Cerisy-la-Salle, September 1983, published later as *Postmodernism; Search for Criteria*, International Circle for Research in Philosophy, Houston, Tex, 1985, with contributions by writers and philosophers; *Postmodernism*, ICA Documents 4, London, 1985, a conference in May of that year which had contributions by Kenneth Frampton and Jean-François Lyotard among others. The conceptual confusion of Post-Modernism in the arts is well shown by two anthologies which discuss it from time to time and elide it with *Late-Modernism: Theories of Contemporary Art*, ed Richard Hertz, Prentice Hall, Englewood Cliffs, NJ, 1985, and *Art After Moderning: Rethinking Representation*, ed with an introduction by Brian Wallis, foreword by Marcia Tucker, The New Museum of Contemporary Art, New York, nd (1985). In literary theory the clarity of postmodernism still remains blurred with Late-Modernism. See for instance Charles Newman, *The Post-Modern Aura, The Act of Fiction in an Age of Inflation*, Northwestern University Press, Evanston, 1985. The works of John Barth (note 19) and Umberto Eco (note 21) are exceptions to this lack of definition.

31 Charles Jencks, 'Post-Modern Classicism – The New Synthesis', *Architectural Design* 5/6, London 1980, p 5.

31 Charles Jencks, 'Free-Style Classicism', *Architectural Design* 1/2, January 1982, especially pp 5-21 and 117-20.

32 See Nicholas Penny, 'Post-Modern Classicism', *Times Literary Supplement*, 3 April 1981 and my response, *TLS*, 24 April, 1981.

33 Gavin Stamp views Post-Modernism as 'Illiterate Vernacular'; see his essay of that title in *The Spectator*, 2 August 1986, pp 15-17.

34 CP Snow's notion of 'two cultures', the literary and scientific communities, has also been articulated in a different way as cultures which are 'highbrow, middle brow and low brow' and again into the seven taste-cultures that Herbert Gans defines in *Popular Culture and High Culture*, Basic Books, New York, 1974, pp 69-103. Market researchers and advertisers group the market place differently again. Depending on what is being measured, each one of these fragmented subcultures has relevance. It may well be that the most unifying force today in a pluralist society is mass-culture: TV, films, newspapers and processed food which most of society consumes. This would explain the fact that the British Royal family enjoys watching 'Dallas' and 'Dynasty' and vice-versa.

35 Arthur Kroker, *The Postmodern Scene, Excremental Culture and Hyper-Aesthetics*, St Martin's Press, New York, 1986, p 8.

36 See David Ray Griffin's introductions to the SUNY series in *Constructive Postmodern Thought*, State University of New York Press; *The Reenchantment of Science, Postmodern Proposals*, 1988; *Spirituality and Society, Postmodern Visions*, 1988; *God and Religion in the Postmodern World, Essays in Postmodern Theology*, 1989; with Beardslee and Holland, *Varieties of Postmodern Theology*, 1989; with Huston Smith, *Primordial Truth and Postmodern Theology*, 1990; *Sacred Interconnections: Postmodern Spirituality, Political Economy, and Art*, 1990. Griffin has set up The Center for the Postmodern World, 3463 State Street, Suite 252 Santa Barbara, Ca 93105.

37 Margaret Rose, *The Post-Modern and The Post-Industrial*, Cambridge University Press, 1991; Jim Collins, *Uncommon Cultures, Popular Culture and Post-Modernism*, Routledge, London, 1989.

38 Paul Davies and John Gribbin, *The Matter Myth*, Viking, London, 1991, pp 226-27.

39 Matthew Fox, *The Four Paths of Creation-Centred Spirituality, Talks by Matthew Fox*, St James's Church, Piccadilly, London, 1987, p 11; also in *Creation Spirituality*, Harper, San Fransisco, 1991, p 28.

40 Matthew Fox, *Original Blessing*, Bear & Co, Santa Fe, N Mex, 1983.

Andreas Huyssen
MAPPING THE POSTMODERN

A Story

In the summer of 1982 I visited the Seventh Documenta in Kassel, Germany, a periodic exhibition which documents the latest trends in contemporary art every four or five years. My then five-year old son Daniel was with me, and he succeeded, unintentionally, in making the latest in postmodernism quite palpable to me. Approaching the Fridericianum, the museum housing the exhibit, we saw a huge and extended wall of rocks, seemingly heaped haphazardly alongside the museum. It was a work by Joseph Beuys, one of the key figures of the postmodern scene for at least a decade. Coming closer we realised that thousands of huge basalt blocks were arranged in a triangle formation the smallest angle of which pointed at a newly planted tree – all of it part of what Beuys calls a social sculpture and what in a more traditional terminology would have been called a form of applied art. Beuys had issued an appeal to the citizens of Kassel, a dismal provincial city rebuilt in concrete after the heavy bombings of the last great war, to plant a tree with each of his 7,000 'planting stones'. The appeal – at least initially – had been enthusiastically received by a populace usually not interested in the latest blessings of the art world. Daniel, for his part, loved the rocks. I watched him climb up and down, across and back again. 'Is this art?' he asked matter-of-factly. I talked to him about Beuys's ecological politics and about the slow death of the German forest (*Waldsterben*) due to acid rain. As he kept moving around on the rocks, listening distractedly, I gave him a few simple concepts about art in the making, sculpture as monument or anti-monument, art for climbing on, and ultimately, art for vanishing –the rocks after all would disappear from the museum site as people would begin to plant the trees.

Later in the museum, however, things turned out quite differently. In the first halls we filed past a golden pillar, actually a metal cylinder entirely covered with golden leaves (by James Lee Byars), and an extended golden wall by Kounellis, with a clothes stand including hat and coat placed before it. Had the artist, as a latter day Wu Tao-Tse, vanished into the wall, into his work, leaving only his hat and coat? No matter how suggestive we might find the juxtaposition of the banal clothes stand and the preciosity of the doorless shining wall, one thing seemed clear: 'Am Golde hängt, zum Golde drängt die Postmoderne'.

Several rooms further on we encountered Mario Merz's spiral table made out of glass, steel, wood and plates of sandstone, with bushlike twigs sticking out of the external parameter of the spiral formation – again, it seemed, an attempt to overlay the typical hard materials of the modernist era, steel and glass, with softer, more 'natural' ones, in this case sandstone and wood. There were connotations of Stonehenge and ritual, domesticated and brought down to living-room size, to be sure. I was trying to hold together in my mind the eclecticism of materials used by Merz with the nostalgic eclecticism of postmodern architecture or the pastiche of expressionism in the painting of the *neuen Wilden*, prominently exhibited in another building of this Documenta show. I was trying, in other words, to spin a red thread through the labyrinth of the postmodern. Then, in a flash, the pattern became clear. As Daniel tried to feel the surfaces and crevices of Merz's work, as he ran his fingers alongside the stone plates and over the glass, a guard rushed over shouting: 'Nicht berühren! Das ist Kunst!' (Don't touch! This is art!) And a while later, tired from so much art, he sat down on Carl André's solid cedar blocks only to be chased away with the admonition that art was not for sitting on.

Here it was again, that old notion of art: no touching, no trespassing. The museum as temple, the artist as prophet, the work as relic and cult object, the halo restored. Suddenly the privileging of gold in this exhibit made a lot of sense. The guards, of course, only performed what Rudi Fuchs, organiser of this Documenta and in touch with current trends, had in mind all along: 'To disentangle art from the diverse pressures and social perversions it has to bear.'[1] The debates of the last fifteen to twenty years about ways of seeing and experiencing contemporary art, about imaging and image making, about the entanglements between avantgarde art, media iconography and advertising seemed to have been wiped out, the slate cleaned for a new romanticism. But then it fits in all too well with, say, the celebrations of the prophetic word in the more recent writings of Peter Handke, with the aura of the 'postmodern' in the New York art scene, with the self-stylisation of the film-maker as *auteur* in *Burden of Dreams*, a recent documentary about the making of Werner Herzog's *Fitzcarraldo*. Think of *Fitzcarraldo*'s closing images – opera on a ship on the Amazon. *Bâteau Ivre* was briefly considered by the Documenta organisers as the title for the exhibit. But while Herzog's worn-out steam boat was indeed a *bâteau ivre* – opera in the jungle, a ship moved across a mountain – the *bâteau ivre* of Kassel was only sobering in its pretentiousness. Consider this, taken from Fuchs's catalogue introduction: 'After all the artist is one of the last practitioners of distinct individuality'. Or, again *Originalton* Fuchs: 'Here, then, begins our exhibition; here is the euphoria of Hölderlin, the quiet logic of TS Eliot, the unfinished dream of Coleridge. When the French traveller who discovered the Niagara Falls returned to New York, none of his sophisticated friends believed his fantastic story. What is your proof, they asked. My proof, he said, is that I have seen it.'[2]

Niagara Falls and Documenta 7 – indeed we have seen it all before. Art as nature, nature as art. The halo Baudelaire once lost on a crowded boulevard is back, the aura restored, Baudelaire, Marx and Benjamin forgotten. The gesture in all of this is patently anti-modern and anti-avantgarde. Sure, one could argue that in his recourse to Hölderlin, Coleridge and Eliot, Fuchs tries to revive the modernist dogma itself – yet another postmodern nostalgia, another sentimental return to a time when art was still art. But what distinguishes this nostalgia from 'the real thing', and what ultimately makes it anti-modernist, is its loss of irony, reflexiveness and self-doubt, its cheerful abandonment of a critical consciousness, its ostentatious self-confidence and the *mise en scène* of its conviction (visible even in the spatial arrangements inside the Fridericianum) that there must be a realm of purity for art, a space beyond those unfortunate 'diverse pressures and social perversions' art has had to bear.[3]

This latest trend within the trajectory of postmodernism, embodied for me in the Documenta 7, rests on an all but total confusion of codes: it is anti-modern and highly eclectic, but dresses up as a return to the modernist tradition; it is anti-avantgarde in that it simply chooses to drop the avantgarde's crucial concern for a new art in an alternative society, but it pretends to be avantgarde in its presentation of current trends; and, in a certain sense, it is even anti-postmodern in that it abandons any reflection of the problems which the exhaustion of high modernism originally brought about, problems which postmodern art, in its better moments, has attempted to address aesthetically and sometimes even politically. Documenta 7 can stand as the perfect aesthetic simulacrum: facile eclecticism combined with aesthetic amnesia and delusions of grandeur. It represents the kind of postmodern restoration of a domesticated modernism which seems to be gaining ground in the age of Kohl-Thatcher-Reagan and it parallels the conservative political attacks on the culture of the 1960s which have increased in volume and viciousness in these past years.

The Problem

If this were all that could be said about postmodernism it would not be worth the trouble of taking up the subject at all. I might just as well stop right here and join the formidable chorus of those who lament the loss of quality and proclaim the decline of the arts since the 1960s. My argument, however, will be a different one. While the recent media hype about postmodernism in architecture and the arts has propelled the phenomenon into the limelight, it has also tended to obscure its long and complex history. Much of my ensuing argument will be based on the premise that what appears on one level as the latest fad, advertising pitch and hollow spectacle is part of a slowly emerging cultural transformation in Western societies, a change in sensibility for which the term 'postmodernism' is actually, at least for now, wholly adequate. The nature and depth of that transformation are debatable, but transformation it is. I don't want to be misunderstood as claiming that there is a wholesale paradigm shift of the cultural, social and economic orders;[4] any such claim clearly would be overblown. But in an important sector of our culture there is a noticeable shift in sensibility, practices and discourse formations which distinguishes a post-modern set of assumptions, experiences and propositions from that of a preceding period. What needs further exploration is whether this transformation has generated genuinely new aesthetic forms in the various arts or whether it mainly recycles techniques and strategies of modernism itself, reinscribing them into an altered cultural context.

Of course, there are good reasons why any attempt to take the postmodern seriously on its own terms meets with so much resistance. It is indeed tempting to dismiss many of the current manifestations of postmodernism as a fraud perpetrated on a gullible public by the New York art market in which reputations are built and gobbled up faster than painters can paint: witness the frenzied brushwork of the new expressionists. It is also easy to argue that much of the contemporary inter-arts, mixed-media and performance culture, which once seemed so vital, is now spinning its wheels and speaking in tongues, relishing, as it were, the eternal recurrence of the *déjà vu*. With good reason we may remain sceptical towards the revival of the Wagnerian *Gesamtkunstwerk* as postmodernism spectacle in Syberberg or Robert Wilson. The current Wagner cult may indeed be a symptom of a happy collusion between the megalomania of the postmodern and that of the premodern on the edge of modernism. The search for the grail, it seems, is on.

But it is almost too easy to ridicule the postmodernism of the current New York art scene or of Documenta 7. Such total rejection will blind us to postmodernism's critical potential which, I believe, also exists, even though it may be difficult to identify.[5] The notion of the art work as critique actually informs some of the more thoughtful condemnations of postmodernism, which is accused of having abandoned the critical stance that once characterised modernism. However, the familiar ideas of what constitutes a critical art (*Parteilichkeit* and vanguardism, *l'art engagé*, critical realism, or the aesthetic of negativity, the refusal of representation, abstraction, reflexiveness) have lost much of their explanatory and normative power in recent decades. This is precisely the dilemma of art in a postmodern age. Nevertheless, I see no reason to jettison the notion of a critical art altogether. The pressures to do so are not new; they have been formidable in capitalist culture ever since romanticism, and if our postmodernity makes it exceedingly difficult to hold on to an older notion of art as critique, then the task is to redefine the possibilities of critique in postmodern terms rather than relegating it to oblivion. If the postmodern is discussed as a historical condition rather than only as style it becomes possible and indeed important to unlock the critical moment in postmodernism itself and to sharpen its cutting edge, however blunt it may seem at first sight. What will no longer do is either to eulogise or to ridicule postmodernism *en bloc*. The postmodern must be salvaged from its champions and from its detractors. This essay is meant to contribute to that project.

In much of the postmodernism debate, a very conventional thought pattern has asserted itself. Either it is said that postmodernism is continuous with modernism, in which case the whole debate opposing the two is specious; or, it is claimed that there is a radical rupture, a break with modernism, which is then evaluated in either positive or negative terms. But the question of historical continuity or discontinuity simply cannot be adequately discussed in terms of such an either/or dichotomy. To have questioned the validity of such dichotomous thought patterns is of course one of the major achievements of Derridean deconstruction. But the poststructuralist notion of endless textuality ultimately cripples any meaningful historical reflection on temporal units shorter than, say, the long wave of metaphysics from Plato to Heidegger or the spread of *modernité* from the mid-nineteenth century to the present. The problem with such historical macro-schemes, in relation to postmodernism, is that they prevent the phenomenon from even coming into focus.

I will therefore take a different route. I will not attempt here to define what postmodernism *is*. The term '*post*modernism' itself should guard us against such an approach as it positions the phenomenon as relational. Modernism as that from which postmodernism is breaking away remains inscribed into the very word with which we describe our distance from modernism. Thus keeping in mind postmodernism's relational nature, I will simply start from the *Selbstverständnis* of the postmodern as it has shaped various discourses since the 1960s. What I hope to provide in this essay is something like a large-scale map of the postmodern which surveys several territories and on which the various postmodern artistic and critical practices could find their aesthetic and political place. Within the trajectory of the postmodern in the United States I will distinguish several phases and directions. My primary aim is to emphasise some of the historical contingencies and pressures that have shaped recent aesthetic and cultural debates but have either been ignored or systematically blocked out in critical theory *à l'américaine*. While drawing on developments in architecture, literature and the visual arts, my focus will be primarily on the critical discourse about the postmodern: postmodernism in relation to, respectively, modernism, the avantgarde, neo-conservatism and poststructuralism. Each of these constellations represents a somewhat separate layer of the postmodern and will be presented as such. And, finally, central elements of the *Begriffsgeschichte* of the term will be discussed in relation to a broader set of questions that have arisen in recent debates about modernism, modernity and the historical avantgarde.[6] A crucial question for me concerns the extent to which modernism and the avantgarde as forms of an adversary culture were nevertheless conceptually and practically bound up with capitalist modernisation and/or with communist vanguardism, that modernisation's twin brother. As I hope this essay will show, postmodernism's critical dimension lies precisely in its radical questioning of those presuppositions which linked modernism and the avantgarde to the mindset of modernisation.

The Exhaustion of the Modernist Movement

Let me begin, then, with some brief remarks about the trajectory and migrations of the term 'postmodernism'. In literary criticism it goes back as far as the late 1950s when it was used by Irving Howe and Harry Levin to lament the levelling off of the modernist movement. Howe and Levin were looking back nostalgically to what already seemed like a richer past. 'Postmodernism' was first used emphatically in the 1960s by literary critics such as Leslie Fiedler and Ihab Hassan who held widely divergent views of what a postmodern literature was. It was only during the early and mid 1970s that the term gained a much wider currency, encompassing first architecture, then dance, theatre, painting, film and music. While the postmodern break with classical modernism was fairly visible in architecture and the visual arts, the notion of a postmodern rupture in literature has been much harder to ascertain. At some point in the late 1970s, 'postmodernism', not without American prodding, migrated to Europe via Paris and Frankfurt. Kristeva and Lyotard took it up in France, Habermas in Germany. In the United States, meanwhile, critics had begun to discuss the interface of postmodernism with French poststructuralism in its peculiar American adaptation, often simply on the assumption that the avantgarde in theory somehow had to be homologous to the avantgarde in literature and the arts. While scepticism about the feasibility of an artistic avantgarde was on the rise in the 1970s, the vitality of theory, despite its many enemies, never seemed in serious doubt. To some, indeed, it appeared as if the cultural energies that had fuelled the art movements of the 1960s were flowing during the 1970s into the body of theory, leaving the artistic enterprise high and dry. While such an observation is at best of impressionistic value and also not quite fair to the arts, it does seem reasonable to say that, with postmodernism's big-band logic of expansion irreversible, the maze of the postmodern became ever more impenetrable. By the early 1980s the modernism/postmodernism constellation in the arts and the modernity/postmodernity constellation in social theory had become one of the most contested terrains in the intellectual life of Western societies. And the terrain is contested precisely because there is so much more at stake than the existence or non-existence of a new artistic style, so much more also than just the 'correct' theoretical line.

Nowhere does the break with modernism seem more obvious than in recent American architecture. Nothing could be further from Mies van der Rohe's functionalist glass curtain walls than the gesture of random historical citation which prevails on so many postmodern facades. Take, for example, Philip Johnson's AT&T highrise, which is appropriately broken up into a neoclassical mid-section, Roman colonnades at the street level and a Chippendale pediment at the top. Indeed, a growing nostalgia for various life forms of the past seems to be a strong undercurrent in the culture of the 1970s and 1980s. And it is tempting to dismiss this historical eclecticism, found not only in architecture, but in the arts, in film, in literature and in the mass culture of recent years, as the cultural equivalent of the neo-conservative nostalgia for the good old days and as a manifest sign of the declining rate of creativity in late capitalism. But is this nostalgia for the past, the often frenzied and exploitative search for usable traditions, and the growing fascination with pre-modern and primitive cultures – is all of this rooted only in the cultural institutions' perpetual need for spectacle and frill, and thus perfectly compatible with the status quo? Or does it perhaps also express some genuine and legitimate dissatisfaction with modernity and the unquestioned belief in the perpetual modernisation of art? If the latter is the case, which I believe it is, then how can the search for alternative traditions, whether emergent or residual, be made culturally productive without yielding to the pressures of conservatism which, with a vicelike grip, lays claim to the very concept of tradition? I am not arguing here that all manifestations of the postmodern recuperation of the past are to be welcomed because somehow they are in tune with the Zeitgeist. I also don't want to be misunderstood as arguing that postmodernism's fashionable repudiation of the high modernist aesthetic and its boredom with the propositions of Marx and Freud, Picasso and Brecht, Kafka and Joyce, Schönberg and Stravinsky are somehow marks of a major cultural advance. Where postmodernism simply jettisons modernism it just yields to the cultural apparatus's demands that it legitimise itself as radically new, and it revives the philistine prejudices modernism faced in its own time.

But even if postmodernism's own propositions don't seem convincing – as embodied, for example, in the buildings by Philip Johnson, Michael Graves and others – that does not mean that continued adherence to an older set of modernist propositions would guarantee the emergence of more convincing buildings or works of art. The recent neo-conservative attempt to reinstate a domesticated version of modernism as the only worthwhile truth of twentieth-century culture – manifest for instance in the 1984 Beckmann exhibit in Berlin and in many articles in Hilton Kramer's *New Criterion* – is a strategy aimed at burying the political and aesthetic critiques of certain forms of modernism which have gained ground since the 1960s. But the problem with modernism is not just the fact that it can be integrated into a conservative ideology of art. After all, that already happened once on a major scale in the 1950s.[7] The larger problem we recognise today, it seems to me, is the closeness of various forms of modernism in its own time to the mindset of modernisation, whether in its capitalist or communist version. Of course, modernism was never a monolithic phenomenon, and it contained *both* the modernisation euphoria of futurism, constructivism and Neue Sachlichkeit and some of the starkest critiques of modernisation in the various modern forms of 'romantic anti-capitalism'.[8] The problem I address in this essay is not what modernism *really was*, but rather how it was perceived retrospectively, what dominant values and knowledge it carried, and how it functioned ideologically and culturally after World War II. It is a specific image of modernism that has become the bone of contention for the postmoderns, and that image has to be reconstructed if we want to understand postmodernism's problematic relationship to the modernist tradition and its claims to difference.

Architecture gives us the most palpable example of the issues at stake. The modernist utopia in the building programmes of the Bauhaus, of Mies, Gropius and Le Corbusier, was part of a heroic attempt after the Great War and the Russian Revolution to rebuild a war-ravaged Europe in the image of the new, and to make building a vital part of the envisioned renewal of society. A new Enlightenment demanded rational design for a rational society, but the new rationality was overlayed with a utopian fervour which ultimately made it veer back into myth – the myth of modernisation. Ruthless denial of the past was as much an essential component of the modern movement as its call for modernisation through standardisation and rationalisation. It is well-known how the modernist utopia shipwrecked on its own internal contradictions and, more importantly, on politics and history.[9] Gropius, Mies and others were forced into exile, Albert Speer took their place in Germany. After 1945, modernist architecture was largely deprived of its social vision and became increasingly an architecture of power and representation. Rather than standing as harbingers and promises of the new life, modernist housing projects became symbols of alienation and dehumanisation, a fate they shared with the assembly line, that other agent of the new which had been greeted with exuberant enthusiasm in the 1920s by Leninists and Fordists alike.

Charles Jencks, one of the most well-known popularising chroniclers of the agony of the modern movement and spokesman for a postmodern architecture, dates modern architecture's symbolic demise July 15, 1972 at 3.32 pm. At that time several slab blocks of St Louis's Pruitt-Igoe Housing (built by Minoru Yamasaki in the 1950s) were dynamited, and the collapse was dramatically displayed on the evening news. The modern machine for living, as Le Corbusier had called it with the technological euphoria so typical of the 1920s, had become unlivable, the modernist experiment, so it seemed, obsolete. Jencks takes pains to distinguish the initial vision of the modern movement from the sins committed in its name later on. And yet, on balance he agrees with those who, since the 1960s, have argued against modernism's hidden dependence on the machine metaphor and the production paradigm, and against its taking the factory as the primary model for all buildings. It has become commonplace in postmodernist circles to favour a reintroduction of mutivalent symbolic dimensions into architecture, a mixing of codes, an appropriation of local vernaculars and regional traditions.[10] Thus Jencks suggests that architects look two ways simultaneously, 'towards the traditional slow-changing codes and particular ethnic meanings of a neighbourhood, and towards the fast-changing codes of architectural fashion and professionalism.'[11] Such schizophrenia, Jencks holds, is symptomatic of the postmodern movement in architecture; and one might well ask whether it does not apply to contemporary culture at large, which increasingly seems to privilege what Bloch called *Ungleichzeitigkeiten* (non-synchronisms),[12] rather than favouring only what Adorno, the theorist of modernism par excellence, described as *der fortgeschrittenste Materialstand der Kunst* (the most advanced state of artistic material). Where such postmodern schizophrenia is creative tension resulting in ambitious and successful buildings, and where conversely, it veers off into an incoherent and arbitary shuffling of styles, will remain a matter of debate. We should also not forget that the mixing of codes, the appropriation of regional traditions and the uses of symbolic dimensions other than the machine were never entirely unknown to the architects of the International Style. In order to arrive at his postmodernism, Jencks ironically had to exacerbate the very view of modernist architecture which he persistently attacks.

One of the most telling documents of the break of postmodernism with the modernist dogma is a book coauthored by Robert Venturi, Denise Scott-Brown and Steven Izenour and entitled *Learning from Las Vegas*. Rereading this book and earlier writings by Venturi from the 1960s today,[13] one is struck by the proximity of Venturi's strategies and solutions to the pop sensibility of those years. Time and again the authors use pop art's break with the austere canon of high modernist painting and pop's uncritical espousal of the commercial vernacular of consumer culture as an inspiration for their work. What Madison Avenue was for Andy Warhol, what the comics and the Western were for Leslie Fielder, the landscape of Las Vegas was for Venturi and his group. The rhetoric of *Learning from Las Vegas* is predicated on the glorification of the billboard strip and of the ruthless shlock of casino culture. In Kenneth Frampton's ironic words, it offers a reading of Las Vegas as 'an authentic outburst of popular phantasy.'[14] I think it would be gratuitous to ridicule such odd notions of cultural populism today. While there is something patently absurd about such propositions, we have to acknowledge the power they mustered to explode the reified dogmas of modernism and to reopen a set of questions which the modernism gospel of the 1940s and 1950s had largely blocked from view: questions of ornament and metaphor in architecture, of figuration and realism in painting, of story and representation in literature, of the body in music and theatre. Pop in the broadest sense was the context in which a notion of the postmodern first took shape, and from the beginning until today, the most significant trends within postmodernism have challenged modernism's relentless hostility to mass culture.

Postmodernism in the 1960s: An American Avantgarde?

I will now suggest a historical distinction between the postmodernism of the 1960s and that of the 1970s and early 1980s. My argument will roughly be this: 1960s and 1970s postmodernism both rejected or criticised a certain version of modernism. Against the codified high modernism of the preceding decades, the postmodernism of the 1960s tried to revitalise the heritage of the European avantgarde and to give it an American form along what one could call in short-hand the Duchamp-Cage-Warhol axis. By the 1970s this avantgardist postmodernism of the 1960s had in turn exhausted its potential, even though some of its manifestations continued well into the new decade. What was new in the 1970s was, on the one hand, the emergence of a culture of eclecticism, a largely affirmative postmodernism which had abandoned any claim to critique, transgression or negation; and, on the other hand, an alternative postmodernism in which resistance, critique and negation of the status quo were redefined in non-modernist and non-avantgardist terms, terms which match the political developments in contemporary culture more effectively than the older theories of modernism. Let me elaborate.

What were the connotations of the term postmodernism in the 1960s? Roughly since the mid 1950s literature and the arts witnessed a rebellion of a new generation of artists such as Rauschenberg and Jasper Johns, Kerouac, Ginsberg and the Beats, Burroughs and Barthelme against the dominance of abstract expressionism, serial music and classical literary modernism.[15] The rebellion of the artists was soon joined by critics such as Susan Sontag, Leslie Fiedler and Ihab Hassan who all vigorously, though in very different ways and to a different degree, argued for the postmodern. Sontag advocated camp and a new sensibility, Fiedler sang the praise of popular literature and genital enlightenment, and Hassan – closer than the others to the moderns – advocated a 'literature of silence', trying to mediate between the 'tradition of the new' and post-war literary developments. By that time, modernism had of course been safely established as the canon in the academy, the museums and the gallery network. In that canon the New York School of abstract expressionism represented the epitome of that long trajectory of the modern which had begun in Paris in the 1850s and 1860s and which had inexorably led to New York – the American victory in culture following on the heels of the victory on the battlefields of World War II. By the 1960s artists and critics alike shared a sense of a fundamentally new situation. The assumed postmodern rupture with the past was felt as a loss: art and literature's claims to truth and human value seemed exhausted, the belief in the constitutive power of the modern imagination just another delusion. Or it was felt as a breakthrough towards an ultimate liberation of instinct and consciousness, onto the global village of McLuhanacy, the new Eden of polymorphous perversity, Paradise Now, as the Living Theater proclaimed it on stage. Thus critics of postmodernism such as Gerald Graff have correctly identified two strains of the postmodern culture of the 1960s: the apocalyptic desperate strain and the visionary celebratory strain, both of which, Graff claims, already existed within modernism.[16] While this is certainly true, it misses an important point. The ire of the postmodernists was directed not so much against modernism as such, but rather against a certain austere image of 'high modernism', as advanced by the New Critics and other custodians of modernist culture. Such a view, which avoids the false dichotomy of choosing either continuity or discontinuity, is supported by a retrospective essay by John Barth. In a 1980 piece in *The Atlantic*, entitled 'The Literature of Replenishment', Barth criticises his own 1968 essay 'The Literature of Exhaustion', which seemed at the time to offer an adequate summary of the apocalyptic strain. Barth now suggests that what his earlier piece was really about 'was the effective "exhaustion" not of language or of literature but of the aesthetic of high modernism.'[17] And he goes on to describe Beckett's *Stories and Texts for Nothing* and Nabokov's *Pale Fire* as late modernist marvels, distinct from such postmodernist writers as Italo Calvino and Gabriel Marquez. Cultural critics like Daniel Bell, on the other hand, would simply claim that the postmodernism of the 1960s was the 'logical culmination of modernist intentions',[18] a view which rephrases Lionel Trilling's despairing observation that the demonstrators of the 1960s were practising modernism in the streets. But my point here is precisely that high modernism had never seen fit to be in the streets in the first place, that its earlier undeniably adversary role was superseded in the 1960s by a very different culture of confrontation in the streets *and* in the art works, and that this culture of confrontation transformed inherited ideological notions of style, form and creativity, artistic autonomy and the imagination to which modernism had by then succumbed. Critics like Bell and Graff saw the rebellion of the late 1950s and the 1960s as continuous with modernism's earlier nihilistic and anarchic strain; rather than seeing it as a postmodernist revolt against classical modernism, they interpreted it as a profusion of modernist impulses into everyday life. And in some sense they were absolutely right, except that this 'success' of modernism fundamentally altered the terms of how modernist culture was to be perceived. Again, my argument here is that the revolt of the 1960s was never a rejection of modernism *per se*, but rather a revolt against that version of modernism which had been domesticated in the 1950s, become part of the liberal-conservative consensus of the times, and which had even been turned into a propaganda weapon in the cultural-political arsenal of Cold War anti-communism. The modernism against which artists rebelled was no longer felt to be an adversary culture. It no longer opposed a dominant class and its world view, nor had it maintained its programmatic purity from contamination by the culture industry. In other words, the revolt sprang precisely from the success of modernism, from the fact that in the United States, as in West Germany and France, for that matter, modernism had been perverted into a form of affirmative culture.

I would go on to argue that the global view which sees the 1960s as part of the modern movement extending from Manet and Baudelaire if not from romanticism, to the present is not able to account for the specifically American character of postmodernism. After all, the term accrued its emphatic connotations in the United States; not in Europe. I would even claim that it could not have been invented in Europe at the time. For a variety of reasons, it would not have made any sense there. West Germany was still busy rediscovering its own moderns who had been burnt and banned during the Third Reich. If anything, the 1960s in West Germany produced a major shift in evaluation and interest from one set of moderns to another: from Benn, Kafka and Thomas Mann to Brecht, the left expressionists and the political writers of the 1920s, from Heidegger and Jaspers to Adorno and Benjamin, from Schönberg and Webern to Eisler, from Kirchner and Beckmann to Grosz and Heartfield. It was a search for alternative cultural traditions within modernity and as such directed against the politics of a depoliticised version of modernism, which had come to provide much needed cultural legitimation for the

Adenauer restoration. During the 1950s, the myths of 'the golden twenties', the 'conservative revolution', and universal existentialist *Angst*, all helped block out and suppress the realities of the fascist past. From the depths of barbarism and the rubble of its cities, West Germany was trying to reclaim a civilised modernity and to find a cultural identity tuned to international modernism which would make others forget Germany's past as predator and pariah of the modern world. Given this context, neither the variations on modernism of the 1950s nor the struggle of the 1960s for alternative democratic and socialist cultural traditions could have possibly been construed as *post-modern*. The very notion of postmodernism has emerged in Germany only since the late 1970s and then not in relation to the culture of the 1960s, but narrowly in relation to recent architectural developments and, perhaps more importantly, in the context of the new social movements and their radical critique of modernity.[19]

In France, too, the 1960s witnessed a return to modernism rather than a step beyond it, even though for different reasons than in Germany, some of which I will discuss in the later section on poststructuralism. In the context of French intellectual life, the term 'postmodernism' was simply not around in the 1960s, and even today it does not seem to imply a major break with modernism as it does in the US.

I would now like to sketch four major characteristics of the early phase of postmodernism which all point to postmodernism's continuity with the international tradition of the modern, yes, but which – and this is my point – also establish American postmodernism as a movement *sui generis*.[20]

First, the postmodernism of the 1960s was characterised by a temporal imagination which displayed a powerful sense of the future and of new frontiers, of rupture and discontinuity, of crisis and generational conflict, an imagination reminiscent of earlier continental avantgarde movements such as dada and surrealism rather than of high modernism. Thus the revival of Marcel Duchamp as godfather of 1960s postmodernism is not historical accident. And yet, the historical constellation in which the postmodernism of the 1960s played itself out (from the Bay of Pigs and the civil rights movement to the campus revolts, the anti-war movement and the counter-culture) makes this avantgarde specifically American, even where its vocabulary of aesthetic forms and techniques was not radically new.

Secondly, the early phase of postmodernism included an iconoclastic attack on what Peter Bürger has tried to capture theoretically as the 'institution art'. By that term Bürger refers first and foremost to the ways in which art's role in society is perceived and defined, and secondly, to ways in which art is produced, marketed, distributed and consumed. In his book *Theory of the Avantgarde* Bürger has argued that the major goal of the historical European avantgarde (dada, early surrealism, the post-revolutionary Russian avantgarde[21]) was to undermine, attack and transform the bourgeois 'institution art' and its ideology of autonomy rather than only changing artistic and literary modes of representation. Bürger's approach to the question of art as institution in bourgeois society goes a long way towards suggesting useful distinctions between modernism and the avantgarde, distinctions which in turn can help us place the American avantgarde of the 1960s. In Bürger's account the European avantgarde was primarily an attack on the highness of high art and on art's separateness from everyday life as it had evolved in nineteenth-century aestheticism and its repudiation of realism. Bürger argues that the avantgarde attempted to reintegrate art and life or, to use his Hegelian-Marxist formula, to sublate art into life and he sees this reintegration attempt, I think correctly, as a major break with the aestheticist tradition of the later nineteenth century. The value of Bürger's account for contemporary American debates is that it permits us to distinguish different stages and different projects within the trajectory of the modern. The usual equation of the avantgarde with modernism can indeed no longer be maintained. Contrary to the avantgarde's intention to merge art and life, modernism always remained bound up with the more traditional notion of the autonomous art work, with the construction of form and meaning (however estranged or ambiguous, displaced or undecidable such meaning might be), and with the specialised status of the aesthetic.[22] The politically important point of Bürger's account for my argument about the 1960s is this: The historical avantgarde's iconoclastic attack on cultural institutions and on traditional modes of representation presupposed a society in which high art played an essential role in legitimising, hegemony, or, to put it in more neutral terms, to support a cultural establishment and its claims to aesthetic knowledge. It had been the achievement of the historical avantgarde to demystify and to undermine the legitimising discourse of high art in European society. The various modernisms of this century, on the other hand, have either maintained or restored versions of high culture, a task which was certainly facilitated by the ultimate and perhaps unavoidable failure of the historical avantgarde to reintegrate art and life. And yet, I would suggest that it was this specific radicalism of the avantgarde, directed against the institutionalisation of high art as a discourse of hegemony, that recommended itself as a source of energy and inspiration to the American postmodernists of the 1960s. Perhaps for the first time in American culture an avantgardist revolt against a tradition of high art and what was perceived as its hegemonic role made political sense. High art had indeed become institutionalised in the burgeoning museum, gallery, concert, record and paperback culture of the 1950s.

Modernism itself had entered the mainstream via mass reproduction and the culture industry. And, during the Kennedy years, high culture even began to take on functions of political representation with Robert Frost and Pablo Casals, Malraux and Stravinsky at the White House. The irony in all of this is that the first time the US had something resembling an 'institution art' in the emphatic European sense, it was modernism itself, the kind of art whose purpose had always been to resist institutionalisation. In the form of happenings, pop vernacular, psychedelic art, acid rock, alternative and street theatre, the postmodernism of the 1960s was groping to recapture the adversary ethos which had nourished modern art in its earlier stages, but which it seemed no longer able to sustain. Of course, the 'success' of the pop avantgarde, which itself had sprung full-blown from advertising in the first place, immediately made it profitable and thus sucked it into a more highly developed culture industry than the earlier European avantgarde ever had to contend with. But despite such cooption through commodification the pop avantgarde retained a certain cutting edge in its proximity to the 1960s culture of confrontation.[23] No matter how deluded about its potential effectiveness, the attack on the institution art was always also an attack on hegemonic social institutions, and the raging battles of the 1960s over whether or not pop was legitimate art prove the point.

Thirdly, many of the early advocates of postmodernism shared the technological optimism of segments of the 1920s avantgarde. What photography and film had been to Vertov and Tretyakov, Brecht, Heartfield and Benjamin in that period, television, video and the computer were for the prophets of a technological aesthetic in the 1960s. McLuhan's cybernetic and technocratic media eschatology and Hassan's praise for 'runaway technology', the 'boundless dispersal by media', 'the computer as substitute consciousness' – all of this combined easily with euphoric visions of a post-industrial society. Even if compared to the equally exuberant technological optimism of the 1920s, it is striking to see in retrospect how uncritically media technology and the cybernetic paradigm were espoused in the 1960s by conservatives, liberals and leftists alike.[24]

The enthusiasm for the new media leads me to the fourth trend within early postmodernism. There emerged a vigorous, though again largely uncritical attempt to validate popular culture as a challenge to the canon of high art, modernist or traditional. This 'populist' trend of the 1960s with its celebration of rock 'n roll and folk music, of the imagery of everyday life and of the multiple forms of popular literature gained much of its energy in the context of the counter-culture and by a next to total abandonment of an earlier American tradition of a critique of modern mass culture. Leslie Fiedler's incantation of the prefix 'post' in his essay 'The New Mutants' had an exhilarating effect at the time.[25] The postmodern harboured the promise of a 'post-white', 'post-male', 'post-humanist' 'post-Puritan' world. It is easy to see how all of Fielder's adjectives aim at the modernist dogma and at the cultural establishment's notion of what Western Civilisation was all about. Susan Sontag's camp aesthetic did much the same. Even though it was less populist, it certainly was as hostile to high modernism. There is a curious contradiction in all this. Fiedler's populism reiterates precisely that adversarial relationship between high art and mass culture which, in the accounts of Clement Greenberg and Theodor W Adorno, was one of the pillars of the modernist dogma Fielder had set out to undermine. Fiedler just takes his position on the other shore, opposite Greenberg and Adorno, as it were, validating the popular and pounding away at 'elitism'. And yet, Fiedler's call to cross the border and close the gap between high art and mass culture as well as his implied political critique of what later came to be called 'eurocentrism' and 'logocentrism' can serve as an important marker for subsequent developments within postmodernism. A new creative relationship between high art and certain forms of mass culture is, to my mind, indeed one of the major marks of difference between high modernism and the art and literature which followed it in the 1970s and 1980s both in Europe and the United States. And it is precisely the recent self-assertion of minority cultures and their emergence into public consciousness which has undermined the modernist belief that high and low culture have to be categorically kept apart; such rigorous segregation simply does not make much sense *within* a given minority culture which has always existed outside in the shadow of the dominant high culture.

In conclusion, I would say that from an American perspective the postmodernism of the 1960s had some of the makings of a genuine avantgarde movement, even if the overall political situation of 1960s America was in no way comparable to that of Berlin or Moscow in the early 1920s when the tenuous and short-lived alliance between avantgardism and vanguard politics was forged. For a number of historical reasons the ethos of artistic avantgardism as iconoclasm, as probing reflection upon the ontological status of art in modern society, as an attempt to forge another life was culturally not yet as exhausted in the US of the 1960s as it was in Europe at the same time. From a European perspective, therefore, it all looked like the endgame of the historical avantgarde rather than like the breakthrough to new frontiers it claimed to be. My point here is that American postmodernism of the 1960s was both: an American avantgarde *and* the endgame of international avantgardism. And I would go on to argue that it is indeed important for the cultural historian to analyse such *Ungleichzeitigkeiten* within modernity and to relate them to the very specific constellations and contexts of national and regional cultures and histories. The view that the culture of modernity is essentially internationalist – with its cutting edge moving in space and time from Paris in the later nineteenth and early twentieth centuries to Moscow and Berlin in the 1920s and to New York in the 1940s – is a view tied to a teleology of modern art whose unspoken subtext is the ideology of modernisation. It is precisely this teleology and ideology of modernisation which has become increasingly problematic in our postmodern age, problematic not so much perhaps in its descriptive powers relating to past events, but certainly in its normative claims.

Postmodernism in the 1970s and 1980s

In some sense, I might argue that what I have mapped so far is really the prehistory of the postmodern. After all, the term postmodernism only gained wide currency in the 1970s while much of the language used to describe the art, architecture and literature of the 1960s was still derived – and plausibly so – from the rhetoric of avantgardism and from what I have called the ideology of modernisation. The cultural developments of the 1970s, however, are sufficiently different to warrant a separate description. One of the major differences, indeed, seems to be that the rhetoric of avantgardism has faded fast in the 1970s so that one can speak perhaps only now of a genuinely post-modern and post-avantgarde culture. Even if, with the benefit of hindsight, future historians of culture were to opt for such a usage of the term, I would still argue that the adversary and critical element in the notion of postmodernism can only be fully grasped if one takes the late 1950s as the starting point of a mapping of the postmodern. If we were to focus only on the 1970s, the adversary moment of the post-modern would be much harder to work out precisely because of the shift within the trajectory of postmodernism that lies somewhere in the fault lines between 'the sixties' and 'the seventies'.

By the mid 1970s, certain basic assumptions of the preceding decade had either vanished or been transformed. The sense of a 'futurist revolt' (Fiedler) was gone. The iconoclastic gestures of the pop, rock and sex avantgardes seemed exhausted since their increasingly commercialised circulation had deprived them of their avantgardist status. The earlier optimism about technology, media and popular culture had given way to more sober and critical assessments: television as pollution rather than panacea. In the years of Watergate and the drawn-out agony of the Vietnam war, of the oil-shock and the dire predictions of the Club of Rome, it was indeed difficult to maintain the confidence and exuberance of the 1960s. Counter-culture, New Left and anti-war movement were ever more frequently denounced as infantile aberrations of American history. It was easy to see that the 1960s were over. But it is more difficult to describe the emerging cultural scene which seemed much more amorphous and scattered than that of the 1960s. One might begin by saying that the battle against the normative pressures of high modernism waged during the 1960s had been successful – too successful, some would argue. While the 1960s could still be discussed in terms of a logical sequence of styles (Pop, Op, Kinetic, Minimal, Concept) or in equally modernist terms of art versus anti-art and non-art, such distinctions have increasingly lost ground in the 1970s.

The situation in the 1970s seems to be characterised rather by an ever wider dispersal and dissemination of artistic practices all working out of the ruins of the modernist edifice, raiding it for ideas, plundering its vocabulary and supplementing it with randomly chosen images and motifs from pre-modern and non-modern cultures as well as from contemporary mass culture. Modernist styles have actually not been abolished, but, as one art critic recently observed, continue 'to enjoy a kind of half-life in mass culture',[26] for instance in advertising, record cover design, furniture and household items, science fiction illustration, window displays, etc. Yet another way of putting it would be to say that all modernist and avantgardist techniques, forms and images are now stored for instant recall in the computerised memory banks of our culture. But the same memory also stores all pre-modernist art as well as the genres, codes and image worlds of popular cultures and modern mass culture. How precisely these enormously expanded capacities for information storage, processing and recall have affected artists and their work remains to be analysed. But one thing seems clear: the great divide that separated high modernism from mass culture and that was codified in the various classical accounts of modernism no longer seems relevant to postmodern artistic or critical sensibilities.

Since the categorical demand for the uncompromising segregation of high and low has lost much of its persuasive power, we may be in a better position now to understand the political pressures and historical contingencies which shaped such accounts in the first place. I would suggest that the primary place of what I am calling the great divide was the age of Stalin and Hitler when the threat of totalitarian control over all culture forged a variety of defensive strategies meant to protect high culture in general, not just modernism. Thus conservative culture critics such as Ortega y Gasset argued that high culture needed to be protected from the 'revolt of the masses'. Left critics like Adorno insisted that genuine art resists its incorporation into the capitalist culture industry which he defined as the total administration of culture from above. And even Lukács, the left critic of modernism *par excellence*, developed his theory of high bourgeois realism not in unison with but in antagonism to the Zhdanovist dogma of socialist realism and its deadly practice of censorship.

It is surely no coincidence that the Western codification of modernism as canon of the twentieth century took place during the 1940s and 1950s, preceding and during the Cold War. I am not reducing the great modernist works, by way of a simple ideology critique of their function, to a ploy in the cultural strategies of the Cold War. What I am suggesting, however, is that the age of Hitler, Stalin and the Cold War produced specific accounts of modernism, such as those of Clement Greenberg and Adorno,[27] whose aesthetic categories cannot be totally divorced from the pressures of that era. And it is in this sense, I would argue, that the logic of modernism advocated by those critics has become an aesthetic dead end to the extent that it has been upheld as rigid guideline for further artistic production and critical evaluation. As against such dogma, the postmodern has indeed opened up new directions and new visions. As the confrontation between 'bad' socialist realism and the 'good' art of the free world began to lose its ideological momentum in an age of *détente*, the whole relationship between modernism and mass culture as well as the problem of realism could be reassessed in less reified terms. While the issue was already raised in the 1960s, eg, in pop art and various forms of documentary literature, it was only in the 1970s that artists increasingly drew on popular or mass cultural forms and genres, overlaying them with modernist and/or avantgardist strategies. A major body of work representing this tendency is the New German Cinema, and here especially the films of Rainer Werner Fassbinder, whose success in the United States can be explained precisely in those terms. It is also no coincidence that the diversity of mass culture was now recognised and analysed by critics who increasingly began to work themselves out from under the modernist dogma that all mass culture is monolithic Kitsch, psychologically regressive and mind-destroying. The possibilities for experimental meshing and mixing of mass culture and modernism seemed promising and produced some of the most successful and ambitious art and literature of the 1970s. Needless to say, it also produced aesthetic failures and fiascos, but then modernism itself did not only produce masterworks.

It was especially the art, writing, film making and criticism of women and minority artists with their recuperation of buried and mutilated traditions, their emphasis on exploring forms of gender- and race-based subjectivity in aesthetic productions and experiences, and their refusal to be limited to standard canonisations, which added a whole new dimension to the critique of high modernism and to the emergence of alternative forms of culture. Thus, we have come to see modernism's imaginary relationship to African and Oriental art as deeply problematic, and will approach, say, contemporary Latin American writers other than by praising them for being good modernists, who, naturally, learned their craft in Paris. Women's criticism has shed some new light on the modernist canon itself from a variety of different feminist perspectives. Without succumbing to the kind of feminine essentialism which is one of the more problematic sides of the feminist enterprise, it just seems obvious that were it not for the critical gaze of feminist criticism, the male determinations and obsessions of Italian futurism, vorticism, Russian constructivism, Neue Sachlichkeit or surrealism would probably still be blocked from our view; and the writings of Marie Luise Fleisser and Ingeborg Bachmann, the paintings of Frida Kahlo would still be known only to a handful of specialists. Of course such new insights can be interpreted in multiple ways, and the debate about gender and sexuality, male and female authorship and reader/ spectatorship in literature and the arts is far from over, its implications for a new image of modernism not yet fully elaborated.

In light of these developments it is somewhat baffling that feminist criticism has so far largely stayed away from the postmodernism debate which is considered not to be pertinent to feminist concerns. The fact that to date only male critics have addressed the problem of modernity/postmodernity, however, does not mean that it does not concern women. I would argue – and here I am in full agreement with Craig Owens[28] that women's art, literature and criticism are an important part of the postmodern culture of the 1970s and 1980s and indeed a measure of the vitality and energy of that culture. Actually, the suspicion is in order that the conservative turn of these past years has indeed something to do with the sociologically significant emergence of various forms of 'otherness' in the cultural sphere, all of which are perceived as a threat to the stability and sanctity of canon and tradition. Current attempts to restore a 1950s version of high modernism for the 1980s certainly point in that direction. And it is in this context that the question of neo-conservatism becomes politically central to the debate about the postmodern.

Habermas and the Question of Neo-Conservatism

Both in Europe and the US, the waning of the 1960s was accompanied by the rise of neo-conservatism, and soon enough there emerged a new constellation characterised by the terms postmodernism and neo-conservatism. Even though their relationship was never fully elaborated, the Left took them to be compatible with each other or even identical, arguing that postmodernism was the kind of affirmative art that could happily coexist with political and cultural neo-conservatism. Until very recently, the question of the postmodern was simply not taken seriously on the Left,[29] not to speak of those traditionalists in the academy or the museum for whom there is still nothing new and worthwhile under the sun since the advent of modernism. The Left's ridiculing of postmodernism was of a piece with its often haughty and dogmatic critique of the counter-cultural impulses of the 1960s. During much of the 1970s, after all, the trashing of the 1960s was as much a pastime of the Left as it was the gospel according to Daniel Bell.

Now, there is no doubt that much of what went under the label of postmodernism in the 1970s is indeed affirmative, not critical, in nature, and often, especially in literature, remarkably similar to tendencies of modernism which it so vocally repudiates. But not all of it is simply affirmative, and the wholesale writing off of postmodernism as a symptom of capitalist culture in decline is reductive, unhistorical and all too reminiscent of Lukács's attacks on modernism in the 1930s. Can one really make such clear-cut distinctions as to uphold modernism, today, as the only valid form of twentieth-century 'realism',[30] an art that is adequate to the *condition moderne*, while simultaneously reserving all the old epitheta – inferior, decadent, pathological – to postmodernism? And isn't it ironic that many of the same critics who will insist on this distinction are the first ones to declare emphatically that modernism already had it all and that there is really nothing new in postmodernism . . .

I would instead argue that in order not to become the Lukács of the postmodern by opposing, today, a 'good' modernism to a 'bad' postmodernism, we try to salvage the postmodern from its assumed total collusion with neo-conservatism wherever possible; and that we explore the question whether postmodernism might not harbour productive contradictions, perhaps even a critical and oppositional potential. If the postmodern is indeed a historical and cultural condition (however transitional or incipient), then oppositional cultural practices and strategies must be located *within* postmodernism, not necessarily in its gleaming facades, to be sure, but neither in some outside ghetto of a properly 'progressive' or a correctly 'aesthetic' art. Just as Marx analysed the culture of modernity dialectically as bringing both progress and destruction,[31] the culture of postmodernity, too, must be grasped in its gains as well as in its losses, in its promises as well as in its depravations; and yet, it may be precisely one of the characteristics of the postmodern that the relationship between progress and destruction of cultural forms, between tradition and modernity can no longer be understood today the same way Marx understood it as the dawn of modernist culture.

It was, of course, Jürgen Habermas's intervention which, for the first time, raised the question of postmodernism's relationship to neo-conservatism in a theoretically and historically complex way. Ironically, however, the effect of Habermas's argument, which identified the postmodern with various forms of conservatism, was to reinforce leftist cultural stereotypes rather than challenge them. In his 1980 Adorno prize lecture,[32] which has become a focal point for the debate, Habermas criticised both conservatism (old, neo and young) and postmodernism for not coming to terms either with the exigencies of culture in late capitalism or with the successes and failures of modernism itself. Significantly, Habermas's notion of modernity – the modernity he wishes to see continued and completed – is purged of modernism's nihilistic and anarchic strain just as his opponents', eg Lyotard's,[33] notion of an aesthetic (post)modernism is determined to liquidate any trace of the enlightened modernity inherited from the eighteenth century which provides the basis for Habermas's notion of modern culture. Rather than rehearsing the theoretical differences between Habermas and Lyotard one more time – a task which Martin Jay has performed admirably in a recent article on 'Habermas and Modernism'[34] – I want to point to the German context of Habermas's reflections which is too readily forgotten in American debates, since Habermas himself refers to it only marginally.

Habermas's attack on postmodern conservatisms took place on the heels of the political *Tendenzwende* of the mid 1970s, the conservative backlash which has affected several Western countries. He could cite an analysis of American neo-conservatism without even having to belabour the point that the neo-conservative strategies to regain cultural hegemony and to wipe out the effect of the 1960s in political and cultural life are very similar in the FRG. But the national contingencies of Habermas's argument are at least as important. He was writing at the tail end of a major thrust of modernisation of German cultural and political life which seemed to have gone awry sometime during the 1970s, producing high levels of disillusionment both with the utopian hopes and the pragmatic promises of 1968/69. Against the growing cynicism, which has then been brilliantly diagnosed and criticised in Peter Sloterdijk's *Kritik der zynischen Vernunft* as a form of 'enlightened false consciousness',[35] Habermas tries to salvage the emancipatory potential of enlightened reason which to him is the *sine qua non* of political democracy. Habermas defends a substantive notion of communicative rationality, especially against those who will collapse reason with domination, believing that by abandoning reason they free themselves from domination. Of course Habermas's whole project of a critical social theory revolves around a defence of enlightened modernity, which is *not* identical with the aesthetic modernism of literary critics and art historians. It is directed simultaneously against political conservatism (neo or old) and against what he perceives, not unlike Adorno, as the cultural irrationality of a post-Nietzschean aestheticism embodied in surrealism and subsequently in much of contemporary French theory. The defence of enlightenment in Germany is and remains an attempt to fend off the reaction from the Right.

During the 1970s, Habermas could observe how German art and literature abandoned the explicit political commitments of the 1960s, a decade often described in Germany as a 'second enlightenment'; how autobiography and *Erfahrungstexte* replaced the documentary experiments in prose and drama of the previous decade; how political poetry and art made way for a new subjectivity, a new romanticism, a new mythology; how a new generation of students and young intellectuals became increasingly weary of theory, left politics and social science, preferring instead to flock towards the revelations of ethnology and myth. Even though Habermas does not address the art and literature of the 1970s directly – with the exception of the late work of Peter Weiss, which is itself an exception – it seems not too much to assume that he interpreted this cultural shift in light of the political *Tendenzwende*. Perhaps his labelling of Foucault and Derrida as young conservatives is as much a response to German cultural developments as it is to the French theorists themselves. Such a speculation may draw plausibility from the fact that since the late 1970s, certain forms of French theory have been quite influential, especially in the subcultures of Berlin and Frankfurt, among those of the younger generation who have turned away from critical theory made in Germany.

It would be only a small step, then, for Habermas to conclude that a post-modern, post-avantgarde art indeed fits in all too smoothly with various forms of conservatism, and is predicated on abandoning the emancipatory project of modernity. But to me, there remains the question of whether these aspects of the 1970s – despite their occasionally high levels of self-indulgence, narcissism and false immediacy – do not also represent a deepening and a constructive displacement of the emancipatory impulses of the 1960s. But one does not have to share Habermas's positions on modernity and modernism to see that he did indeed raise the most important issues at stake in a form that avoided the usual apologies and facile polemics about modernity and post-modernity.

His questions were these: How does postmodernism relate to modernism? How are political conservatism, cultural eclecticism or pluralism, tradition, modernity and anti-modernity interrelated in contemporary Western culture? To what extent can the cultural and social formation of the 1970s be characterised as postmodern? And, further, to what extent is postmodernism a revolt against reason and enlightenment, and at what point do such revolts become reactionary – a question heavily loaded with the weight of recent German history? In comparison, the standard American accounts of postmodernism too often remain entirely tied to questions of aesthetic style or poetics; the occasional nod towards theories of a post-industrial society is usually intended as a reminder that any form of Marxist or neo-Marxist thought is simply obsolete. In the American debate, three positions can be schematically outlined. Postmodernism is dismissed outright as a fraud and modernism held up as the universal truth, a view which reflects the thinking of the 1950s. Or modernism is condemned as elitist and postmodernism praised as populist, a view which reflects the thinking of the 1960s. Or there is the truly 1970s proposition that 'anything goes', which is consumer capitalism's cynical version of 'nothing works',but which at least recognises that the older dichotomies no longer work. Inevitably, none of these positions ever reached the level of Habermas's interrogation.

However, there were problems not so much with the questions Habermas raised, as with some of the answers he suggested. Thus his attack on Foucault and Derrida as young conservatives drew immediate fire from poststructuralist quarters, where the reproach was turned around and Habermas himself was labelled a conservative. At this point, the debate was quickly reduced to the silly question: 'Mirror, mirror on the wall, who is the least conservative of us all?' And yet, the battle between 'Frankfurters and French fries', as Rainer Nägele once referred to it, is instructive because it highlights two fundamentally different visions of modernity. The French vision of modernity begins with Nietzsche and Mallarmé and is thus quite close to what literary criticism describes as modernism. Modernity for the French is primarily – though by no means exclusively – an aesthetic question relating to the energies released by the deliberate destruction of language and other forms of representation. For Habermas, on the other hand, modernity goes back to the best traditions of the Enlightenment which he tries to salvage and to reinscribe into the present philosophical discourse in a new form. In this, Habermas differs radically from an earlier generation of Frankfurt School critics, Adorno and Horkheimer who, in *The Dialectic of Enlightenment*, developed a view of modernity which seems to be much closer in sensibility to current French theory than to Habermas. But even though Adorno and Horkheimer's assessment of the enlightenment was so much more pessimistic than Habermas's,[36] they also held on to a substantive notion of reason and subjectivity which much of French theory has abandoned. It seems that in the context of the French discourse, enlightenment is simply identified with a history of terror and incarceration that reaches from the Jacobins via the *métarécits* of Hegel and Marx to the Soviet Gulag. I think Habermas is right in rejecting that view as too limited and as politically dangerous. Auschwitz, after all, did *not* result from too much enlightened reason – even though it was organised as a perfectly rationalised death factory – but from a violent anti-enlightenment and anti-modern affect, which exploited modernity ruthlessly for its own purposes. At the same time, Habermas's turn against the French post-Nietzschean vision of *modernité* as simply anti-modern or, as it were, postmodern, itself implies too limited an account of modernity, at least as far as aesthetic modernity is concerned.

In the uproar over Habermas's attack on the French poststructuralists, the American and European neo-conservatives were all but forgotten, but I think we should at least take cognisance of what cultural neo-conservatives actually say about postmodernism. The answer is fairly simple and straightforward: they reject it and they think it is dangerous. Two examples: Daniel Bell, whose book on the post-industrial society has been quoted time and again as supporting sociological evidence by advocates of postmodernism, actually rejects postmodernism as a dangerous popularisation of the modernist aesthetic. Bell's modernism only aims at aesthetic pleasure, immediate gratification and intensity of experience, all of which, to him, promote hedonism and anarchy. It is easy to see how such a jaundiced view of modernism is quite under the spell of those 'terrible' 1960s and cannot at all be reconciled with the austere high modernism of a Kafka, a Schönberg or a TS Eliot. At any rate, Bell sees modernism as something like an earlier society's chemical waste deposits which, during the 1960s, began to spill over, not unlike Love Canal, into the mainstream of culture, polluting it to the core. Ultimately, Bell argues in *The Cultural Contradictions of Capitalism*, modernism and postmodernism together are responsible for the crisis of contemporary capitalism.[37] Bell – a postmodernist? Certainly not in the aesthetic sense, for Bell actually shares Habermas's rejection of the nihilistic and aestheticist trend within modernist/ postmodernist culture. But Habermas may have been right in the broader political sense. For Bell's critique of contemporary capitalist culture is energised by a vision of a society in which the values and norms of everyday life would no longer be infected by aesthetic modernism, a society which, within Bell's framework, one might have to call post-modern. But any such reflection on neo-conservatism as a form of anti-liberal, anti-progressive postmodernity remains beside the point. Given the aesthetic force-field of the term postmodernism, no neo-conservative today would dream of identifying the neo-conservative project as postmodern.

On the contrary, cultural neo-conservatives often appear as the last-ditch defenders and champions of modernism. Thus in the editorial to the first issue of *The New Criterion* and in an accompanying essay entitled 'Postmodern: Art and Culture in the 1980s',[38] Hilton Kramer rejects the postmodern and counters it with a nostalgic call for the restoration of modernist standards of quality. Differences between Bell's and Kramer's accounts of modernism notwithstanding, their assessment of postmodernism is identical. In the culture of the 1970s, they will only see loss of quality, dissolution of the imagination, decline of standards and values and the triumph of nihilism. But their agenda is not art history. Their agenda is political. Bell argues that postmodernism 'undermines the social structure itself by striking at the motivational and psychic-reward system which has sustained it.'[39] Kramer attacks the politicisation of culture which, in his view, the 1970s have inherited from the 1960s, that 'insidious assault on the mind'. And like Rudi Fuchs and the 1982 Documenta, he goes on to shove art back into the closet of autonomy and high seriousness where it is supposed to uphold the new criterion of truth. Hilton Kramer – a postmodernist? No, Habermas was simply wrong, it seems, in his linkage of the post-modern with neo-conservatism. But again the situation is more complex than it seems. For Habermas, modernity means critique, enlightenment and human emancipation, and he is not willing to jettison this political impulse because doing so would terminate left politics once and for all. Contrary to Habermas, the neo-conservative resorts to an established tradition of standards and values which are immune to criticism and change. To Habermas, even Hilton Kramer's neo-conservative defence of a modernism deprived of its adversary cutting edge would have to appear as post-modern, post-modern in the sense of anti-modern. The question in all of this is absolutely not whether the classics of modernism are or are not great works of art. Only a fool could deny that they are. But a problem does surface when their greatness is used as unsurpassable model and appealed to in order to stifle contemporary artistic production. Where that happens, modernism itself is pressed into the service of anti-modern resentment, a figure of discourse which has a long history in the multiple *querelles des anciens et des modernes*.

The only place where Habermas could rest assured of neo-conservative applause is in his attack on Foucault and Derrida. Any such applause, however, would carry the proviso that neither Foucault nor Derrida be associated with conservatism. And yet, Habermas was right, in a sense, to connect the postmodernism problematic with poststructuralism. Roughly since the late 1970s, debates about aesthetic postmodernism and poststructuralist criticism have intersected in the US. The relentless hostility of neo-conservatives to both poststructuralism and postmodernism may not prove the point, but it is certainly suggestive. Thus the February 1984 issue of *The New Criterion* contains a report by Hilton Kramer on the Modern Language Association's centennial convention last December in New York, and the report is polemically entitled 'The MLA Centennial Follies'. The major target of the polemic is precisely French poststructuralism and its America appropriation. But the point is not the quality or the lack thereof in certain presentations at the convention. Again, the real issue is a political one. Deconstruction, feminist criticism, Marxist criticism, all lumped together as undesirable aliens, are said to have subverted American intellectual life via the academy. Reading Kramer, the cultural apocalypse seems near, and there would be no reason for surprise if *The New Criterion* were soon to call for an import quota on foreign theory.

What, then, can one conclude from these ideological skirmishes for a mapping of postmodernism in the 1970s and 1980s? First, Habermas was both right and wrong about the collusion of conservative political vision of a post-modern society freed from all aesthetic, ie, hedonistic, modernist and postmodernist subversions, or whether the issue is aesthetic postmodernism. Secondly, Habermas and the neo-conservatives are right in insisting that postmodernism is not so much a question of style as it is a question of politics and culture at large. The neo-conservative lament about the politicisation of culture since the 1960s is only ironic in this context since they themselves have a thoroughly political notion of culture. Thirdly, the neo-conservatives are also right in suggesting that there are continuities between the oppositional culture of the 1960s and that of the 1970s. But their obsessive fixation on the 1960s, which they try to purge from the history books, blinds them to what is different and new in the cultural developments of the 1970s. And, fourthly, the attack on poststructuralism by Habermas and the American neo-conservatives raises the question of what to make of that fascinating interweaving and intersecting of poststructuralism with postmodernism, a phenomenon that is much more relevant in the US than in France. It is to this question that I will now turn in my discussion of the critical discourse of American postmodernism in the 1970s and 1980s.

Poststructuralism: Modern or Postmodern?

The neo-conservative hostility towards both is not really enough to establish a substantive link between postmodernism and poststructuralism; and it may indeed be more difficult to establish such a link than it would seem at first. Certainly, since the late 1970s we have seen a consensus emerge in the US that if postmodernism represents the contemporary 'avantgarde' in the arts, poststructuralism must be its equivalent in 'critical theory'.[40] Such a parallelisation is itself favoured by theories and practices of textuality and intertextuality which blur the boundaries between the literary and the critical text, and thus it is not surprising that the names of the French *maîtres penseurs* of our time occur with striking regularity in the discourse on the postmodern.[41] On a superficial level, the parallels seem indeed obvious. Just as postmodern art and literature have taken the place of an earlier modernism as the major trend of our times, poststructuralist criticism has decisively passed beyond the tenets of its major predecessor, the New Criticism. And just as the New Critics championed modernism, so the story goes, poststructuralism – as one of the most vital forces of the intellectual life of the 1970s – must somehow be allied with the art and literature of its own time, ie, with postmodernism.[42] Actually, such thinking, which is quite prevalent if not always made explicit, gives us a first indication of how American postmodernism still lives in the shadow of the moderns. For there is no theoretical or historical reason to elevate the synchronism of the New Criticism with high modernism into norm or dogma. Mere simultaneity of critical and artistic discourse formations does not *per se* mean that they have to overlap, unless, of course, the boundaries between them are intentionally dismantled, as they are in modernist and postmodernist literature as well as in poststructuralist discourse.

And yet, however much postmodernism and poststructuralism in the US may overlap and mesh, they are far from identical or even homologous. I do not question that the theoretical discourse of the 1970s has had a profound impact on the work of a considerable number of artists both in Europe and in the US. What I do question, however, is the way in which this impact is automatically evaluated in the US as postmodern and thus sucked into the orbit of the kind of critical discourse that emphasises radical rupture and discontinuity. Actually, both in France and in the US, poststructuralism is much closer to modernism than is usually assumed by the advocates of postmodernism. The distance that does exist between the critical discourses of the New Criticism and poststructuralism (a constellation which is only pertinent in the US, not in France) is not identical with the differences between modernism and postmodernism. I will argue that poststructuralism is primarily a discourse of and about modernism,[43] and that if we are to locate the postmodern in poststructuralism it will have to be found in the ways various forms of poststructuralism have opened up new problematics in modernism and have reinscribed modernism into the discourse formations of our own time.

Let me elaborate my view that poststructuralism can be perceived, to a significant degree, as a theory of modernism. I will limit myself here to certain points that relate back to my discussion of the modernism/postmodernism constellation in the 1960s and 1970s: the questions of aestheticism and mass culture, subjectivity and gender.

If it is true that postmodernity is a historical condition making it sufficiently unique and different from modernity, then it is striking to see how deeply the poststructuralist critical discourse – in its obsession with *écriture* and writing, allegory and rhetoric, and in its displacement of revolution and politics to the aesthetic – is embedded in that very modernist tradition which, at least in American eyes, it presumably transcends. What we find time and again is that American poststructuralist writers and critics emphatically privilege aesthetic innovation and experiment; that they call for self-reflexiveness, not, to be sure, of the author-subject, but of the text; that they purge life, reality, history, society from the work of art and its reception, and construct a new autonomy, based on a pristine notion of textuality, a new art for art's sake which is presumably the only kind possible after the failure of all and any commitment. The insight that the subject is constituted in language and the notion that there is nothing outside the text has led to the privileging of the aesthetic and the linguistic which aestheticism has always promoted to justify its imperial claims. The list of 'no longer possibles' (realism, representation, subjectivity, history, etc, etc) is as long in poststructuralism as it used to be in modernism, and it is very similar indeed.

Much recent writing has challenged the American domestication of French poststructuralism.[44] But it is not enough to claim that in the transfer to the US, French theory lost the political edge it has in France. The fact is that even in France the political implications of certain forms of poststructuralism are hotly debated and in doubt.[45] It is not just the institutional pressures of American literary criticism which have depoliticised French theory; the aestheticist trend *within* poststructuralism itself has facilitated the peculiar American reception. Thus it is no coincidence that the politically weakest body of French writing (Derrida and the late Barthes) has been privileged in American literature departments over the more politically intended projects of Foucault and Baudrillard, Kristeva and Lyotard. But even in the more politically conscious and self-conscious theoretical writing in France, the tradition of modernist aestheticism – mediated through an extremely selective reading of Nietzsche – is so powerful a presence that the notion of a radical rupture between the modern and the postmodern cannot possibly make much sense. It is furthermore striking that despite the considerable differences between the various poststructuralist projects, none of them seems informed in any substantial way by postmodernist works of art. Rarely, if ever, do they even address postmodernist works. In itself, this does not vitiate the power of the theory. But it does make for a kind of dubbing where the poststructuralist language is not in sync with the lips and movements of the postmodern body. There is no doubt that centre stage in critical theory is held by the classical modernists: Flaubert, Proust and Bataille in Barthes; Nietzsche and Heidegger, Mallarmé and Artaud in Derrida; Nietzsche, Magritte and Bataille in Foucault; Mallarmé and Lautréamont, Joyce and Artaud in Kristeva; Freud in Lacan; Brecht in Althusser and Macherey, and so on *ad infinitum*. The enemies still are realism and representation, mass culture and standardisation, grammar, communication and the presumably all-powerful homogenising pressures of the modern State.

I think we must begin to entertain the notion that rather than offering a *theory of postmodernity* and developing an analysis of contemporary culture, French theory provides us primarily with an *archeology of modernity*, a theory of modernism at the stage of its exhaustion. It is as if the creative powers of modernism had migrated into theory and come to full self-consciousness in the poststructuralist text – the owl of Minerva spreading its wings at the fall of dusk. Poststructuralism offers a theory of modernism characterised by *Nachträglichkeit*, both in the psychoanalytic and the historical sense. Despite its ties to the tradition of modernist aestheticism, it offers a reading of modernism which differs substantially from those offered by the New Critics, by Adorno or by Greenberg. It is no longer the modernism of 'the age of anxiety', the ascetic and tortured modernism of a Kafka, a modernism of negativity and alienation, ambiguity and abstraction, the modernism of the closed and finished work of art. Rather, it is a modernism of playful transgression, of an unlimited weaving of textuality, a modernism all confident in its rejection of representation and reality, in its denial of the subject, of history, and of the subject of history; a modernism quite dogmatic in its rejection of presence and in its unending praise of lacks and absences, deferrals and traces which produce, presumably, not anxiety but, in Roland Barthes's terms, *jouissance*, bliss.[46]

But if poststructuralism can be seen as the *revenant* of modernism in the guise of theory, then that would also be precisely what makes it postmodern. It is a postmodernism that works itself out not as a rejection of modernism, but rather as a retrospective reading which, in some cases, is fully aware of modernism's limitations and failed political ambitions. The dilemma of modernism had been its inability, despite the best intentions, to mount an effective critique of bourgeois modernity and modernisation. The fate of the historical avantgarde especially had proven how modern art, even where it ventured beyond art for art's sake, was ultimately forced back into the aesthetic realm. Thus the gesture of poststructuralism, to the extent that it abandons all pretence to a critique that would go beyond language games, beyond epistemology and the aesthetic, seems at least plausible and logical. It certainly frees art and literature from that overload of responsibilities – to change life, change society, change the world – on which the historical avantgarde shipwrecked, and which lived on in France through the 1950s and 1960s embodied in the figure of Jean Paul Sartre. Seen in this light, poststructuralism seems to seal the fate of the modernist project which, even where it limited itself to the aesthetic sphere, always upheld a vision of a redemption of modern life through culture. That such visions are no longer possible to sustain may be at the heart of the postmodern condition, and it may ultimately vitiate the poststructuralist attempt to salvage aesthetic modernism for the late twentieth century. At any rate, it all begins to ring false when poststructuralism presents itself, as it frequently does in American writings, as the latest 'avantgarde' in criticism, thus ironically assuming, in its institutional *Selbstverständnis*, the kind of teleological posturing which poststructuralism itself has done so much to criticise.

But even where such pretence to academic avantgardism is not the issue, one may well ask whether the theoretically sustained self-limitation to language and textuality has not been too high a price to pay; and whether it is not this self-limitation (with all it entails) which makes this poststructuralist modernism look like the atrophy of an earlier aestheticism rather than its innovative transformation. I say atrophy because the turn-of-the-century European aestheticism could still hope to establish a realm of beauty in opposition to what it perceived as the vulgarities of everyday bourgeois life, an artificial paradise thoroughly hostile to official politics and the kind of jingoism known in Germany as *Hurrapatriotismus*. Such an adversary function of aestheticism, however, can hardly be maintained at a time when capital itself has taken the aesthetic straight into the commodity in the form of styling, advertising and packaging. In an age of commodity aesthetics, aestheticism itself has become questionable either as an adversary or as a hibernating strategy. To insist on the adversary function of *écriture* and of breaking linguistic codes when every second ad bristles with domesticated avantgardist and modernist strategies strikes me as caught precisely in that very overestimation of art's transformative function for society which is the signature of an earlier, modernist, age. Unless, of course *écriture* is merely practiced as a glass bead game in happy, resigned, or cynical isolation from the realm the uninitiated keep calling reality.

Take the later Roland Barthes.[47] His *The Pleasure of the Text* has become a major, almost canonical formulation of the postmodern for many American literary critics who may not want to remember that already twenty years ago Susan Sontag had called for an erotics of art intended to replace the stuffy and stifling project of academic interpretation. Whatever the differences between Barthes's *jouissance* and Sontag's erotics (the rigours of New Criticism and structuralism being the respective *Feindbilder*), Sontag's gesture, at the time, was a relatively radical one precisely in that it insisted on presence, on a sensual experience of cultural artifacts; in that it attacked rather than legitimised a socially sanctioned canon whose prime values were objectivity and distance, coolness and irony; and in that it licensed the flight from the lofty horizons of high culture into the netherlands of pop and camp.

Barthes, on the other hand, positions himself safely within high culture and the modernist canon, maintaining equal distance from the reactionary Right which champions anti-intellectual pleasures and the pleasure of anti-intellectualism, and the boring Left which favours knowledge, commitment, combat, and disdains hedonism. The Left may indeed have forgotten, as Barthes claims, the cigars of Marx and Brecht.[48] But however convincing cigars may or may not be as signifiers of hedonism, Barthes himself certainly forgets Brecht's constant and purposeful immersion in popular and mass culture. Barthes's very un-Brechtian distinction between *plaisir* and *jouissance* – which he simultaneously makes and unmakes[49] – reiterates one of the most tired topoi of the modernist aesthetic and of bourgeois culture at large: there are the lower pleasures for the rabble, ie, mass culture, and then there is the *nouvelle cuisine* of the pleasure of the text, of *jouissance*. Barthes himself describes *jouissance* as a 'mandarin praxis',[50] as a conscious retreat, and he describes modern mass culture in the most simplistic terms as petit-bourgeois. Thus his appraisal of *jouissance* depends on the adoption of that traditional view of mass culture that the Right and the Left, both of which he so emphatically rejects, have shared over the decades.

This becomes even more explicit in *The Pleasure of the Text* where we read: 'The bastard form of mass culture is humiliated repetition: content, ideological schema, the blurring of contradictions – these are repeated, but the superficial forms are varied: always new books, new programmes, new films, news items, but always the same meaning.'[51] Word for word, such sentences could have been written by Adorno in the 1940s. But, then, everybody knows that Adorno's was a theory of modernism, not of postmodernism. Or was it? Given the ravenous eclecticism of postmodernism, it has recently become fashionable to include even Adorno and Benjamin into the canon of postmodernists *avant la lettre* – truly a case of the critical text writing itself without the interference of any historical consciousness whatsoever. Yet the closeness of some of Barthes's basic propositions to the modernist aesthetic could make such a rapprochement plausible. But then one might want to stop talking of postmodernism altogether, and take Barthes's writing for what it is: a theory of modernism which manages to turn the dung of post-68 political disillusionment into the gold of aesthetic bliss. The melancholy science of Critical Theory has been transformed miraculously into a new 'gay science', but it still is, essentially, a theory of modernist literature.

Barthes and his American fans ostensibly reject the modernist notion of negativity replacing it with play, bliss, *jouissance*, ie, with a critical form of affirmation. But the very distinction between the *jouissance* provided by the modernist, 'writerly' text and the mere pleasure (*plaisir*) provided by 'the text that contents, fills, grants euphoria',[52] reintroduces, through the back door, the same high culture/low culture divide and the same type of evaluations which were constitutive of classical modernism. The negativity of Adorno's aesthetic was predicated on the consciousness of the mental and sensual depravations of modern mass culture and on his relentless hostility to a society which needs such depravation to reproduce itself. The euphoric American appropriation of Barthes's *jouissance* is predicated on ignoring such problems and enjoying, not unlike the 1984 yuppies, the pleasures of writerly connoisseurship and textual gentrification. That, indeed, may be a reason why Barthes has hit a nerve in the American academy of the Reagan years, making him the favourite son who has finally abandoned his earlier radicalism and come to embrace the finer pleasures of life, pardon, the text.[53] But the problems with the older theories of a modernism of negativity are not solved by somersaulting from anxiety and alienation into the bliss of *jouissance*. Such a leap diminishes the wrenching experiences of modernity articulated in modernist art and literature; it remains bound to the modernist paradigm by way of simple reversal; and it does very little to elucidate the problem of the postmodern.

Just as Barthes's theoretical distinctions between *plaisir* and *jouissance*, the readerly and the writerly text, remain within the orbit of modernist aesthetics, so the predominant poststructuralist notions about authorship and subjectivity reiterate propositions known from modernism itself. A few brief comments will have to suffice.

In a discussion of Flaubert and the writerly, ie, modernist, text, Barthes writes: 'He [Flaubert] does not stop the play of codes (or stops it only partially), so that (and this is indubitably the proof of writing) *one never knows if he is responsible for what he writes* (if there is a subject *behind* his language); for the very being of writing (the meaning of the labour that constitutes it) is to keep the question *Who is speaking?* from ever being answered.'[54] A similarly prescriptive denial of authorial subjectivity underlies Foucault's discourse analysis. Thus Foucault ends his influential essay 'What is an Author?' by asking rhetorically 'What matter who's speaking?' Foucault's 'murmur of indifference'[55] affects both the writing and the speaking subject, and the argument assumes its full polemical force with the much broader anti-humanist proposition, inherited from structuralism, of the 'death of the subject'. But none of this is more than a further elaboration of the modernist critique of traditional idealist and romantic notions of authorship and authenticity, originality and intentionality, self-centred subjectivity and personal identity. More importantly, it seems to me that as a postmodern, having gone through the modernist purgatory, I would ask different questions. Isn't the 'death of the subject/author' position tied by mere reversal to the very ideology that invariably glorifies the artist as genius, whether for marketing purposes or out of conviction and habit? Hasn't capitalist modernisation itself fragmented and dissolved bourgeois subjectivity and authorship, thus making attacks on such notions somewhat quixotic? And finally, doesn't poststructuralism, where it simply denies the subject altogether, jettison the chance of challenging the *ideology of the subject* (as male, white and middle-class) by developing alternative and different notions of subjectivity?

To reject the validity of the question Who is writing? or Who is speaking? is simply no longer a radical position in 1984. It merely duplicates on the level of aesthetics and theory what capitalism as a system of exchange relations produces tendentially in everyday life: the denial of subjectivity in the very process of its construction. Poststructuralism thus attacks the appearance of capitalist culture – individualism writ large – but misses its essence; like modernism, it is always also in sync with rather than opposed to the real processes of modernisation.

The postmoderns have recognised this dilemma. They counter the modernist litany of the death of the subject by working towards new theories and practices of speaking, writing and acting subjects.[56] The question of how codes, texts, images and other cultural artifacts constitute subjectivity is increasingly being raised as an always already historical question. And to raise the question of subjectivity at all no longer carries the stigma of being caught in the trap of bourgeois or petit-bourgeois ideology; the discourse of subjectivity has been cut loose from its moorings in bourgeois individualism. It is certainly no accident that questions of subjectivity and authorship have resurfaced with a vengeance in the postmodern text. After all, it *does* matter who is speaking or writing.

Summing up, then, we face the paradox that a body of theories of modernism and modernity, developed in France since the 1960s, has come to be viewed, in the US, as the embodiment of the postmodern theory. In a certain sense, this development is perfectly logical. Poststructuralism's readings of modernism are new and exciting enough to be considered somehow beyond modernism as it has been perceived before; in this way poststructuralist criticism in the US yields to the very real pressures of the postmodern. But against any facile conflation of poststructuralism with the postmodern, we must insist on the fundamental non-identity of the two phenomena. In America, too, poststructuralism offers a theory of modernism, not a theory of the postmodern.

As to the French theorists themselves, they rarely speak of the postmodern. Lyotard's *La Condition postmoderne*, we must remember, is the exception not the rule.[57] What the French explicitly analyse and reflect upon is *le texte moderne* and *la modernité*. Where they talk about the postmodern at all, as in the cases of Lyotard and Kristeva,[58] the question seems to have been prompted by American friends, and the discussion almost immediately and invariably turns back to problems of the modernist aesthetic. For Kristeva, the question of postmodernism is the question of how anything can be written in the twentieth century and how we can talk about this writing. She goes on to say that postmodernism is 'that literature which writes itself with the more or less conscious intention of expanding the signifiable and thus the human realm.'[59] With the Bataillean formulation of writing-as-experience of limits, she sees the major writing since Mallarmé and Joyce, Artaud and Burroughs as the 'exploration of the typical imaginary relationship, that to the mother, through the most radical and problematic aspect of this relationship, language.'[60] Kristeva's is a fascinating and novel approach to the question of modernist literature, and one that understands itself as a political intervention. But it does not yield much for an exploration of the differences between modernity and postmodernity. Thus it cannot surprise that Kristeva still shares with Barthes and the classical theorists of modernism an aversion to the media whose function, she claims, is to collectivise all systems of signs thus enforcing contemporary society's general tendency towards uniformity.

Lyotard, who like Kristeva and unlike the deconstructionists is a political thinker, defines the postmodern, in his essay, 'Answering the Question: What is Postmodernism?'. as a recurring stage within the modern itself. He turns to the Kantian sublime for a theory of the nonrepresentable essential to modern art and literature. Paramount are his interest in rejecting representation, which is linked to terror and totalitarianism, and his demand for radical experimentation in the arts. At first sight, the turn to Kant seems plausible in the sense that Kant's autonomy aesthetic and notion of 'disinterested pleasure' stand at the threshold of a modernist aesthetic, at a crucial juncture of that differentiation of spheres which has been so important in social thought from Weber to Habermas. And yet, the turn to Kant's sublime forgets that the eighteenth-century fascination with the sublime of the universe, the cosmos, expresses precisely that very desire of totality and representation which Lyotard so abhors and persistently criticises in Habermas's work.[61] Perhaps Lyotard's text says more here than it means to. If historically the notion of the sublime harbours a secret desire for totality, then perhaps Lyotard's sublime can be read as an attempt to totalise the aesthetic realm by fusing it with all other spheres of life, thus wiping out the differentiations between the aesthetic realm and the life-world on which Kant did after all insist. At any rate, it is no coincidence that the first moderns in Germany, the Jena romantics, built their aesthetic strategies of the fragment precisely on a rejection of the sublime which had to them become a sign of the falseness of bourgeois accommodation to absolutist culture. Even today, the sublime has not lost its link with terror which, in Lyotard's reading, it opposes. For what would be more sublime and unrepresentable than the nuclear holocaust, the bomb being the signifier of an ultimate sublime. But apart from the question whether or not the sublime is an adequate aesthetic category to theorise contemporary art and literature, it is clear that in Lyotard's essay the postmodern as aesthetic phenomenon is not seen as distinct from modernism. The crucial historical distinction which Lyotard offers in *La Condition postmoderne* is that between the *métarécits* of liberation (the French tradition of enlightened modernity) and of totality (the German Hegelian/Marxist tradition) on the one hand, and the modernist experimental discourse of language games on the other. Enlightened modernity and its presumable consequences are pitted against aesthetic modernism. The irony in all of this, as Fred Jameson has remarked,[62] is that Lyotard's commitment to radical experimentation is politically 'very closely related to the conception of the revolutionary nature of high modernism that Habermas faithfully inherited from the Frankfurt School'.

No doubt, there are historically and intellectually specific reasons for the French resistance to acknowledging the problem of the postmodern as a historical problem of the twentieth century. At the same time, the force of the French rereading of modernism proper is itself shaped by the pressures of the 1960s and 1970s, and it has thus raised many of the questions pertinent to the culture of our own time. But it has done very little towards illuminating an emerging postmodern culture, and it has largely remained blind to or uninterested in many of the most promising artistic endeavours today. French theory of the 1960s and 1970s has offered us exhilarating fireworks which illuminate a crucial segment of the trajectory of modernism, but, as appropriate with fireworks, after dusk has fallen. This view is borne out by none less than Michel Foucault who, in the late 1970s, criticised his own earlier fascination with language and epistemology as a limited project of an earlier decade: 'The whole relentless theorisation of writing which we saw in the 1960s was doubtless only a swansong.'[63] Swansong of modernism indeed; but as such already a moment of the postmodern. Foucault's view of the intellectual movement of the 1960s as a swansong, it seems to me, is closer to the truth than its American rewriting, during the 1970s, as the latest avantgarde.

Whither Postmodernism?

The cultural history of the 1970s still has to be written, and the various postmodernisms in art, literature, dance, theatre, architecture, film, video, and music will have to be discussed separately and in detail. All I want to do now is to offer a framework for relating some recent cultural and political changes to postmodernism, changes which already lie outside the conceptual network of 'modernism/avantgardism' and have so far rarely been included in the postmodernism debate.[64]

I would argue that the contemporary arts – in the widest possible sense, whether they call themselves postmodernist or reject that label – can no longer be regarded as just another phase in the sequence of modernist and avantgardist movements which began in Paris in the 1850s and 1860s and which maintained an ethos of cultural progress and vanguardism through the 1960s. On this level, postmodernism cannot be regarded simply as a sequel to modernism, as the latest step in the never ending revolt of modernism against itself. The postmodern sensibility of our time is different both from modernism *and* avantgardism precisely in that it raises the question of cultural tradition and conservation in the most fundamental way as an aesthetic and a political issue. It doesn't always do it successfully, and often does it exploitatively. And yet, my main point about contemporary postmodernism is that it operates in a field of tension between tradition and innovation, conservation and renewal, mass culture and high art, in which the second terms are no longer automatically privileged over the first; a field of tension which can no longer be grasped in categories such as progress vs reaction, Left vs Right, present vs past, modernism vs realism, abstraction vs representation, avantgarde vs Kitsch. The fact that such dichotomies, which after all are central to the classical accounts of modernism, have broken down is part of the shift I have been trying to describe. I could also state the shift in the following terms: Modernism and the avantgarde were always closely related to social and industrial modernisation. They were related to it as an adversary culture, yes, but they drew their energies, not unlike Poe's *Man of the Crown*, from their proximity to the crises brought about by modernisation and progress. Modernisation – such was the widely held belief, even when the word was not around – had to be traversed. There was a vision of emerging on the other side. The modern was a world-scale drama played out on the European and American stage, with mythic modern man as its hero and with modern art as a driving force, just as Saint-Simon had envisioned it already in 1825. Such heroic visions of modernity and of art as a force of social change (or, for that matter, resistance to undesired change) are a thing of the past, admirable for sure, but no longer in tune with current sensibilities, except perhaps with an emerging apocalyptic sensibility as the flip side of modernist heroism.

Seen in this light, postmodernism at its deepest level represents not just another crisis within the perpetual cycle of boom and bust, exhaustion and renewal, which has characterised the trajectory of modernist culture. It rather represents a new type of crisis *of* that modernist culture itself. Of course, this claim has been made before, and fascism indeed was a formidable crisis *of* modernist culture. But fascism was never the alternative to modernity it pretended to be, and our situation today is very different from that of the Weimar Republic in its agony. It was only in the 1970s that the historical limits of modernism, modernity and modernisation came into sharp focus. The growing sense that we are not bound to *complete* the project of modernity (Habermas's phrase) and still do not necessarily have to lapse into irrationality or into apocalyptic frenzy, the sense that art is not exclusively pursuing some telos of abstraction, non-representation and sublimity – all of this has opened up a host of possibilities for creative endeavours today. And in certain ways it has altered our views of modernism itself. Rather than being bound to a one-way history of modernism which interprets it as a logical unfolding towards some imaginary goal, and which thus is based on a whole series of exclusions, we are beginning to explore its contradictions and contingencies, its tensions and internal resistances to its own 'forward' movement. Postmodernism is far from making modernism obsolete. On the contrary, it casts a new light on it and appropriates many of its aesthetic strategies and techniques inserting them and making them work in new constellations. What has become obsolete, however, are those codifications of modernism in critical discourse which, however subliminally, are based on a teleological view of progress and modernisation. Ironically, these normative and often reductive codifications have actually prepared the ground for that repudiation of modernism which goes by the name of the postmodern. Confronted with the critic who argues that this or that novel is not up to the latest in narrative technique, that it is regressive, behind the times and thus uninteresting, the postmodernist is right in rejecting modernism. But such rejection affects only that trend within modernism which has been codified into a narrow dogma, not modernism as such. In some ways, the story of modernism and postmodernism is like the story of the hedgehog and the hare: the hare could not win because there always was more than just one hedgehog. But the hare was still the better runner . . .

The crisis of modernism is more than just a crisis of those trends within it which tie it to the ideology of modernisation. In the age of late capitalism, it is also a new crisis of art's relationship to society. At their most emphatic, modernism and avantgardism attributed to art a privileged status in the processes of social change. Even the aestheticist withdrawal from the concern of social change is still bound to it by virtue of its denial of the status quo and the construction of an artificial paradise of exquisite beauty. When social change seemed beyond grasp or took an undesired turn, art was still privileged as the only authentic voice of critique and protest, even when it seemed to withdraw into itself. The classical accounts of high modernism attest to that fact. To admit that these were heroic illusions – perhaps even necessary illusions in art's struggle to survive in dignity in a capitalist society – is not to deny the importance of art in social life.

But modernism's running feud with mass society and mass culture as well as the avantgarde's attack on high art as a support system of cultural hegemony always took place on the pedestal of high art itself. And certainly that is where the avantgarde has been installed after its failure, in the 1920s, to create a more encompassing space for art in social life. To continue to demand today that high art leave the pedestal and relocate elsewhere (wherever that might be) is to pose the problem in obsolete terms. The pedestal of high art and high culture no longer occupies the privileged space it used to, just as the cohesion of the class which erected its monuments on that pedestal is a thing of the past; recent conservative attempts in a number of Western countries to restore the dignity of the classics of Western Civilisation, from Plato via Adam Smith to the high modernists, and to send students back to the basics, prove the point. I am not saying here that the pedestal of high art does not exist any more. Of course it does, but it is not what it used to be. Since the 1960s, artistic activities have become much more diffuse and harder to contain in safe categories or stable institutions such as the academy, the museum or even the established gallery network. To some, this dispersal of cultural and artistic practices and activities will involve a sense of loss and disorientation; others will experience it as a new freedom, a cultural liberation. Neither may be entirely wrong, but we should recognise that it was not only recent theory or criticism that deprived the univalent, exclusive and totalising accounts of modernism and of their hegemonic role. It was the activities of artists, writers, film makers, architects, and performers that have propelled us beyond a narrow vision of modernism and given us a new lease on modernism itself.

In political terms, the erosion of the triple dogma modernism/modernity/avantgardism can be contextually related to the emergence of the problematic of 'otherness', which has asserted itself in the socio-political sphere as much as in the cultural sphere. I cannot discuss here the various and multiple forms of otherness as they emerge from differences in subjectivity, gender and sexuality, race and class, temporal *Ungleichzeitigkeiten* and spatial geographic locations and dislocations. But I want to mention at least four recent phenomena which, in my mind, are and will remain constitutive of postmodern culture for some time to come.

Despite all its noble aspirations and achievements, we have come to recognise that the culture of enlightened modernity has also always (though by no means exclusively) been a culture of inner and outer imperialism, a reading already offered by Adorno and Horkheimer in the 1940s and an insight not unfamiliar to those of our ancestors involved in the multitude of struggles against rampant modernisation. Such imperialism, which works inside and outside, on the micro and macro levels, no longer goes unchallenged either politically, economically or culturally. Whether these challenges will usher in a more habitable, less violent and more democratic world remains to be seen, and it is easy to be sceptical. But enlightened cynicism is as insufficient an answer as blue-eyed enthusiasm for peace and nature.

The women's movement has led to some significant changes in social structure and cultural attitudes which must be sustained even in the face of the recent grotesque revival of American machismo. Directly and indirectly, the women's movement has nourished the emergence of women as a self-confident and creative force in the arts, in literature, film and criticism. The ways in which we now raise questions of gender and sexuality, reading and writing, subjectivity and enunciation, voice and performance are unthinkable without the impact of feminism, even though many of these activities may take place on the margin or even outside the movement proper. Feminist critics have also contributed substantially to revisions of the history of modernism, not just by unearthing forgotten artists, but also by approaching the male modernists in novel ways. This is true also of the 'new French feminists' and their theorisation of the feminine in modernist writing, even though they often insist on maintaining a polemical distance from an American-type feminism.[65]

During the 1970s, questions of ecology and environment have deepened from single-issue politics to a broad critique of modernity and modernisation, a trend which is politically and culturally much stronger in West Germany than in the US. A new ecological sensibility manifests itself not only in political and regional subcultures, in alternative life-styles and the new social movements in Europe, but it also affects art and literature in a variety of ways: the work of Joseph Beuys, certain land art projects, Christo's California running fence, the new nature poetry, the return to local traditions, dialects and so on. It was especially due to the growing ecological sensibility that the link between certain forms of modernism and technological modernisation has come under critical scrutiny.

There is a growing awareness that other cultures, non-European, non-Western cultures must be met by means other than conquest or domination, as Paul Ricoeur put it more than twenty years ago, and that the erotic and aesthetic fascination with 'the Orient' – so prominent in Western culture, including modernism – is deeply problematic. This awareness will have to translate into a type of intellectual work very different from that of the modernist intellectual who typically spoke with the confidence of standing at the cutting edge of time and of being able to speak for others. Foucault's notion of the local and specific intellectual as opposed to the 'universal' intellectual of modernity may provide a way out of the dilemma of being locked into our own culture and traditions while simultaneously recognising their limitations.

In conclusion, it is easy to see that a postmodernist culture emerging from these political, social and cultural constellations will have to be a postmodernism of resistance, including resistance to that easy postmodernism of the 'anything goes' variety. Resistance will always have to be specific and contingent upon the cultural field within which it operates. It cannot be defined simply in terms of negativity or non-identity à la Adorno, nor will the litanies of a totalising, collective project suffice. At the same time, the very notion of resistance may itself be problematic in its simple opposition to affirmation. After all, there are affirmative forms of resistance and resisting forms of affirmation. But this may be more a semantic problem than a problem of practice. And it should not keep us from making judgments. How such resistance can be articulated in art works in a way that would satisfy the needs of the political *and* those of the aesthetic, of the producers and of the recipients, cannot be prescribed, and it will remain open to trial, error and debate. But it is time to abandon that dead-end dichotomy of politics and aesthetics which for too long has dominated accounts of modernism, including the aesthetics trend within poststructuralism. The point is not to eliminate the productive tension between the political and the aesthetic, between history and the text, between engagement and the mission of art. The point is to heighten that tension, even to rediscover it and to bring it back into focus in the arts as well as in criticism. No matter how troubling it may be, the landscape of the postmodern surrounds us. It simultaneously delimits and opens our horizons. It's our problem and our hope.

NOTES

Earlier verions of this article were presented at the XVIIth World Congress of Philosophy in Montreal, August 1983, and at a conference on 'The Question of the Postmodern: Criticism/Literature/Culture' organised at Cornell University by Michael Hays, April 1984.

1 Catalogue, *Documenta 7*, Paul Dierichs, Kassel, nd, 1982, p XV.

2 Ibid.

3 Of course, this is not meant as a 'fair' evaluation of the show or of all the works exhibited in it. It should be clear that what I am concerned with here is the dramaturgy of the show, the way it was conceptualised and presented to the public. For a more comprehensive discussion of Documenta 7, see Benjamin HD Buchloch, 'Documenta 7: A Dictionary of Received Ideas', *October* 22, Fall 1982, pp 105-126.

4 On this question see Fredric Jameson, 'Postmodernism or the Cultural Logic of Late Capitalism', *New Left Review* 146, July-August 1984, pp 53-92, whose attempt to identify postmodernism with a new stage in the developmental logic of capital, I feel, overstates the case.

5 For a distinction between a critical and an affirmative postmodernism, see Hal Foster's introduction to *The Anti-Aesthetic*, Bay Press, Port Townsend, Wash, 1984. Foster's new essay in this issue, however, indicates a change of mind with regard to the critical potential of postmodernism.

6 For an earlier attempt to give a *Begriffsgeschichte* of postmodernism in literature, see the various essays in

Amerikastudien 22:1, 1977, pp 9-46 (includes a valuable bibliography). Cf also Ihab Hassan, *The Dismemberment of Orpheus*, second edn, University of Wisconsin Press, Madison, 1982, especially the new 'Postface 1982: Toward a Concept of Postmodernism', pp 259-271. The debate about modernity and modernisation in history and the social sciences is too broad to document here; for an excellent survey of the pertinent literature, see Hans-Ulrich Wehler, *Modernisierungstheorie und Geschichte*, Vandenhoeck & Ruprecht, Göttingen, 1975. On the question of modernity and the arts, see Matei Calinescu, *Faces of Modernity*, Indiana University Press, Bloomington, 1977; Marshal Berman, *All that is Solid Melts into Air: The Experience of Modernity*, Simon & Schuster, New York; Eugene Lunn, *Marxism and Modernism*, University of California Press, Berkeley and Los Angeles, 1982; Peter Bürger, *Theory of the Avantgarde*, University of Minnesota Press, Minneapolis, 1984. Also important for this debate is the recent work by cultural historians on specific sites and their culture, eg Carl Schorske's and Robert Waissenberger's work on fin-de-siècle Vienna, Peter Gay's and John Willett's work on the Weimar Republic, and, for a discussion of American anti-modernism at the turn of the century, TJ Jackson Lears, *No Place of Grace*, Pantheon, New York, 1981.

7 On the ideological and political function of modernism in the 1950s cf Jost Hermand, 'Modernism Restored: West German Painting in the 1950s', *NGC* 32, Spring/Summer 1984; and Serge Guilbaut, *How New York Stole the Idea of Modern Art*, Chicago University Press, 1983.

8 For a thorough discussion of this concept see Robert Sayre and Michel Löwry, 'Figures of Romantic Anti-Capitalism', *NGC* 32.

9 For an excellent discussion of the politics of architecture in the Weimar Republic see the exhibition catalogue *Wem gehört die Welt: Kunst und Gesellschaft in der Weimarer Republik*, Neue Gesellschaft für bildende Kunst, Berlin, 1977, pp 38-157. Cf also Robert Hughes, 'Trouble in Utopia', *The Shock of the New*, Alfred A Knopf, New York, 1981, pp 164-211.

10 The fact that such strategies can cut different ways politically is shown by Kenneth Frampton in his essay 'Towards a Critical Regionalism', *Anti-Aesthetic*, ed Foster, pp 23-38.

11 Charles Jencks, *The Language of Postmodern Architecture*, Rizzoli, New York, 1977, p 97.

12 For Bloch's concept of *Ungleichzeitigkeit*, see his 'Non-Synchronism and the Obligation to its Dialectics', and Anson Rabinbach, 'Ernst Bloch's *Heritage of our Times* and Fascism', *NGC* 11, Spring 1977, pp 5-38.

13 Robert Venturi, Denise Scott Brown, Steven Izenour, *Learning from Las Vegas*, MIT Press, Cambridge, 1972. Cf also the earlier study by Venturi, *Complexity and Contradiction in Architecture*, Museum of Modern Art, New York, 1966.

14 Kenneth Frampton, *Modern Architecture: A Critical History*, Oxford University Press, New York and Toronto, 1980, p 290.

15 I am mainly concerned here with the *Selbstverständnis* of the artists, and not with the question of whether their work really went beyond modernism or whether it was in all cases politically 'progressive'. On the politics of the Beat rebellion see Barbara Ehrenreich, *The Hearts of Men*, Doubleday, New York, 1984, especially pp 52-67.

16 Gerald Graff, 'The Myth of the Postmodern Breakthrough', *Literature Against Itself*, Chicago University Press, 1979, pp 31-62.

17 John Barth, 'The Literature of Replenishment: Postmodernist Fiction', *Atlantic Monthly*, January 1980.

18 Daniel Bell, *The Cultural Contradictions of Capitalism*, Basic Books, New York, 1976, p 51.

19 The specific connotations the notion of postmodernity has taken on in the German peace and anti-nuke movements as well as within the Green Party will not be discussed here, as this article is primarily concerned with the American debate. In German intellectual life, the work of Peter Sloterdijk is eminently relevant for these issues, although Sloterdijk does not use the word 'postmodern'; Peter Sloterdijk, *Kritik der zynischen Vernunft*, 2 vols, Suhrkamp, Frankfurt am Main, 1983. Equally pertinent is the peculiar German reception of French theory, especially of Foucault, Baudrillard, and Lyotard; see for example *Der Tod der Moderne. Eine Diskussion*, Konkursbuchverlag, Tübingen, 1983. On the apocalyptic shading of the postmodern in Germany see Ulrich Horstmann, *Das Untier. Konturen einer Philosophie der Menschenflucht*, Medusa, Wien-Berlin, 1983.

20 The following section will draw on arguments developed less fully in my earlier article entitled 'The Search for Tradition: Avantgarde and Postmodernism in the 1970s', *NGC* 22, Winter 1981, pp 23-40.

21 Peter Bürger, *Theory of the Avantgarde*, University of Minnesota Press, Minneapolis, 1984. The fact that Bürger reserves the term avantgarde for mainly these three movements may strike the American reader as idiosyncratic or as unnecessarily limited unless the place of the argument within the tradition of twentieth-century German aesthetic thought from Brecht and Benjamin to Adorno is understood.

22 This difference between modernism and the avantgarde was one of the pivotal points of disagreement between Benjamin and Adorno in the 1930s, a debate to which Bürger owes a lot. Confronted with the successful fusion of aesthetics, politics and everyday life in fascist Germany, Adorno condemned the avantgarde's intention to merge art with life and continued to insist, in best modernist fashion, on the autonomy of art; Benjamin on the other hand, looking backwards to the radical experiments in Paris, Moscow and

Berlin in the 1920s, found a messianic promise in the avantgarde, especially in surrealism, a fact which may help explain Benjamin's strange (and, I think, mistaken) appropriation in the US as a postmodern critic *avant la lettre*.

23 Cf my essay 'The Cultural Politics of Pop', *NGC* 4, Winter 1975, pp 77-97. From a different perspective, Dick Hebdige developed a similar argument about British pop culture at a talk he gave in 1983 at the Center for Twentieth Century Studies at the University of Wisconsin-Milwaukee.

24 The Left's fascination with the media was perhaps more pronounced in Germany than it was in the US. Those were the years when Brecht's radio theory and Benjamin's 'The Work of Art in the Age of Mechanical Reproduction' became cult texts. See, for example, Hans Magnus Enzensberger, 'Baukasten zu einer Theorie der Medien', *Kursbuch* 20, March 1970, pp 159-86. Reprinted in HME, *Palaver*, Suhrkamp, Frankfurt am Main, 1974. The old belief in the democratising potential of the media is also intimated on the last pages of Lyotard's *The Postmodern Condition*, not in relation to radio, film or television, but in relation to computers.

25 Leslie Fiedler, 'The New Mutants', 1965, *A Fiedler Reader*, Stein & Day, New York, 1977, pp 189-210.

26 Edward Lucie-Smith, *Art in the Seventies*, Cornell University Press, Ithaca, 1980, p 11.

27 For a lucid discussion of Greenberg's theory of modern art in its historical context see TJ Clark, 'Clement Greenberg's Theory of Art', *Critical Inquiry* 9:1, September 1982, pp 139-56. For a different view of Greenberg see Ingeborg Hoesterey, 'Die Moderne am Ende? Zu den ästhetischen Positionen von Jürgen Habermas und Clement Greenberg', *Zeitschrift für Ästhetik und allgemeine Kunstwissenschaft* 29:2, 1984. On Adorno's theory of modernism see Eugene Lunn, *Marxism and Modernism*; Peter Bürger, *Vermittlung – Rezeption – Funktion*, Suhrkamp, Frankfurt am Main, 1979, especially pp 79-92; eds Burkhardt Lindner and W Martin Lüdke, *Materialien zur ästhetischen Theorie: Th W Adornos Konstruktion der Moderne*, Suhrkamp, Frankfurt am Main, 1980. Cf also my essay 'Adorno in Reverse: From Hollywood to Richard Wagner', *NGC* 29, Spring-Summer, 1982, pp 8-38.

28 See Craig Owens, 'The Discourse of Others', *Anti-Aesthetic*, ed Foster, pp 65-90.

29 It is with the recent publications by Fred Jameson and Hal Foster's *The Anti-Aesthetic* that things have begun to change.

30 Of course, those who hold this view will not utter the word 'realism' as it is tarnished by its traditionally close association with the notions of 'reflection', 'representation' and a transparent reality; but the persuasive power of the modernist doctrine owes much to the underlying idea that only modernist art and literature are somehow adequate to our time.

31 For a work that remains very much in the orbit of Marx's notion of modernity and tied to the political and cultural impulses of the American 1960s see Marshall Berman, *All That is Solid Melts Into the Air: the Experience of Modernity*. For a critique of Berman see David Bathrick's review essay in *NGC* 33, Fall, 1984.

32 Jürgen Habermas, 'Modernity versus Postmodernity', *NGC* 22, Winter, 1981, pp 3-14. Reprinted in *The Anti-Aesthetic*, ed Foster.

33 Jean-François Lyotard, 'Answering the Question: What Is Postmodernism?' *The Postmodern Condition*, University of Minnesota Press, Minneapolis, 1984, pp 71-82.

34 Martin Jay, 'Habermas and Modernism', *Praxis International* 4:1, April 1984, pp 1-14. Cf in the same issue Richard Rorty, 'Habermas and Lyotard on Postmodernity', pp 32-44.

35 Peter Sloterdijk, *Kritik der zynischen Vernunft*. The first two chapters of Sloterdijk's essay appear in English in this issue. Sloterdijk himself tries to salvage the emancipatory potential of reason in ways fundamentally different from Habermas, ways which could indeed be called postmodern. For a brief, but incisive discussion in English of Sloterdijk's work see Leslie A Adelson, 'Against the Enlightenment: A Theory with Teeth for the 1980s', *German Quarterly* 57:4, Fall 1984, pp 625-31.

36 Cf Jürgen Habermas, 'The Entwinement of Myth and Enlightenment, Rereading *Dialectic of Enlightenment*', *NGC* 26, Spring-Summer, 1982, pp 13-30.

37 Of course there is another line of argument in the book which does link the crisis of capitalist culture to economic developments. But I think that as a rendering of Bell's polemical stance the above description is valid.

38 The Editors, 'A Note on The New Criterion', *The New Criterion* 1:1, September 1982, pp 1-5. Hilton Kramer, 'Postmodern: Art and Culture in the 1980s', ibid, pp 36-42.

39 Bell, *Cultural Contradictions of Capitalism*, p 54.

40 I follow the current usage in which the term 'critical theory' refers to a multitude of recent theoretical and interdisciplinary endeavours in the humanities. Originally, Critical Theory was a much more focused term that referred to the theory developed by the Frankfurt School since the 1930s. Today, however, the critical theory of the Frankfurt School is itself only a part of an expanded field of critical theories, and this may ultimately benefit its reinscription in contemporary critical discourse.

41 The same is not always true the other way round, however. Thus American practitioners of deconstruction usually are not very eager to address the problem of the postmodern. Actually, American deconstruction, such as practised by the late Paul de Man, seems altogether unwilling to grant a distinction between the

modern and the postmodern at all. Where de Man addresses the problem of modernity directly, as in his seminal essay 'Literary History and Literary Modernity' in *Blindness and Insight*, he projects characteristics and insights of modernism back into the past so that ultimately all literature becomes, in a sense, essentially modernist.

42 A cautionary note may be in order here. The term poststructuralism is by now about as amorphous as 'postmodernism', and it encompasses a variety of quite different theoretical endeavours. For the purposes of my discussion, however, the differences can be bracketed temporarily in order to approach certain similarities between different poststructuralist projects.

43 This part of the argument draws on the work about Foucault by John Rajchman, 'Foucault, or the Ends of Modernism', *October* 24, Spring 1983, pp 37-62, and on the discussion of Derrida as a theorist of modernism in Jochen Schulte-Sasse's introduction to Peter Bürger, *Theory of the Avantgarde*.

44 Jonathan Arac, Wlad Godzich, Wallace Martin, ed *The Yale Critics: Deconstruction in America*, University of Minnesota Press, Minneapolis, 1983.

45 See Nancy Fraser's article in *NGC* 33, Fall, 1984.

46 'Bliss' is an inadequate rendering of *Jouissance* as the English term lacks the crucial bodily and hedonistic connotations of the French word.

47 My intention is not to reduce Barthes to the positions taken in his later work. The American success of this work, however, makes it permissible to treat it as a symptom, or, if you will, as a '*mythologie*'.

48 Roland Barthes, *The Pleasure of the Text*, Hill & Wang, New York, 1975, p 22.

49 See Tania Modleski, 'The Terror of Pleasure: The Contemporary Horror Film and Postmodern Theory', paper given at a conference on mass culture, Center for Twentieth Century Studies, University of Wisconsin-Milwaukee, April 1984.

50 Barthes, *Pleasure of the Text*, p 38.

51 Ibid, p 41 f.

52 Ibid, p 14.

53 Thus the fate of pleasure according to Barthes was extensively discussed at the 1983 MLA forum while an hour later, in a session on the future of literary criticism, various speakers extolled the emergence of a new historical criticism. This, it seems to me, marks an important line of conflict and tension in the current litcrit scene in the US.

54 Roland Barthes, *S/Z*, Hill & Wang, New York, 1974, p 140.

55 Michel Foucault, 'What Is an Author?' *Language, Counter-memory, Practice*, Cornell University Press, Ithaca, 1977, p 138.

56 This shift in interest back to questions of subjectivity is actually also present in some of the later poststructuralist writings, for instance in Kristeva's work on the symbolic and the semiotic and in Foucault's work on sexuality. On Foucault see Biddy Martin, 'Feminism, Criticism, and Foucault', *NGC* 27, Fall, 1982, pp 3-30. On the relevance of Kristeva's work for the American context see Alice Jardine, 'Theories of the Feminine', *Enclitic* 4:2, Fall 1980, pp 5-15; and 'Pre-Texts for the Transatlantic Feminist', *Yale French Studies* 62, 1981, pp 220-36. Cf also Teresa de Lauretis, *Alice Doesn't: Feminism, Semiotics, Cinema*, Indiana University Press, Bloomington, 1984, especially chap 6 'Semiotics and Experience'.

57 Jean-François Lyotard, *La Condition postmoderne*, Minuit, Paris, 1979. English translation, *The Postmodern Condition*, University of Minnesota Press, 1984.

58 The English translation of *La Condition postmoderne* includes the essay, important for the aesthetic debate, 'Answering the Question: What is Postmodernism?' For Kristeva's statement on the postmodern see 'Postmodernism?' *Bucknell Review* 25:11, 1980, pp 136-41.

59 Kristeva, 'Postmodernism?', p 137.

60 Ibid, p 139 f.

61 In fact *The Postmodern Condition* is a sustained attack on the intellectual and political traditions of the Enlightenment embodied for Lyotard in the work of Jürgen Habermas.

62 Fredric Jameson, 'Foreword', Lyotard, *The Postmodern Condition*, p XVI.

63 Michel Foucault, 'Truth and Power', *Power/Knowledge*, Pantheon, New York, 1980, p 127.

64 The major exception is Craig Owens, 'The Discourse of Others', *Anti-Aesthetic*, ed Foster, pp 65-98.

65 Cf Elaine Marks and Isabelle de Courtivron, ed *New French Feminisms*, University of Massachusetts Press, Amherst, 1980. For a critical view of French theories of the feminine cf the work by Alice Jardine cited in note 56 and her essay 'Gynesis', *Diacritics* 12:2, Summer, 1982, pp 54-65.

From *After the Great Divide*, Macmillan, London, 1984. First published in *New German Critique* 33, Fall 1984, 5-52.

Umberto Eco
POSTSCRIPT TO *THE NAME OF THE ROSE*
POSTMODERNISM, IRONY, THE ENJOYABLE

Between 1965 and today, two ideas have been definitively clarified: that plot could be found also in the form of quotation of other plots, and that the quotation could be less escapist than the plot quoted. In 1971 I edited the *Almanacco Bompiani*, celebrating 'The Return to the Plot', though this return was via an ironic re-examination (not without admiration) of Ponson du Terrail and Eugène Sue, and admiration (with very little irony) of some of the great pages of Dumas. The real problem at stake then was, could there be a novel that was not escapist and, nevertheless, still enjoyable?

This link, and the rediscovery not only of plot but also of enjoyability, was to be realised by the American theorists of postmodernism.

Unfortunately, 'postmodern' is a term *bon à tout faire*. I have the impression that it is applied today to anything the user of the term happens to like. Further, there seems to be an attempt to make it increasingly retroactive: first it was apparently applied to certain writers or artists active in the last twenty years, then gradually it reached the beginning of the century, then still further back. And this reverse procedure continues; soon the postmodern category will include Homer.

Actually, I believe that postmodernism is not a trend to be chronologically defined, but, rather, an ideal category or, better still, a *Kunstwollen*, a way of operating. We could say that every period has its own postmodernism, just as every period would have its own mannerism (and, in fact, I wonder if postmodernism is not the modern name for mannerism as metahistorical category). I believe that in every period there are moments of crisis like those described by Nietzsche in his *Thoughts Out of Season*, in which he wrote about the harm done by historical studies. The past conditions us, harries us, blackmails us. The historic avant-garde (but here I would also consider avant-garde a metahistorical category) tries to settle scores with the past. 'Down with moonlight' – a futurist slogan – is a platform typical of every avant-garde; you have only to replace 'moonlight' with whatever noun is suitable. The avant-garde destroys, defaces the past: *Les Demoiselles d'Avignon* is a typical avant-garde act. Then the avant-garde goes further, destroys the figure, cancels it, arrives at the abstract, the informal, the white canvas, the slashed canvas, the charred canvas. In architecture and the visual arts, it will be the curtain wall, the building as stele, pure parallelepiped, minimal art; in literature, the destruction of the flow of discourse, the Burroughs-like collage, silence, the white page; in music, the passage from atonality to noise to absolute silence (in this sense, the early Cage is modern).

But the moment comes when the avant-garde (the modern) can go no further; because it has produced a metalanguage that speaks of its impossible texts (conceptual art). The postmodern reply to the modern consists of recognising that the past, since it cannot really be destroyed, because its destruction leads to silence, must be revisited: but with irony, not innocently. I think of the postmodern attitude as that of a man who loves a very cultivated woman and knows he cannot say to her, 'I love you madly,' because he knows that she knows (and that she knows that he knows) that these words have already been written by Barbara Cartland. Still, there is a solution. He can say, 'As Barbara Cartland would put it, I love you madly.' At this point, having avoided false innocence, having said clearly that it is no longer possible to speak innocently, he will nevertheless have said what he wanted to say to the woman: that he loves her, but he loves her in an age of lost innocence. If the woman goes along with this she will have received a declaration of love all the same. Neither of the two speakers will feel innocent, both will have accepted the challenge of the past, of the already said, which cannot be eliminated; both will consciously and with pleasure play the game of irony . . . But both will have succeeded, once again, in speaking of love.

Irony, metalinguistic play, enunciation squared. Thus, with the modern, anyone who does not understand the game can only reject it, but with the postmodern, it is possible not to understand the game and yet to take it seriously. Which is, after all, the quality (the risk) of irony. There is always someone who takes ironic discourse seriously. I think that the collages of Picasso, Juan Gris, and Braque were modern: this is why normal people would not accept them. On the other hand, the collages of Max Ernst, who pasted together bits of nineteenth-century engravings, were postmodern: they can be read as fantastic stories, as the telling of dreams, without any awareness that they amount to a discussion of the nature of engraving, and perhaps even of collage. If 'postmodern' means this, it is clear why Sterne and Rabelais were postmodern, why Borges surely is, and why in the same artist the modern moment and the postmodern moment can coexist, or alternate, or follow each other closely. Look at Joyce. The *Portrait* is the story of an attempt at the Modern. *Dubliners*, even if it comes before, is more modern than *Portrait*. *Ulysses* is on the borderline. *Finnegans Wake* is already postmodern, or at least it initiates the postmodern discourses: it demands, in order to be understood, not the negation of the already said, but its ironic rethinking.

On the subject of the postmodern nearly everything has been said (namely, in essays like 'The Literature of Exhaustion' by John Barth, which dates from 1967). Not that I am entirely in agreement with the grades that the theoreticians of postmodernism (Barth included) give to writers and artists, establishing who is postmodern and who has not yet made it. But I am interested in the theorem that the trend's theoreticians derive from their premises:

My ideal postmodernist author neither merely repudiates nor merely imitates either his twentieth-century modernist parents or his nineteenth-century premodernist grandparents. He has the first half of our century under his belt, but not on his back . . . He may not hope to reach and move the devotees of James Michener and Irving Wallace – not to mention the lobotomised mass-media illiterates. But he *should* hope to reach and delight, at least part of the time, beyond the circle of what Mann used to call the Early Christians: professional devotees of high art . . . The ideal postmodernist novel will somehow rise above the quarrel between realism and irrealism, formalism and 'contentism', pure and committed literature, coterie fiction and junk fiction . . . My own analogy would be with good jazz or classical music: one finds much on successive listenings or close examination of the score that one didn't catch the first time through; but the first time through should be so ravishing – and not just to specialists – that one delights in the replay.

This is what Barth wrote in 1980, resuming the discussion, but this time under the title 'The Literature of Replenishment: Postmodernist Fiction'. Naturally, the subject can be discussed further, with greater taste for paradox; and this is what Leslie Fiedler does. In 1980 *Salmagundi* (no 50-51) published a debate between Fiedler and other American authors. Fiedler, obviously, is out to provoke. He praises *The Last of the Mohicans*, adventure stories, Gothic novels, junk scorned by critics that was nevertheless able to create myths and capture the imagination of more than one generation. He wonders if something like *Uncle Tom's Cabin* will ever appear again, a book that can be read with equal passion in the kitchen, the living room, and the nursery. He includes Shakespeare among those who knew how to amuse, along with *Gone with the Wind.* We all know he is too keen a critic to believe these things. He simply wants to break down the barrier that has been erected between art and enjoyability. He feels that today reaching a vast public and capturing its dreams perhaps means acting as the avant-garde, and he still leaves us free to say that capturing readers' dreams does not necessarily mean encouraging escape: it can also mean haunting them.

Linda Hutcheon
THEORISING THE POSTMODERN
TOWARDS A POETICS

> Clearly, then, the time has come to theorise the term [postmodernism], if not to
> define it, before it fades from awkward neologism to derelict cliché without ever
> attaining to the dignity of a cultural concept. (Ihab Hassan)

Of all the terms bandied about in both current cultural theory and contemporary writing
on the arts, postmodernism must be the most over- and under-defined. It is usually
accompanied by a grand flourish of negativised rhetoric: we hear of discontinuity,
disruption, dislocation, decentring, indeterminacy, and anti-totalisation. What all of
these words literally do (precisely by their disavowing prefixes – *dis, de, in, anti*) is
incorporate that which they aim to contest – as does, I suppose, the term postmodernism
itself. I point to this simple verbal fact in order to begin 'theorising' the cultural
enterprise to which we seem to have given such a provocative label. Given all the
confusion and vagueness associated with the term itself,[1] I would like to begin by
arguing that, for me, postmodernism is a contradictory phenomenon, one that uses and
abuses, installs and then subverts, the very concepts it challenges – be it in architecture,
literature, painting, sculpture, film, video, dance, TV, music, philosophy, aesthetic
theory, psychoanalysis, linguistics, or historiography. These are some of the realms
from which my 'theorising' will proceed, and my examples will always be specific,
because what I want to avoid are those polemical generalisations – often by those
inimical to postmodernism[2] – that leave us guessing about just what it is that is being
called postmodernist, though never in doubt as to its undesirability. Some assume a
generally accepted 'tacit definition';[3] others locate the beast by temporal (after 1945?
1968? 1970? 1980?) or economic signposting (late capitalism). But in as pluralist and
fragmented a culture as that of the western world today, such designations are not
terribly useful if they intend to generalise about all the vagaries of our culture. After all,
what does television's 'Dallas' have in common with the architecture of Ricardo Bofill?
What does John Cage's music share with a play (or film) like *Amadeus*?

In other words, postmodernism cannot simply be used as a synonym for the
contemporary.[4] And it does not really describe an international cultural phenomenon,
for it is primarily European and American (North and South). Although the concept of
modernism is largely an Anglo-American one,[5] this should not limit the poetics of
postmodernism to that culture, especially since those who would argue that very stand
are usually the ones to find room to sneak in the French *nouveau roman*.[6] And almost
everyone[7] wants to be sure to include what Severo Sarduy[8] has labelled – not postmodern
– but 'neo-baroque' in a Spanish culture where 'modernism' has a rather different
meaning.

I offer instead, then, a specific, if polemical, start from which to operate: as a cultural
activity that can be discerned in most art forms and many currents of thought today,
what I want to call postmodernism is fundamentally contradictory, resolutely historical,

and inescapably political. Its contradictions may well be those of late capitalist society, but whatever the cause, these contradictions are certainly manifest in the important postmodern concept of 'the presence of the past'. This was the title given to the 1980 Venice Biennale which marked the institutional recognition of postmodernism in architecture. Italian architect Paolo Portoghesi's[9] analysis of the twenty facades of the 'Strada Novissima' – whose very newness lay paradoxically in its historical parody – shows how architecture has been rethinking modernism's purist break with history. This is not a nostalgic return; it is a critical revisiting, an ironic dialogue with the past of both art and society, a recalling of a critically shared vocabulary of architectural forms. 'The past whose presence we claim is not a golden age to be recuperated', argues Portoghesi.[10] Its aesthetic forms and its social formations are problematised by critical reflection. The same is true of the postmodernist rethinking of figurative painting in art and historical narrative in fiction and poetry: it is always a critical reworking, never a nostalgic 'return'.[11] Herein lies the governing role of – irony in postmodernism. Stanley Tigerman's dialogue with history in his projects for family houses modelled on Raphael's palatial Villa Madama is an ironic one: his miniaturisation of the monumental forces a rethinking of the social function of architecture – both then and now.

Because it is contradictory and works within the very systems it attempts to subvert, postmodernism can probably not be considered a new paradigm (even in some extension of the Kuhnian sense of the term). It has not replaced liberal humanism, even if it has seriously challenged it. It may mark, however, the site of the struggle of the emergence of something new. The manifestations in art of this struggle may be those almost undefinable and certainly bizarre works like Terry Gilliam's film *Brazil*. The postmodern ironic rethinking of history is here textualised in the many general parodic references to other movies: *A Clockwork Orange*, 1984, Gilliam's own *Time Bandits* and Monty Python sketches, and Japanese epics, to name but a few. The more specific parodic recalls range from *Star Wars'* Darth Vadar to the Odessa Steps sequence of Eisenstein's *Battleship Potemkin*. In *Brazil*, however, the famous shot of the baby carriage on the steps is replaced by one of a floor cleaner, and the result is to reduce epic tragedy to the bathos of the mechanical and debased. Along with this ironic reworking of the history of film comes a temporal historical warp: the movie is set, we are told, at 8:49 am, sometime in the twentieth century. The decor does not help us identify the time more precisely. The fashions mix the absurdly futuristic with 1930s styling; an oddly old-fashioned and dingy setting belies the omnipresence of computers – though even they are not the sleekly designed creatures of today. Among the other typically postmodern contradictions in this movie is the co-existence of heterogeneous filmic genres: fantasy Utopia and grim dystopia; absurd slapstick comedy and tragedy (the Tuttle/Buttle mix-up); the romantic adventure tale and the political documentary.

While all forms of contemporary art and thought offer examples of this kind of postmodernist contradiction, this book (like most others on the subject) will be 'privileging' the novel genre, and one form in particular, a form that I want to call 'historiographic metafiction'. By this I mean those well-known and popular novels which are both intensely self-reflexive and yet paradoxically also lay claim to historical events and personages: *The French Lieutenant's Woman*, *Midnight's Children*, *Ragtime*, *Legs*, *G*, *Famous Last Words*. In most of the critical work on postmodernism, it is narrative – be it in literature, history, or theory – that has usually been the major focus of attention. Historiographic metafiction incorporates all three of these domains: that is, its theoretical self-awareness of history and fiction as human constructs (historio*graphic* *meta*fiction) is made the grounds for its rethinking and reworking of the forms and contents of the past. This kind of fiction has often been noticed by critics, but its paradigmatic quality has been passed by: it is commonly labelled in terms of something else – for example as 'midfiction'[12] or 'paramodernist'.[13] Such labelling is another mark of the inherent contradictoriness of historiographic metafiction, for it always works *within* conventions in order to subvert them. It is not just metafictional; nor is it just another version of the historical novel or the non-fictional novel. Gabriel García Marquez's *One Hundred Years of Solitude* has often been discussed in exactly the contradictory terms that I think define postmodernism. For example Larry McCaffery sees it as both metafictionally self-reflexive and yet speaking to us powerfully about real political and historical realities: 'It has thus become a kind of model for the contemporary writer, being self-conscious about its literary heritage and about the limits of mimesis . . . but yet managing to reconnect its readers to the world outside the page.'[14] What McCaffery here adds as almost an afterthought at the end of his book, *The Metafictional Muse*, is in many ways my starting point.

Most theorists of postmodernism who see it as a 'cultural dominant'[15] agree that it is characterised by the results of late-capitalist dissolution of bourgeois hegemony and the development of mass culture.[16] I would agree and, in fact, argue that the increasing uniformisation of mass culture is one of the totalising forces that postmodernism exists to challenge. Challenge, but not deny. But it does seek to assert difference, not homogeneous identity. Of course, the very concept of difference could be said to entail a typically postmodern contradiction: 'difference', unlike 'otherness', has no exact opposite against which to define itself. Thomas Pynchon allegorises otherness in *Gravity's Rainbow* through the single, if anarchic, 'we-system' that exists as the counterforce of the totalising 'They-system' (though also implicated in it). Postmodern difference or rather differences, in the plural are always multiple and provisional.

Postmodern culture, then, has a contradictory relationship to what we usually label our dominant, liberal humanist culture. It does not deny it, as some have asserted.[17] Instead, it contests it from within its own assumptions. Modernists like Eliot and Joyce have usually been seen as profoundly humanistic[18] in their paradoxical desire for stable aesthetic and moral values, even in the face of their realisation of the inevitable absence of such universals. Postmodernism differs from this, not in its humanistic contradictions, but in the provisionality of its response to them; it refuses to posit any structure or, what Lyotard calls, master narrative[19] – such as art or myth – which, for such modernists, would have been consolatory. It argues that such systems are indeed attractive, perhaps even necessary; but this does not make them any the less illusory. For Lyotard, postmodernism is characterised by exactly this kind of incredulity towards master or meta-narratives: those who lament the 'loss of meaning' in the world or in art are really mourning the fact that knowledge is no longer primarily narrative knowledge of this kind.[20] This does not mean that knowledge somehow disappears. There is no radically new paradigm here, even if there is change.

It is no longer big news that the master narratives of bourgeois liberalism are under attack. There is a long history of many such sceptical sieges to positivism and humanism, and today's footsoldiers of theory – Foucault, Derrida, Habermas, Vattimo, Baudrillard – follow in the footsteps of Nietzsche, Heidegger, Marx, and Freud, to name but a few, in their attempts to challenge the empiricist, rationalist, humanist assumptions of our cultural systems, including those of science.[21] Foucault's early rethinking of the history of ideas in terms of an 'archaeology' (in *The Order of Things*, 1970; *The Archaeology of Knowledge*, 1972) that might stand outside the universalising assumptions of humanism is one such attempt, whatever its obvious weaknesses. So is Derrida's more radical contesting of Cartesian and Platonic views of the mind as a system of closed meanings.[22] Like Gianni Vattimo's *pensiero debole* (weak thought),[23] these challenges characteristically operate in clearly paradoxical terms, knowing that to claim epistemological authority is to be caught up in what they seek to displace. The same applies to Habermas's work, though it often appears somewhat less radical in its determined desire to work from within the system of 'Enlightenment' rationality and yet manage to critique it at the same time. This is what Lyotard has attacked as just another totalising narrative.[24] And Jameson has argued that both Lyotard and Habermas are resting their arguments on different but equally strong legitimising 'narrative archetypes'.[25]

This game of meta-narrative one-upmanship could go on and on, since arguably Jameson's Marxism leaves him vulnerable too. But this is not the point. What is important in all these internalised challenges to humanism is the interrogating of the notion of consensus. Whatever narratives or systems that once allowed us to think we could unproblematically and universally define public agreement have now been questioned by the acknowledgement of differences – in theory and in artistic practice. In its most extreme formulation, the result is that consensus becomes the illusion of consensus, whether it be defined in terms of minority (educated, sensitive elitist) or mass (commercial, popular, conventional) culture, for *both* are manifestations of late capitalist, bourgeois, informational, postindustrial society, a society in which social reality is structured by discourses (in the plural) – or so postmodernism endeavours to teach.

What this means is that the familiar humanist separation of art and life (or, human imagination and order *versus* chaos and disorder) no longer holds . . . Postmodernist contradictory art still installs that order, but it then uses it to demystify our everyday processes of structuring chaos, of imparting or assigning meaning.[26] For example, within a positivistic frame of reference, photographs could be accepted as neutral representations, as technological windows on the world. In the postmodern photos of Heribert Berkert or Ger Dekkers, they still represent (for they cannot avoid reference) but what they represent is self-consciously shown to be highly filtered by the discursive and aesthetic assumptions of the camera-holder.[27] While not wanting to go as far as Morse Peckham[28] and argue that the arts are somehow 'biologically' necessary for social change, I would like to suggest that, in its very contradictions, postmodernist art (like Brecht's epic theatre) might be able to dramatise and even provoke change from within. It is not that the modernist world was 'a world in need of mending' and the postmodernist one 'beyond repair'.[29] Postmodernism works to show that all repairs are human constructs, but that, from that very fact, they derive their value as well as their limitation. All repairs are both comforting and illusory. Postmodernist interrogations of humanist certainties live within this kind of contradiction.

Perhaps it is another inheritance from the 1960s to believe that challenging and questioning are positive values (even if solutions to problems are not offered), for the knowledge derived from such inquiry may be the only possible condition of change. In the late 1950s in *Mythologies*,[30] Roland Barthes had prefigured this kind of thinking in his Brechtian challenges to all that is 'natural' or 'goes without saying' in our culture – that is, all that is considered universal and eternal, and therefore unchangeable. He suggested the need to question and demystify first, and then work for change. The 1960s were the time of ideological formation for many of the postmodernist thinkers and artists of the 1980s and it is now that we can see the results of that formation.

Perhaps, as some have argued, the 1960s themselves (that is, at the time) produced no enduring innovation in aesthetics, but I would argue that they did provide the background, though not the definition, of the postmodern,[31] for they were crucial in developing a different concept of the possible function of art, one that would contest the 'Arnoldian' or humanist moral view with its potentially elitist class bias.[32] One of the functions of art in mass culture, argued Susan Sontag, would be to 'modify consciousness'.[33] And many cultural commentators since have argued that the energies of the 1960s have changed the framework and structure of how we consider art.[34] The conservatism of the late 1970s and 1980s may have their impact when the thinkers and artists being formed now begin to produce their work,[35] but to call Foucault or Lyotard a neo-conservative – as did Habermas[36] – is historically and ideologically inaccurate.[37]

The political, social, and intellectual experience of the 1960s helped make it possible for postmodernism to be seen as what Kristeva calls 'writing-as-experience-of-limits':[38] limits of language, of subjectivity, of sexual identity, and we might also add: of systematisation and uniformisation. This interrogating (and even pushing) of limits has contributed to the 'crisis in legitimation' that Lyotard and Habermas see (differently) as part of the postmodern condition. It has certainly meant a rethinking and putting into question of the bases of our western modes of thinking that we usually label, perhaps rather too generally, as liberal humanism.

Modelling the Postmodern: Parody and Politics

That postmodern theses have deep roots in the present human condition is confirmed today in the document on architecture issued by the Polish union Solidarity. This text accuses the modern city of being the product of an alliance between bureaucracy and totalitarianism, and singles out the great error of modern architecture in the break of historical continuity. Solidarity's words should be meditated upon, especially by those who have confused a great movement of collective consciousness [postmodernism] with a passing fashion. (Paolo Portoghesi)

We have seen that what both its supporters and its detractors seem to want to call 'postmodernism' in art today – be it in video, dance, literature, painting, music, architecture, or any other form – seems to be art marked paradoxically by both history and an internalised, self-reflexive investigation of the nature, the limits, and the possibilities of the discourse of art. On the surface, postmodernism's main interest might seem to be in the processes of its own production and reception, as well as in its own parodic relation to the art of the past. But I want to argue that it is precisely parody – that seemingly introverted formalism – that paradoxically brings about a direct confrontation with the problem of the relation of the aesthetic to a world of significance external to itself, to a discursive world of socially defined meaning systems (past and present) – in other words, to the political and the historical.

My focus in this chapter will be on what I think offers the best model for a poetics of postmodernism: postmodern architecture, the one art form in which the label seems to refer, uncontested, to a generally agreed upon corpus of works. Throughout, my (non-specialist) discussion will be clearly indebted to the work of architect/theorists like Charles Jencks and Paolo Portoghesi, the major voices in the postmodern debates. This will be my model, because the characteristics of this architecture are also those of postmodernism at large – from historiographic metafictions like Christa Wolf's *Cassandra* or EL Doctorow's *The Book of Daniel* to metafilmic historical movies like Peter Greenaway's *The Draughtsman's Contract*, from the video art of Douglas Davis to the photography of Vincent Leo. And all of these art works share one major contradictory characteristic: they are all overtly historical and unavoidably political, precisely because they are formally parodic. I will argue throughout this study that postmodernism is a fundamentally contradictory enterprise: its art forms (and its theory) at once use and abuse, install and then destabilise convention in parodic ways, self-consciously pointing both to their own inherent paradoxes and provisionality and, of course, to their critical or ironic re-reading of the art of the past. In implicitly contesting in this way such concepts as aesthetic originality and textual closure, postmodernist art offers a new model for mapping the borderland between art and the world, a model that works from a position within both and yet not totally within either, a model that is profoundly implicated in, yet still capable of criticising, that which it seeks to describe.

As we have seen, such a paradoxical model of *post*modernism is consistent with the very name of the label for postmodernism signals its contradictory dependence upon and independence from the modernism that both historically preceded it and literally made it possible. Philip Johnson probably could not have built the postmodern Transco Tower in Houston if he had not first designed the modernist purist form of Pennzoil Place – and if he had not begun his career as an architectural historian. All architects know that, by their art's very nature as the shaper of public space, the act of designing a building is an unavoidably social act. Parodic references to the history of architecture textually reinstate a dialogue with the past and – perhaps inescapably – with the social and ideological context in which architecture is (and has been) both produced and lived. In using parody in this way, postmodernist forms want to work towards a public discourse that would overtly eschew modernist aestheticism and hermeticism and its attendant political self-marginalisation.

I am fully aware that my last sentence constitutes a kind of 'red flag' in the light of the debate on postmodernism being argued out on the pages of the *New Left Review*. We have seen that, in reply to Fredric Jameson's 'Postmodernism, Or The Cultural Logic of Late Capitalism',[39] Terry Eagleton found himself in an oddly inverted Lukácian position, championing that same hermetic modernism (which Lukács had denigrated) in his rush to join the now fashionable attack on postmodernism. Without ever really giving an example of what to him would be an actual postmodernist work of art (as if there were not considerable disagreement on this topic in both theory and practice), Eagleton simply states that postmodernism will not do, that the only way to develop an 'authentically political art in our own time' would be to combine somehow the revolutionary avant-garde with modernism:

> An art today which, having learnt from the openly committed character of avant-garde culture, might cast the contradictions of modernism in a more explicitly political light, could do so effectively only if it had also learnt its lesson from modernism too – learnt, that is to say, that the 'political' itself is a question of the emergence of a transformed rationality, and if it is not presented as such will still seem part of the very tradition from which the adventurously modern is still striving to free itself.[40]

But, were Eagleton to look at actual postmodernist art today – and at architecture, in particular – he would see that the art for which he calls already exists. Postmodernist art is precisely that which casts 'the contradictions of modernism in an explicitly political light'. In fact, as architect Paolo Portoghesi reminds us, it has arisen from the very conjunction of modernist and avant-garde politics and forms.[41] But it also suggests that we must be critically conscious of the myths of both the modernists and the late-romantic avant-garde. The 'elitism' of Dada and of Eliot's verse is exactly what postmodernism paradoxically seeks to exploit and to undercut. But the theorist/practitioners of postmodernism in all the arts – from Umberto Eco to Karlheinz Stockhausen – are emphatic in their commitment to the formation (or recollection) of a more generally shared collective aesthetic code. They insist: 'It is not just the cry of rage of a minority of intellectuals who want to teach others how to live, and who celebrate their own solitude and separateness.'[42]

Furthermore, Edward Said has argued that we must realise that all art is discourse-specific, that it is to some degree 'worldly', even when it appears to deny any such connection.[43] The paradox of postmodernist parody is that it is not essentially depthless, trivial kitsch, as Eagleton[44] and Jameson[45] both believe, but rather that it can and does lead to a vision of inter-connectedness: 'illuminating itself, the artwork simultaneously casts light on the workings of aesthetic conceptualisation and on art's sociological situation.'[46] Postmodernist ironic recall of history is neither nostalgia nor aesthetic cannibalisation.[47] Nor can it be reduced to the glibly decorative.[48]

It is true, however, as we shall see at length in Part II, that postmodern art does not offer what Jameson desires – 'genuine historicity' – that is, in his terms, 'our social, historical and existential present and the past as 'referent' or as 'ultimate objects'. But its deliberate refusal to do so is not a naive one: what postmodernism does is to contest the very possibility of our ever being able to know the 'ultimate objects' of the past. It teaches and enacts the recognition of the fact that the social, historical, and existential 'reality' of the past is discursive reality when it is used as the referent of art, and so the only 'genuine historicity' becomes that which would openly acknowledge its own discursive, contingent identity. The past as referent is not bracketed or effaced, as Jameson would like to believe: it is incorporated and modified, given new and different life and meaning. This is the lesson taught by postmodernist art today. In other words, even the most self-conscious and parodic of contemporary works do not try to escape, but indeed foreground, the historical, social, ideological contexts in which they have existed and continue to exist. This is as true of music as of painting; it is as valid for literature as it is for architecture.

It is not surprising that a post-Saussurian kind of pragmatics or semiotics has had a strong appeal for those studying this kind of parodic art. Postmodernism self-consciously demands that the 'justifying premises and structural bases' of its modes of 'speaking' be investigated to see what permits, shapes, and generates what is 'spoken'.[49] According to one important, but often neglected aspect of the Saussurian model, language is a social contract: everything that is presented and thus received through language is already loaded with meaning inherent in the conceptual patterns of the speaker's culture. In an extension of the meaning of 'language', we could say that the *langue* of architecture is in some ways no different from that of ordinary language: no single individual can alter it at his or her own will; it embodies certain culturally accepted values and meanings; it has to be learned in some detail by users before it can be employed effectively.[50] The architecture of the 1970s and 1980s has been marked by a deliberate challenge to the conventions and underlying assumptions of that *langue*, but it is a typically postmodern and self-conscious challenge offered from *within* those very conventions and assumptions.

Whatever modernism's historical and social ideals at its inception, by the end of the Second World War its innovatory promises had become symbols and causes – of alienation and dehumanisation. Modernism in architecture had begun as a 'heroic attempt after the Great War and the Russian Revolution to rebuild a war-ravaged Europe in the image of the new, and to make building a vital part of the envisioned renewal of society'.[51] In reaction against what modernist ahistoricism then led to, however, postmodern parodic revisitations of the history of architecture interrogate the modernist totalising ideal of progress through rationality and purist form.[52]

As a way of textually incorporating the history of art, parody is the formal analogue to the dialogue of past and present that silently but unavoidably goes on at a social level in architecture, because the relation of form to function, shape to use of space, is not a new problem for architects. It is in this way that parodic postmodern buildings can be said to parallel, in their form and their explicitly social contextualising, contemporary challenges on the level of theory. Any study of the actual aesthetic *practice* of postmodernism quickly makes clear its role in the crises of *theoretical* legitimation that have come to our attention in the now infamous Lyotard-Habermas-Rorty debate.[53] Perhaps it is at this level that the ideological status of postmodernist art should be argued out, instead of at that of an understandable, if knee-jerk, reaction against its implication in the mass culture of late capitalism.

To rage, as so many do, following Adorno, against mass culture as only a negative force may be, as one architect/critic has remarked, 'simply continuing to use an aristocratic viewpoint and not knowing how to grasp the liberating result and the egalitarian charge of this [postmodernist] profanation of the myth' of elitist romantic/modernist originality and unique genius.[54] In fact the architecture of the 1970s from the start signalled a conscious move away from the modern movement or the International Style as much for overtly ideological as for aesthetic reasons. The social failure of the great modernist housing projects and the inevitable economic association of 'heroic' modernism with large corporations combined to create a demand for new architectural forms that would reflect a changed and changing social awareness. These new forms were not, by any means, monolithic. They did, however, mark a shared return to such rejected forms as the vernacular (that is, to local needs and local architectural traditions), to decoration and a certain individualism in design, and, most importantly, to the past, to history. Modernism's great purist monuments to the corporate elite and to the cultural seats of power (museums, theatres) gave way, for example, to the Centre Pompidou's (at least stated) desire to make culture part of the business of everyday living.

What soon became labelled as *post*modernism challenged the survival of modernism by contesting its claims to universality: its transhistorical assertions of value were no longer seen as based – as claimed – on reason or logic, but rather on a solid alliance with power, with what Portoghesi calls its 'identification with the productive logic of the industrial system'.[55] In addition, any feeling of 'inevitability'[56] of form was shown to be historically and culturally determined. The 'inevitable' was not eternal, but learned. Peter Eisenman's houses deliberately undercut our 'natural' reactions to space in order to reveal to us that these reactions are, in fact, cultural. And, just as modernism (oedipally) had to reject historicism and to pretend to a parthenogenetic birth fit for the new machine age, so postmodernism, in reaction, returned to history, to what I have been calling 'parody', to give architecture back its traditional social and historical dimension, though with a new twist this time.

What I mean by 'parody' here – as elsewhere in this study – is *not* the ridiculing imitation of the standard theories and definitions that are rooted in eighteenth-century theories of wit. The collective weight of parodic practice suggests a redefinition of parody as repetition with critical distance that allows ironic signalling of difference at the very heart of similarity. In historiographic metafiction, in film, in painting, in music, and in architecture, this parody paradoxically enacts both change and cultural continuity: the Greek prefix *para* can mean both 'counter' or 'against' and 'near' or 'beside'. Jameson argues that in postmodernism 'parody finds itself without a vocation',[57] replaced by pastiche, which he (bound by a definition of parody as ridiculing imitation) sees as neutral or blank parody. But the looking to both the aesthetic and historical past in postmodernist architecture is anything but what Jameson describes as pastiche, that is 'the random cannibalisation of all the styles of the past, the play of random stylistic allusion'. There is absolutely nothing random or 'without principle' in the parodic recall and re-examination of the past by architects like Charles Moore or Ricardo Bofill. To include irony and play is never necessarily to exclude seriousness and purpose in postmodernist art. To misunderstand this is to misunderstand the nature of much contemporary aesthetic production – even if it does make for neater theorising.

> O beautiful, for spacious skies, for amber waves of grain, has there ever been another place on earth where so many people of wealth and power have paid for and put up with so much architecture they detested as within thy blessed borders today? (Tom Wolfe)

In order to understand why ironic parody should, seemingly paradoxically, become such an important form of postmodernist architecture's desire to reinstate a 'worldly' connection for its discourse, we should remind ourselves of what the tyranny of 'heroic' or high modernism has meant in the twentieth century. There have been two kinds of reactions to this modernist hegemony: those from architects themselves and those from the public at large. Perhaps the most eloquent and polemical of the recent public responses has been that of Tom Wolfe in his *From Bauhaus to Our House*, which opens with the wonderfully parodic American lament quoted above. Wolfe's is a negative aesthetic response to what he amusingly calls 'the whiteness & lightness & leanness & cleanness & bareness & spareness of it all'.[58] But it is also an ideological rejection of what can only be called the modernist architects' 'policing' of the impulses of both the clients and the tenants of their buildings. This is the tyranny of the European theorists working in their 'compounds' (be they the Bauhaus or, later, the American universities). This is a tyranny – both moral and aesthetic – over American clients. In Wolfe's terms: 'No alterations, special orders, or loud talk from the client permitted. We know best. We have exclusive possession of the true vision of the future of architecture.'[59] The clients – even if they did foot the bill – were still considered the 'bourgeois' to be despised and, if possible, confounded by the architectural clerisy's elitist esoteric theories.

The *users* of the buildings were also to be controlled. Although Gropius and Le Corbusier both designed workers' housing, neither seems to have felt the need to consult those who would live there: it must have been tacitly assumed that the intellectually underdeveloped would allow the architects to arrange their lives for them. Not surprisingly, many of the worker housing projects of high modernism, like the infamous Pruitt-Igoe one in St Louis, degenerated into shabby welfare housing and were finally and literally blown up, when their social failure was acknowledged. Similarly those so-called non-bourgeois concrete and glass skyscraper apartment buildings and hotels became the housing of the bourgeois – the only ones who could afford to live there. But the control of the architect was often even more extreme: in the Seagram Building, Mies allowed only white blinds on the plate-glass windows and demanded that these be left in only one of three positions, open, shut, or half-way.

Modernist architects seemed to set themselves up in one of two privileged positions with regard to the groups that were actually to occupy their designs. One position is what George Baird has called that of the *Gesamtkünstler* who took for granted an ability to enhance the lives of the future tenants by dramatically heightening their experience of their environment.[60] This position is one over and above them; the attitude is a paternalistic one towards the tenant/child. On the other hand, some modernists saw themselves as, in Baird's terms, the 'life-conditioners'. Not above, but now outside the experience of the tenant, the scientistic architect regarded the tenant as object and the building as an experiment. Be the stance one of indifference or arrogance, it is certainly not hard to see how it could come to be labelled as elitist. And one need only recall Le Corbusier's oddly Platonic Nietzschean view of society controlled by the enlightened businessman and the architect, both the products of an impersonal, universal, transhistorical force symbolised by the machine. The lessons of the past were rejected in the name of this new brand of liberal elitism or idealistic paternalism.[61] Although Le Corbusier saw himself as the apolitical technocrat, the ideological assumptions behind his aesthetic theories of purist rationality might be seen to have played a role in his collaboration with the Vichy government and the failure, in practical terms, of his rather simplistic theory of social good through pure form. We must, of course, beware of making our own simplistic associations of architectural style and single ideologies. Portoghesi reminds us that 'History proves that forms and models survive the type of power that produced them, and that their meaning changes in time according to the social use that is made of them'.[62] And such was indeed the case with the modernist premises which postmodernism used – but transformed.

What we should not forget is that the act of designing and building is always a gesture in a social context,[63] and this is one of the ways in which formal parody meets social history. Architecture has both an aesthetic (form) and social (use) dimension. The odd combination of the empirical and the rational in modernist theory was meant to suggest a scientific determinism that was to combat the cumulative power and weight of all that had been inherited from the past. Faith in the rational, scientific mastery of reality implicitly – then explicitly – denied the inherited, evolved cultural continuity of history. It is perhaps a loss of faith in these modernist values that has led to postmodernist architecture today. The practitioners of this new mode form an eclectic grouping, sharing only a sense of the past (though not a 'random' one) and a desire to return to the idea of architecture as both communication and community (despite the fact that both of these concepts, from a postmodern perspective, now have a distinctly problematic and decentralised ring to them). The two major theoretical spokesmen of this mixed group have been Paolo Portoghesi and Charles Jencks – both practising architects.

As early as 1974, in *Le inibizioni dell'architettura moderna*, Portoghesi argued for the return of architecture to its roots in practical needs and in the (now problematised) aesthetic and social sense of continuity and community. Memory is central to this linking of the *past* with the *lived*. As an architect working in Rome, Portoghesi cannot avoid direct confrontation with the layers of history in his city and with the example of the baroque architects before him. History is not, however, a repository of models: he is not interested in copying or in straight revivalism. Like all the post*modernists* (and this is the reason for the label) he knows he cannot totally reject modernism, especially its material and technological advances, but he wants to integrate with these positive aspects of the immediate past the equally positive aspects of the more remote and repressed history of forms. All must be used; all must also be put into question, as architecture 'writes' history through its modern re-contextualising of the forms of the past. Surely this is exactly what Jameson and Eagleton are calling for,[64] but failing to see in postmodernist architecture, where the collective architectural language of postmodernism is put into ironic contact with 'the entire historical series of its past experiences' in order to create an art that is 'paradoxical and ambiguous but vital'.[65] (Portoghesi refuses to limit this historical borrowing to post-industrial periods and has been accused of being reactionary for it.[66])

An example might make clearer the form taken by this kind of historical interrogation or ironic contamination of the present by the past. Portoghesi's early (1959-60) Casa Baldi is a direct parody (in the sense of repetition with ironic distance) of Michelangelo's Capella Sforza in S Maria Maggiore. The exact structural echoing is made parodic – that is ironically different – by the use of new materials: vertically placed bricks and stones, instead of plaster. In addition, the church's interior shaping of corners has become the house's exterior form. Another kind of formal echoing occurs in the relation of this building to its environment. Portoghesi inverts the eighteenth-century taste for inserting ruins into the garden: the nearby (real) Roman ruins, overrun with vegetation, are echoed in his allowing nature to overrun the house as well. In his other designs, Portoghesi re-contextualises and (literally) inverts the forms of the past in an even more radical way: a baroque church ceiling (in Borgo d'Ale) can become the basis of a Portoghesi floorplan – ironically that of the Royal Palace of Amman.

The implication of this kind of relationship to the historical forms of the past is perhaps best expressed by architect Aldo van Eyck:

Man, after all, has been accommodating himself physically in this world for thousands of years. His natural genius has neither increased nor decreased during that time. It is obvious that the full scope of this enormous environmental experience cannot be contained in the present unless we telescope the past, ie the entire human effort, into it. This is not historical indulgence in a limited sense, not a question of travelling back, but merely of being aware of what 'exists' in the present – what has travelled into it.[67]

The naivety of modernism's ideologically and aesthetically motivated rejection of the past (in the name of the future) is not countered here by an equally naive antiquarianism, as Jameson and Eagleton assert. On the contrary, what does start to look naive, as I suggested in the last chapter, is this reductive notion that any recall of the past must, by definition, be sentimental nostalgia.

By its doubly parodic, double coding (that is, as parodic of both modernism and something else), postmodernist architecture also allows for that which was rejected as uncontrollable and deceitful by both modernism's *Gesamtkünstler* and its 'life-conditioner': that is, ambiguity and irony. Architects see themselves as no longer above or outside the experience of the users of their buildings; they are now in it, subject to its echoing history and its multivalent meanings – both the results of the 'recycling and creative transformation of any number of prototypes which [have] survived in the western world for centuries'.[68] In Portoghesi's words: 'It is the loss of memory, not the cult of memory, that will make us prisoners of the past'.[69] To disregard the collective memory of architecture is to risk making the mistakes of modernism and its ideology of the myth of social reform through purity of structure. Jane Jacobs has clearly documented the failure of this myth in her *Death and Life of Great American Cities*,[70] and even the opponents of postmodernism agree on the social and aesthetic effects of modernism on major urban centres.

Yet postmodernism does not entirely negate modernism. It cannot. What it does do is interpret it freely; it 'critically reviews it for its glories and its errors'.[71] Thus modernism's dogmatic reductionism, its inability to deal with ambiguity and irony, and its denial of the validity of the past were all issues that were seriously examined and found wanting. Postmodernism attempts to be historically aware, hybrid, and inclusive. Seemingly inexhaustible historical and social curiosity and a provisional and paradoxical stance (somewhat ironic, yet involved) replace the prophetic, prescriptive posture of the great masters of modernism. An example of this new collaborative position would be Robert

Pirzio Biroli's rebuilding of the Town Hall in Venzone, Italy following a recent earthquake. An elegant re-reading of the local structural models (mostly Palladian) of the Veneto region is here filtered through both the modernist technology best suited to a structure built in a seismic area and the particular needs of a modern administrative centre. Even more significantly, perhaps, this building was designed with the help of a co-operative formed by the inhabitants of the destroyed village – who also literally worked at the rebuilding themselves. Here memory played a central role: both the material and cultural memory of the users of the site and the collective architectural memory of the place (and architect).

This is not to deny that there is also kitsch, kitsch that is being labelled as postmodernism: the tacking of classical arches onto the front of modernist skyscrapers, for instance. This trendy attempt to capitalise on the popularity of postmodern historicism is not the same as postmodernism itself, but is a sign of its (perhaps inevitable) commodification. Just as modernist techniques and forms became debased by dilution and commercialisation, so the same has happened to the postmodern. This does not, however, undermine the positive potential value of postmodernist architecture as a whole and its salutary and necessary critique of some of the 'unexamined cant' of modernism.[72] A young Toronto architect, Bruce Kuwabara, recently pointed to the importance of the postmodern breaking up of modernist dogma and its reconsideration of the urban heritage of the city.[73] Another architect, Eberhardt Zeidler, has compared this postmodern shattering of the doxa to that of mannerism's challenge to the classical order of architecture.[74] Neither is in itself radically new, but both open things up to the possibility of the new.

There are always two ways of reading the contradictions of postmodernism, though. What Tom Wolfe sees as postmodernism's failure to break completely with modernism is interpreted by Portoghesi as a necessary and often even affectionate 'dialogue with a father'.[75] What Wolfe sees as Robert Venturi's empty ironic references, Portoghesi sees as a way of involving the decoding observer in the process of meaning-generating through ambiguity and multivalence.[76] It is also a way to mark an ideological stance: the Venturis, in their work on Las Vegas, for instance, can be seen – as Jencks notes – to

> express, in a gentle way, a mixed appreciation for the American Way of Life. Grudging respect, not total acceptance. They don't share all the values of a consumer society, but they want to speak to this society, even if partially in dissent.[77]

What to Wolfe is just camp historical reference in the work of Charles Moore is seen by Portoghesi as revealing the nearly limitless possibilities for recycling historic forms.[78] Moore's famous Piazza d'Italia in New Orleans is perhaps the best example of what novelist John Fowles once called both a homage and a kind of ironic thumbed nose to the past.[79] With none of modernism's iconoclasm, this parodic project shows both its critical awareness and its love of history by giving new meaning to old forms, though often not without irony. We are clearly dealing here with classical forms and ornamentation, but with a new and different twist: there is no hand-crafted decoration at all (this is not a celebration of romantic individuality or even gothic craftsmanship). The ornamentation is here, but it is of a new kind, one that partakes, in fact, of the machine-tooled impersonality and standardisation of modernism.

Because this is a public area for the Italian community of the city, Moore encodes signs of local Italian ethnic identity – from Latin inscriptions to a parody of the Trevi fountain. That particular corner of Rome is a complex mix of theatrical stage, palace, sculpture, and nature (rocks and water). In Moore's parodic rendition, the same elements are retained, but are now executed in new media. Sometimes even structures are refashioned and 're-functioned': a Tuscan column becomes a fountain, with water running down it. Despite the use of modernist materials like neon, concrete, and stainless steel, there is still a challenge to modernism. This appears not just in the eclectic (but never random) classical echoing, but also in the use of colour and ornament in general. The same challenge is also to be seen in the deliberate contextualising of the piazza into the local architecture. From a nearby skyscraper, Moore took the black and white colouring of the concentric rings, themselves reminiscent of the Place des Victoires in Paris. But what he did with these rings is new: the bull's-eye form draws the eye towards the centre, leading us to expect symmetry. But this symmetry is denied by the incompletion of the circles. As in much postmodernist art, the eye is invited to complete the form for itself; such counter-expectation urges us to be active, not passive, viewers.

In another implicitly anti-modernist gesture, Moore takes the actual social use of the square into account. The shape that interrupts the concentric circles is a familiar boot-shaped map of Italy, with Sicily at the point of the bull's eye. Such a focus is apt because most of the Italians in New Orleans are, in fact, Sicilian. On that spot there is a podium for speeches on St Joseph's day. Piazza d'Italia is meant as a return to the idea of architecture as intimately related to the *res publica*, and the awareness of this social and political function is reflected in its echoing of classical forms – that is, an echoing of a familiar and accessible public idiom. In an implied attack on the earnest seriousness of high modernism, such relevance and function here go together with irony: the boot-shape is constructed as a new Trevi fountain, a cascade of broken forms in which (when it works properly) water flows from the highest point (the Alps) to the lowest, along the Po, Arno, and Tiber rivers. This celebration of ethnic public identity is brought about by a formal reworking of the structures and functions of both classical and modernist architecture. The dialogue of past and present, of old and new, is what gives formal expression to a belief in change within continuity. The obscurity and hermeticism of modernism are abandoned for a direct engagement of the viewer in the processes of signification through re-contextualised social and historical references.

> Those who fear a wave of permissiveness would do well to remember that the ironic use of quotation and the archaeological artifact as an *objet trouvé* are discoveries of the figurative avant-garde of the twenties that have landed on the island of architecture sixty years late. (Paolo Portoghesi)

The other major theorist of postmodernism has been Charles Jencks, upon whose descriptions of Moore's work I have just been drawing. Influenced by modern semiotics, Jencks sees architecture as conveying meaning through language and convention. It is in this context that he situates the parodic recall of the past, the context of the need to look to history to enlarge the available vocabulary of forms. His description of Robert Stern's design for the Chicago Tribune Tower is typical in revealing his interest in the language and rhetoric of architecture:

> The skycolumn, one of the oldest metaphors for the tall building, is used very effectively here to accentuate the vertical dimension and emphasise the top. Unlike the [Adolf] Loos [1922] entry, from which Stern's tower derives, it ends with a flourish ... Unlike the Michelangelo pilasters [from the Palazzo Farnese in Rome], to which it also relates, it sets horizontal and vertical faces into extreme opposition by changing the colour and texture ... the building seems to ripple and then burst upwards towards its 'shower' of grey, gold, white and red – its

entablature and advertisement. Since the building is to be made from coloured glass, one would experience an odd oxymoronic contradiction – 'glass/masonry' – that, in a way, is as odd as the basic conceit: the skycolumn which supports the sky.[80]

The pun on newspaper columns is deliberate; the black and white of the building are meant to suggest print lines and, of course, the *Chicago Tribune* is red/read all over. The same punning occurs in Thomas Vreeland's World Savings and Loan Association building in California. The formal echoing of the black and white marble stripes of the campanile of the Cathedral in Sienna gives an ironic religious edge to the bank building's large and simple sign: 'World Savings'.

That such a complex combination of verbal and architectural languages also has direct social implications goes without saying to Jencks. Even without the verbal connection, the ideological dimension is clear. For instance, in his discussion of late-modern architecture (which Jameson confuses with postmodernism[81]), Jencks points out how the 'Slick-Tech' forms of 'Corporate Efficiency' imply effortless mechanical control of the users of the buildings.[82] But this industrial aesthetic of utility, exchange, and efficiency has been challenged by a postmodernist return to the historical and semantic awareness of architecture's relationship to the *res publica*, for example, with its very different associations of communal power, political process, and social vision.[83] In other words, the self-reflexive parodic introversion suggested by a turning to the aesthetic past is itself what makes possible an ideological and social intervention. Philip Johnson returned the city street to its users in the plaza of his AT&T Building in New York precisely through his parodic historical recalling of the *loggia* as shared public space.

There are obviously borderline cases, however, where the contradictions of the postmodern use and abuse of conventions may, in fact, be rather problematic. Jencks has trouble dealing with Michael Graves's Fargo/Moorhead Cultural Bridge with its admitted echoes of Ledoux, Castle Howard, Serliana, Wilson's architecture at Kew, Asplund, Borromini, and others. He adds other parodic reworkings which Graves does not mention, but which he himself notices: of modernist concrete construction, of mannerist broken pediments, and of cubist colours. Jencks acknowledges that the meaning of these historical references would likely be lost on the average citizen of the American mid-west. He seems to want to call this esoteric, private game-playing, but then stops and claims, after all, that 'there is a general penumbra of historical meaning which would, I believe, be perceived'.[84] Like all parody, postmodernist architecture can certainly be elitist, if the codes necessary for its comprehension are not shared by both encoder and decoder. But the frequent use of a very common and easily recognised idiom – often that of classical architecture – works to combat such exclusiveness.

In 'postmodern Classicism', to use Jencks's phrase, such explicit clues as columns and arches should be obvious enough to counteract any tendency to privacy of meaning. Like the 'misprision' of Harold Bloom's poets,[85] burdened by the 'anxiety of influence', postmodern classicists 'try hard to misread their classicism in a way which is still functional, appropriate and understandable'.[86] It is this concern for 'being under-stood' that replaces the modernist concern for purism of form. The search is now for a public discourse that will articulate the present in terms of the 'presentness' of the past and of the social placement of art in cultural discourse – then and now. Parody of the classical tradition offers a set of references that not only remain meaningful to the public but also continue to be compositionally useful to architects.

Parody of this kind, then, is one way of making the link between art and what Said calls the 'world', though it appears on the surface to be distinctly introverted, to be only a form of inter-art traffic. It is significant that postmodernist architects do not often use the term parody to describe their ironically recontextualised echoing of the forms of the past. I think this is because of the negative connotations of trivialisation caused by the retention of an historically limited definition of parody as ridiculing imitation. It is to this limitation of the meaning of parody that Jameson falls prey. But there appear to be many possible pragmatic positions and strategies open to parody today – at least if we examine actual contemporary works of art: from reverence to mockery. And it is this very range that postmodernist architecture illustrates so well. The mockery is something we always associate with parody; but the deference is another story. Nevertheless, deference is exactly what architects like Thomas Gordon Smith suggest in their loving, if ironic, refunctioning of previous architectural conventions.

Smith's Matthews Street House project in San Francisco incorporates into an unremarkable stucco bungalow the front of a quite remarkable asymmetrical temple, with a Michelangelesque broken pediment. The single column in the middle of the garden is a parody of a historically previous habit of setting classical ruins in the garden or grounds of grand homes. (It is also, therefore, an ironic comment on the modern vulgarisation of this habit: the presence of flamingos, dwarves, and lawn jockeys.) What is interesting, though, is that this column is precisely the one that is missing from the portico of the house. This is clearly not straight nostalgic revivalism (like Quinlan Terry's upper-class English country houses). It is closer to Martin Johnson's more extreme Ovenden House, with its definitely ironic echoes of the Victorian polychromatic church, of flying buttresses, and of medieval gunslits in its thick masonry. Parodic echoing of the past, even with this kind of irony, can still be deferential. It is in this way that postmodern parody marks its paradoxical doubleness of both continuity and change, both authority and transgression. Postmodernist parody, be it in architecture, literature, painting, film, or music, uses its historical memory, its aesthetic introversion, to signal that this kind of self-reflexive discourse is always inextricably bound to social discourse. In Charles Russell's words, the greatest contribution of postmodernism has been a recognition of the fact that 'any particular meaning system in society takes its place amongst – and receives social validation from – the total pattern of semiotic systems that structure society'.[87] If the self-conscious formalism of modernism in many of the arts led to the isolation of art from the social context, then postmodernism's even more self-reflexive parodic formalism reveals that it is art as discourse that is what is intimately connected to the political and the social.

Parody has perhaps come to be a privileged mode of postmodern formal self-reflexivity because its paradoxical incorporation of the past into its very structures often points to these ideological contexts somewhat more obviously, more didactically, than other forms. Parody seems to offer a perspective on the present and the past which allows an artist to speak *to* a discourse from *within* it, but without being totally recuperated by it. Parody appears to have become, for this reason, the mode of what I have called the 'ex-centric', of those who are marginalised by a dominant ideology. This is clearly true of contemporary architects trying to combat the hegemony of modernism in our century. But parody has also been a favourite postmodern literary form of writers in places like Ireland and Canada, working as they do from both inside and outside a culturally different and dominant context. And parody has certainly become a most popular and effective strategy of the other ex-centrics – of black, ethnic, gay, and feminist artists – trying to come to terms with and to respond, critically and creatively, to the still predominantly white, heterosexual, male culture in which they find themselves. For both artists and their audiences, parody sets up a dialogical relation between identification and distance. Like Brecht's *Verfremdungseffekt*, parody works to distance and, at the same time, to involve both artist and audience in a participatory hermeneutic activity. *Pace* Eagleton and Jameson, only on a very abstract level of theoretical analysis – one which ignores actual works of art – can it be dismissed as a trivial and depthless mode.

David Caute has argued that if art wants to make us question the 'world', it must question and expose itself first, and it must do so in the name of public action.[88] Like it or not, contemporary architecture cannot evade its representative social function. As Jencks explains: 'Not only does it express the values (and land values) of a society, but also its ideologies, hopes, fears, religion, social structure, and metaphysics.'[89] Because architecture both is and represents this state of affairs, it may be the most overt and easily studied example of postmodernist discourse, a discourse which may, in Charles Russell's words, perhaps at first appear to be merely the next logical step in accepted art history, but which subsequently must be seen as revealing the fatal limitations of current patterns of seeing or reading, and as having, in fact, effected a fundamental transformation of the practices of art.[90]

Postmodern architecture seems to me to be paradigmatic of our seeming urgent need, in both artistic theory and practice, to investigate the relation of ideology and power to all of our present discursive structures, and it is for this reason that I will be using it as my model throughout this study.

NOTES

1 See Janet Paterson, 'Le Roman "Postmoderne": mise au point et perspectives', *Canadian Review of Comparative Literature* 13, 2, pp 238-55.

2 Fredric Jameson, 'Postmodernism, Or The Cultural Logic of Late Capitalism', *New Left Review* 146, 1984, pp 53-92 (an extract is reproduced in this volume); Terry Eagleton, 'Capitalism, Modernism and Postmodernism', *New Left Review* 152, 1985, pp 60-73; Charles Newman, *The Post-Modern Aura: The Act of Fiction in an Age of Inflation*, Northwestern University Press, Evanston, Ill, 1985.

3 Charles Caramello, *Silverless Mirrors: Book, Self and Postmodern American Fiction*, University Presses of Florida, Tallahassee, 1983.

4 Cf Arthur Kroker and David Cooke, *The Postmodern Scene: Excremental Culture and Hyper-Aesthetics*, New World Perspectives, Montreal, 1986.

5 Susan Rubin Suleiman, 'Naming a Difference: Reflections on "Modernism versus Postmodernism" in Literature', *Approaching Postmodernism*, ed Dowe Fokkema and Hans Bertens, John Benjamins, Amsterdam and Philadelphia, Pa, 1986, pp 255-70.

6 Alan Wilde, *Horizons of Assent: Modernism, Postmodernism, and the Ironic Imagination*, John Hopkins University Press, Baltimore, Md, 1981; Christine Brooke-Rose, *A Rhetoric of the Unreal: Studies in Narrative and Structure, Especially of the Fantastic*, Cambridge University Press, Cambridge and New York, 1981; David Lodge, *The Modes of Modern Writing: Metaphor, Metonymy, and the Typology of Modern Literature*, Edward Arnold, London, 1977.

7 Eg John Barth, 'The Literature of Replenishment: Postmodernist Fiction', *The Atlantic* 145, 1, pp 65-71 (reproduced in this volume).

8 Severo Sarduy, 'El barroco y el neobarroco', *América Latina en su Literatura*, ed César Fernández Moreno, 2nd ed, Siglo XXI, Buenos Aires, 1974, pp 167-84.

9 Paolo Portoghesi, *Postmodern: The Architecture of the Postindustrial Society*, Rizzoli, New York, 1983.

10 Ibid, p 26.

11 See Marjorie Perloff, *The Dance of the Intellect: Studies in the Poetry of the Pound Tradition*, Cambridge University Press, 1985.

12 Wilde, *Horizons of Assent*.

13 Carl Darryl Malmgren, *Fictional Space in the Modernist and Postmodernist American Novel*, Bucknell University Press, Lewisburg, Pa, 1985.

14 Larry McCaffery, *The Metafictional Muse*, University of Pittsburgh Press, 1982, p 264.

15 Jameson, 'Cultural Logic', p 56.

16 Ibid, via Henri Lefebvre, *La Vie quotidienne dans le monde moderne*, Gallimard, Paris, 1968; Charles Russell, 'The Context of the Concept', *Romanticism, Modernism, Postmodernism*, ed Harry R Garvin, Bucknell University Press, Lewisburg, Pa; Associated University Press, London, 1980, 181-93; Donald D Egbert, *Social Radicalism and the Arts*, Knopf, New York, 1970; Matei Calinescu, *Faces of Modernity*, Indiana University Press, Bloomington, 1977.

17 Newman, *Postmodern Aura*, p 42; Richard E Palmer, 'Postmodernity and Hermeneutics', *Boundary* 2 5, 2, 1977 pp 636-93.

18 Eg Daniel Stern, 'The Mysterious New Novel', in *Liberations: New Essays on the Humanities in Revolution*, ed Ihab Hassan, Wesleyan University Press, Middletown, Conn, 1971, p 26.

19 Jean-François Lyotard, *The Postmodern Condition: A Report on Knowledge*, trans Geoff Bennington and Brian Massumi, University of Minnesota Press, Minneapolis, 1984.

20 Ibid, p 26.

21 Joseph F Graham, 'Critical Persuasion: In Response to Stanley Fish', *The Question of Textuality: Strategies of Reading in Contemporary American Criticism*, ed William V Spanos, Paul A Bové and Daniel O'Hara, Indiana University Press, Bloomington, 1982, p 148; Stephen Toulmin, *Human Understanding*, Princeton University Press, Princeton, NJ, 1972.

22 See Bernard Harrison, 'Deconstructing Derrida', *Comparative Criticism* 7, 1985, pp 3-24.

23 Gianni Vattimo, 'Dialettica, differenza, pensiero debole', *Il Pensiero Debole*, ed Gianni Vattimo and Pier Aldo Rovatti Feltrinelli, Milan, 1983; *La fine della modernità: Nichilismo ed ermeneutica nella cultura postmoderna*, Garzanti, Milan, 1985.

24 Jean-François Lyotard, 'Answering the Question: What is Postmodernism?', trans Régis Durand, *Postmodern Condition*.

25 Fredric Jameson, 'Foreword', ibid, pp vii-xi.

26 Theo D'Haen, *Text to Reader: A Communicative Approach to Fowles, Barth, Cortázar and Boon*, John Benjamins, Amsterdam, 1983.

27 Douglas Davis, *Artculture: Essays on the Post-Modern*, Harper and Row, New York, 1977.

28 Morse Peckham, *Man's Rage for Chaos: Biology, Behaviour and the Arts*, Chilton Books, Philadelphia, Pa, 1965.

29 Wilde, *Horizons of Assent*, p 131.

30 Roland Barthes, *Mythologies*, trans Annette Lavers, Granada, London, 1973.

31 Cf Hans Bertens, 'The Postmodern *Weltanschauung* and its Relation with Modernism: An Introductory Survey', *Approaching Postmodernism*, ed Dowe Fokkema and Hans Bertens, John Benjamins, Amsterdam and Philadelphia, Pa, 1986, p 17.

32 See Raymond Williams, *Culture and Society 1780-1950*, Doubleday, Garden City, NY, 1960, p xiii.

33 Susan Sontag, *Against Interpretation and Other Essays*, Dell, New York, 1967, p 304.

34 Richard Wasson, 'From Priest to Prometheus: Culture and Criticism in the Post-Modernist Period', *Journal of Modern Literature* 3, 5, pp 1,188-202.

35 Cf McCaffery, *Metafictional Muse*.

36 Jurgen Habermas, 'Modernity – An Incomplete Project', *The Anti-Aesthetic: Essays on Postmodern Culture*, ed Hal Foster, Bay Press, Port Townsend, Wash, 1983, pp 3-15.

37 See also Matei Calinescu, 'Postmodernism and Some Paradoxes of Periodization', *Approaching Postmodernism*, ed Fokkema and Bertens, p 246; Anthony Giddens, 'Modernism and Post-Modernism', *New German Critique* 22, pp 15-18.

38 Julia Kristeva, 'Postmodernism?' *Romanticism, Modernism, Postmodernism*, ed Harry R Garvin, Bucknell University Press, Lewisburg, Pa; Associated University Press, London, 1980, p 137.

39 Jameson, *'Cultural Logic'*.

40 Eagleton, 'Capitalism, Modernism and Postmodernism', p 72.

41 Portoghesi, *Architecture of the Postindustrial Society*, p 35.

42 Ibid, p 81.

43 Edward Said, *The World, the Text and the Critic*, Harvard University Press, Cambridge, Mass, 1983, p 4.

44 Eagleton, 'Capitalism, Modernism and Postmodernism', pp 61, 68.

45 Jameson, 'Cultural Logic', p 85.

46 Russell, 'Context of the Concept', p 189.

47 Jameson, 'Cultural Logic', p 67.

48 Cf Kenneth Frampton, 'Towards a Critical Regionalism: Six Points for an Architecture of Resistance', *Anti-Aesthetic: Essays on Postmodern Culture*, ed Foster.

49 Russell, 'Context of the Concept', p 186.

50 Geoffrey Broadbent, 'Meaning into Architecture', *Meaning in Architecture*, Charles Jencks and George Baird, Braziller, New York, 1969, p 51.

51 Andreas Huyssen, *After the Great Divide: Modernism, Mass Culture, Postmodernism*, Indiana University Press, Bloomington, 1986, p 186.

52 Jean-François Lyotard, *Le Postmoderne expliqué aux enfants: Correspondance 1982-1985*, Galilée, Paris, 1986, p 120.

53 See Lyotard, *Postmodern Condition;* Habermas, 'Modernity – An Incomplete Project'; Richard Rorty, 'Habermas, Lyotard et la postmodernité', *Critique* 442, 1984, pp 181-97.

54 Portoghesi, *Architecture of the Postindustrial Society*, p 28.

55 Paolo Portoghesi, *After Modern Architecture*, trans Meg Shore, Rizzoli, New York, 1982, p 3.

56 William Hubbard, *Complicity and Conviction: Steps Toward an Architecture of Convention*, MIT Press, Cambridge, Mass and London, 1980.

57 Jameson, 'Cultural Logic', p 65.

58 Tom Wolfe, *From Bauhaus to Our House*, Farrar, Strauss, & Giroux, New York, 1981, p 4.

59 Ibid, p 17.

60 George Baird, '"La Dimension Amoureuse" in Architecture', *Meaning in Architecture*, Jencks and Baird, Braziller, New York, 1969.

61 Charles Jencks, *Le Corbusier and the Tragic View of Architecture*, Allen Lane, London, 1973, pp 51-54, 72.

62 Portoghesi, *Architecture of the Postindustrial Society*.

63 Baird, '"La Dimension Amoureuse" in Architecture', p 81.

64 Jameson, 'Cultural Logic', p 85; Eagleton, 'Capitalism, Modernism and Postmodernism', p 73.

65 Portoghesi, *Architecture of the Postindustrial Society*, pp 10-11.

66 Frampton, 'Towards a Critical Regionalism', p 20.

67 Aldo van Eyck, 'The Interior of Time', *Meaning in Architecture*, Jencks and Baird, p 171.

68 Portoghesi, *After Modern Architecture*, p 5.

69 Ibid, p 111.

70 Jane Jacobs, *Death and Life of American Cities*, Vintage, New York, 1961.

71 Portoghesi, *After Modern Architecture*, p 28.

72 Hubbard, *Complicity and Conviction*, p 8.

73 Bruce Kuwabara, 'A Problem for Post-Modern Architecture: Which Heritage to Preserve?', panel at University College Symposium on 'Our Postmodern Heritage', Toronto, 1987.

74 Eberhardt Zeidler, 'Post-Modernism: From the Past into the Future' panel at University College Symposium on 'Our Postmodern Heritage', Toronto, 1987.

75 Tom Wolfe, *Bauhaus to Our House*, p 127-29; Portoghesi, *After Modern Architecture*, p 80.

76 Portoghesi, *After Modern Architecture*, p 86.

77 Charles Jencks, *The Language of Postmodern Architecture*, Academy, London, 1977, p 70.

78 Portoghesi, *After Modern Architecture*, p 77.

79 John Fowles, *The Ebony Tower*, Little, Brown, Boston, Mass and Toronto, 1974.

80 Charles Jencks, *Post-Modern Classicism: The New Synthesis*, Academy, London, 1980, p 35

81 Jameson, 'Cultural Logic', p 80-83.

82 Charles Jencks, *Architecture Today*, Abrams, New York, 1982, p 50.

83 Ibid, p 92.

84 Charles Jencks, *Late-Modern Architecture and Other Essays*, Academy, London, 1980.

85 Harold Bloom, *The Anxiety of Influence*, Oxford University Press, New York, 1973.

86 Jencks, *Post-Modern Classicism*, p 12.

87 Russell, 'Context of the Concept', p 197.

88 David Caute, *The Illusion*, Harper and Row, New York, 1972.

89 Jencks, *Architecture Today*, p 178; see also Jameson, 'Cultural Logic', p 56.

88 Russell, 'Context of the Concept', p 182.

From *A Poetics of Postmodernism, History, Theory, Fiction,* Routledge, New York and London, 1988.

Jim Collins
POST-MODERNISM AS CULMINATION
THE AESTHETIC POLITICS OF DECENTRED CULTURES

The goal of this study is to explore the nature of popular narratives and the ideologies they promote once an 'official' or 'common' culture begins to fragment and various discourses begin to compete for the same or overlapping functions within the same semiotic context. Much of what I say about the tensions between narratives, the overall lack of 'cultural orchestration', and the basic decentring of culture has been ascribed specifically to Post-Modernism both as a movement and as a 'condition'. While I refer to Post-Modernist texts throughout this work, here a full-scale discussion of its most distinctive characteristics is essential as a way of understanding how those characteristics are not sudden developments, but the culmination of processes that were at work even in the pre-Modernist period. The debate over Post-Modernism has been highly politicised, and a thorough examination of the key points of conflict should clarify the politics of such decentring as a style, a cultural context, and a critical approach.

In true Post-Modernist fashion this chapter will juxtapose radically opposing positions concerning the nature of Post-Modernism coming from both critics and artists of various media – Jean Louis Baudrillard, Jean-François Lyotard, Fredric Jameson, Charles Jencks, Charles Moore, Manuel Puig, Hans-Jürgen Syberberg. This multi-media, multi-discourse combination is necessary for a number of reasons. First, the vast majority of theorising done on Post-Modernism has been extremely polemical and, unfortunately, extremely narrow in its scope, thereby producing only distorted notions about what it is as an artistic movement as well as a cultural milieu. Second, the comparative approach will establish the sites of conflict in the debate on Post-Modernism and evaluate many of the charges made against it: specifically that it annihilates artistic 'difference', demolishes narrative, abolishes subjectivity, and just plain denies 'history'. Third, the multi-media approach has become necessary if for no other reason than that so many of the artworks in question are explicitly or implicitly a reaction to the interpenetration of various modes of encoding and decoding used by and for different media. Fourth, the analysis of textual practices in tandem with critical theory is virtually unavoidable because the distinctions between primary and secondary texts have become increasingly difficult to make since the former has very often made the latter a constitutive element of the text itself. Lastly, any thorough discussion of Post-Modernism must examine the diversity of styles and positions taken by different discourses because one of its chief defining factors is that it is a context without a *Zeitgeist*, and therefore the conflicts and gaps between these discourses are a central part of that which differentiates that context from preceding ones.

While critical opinion on Post-Modernism may be sharply divided, the elaborate attacks and defences have one common denominator – the establishment of a dialogic relationship between Modernism and Post-Modernism, in which one must be the clear force of artistic and cultural good, and the other must threaten the future of civilisation. The resulting distinctions between the two movements/moments have tended towards the hyperbolic. Nevertheless, most of them remain valuable, since the only real 'mistaken' opinion in this debate is one that fails to recognise that the substantial stylistic and ideological differences between the two reflect radical differences in the cultures they envision. As Andreas Huyssen has said, 'Post-Modernism at its deepest level represents not just another crisis within the perpetual cycle of boom and bust, exhaustion and renewal, which has characterised the trajectory of modernist culture. It rather represents a new type of crisis *of* that modernist culture itself'.[1]

Dominant for Whom? The Last Train to Zeitgeist

Perhaps the best way to begin a discussion of Post-Modernism is to consider how it has already been 'historicised', since the problems implicit in such attempts reveal the complexity of the contemporary situation and its resistance to traditional modes of historiography. The vast majority of histories of cultural production have concentrated on the evolution of 'dominant' styles; Stefano Tani's study of the Post-Modernist detective novel is a perfect case in point.[2] Tani contends that the history of detective fiction is the shifting of 'dominants' in dialectical fashion. The British (White Glove) detective novel was dominant until replaced by the American hard-boiled, which was dominant until replaced by the Post-Modernist detective novel. He invokes Yuri Tynjanov's stages of literary change as the theoretical foundation for this evolution – ie the 'automatised constructive principle' is replaced by the 'opposite constructive principle', which then becomes 'automatised' and so on. The emphasis on the changing 'dominant' may well provide an explanation for the evolution of certain genres, but it does so only by minimising their heterogeneity at any given point.

According to Tani, now that the Post-Modernist detective novels have become the new dominant, earlier forms such as the White Glove and hard-boiled have faded into oblivion. Quite the opposite is actually the case. How does this evolving dominant mode of literary history account for not only the very active continuation of both traditions by very popular contemporary authors (eg Martha Grimes, PD James, Robert Parker, Elmore Leonard), but also the continued popularity of Sayers, Hammett, and company through regular re-editions and new adaptations of these novels on radio, television, film, etc? The persistence and continuation of earlier forms of detective fiction now supposedly non-dominant (and therefore dead or dying) can be seen in the popularity of their reactivations, eg Nicholas Meyer's *The Seven Per-Cent-Solution* (1974), Julian Symons's *The Black Heath Poisonings* (1978) and *Three Pipe Problem* (1975). This last text in particular epitomises the spirit of these reactivations. *Three Pipe Problem* focuses on an actor portraying Sherlock Holmes on a TV series who, because of his ability to bring Holmesian standards to the present, eventually solves an actual murder in modern London – 'in character', as it were. His popularity, and the popularity of all such recreations of Holmes or Marlowe or Spade, suggests that these earlier supposedly non-dominant forms continue to fulfil a function for the modern reading publics.

That so many texts from so many different stages in the history of detective fiction continue to enjoy simultaneous popularity, especially over the last decade, suggests the insufficiency of the alternating dominant model to describe the Post-Modernist situation. The Tani/Tynjanov model is essentially evaluative; it may describe the radically new or avant-garde of a given period, but not indicate what is actually 'dominant' either in regard to production or consumption. This is particularly obvious when Tani suggests that Post-Modernism is the new 'dominant' in detective fiction. Dominant for whom?

What differentiates Post-Modernism from earlier periods is that while a specific style may be identifiable, its circulation and popularity do not define what is distinctive about

the period. In other words, there is indeed a Post-Modernist textual *practice* in literature, film, architecture, etc, but what distinguishes the Post-Modernist context is the
simultaneous presence of that style along with Modernist, pre-Modernist, and non-
Modernist styles – all enjoying significant degrees of popularity with different audiences
and institutions within a specific culture. While this co-presence of competing styles
could be found in the Modernist period as well, Post-Modernism departs from its
predecessors in that as a textual practice it actually incorporates the heterogeneity of
those conflicting styles, rather than simply asserting itself as the newest radical
alternative seeking to render all conflicting modes of representation obsolete. As a style,
then, Post-Modernism can become 'dominant' only in localised situations; Post-
Modernism's recognition that culture has become a multiplicity of competing signs
necessarily prevents it from asserting total stylistic 'dominance' – to do so would violate
one of the constitutive principles of the movement. *Diva* may be a Post-Modernist text,
but the truly Post-Modernist context is one in which Beineix's film plays on the cable
movie-channel Cinemax, while *Murder, She Wrote* and *Mickey Spillane's Mike Hammer*
run on opposite network channels.

The presence of tensions between conflicting types of representations, a presence
that one finds incorporated in Post-Modernist texts and thoroughly ingrained in the
Post-Modernist context problematises the Tani/Tynjanov approach – as well as all other
histories that seek to minimise heterogeneity in pursuit of a dominant style, collective
spirit, or any other such unitary conception. The common denominator of all such
histories, from Oswald Spengler's *The Decline of the West* to Will Wright's *Six Guns in
Society*, has been the privileging of homogeneous structures that allow historians to
draw rather neat generalisations that support far more grandiose claims about a culture
'as a whole'. Emphasis has been placed repeatedly on the diachronic changes between
periods, movements, moods, etc, instead of on synchronic tensions within those
subdivisions – which would naturally undermine any unitary formulations concerning a
particular period's representation of itself in a specific time.

Traditional histories of artistic production have failed to account for its heterogeneity
in decentred cultures because time and culture have been treated as if they were
uniform. Siegfried Kracauer describes this problem quite succinctly: 'Under the spell of
the homogeneity and irreversible direction of chronological time, conventional
historiography tends to focus on what is believed to be more or less a continuous large
scale sequence of events and to follow the course of these units through the centuries.'[3]
The chief way to break this spell is to begin with a different set of priorities – specifically
that most periods (particularly since the eighteenth century) are a 'mixture of inconsistent
elements', and that different art forms, discourses, etc, all have their own history as well
as a societal history. Fundamental changes in the Western may run parallel to changes in
American capitalism, but the musical and the crime film either run counter to such
changes or demonstrate no awareness of them whatsoever. To account for these
differences, histories (not only of Post-Modernism, but of any cultural production since
the end of the eighteenth century) that have been predicated on theories of evolution,
mass consciousness, or *Zeitgeist*, must be replaced by histories that emphasise synchronic
tensions, the fragmentation of mass consciousness, and the possibility of more than one
Zeitgeist per culture.

Kracauer describes the on going process that culminates in Post-Modernism quite
effectively when he claims that 'the upshot is that the period, so to speak, disintegrates
before our eyes. From a meaningful spatiotemporal unit it turns into a kind of meeting
place for chance encounters – something like the waiting room of a railway station'. The

waiting-room analogy can be fruitful only if further elaborated. In decentred cultures, various narrative discourses may originate within the same space, but they depart on different trains for different destinations. To make one discourse or traveller the representative of all travellers and assume they are all headed in the same direction on the same train, based on an individual itinerary, can only lead to a basic misrepresentation of that situation. At different times during the day, of course, such assumptions may be relatively safe (eg at five o'clock, commuters in large numbers will all be headed towards the suburbs). One can also formulate assumptions based on representative texts more safely in certain cultural circumstances than in others (eg during World War II, virtually every genre in Hollywood incorporated the 'War Effort' in one way or another). In other words, homogeneity of artistic production is not an impossibility; in a specific situation it may be inevitable. But to presuppose homogeneity in every situation leads to fundamentally reductive and, in the long run, thoroughly misleading characterisations of that culture; this is clearly the case regarding Post-Modernism.

Difference and Belief: But Oh! the Difference to Them

The notion of culture as a semiotic train station without a *Zeitgeist* has been judged unacceptable by many cultural theorists and has been cause for many vehement attacks on the 'chaotic' nature of Post-Modernist cultures. Much has been made of the technological revolution's impact on production and consumption of film and television, but the changes wrought by this revolution have had little impact on the presuppositions of most cultural studies. The force of these changes has all too often been measured by models of society and cultural production developed in the nineteenth century. Jean Baudrillard's belief in a basic implosion of meaning in a technological age exemplifies the use of nineteenth-century models to account for cultural production in post-industrial, post-technological-revolution societies.[4] He insists that the constant bombardment of the individual by so many different sources of information has led to 'the relentless destructuring of the *social*'. Baudrillard seeks the lack of coordination of these sources as pure entropy, yet they appear so only if one's model for the State is one in which some agency somehow coordinates all cultural activity into a cohesive, centralised whole. He contends that 'information, in all its forms, instead of intensifying or even creating the 'social relationship' is, on the contrary, an entropic process, a modality of the extinction of the social'. He confuses decentralised activity with pure entropy, as if once coordination and centralisation have faded 'the social' no longer exists.

But as Kenneth Roberts[5] and others have argued, the fragmentation of traditional categories of class solidarity results not in entropy, but in realignment along different, specifically twentieth-century lines. Underlying all of Baudrillard's claims is a basically Adorno-like combination of nostalgia and paranoia: 'Whatever its content . . . the objective of information is always to circulate meaning, to *subjugate the masses to meaning*. . . . There is a kind of reverse shamming among the masses, and in each of us, at the individual level, which corresponds to that travesty of meaning and communication in which we are *imprisoned by the system*'. As in Adorno, one finds in Baudrillard this basic distrust of the mass media culture created by technological change, with authentic 'social relationships' existing only in the Paradise Lost of the pre-technological age.

The inability of this fundamentally nostalgic position to account for a decentred, but not entropic techno-culture becomes clear in Baudrillard's belief that 'the masses do not choose, do not produce differences, but indifference. . . . Yet it is not meaning or the increase of meaning that produces intense pleasure. It is rather its neutralisation that fascinates us'. The masses respond to the bombardment of signs 'by reducing all articulate discourse to a single irrational groundless dimension in which signs lose their meaning and subside into exhausted fascination'. Yet Baudrillard offers a poor case for this indifference in the masses and their refusal to differentiate or make choices. Where is this mass indifference, this mass recognition that somehow it's all just the same difference. Does it really make no difference to a housewife whether she reads Rosemary Rodgers or Thomas Pynchon, or to a teenager whether he or she watches MTV or Mutual of Omaha's *Wild Kingdom?* Signs may be exhausted for Baudrillard, but are they for everyone?

The problem is that 'the masses' for Baudrillard are always a unitary quantity – *they* think this, or *they* believe that as *one* undifferentiated body. The failure to recognise the persistence of belief in differences within the masses is most obvious in Baudrillard's misappropriation of Mannoni's 'je sais bien, mais quand même'. He asserts, 'One both believes it and doesn't believe it at the same time, without questioning it seriously, an attitude that may be summed up in the phrase: "Yes, I know, but all the same." For Baudrillard the phrase signifies an intellectual shrug of the shoulders, yet for Mannoni the phrase describes the basis of fetishistic belief which, if anything, means the insistence on differentiation, the denial of neutrality.[6] The basis for fetishistic pleasure is always a specific object, and, as such, totally contradicts formats – the 'monster'-sized paperback novel, the multi-volume family saga series, etc. Obviously, the multi-volume, continuing saga was an established tradition by the nineteenth century, so this, in and of itself, is hardly a new phenomenon; but its re-emergence and ubiquity next to cash registers in supermarkets throughout the nation can hardly be seen as a sign that narrative is somehow dying or losing its force in contemporary culture.

That the opposite is indeed in effect, that the power of narrative has not only persisted, but intensified, can be seen in the narrativisation of non-narrative discourses. The most striking example is, of course, rock music, especially in video form. Rock lyrics since their inception have tended to tell stories, but the ballad form (in its strictest definition) was always far more common in folk, country, and blues music. The most significant change has not been in the lyrics as such, but rather in the actual presentation of rock music; here, the performance mode of the sixties has been completely transformed into a narrative mode of the eighties. A significant percentage of rock videos have either done away with outright performance, or placed it entirely within a narrative context, so that very few videos maintain anything like a 'concert' aesthetic. (There are, of course, significant exceptions – Bruce Springsteen's *Dancing in the Dark* (1985), Robert Palmer's *Addicted to Love* (1986).) Most surprising about this transition is that very often, even though narrativisation appears entirely unjustified by the song lyrics, the band members 'act out' those lyrics (often in period costumes and settings); videos such as these are attempting to narrativise, spatially and temporally, songs about atemporal 'states of consciousness'. It is difficult to imagine a quintessentially sixties band like Crosby, Stills, Nash, and Young acting out *Ohio* (1971) (even though the lyrics appear ripe for narrativising), because the dominant mode of presentation remained the rock concert festival, and the dominant modes of dissemination remained largely non-narrative media – radio, record album, television variety shows, etc. Now that one of the major modes of dissemination has become television, it has developed its own narrative format (the four to five minute mini-narrative) to compete with the narrative on the channels that surround it. It comes as no surprise that a recent Neil Young video *Touch the Night* (1987) is completely narrativised, with Young acting the role of a local newscaster in full make-up and costume that completely disguise his recognisable stage image.

Lyotard's notion of 'micro-narratives' used as the basis of legitimation of various forms of discourse, scientific as well as non-scientific, would be especially useful were his notion of narrative legitimation not oversimplified and ahistorical.[8] In his discussion of scientific and narrative 'knowledge', he claims that 'narrative knowledge does not give priority to the question of its own legitimation and that it certifies itself in the pragmatics of its own transmission without having recourse to argument or proof'. While narrative may not utilise the same type of proof as scientific discourse, the history of narrative since the eighteenth century has been one in which strategies of legitimation have become increasingly sophisticated as narrative has continued to differentiate itself into multiple, often conflicting discourses. Lyotard's conception of narrative here would appear to be based on a primitive storytelling situation around the proverbial camp-fire where one storyteller told one body of tales to an extremely homogeneous audience. The ramifications of this conception of narrative (and its transmission) are especially serious, since it presupposes not only a grand uniformity to narrative, but to cultural production as a whole, excluding the *philosophe* tradition and the radical avant-garde.

The Post-Modernist condition posited by Lyotard, with its fragmentation and decentring, can only appear to be a radically new *episteme* rather than the culmination of processes at work within popular culture for the past two centuries. Lyotard asserts, like Jameson, that 'grand narratives' have disappeared, but the two questions that need to be asked at this point are whether such 'grand' or 'master' narratives actually did exist for entire cultures once narrative and audience begin to fragment (ie since the disintegration of the public sphere in the eighteenth century), and whether the absence of the alleged 'master narratives' has produced only a greater reliance on narratives insisting on their ability to explain fragmentary existence to fragmentary audiences. For Lyotard, the only hope for this 'chaotic' culture is that which resists commodification – the avant-garde of the high Modernist period. Belief, differentiation, and narrative have not only survived, but intensified in contemporary cultures; but since they are supposedly commodified, they are, for Lyotard, therefore invalid.

And the Radical Avant-Garde Shall Make You Free, or 'Cigarettes and Whisky and Commodification'

One of the most frequent attacks on the chaotic nature of Post-Modernist culture has taken the form of an elaborate apology for Modernism, where an 'authentic' avant-garde still existed. In the appendix to *The Post-Modern Condition*, Lyotard dismisses the eclecticism of this movement as 'the degree zero of contemporary general culture', as 'kitsch' that 'panders' in the 'absence of aesthetic criteria'. Likewise, Jameson rejects Post-Modernism because it is 'sheer heterogeneity, random difference, a co-existence of a host of distinct forces whose effectivity is undecidable.'[9] This shared paranoia concerning heterogeneity and the lack of absolute aesthetic criteria reveals several of the basic limitations of both of these essays, especially their nostalgia for the Paradise Lost of the homogeneous culture, and the Marxists'/avant-gardists' ability to stand in opposition to it, making easy, yet absolute value judgments – rather like a counter-cultural Salvation Army beating its moralistic drum about the wickedness of the dominant culture.

The cornerstone of this elaborate defense of what Jameson calls the 'High Modernists' is a fascination with the then still operative category of 'personal expression', which is now seemingly lost for ever. The Post-Modern world, Jameson insists, means the end of 'style, in the sense of the unique and the personal, the end of the distinctive individual brushstroke which results in the collapse of the high modernist ideology of style – what is as unique and unmistakeable as your own fingerprints, as incomparable as your own body' ('Post-Modernism', 1984). The choice of terms used here to characterise this cultural crisis suggests that what Jameson considers High Modernism bears a striking resemblance to High Romanticism as it has been transformed and carried into the twentieth century. The obsession with the absolute uniqueness of self and style, carried to the point where a quasi-private language (as individual as a fingerprint) becomes the ideal mode of expression, is a common thread that ties Chateaubriand's *René* (1802) to Barthes's *Fragments d'un discours amoureux* (1977). The twentieth-century artist must occupy the position of perpetual, enlightened outsider. Popular culture in such a scenario serves only as a vapid background against which the personal expression of the artist stands out in bold relief.

The chief crime of Post-Modernism, then, would appear to be its robbing the Modernist/Romantic of the neat binary oppositions which made their status so easily definable. Jameson claims that our contemporary society 'reflects not only the absence of any great collective project, but also the unavailability of the older national language itself' ('Post-Modernism', 1984). There are two enormous problems with this assertion. First, is Jameson really bemoaning the loss of a common national language for its own sake, or rather as a monolith which allows individual oppositional values to stand out clearly against it? When Jameson moves his argument into the realm of contemporary architecture, his preference for Modernists such as Mies van der Rohe becomes explicit, but Mies's architecture (which will be discussed in greater detail below) and that of the International Style as a whole was conceived as a radical break with the impoverished 'national' architecture that served as the status quo. The International Style office building was never intended to blend into the 'vernacular' architecture, but rather to serve as an affront to it, a disjunctive break with its surroundings.

The second, and more fundamental problem here concerning the mythic 'national language' is that it was never (as Bakhtin has argued so convincingly) the univocal, homogeneous entity that linguists and theoreticians have assumed it to be.[10] If anything, the centripetal and centrifugal forces Bakhtin describes, the intersection of various specialised discourses and dialects could be described as a kind of radical eclecticism, the 'sheer heterogeneity' that so repulses Jameson. No simple binary oppositions can exist within the 'heteroglot' nature of culture, nor can any one agency decide on the 'effectivity' of all cultural production in a once and for all manner for entire publics.

The attacks levelled against Post-Modernism by Jameson, Terry Eagleton[11] and their disciples call out for the same kind of symptomatic reading that Eagleton does of the Scrutiny group or the New Critics.[12] Eagleton's rejection of Post-Modernism is total, with many a specific textual example to mar the effect. This wholesale rejection reveals the latent Romanticism not only of the High Modernists they praise, but of Marxist critics as well. This becomes most obvious in the fetishising of alienation as a positive value in and of itself, as if somehow, Post-Modernism as a movement has ruined all the fun of being alienated. Eagleton asserts that the 'depthless, styleless, dehistoricised, decathected surfaces of Post-Modernist culture are not meant to signify alienation, for the very concept of alienation must necessarily posit a dream of authenticity which Post-Modernism finds unintelligible' (1986).

But what is really dehistoricised here? Is it Post-Modernism, or this vision of 'authenticity' which floats above various cultures like some sort of representational El Dorado transcending all signification? This 'authenticity' is remarkably similar to the

Romantics' notion of 'individual genius', in that both exist as semiotic, sanctified categories predicated on alienation. This merging of Romanticism and Marxism becomes apparent in Eagleton's only specific example of the dreaded Post-Modernism – 'Mayakovksy's poetry readings in the factory yard become Warhol's shoes and soup cans'. The Mayakovksy image epitomises the conflation of Romanticism and Marxism – Chateaubriand Meets the Noble Savages of the Working Jungle.

For Neo-Romantic Marxists, perhaps, the most significant and unacceptable ramification of this decentred and heteroglot culture is that within such a context any number of different aspects of popular culture must cease to operate as mere backdrops for theory and must actually assume a critical function that is normally reserved for avant-garde or radical cultural analysis. Jameson's rejection of popular culture as a vehicle for such a function is most obvious in 'Reification and Utopia in Mass Culture' where he comes very close to the Frankfurt School in his characterisation of these twin functions.[13] On one level, the essay might appear a rather lukewarm apology for popular culture, since he acknowledges that 'even the most degraded type of mass culture remains implicitly negative and critical of the social order from which, as a product and a commodity, it springs'. But the utopian value is there only because 'they cannot manipulate unless they offer some genuine shred of content as a fantasy bribe to the public about to be so manipulated'. He summarises his position in the following manner:

> We will now suggest that anxiety and hope are two faces of the same *collective consciousness* so that the works of mass culture, even if their function lies in the legitimation of the existing order – or some worse one – cannot do their job without deflecting *in the latter's service* the deepest and most fundamental hopes and fantasies of the collectivity to which they can therefore, no matter in how distorted a fashion, be found to have given voice [emphasis mine].

Popular movies and films, then, may have a utopian/critical dimension, but it is entirely produced and managed by the existing order. The presuppositions here reflect a rigidly monolithic society – the collective consciousness, the collectivity, which orchestrates all cultural production quite effectively – all, of course, except for the avant-garde and radical social theorists who somehow stand above this manipulation. The notion that popular culture may be heterogeneous and therefore take a critical position regarding the society which produces it simply cannot be allowed within the Culture as Grand Hotel scenario.

Underlying this rejection of a 'mass culture' is the belief that the commodification of cultural phenomena has meant their subjugation to the dominant order, and therefore their invalidation as 'genuine' expressions of anything other than that of the multi-national corporations which produce them. The commodity status of both popular and Post-Modernist texts appears to be their 'original sin' according to Jameson and Eagleton, that which makes them inferior works of art, somehow tainted by the filthy lucre one must pay in order to appreciate them. The foundation for this, of course, is a nostalgia for a Golden Age of 'folk' culture. Jameson states in unequivocal terms, 'The commodity production of contemporary or industrial mass culture has nothing whatsoever to do, and nothing in common, with older forms of popular or folk art' (1979).

Only the Modernist text remains somehow admirable in this, since it utilises various strategies to resist commodification, usually by resisting the use of codes comprehensible to its audience (which ironically suggests an extremely 'privatised' rather than 'folk' aesthetic – the 'fingerprint' instead of the 'carnival'). But the contention that commodification suddenly tainted all cultural production starting somewhere in the nineteenth century, and then just plain ruined it in the twentieth century is fraught with a number of historical problems. The argument that art has become commodified, and therefore less aesthetically and politically pleasing than it had been before, has been made by innumerable critics from a wide variety of critical perspectives and has been located, interestingly enough, at different time periods. One could argue quite convincingly, as John Berger and others have done, that the key transition phase was the replacement of the fresco by easel-painting as the dominant mode of European painting.[14] The industrial revolution is another commonly chosen phase, as is the arrival of supposedly 'late' capitalism somewhere after World War II. The variation in the dates chosen for the Age of Commodification does not suggest that such transitions have not occurred, but instead problematises the alleged impact – since so much of the cultural production that has been valorised by one theorist as pre-commodified has been vilified as post-commodified by another. Such discrepancies suggest that the impact of commodification is hardly as far-reaching or one-dimensional as many would have it, since its impact and temporal dimensions appear to depend more on the scenario of the historian than any kind of episteme-shattering moment in the evolution of material production.

One of the more perplexing developments that has occurred in theorising the 'history' of commodification has been the admiration for pre-capitalist modes of financing artistic activities, resulting in rather odd apologies for patronage rather than public support. Jameson's work once again summarises this position quite effectively. In the pre-capitalist period:

The relationship between artist and public was still in one way or another a social institution and a concrete social and interpersonal relationship with its own validation and specificity. With the coming of the market, this institutional status of artistic consumption and production vanishes: art becomes one more branch of commodity production, the artist loses all social status and faces the options of becoming a *poète maudit* or a journalist. The relationship to the public is problematised and the latter becomes a virtual 'public introuvable' (1979).

The 'social status' is truly problematic here, since that status, when not dependent upon a paying public, depended entirely upon a patronage system in which the artist's status was carefully proscribed (as countless forewords in sixteenth- and seventeenth-century volumes of literature will attest), thoroughly 'institutionalised' within a carefully orchestrated system. With the shift from patron to public support did indeed come a fundamental change in the relationship between artist and public – but rather than de-institutionalisation, it must be understood as a de-stabilisation of the entire exchange, one which changed the pre-established relationships (both in the constitution of the audience and the hierarchy of discourses [à la Mukarovsky]) that had institutionalised *what* was read *by whom* for *what* reason. The public does not become *introuvable*, nor *invisible*, but *infixible* in its fragmentation into shifting reading publics consuming competing modes of narrative discourse.

Eagleton virtually makes commodification and Post-Modernism coterminous, since the latter to his mind is merely the end result of processes begun in the former. Although critical of Modernism as a movement for a number of reasons, Eagleton praises it for at least resisting commodification, whereas Post-Modernism simply embraces it wholeheartedly – 'Post-Modernist culture will dissolve its own boundaries and become co-extensive with ordinary commodified life itself' (1986). For Eagleton, commodification has replaced the 'public sphere' of the eighteenth century in a bastardised form, making the product rather than the opinions of the learned community the basis for a sense of common culture.

Yet this shift from public sphere to commodified sphere is challenged by works which thematise commodification in the former period. Perhaps the best example of this is William Hogarth's 'The Battle of the Pictures' (1744). While this print was no doubt inspired by Jonathan Swift's 'The Battle of the Books' (1704), the conflict is situated in a different terrain here. Swift's battle was located entirely 'within the library', as it were, and combat between the ancients and the moderns remains an idealist struggle. Hogarth's engraving also includes such conflicts, but places them within a materialist context that acknowledges in explicit detail that his own works are products as well as artistic creations. Designed as a bidder's ticket for an auction of his own paintings, the engraving represents the struggle between his own work and the invading foreign paintings, the former depicting scenes of British life, the latter all of a religious-mythological nature. The foreign paintings are assembly-line products, emphasised not only by their stockpile arrangement, but by the 'Dto' (for 'ditto') designation in the upper right-hand corner of each, and the auctioneer's gavel as their battle-flag. Behind them sits a building (the auction house or the House of Commerce), as poorly designed as these paintings, with 'PUFS' (as in 'puffed up') on its weather-vane, and a ludicrously over-framed portrait by the door. At the far right, British paintings emanate from Hogarth's own studio, and the weather-vane is balanced at the opposite corner by the palette and brushes of the artist. The opposition could hardly be more clear-cut, and one could quite easily construct a reading in pure Frankfurt School fashion that would see 'Commodity attacking Pure Art', or 'Creativity Defeated by Mass Production'.

Yet the choice of images within the engraving stresses the naivety of such a reading. The Hogarth works which are clearly identifiable within his studio all come from *The Harlot's Progress*, *The Rake's Progress*, and *Marriage à la Mode*, three series which focus explicitly on characters completely consumed and defined by their material circumstances. The painting on the easel, for example, is the second picture from *Marriage à la Mode*, in which the commodified nature of contemporary British society is emphasised by a loveless marriage of financial convenience, and the actual representation of bank notes and bills in the hand of a valet (obscured, not coincidentally, by an 'attacking' European painting of Van Eyck's *The Aldobrandini Marriage*).

The conflict between the two representations of marriages – one mythological, one realist – is central because it depicts the struggle between two different styles (in perhaps the most explicit kind of intertextuality imaginable), but also the differences in the societies there depicted. Rather than set up an idealistic landscape that transcends the vulgarity of commodified art, and by extension commodified existence, Hogarth's engraving acknowledges that the commodification of art is simply part of a commodified society and that within such a context conflict becomes a fact of existence. To extrapolate Hogarth's message for today's artworld, the appropriate gesture on the part of the artist is to engage actively in such representational battles rather than attempt a utopian transcendence through mythology or Modernism.

In addition to the historical limitations of the Age of Commodification argument, a serious theoretical problem undermines the obsession with commodification as the underlying evil of all cultural production beginning sometime after the sack of Rome. The emphasis placed on commodification presupposes the uniformity of intentions and functions, as well as its subservience to one set of interests, specifically those of the ruling class. But as Paul Hirst has so persuasively argued, the interests of that class are hardly as unified as they might appear, and even more importantly, there is no necessary link between those interests and cultural production as a whole – 'There is no necessary relation between the conditions of existence of the means of representation and what is produced by the action of those means, no necessity that they *represent those conditions*.[15] Althusser's dictum that the role of ideology is to reproduce the means of production is accurate, but only if applied at the level of the individual commodity – ie the goal of the detective novel is to construct specific detective subjects, thereby reproducing the demand for the production of detective fiction as a privileged mode of organising experience. That individual commodities altruistically work in harmony for the greater good of the system as a whole would necessitate an enormous degree of orchestration of those commodities and a strict uniformity of purpose. As commodities, they may indeed have one common goal – to be consumed – but in the attainment of that goal they may take different forms that problematise the construction of a uniform subjectivity and fail to exhibit any kind of integration or coordination of design.

In other words, commodification may not only be a fact of life as well as a fact of art in the twentieth century, but its lack of orchestration, specifically within a Post-Modernist context, has so thoroughly negated its homogenising force that it can produce only decentred subjects. We may indeed be constantly encouraged to define ourselves through commodities, but the absence of coordination in such a process results in our being asked to define ourselves in quite different ways, thereby producing anything but a uniform subjectivity.

Post-Modernism as Popular Semiotic, or 'We Built This City on Rock and Roll'

What, then, is Post-Modernism's alternative to the High Romantic/High Modernist dismissal of all commodified art (especially popular culture) and to the insistence that a decentred culture can only be sheer heterogeneity without purpose? According to many of its critics, it could not possibly have an alternative because it is so thoroughly without politics, or any kind of coherent critical theory. The following passage from Jameson's attack on the movement expresses this attitude: [the] 'complacent eclecticism of Post-Modern architecture which randomly and *without principle* but with gusto cannibalises all the architectural styles of the past and combines them in over-stimulating ensembles' ['Post-Modernism', 1984, emphasis mine].

That the movement's juxtapositions are without principle will come as somewhat of a surprise to anyone familiar with the various manifestos written by Post-Modernist architects over the past two decades. Their detractors would have us believe that Post-Modern artists are glitz-loving barbarians, utterly devoid of theoretical foundation or without any grasp of what made High-Modernism so 'special'. Yet nothing could be less accurate. Since the early sixties countless articles, conferences, and book-length treatises have appeared which have tried to establish not only a theoretical common ground among Post-Modernists, but a pragmatic agenda concerning its place within the larger context of urban planning – an issue which seldom seems to have troubled the High Modernists. Perhaps most telling, three of the most important book-length studies – Peter Blake's *Form Follows Fiasco: Why Modern Architecture Hasn't Worked* (1974), Paolo Portoghesi's *After Modern Architecture* (1982), and Charles Jencks's *The Language of Post-Modern Architecture* (1977) – were written by figures who were formerly confirmed Modernist architects and critics. In each case, one finds the move to Post-Modernism motivated by a thoroughgoing rejection of Modernism as an aesthetic and political dead end – hardly a fad pursued by irresponsible philistines!

A brief discussion of Jencks's work becomes essential here because his position concerning the shift from Modernism to Post-Modernism represents a significant alternative to the Baudrillard-Lyotard-Jameson perspective. His analysis of this shift and his attempts to define the differences between the two movements semiotically are also extremely relevant to our understanding of film and literary texts; Jencks describes not just architectural stylistics, but larger issues concerning the context that produced that shift. Lyotard and Jameson both making passing reference to Jencks, yet both significantly omit discussion of his most devastating attacks on Modernism and the avant-garde.

Jencks makes the crucial point that while Modernism depended on the elite coding of professional architecture, Post-Modernism's primary distinguishing characteristic is that it is 'double-coded';[16] it respects both the professional and popular codes simultaneously, thereby speaking a 'language' that can be understood by two quite different groups through its uses of signifiers accessible to both professional and layman. Architecture is not a quasi-private artistic language, but an avowedly 'public language', in which the architect is not a 'saviour/doctor', but a 'representative and activist'. According to Jencks, the collapse of Modernist architecture as a whole was inevitable because from its inception it was a movement that demonstrated indifference – if not outright contempt – for the context and eventual inhabitants of its designs. Its emphasis on purely formal concerns led to a fetishising of the means of production, and, as a result, to the development – under Mies van der Rohe – of a 'universal grammar of steel I-beams' that was seemingly appropriate for any function (whether office building, housing complex, schools, churches, etc) and any culture (war-ravaged Europe, thriving business centres in the United States, etc).

The relevance of these statements to narrative and ideological theory since the late sixties is nothing short of uncanny, since 'radical signifying practice' has served in many significant ways as the literary and filmic equivalent of an 'International Style' in architecture, with all the accompanying limitations. In both, one finds the valorisation of the means of production as an end in itself, as well as an apparent disregard for their function within a special cultural context. This led to the creation of a pseudo-pantheon, however unintentional, by the *Tel Quel/Screen/Cinéthique/Cahiers due cinéma* combines, of those writers and filmmakers whose work epitomises 'radical signifying practice' down through the ages – thereby producing a culturally transcendent radical avant-garde that somehow manages to link Rabelais, the Marquis de Sade, Lautrémont, Godard, and Straub as proponents of the same 'International Style', linked by the same 'grammar' (ie the endless 'play' of signifiers). In both its architectural and literary/filmic versions, the International Style was utopian and acontextual, a kind of second-order Esperanto that would signify 'radical other' or 'oppositional voice' regardless of situation. Jencks sums up the problem quite succinctly by insisting that Modernists had a rigorous theorised *univalent* style, but no theory at all of city planning (1984). In much the same way, 'Tel Quelisme' advocated, quite brilliantly, a radical mode of signification, but had only the most utopian, ill-defined notions of how this would have any far-reaching impact on the cultures which surrounded it.

The alternative to the 'universal grammar' of the International Style has been the determination on the part of Post-Modernists to develop a 'neo-vernacular'. The use of the term 'vernacular' is especially interesting here, since it clearly states a different programme from that of the International Style. The latter is the 'classical' language of the twentieth century, the 'universal' language of an intellectual elite; it is self-consciously demarcated as a special means of communication transcending the common 'babble' of local ethnic cultures.

A renewed interest in the vernacular and the recognition of its political effectivity are made explicit in Fernando Solanas's Post-Modernist film *Tangos, the Exile of Gardel* (1985). The film follows the lives of several Argentinian exiles living in Paris (before the fall of the Argentinian military dictatorship) as they try to produce a 'Tangody' – part comedy, part tragedy, part tango. The tango serves as the basis for their collective creation because it is that form which allows them to preserve their national identity in regard to their exiled existence within France, as well as their refusal to acknowledge the legitimacy of the sitting government in Argentina.

Solanas's emphasis on a vernacular art form like the tango marks a significant departure from his earlier documentary *The Hour of the Furnaces* (1967), which insisted that a materialist film-making style based on radical signifying practice – the filmic equivalent of the International Style – was the only way to combat colonisation by North American media. By adopting the tango as a new, preferred weapon in the war for national identity, Solanas bases his film on the same kind of 'double-coding' that Jencks ascribes to Post-Modern architecture. *Tango* addresses an elite audience in its use of specific codes associated with art cinema – direct address to the camera, nonlinear narrative, a very fluid relationship between diegesis and actual performance, homages to other films, etc. But he also addresses a broader, more general, but specifically Argentinian audience through the use of the tango and the domestic/familial problems of his principal actors. The point here is that the vernacular form itself must be seen as political. Near the end of the film Gerardo, the professor, is visited in his sick-bed by two figures – San Martin, the general who liberated Argentina from Spain, and Gardel, the most famous of all tango singers – both of whom died in exile in France. Within the space of Gerardo's room, the three men converse in a triangle with the professor placed directly between the two visitors. This scene functions as a synthesis of Solanas's 'tangody': to be Argentinian is to become engaged with both political history and popular culture, each serving as a source of instruction for the professor in his desire to maintain his Argentinian identity. Most importantly, Solanas's use of the tango is not mere nostalgia for a lost 'folk' culture; Gardel's status as a *recording* star is repeatedly foregrounded in the film. His records, like Solanas's film, represent the possibility of the vernacular within mass media, a vernacular that maintains its force and authenticity despite its commodity status.

The development of a neo-vernacular has been accompanied by increased emphasis on contextualism and participatory design. Architects like Ralph Erskine, Lucien Kroll, and Charles Moore have completely reversed the Modernist aesthetic of simply inserting the genius-architects' plans into cities without undue concern about their reception or appropriateness. When Erskine was commissioned to design the Byker housing community outside of Newcastle, he actively solicited the participation of the inhabitants in the planning of the project; he set up an office in a flower shop and made that space the local 'lost and found' as a way of understanding the non-architectural codes at work within a very specific community. In much the same way, Kroll, while designing buildings at Louvain University, directly involved students by breaking them into teams responsible for developing their own design concerns as well as arriving at a group consensus.

Where the International Style building was architecture 'from above', and obedient to the pre-existent principles of the universal grammar, these Post-Modernist projects were developed from within, in a purposefully ad hoc fashion calculated to meet the desires of a specific spatial and temporal context. The dynamics of such an exchange between Post-Modernist architects and the communities they design for is perfectly illustrated by the working methods of Charles Moore and the Centerbrook group. One of their most recent projects, the Cedar Rapids Art Museum, is a case in point. This project involved the development of a hybrid structure – converting an older Carnegie Library into an art museum and building an extensive addition onto that building that would coordinate stylistically with that library and the surrounding downtown area.

The design of the museum was from the earliest stages an interactive process based on the solicitation and incorporation of community opinion. A series of five workshops were conducted over the course of a week, making it not only an interactive, but additive process in which the exchange of ideas continued from one step to the next. Participants in these sessions were issued 'Workshop Books' designed to elicit as much oral and written commentary as possible. For the first sitewalk, for example, participants were to respond to specific questions about the site location, its eventual users, its relationship to the surrounding area, etc. The 'Beauty Contest' conducted at the second workshop consisted of an eighty-image slide show in which the participants indicated in their workshop books first whether they liked the image, and then whether they felt it appropriate as a model for their museum. After initial designs were executed based on these responses, participants were asked to suggest further alterations so that the process continued to be interactive.

The accusation that Post-Modernist style has no social responsibility appears rather ludicrous coming from Modernists or their admirers, since this kind of social intervention by architects – this self-conscious attempt to integrate themselves into the microcultures they design for – was impossible within the International Style, with its semiotically impossible 'universal grammar'. Modernists have rejected participatory architectural design as mere gimmickry or have dismissed its premise as counterproductive to artistic excellence. While the 'genuineness' of this activity can of course be questioned by its critics, the fact remains that Modernist architects disdained any such activity, preferring to maintain the purity of single-coded architectural language for a coterie of architects and critics. Participatory architecture may indeed be accused of false populism, but no one could ever accuse the International Style of false elitism. Not all Post-Modernist buildings will be founded on such participatory and integrationist principles, but the community activity Moore and his associates encourage clearly indicates a radically different orientation – beginning not from a pre-existent grammar (no matter how avant-garde), but from specific spatial and cultural contexts.

The move toward recontextualisation in Post-Modernist art has necessarily been accompanied by a renewed interest in the historical traditions that preceded it. Jameson attacks this tendency rather vociferously, dismissing it as mere 'cannibalisation', or rejecting it entirely as a reactionary 'nostalgia mode' ('Post-Modernism', 1984). His attack on Post-Modernism's use or abuse of history is especially puzzling, since, in the first place, Post-Modernism's use of past styles is not haphazard activity, but carefully executed juxtaposition for specific effect; and, in the second place, historical consciousness was hardly a defining feature of the Modernists. Paolo Portoghesi has compared the outright rejection of historical tradition (especially indigenous ones) by the Modernist movement to the myth of Lot's wife – that by turning around to see from whence they came they could only turn into a pillar of salt (as opposed to a pillar of I-beams).[17] The universal grammar of the International Style (in architecture as well as in film and literature) was founded on a temporality that denied the past and sealed off any further development in the future (a closure that its admirers have tried to insure), resulting in a perpetually transcendent 'modern' nether-world.

Portoghesi summarises this situation most effectively when he discusses the obsession with 'purity' that led the Modernists to opt for a pure Euclidean geometry as the basis for their designs:

This radical choice interrupted a continuous process based on the recycling and creative transformation of any number of prototypes which had survived in the Western world for centuries.... In reality the destruction of morphological continuity was a revolution of methods and ideas. The result, as we shall see, was the creation of a culture incapable of evolution and renewal ... an iron cage, a labyrinth without exit, in which a search for the new, for the different has produced a tragic uniformity, a trail of ashes.

Rather than a mere expression of nostalgia, Post-Modernism may be seen as an attempt to recover the morphological continuity of specific cultures. In his film criticism, Jameson quite brilliantly exposes the counter-productive dimensions of a 'retro' culture that simply resurrects past styles in films like Lawrence Kasdan's *Body Heat* (1981) or Steven Spielberg's *Raiders of the Lost Ark* (1981). The revivalism at work in these texts has indeed become a kind of industry unto itself which cross-cuts a variety of media – nowhere more obviously than in the fashion and interior design collections of Ralph Lauren that allow individuals to become metteurs-en-scène of their own existence, turning their households into movie sets, complete with the appropriate clothing and furniture to recreate the Wild West or Edwardian England. But this simple revivalism does not describe the complex 'layering' of past styles found in a film like Ridley Scott's *Blade Runner* (1982).

Where the Ralph Lauren interior has one goal – to create a hermetically sealed time-capsule devoid of anachronism that might come from the present – Scott's film is founded on the simultaneous presence of multiple time frames and modes of image-making antithetical to such revivalism. Throughout *Blade Runner*, director Ridley Scott and production designers Lawrence Paull and Syd Mead explicitly visualise the successive layers of urban history by juxtaposing images drawn from William Hogarth, Edward Hopper, Frank Lloyd Wright, Moebius, and Michael Graves. The distinctiveness of *Blade Runner's* vision of the future is this 'archaeological' attitude toward the past, which exposes the layers of sedimented representations – the city-scape is simultaneously archaic, early Modern, and futuristic. In much the same way the androids become invested with the accumulated functions that the 'other' has served for those cultures, appearing to be simultaneously the Fallen Angel, Wagnerian superman, exploited minority, and technology gone berserk.

The use of past styles in this case is motivated not by a simple escapism, but by a desire to understand our culture and ourselves as products of previous codings. In her article on the semiotics of fashion, Kaja Silverman defends a 'retro' dressing (the wearing of vintage clothing) because

> it inserts its wearer into a complex network of cultural and historical references . . . by putting quotation marks around the garments it revitalises, it makes clear that the past is available to us only in a textual form, and through the mediation of the present. . . . It is thus a highly visible way of acknowledging that its wearer's identity has been shaped by decades of representational activity, and that no cultural project can ever 'start from zero'.[18]

Modernist and Post-Modernist texts differ fundamentally, then, in their respective attitudes toward the 'already said'. The former constructs a dialogic relationship with previous representations only to reject them as outmoded, resulting in a semiotic zero-sum game. The latter constructs an entirely different relationship with the accumulated representational activity, recognising that this activity cannot be conjured away by a sudden rupture because it forms the very fabric of our 'structures of feeling'. Post-Modernist texts acknowledge that 'meaning', 'identity', etc, are complicated not only by the decentred nature of current political production, but also by the co-presence of previous representations persisting through mass media – specifically television, which presents it own morphological continuity on a daily basis. In concentrating on synchronic tensions rather than diachronic breaks, the Post-Modernist text constructs *polylogic* rather than dialogic relationships with multiple 'already said' where the relationship between past and present coding is based on interaction and transformation instead of simple rejection.

The temporality that the Modernists laboured to create was a quasi-perpetual present, hermetically sealed against historical antecedent or eventual change. This attempt to establish thoroughly ahistorical time frames is especially obvious in the way time has been handled in Modernist fiction. Jameson sees a concern with 'time and temporality' as one of the distinguishing features of the High Modernists, a feature that has supposedly been replaced by an aesthetic of 'space' in Post-Modernism. Yet this emphasis on temporality is a direct manifestation of the desire to construct a hermetically sealed private world. High Modernists, from Marcel Proust to Jean-Paul Sartre to Michel Butor, made temporality a thoroughly subjectivised order, consistently opposed to the public notion of time that was exposed as empty, bogus, or superficial. Butor's *L'Emploi du temps* (1956) serves as a particularly relevant example, since the narrator's obsession with his intensely personal ordering of time is what defines him as a character, what he used to keep himself separate from the city around him. This tendency is taken to its inevitable conclusion in Roger Laporte's *Fugue* (1970), in which subjective time is no longer set in opposition to public time, but rather replaces it altogether, the only temporality being the time of the writing of the book itself. The High Modernist notion of time and history, then (in literature, film, and architecture), was subsumed entirely to 'personal expression'. Not coincidentally, the chief narrative mode of both the Romantics and the Modernists was the first-person confession; in both cases personal expression creates a private temporality that, in effect, kills history by making the main character step out of it into the time frame of his or her own creation.

The problem of temporality vs historical consciousness leads to a large problem with Modernism itself, or more specifically, in the criticism devoted to it. The central contradiction within the International Style in its various media was a simultaneous fascination with the personal expression of a few Modernist/Romantics and the 'universal grammar' that supposedly unified the movement. But the tension between the individual style (as unique as a set of fingerprints) and the universal aesthetic remains unresolvable semiotically. The former presupposes a virtually private language and the latter presupposes a 'natural' one, having the same meanings and resonances regardless of cultural context. Either assertion by itself is based on rather questionable, decidedly non-semiotic foundations; but the successful combination of the two is simply an impossibility, since the presence of an intensely 'personal' style becomes possible only at the expense of the universal. What occurred instead of the harmonious merger of the two was the promotion *as* universal of an elitism masquerading as a utopian signifying practice, regardless of context or reception.

The emphasis placed on cultural context by so many Post-Modernist artists is due, according to Jencks, to the fact that Post-Modernism, which has 'developed from semiotic research, looks at the abstract notion of taste and its coding and then takes up a situational position, ie no code is inherently better than any other, and therefore the subculture being designed for must be identified before one code can be chosen rather than another' (1984). Coding as a concept has traditionally either been ignored in relation to High Modernists (the notion that 'personal genius' transcends commonplace communication), or defined negatively (codes exist only to be broken by 'personal genius'. The semiotic basis of Post-Modernism (no matter how consciously or uncon-sciously theorised), with its emphasis on the vernacular, the ad hoc, and the conventional, rejects any mode of communication predicated on the 'personal' or the 'universal', since neither can exist within a semiotic framework.

That the work of Post-Modernist architects (especially Jencks, Moore, Robert Venturi, etc) has been labelled 'neo-conservative' by Modernist partisans like Hal Foster is especially interesting, given the former group's insistence on making architecture an explicitly 'public' language based on semiotics rather than Romantic conceptions. Foster, in particular, sees the Post-Modernist attempt to connect up with the cultural heritage and traditions of a particular society as necessarily reactionary, since it is a programme that seeks to recoup the ruptures of modernism and restore the continuity with historical forms.[19] The choice of words here is telling: 'rupturing' is the valorised activity, while historical/cultural continuity' functions only as an uninteresting background for that activity. The cult of the individual genius, whether called Romanticism or Modernism, for Modernist apologists, remains firmly in place.

But which is the 'neo-conservative' stance, the fascination with the 'ruptures' produced by enlightened artists, or the attempt to produce an architectural language understandable to its inhabitants? Huyssen makes the essential point that 'contemporary Post-Modernism . . . operates in a field of tension between tradition and innovation, conservation and renewal, mass culture and high art, in which the second terms are no longer automatically privileged over the first: a field of tension which can no longer be grasped in categories such as progress vs reaction, left vs right, present vs past, modernism vs realism, abstraction vs representation, avant-garde vs kitsch.'[20] For the avant-garde to be meaningful it must remain a relative term, yet those so desperate to label Post-Modernism as 'neo-conservative' would de-relativise it by insisting that Modernism is the perpetual avant-garde, outside that field of tension, resulting in a frozen set of stylistic features that are supposedly able to provide the 'shock of the new' throughout infinity, when they actually remain as fresh as Miss Havisham and her wedding cake, attempting to step outside of time as the only alternative to having been rejected.

Eclecticism as Interrogation: Text as Site
The high priority placed on eclecticism by Post-Modernists is a direct rejection of the purity of the International Style in its various incarnations in different media – a purity which, by its very nature would deny the existence of a semiotic context, both in its rigorous dismissal of all other styles and its indifference to the eventual users. The issue of eclecticism becomes perhaps the central issue in the debate over Post-Modernism, since it is not only a matter of stylistics, but politics, in regard to both textual practice and the critical approaches that have been brought to bear. Its detractors have considered this eclecticism 'casual' or 'schizophrenic', a veritable 'non-style' devoid of personal artistry or authentic judgment. Its defenders, on the other hand, have argued that it is a style and an ideology which 'builds in' the fragmentation and conflicted nature of contemporary culture – just as the perfect symmetry of Georgian architecture represented eighteenth-century culture's perception of itself.

In his discussion of the Stuttgart Museum designed by James Stirling, Jencks stresses the confrontation within the architecture of classical motifs, German Romanesque, and ultra-modern, resulting in a thoroughly Post-Modern design that 'confronts tradition and modern technology giving neither a supreme role. . . . They both feel the present condition of culture – and the Stuttgart buildings are cultural institutions – demands a juxtaposition of connecting ideologies, not a resolution' (1984). The lack of resolution becomes not a 'non-style', but the only accurate way to reflect the cultural conflicts which have produced these texts. Eclecticism, then, must be seen as a decidedly 'radical' feature of Post-Modernism, as these sorts of juxtapositions establish not only a design, but a specific view of the subject, society, and the functions that cultural production has in constructing the relationship between the two.

The emphasis placed on juxtapositions of conflicting discourses has become a distinguishing feature of Post-Modernist architecture, but similar types of juxtapositions are central to literary and film texts as well. Manuel Puig's *Kiss of the Spiderwoman* is a prime literary example of making conflicting styles and ideologies the basic structuring principle of the text as a whole.[21] Throughout the novel the dialogue between the cell mates (Molina, the homosexual, and Valentin, the political activist) is redoubled on the format of the pages themselves, the top section devoted to Molina's narratives, the bottom section containing an ongoing essay for each chapter. Throughout these double-tracked pages, the pulp romances and films of Molina appear to operate in perfect counterpoint to the erudite essays below: each functioning according to the modalities and prohibitions (in the Foucauldian sense) of its own discourse, each taking apparently very different views of desire – one romanticised in the extreme, the other clinical in the extreme. The prisoners, in their conversations, only stress these disjunctions. Valentin orders Molina not to tell the stories during the day since 'it's better at night, during the day I don't want to be thinking about such trivia. I've got more important things to think about'.[22] Specifically, Valentin means reading the sort of essays one finds at the bottom of each page. The tensions between the two discourses must be confronted by the reader quite actively due to the difficulty in the actual reading of the text. Should we read the narrative and the essays simultaneously, or read each to its conclusion, and then go back to the other track and read it as a whole? Either way, the reader must confront the conflicting discourses in a more direct way than in, say, Julio Cortázar's *Hopscotch* (1963; trans 1966), where the hopscotching activity becomes a matter of temporal rather than discursive juxtaposition.

The most significant feature of the discursive juxtapositionings of *Kiss of the Spiderwoman*, however, is that their points of contact, as well as their points of departure are consistently foregrounded by the dialogic structure. These juxtapositions are discursive in a three-fold manner: first in the Foucauldian sense, but also in a doubly Benvenistean sense, in that a 'discursive' exchange occurs between those modes of representation as well as between the text and the reader/viewer. As the novel progresses it becomes increasingly clear that both men are victims of repression by the same totalitarian regime, and that both the narratives and the essays stress the primacy of desire. The confluence of the two tracks is most explicit when late in the novel the men come together, emotionally as well as physically. At that point, the essay track draws the explicit parallel, 'Marcuse points out that the social function of the homosexual is analogous to that of a critical philosopher since his very presence is a constant reminder of the repressed elements of society.' The power that Molina's stories and songs have to represent 'real-life' situations also becomes increasingly evident as the novel progresses. Valentin remains derisive about Molina's material, but then admits, 'Know something? There I was laughing at your bolero, but the letter I got today says just what the bolero says.' Molina insists, 'Listen, big man, don't you know by now boleros contain tremendous truths, which is why I like them'. The novel as a whole proves Molina correct in a rather bitterly ironic way. In one of Molina's later stories he has character sing, 'Even though you're . . . a prisoner in your solitude your heart whispers still I love you', foreshadowing quite perfectly the end of the novel when Valentin whispers exactly that before (after?) he dies from his torture.

Puig's use of discursive juxtaposition in *Kiss of the Spiderwoman* epitomises one of the fundamental tenets of Post-Modernism – that only by confronting the conflicting discourses we use to structure experience can we begin to understand what is actually at stake in the structuring process. Only then may we begin to see that no hierarchy of discourses or 'cultural orchestration' makes that process automatic in contemporary cultures. The Post-Modernist aim, then, is not haphazard 'pastiche', motivated only by perversity, but specific juxtapositions for particular purposes. Charles Moore's Piazza d'Italia in New Orleans is a perfect architectural example of this. His design for an Italian cultural centre incorporates Roman arches, neon bars, and skyscrapers, utilising stone as well as highly polished aluminium in its various columns. But the juxtapositions here are not without a precise guiding principle. Moore has included most of the important styles that have been used within the Italian city-space since ancient Rome. This combination of seemingly contradictory styles makes perfect sense, given the Piazza d'Italia's function as a centre intended to celebrate cultural traditions in the 1980s. It is an avowedly contemporary work 'built' on past styles. Like *Kiss of the Spiderwoman*, the work juxtaposes disparate styles and foregrounds the unresolvable tensions between them, but also unifies these juxtapositions around a well-defined theme (repressed desire in *Spiderwoman* and Italian culture in the Piazza d'Italia). Where Modernism sought to replace outmoded styles entirely with another 'radical' one, Post-Modern texts, like these by Puig and Moore, emphasise the question of style itself as a way of coming to terms with the traditions of the past as well as the discursive and ideological conflicts in the present.

This gesture has been developed most elaborately in Hans-Jürgen Syberberg's *Parsifal* (1984), also structured around a series of discursive juxtapositions. While his project may be similar to Moore's, it takes a more overtly critical view of the particular cultural heritage which unifies the work's juxtapositions. While the film ostensibly presents a performance of the Wagner opera, Syberberg turns his production into a kind of filmic 'Piazza Germania', in which the opera's visualisation becomes a 'site' where a range of German cultural traditions (political, sexual, artistic, etc) interconnect simultaneously. Syberberg makes Wagner's *Parsifal* the lynchpin of a cultural continuum by emphasising, at one and the same time, traditions which lead back to medieval times as well as traditions which lead forward into the 1980s. To make the opera into this kind of 'site', Syberberg emphasises conflicts between various of its stagings. Using back-projection, inserted photographs, and drawings, he repeatedly, within the space of the image, contrasts his own filmic production with the famous Bayreuth productions of 1882 and 1951, as well as with Fritz Lang's *Siegfried* (1922-24), and a puppet show modelled on the original singers who created the featured roles. In so doing, Syberberg is not only juxtaposing multiple productions, but multiple modes of representation – photos, puppet shows, highly stylised sets, minimalist sets, symbolic considerations, illuminated manuscripts, the score itself, etc. Likewise, Syberberg's treatment of the figure of Wagner takes on different forms, reflecting various popular conceptions of this composer: crucified artist, Romantic poseur, radical theoretician, a decapitated head, a death mask, etc.

There is one shot in *Parsifal* which encapsulates the whole of the activity of the film: the long tracking shot that leads into the Grail Hall. The camera moves past a seemingly endless series of flags and banners from German history, from the medieval to the nineteenth century up to the swastika. The historical/cultural continuum is clearly drawn here: *Parsifal* the opera is a product of the nineteenth century and it recreates a medieval myth which itself is appropriated as a myth for fascism in the twentieth century. Throughout the film, the discursive juxtapositions lead us to a major conclusion about the opera; for us today, *Parsifal* cannot be looked at merely as a classic, or even as a radical, new production of a classic, but rather it must be seen as the assemblage of all its past and present incarnations and appropriations. *Parsifal* is both the fulfilment of the Grail brotherhood and the foreshadowing of the Nazi brotherhood. What Thomas Elsaesser says of *Ludwig* (1972) in his compelling essay on Syberberg applies perfectly to this later film:

> Syberberg's film is not a mimesis or representation as much as an interpretation in the biblical sense of exegesis, it is a 'reading' of German history which might with such justification, be called a hermeneutics of the texts that make up history, before it is narrativised, unified, and pressed into the unilinear flow of realist narrative. It is in the very nature of this kind of interrogation and interpretation that it not only 'deconstructs' our view of history but also the cinematic space of representation.[23]

Juxtaposition as interrogation is characterised in Moore, Puig, and Syberberg by a careful, purposeful consideration of representational alternatives – rather than by simple pastiche or the 'plundering' of history of art as though it were an attic filled with the artifacts of one's ancestors. The key point here is that the discursive juxtapositions do not result in an 'emptying out' of all styles (where hyper-awareness of the multiple possibilities would somehow make any one style an impoverished dead end or their combination mere pastiche). Exactly the opposite is the case in texts such as *The Kiss of the Spiderwoman, Parsifal, The White Hotel, Tangos, the Exile of Gardel, The Name of the Rose, Diva*, Moore's Piazza or Stirling's Stuttgart Gallery; in each of these cases, a precise combination of styles forms the basis of a productive engagement with antecedent and contemporary modes of organising experience as a way of making sense of life in decentred cultures.

Linda Hutcheon makes the crucial point that the parody that supposedly defines Post-Modern textuality is not a uniform perspective, since 'parody, paradoxically, exacts both change and cultural continuity; the Greek prefix *paras* can mean both counter and against *and* near or beside'.[24] That Post-Modernist texts employ eclectic combinations in order to produce meaning (as opposed to frustrating it), is perhaps best illustrated by the Kokuku sequence in Laurie Anderson's *Home of the Brave*. Two musicians sit before their guitars, playing them with forks, screwdrivers, etc, while directly above them on the rear screen, a series of simple drawings of objects are intercut with a series of Chinese characters – *conjis*, considered to be some of the earliest examples of symbolic signs (in the Peircean sense). In the foreground, an Oriental musician sits before an ancient form of the guitar; he is telling a story. The song's title, 'Kokuku' signifies place of origin, and the composite space emphasises the creation of meaning, in which sounds become meaningful as symbols. Throughout *Home of the Brave* and other Post-Modernist texts, the production of meaning depends upon a direct engagement with the 'already said', which is neither a nihilistic emptying out nor a revivalist resuscitation of that already said.

The Functions of Criticism: The Semiotic Glut and the Musée Imaginaire

Within decentred cultures, no *Zeitgeist* can emerge as a dominant; nor can any one institution – whether the university or prime-time television – be considered the sole 'official' culture responsible for establishing aesthetic ideological standards for entire societies. Throughout this study, I have discussed the shortcomings of the 'Grand Hotel' conception of culture. I have argued that just as the organised cabal of mass culture czars seems quaintly out of date in contemporary culture, so too does the notion that any one group of scholars or critics could serve as its inverted, negating image – ie a master control room where Adorno-ites would establish official standards for what constitutes 'culture' for entire societies and somehow enforce them in an all-pervasive manner. Just as the advent of Post-Modernist culture has not meant the end of 'oppositional' art, it also does not mean the end of aesthetic judgment. The Post-Modernisms represented by Moore, Puig, and Syberberg, for instance, are vehiculations of very precise aesthetic judgments, judgments in which critical dialogue about conflicting styles becomes a structuring principle of the text. Aesthetic judgment is not, therefore, ignored, but redefined and relocated at the junctures between opposing discourses, where critical, ethical, and ideological decisions are made. Post-Modernist judgment is not formulated from out of an acontextual, a-vernacular set of transcendent principles that might constitute a 'universal grammar' of genius. Consequently, it does mean the end of any uniform conception of 'the best that has been thought and said', or of any easy binary relations between two opposing sets (each equally uniform). Most critiques of Post-Modernism – similar to Adorno's attack on the 'culture industry as an attack that so clearly informs these later critiques – are themselves written in a 'nostalgia mode', essentially a nostalgia for a culture where the oppositional version of the 'best that has been thought and said' was easily determinable and easily championed. Ironically, the anti-Post-Modernist nostalgia appears to be for a Panopticon Lost, where societies were supposedly centralised and homogeneous, but oppositional voices knew their own and endlessly plotted utopian prison breaks from out of officially Oppositional Cells.

The advent of Post-Modernist textual practice, and, more importantly, the Post-Modernist cultural context, makes ideological analysis more essential than it has ever been before in the decoding and evaluating of those diverse messages. In his eloquent conclusion to *The Function of Criticism*, Terry Eagleton insists that the role of the contemporary critic should be a traditional one – to be concerned with the interrelationships between symbolic processes and the social production of subjectivity.

> For it is surely becoming apparent that without a more profound understanding of such symbolic processes, through which political power is deployed, reinforced, resisted, at times subverted, we shall be incapable of unlocking the most lethal power-struggle now confronting us. Modern criticism was born of a struggle against the absolutist state; unless its future is now defined as a struggle against the bourgeois it might have no future at all.

While Eagleton is quite correct in outlining the project and recognising the stakes involved, the question that arises is whether this can be done effectively if it is based on problematic preconceptions about how cultural production creates our perception of that bourgeois state. The project would appear, if anything, doomed to failure if its attitude toward so much of that cultural production is outright rejection. Criticism must be evaluative in this context, but it becomes ineffectual when it degenerates into a 'nostalgia mode' for cultures lost. The survival of Marxist cultural analysis is truly in jeopardy if its treatment of contemporary culture (specifically in regard to popular culture and Post-Modernism) amounts to self-righteous dismissal. The inevitable and ironic result of such a stance is a bizarre temporality that inverts the temporality of the Modernism it admires; in its nostalgia for the past and its utopian visions of the future, it constructs not a perpetual present, but an 'absent present'.

The denial of Post-Modernism is symptomatic of a much broader problem concerning the relevance and the efficacy of Marxist analysis in the present conjuncture. Eagleton points to Raymond Williams as a kind of model of what the contemporary critic should be, and in doing so compares him to Wordsworth, leading to an explicit comparison of the Socialist Critic and the Romantic Poet:

> Socialist criticism cannot conjure a counter public sphere into existence; on the contrary, that criticism cannot itself fully exist until such a sphere has been fashioned: Until that time the socialist critic will remain stranded between sage and man of letters, combining the critical dissociation of the former with the practical, engaged, wide-ranging activity of the latter.

Williams indeed managed to maintain a balance between the two roles. But in their self-consciously dissociated stances, Jameson, Eagleton, and Foster appear to be adopting the role of the romantic 'sage' far too whole-heartedly. Eagleton's own epitaph for the Romantic sage describes, ironically, his own position vis-à-vis Post-Modernist cultures:

> No critique which does not establish such an implacable distance between itself and the social order, which does not launch its utterances from some other different place, is likely to escape incorporation; but that powerfully enabling distance is also Romanticism's tragedy, as the imagination joyfully transcends the actual only to consume itself and the world in its own guilt-stricken self-isolation.

Eagleton here performs (unwittingly) a brilliant self-diagnosis. The search for one great counter-public sphere is doomed to be fruitless, due to the cultural fragmentation produced by the heterogeneity of encoding and decoding strategies at work within a given society. But even if the creation of such a sphere were a possibility, would the outright dismissal of all that is tainted by commodification – especially popular and Post-Modernist texts – be an appropriate way to begin constructing it (considering the determination of these texts to use the most accessible codes for non-elite audiences)? Could such a sphere ever exist between anything but latter-day dissociated sages?

The issue of subject construction should indeed remain the central problematic in ideological analysis, but, here again, we can hope to understand the complexity of the processes involved in current context only if we go beyond simple denunciation. It is frequently argued that the individual self has been annihilated by Post-Modernism since it is no longer a centred subject; yet this presupposes that subjectivity is impossible without a rigorous homogeneity of all ideological messages within a given context. In fact, in a world defined by competitive interpellation, the subject is seldom answering one uniform 'call', but, rather, being hailed by multiple, competing messages all issued simultaneously. The 'disappearing self' criticism is common, but it fails to take into account the centring power of individual discourses, or the power of individuals to make choices regarding those discourses.

Eagleton acknowledges that the centred subject has become in some ways inappropriate, but argues that this has not led to its complete disappearance – 'The subject of late capitalism . . . is neither simply the self-regulating synthetic agent posited by classical humanist ideology, nor merely a decentred network of desire, but a contradictory amalgam of the two' (1986). Eagleton does not fully pursue the causes of this 'contradictory amalgam', yet the existence of such a contradictory situation is itself a product of the conflicting ideological messages being processed by those subjects on a daily basis. While a unitary culture may have disappeared, unitary discourses constructing very specific subjects have only intensified. The category of the subject remains highly viable in large part because it has never been so hotly contested.

The function of criticism vis-à-vis subject construction must be thoroughly reconceived if it is to have any significant impact in contemporary society. In discussing the influence of new technologies on Post-Modernist practice, Jencks states,

We can reproduce fragmented experiences of different cultures and, since all the media have been doing this for fifteen years our sensibility has been modified. Thanks to colour magazines, travel, and Kodak, Everyman has a well-stocked *musée imaginaire* and is a potential eclectic. At least he is exposed to a plurality of other cultures and he can make choices and discriminations from this wide corpus, whereas previous cultures have stuck with what they'd inherited. (1984)

This point contains several ramifications for subject construction. The image of the *musée imaginaire* is especially useful since it suggests not only the stockpiling, but purposeful arrangement of the signs which bombard us constantly (even if Jencks's list seems paltry at best and emphasises only the international nature of such a *musée* without acknowledging the diversified nature of the 'national' collection). Here the activity *of* the subject is as important as activity *on* the subject, whereas previous conceptions of the subject have emphasised only the latter. Due to the bombardment of conflicting messages the individual subject *must* be engaged in processes of selection and arrangement. Not that subjects are completely 'free to choose' as an independent agent, unconstructed by the very messages they come into contact with, or that a range of choices doesn't change drastically from society to society. Nevertheless, to deny that a selection process hasn't been made mandatory by that bombardment is to posit an absurdly simplified subject, strapped down with eyes pryed open like Alex in Anthony Burgess's *A Clockwork Orange* (1963), force-fed a carefully orchestrated series of images. But the lack of orchestration of cultural production is precisely what makes such an imagined spectator ludicrously outmoded.

The situation, then, is not a 'democratic' plurality, where aesthetic and ideological alternatives are carefully arranged in a kind of laissez-faire smorgasbord. Instead, a semiotic glut necessitates the arrangement, even hierarchising of conflicting discourses by individual subjects at a localised level. The bombardment of signs has produced, by no preconceived design whatsoever, a subject who is engaged in the process of being interpellated while simultaneously arranging those messages – as if the lack of cultural orchestration has produced a subject who must act as curator of his or her *musée imaginaire*.

This lack of uniformity in interpellation necessitates a new conception of the subject, defined by activity rather than passivity, by selection rather than simple reception. Jencks's image of the *musée imaginaire* suggests that *bricolage* is one of the distinguishing characteristics of life in Post-Modern cultures. In *Subculture*, Dick Hebdige utilises the term *bricolage* to describe how individuals manipulate disparate cultural phenomena in order to explain their world to themselves in satisfactory ways (restricting it to explicitly subcultural groups).[25] Hebdige's use of this term in relation to technologically sophisticated cultures is a significant move, since he demonstrates effectively that bricolage as an activity cannot be limited to primitive, pre-literate societies. If anything, its appearance within subcultural groups reflects an extremely refined understanding of complicated semiotic environments. I believe this notion of bricolage may be pursued even further; characters in Joe Dante's *Explorers* or Puig's *Kiss of the Spiderwoman* can hardly be considered subcultural in the same way as punks or Rastafarians, yet their manipulation of signs (in locally meaningful structures) involves the same kind of ad hoc arrangements.

Within media-saturated cultures where no overarching, pan-cultural distinctions between official and unofficial, mainstream and avant-garde are in effect, bricolage becomes the inevitable response to semiotic overload. It should not, therefore, be reserved for sub-cultural activity, but should be applied to all kinds of micro-cultural activity. This is not to suggest that individual discourses and institutions within our cultures do not attempt to provide totalising modes of organising experience; the decentring of the subject that typifies Post-Modernism is the direct result of the simultaneous appearance of multiple centres, multiple unified subject positions that are often fundamentally incompatible with one another. The situation is not unlike that conceived by Thomas Pynchon in *The Crying of Lot 49* (1966), where Oedipa Maas searches for the signs of an underground communication system only to uncover an endless proliferation of subcultural languages – at which point she realises that what she thought was marginal is instead endemic; that to be alienated from some imaginary central language has itself become central; that everyone has become a potential *bricoleur* in a sense, because everyone is caught in that endless 'roar of relays'.

The project of contemporary criticism as outlined by Eagleton is then imperative, but it lacks a third component. In addition to an understanding of symbolic processes and subject construction, we need a theory of the subject that emphasises the activities undertaken by that subject when faced with conflicting cultural messages. The function of the critic cannot be limited merely to showing his or her readers the error of their culture's ways; it must instead sensitise readers and students to the processes involved in the production of subjectivity. Unless we emphasise the active role all people may play in that production, criticism remains a 'spectator sport' for an increasingly smaller audience. The activity of the critic, then, must be directly linked to the activity of subject production; the critic's activity, undertaken in a specific cultural context, should serve as a model for the latter. In *The Cheese and the Worms*, Carlo Ginzburg elucidates in thorough detail how, in the sixteenth century, Menocchio constructed what amounted to a *cosmogonie imaginaire* through his distinctive decodings of the texts he had read. In our technologically sophisticated age, where the bombardment of diverse sign systems will only continue to intensify (as will the individual's ability to manipulate them with VCRs and remote-control devices), the proliferation of techno-Menocchios becomes inevitable. Umberto Eco summarises the situation in the following manner:

> What radio and television are today, we know – incontrollable plurality of messages that each individual uses to make up his own composition with the remote control switch. The consumer's freedom may not have increased, but surely the way to teach him to be free and controlled has changed.[26]

The opponents of Post-Modernism have been especially critical of the notion that individual subjects are capable of making selective decisions in the face of this semiotic glut, preferring to dispense with the issue by insisting that this 'free to choose' mentality plays directly into the 'free market' ideology. But such a move, in addition to being sadly reductive, only brackets the central issue – what is the individual subject to *do* in such a context? Of course, it is quite possible to link the making of choices to capitalist ideology as a whole. But one can just as easily conceive of the ability to choose in quite another way, as *heretical* action (since the Greek root for heretic means 'able to choose'). For Post-Modernism as a cultural programme to succeed critically, and have the kind of widespread impact that the private languages of High Modernism never did, heretical activity must be conducted on three interrelated fronts. As a particular type of textual practice or 'style', Post-Modernist artists must continue to violate the precepts of Modernism as a way of demonstrating the possibility that 'multiple aesthetics' are appropriate for different publics within a given culture at the same time. Critical practice must likewise be heretical, by conducting a complete re-examination of all the 'givens' of cultural analysis – especially those that depend on outmoded categories and scenarios that are more appropriate to pre-industrial societies. But the most important of these fronts is the heretical activity of individual subjects who can strike a balance between involvement and critical distance so long as they recognise that they are not only able to choose, but *impelled* to choose if they hope to gain any control of their cultures.

NOTES

1 Andreas Huyssen, *After The Great Divide: Modernism, Mass Culture, Post-Modernism*, Indiana University Press, Bloomington, 1986, p 217.

2 Stefano Tani, *The Doomed Detective: The Contribution of the Detective Novel to Post-Modern American and Italian Fiction*, Southern Illinois University Press, Carbondale, 1984.

3 Siegfried Kracauer, *History: The Last Things Before the Last*, Oxford University Press, New York, 1969.

4 Jean Baudrillard, 'The Implosion of Meaning in the Media and the Information of the Social in the Masses', *Myths of Information: Technologic and Post-Industrial Culture*, ed Kathleen Woodward, Coda Press, Madison, 1980, pp 137-48.

5 Kenneth Roberts et al, *The Fragmentary Class Structure*, Heinemann, London, 1977.

6 Octave Mannoni, *Clefs pour l'Imaginaire ou L'Autre Scène*, Editions due Seuil, Paris, 1969.

7 Fredric Jameson, 'Introduction', *The Postmodern Condition: A Report on Knowledge*, by Jean-François Lyotard, University of Minnesota Press, Minneapolis, 1984.

8 Jean-François Lyotard, *The Postmodern Condition: A Report on Knowledge*, University of Minnesota Press, Minneapolis, 1984.

9 Fredric Jameson, 'Post-Modernism, or The Cultural Logic of Late Capitalism', *New Left Review* 146, July-August 1984, p 57.

10 Mikhail Bakhtin, 'Discourse in the Novel', *The Dialogic Imagination*, ed Michael Holquist, University of Texas Press, Austin, 1981, pp 259-422.

11 Terry Eagleton, 'Capitalism, Modernism, Post-Modernism', *Against the Grain*, Verso, London, 1986, pp 131-48.

12 Terry Eagleton, *The Function of Criticism*, Verso/New Left Books, London, 1984.

13 Fredric Jameson, 'Reification and Utopia in Mass Culture', *Social Text*, Winter 1979.

14 John Berger, *Ways of Seeing*, Penguin, London, 1972.

15 Paul Hirst, *On Law and Ideology*, Macmillan Press, New York, 1981.

16 Charles Jencks, *The Language of Post-Modern Architecture*, Rizzoli, New York, 1984. See also Charles Jencks, *What is Post-Modernism?* Academy, London/St Martin's Press, New York, 1986; and *Charles Jencks, Architecture and Urbanism*, extra edition, A&U Publishing Company, Tokyo, January 1986.

17 Paolo Portoghesi, *After Modern Architecture*, Rizzoli, New York, 1982.

18 Kaja Silverman, 'Fragments of a Fashionable Discourse', *Studies in Entertainment: Critical Approaches to Mass Culture*, ed Tania Modleski, Indiana University Press, Bloomington, 1986, p 150-51.

19 Hal Foster, 'Post Modern Polemics', *Recodings: Art, Spectacle, Cultural Politics*, Bay Press, Port Townsend, 1985, p 125.

20 Huyssen, *After The Great Divide*, p 216.

21 For another discussion of this novel in relation to theories of popular culture see Tania Modleski, 'Femininity as Mas(s)querade A Feminist Approach to Mass Culture', *High Theory/Low Culture*, ed Colin MacCabe, St Martin's Press, New York, 1987, pp 37-52.

22 Manuel Puig, *Kiss of The Spiderwoman*, Vintage Books, New York, 1980, p 9.

23 Thomas Elsaesser, 'Myth as Phantasmagoria of History: HJ Syberberg, Cinema and Representation', *New German Critique* 24-25, Fall/Winter 1981-82.

24 Linda Hutcheon, 'The Politics of Post Modernism: Parody and History', *Cultural Critique*, Winter 1986-87, pp 179-208.

25 Dick Hebdige, *Subculture: The Meaning of Style*, Methuen, New York, 1979.

26 Umberto Eco, *Travels in Hyperreality*, Harcourt, Brace, Jovanovich, New York, 1986, p 148.

Reprinted from Jim Collins, *Uncommon Cultures*, Routledge, New York and London, 1989. © 1989 Routledge, Chapman and Hall. A condensed version of this chapter appeared in *Screen* 28, No 2, Spring 1987.

Margaret Rose
DEFINING THE POST-MODERN

Dick Hebdige opens the section on post-modernism in his *Hiding in the Light: On Images and Things* of 1988 with the statement that 'The success of the term postmodernism . . . has generated its own problems', and that

> It becomes more and more difficult as the 1980s wear on to specify exactly what it is that 'postmodernism' is supposed to refer to as the term gets stretched in all directions across different debates, different disciplinary and discursive boundaries, as different factions seek to make it their own, using it to designate a plethora of incommensurable objects, tendencies, emergencies.[1]

Despite this and other similar complaints,[2] there is, however, no necessary reason why some of the 'factional' or other differences behind the variety of definitions of post-modernism and the post-modern in general which we now have may not be defined as such, and the different meanings which have been given the term be categorised more succinctly. One major source for the idea that post-modernism is a movement in which 'anything goes' is, in fact, to be found in an attack by the French theorist Lyotard on a rival concept of post-modernism, which, in addition, cannot be said to describe its target accurately.[3]

Many (although certainly not all) recent discussions of post-modernism have also followed Lyotard's writings on the subject in some regard. Hebdige himself, for example, goes on after summarising a variety of uses of the term 'postmodernism' to use it, without specifically saying so, in the Lyotardian sense of a critique of meta-narratives,[4] when he claims that his following overview of the term will entail his 'going against the spirit of postmodernism', understood as being 'founded in the renunciation of claims to mastery and dominant specularity'.[5]

While the 'renunciation of claims to mastery' evokes Lyotard's deconstruction of the 'meta-narratives' of modernity, the positing of a 'dominant specularity' as yet another target of the post-modernist also recalls the terminology of works such as Guy Debord's *Society of the Spectacle* of 1967; and the use of it by Jean Baudrillard in his contribution to Hal Foster's *Postmodern Culture*[6] or his 'The Orders of Simulacra' of 1975. In this latter text Baudrillard had not only spoken of the 'burlesque spectacle' of the political class,[7] but had also divided history into three dominant 'orders of appearance' since the Renaissance: of *Counterfeit* for the period from the Renaissance to the industrial revolution; *Production* for the industrial era; and *Simulation* for the current phase, in which reality is said to be continuously overtaken by its images and to be ruled by indeterminacy.[8] While Baudrillard had been speaking here, as elsewhere, largely of the modern world, rather than of something termed the post-modern (or 'postmodern'), one theorist of post-modernism writing prior to both Hebdige and Lyotard, Ihab Hassan, will be seen to have taken the post-modern age to be an age of 'indeterminacy', while others, such as Fredric Jameson, will be seen to have echoed Baudrillard in viewing the present age as a 'neo-capitalist cybernetic order' which aims at total control.[9]

Hebdige's commentary on post-modernism also continues in a Baudrillardian vein when he claims that 'postmodernity is modernity without the hopes and dreams which made modernity bearable'[10] and adds that 'it is a hydra-headed, decentred condition in which we get dragged along from pillar to post across a succession of reflecting surfaces, drawn by the call of the wild signifier'.[11] Further to this we shall see later that Hebdige's description of post-modernism as 'bricolage, pastiche, allegory, and the hyperspace of the new architecture'[12] echoes a 'Baudrillardian' characterisation of post-modernism by Fredric Jameson which has projected characteristics onto post-modern-ism[13] which others, such as Charles Jencks, have preferred to describe as 'Late-Modern' rather than as 'Post-Modern'.[14]

Although it gives a somewhat broader account of the concept of the post-modern than Hebdige's survey, and those like it,[15] the Oxford English Dictionary's (OED) Supplement of 1982 was of necessity also too restricted in its coverage of the use of the term to give all the details required for an accurate history of it or of the sometimes related term 'post-modernism'.[16]

The OED Supplement's entry begins:

> **post-mo.dern**, a. Also **post-Modern**. (POST-B. 1b.) Subsequent to, or later than, what is 'modern'; spec. in the arts, esp. Archit., applied to a movement in reaction against that designated 'modern' (cf. MODERN a. 2h.)[17] Hence **post-mo.dernism**, **post-mo.dernist**, a. and sb.

Despite the generally scientific appearance of the above entry, it contains a number of problems which the reader aware of the possible variety of definitions of the post-modern may already have been able to discern. Firstly, the word 'post-modern' is not always thought to be subsequent to or later than the 'modern', but may both be contemporary with it, or, as in the writings of Lyotard, 'prior' to the modern. Secondly, although one other theorist of post-modernism, Charles Jencks, has questioned the sense of Lyotard's claims, he himself has not seen the post-modern in architecture as simply a reaction against the 'modern', but has described it as a 'double-coding' of the modern style with some other style or 'code'.[18]

Further to the above, the OED Supplement's cross-reference to its '2h' definition of the 'modern' in its characterisation of the 'post-modern' as, 'with reference to the arts and architecture', a 'movement in reaction against that designated "modern"', creates some problems not only on account of its conflation of the terms 'modern' and 'modernism' in its application of the former to the arts, where the two terms might not always be able to describe the same phenomena, but also because its 2h definition of the modern has described the 'modern' in terms of its 'departure from or . . . repudiation of accepted or traditional styles and values'.[19] Hence we have a definition of the post-modern which not only describes it negatively as a reaction against the modern, but which also relates it to a description of the modern which sees it too in negative terms as a reaction against other traditions. Although the latter may be true for some modernisms, it is not the only aspect of the modern, or of modernism, which has been addressed by post-modernists who have reacted specifically to modernist alternatives to other traditions as well as to modernist rejections of the past.

Other problems abound in giving a history of today's usage of the term post-modern. The OED Supplement's reference to Joseph Hudnut's use of the term post-modern in relation to architecture (which the dictionary's entry goes on to date as being from 1949 and as the earliest use of the term 'post-modern', whereas it is in fact used by Hudnut from at least 1945 on, and by others prior to that)[20] is, for example, to a concept of 'post-modern' architecture as mass-produced prefabricated building which would today be rejected by many post-modernist architects as describing an 'ultra-modern' rather than a 'post-modern' form of architecture.[21] Further to this, the quotation given by the diction- ary entry from Hudnut gives little idea of the application of the term to the prefabricated house in his article: 'He shall be a modern owner, a post-modern owner, if such a thing is conceivable. Free from all sentimentality or fantasy or caprice.'[22]

Hudnut had published these words in an article of 1945 entitled 'the post-modern house' as well as in a 1949 collection of essays entitled *Architecture and the Spirit of Man*.[23] The passage from which they are taken reads in full:

> I shall not imagine for my future house a romantic owner, nor shall I defend my client's preferences as those foibles and aberrations usually referred to as 'human nature'. No, he shall be a modern owner, a post-modern owner, if such a thing is conceivable. Free from all sentimentality or fantasy or caprice, his vision, his tastes, his habits of thought shall be those most necessary to a collective-industrial scheme of life; the world shall, if it pleases him, appear as a system of casual sequences transformed each day by the cumulative miracles of science. Even so he will claim for himself some inner experiences, free from outward control, unprofaned by the collective conscience. That opportunity, when the universe is socialised, mechanised and standardised, will yet be discoverable in the home. Though his house is the most precise product of modern processes there will be entrenched within it this ancient loyalty invulnerable against the siege of our machines. It will be the architect's task, as it is today, to comprehend that loyalty – to comprehend it more firmly than anyone else – and, undefeated by all the armaments of industry, to bring it out in its true and beautiful character.[24]

I have quoted this passage at length because there are several points made in it which are of interest for understanding Hudnut's concept of the post-modern. Firstly, the concept of the post-modern is clearly used to describe what could also be denoted in Hudnut's own terms a modern or ultra-modern owner. Secondly, Hudnut had spoken in the opening of his 1945 article on the 'post-modern house' of the 'prefabricated' hut or house as the house of the future,[25] and had also suggested in his 1949 text that his vision had been produced by 'thinking about those factory-built houses, pure products of technological research and manufacture, which are promised us as soon as a few remaining details of finance and distribution are worked out'.[26] As Hudnut envisaged these houses in 1949 they were to be 'pressed by giant machines out of plastics or chromium steel, pouring out of assembly lines by the tens of thousands, delivered anywhere in response to a telephone call, and upon delivery made ready for occupancy by the simple process of tightening a screw'.[27] After flying over a parking lot beside a baseball stadium, Hudnut had also been inspired to see the thousands of automobiles parked there in herringbone patterns as a foreshadowing of those future suburbs in which 'every family will have each its standardised mass-produced and movable shell, indistinguishable from those of its thousand neighbours except by a choice of paint and the (relative) ambitions of their owners to be housed in the latest model'.[28]

In addition to this, Hudnut's post-modern owner's house is described in his conclusion as the epitome of the results of 'the cumulative miracles of science', which might even be termed the forces of 'modernisation', given that Hudnut had also spoken in his article of the coming of a 'collective-industrial scheme of life' which now appears to have looked back to the relations of modern industrial society rather than forward to any new 'post-industrial' scheme of things similar to those spoken of by Jencks in his writings on the post-modern in architecture.[29] For this reason too Hudnut's vision could be said to be 'ultra' rather than 'post'-modern. Only when Hudnut goes on to speak of the architect as providing an antidote to the machine, by providing the way of bringing out the 'true and beautiful character' of the post-modern house, might we in fact find something which looks forward to at least some of the post-modern architectural theory of the 1970s.

Charles Jencks has even written of Hudnut in his *What is Post-Modernism?* of 1986 that he had 'introduced the term "Post-Modernism" into the "architectural subconscious"', and, in being at Harvard with Walter Gropius, 'may have wished to give this pioneer of the Modern Movement a few sleepless nights'.[30] Although Jencks does not refer specifically to the passage, Hudnut's 1945 article had also contained the statement that while the author would not advise a return to 'that harlequinade of Colonial, Regency, French Provincial, Tudor and Small Italian Villa which adds such dreary variety to our suburban landscapes', he sometimes thought 'that the eclectic soul of these suburbs is, by intuition if not by understanding, nearer the heart of architecture than those rigid minds which understand nothing but the economics of shelter and the arid technicalities of construction'.[31] In that the Modern Movement had not yet achieved all it should achieve for Hudnut, who also wrote that 'we have not yet learned to give them [ie the modern techniques and motives] any persuasive meanings',[32] he may well have placed the concept of the post-modern into the 'architectural subconscious', as suggested by Jencks.[33] At the same time it has also to be noted that Hudnut was writing in the 1940s largely within the debates of his time, and that, while critical of the distortion of modernism into pure functionalism, still saw many of the ideals of the Modern Movement as being basically sound.[34] Added to this it must again be recalled that Hudnut has used the term post-modern itself not to describe a better alternative to the modern, but to describe an ultra-functionalist version of the modern house. If Hudnut is to be understood to have sought to give his Modernist colleagues 'a scare' with his vision of the 'post-modern house' of the coming years it was therefore with what might now be seen as a dystopian vision of what their modernism could degenerate into, rather than with a utopian insight into any of the post-modern alternatives recommended by post-modernist architects of today.

Although Arnold J Toynbee had used the term post-modern in several volumes of his *A Study of History* of 1939 and 1954, and it had also been used in the 1946 DC Somervell abridgement of the early volumes of 1939 written prior to Hudnut's articles, it is only to his *Historian's Approach to Religion* of 1956 to which the *OED* entry next makes reference, and again without giving an explanation of the specific meaning of the term there.[35] In addition to using the term post-modern in his 1956 text to describe the changes experienced by Western civilisation since the end of the nineteenth century, Toynbee had used it in volume V of his *A Study of History* of 1939 to describe the age inaugurated by the war of 1914-18.[36] Only after the end of the Second World War had Toynbee gone on to apply it, as indicated by DC Somervell's abridgement of the first six volumes of that work of 1946,[37] to the period of Western civilisation from 1875 on.[38] While this is the period to which the term 'post-Modern' is attached by Toynbee in the post-World War Two volumes of his *A Study of History* of 1954,[39] it should be noted that when that period is mentioned in volume I of 1934, at the place related to that in which the term 'Post-Modern' appears in Somervell's abridgement of 1946, the term 'Post-Modern' is not used.[40]

Further to being used in the post-war volumes of Toynbee's *A Study of History* to describe the period from the end of the nineteenth century, the term post-modern (now written 'post-Modern') had been used by Toynbee in those volumes to describe the rise of an industrial urban working class, and after the term 'Modern' had been used by him to describe the 'middle classes' of Western civilisation. Toynbee wrote, for example, in volume VIII of his *A Study of History*:

> The most significant of the conclusions that suggest themselves is that the word 'modern' in the term 'Modern Western Civilisation', can, without inaccuracy, be given a more precise and concrete connotation by being translated 'middle class'. Western communities became 'modern' in the accepted Modern Western meaning of the word, just as soon as they had succeeded in producing a bourgeoisie that was both numerous enough and competent enough to become the predominant element in Society. We think of the new chapter of Western history that opened at the turn of the fifteenth and sixteenth centuries as being 'modern' *par excellence* because, for the next four centuries and more, until the opening of a 'post-Modern Age' at the turn of the nineteenth and twentieth centuries, the middle class was in the saddle in the larger and more prominent part of the Western World as a whole.

Toynbee added:

> This definition of the Modern Western culture as being a phase of Western cultural development that is distinguished by the ascendancy of the middle class throws light on the conditions under which, before the advent in the West of a post-Modern Age marked by the rise of an industrial urban working class, any alien recipients of this Modern Western culture would be likely to be successful in making it their own. During the currency of the Modern Age of Western history the ability of aliens to become Westerners would be proportionate to their capacity for entering into the middle-class Western way of life.[41]

As later notes will show, to Toynbee the 'post-Modern Age' was also to be marked not only by the rise of a new industrial urban working class in the West, but by both the rise of other nations and their proletariats and the rise of a variety of 'post-Christian' religious cults as well as sciences.

While Charles Jencks has written in his *Post-Modernism: The New Classicism in Art and Architecture* of 1987 that the term post-modern had also acquired an element of Spenglerian doom in Toynbee's *A Study of History* in being used there to refer to 'the end of Western dominance, Christian culture and individualism',[42] it should also be noted that Toynbee had used the term in post-Second World War (1954) volumes of his *History* which he himself saw as optimistic rather than pessimistic. Toynbee wrote, for instance, in the opening of the chapter on 'Law and Freedom in History' of volume IX of his *A Study of History* that when he was planning his study in the summer of 1927 he had seen that he would have to 'grapple with the problem of the respective roles of Law and Freedom in human history before he could attempt to win a Pisgah sight of the prospects of the Western Civilisation'. It was, however, only in June 1950 when, after a seven-years-long interruption extending over the years 1939 to 1946, he at last reached this point in the writing of the book, that he found himself working in a new atmosphere that was 'decidedly more congenial to his theme'.

Toynbee's discussion of the 'post-Modern' age is also carried out largely in this post-war work, where he dates the post-modern period from the end of the nineteenth century.[43] Further to this, these post-war volumes by Toynbee had also criticised those who had taken the end of their own period to be the end of history as such.[44] This criticism was directed, moreover, against both the 'complacent' view that a period was as good as could be (Toynbee quotes Sellar and Yeatman's ironic *1066 and All That* of 1930: 'History is now at an end; this History is therefore final'[45]) and the 'antithetical' view that things were so bad that nothing new could arise.

While Toynbee counters the first view by pointing out that a 'post-Modern Age' was to follow the 'Modern' which would bring 'new tragedies as well as new developments', he counters the second by pointing out that the pessimistic view of the end of history is as 'subjective' and 'egocentric' as the former.[46] Both views, the complacent view that no further improvement is needed in history, and the pessimistic view that history itself is some way 'at an end', look no further than the view-point of the viewer for Toynbee, and are described by him as 'rationalisations of feelings that are irrationally subjective'.[47] Following this discussion, Toynbee adds that in 'studying the breakdowns of civilisations, we found that the cause was, in every case, some failure of self-determination, and that, when human beings thus lost control over their own destinies, this social disaster usually turned out to have been the consequence of a moral aberration'.[48]

Although the question of Spengler's pessimism is complex, the conclusion of his *Decline of the West* that 'a task that historic necessity has set *will* be accomplished with the individual or against him' may also be said to present a much more pessimistic view of the possibility of individual intervention in the direction of history than that suggested by Toynbee.[49]

Further examples of the use of the term 'post-modern' given by the *OED* include C Wright Mills's use of it in his *The Sociological Imagination* of 1959 to describe a new 'Fourth Epoch' after the 'Modern Age';[50] Leslie Fiedler's 1965 reference to post-modernist literature (again the quotation given by the dictionary is not very explanatory, being Fiedler's sentence: 'I am not now interested in analysing . . . the diction and imagery which have passed from Science Fiction into post-Modernist literature');[51] Frank Kermode's 1966 remarks that Pop Fiction demonstrates 'a growing sense of the irrelevance of the past', and that 'post-Modernists are catching on';[52] Nikolaus Pevsner's reference in *The Listener* of 29 December 1966, to a 'new style', a 'successor' to his 'International Modern' of the 1930s which he 'was tempted to call . . . a post-modern style';[53] a reference in the *New York Review of Books* of 28 April 1977 to 'the post-modernist demand for the abolition of art and its assimilation to "reality";[54] two somewhat different remarks in the *Journal of the Royal Society of Arts* of November 1979 to 'Post-Modern architects [who] use motifs . . . in questionable taste', and to 'Post-Modernists who have substituted the body metaphor for the machine metaphor'; a reference in *Time* of January 1979 to Philip Johnson as 'the nearest Post-Modernism has to a senior partner'; and another, finally, to *The Times Higher Education Supplement* of 7 March 1980 in which 'Postmodernism, structuralism, and neo-dada' are all said to represent 'a reaction against modernism'.

Several of these uses of the term post-modernism will be discussed at greater length, or referred to again in either text or notes, presently. Other early uses of the term not listed by the *OED* have included several given by Michael Koehler in his article entitled '"Postmodernismus": Ein begriffsgeschichtlicher Ueberblick', which was completed in November 1976 and published in 1977.[55] Here Koehler drew attention to the use made of the term and its variants by the professor Federico de Onis in 1934, the anthologist Dudley Fitts in 1942 (although the use ascribed to Fitts is attributed by Fitts himself to his assistant HR Hays), Arnold J Toynbee (whose usage of the term post-modern Koehler dates only from 1947), Charles Olson (in the years between 1950 and 1958), Irving Howe (1959), Harry Levin (1960), Leslie Fiedler (1965) and John Perreault,[56] as well as Amitai Etzioni in his *The Active Society* of 1968,[57] Ihab Hassan in his *The Dismemberment of Orpheus* and 'POSTmodernISM' essay of 1971,[58] and Ralph Cohen in his autumn 1971 edition of *New Literary History* in which Hassan's 'POSTmodernISM' essay was published.[59]

Details of Koehler's own assessment of these varying definitions will be given presently. First of all it has, however, to be noted that Koehler has not only given one of the most extensive surveys of the term 'postmodernism' (as it is written in the brief abstract in English which precedes his essay), but has also referred us to one of its earliest uses in his documentation of the 1934 use made of it by de Onis.[60]

Koehler writes of de Onis's *Antologica de la poesia española e hispanoamericano* (Madrid 1934) that its Introduction had dated Modernism from the years 1896 to 1905 and had added two other phases to it, of 'postmodernismo' (of 1905 to 1914) and 'ultramodernismo' (of 1914 to 1932). While the first had been defined as a reaction to the 'excesses' of modernism (de Onis describes it as a 'reining in' of modernist excesses which sometimes resulted in more prosaic or ironic works), the second had been seen as an attempt to extend the 'Modernist search for poetic innovation and freedom'.[61]

Further to de Onis's use of the term 'postmodernismo' to describe works of Spanish and Latin-American verse which could be said to be reacting to the excesses of modernism, the anthologist and poet Dudley Fitts's *Anthology of Contemporary Latin American Poetry* of 1942 had also used the term 'post-modernism' in its 'Note' on the Mexican poet Enrique Gonzalez Martinez:

He more than any other single force, is responsible for the revolt against the decorative rhetoric of the school of Ruben Dario. From his work – stripped, hard, clear – the new poets derive much of their strength. It is not exaggeration to say that his sonnet on the Swan, used as a general epigraph for this anthology, is the manifesto of post-Modernism – one of the significant landmarks in world literature.[62]

While, according to Fitts's Preface, the Notes to his anthology had been written by HR Hays,[63] it is also clear from the Preface that Fitts had agreed with them.[64] As indicated in the Note just cited, Fitts's anthology had also used Martinez's sonnet as a 'general epigraph':

THEN TWIST THE NECK OF THIS DELUSIVE SWAN
Then twist the neck of this delusive swan,
white stress upon the fountain's overflow,
that merely drifts in grace and cannot know
the reed's green soul and the mute cry of stone.

Avoid all form, all speech, that does not go
shifting its beat in secret unison
with life . . . Love life to adoration!
Let life accept the homage you bestow.

See how the sapient owl, winging the gap
from high Olympus, even from Pallas' lap,
closes upon this tree its noiseless flight . . .

Here is no swan's grace. But an unquiet stare
interprets through the penetrable air
the inscrutable volume of the silent night.[65]

In addition to using Martinez's poem as the epigraph for his anthology, Fitts had spoken in his Preface of how the anthology was an introductory survey of Latin-American poetry since the death, in 1916, of Ruben Dario, and of how the reaction to the Dario tradition since then was prefigured in Enrique Gonzalez Martinez's sonnet.[66] Although this might be taken to extend the dates of the 'postmodernismo' spoken of by de Onis as taking place only between 1905 and 1914, Fitts continued to speak of the movement prefigured by Martinez's sonnet in terms comparable to those used by de Onis to describe 'postmodernismo':

> The new verse is tougher, more intellectualised: its symbol is the 'sapient owl', as opposed to the graceful but vague and somewhat decadent Swan so beloved by Dario and his precursors among the French symbolists. Native themes and native rhythms – whether Indian, Afro-Antillean or Gaucho – have energised it, transforming it into something that is peculiarly American and wholly of our own time. It has never lost the profound tones of its European ancestry, but it speaks to us with a voice that is authentically its own. Poetry, after long absence, has returned to the people.

Here the modernism of which Fitts speaks is not the modernism to which Joseph Hudnut will refer in his articles on the 'post-modern' house of the 1940s but the decorative Symbolism of the end of the nineteenth century.[67] Despite this, both Hudnut's 'post-modernism' and the 'post-modernism' spoken of by de Onis and Fitts/Hays may be said to share the common element of a lack of sentimentality and decorativeness because the post-modernism of which de Onis and Fitts/Hays have spoken was conceived of as a *reaction to* a late nineteenth-century decorative modernism, while Hudnut's post-modern house may be understood as an *extension of* the abstract and decoration-free ('less is more') modernism of the International Style and its offshoots.[68] Here we may again note that the term post-modernism will always need to be read alongside the author's understanding of both modernism and the prefix 'post'.

Michael Koehler concludes his survey of the term 'post-modernism' with the statement that it not only shows that there is still no agreement over that which may be counted as 'post-modern', but that one of the reasons for this is the double meaning of the concept of the 'modern' period. This, Koehler writes, can be used as a synonym for 'die Neuzeit' (literally, 'the new age', although it is usually translated as 'the modern period' or 'modern times'), which for Koehler refers to the time since the European Renaissance, from around 1500,[69] or it can be used to designate the most recent historical period from around 1900 and is then concurrent with the cultural concept of modernism. As has just been seen from our comparison of the uses of the term post-modernism by de Onis and Hudnut, this 'cultural concept of modernism' can itself be divided into several different periods and movements – from, for instance, Symbolism to Abstractionism, Expressionism, Surrealism or any other such modern '-ism' selected by the theorist. Further to this, several other meanings of the term modern could be added to those given by Koehler, such as, for instance, those given it in the phrase describing 'the battle of the ancients and the moderns' from the late seventeenth century on.[70]

Koehler himself continues to argue from his set of alternatives that while Toynbee and Olson may be said to have used the word 'modern' in the first sense given by him (to refer, that is, to a modern period dating from around 1500),[71] they have produced confusion by using the word post-modern to cover a period in which modernism was also born and developed.[72] Koehler adds that this use of the term post-modern is therefore comparable with all those theories which contest the view that the most recent art has broken with the paradigm of modernism. Whether this is either an accurate or a helpful view of Arnold Toynbee's position may, however, be questioned, especially as although Toynbee had used the term 'post-Modern' to refer to a new 'post-Middle class' age, he had continued to see the middle class as the force behind the production of 'Modern' art of both archaic and futurist kinds and to criticise both those types of art.[73]

While it is clear that the question of whether a new 'post-Modernist' art might still arise from the 'post-Modern Age' and its proletariats was one left unanswered by Toynbee, it is also clear that he believed that there was much in existing modernist art which needed to be changed.[74]

One other point which needs to be made here, and which Koehler himself suggests in a footnote,[75] is also that a comparison of Toynbee's views on the 'post-Modern' with more recent views on post-modernism and its relationship to modernism is problematic in that the 'post-modernist' art spoken of in the last two decades was not only unknown to Toynbee, but is inclusive of a great many reactions to, and extensions of, a variety of modernisms.

From the subject described above, Koehler goes on to speak of those theories which have equated the modern with modernism[76] and to detail those by, for example, Irving Howe and Harry Levin which date the end of the modern period from the end of World War Two. According to Koehler the years of the 1950s then see a reaction to the extremes of modernist Formalism and a return to Realism which is not so evident in the more 'avantgarde' 1960s, which, Koehler suggests (in an echo of de Onis's terminology), might rather be seen as 'ultra-modern' if the 1950s are to be described as post-modern.

One other hypothesis – which Koehler sees as having been put by Leslie Fiedler and Ihab Hassan – views, by contrast, the 1960s as representative of a 'postmodern sensibility'. (In fact, Hassan will be seen to have taken his 'postmodernism' back much further than this.) According to this view, continues Koehler, the 1950s are seen as being only an early phase of 'postmodernity'.[77]

For Koehler this approach also revolts against the canonisation of a classical modernism which suppresses the 'aesthetic praxis' of 'alternative' modern 'traditions' such as Dadaism and Surrealism. Koehler adds, however, that 'insofar as the "post" in "postmodern" does not just imply a temporal relation, but also designates a break with the preceding style', this approach leads to an 'internal contradiction', for here 'the postmodernism in question breaks only with the conventions of the (so-called) classical Modern, but not with its "alternative" tradition'. Although it could be argued (as others have since Koehler) that the term post-modern need not necessarily designate a total break with the modern (or 'post-modernism' with 'modernism') in the first place,[78] Koehler goes on to conclude from the above that the 1960s should be seen as 'late modern' rather than as 'postmodern'.[79]

The argument over whether a movement is 'late' or 'post'-modern is also one around which several post-modernist debates have circled since Koehler wrote his article. As we shall see, they include the contributions made by Charles Jencks that the 'Post-Modern' in both art and architecture involves a 'double-coding' of the 'Modern' with other 'codes' where the 'Late-Modern' does not, and that theories of the post-modern which do not see it as aiming to double-code the modern with another code, but as simply 'deconstructing' the modern, should themselves only be seen as being 'late modern'.[80]

Koehler's last alternative, and preferred, view of the post-modern is that of a 'model' which would cover the last two decades from the point of view of two 'sometimes intersecting developments'. During the 1950s, Koehler claims, a 'traditionalism' born of the 'modern classics' was dominant, but at the same time a 'Neo-Avantgardism' developed from the premises of Dadaism and Surrealism which finally 'wore itself out' in the 1960s.[81] In the second half of that period a new sensibility was evident which was, however, no longer in harmony with either of the modernisms previously mentioned.

Koehler adds that this 'tentative postmodernism' only begins to take form in the 1970s, but is still not easy to define. For Koehler the 'postmodern' thus begins only after 1970, and the period from 1945 to 1970 must therefore be called 'late modern'.

Despite the above vagueness over the nature of the 'postmodern', as well as some lack of clarity in Koehler's text over the boundaries between the words 'postmodern', 'postmodernity' and 'postmodernism',[82] and some minor errors,[83] it must still be seen as one of the earliest systematic attempts to give a history of the term post-modernism, although it may also now seem ironic, given the growth of post-modernist architecture in recent years and the use of the term post-modern in theoretical writings on the subject of architecture from at least 1945 on, that the one field omitted from its survey was that of architecture.[84]

Amongst the other early uses of the term post-modernism not listed by either the *OED Supplement* of 1982 or by Koehler in his 1977 essay[85] is, moreover, one by the Australian art historian Bernard Smith which may well be one of the first twentieth-century applications of the term to the visual arts.[86] Smith (who had been reading Toynbee's *A Study of History* through the war years[87]) had used the word 'post-Modernist' in the Conclusion of his *Place, Taste and Tradition* of 1945 (the text of which was completed in February 1944) with reference to the emergence of a new social and political realism in the Australian work of the artists Noel Counihan, Josl Bergner and Victor O'Connor. This 'new' form of Realism (in which elements from Expressionism and other twentieth-century styles mixed with the realistic depiction of the subject-matter of poverty and labour) represented for Smith a move away from modernist abstract art, as well as a reaction to what he saw to be the 'l'art pour l'art' mentality of many of the modernists of the twentieth century,'[88] and was described by him as having arisen in the 'post-Modernist world' of the 1940s.[89]

In addition to the above, the 'post-Modernist' Realism of Counihan, Bergner and O'Connor was also described by Smith as having arisen in the place of the prophecies for a 'Post-Byzantine' form of modernism which would see the latter reduced further to the cold geometric forms favoured by Abstractionists. Here Smith was speaking in particular of a prophecy by Clive Bell and Pitirim Sorokin that modernism would develop into a 'sort of Post-Byzantinism that would catch the 'spirit' of machinery in a vague symbolic fashion, in abstract geometric forms'.[90]

Further to referring us to the theories of Bell and Sorokin, Smith's use of the term 'Post-Byzantine' again recalls the work of Arnold J Toynbee in that the latter had both described the contemporary world as a 'machine age' in the pre-World War Two volumes of his *A Study of History* and used the word 'Byzantine' in his fifth volume of 1939 to describe the 'archaism' of movements such as that of the 'Pre-Raphaelites' and 'Neo-Gothicists'.[91] Following Toynbee's use of the term 'Byzantine' to describe those forms of modernism which he thought to be 'archaic', Smith had used the term 'Post-Byzantine' to designate the reaction of modernist abstractionist against the 'Byzantine'. While de Onis's and Fitts/Hays's post-modernisms could be said to share some characteristics with that which Smith has termed 'Post-Byzantine' art, of, for instance, a reaction against earlier modernist Symbolist art, Smith's chosen category of 'post-Modernist' art is understood as standing in contrast to the cold abstractions of the 'Post-Byzantine'. Put in summary this could read:

Toynbee (1939): Post-World War One = *Post-Modern Age; Modern Art* = either Byzantine Archaism (Neo-Gothic or Pre-Raphaelite) or Futurism;

De Onis (1934) and Fitts/Hays (1942): 'postmodernismo' poetry = a reaction to earlier Modernist decorativeness;

Hudnut (1945): the '*post-modern* house' = (1) extension of Modern Movement functionalism and lack of decorativeness, and (2) in need of architect's sensibility; *Smith (1945)*: modern '*Post-Byzantine*' Art = a reaction to decorativeness and a move towards greater action; '*Post-Modernist*' Art (of the 1940s) = a reaction against Modernist abstraction.[92]

Here the Modernism to which de Onis and Fitts/Hays's 'postmodernismo' was an alternative may be aligned (though not equated) with the Byzantine Archaism condemned by Toynbee[93] and their 'postmodernist' alternatives compared with the 'post-byzantinism' to which Smith's 'post-Modernism' was seen by him to have acted as an alternative.[94] Although the Realism described by Smith as 'post-Modernist' in 1944 might now be described as a modern form of nineteenth-century social realism, and, hence, as also carrying on a tradition of modernism which existed prior to abstract modernism,[95] the use made by Smith of the term 'post-Modernism' in 1944/5 to describe a reaction to abstract modernism has also been echoed, despite Smith's own more recent condemnation of contemporary post-modernism,[96] in some contemporary uses of the term post-modernism and its concomitants in the fields of both art and architecture to denote a turning-away from the modernist obsession with abstraction.[97]

This is true, for example, of Achille Bonito Oliva's concept of the 'transavantgarde', as well as of some other contemporary concepts of post-modernist art. Further to this, Michael Koehler's history of the term 'postmodern' refers to the American art critic John Perreault as having used the term in the mid 1960s for art works which 'did not seem to fit within the rules of modernism in art' or which revived 'art styles "wiped out" by modernism', or 'Anti-Object Art' or 'what have you'.[98] As with some later concepts of 'post-modernism', such accounts of post-modernist art have also thought it legitimate for that art to go back to movements prior to modernism as well as to go beyond them. Whether the work of Counihan, Bergner or O'Connor could be said to be 'post-modernist' in any of the contemporary senses given the word by those discussed in the following chapters could, however, be questioned on the basis of the absence of other basic criteria listed for today's 'post-modernisms' or 'transavantgardes', such as the ironic awareness that all the modernist styles of the past are now historic and archaic rather than truly of the present, and that any opposition to modernist abstraction should also be aware of the naivety of many 'pre-abstractionist' concepts of representation or Realism.

Many of the early uses of the terms post-modern and post-modernism discussed here have also become outdated now because that which was for them post-modern has come to be seen in more recent years as a part of a now historical modern period. Whether current uses of the term will prove to have a better foot-hold in history remains to be seen, but they do at least seem at this point of time to have a wider distribution than that enjoyed by those of the 1930s and 1940s in their time.

NOTES

1 See Dick Hebdige, *Hiding in the Light: on Images and Things*, London and New York, 1988, pp 181 ff.

2 See, for example, Ihab Hassan, 'The Question of Postmodernism', *Romanticism, Modernism, Postmodernism*, ed Harry R Garvin, *Bucknell Review 25*, 2, London and Toronto, 1980, p 120; Wallace Martin, 'Postmodernism: Ultima Thule or Seim Anew?', *Romanticism, Modernism, Postmodernism*, ed Garvin, p 145.

3 Ironically, the term 'anything goes' may more accurately describe Lyotard's relativistic stance, although even here a close analysis of his position will show that not everything 'does go', and especially when he is speaking of targets of his post-modernism which he has described as modernist 'metanarratives'.

4 The spelling of the term post-modernism without its hyphen is often an indication that the user is following deconstructionist post-modernist theories, although some editorial intervention may also be responsible.

(And see also note 18 on other reasons for the form 'postmodernism'.) Other 'tracers' (to use a term suggested to me by Charles Jencks to refer to words or concepts from which the origins or theoretical underpinnings may be traced) include the designation, following Jameson, of the Portman Bonaventure Hotel as post-modern rather than late-modern, the use of concepts such as 'hyperreality' or 'normless pastiche', and the use, following Hassan, of the concept of indeterminacy. As with all tracings of ideas, other factors involved in the use of similar ideas, such as chance or misunderstanding, will also have to be taken into account, although in most cases there will be other factors involved, such as a direct reference to an author or to his or her other ideas, which may support the use of a 'tracer' in the above manner.

5 Hebdige, *Hiding in the Light*, p 183.

6 See Jean Baudrillard, 'The Ecstasy of Communication', *The Anti-Aesthetic*, ed Hal Foster, Port Townsend, Wash, 1983.

7 Jean Baudrillard, 'The Orders of Simulacra', trans Philip Beitchmann, *Simulations*, New York, 1983, p 128.

8 Baudrillard, *Simulations*, p 83 and pp 103 ff.

9 Ibid, p 111.

10 Hebdige, *Hiding in the Light*, p 195.

11 Ibid.

12 Ibid.

13 Hebdige is not altogether uncritical of Baudrillard's attitudes to contemporary society and its culture (see, for example, Hebdige, *Hiding in the Light*, pp 176, 253, note 6), but does take over many of Baudrillard's characterisations of the latter for his depiction of the post-modern and from either Baudrillard himself (see Hebdige p 253 for examples of his reading of Baudrillard) or from other readers of Baudrillard such as Fredric Jameson. (See for example, Hebdige, *Hiding in the Light*, top of p 254.)

14 Hebdige's discussion of the theories of post-modernism also revolves in general around the figures of Lyotard, Baudrillard, Habermas and Richard Rorty, rather than theorists of post-modern architecture such as Jencks.

15 Mike Featherstone's introductory essay to the special issue of *Theory, Culture & Society* on post-modernism of June 1988 (vol 5, nos 2-3, pp 195-215), 'In Pursuit of the Postmodern: an Introduction', also provides a list of 'definers' of post-modernism on its p 203, which brings together several different schools of thought about the subject without always making their separate identities clear.

16 See the *Oxford English Dictionary Supplement* (Oxford, 1982), vol III, p 698, or the *Oxford English Dictionary*, 2nd edn (Oxford, 1989), vol XII, p 201. The dictionary's coverage of the history of the term is not only limited by the space allotted it, but by its omission of texts such as those by Charles Jencks on post-modern architecture.

17 Here the dictionary refers to its previous definition of the term modern (in col II of the supplement to the 1st edn, p 993; or the 2nd edn, vol IX, p 948) as being 'of a movement in art or architecture, or the works produced by such a movement: characterised by a departure from or a repudiation of accepted or traditional styles and values'. As noted earlier, the derivation of the word modern from the Latin for 'today' or 'just now', is given in vol VI of the *OED*, 1st edn, p 573, and may also be found in the new, second, edition in vol IX, pp 947-48.

18 The term 'double-coding' is used by Jencks at least from 1978 on (in the 2nd edn of his *The Language of Post-Modern Architecture*), and refers to how the post-modern building may use both a 'Modern' code (described as a code because it, like other architectural styles, is understood as sending out messages to its users in a similar way to other codes or speech acts) and at least one other style or code (such as, for example, the classical codes used in Stirling, Wilford and Associates' new Stuttgart State Gallery). While Jencks uses the hyphenated term 'Post-Modern' from at least 1977 on, and then together with the term 'Post-Modernism', Hassan, Lyotard, Jameson and other recent critics will be seen to have spoken of 'postmodernism'. One other form of the word 'post-Modernism' has also been used by Leslie Fiedler (in 1965) and by Bernard Smith (in 1945), while Arnold J Toynbee had used the spelling 'post-Modern' from at least 1954 on. Sometimes the particular form taken by the word has also been influenced by the form taken by it in the language from which it has been translated (such as, for example, Spanish, French or German) in which hyphens are not used, although, as pointed out in the preceding note 4, it may also follow, in other instances, from the particular canon of post-modernist theory being supported by the user in question. Except where quoting from a particular usage, this text will use the form given in the *OED* of the hyphenation 'post-modern' as being the most correct form for usage in English.

19 See the previous note 17.

20 Hudnut had used the term in 1945 in an article entitled 'the post-modern house' in the *Architectural Record*

97, May 1945, pp 70-75. The article was also published in the *Royal Architectural Institute of Canada Journal* 22, pp 135-40. (See also note 23 below.)

21 To my knowledge, no self-professed post-modern architect of recent times has described the prefabricated houses as post-modern on that basis alone. When Charles Jencks illustrates his partly prefabricated Garagia Rotunda of 1977 in the fifth edition of his *The Language of Post-Modern Architecture*, p 120, he describes it as 'Architecture as prefabrication plus cosmetics'. And see also Lucien Kroll's condemnation of the prefabricated house as a product of modernism in his *The Architecture of Complexity* of 1983, trans Peter Blundell Jones, London, 1986, p 10.

22 The *OED* is quoting p 119 of Joseph Hudnut's *Architecture and the Spirit of Man*, Harvard, 1949. The misleading nature of the *OED*'s entry on Hudnut's usage of the word post-modern may also be reflected in Frank Kermode's interpretation of its 1949 usage in his *History and Value*, (Oxford 1988, p 129) to refer to 'a kind of architecture that came later than, and reacted against, the Modern Movement in that field'.

23 See the previous note 20 for details of Hudnut's 1945 article. It was a slightly different version of that article that was published by Hudnut in his *Architecture and the Spirit of Man*, pp 108-19, under the same title of 'the post-modern house'.

24 Hudnut, 'the post-modern house', 1945, p 75; and 1949, p 119.

25 Hudnut had begun his 1945 article with the words: 'I have been thinking about that cloud burst of new houses which as soon as the war is ended is going to cover the hills and valleys of New England with so many square miles of prefabricated happiness' (see Hudnut, 'the post-modern house', 1945, p 70).

26 Hudnut, 'the post-modern house', 1949, p 108.

27 Ibid.

28 Ibid.

29 Toynbee's descriptions of the 'post-Modern Age' in the post-war (1954) volumes of his *A Study of History* also characterise it as 'collective industrial' in a way which makes it seem fixed in a stage prior to the post-industrial as described by Bell and others in more recent years.

30 See Charles Jencks, *What is Post-Modernism?* London, 1986, p 14. Jencks also refers to Hudnut in a 'Foot-Note' to the introductions of the 1978 and following revised editions of his *The Language of Post-Modern Architecture* of 1977 as having made 'what appears to be' the 'first use of Post-Modern in an architectural context'. See Jencks, *Language of Post-Modern Architecture*, 4th revised enlarged edition, London, 1984, p 8.

31 See Hudnut, 'the post-modern house', 1945, pp 72-73. Hudnut had, however, also added on p 73 with regard to the 'harlequinade' of styles used in the suburbs that he thought 'that that adventure is at an end'.

32 Ibid, p 73. One of the criteria for post-modernism suggested by Jencks is that it give meaning to its techniques and motives.

33 Jencks has also criticised modern architecture's belief in the 'myth of the machine aesthetic'. See, for example, his 1975 article 'The Rise of Post Modern Architecture' in the *Architectural Association Quarterly* 7, no 4, p 6: 'What is modern architecture based on? Why . . . the myth of the machine aesthetic, an abstract language, geometry and good taste.'

34 Although Gropius had also experimented with prefabricated housing in America, Hudnut had defended him and other founders of the Modern Movement in architecture for their ideals, while also criticising those who had 'distorted' the latter into a 'cold and uncompromising functionalism' in his 1945 article, 'the post-modern house', pp 73-74. In addition to such statements, Hudnut's 1949 collection of essays also contains passages where he defends the 'modernist dictum' that 'form follows function'. (See Hudnut, 'the post-modern house', pp 113, 13.

35 Toynbee's use of the term post-modern will be discussed more fully presently. In being used as early as 1939 it predates Hudnut's usage rather than the other way around as suggested by the *OED*. Even earlier uses of the term will, however, also be dealt with in this essay in following pages.

36 See Arnold J Toynbee, *A Study of History*, vol V, London, 1939, p 43.

37 *A Study of History by Arnold J Toynbee*, abridged by DC Somervell, Oxford, 1946, p 39.

38 As suggested in the text, the first use of the term 'post-Modern' to denote the period from 1875 on in Toynbee's own *A Study of History* is only to be found in the post-war volumes published in 1954. When used in Somervell's abridgement to describe the period from 1875 on the term 'Post-Modern' is also followed by a question-mark.

39 See note 37 above.

40 Somervell's abridgement was completed in 1946 and approved by Toynbee. The use of the term 'Post-Modern' in the abridgement with a question-mark may mean that Somervell thought that this was the direction which Toynbee's work was taking in the post-war years.

41 Toynbee, *A Study of History*, vol VIII, p 338. Toynbee also makes some references to Western architecture of pp 374-75 of vol VIII, and describes the 'sky-scrapers' of the twentieth century as 'Modern Neo-Gothic'. Previously (see, for example, Somervell, *A Study of History*, pp 507-08, or Toynbee, *A Study of History*, vol VI, 1939, pp 60-61), Toynbee had also attacked both the 'Gothic revival' in 'modern' architecture as a decadent archaism, and (Somervell, *A Study of History*, pp 446-47 or Toynbee, *A Study of History*, vol V, 1939, p 482) the modern commercialisation of art. Both were signs of decay for Toynbee, who also went on to condemn the 'Futurist' destruction of the heritage of the past as equally damaging. (See, for example, Somervell, *A Study of History*, p 519, or Toynbee, *A Study of History*, vol VI, pp 115 ff.)

42 See Charles Jencks, *Post-Modernism: the New Classicism in Art and Architecture*, London, 1987, p 13, and also Jencks's foreword to his *What is Post-Modernism?*, 1986, p 3.

43 See also Toynbee, *A Study of History*, vol IX, p 235.

44 Ibid, p 421.

45 Ibid; and see the 'Compulsory Preface' of *1066 and All That* for the line quoted by Toynbee. The 'end of History' ironically referred to as such by Sellar and Yeatman was marked in their text by the rise of America to 'top nation' status after the end of the Great War of 1914-18: 'America was thus clearly top nation, and History came to a.'

46 See Toynbee, *A Study of History*, vol IX, p 436. A 'pessimistic' view of history has also been ascribed to Jean Baudrillard in more recent times. Douglas Kellner, for example, has described Baudrillard as preaching a 'nihilism' which is 'without joy, without energy, without hope for a better future'. See Douglas Kellner, 'Postmodernism as a Social Theory', *Theory, Culture and Society* 5, nos 2-3, June 1988, p 247. Baudrillard also writes in his 'The Orders of Simulacra', *Simulations*, p 111, of the 'new age of the simulacrum', that 'It is the end of a history in which successively, God, Man, Progress and History itself die to profit the code, in which transcendence dies to profit immanence.' Baudrillard adds (ibid p 112) that 'In its indefinite reproduction . . . the system puts an end to the myth of its origin and to all the referential values it has itself secreted along the way.'

47 Toynbee, *A Study of History*, vol IX, p 436, takes the British historian Edward Gibbon as an exemplar of the optimistic view of modern history and the French writer Paul Valéry as an exemplar of the pessimist. Toynbee adds (ibid, p 438) that 'pessimism . . . was no more proof than optimism against the possibility of being refuted by events'. Toynbee continues (ibid, p 439): 'The pessimist's error of mistaking dawn for nightfall may be rarer than the optimist's error of mistaking sunset for noon' – but it is still an error'.

48 Ibid, p 441.

49 See Oswald Spengler, *The Decline of the West*, translated by Charles Francis Atkinson, London, 1971, p 507. In contrast to Spengler, Toynbee had written of the role of the individual in society in the 1946 DC Somervell abridgement of his *A Study of History*, pp 576-77, that the 'source of action' is 'in the individuals'. (And see also the text referred to in note 48 above as well as Toynbee's specific criticisms of Spengler's belief in the omnipotence of necessity on, for example, p 168 of vol IX of his *A Study of History*.) Here it is also interesting to note that Rudolf Pannwitz's 1917 use of the term 'post-modern' (as referred to by Wolfgang Welsch, *Unsere postmoderne Moderne*, Weinheim, 1988, pp 12 f) had occurred in a work entitled 'Die Krisis der europacischen Kulture' ('The Crisis of European Culture'), published just prior to Spengler's *Decline of the West* and had been used to describe a type of human who was outwardly tough but inwardly decadent. By contrast to Toynbee, Jean Baudrillard's contribution to Hal Foster's *Postmodern Culture*, his essay 'The Ecstasy of Communication', concludes (p 133) in a pessimistic as well as fanciful manner on the agency of the human subject: 'He can no longer produce the limits of his own being, can no longer produce himself as a mirror. He is now only a pure screen, a switching centre for all the networks of influence.'

50 See C Wright Mills, *The Sociological Imagination*, Harmondsworth, 1983, pp 184 ff. Mills characterises the 'Fourth Epoch' as one in which the liberalism and socialism 'born of the Enlightenment' have both 'virtually collapsed as adequate explanations of the world'; 'the ideas of freedom and reason have become moot'; and 'increased rationality may not be assumed to make for increased reason.'

51 See Leslie Fiedler, 'The New Mutants', *Partisan Review*, 1965, p 508, or in *Collected Essays of Leslie Fiedler*, vol II, New York, 1971, pp 379-400. Just prior to this passage Fiedler had been referring to the influence of science fiction on Wilhelm Reich, Buckminster Fuller, Marshal McLuhan and ('perhaps') Norman O Brown as well as on writers such as William Golding, Anthony Burgess, William Burroughs, Kurt Vonnegut, Jr, Harry Matthews and John Barth. The passage quoted by the *OED* had continued: 'but rather in coming to terms with the prophetic content common to both; with the myth rather than the modes of Science Fiction'. Fiedler had then proceeded (*Collected Essays*, p 382) to describe that myth as 'quite simply the myth of the end of man', and, more specifically, as the idea of turning humans into newly irrational, and even 'barbaric' beings, or,

that is, 'the new mutants', and had then also gone on to speak at length of the new 'post-modernist' irrationality, cultism and antipathy to the precepts of the Protestant work ethic which he found to be already evident in the 1960s. Later, in an article published in *Playboy* in December 1969 entitled 'Cross the Border – Close the Gap', Fiedler also spoke of 'Post-Modernist' literature as closing the gap between 'High' and Pop literature to align itself with the latter and its subservient (parodistic and other) forms as the culture of the present, and of the need created thereby for a new 'Post-Modernist criticism', able to make judgments 'about the "goodness" and "badness" of art quite separated from distinctions between "high" and "low" with their concealed class bias'.

52 In *Encounter*, vol 26 no 4, April 1966, p 73. Here Kermode was referring, however, largely to Fielder's use of the term, and did not entirely agree with Fielder's assessment that something so new was happening in literature.

53 Nikolaus Pevsner's December 1966 remarks were made in *The Listener*, 29 December 1966, p 955, following a discussion of the buildings of Churchill College Cambridge and referred to architecture of the 1950s and 1960s which Jencks and others have since described as 'late-modern'. Pevsner's second article in *The Listener*, 5 January 1967, pp 7-9, was, however, to include some buildings in his new category which Jencks will at least classify as both late-modern and post-modern, such as Eero Saarinen's TWA Terminal and Joorn Utzon's Sydney Opera House. (See, for example, the entries on Saarinen and Utzon in Charles Jencks, *The Language of Post-Modern Architecture*, and his *Architecture Today*, London 1988, as well as the latter's 'evolutionary trees' of 'Late-Modernism' and 'Post-Modernism' on its pp 20, 110.)

54 Although clearer than some of the other quotations, it should be noted that this is again a reference to a particular view of post-modernism, and not one which can be generalised to cover all forms for post-modernism.

55 Michael Koehler's '"Postmodernismus": ein begriffsgeschichtlicher Uerberblick' is published in *Amerikastudien* 22, 1, 1977, pp 8-18. An editorial note to Koehler's article on its p 8 also refers the reader to the next article in the journal by Gerhard Hoffmann, Alfred Hornung and Ruediger Kunow, '"Modern", "Postmodern" and "Contemporary" as Criteria for the Analysis of 20th-Century Literature', in *Amerikastudien* 22, 1 (1997), pp 19-46, for further bibliographic information.

56 Hoffmann, Hornung and Kunow, '"Modern", "Postmodern" and "Contemporary"', p 45, list the following papers by Olson: 'The Act of Writing in the Context of Post-Modern Man' of 1952; 'The Present is Prologue' of 1955; 'Definitions by Undoings' of 1956; and 'Equal, That Is, To the Real Itself of 1958'. Koehler, '"Postmodernismus"', p 11, also sees Olson as following Toynbee in dating the post-modern from the last quarter of the nineteenth century. (See also the following notes on Toynbee in this chapter.) The reference given by Koehler for Harry Levin's usage is his 'What is Modernism?' in the *Massachusetts Review* of 1960, for Howe his 'Mass Society and Postmodern Fiction' in the *Partisan Review* of 1959, and for Fiedler his 'The New Mutants' in the *Partisan Review* of 1965. While Howe's essay is summarised as describing the new mass society as eliminating many of the moral and aesthetic bases on which classical modernism had been based, Levin's text is described as contrasting the ('postmodern') fiction which he saw to be popularising the achievements of the more experimental modernists of earlier times with the more innovatory nature of the latter. Both are thus seen by Koehler to have used the term post-modern in a negative manner to mourn the demise of modernism. (Further reference to Perreault, whose use of the term occurred in articles in the *Village Voice*, New York, will be made presently.)

57 Amitai Etzioni's *The Active Society: a Theory of Societal and Political Processes* (London and New York, 1968) describes the modern period as having 'ended with the radical transformation of the technologies of communication, knowledge and energy that followed World War Two', and dates the onset of the 'post-modern period' at 1945. Later Etzioni also goes on to claim that the post-modern is similar to the 'late-modern' in some important respects, but still gives some differences, such as that just quoted, by which other theorists will also come to classify the 'post-industrial' society as different from the 'industrial' society.

58 This article has recently been republished in Hassan's *The Postmodern Turn*, 1987.

59 The issue of the journal was entitled 'Modernism and Postmodernism: Inquiries, Reflections and Speculations' and was vol 3, no 1, autumn 1971. Cohen is quoted by Koehler, '"Post-modernismus"', p 14 as saying that 'The issue was planned as an attempt to deal with contemporary avantgarde movements' and that Cohen had decided on the term 'post-modern' 'as the best way to distinguish them from past movements of the avant-garde'. Other journals mentioned by Koehler as having used the term 'post-modern' include *Boundary 2* of 1972, *Triquarterly* of autumn 1973 and spring 1975, the *Journal of Modern Literature* of July 1974, the *New York Drama Review* of March 1975, and the *Hudson Review* of autumn 1973.

60 The *OED* entry referred to earlier was, of course, dealing with uses of the term in English. Although

Koehler is also able to suggest that the word post-modernism may have entered the English language through the translation of the term 'postmodernismo' in Dudley Fitts's 1942 anthology of contemporary Latin-American verse, it has already been seen in this chapter that an even earlier use in English of the term post-modern (if not of post-modernism) can be found in the early (1939) volumes of Arnold Toynbee's *A Study of History*, which Koehler has not mentioned in his survey. As suggested above, and as stated in the notes to the Preface, other claims for terms being prior to de Onis's, such as that made for John Watkins Chapman's in the 1870s, should also be able to show that the use was of some influence or significance.

61 See Koehler, '"Postmodernismus"', p 10, and Federico de Onis, *Antologia de la Poesia española e hispanoamericana (1882-1932)*, Madrid, 1934, pp xviii-xix. I should also like to take the opportunity here to thank Dr Michael Hoskin, Fellow of Churchill College Cambridge, for his assistance with the translation of these pages.

62 See Dudley Fitts, *Anthology of Contemporary Latin-American Poetry*, London and Norfolk, Conn, 1947, p 609, or the 1942 edn, p 601.

63 Ibid, 1947, p xix. (Koehler makes no mention of Hays, and attributes the use of the term 'postmodernism' in Fitts's anthology to Fitts alone.)

64 Fitts's Preface, ibid, also acknowledges his debt to Federico de Onis.

65 Epigraph to Fitts's anthology, trans John Peale Bishop.

66 Fitts, *Anthology of Contemporary Latin-American Poetry*, p xi.

67 See the preceding pages on Hudnut. While Hudnut's 'post-modern' house may be understood as representing an exaggeration of the functionalist ideas of the modern International Style, the 'post-modernismo' of which de Onis and Fitts speak is presented by them as a reaction to an excessively decorated form of Modernism. In consequence, both Hudnut's and de Onis and Fitts's concepts of post-modernism may now be understood as being similar in their evocation of a lack of decoration, and in this both will also be seen to be very different from contemporary applications of the term post-modernism to architecture where post-modern architecture is understood as countering the lack of decoration of the modern International Style.

68 See also note 67 above. The quotation 'less is more' is from Mies van der Rohe.

69 See Koehler, '"Postmodernismus"', pp 16 f, and also the earlier discussion of the use of the term modern to cover this period in the Introduction and its first note.

70 Jencks writes of this quarrel in his 'The New Classicism and its Emergent Rules', in *Architectural Design* 58, nos 1/2, 1988, Profile 70, p 24, that it may also be said to have led to the 'struggle between Modernists of all brands that is still with us today'; and see also on this and other issues relating to the definition of modernity and modernism, Matei Calinescu's *Five Faces of Modernity*, Durham, NC, 1987. This work, which I saw only after completing the body of this manuscript, also has an interesting discussion of de Onis on modernism and post-modernism, as well as of the avant-garde. Calinescu's final (1986) chapter on post-modernism is, however, rather more problematical in its apparent conflation (following Linda Hutcheon), on its p 285, of the double-coding which I described as a characteristic of literary parody in my *Parody/Metafiction*, London, 1979, (a book used by Hutcheon together with several other works for her work on both parody and post-modernism, though not referred to by Calinescu) and the double-coding of which Charles Jencks speaks with reference to post-modern architecture.

71 But see also the earlier discussion of Toynbee's usage of the term post-modern to describe the post-1914 years in 1939, and the post-1875 period in his later texts.

72 Koehler, '"Postmodernismus"', p 16: 'diese "Postmoderne" schliesst den Modernismus schon in seiner ganzen Dauer ein'. As noted previously, Koehler, however, has only made mention of Toynbee's post-World War Two dating of the 'Post-Modern Age' as being from 1875 on, and has made no mention of Toynbee's earlier 1939 dating of it as being from 1914 onwards.

73 See the previous pages on Toynbee for further discussion of his views, as well as both the discussion of Toynbee's views on Modernist art in the pages on Bernard Smith's use of the term 'post-Modernism' at the end of this chapter and the following note 74.

74 In addition to condemning both 'futurist' and 'archaic' types of art of the Modern and 'Post-Modern' (that is, for him, post-1975) periods in his *A Study of History*, Toynbee was also to put Frank Lloyd Wright's 'Mayan-style' Imperial Hotel in Tokyo in the same class of archaic art as nineteenth-century Pre-Raphaelite painting in his later article 'Art: Communicative or Esoteric?', in the collection *On the Future of Art*, introduced by Edward F Fry (New York, 1970), p 18. While Toynbee condemned such historicising art as esoteric in a way which suggests that he might also have been antipathetic to much of the post-modernist architecture of recent years, he had also both criticised the role played by modern specialisation in the creation of such

esotericism and argued for an increased valuation of communication in much the same way as some 'historicising' (and other) post-modernist architects and architectural theorists have done, and in a way which suggests that even if he were not to agree with the solutions provided by the latter, he had agreed with their analyses of the problems of both modernity and modernism. (And see also chapter 2 on Arthur J Penty's criticisms of modernist specialisation and chapter 4 on the writings of Charles Jencks on post-modernist architecture.)

75 See Koehler, "'Postmodernismus'", p 16, note 17.

76 See ibid, p 17.

77 Koehler sometimes shifts from speaking of 'postmodernism' to speak of either the 'postmodern' or 'postmodernity' without fully defining the differences between these terms.

78 See, for example, the pages on Jencks in this chapter.

79 See Koehler, "'Postmodernismus'", p 17 and following.

80 Jencks is, however, unlike Koehler in seeing the late-modern and post-modern as running concurrently from the 1960s on; where Koehler, as explained in the following paragraphs of the text, sees the latter as developing largely from the time when the other has worn itself out. As suggested elsewhere, it may also be because others have assumed the post-modern architecture of which Jencks has spoken to have followed the late-modern from the 1960s on, rather than to have run concurrently with it, that they have accepted Jameson's designation of Portman's 1970s Bonaventure Hotel as post-modern.

81 Like several other German critics (including Habermas) Koehler also appears to have taken up some of the ideas put forward by Peter Bürger in his *Theory of the Avant-Garde*, Manchester and Minneapolis, 1984. Like Bürger (and Habermas after him) Koehler chooses, for instance, the Surrealists and Dadaists as representative of the modern avant-garde (instead of, say, the Russian Constructivists of the 1920s), and then goes on to speak somewhat arbitrarily of these chosen groups. For further discussion of the concept of the avant-garde, and a critique of the restrictiveness of the Bürger view on it, see also the following chapters 3 and 4.

82 See note 77, above.

83 Namely the attribution to Fitts rather than to Hays of the use of the term 'postmodernism' in Fitts's 1942 anthology; the dating of Toynbee's usage of the term 'post-Modern' at 1947; and the interpretation of Hassan's periodisation of 'postmodernism'.

84 Although Charles Jencks's influential book *The Language of Post-Modern Architecture* only appeared first in 1977, the year in which Koehler's article was published, he had used the word post-modern in an architectural essay of 1975 (see note 33), while other uses of the term had, as noted previously, also been applied to architecture in earlier years by both Joseph Hudnut (in 1945) and by Nikolaus Pevsner (in the 1960s). Like Koehler, several other commentators on the concept of the post-modern have also continued to ignore or avoid architectural uses of the term, especially when writing of either literature or French literary theory, although it has also been suggested by others that architecture is the area where the term has been most clearly defined and used, and especially when applied to architecture of the 1960s and after, which has consciously shared some of the precepts of the concepts in question.

85 Apart from the missing architectural references mentioned in note above, Koehler's survey has been seen by Hans Bertens in his essay, 'The Postmodern Weltanschauung and its Relation to Modernism: an Introductory Survey', in Douwe Fokkema and Hans Bertens, ed *Approaching Postmodernism*, (Amsterdam and Philadelphia, 1986, pp 9-51) to have omitted references to the American poet Randall Jarrell's use of the term in a review of Robert Lowell's *Lord Weary's Castle* of 1946, and to John Berryman's use of it following Jarrell as well as several later uses. (See Fokkema and Bertens, *Approaching Postmodernism*, pp 12 ff.)

86 Koehler's references to the use of the term 'postmodernism' in visual art criticism include that to John Perreault mentioned previously, and to Brian O'Doherty's May-June 1971 edition of *Art in America*, in which he had put the question 'What is Post-modernism?'. Koehler adds, however, that the question was largely rhetorical, as O'Doherty could give 'no satisfactory answer'. (See Koehler, "'Postmodernismus'", p 13.)

87 Bernard Smith provided this information when I asked him in April 1989 about his use of the term 'post-Modernist'. As noted previously, Arnold J Toynbee had used the term 'Post-Modern' in volume V of his *A Study of History* of 1939, p 43 to describe the period following World War One, while he later wrote it in the form 'post-Modern' in the 1954 volumes of his study to refer to the new 'post-middle class' age following the year 1875. Although written before the publication of these later volumes of Toynbee's study, Smith's 'post-Modernism' also appears to be dealing with a 'post-bourgeois' set of artists, in so far as all of those listed by Smith had some connection with communist or socialist beliefs, while their art was concerned with the depiction of workers and the impoverished and their conditions, rather than with what was understood to be a middle-class way of life.

88 See, for example, Bernard Smith, *Place, Taste and Tradition*, Oxford, 1979, p 277.

89 Ibid, p 255.

90 See Smith, ibid, pp 270-1.

91 See Toynbee, *A Study of History*, volume V, p 482.

92 Later, in April 1989, after writing an attack on contemporary post-modernism (see the following note 99), Smith claimed that he had used the word 'post-Modernism' in 1944/5 because the art to which it was applied appeared to be doing something different from other modernist works. (And see also the following note 95.)

93 See the previous pages on Toynbee for further explanation of this point.

94 While Koehler has also claimed ('"Postmodernismus'", p 9) that the use of the prefix 'post' had become more frequent following its use in the term 'post-war' (dated by the *OED* from 1908, one other use of the prefix 'post' in art criticism had been the use of it in the term 'Post-Impressionism' from around the same time.

95 The styles of Counihan, Bergner and O'Conner had, as Smith has noted, combined elements of modernist Expressionism with subject matter typical of Social Realism. For Smith (conversation of April 1989) their 'post-Modernism had therefore seemed to be doing something different from 'other forms of Modernism'. By the time of Smith's *Australian Painting* 1733-1970 (Oxford, 1962) (see pp 233-9 of the 2nd edn of 1971) the Social Realism discussed above is, however, being described as something which 'as a creative trend in Australian art barely survived the war' and the post-war years as ones which did not favour a realistic approach to art'.

96 Smith could not at first recall having used the term 'post-Modernism' in his 1945 text when asked about it in April 1989, and had by then also used it in a review of Peter Fuller's *Theoria* (in *Australian Society*, March 1989, p 41) to write that 'a central weakness of post-modernism has been to treat tradition as a load of old junk to be dismissed or ruthlessly exploited'.

97 Here it should, however, also be noted that Smith's final target in his 1944/5 work was not simply modernist abstraction but the fascism of the time and its aesthetics. Hence Smith concluded his 1945 book (*Place, Taste and Tradition*, pp 280-1) by quoting from Melvin Rader's attack on Fascist aesthetics in his *No Compromise* of 1939: 'It is important to remember that there is a tradition, embodied in the works of men like Ruskin, Morris, Wright, Gropius, and Mumford, which insists upon the democratic functional and collective nature of art.'

98 Koehler, '"Postmodernismus'", p 13.

From *The Postmodern and the Post-Industrial, A Critical Analysis*, Cambridge University Press, 1991.

CHAPTER TWO

LATE MODERNISM AS POSTMODERNISM

Richard Rogers, Lloyds Building, London, 1979-84

Jean-François Lyotard
ANSWERING THE QUESTION: WHAT IS POSTMODERNISM?

Introduction

The object of this study is the condition of knowledge in the most highly developed societies. I have decided to use the word *postmodern* to describe that condition. The word is in current use on the American continent among sociologists and critics; it designates the state of our culture following the transformations which, since the end of the nineteenth century, have altered the game rules for science, literature, and the arts. The present study will place these transformations in the context of the crisis of narratives.

Science has always been in conflict with narratives. Judged by the yardstick of science, the majority of them prove to be fables. But to the extent that science does not restrict itself to stating useful regularities and seeks the truth, it is obliged to legitimate the rules of its own game. It then produces a discourse of legitimation with respect to its own status, a discourse called philosophy. I will use the term *modern* to designate any science that legitimates itself with reference to a metadiscourse of this kind making an explicit appeal to some grand narrative, such as the dialectics of Spirit, the hermeneutics of meaning, the emancipation of the rational or working subject, or the creation of wealth. For example, the rule of consensus between the sender and addressee of a statement with truth-value is deemed acceptable if it is cast in terms of a possible unanimity between rational minds: this is the Enlightenment narrative, in which the hero of knowledge works towards a good ethico-political end – universal peace. As can be seen from this example, if a metanarrative implying a philosophy of history is used to legitimate knowledge, questions are raised concerning the validity of the institutions governing the social bond: these must be legitimated as well. Thus justice is consigned to the grand narrative in the same way as truth.

Simplifying to the extreme, I define postmodern as incredulity toward metanarratives. This incredulity is undoubtedly a product of progress in the sciences: but that progress in turn presupposes it. To the obsolescence of the metanarrative apparatus of legitimation corresponds, most notably, the crisis of metaphysical philosophy and of the university institution which in the past relied on it. The narrative function is losing its functors, its great hero, its great danger, its great goal. It is being dispersed in clouds of narrative language elements – narrative, but also denotative, prescriptive, descriptive and so on. Conveyed within each cloud are pragmatic valencies specific to its kind. Each of us lives at the intersection of many of these. However, we do not necessarily establish stable language combinations, and the properties of the ones we do establish are not necessarily communicable.

The decision makers, however, attempt to manage these clouds of sociality according to their input/output matrices, following a logic which implies that their elements are commensurable and that the whole is determinable. They allocate our lives for the growth of power. In matters of social justice and of scientific truth alike, the legitimation of that power is based on its optimising the system's performance – efficiency. The application of this criterion to all of our games necessarily entails a certain level of terror, whether soft or hard: be operational (that is, commensurable) or disappear.

The logic of maximum performance is no doubt inconsistent in many ways, particularly with respect to contradiction in the socio-economic field: it demands both less work (to lower production costs) and more (to lessen the social burden of the idle population). But our incredulity is now such that we no longer expect salvation to rise from these inconsistencies, as did Marx.

Still, the postmodern condition is as much a stranger to disenchantment as it is to the blind positivity of delegitimation. Where, after the metanarratives, can legitimacy reside? The operativity criterion is technological; it has no relevance for judging what is true or just. Is legitimacy to be found in consensus obtained through discussion, as Jürgen Habermas thinks? Such consensus does violence to the heterogeneity of language games. And invention is always born of dissension. Postmodern knowledge is not simply a tool of the authorities; it refines our sensitivity to differences and reinforces our ability to tolerate the incommensurable. Its principle is not the expert's homology, but the inventor's paralogy.

Here is the question: is a legitimation of the social bond, a just society, feasible in terms of a paradox analogous to that of scientific activity? What would such a paradox be?

The text that follows is an occasional one. It is a report on knowledge in the most highly developed societies and was presented to the Conseil des Universités of the government of Quebec at the request of its president. I would like to thank him for his kindness in allowing its publication.

It remains to be said that the author of the report is a philosopher, not an expert. The latter knows what he knows and what he does not know: the former does not. One concludes, the other questions – two very different language games. I combine them here with the result that neither quite succeeds.

The philosopher at least can console himself with the thought that the formal and pragmatic analysis of certain philosophical and ethico-political discourses of legitimation, which underlies the report, will subsequently see the light of day. The report will have served to introduce that analysis from a somewhat sociologising slant, one that truncates but at the same time situates it.

Such as it is, I dedicate this report to the Institut Polytechnique de Philosophie of the Université de Paris VIII (Vincennes) – at this very postmodern moment that finds the University nearing what may be its end, while the Institute may just be beginning.

The Field: Knowledge in Computerised Societies

Our working hypothesis is that the status of knowledge is altered as societies enter what is known as the postindustrial age and cultures enter what is known as the postmodern age.[1] This transition has been under way since at least the end of the 1950s, which for Europe marks the completion of reconstruction. The pace is faster or slower depending on the country, and within countries it varies according to the sector of activity: the general situation is one of temporal disjunction which makes sketching an overview difficult.[2] A portion of the description would necessarily be conjectural. At any rate, we know that it is unwise to put too much faith in futurology.[3]

Rather than painting a picture that would inevitably remain incomplete, I will take as my point of departure a single feature, one that immediately defines our object of study. Scientific knowledge is a kind of discourse. And it is fair to say that for the last forty years the 'leading' sciences and technologies have had to do with language: phonology and theories of linguistics,[4] problems of communication and cybernetics,[5] modern theories of algebra and informatics,[6] computers and their languages,[7] problems of translation and the search for areas of compatibility among computer languages,[8] problems of information storage and data banks,[9] telematics and the perfection of intelligent terminals,[10] paradoxology.[11] The facts speak for themselves (and this list is not exhaustive).

These technological transformations can be expected to have a considerable impact on knowledge. Its two principle functions – research and the transmission of acquired learning – are already feeling the effect, or will in future. With respect to the first function, genetics provides an example that is accessible to the layman: it owes its theoretical paradigm to cybernetics. Many other examples could be cited. As for the second function, it is common knowledge that the miniaturisation and commercialisation of machines is already changing the way in which learning is acquired, classified, made available and exploited.[12] It is reasonable to suppose that the proliferation of information-processing machines is having, and will continue to have, as much of an effect on the circulation of learning as did advancements in human circulation (transportation systems) and later, in the circulation of sounds and visual images (the media).[13]

The nature of knowledge cannot survive unchanged within this context of general transformation. It can fit into the new channels, and become operational, only if learning is translated into quantities of information.[14] We can predict that anything in the constituted body of knowledge that is not translatable in this way will be abandoned and that the direction of new research will be dictated by the possibility of its eventual results being translatable into computer language. The 'producers' and users of knowledge must now, and will have to, possess the means of translating into these languages whatever they want to invent or learn. Research on translating machines is already well advanced.[15] Along with the hegemony of computers comes a certain logic, and therefore a certain set of prescriptions determining which statements are accepted as 'knowledge' statements.

We may thus expect a thorough exteriorisation of knowledge with respect to the 'knower', at whatever point he or she may occupy in the knowledge process. The old principle that the acquisition of knowledge is indissociable from the training (Bildung) of minds, or even of individuals, is becoming obsolete and will become ever more so. The relationship of the suppliers and users of knowledge to the knowledge they supply and use is now tending, and will increasingly tend, to assume the form already taken by the relationship of commodity producers and consumers to the commodities they produce and consume – that is, the form of value. Knowledge is and will be produced in order to be sold, it is and will be consumed in order to be valorised in a new production: in both cases, the goal is exchange. Knowledge ceases to be an end in itself, it loses its 'use-value'.[16]

It is widely accepted that knowledge has become the principle force of production over the last few decades;[17] this has already had a noticeable effect on the composition of the work force of the most highly developed countries[18] and constitutes that major bottleneck for the developing countries. In the postindustrial and postmodern age, science will maintain and no doubt strengthen its preeminence in the arsenal of productive capacities of the nation-states. Indeed, this situation is one of the reasons leading to the conclusion that the gap between developed and developing countries will grow ever wider in the future.[19]

But this aspect of the problem should not be allowed to overshadow the other, which is complementary to it. Knowledge in the form of an informational commodity indispensable to productive power is already, and will continue to be, a major – perhaps *the* major – stake in the worldwide competition for power. It is conceivable that the nation-states will one day fight for control of information, just as they battled in the past for control over territory, and afterwards for control of access to and exploitation of raw materials and cheap labour. A new field is opened for industrial and commercial strategies on the one hand, and political and military strategies on the other.[20]

However, the perspective I have outlined above is not as simple as I have made it appear. For the mercantilisation of knowledge is bound to affect the privilege the nation-states have enjoyed, and still enjoy, with respect to the production and distribution of learning. The notion that learning falls within the purview of the State, as the brain or mind of society, will become more and more outdated with the increasing strength of the opposing principle, according to which society exists and progresses only if the messages circulating within it are rich in information and easy to decode. The ideology of communicational 'transparency', which goes hand in hand with the commercialisation of knowledge, will begin to perceive the State as a factor of opacity and 'noise'. It is from this point of view that the problem of the relationship between economic and State powers threatens to arise with a new urgency.

Already in the last few decades, economic powers have reached the point of imperilling the stability of the State through new forms of the circulation of capital that go by the generic name of *multinational corporations*. These new forms of circulation imply that investment decisions have, at least in part, passed beyond the control of the nation-states.[21] The question threatens to become even more thorny with the development of computer technology and telematics. Suppose, for example, that a firm such as IBM is authorised to occupy a belt in the earth's orbital field and launch communications satellites or satellites housing data banks. Who will have access to them? Who will determine which channels or data are forbidden? The State? Or will the State simply be one user among others? New legal issues will be raised, and with them the question: 'who will know?'

Transformation in the nature of knowledge, then, could well have repercussions on the existing public powers, forcing them to reconsider their relations (both de jure and de facto) with the large corporations and, more generally, with civil society. The reopening of the world market, a return to vigorous economic competition, the breakdown of the hegemony of American capitalism, the decline of the socialist alternative, a probable opening of the Chinese market – these and many other factors are already, at the end of the 1970s, preparing States for a serious reappraisal of the role they have been accustomed to playing since the 1930s: that of gilding, or even directing investments.[22] In this light, the new technologies can only increase the urgency of such a reexamination, since they make the information used in decision making (and therefore the means of control) even more mobile and subject to piracy.

It is not hard to visualise learning circulating along the same lines as money, instead of for its 'educational' value or political (administrative, diplomatic, military) importance; the pertinent distinction would no longer be between knowledge and ignorance, but rather, as is the case with money, between 'payment knowledge' and 'investment knowledge' – in other words, between units of knowledge exchanged in a daily maintenance framework (the reconstitution of the work force, 'survival') versus funds of knowledge dedicated to optimising the performance of a project.

If this were the case, communicational transparency would be similar to liberalism. Liberalism does not preclude an organisation of the flow of money in which some channels are used in decision making while others are only good for the payment of debts. One could similarly imagine flows of knowledge travelling along identical channels of identical nature, some of which would be reserved for the 'decision makers', while the others would be used to repay each person's perpetual debt with respect to the social bond . . .

ANSWERING THE QUESTION: WHAT IS POSTMODERNISM?
A Demand

This is a period of slackening – I refer to the colour of the times. From every direction we are being urged to put an end to experimentation, in the arts and elsewhere. I have read an art historian who extols realism and is militant for the advent of a new subjectivity. I have read an art critic who packages and sells 'Transavantgardism' in the marketplace of painting. I have read that under the name postmodernism, architects are getting rid of the Bauhaus project, throwing out the baby of experimentation with the bathwater of functionalism. I have read that a new philosopher is discovering what he drolly calls Judaeo-Christianism, and intends by it to put an end to the impiety which we are supposed to have spread. I have read in a French weekly that some are displeased with *Mille Plateaux* (by Deleuze and Guattari) because they expect, especially when reading a work of philosophy, to be gratified with a little sense. I have read from the pen of a reputable historian that writers and thinkers of the 1960 and 1970 avant-gardes spread a reign of terror in the use of language, and that the conditions for a fruitful exchange must be restored by imposing on the intellectuals a common way of speaking, that of the historians. I have been reading a young philosopher of language who complains that Continental thinking, under the challenge of speaking machines, has surrendered to the machines the concern for reality, that it has substituted for the referential paradigm that of 'adlinguisticity' (one who speaks about speech, writes about writing, intertextuality), and who thinks that the time has now come to restore a solid anchorage of language in the referent. I have read a talented theatrologist for whom postmodernism, with its games and fantasies, carries very little weight in front of political authority, especially when a worried public opinion encourages authority to a politics of totalitarian surveillance in the face of nuclear warfare threats.

I have read a thinker of repute who defends modernity against those he calls the neoconservatives. Under the banner of postmodernism, the latter would like, he believes, to get rid of the uncompleted project of modernism, that of the Enlightenment. Even the last advocates of *Aufklärung*, such as Popper and Adorno, were only able, according to him, to defend the project in a few particular spheres of life – that of politics for the author of *The Open Society*, and that of art for the author of *Ästhetische Theorie*. Jürgen Habermas (everyone has recognised him) thinks that if modernity has failed, it is in allowing the totality of life to be splintered into independent specialities which are left to the narrow competence of experts, while the concrete individual experiences 'desublimated meaning' and 'destructured form', not as a liberation but in the mode of that immense *ennui* which Baudelaire described over a century ago.

Following a prescription of Albrecht Wellmer, Habermas considers that the remedy for this splintering of culture and its separation from life can only come from 'changing the status of aesthetic experience when it no longer primarily expressed in judgments of taste', but when it is 'used to explore a living historical situation', that is, when 'it is put in relation with problems of existence'. For this experience then 'becomes a part of a language game which is no longer that of aesthetic criticism'; it takes part 'in cognitive processes and normative expectations'; 'it alters the manner in which those different moments *refer* to one another'. What Habermas requires from the arts and the experiences they provide is, in short, to bridge the gap between cognitive, ethical and political discourses, thus opening the way to unity of experience.

My question is to determine what sort of unity Habermas has in mind. Is the aim of the project of modernity the constitution of sociocultural unity within which all the elements of daily life and of thought would take their places as in an organic whole? Or does the passage that has to be charted between heterogeneous language games – those of cognition, of ethics, of politics – belong to a different order from that? And if so, would it be capable of effecting synthesis between them?

The first hypothesis, of a Hegelian inspiration, does not challenge the notion of a dialectically totalising *experience*, the second is closer to the spirit of Kant's *Critique of Judgment;* but must be submitted, like the *Critique,* to that severe re-examination which postmodernity imposes on the thought of the Enlightenment, on the idea of a unitary end of history and of a subject. It is this critique not only Wittgenstein and Adorno have initiated, but also a few other thinkers (French or other) who do not have the honour to be read by Professor Habermas – which at least saves them from getting a poor grade for their neoconservatism.

Realism

The demands I began by citing are not all equivalent. They can even be contradictory. Some are made in the name of postmodernism, others in order to combat it. It is not necessarily the same thing to formulate a demand for some referent (and objective reality), for some sense (and credible transcendence), for an addressee (and audience), or an addressor (and subjective expressiveness) or for some communicational consensus (and a general code of exchanges such as the genre of historical discourse). But in the diverse invitations to suspend artistic experimentation, there is an identical call for order, a desire for unity, for identity, for security, or popularity (in the sense of *Öffentlichkeit,* of 'finding a public'). Artists and writers must be brought back into the bosom of community, or at least, if the latter is considered to be ill, they must be assigned the task of healing it.

There is an irrefutable sign of this common disposition: it is that for all those writers nothing is more urgent than to liquidate the heritage of the avant-gardes. Such is the case, in particular, of the so-called transavantgardism. The answers given by Achille Bonito Oliva to the questions asked by Bernard Lamarche-Vadel and Michel Enric leave no room for doubt about this. By putting the avant-gardes through a mixing process, the artist and critic feel more confident that they can suppress them than by launching a frontal attack. For they can pass off the most cynical eclecticism as a way of going beyond the fragmentary character of the preceding experiments; whereas if they openly turned their backs on them, they would run the risk of appearing ridiculously neoacademic. The *Salons* and the *Académies,* at the time when the bourgeoisie was establishing itself in history, were able to function as purgation and to grant awards for good plastic and literary conduct under the cover of realism. But capitalism inherently possesses the power to derealise familiar objects, social roles, and institutions to such a degree that the so-called realistic representations can no longer evoke reality except as nostalgia or mockery, as an occasion for suffering rather than for satisfaction. Classicism seems to be ruled out in a world in which reality is so destabilised that it offers no occasion for experience but one for ratings and experimentation.

This theme is familiar to all readers of Walter Benjamin. But it is necessary to assess its exact reach. Photography did not appear as a challenge to painting from the outside, any more than industrial cinema did to narrative literature. The former was only putting the final touch to the programme of ordering the visible elaborated by the quattrocento; while the latter was the last step in rounding off diachronies as organic wholes, which had been the ideal of the great novels of education since the eighteenth century. That the mechanical and the industrial should appear as substitutes for hand or craft was not in itself a disaster – except if one believes that art is in its essence the expression of an individuality of genius assisted by an elite craftsmanship.

The challenge lay essentially in that photographic and cinematographic processes can accomplish better, faster, and with a circulation a hundred thousand times larger than narrative or pictorial realism, the task which academicism had assigned to realism: to preserve various consciousnesses from doubt. Industrial photography and cinema will be superior to painting and the novel whenever the objective is to stabilise the referent, to arrange it according to a point of view which endows it with a recognisable meaning, to reproduce the syntax and vocabulary which enable the addressee to decipher images and sequences quickly, and so to arrive easily at the consciousness of his own identity as well as the approval which he thereby receives from others – since such structures of images and sequences constitute a communication code among all of them. This is the way the effects of reality, or if one prefers, the fantasies of realism, multiply.

If they too do not wish to become supporters (of minor importance at that) of what exists, the painter and novelist must refuse to lend themselves to such therapeutic uses. They must question the rules of the art of painting or of narrative as they have learned and received them from their predecessors. Soon those rules must appear to them as a means to deceive, to seduce, and to reassure, which makes it impossible for them to be 'true'. Under the common name of painting and literature, an unprecedented split is taking place. Those who refuse to re-examine the rules of art pursue successful careers in mass conformism by communicating, by means of the 'correct rules', the endemic desire for reality with objects and situations capable of gratifying it. Pornography is the use of photography and film to such an end. It is becoming a general model for the visual or narrative arts which have not met the challenge of the mass media.

As for the artists and writers who question the rules of plastic and narrative arts and possibly share their suspicions by circulating their work, they are destined to have little credibility in the eyes of those concerned with 'reality' and 'identity'; they have no guarantee of an audience. Thus it is possible to ascribe the dialectics of the avant-gardes to the challenge posed by the realisms of industry and mass communication to painting and the narrative arts. Duchamp's 'ready made' does nothing but actively and parodistically signify this constant process of dispossession of the craft of painting or even of being an artist. As Thierry de Duve penetratingly observes, the modern aesthetic question is not 'What is beautiful?' but 'What can be said to be art (and literature)?'

Realism, whose only definition is that it intends to avoid the question of reality implicated in that of art, always stands somewhere between academicism and kitsch. When power assumes the name of a party, realism and its neoclassical complement triumph over the experimental avant-garde by slandering and banning it – that is, provided the 'correct' images, the 'correct' narratives, the 'correct' forms which the party requests, selects, and propagates can find a public to desire them as the appropriate remedy for the anxiety and depression that the public experiences. The demand for reality – that is, for unity, simplicity, communicability, etc – did not have the same intensity nor the same continuity in German society between the two world wars and in Russian society after the Revolution: this provides a basis for a distinction between Nazi and Stalinist realism.

What is clear, however, is that when it is launched by the political apparatus, the attack on artistic experimentation is specifically reactionary: aesthetic judgment would only be required to decide whether such or such work is in conformity with the established rules of the beautiful. Instead of the work of art having to investigate what makes it an art object and whether it will be able to find an audience, political academicism possesses and imposes a priori criteria of the beautiful, which designate some works and a public at a stroke and forever. The use of categories in aesthetic judgment would thus be of the same nature as in cognitive judgment. To speak like Kant, both would be determining judgments: the expression is 'well formed' first in the understanding, then the only cases retained in experience are those which can be subsumed under this expression.

When power is that of capital and not that of a party, the 'transavantgardist' or 'postmodern' (in Jencks's sense) solution proves to be better adapted than the anti-modern solution. Eclecticism is the degree zero of contemporary general culture: one listens to reggae, watches a Western, eats McDonald's food for lunch and local cuisine for dinner, wears Paris perfume in Tokyo and 'retro' clothes in Hong Kong; knowledge is a matter for TV games. It is easy to find a public for eclectic works. By becoming kitsch, art panders to the confusion which reigns in the 'taste' of the patrons. Artists, gallery owners, critics, and public wallow together in the 'anything goes', and the epoch is one of slackening. But this realism of the 'anything goes' is in fact that of money; in the absence of aesthetic criteria, it remains possible and useful to assess the value of works of art according to the profits they yield. Such realism accommodates all tendencies, just as capital accommodates all 'needs', providing that the tendencies and needs have purchasing power. As for taste, there is no need to be delicate when one speculates or entertains oneself.

Artistic and literary research is doubly threatened, once by the 'cultural policy' and once by the art and book market. What is advised, sometimes through one channel, sometimes through the other, is to offer works which, first, are relative to subjects which exist in the eyes of the public they address, and second, works so made ('well made') that the public will recognise what they are about, will understand what is signified, will be able to give or refuse its approval knowingly, and if possible, even to derive from such work a certain amount of comfort.

The interpretation which has just been given of the contact between the industrial and mechanical arts, and literature and the fine arts is correct in its outline, but it remains narrowly sociologising and historicising – in other words, one-sided. Stepping over Benjamin's and Adorno's reticences, it must be recalled that science and industry are no more free of the suspicion which concerns reality than are art and writing. To believe otherwise would be to entertain an excessively humanistic notion of the mephistophelian functionalism of sciences and technologies. There is no denying the dominant existence today of techno-science, that is, the massive subordination of cognitive statements to the finality of the best possible performance, which is the technological criterion. But the mechanical and the industrial, especially when they enter fields traditionally reserved for artists, are carrying with them much more than power effects. The objects and the thoughts which originate in scientific knowledge and the capitalist economy convey with them one of the rules which supports their possibility: the rule that there is no reality unless testified by a census between partners over a certain knowledge and certain commitments.

This rule is of no little consequence. It is the imprint left on the politics of the scientist and the trustee of capital by a kind of flight of reality out of the metaphysical, religious, and political certainties that the mind believed it held. This withdrawal is absolutely necessary to the emergence of science and capitalism. No industry is possible without a suspicion of the Aristotelian theory of motion, no industry without a refutation of corporatism, of mercantilism, and of physiocracy. Modernity, in whatever age it appears, cannot exist without a shattering of belief and without discovery of the 'lack of reality' of reality, together with the invention of other realities.

What does this 'lack of reality' signify if one tries to free it from a narrowly historicised interpretation? The phrase is of course akin to what Nietzsche calls nihilism. But I see a much earlier modulation of Nietzschean perspectivism in the Kantian theme of the sublime. I think in particular that it is in the aesthetic of the sublime that modern art (including literature) finds its impetus and theology of the avant-gardes finds its axioms.

The sublime sentiment, which is also the sentiment of the sublime, is according to Kant, a strong and equivocal emotion: it carries with it both pleasure and pain. Better still, in it pleasure derives from pain. Within the tradition of the subject, which comes from Augustine and Descartes and which Kant does not radically challenge, this, contradiction, which some would call neurosis or masochism, develops as a conflict between the faculties of a subject, the faculty to conceive of something and the faculty to 'present' something. Knowledge exists if, first, the statement is intelligible, and second, if 'cases' can be derived from the experience which 'corresponds' to it. Beauty exists if a certain 'case' (the work of art), given first, by the sensibility without any conceptual determination, the sentiment of pleasure independent of any interest the work may elicit, appeals to the principle of a universal consensus (which may never be attained).

Taste, therefore, testifies that between the capacity to conceive and the capacity to present an object corresponding to the concept, an undetermined agreement, without rules, giving rise to a judgment which Kant calls reflective, may be experienced as pleasure. The sublime is a different sentiment. It takes place, on the contrary, when the imagination fails to present an object which might, if only in principle, come to match a concept. We have the Idea of the world (the totality of what is), but we do not have the capacity to show an example of it. We have the idea of the simple (that which cannot be broken down, decomposed), but we cannot illustrate it with a sensible object which would be a 'case' of it. We can conceive the infinitely great, the infinitely powerful, but every presentation of an object destined to 'make visible' this absolute greatness or power appears to us painfully inadequate. Those are Ideas of which no presentation is possible. Therefore, they impart no knowledge about reality (experience); they also prevent the free union of the faculties which gives rise to the sentiment of the beautiful; and they prevent the formation and the stabilisation of taste. They can be said to be unpresentable.

I shall call modern the art which devotes its 'little technical expertise' (son 'petit technique'), as Diderot used to say, to present the fact that the unpresentable exists. To make visible that there is something which can be conceived and which can neither be seen nor made visible: this is what is at stake in modern painting. But how to make visible that there is something which cannot be seen? Kant himself shows the way when he names 'formlessness, the absence of form', as a possible index to the unpresentable. He also says of the empty 'abstraction' which the imagination experiences when in search for a presentation of the infinite (another unpresentable): this abstraction itself is like a presentation of the infinite, its 'negative presentation'. He cites the commandment, 'Thou shalt not make graven images' (Exodus), as the most sublime passage in the Bible in that it forbids all presentation of the Absolute. Little needs to be added to those observations to outline an aesthetic of sublime paintings. As painting, it will of course 'present' something though negatively; it will therefore avoid figuration or representation. It will be 'white' like one of Malevitch's squares; it will enable us to see only by making it impossible to see; it will please only by causing pain. One recognises in those instructions the axioms of avant-gardes in painting, inasmuch as they devote themselves to making an allusion to the unpresentable by means of visible presentations. The systems in the name of which, or with which, this task has been able to support or to justify itself deserve the greatest attention; but they can originate only in the vocation of the sublime in order to legitimise it, that is, to conceal it. They remain inexplicable without the incommensurability of reality to concept which is implied in the Kantian philosophy of the sublime.

It is not my intention to analyse here in detail the manner in which the various avant-gardes have, so to speak, humbled and disqualified reality by examining the pictorial techniques which are so many devices to make us believe in it. Local tone, drawing, the mixing of colours, linear perspective, the nature of the support and that of the instrument, the treatment, the display, the museum: the avant-gardes are perpetually flushing out artifices of presentation which make it possible to subordinate thought to the gaze and to turn it away from the unpresentable. If Habermas, like Marcuse, understands this task of derealisation as an aspect of the (repressive) 'desublimation' which characterises the avant-garde, it is because he confuses the Kantian sublime with Freudian sublimation, and because aesthetics has remained for him that of the beautiful.

The Postmodern

What, then, is the postmodern? What place does it or does it not occupy in the vertiginous work of the questions hurled at the rules of image and narration? It is undoubtedly a part of the modern. All that has been received, if only yesterday (*modo, modo*, Petronius used to say), must be suspected. What space does Cézanne challenge? The Impressionists'. What object do Picasso and Braque attack? Cézanne's. What presupposition does Duchamp break with in 1912? That which says one must make a painting, be it cubist. And Buren questions that other presupposition which he believes had survived untouched by the work of Duchamp: the place of presentation of the work. In an amazing acceleration, the generations precipitate themselves. A work can become modern only if it is first postmodern. Postmodernism thus understood is not modernism at its end but in the nascent state, and this state is constant.

Yet I would like not to remain with this slightly mechanistic meaning of the word. If it is true that modernity takes place in the withdrawal of the real and according to the sublime relation between the presentable and the conceivable, it is possible, within this relation, to distinguish two modes (to use the musician's language). The emphasis can be placed on the powerlessness of the faculty of presentation, on the nostalgia for presence felt by the human subject, on the obscure and futile will which inhabits him in spite of everything. The emphasis can be placed, rather, on the power of the faculty to conceive, on its 'inhumanity' so to speak (it was the quality Apollinaire demanded of modern artists), since it is not the business of our understanding whether or not human sensibility or imagination can match what it conceives. The emphasis can also be placed on the increase of being and the jubilation which result from the invention of new rules of the game, be it pictorial, artistic, or any other. What I have in mind will become clear if we dispose very schematically a few names on the chessboard of the history of avant-gardes: on the side of melancholia, the German Expressionists, and on the side of *novatio*, Braque and Picasso, on the former Malevitch and on the latter Lissitsky, on the one Chirico and on the other Duchamp. The nuance which distinguishes these two modes may be infinitesimal; they often coexist in the same piece, are almost indistinguishable; and yet they testify to a difference (*un différend*) on which the fate of thought depends and will depend for a long time, between regret and assay.

The work of Proust and that of Joyce both allude to something which does not allow itself to be made present. Allusion, to which Paolo Fabbri recently called my attention, is perhaps a form of expression indispensable to the works which belong to an aesthetic of the sublime. In Proust, what is being eluded as the price to pay for this allusion is the identity of consciousness, a victim to the excess of time (*au trop de temps*). But in Joyce, it is the identity of writing which is the victim of an excess of the book (*au trop de livre*) or of literature.

Proust calls forth the unpresentable by means of a language unaltered in its syntax and vocabulary and of a writing which in many of its operators still belongs to the genre of novelistic narration. The literary institution, as Proust inherits it from Balzac and Flaubert, is admittedly subverted in that the hero is no longer a character but the inner consciousness of time and in that the diegetic diachrony, already damaged by Flaubert is here put in question because of the narrative voice. Nevertheless, the unity of the book, the odyssey of that consciousness, even if it is deferred from chapter to chapter, is not seriously challenged: the identity of the writing with itself throughout the labyrinth of the interminable narration is enough to connote such unity, which has been compared to that of *The Phenomenology of Mind*.

Joyce allows the unpresentable to become perceptible in his writing itself, in the signifier. The whole range of available narrative and even stylistic operators is put into play without concern for the unity of the whole, and new operators are tried. The grammar and vocabulary of literary language are no longer accepted as given; rather, they appear as academic forms, as rituals originating in piety (as Nietzsche said) which prevent the unpresentable from being put forward.

Here, then, lies the difference: modern aesthetics is an aesthetic of the sublime, though a nostalgic one. It allows the unpresentable to be put forward only as the missing contents; but the form, because of its recognisable consistency, continues to offer to the reader or viewer matter for solace and pleasure. Yet these sentiments do not constitute the real sublime sentiment, which is in an intrinsic combination of pleasure and pain: the pleasure that reason should exceed all presentation, the pain that imagination or sensibility should not be equal to the concept.

The postmodern would be that which, in the modern, puts forward the unpresentable in presentation itself; that which denies itself the solace of good forms, the consensus of a taste which would make it possible to share collectively the nostalgia for the unattainable; that which searches for new presentations, not in order to enjoy them but in order to impart a stronger sense of the unpresentable. A postmodern artist or writer is in the position of a philosopher: the text he writes, the work he produces are not in principle governed by pre-established rules, and they cannot be judged according to a determining judgment, by applying familiar categories to the text or to the work. Those rules and categories are what the work of art itself is looking for. The artist and the writer, then, are working without rules in order to formulate the rules of what *will have been done*. Hence the fact that work and text have the characters of an *event*; hence also, they always come too late for their author, or, what amounts to the same thing, their being put into work, their realisation (*mise en oeuvre*) always begin too soon. *Post modern* would have to be understood according to the paradox of the future (*post*) anterior (*modo*).

It seems to me that the essay (Montaigne) is postmodern, while the fragment (*The Athaeneum*) is modern.

Finally, it must be clear that it is our business not to supply reality but to invent allusions to the conceivable which cannot be presented. And it is not to be expected that this task will effect the last reconciliation between language games (which, under the name of faculties, Kant knew to be separated by a chasm), and that only the transcendental illusion (that of Hegel) can hope to totalise them into a real unity. But Kant also knew that the price to pay for such an illusion is terror. The nineteenth and twentieth centuries have given us as much terror as we can take. We have paid a high enough price for the nostalgia of the whole and the one, for the reconciliation of the concept and the sensible, of the transparent and the communicable experience. Under the general demand for slackening and for appeasement, we can hear the mutterings of the desire for a return of terror for the realisation of the fantasy to seize reality. The answer is: Let us wage a war on totality; let us be witnesses to the unpresentable; let us activate the differences and save the honour of the name.

NOTES

1 Alain Touraine, *La Société postindustrielle*, Denoël, Paris, 1969; Eng trans Leonard Mayhew, *The Post-Industrial Society*, Wildwood House, London, 1974; Daniel Bell, *The Coming of the Post-Industrial Society*, Basic Books, New York, 1973; Ihab Hassan, *The Dismemberment of Orpheus: Toward a Post Modern Literature*, Oxford University Press, New York, 1971; Michel Benamou and Charles Caramello, ed *Performance in Postmodern Culture*, Center for Twentieth Century Studies & Coda Press, Wisconsin, 1977; M Köhler, 'Postmodernismus: ein begriffgeschichtlicher Überblick', *Amerikastudien* 22, 1, 1977.

2 An already classic literary expression of this is provided in Michel Butor, *Mobile: Etude pour une représentation des Etats-Unis*, Gallimard, Paris, 1962.

3 Jib Fowles, ed *Handbook of Futures Research*, Greenwood Press, Westport, Conn, 1978.

4 Nikolai S Trubetskoi, *Grunszüge der Phonologie*, Travaux du cercle linguistique de Prague, vol 7, 1939; Eng trans Christiane Bultaxe, Principles of Phonology, University of California Press, Berkeley, Calif, 1969.

5 Norbert Wiener, *Cybernetics and Society: The Human Use of Human Beings*, Houghton Miflin, Boston, 1949; William Ross Ashby, *An Introduction to Cybernetics*, Chapman & Hall, London, 1956.

6 See the work of Johannes von Neumann, 1903-57.

7 S Bellert, 'La Formalisation des systèmes cybernétiques', *Le Concept d'information dans la science contemporaine*, Minuit, Paris, 1965.

8 Georges Mounin, *Les Problèmes théoriques de la traduction*, Gallimard, Paris, 1963. The computer revolution dates from 1965, with the new generation of IBM 360s: R Moch, 'Le Tournant informatique', Documents contributifs, Annex 4, *l'Information de la société*, La Documentation française, Paris, 1978; RM Ashby, 'La Seconde Génération de la micro-électronique', *La Recherche* 2, June 1970, pp 127 ff.

9 CL Gaudfernan and A Taib, 'Glossaire', in P Nora and A Mine, *L'Information de la société*, La Documentation française, Paris, 1978; R Béca, 'Les Banques de donnés', *Nouvelle informatique et nouvelle croissance*, Anex 1, *L'Informatisation de la société*.

10 L Joyeux, 'Les Applications avancées de l'informatique', *Documents contributifs*. Home terminals (Integrated Video Terminals) will be commercialised before 1984 and will cost about $1,400, according to a report of the International Resource Development: *The Home Terminal*, IRD Press, Conn, 1979.

11 Paul Watzlawick, Janet Helmick-Beavin, Don D Jackson, *Pragmatics of Human Communication: A Study of Interactional Patterns, Pathologies, and Paradoxes*, Norton, New York, 1967.

12 JM Treille, of the Groupe d'analyse et de prospective des systèmes économiques et technologiques (GAPSET), states that, 'Not enough has been said about the new possibilities for disseminating stored information, in particular using semiconductor and laser technology. . . . Soon everyone will be able to store information cheaply wherever he wishes, and, further, will be able to process it autonomously' (*La Semaine media* 16, 16 February 1979). According to a study by the National Science Foundation, more than one high school student in two has ready access to the services of a computer, and all schools will have one in the early 1980s (*La Semaine media* 13, 25 January 1979).

13 L Brunel, *Des Machines et des hommes*, Québec Science, Montréal, 1978: Jean-Louis Missika and Dominique Wolton, *Les résaux pensants*, Librairie technique et documentaire, 1978. The use of videoconferences

between the province of Quebec and France is becoming routine: in November and December 1978 the fourth series of videoconferences (relayed by the satellite 'Symphonie') took place between Quebec and Montreal on the one hand, and Paris (Université Paris Nord and the Beaubourg Centre) on the other (*La Semaine media* 5, 30 November 1978). Another example is provided by electronic journalism. The three big American networks (ABC, NBC and CBS) have increased the number of production studios around the world to the extent that almost all the events that occur can now be processed electronically and transmitted to the United States by satellite. Only the Moscow offices still work on film, which is sent to Frankfurt for satellite transmission. London has become the great 'packing point' (*La Semaine média* 20, 15 March 1979).

14 The unit of information is the bit. For these definition see Gaudefernan and Taib, 'Glossaire'. This is discussed in René Thom, 'Un Protée de la sémantique: l'information' (1973), *Modèles mathématique de la morphogenèse*, Union Générale d'Edition, Paris, 1974. In particular, the transcription of messages into code allows ambiguities to be eliminated: see Watzlawick et al, *Pragmatics of Human Communications*, p 98.

15 The firms Craig and Lexicon have announced the commercial production of pocket translators: four modules for four different languages with simultaneous reception, each containing 1,500 words with memory. Weidner Communication Systems Inc produces a Multilingual Word Processor that allows the capacity of an average translator to be increased from 600 to 2,400 words per hour. It includes a triple memory: bilingual dictionary, dictionary of synonyms, grammatical index (*La Semaine media* 6, 6 December 1978, p 5).

16 Jürgen Habermas, *Erkenntnis und Interesse*, Suhrkamp, Frankfurt, 1968; trans Jeremy Shapiro, *Knowledge and Human Interests*, Beacon, Boston, 1971.

17 'Man's understanding of nature and his mastery over it by virtue of his presence as a social body . . . appears as the great foundation-stone [*Grundpfeiler*] of production and of wealth', so that 'general social knowledge becomes a *direct force of production*', writes Marx in the *Grundrisse* (1857-58), Dierz Verlag, Berlin, 1953, p 593; trans Martin Nicolaus, Vintage, New York, 1973, p 705. However, Marx concedes that it is not 'only in the form of knowledge, but also as immediate organs of social practice that learning becomes force, in other words, as machines: machines are '*organs of the human brain created by the human hand;* the power of knowledge, objectified' (p 706). See Paul Mattick, *Marx and Keynes, The Limits of the Mixed Economy*, Extending Horizons Books, Boston, 1969. This point is discussed in Lyotard, 'La place de l'alienation dans le retournement marxist' (1969), *Dérive à partir de Marx et Freud*, Union Générale d'Edition, Paris, 1973, pp 78-166.

18 The composition of the labour force in the United States changed as follows over a twenty-year period (1950-71):

	1950	1971
Factory, service sector, or agricultural workers	62.5%	51.4%
Professionals and technicians	7.5	14.2
White-collar	30.0	34.0

(*Statistical Abstracts*, 1971)

19 Because of the time required for the 'fabrication' of a high-level technician or the average scientist in comparison to the time needed to extract raw materials and transfer money-capital. At the end of the 1960s, Mattick estimated the net rate of investments in underdeveloped countries at 3-5% of the GNP and at 10-15% in the developed countries (*Marx and Keynes*, p 248).

20 Nora and Mine, *L'Informatisation de la société*, especially pt 1, 'Les défis', Y Stourdzé, 'Les Etats-Unis et la guerre des communications', *Le Monde*, 13-15 December 1978. In 1979, the value of the world market of telecommunications devices was $30 billion; it is estimated that in ten years it will reach $68 billion (*La Semaine media* 19, 8 March 1979).

21 F De Combret, 'Le redéploiement industriel', *Le Monde*, April 1978; M Lepage, *Demain le capitalisme*, Le Livre de Poche, Paris, 1979; Alain Cotta, *La France et l'impératif mondial*, Presses Universitaires de France, Paris, 1978.

22 It is a matter of 'weakening the administration', of reaching the 'minimal state'. This is the decline of the Welfare State, which is accompanying the 'crisis' that began in 1974.

From *La Condition postmoderne: Rapport sur le savoir*, Les Editions de Minuit, Paris, 1979; translated by Geoff Bennington and Brian Massumi, © 1984, University of Minnesota Press and Manchester University Press; 'Answering the Question: What is Postmodernism?' translated by Régis Durand, from *Innovation/ Renovation*, edited by Ihab Hassan, University of Wisconsin Press, 1983. 'Réponse à la question: qu'est-ce que le postmodernisme?' was first published in *Critique* 419, April 1982.

Jean Baudrillard
THE ECSTASY OF COMMUNICATION

There is no longer any system of objects. My first book contains a critique of the object as obvious fact, substance, reality, use value.[1] There the object was taken as sign but as sign heavy with meaning. In this critique two principle logics interfered with each other: a *phantasmatic logic* that referred principally to psychoanalysis – its identification, projections, and the entire imaginary realm of transcendence, power and sexuality operating at the level of objects and the environment, with a privilege accorded to the house/automobile axis (immanence/transcendence); and a *differential social logic* that made distinctions by referring to a sociology, itself derived from anthropology (consumption as the production of signs, differentiation, status and prestige). Behind these logics, in some way descriptive and analytic, there was already the dream of symbolic exchange, a dream of the status of the object and consumption beyond exchange and use, beyond value and equivalence. In other words, a *sacrificial logic* of consumption, gift, expenditure (*dépense*), potlatch, and the accursed portion.[2]

In a certain way all this still exists, and yet in other respects it is all disappearing. The description of this whole intimate universe – projective, imaginary and symbolic – still corresponded to the object's status as mirror of the subject, and that in turn to the imaginary depths of the mirror and 'scene': there is a domestic scene, a scene of interiority, a private space-time (correlative, moreover, to a public space). The oppositions subject/object and public/private were still meaningful. This was the era of the discovery and exploration of daily life, this other scene emerging in the shadow of the historic scene, with the former receiving more and more symbolic investment as the latter was politically disinvested.

But today the scene and mirror no longer exist; instead, there is a screen and network. In place of the reflexive transcendence of mirror and scene, there is a nonreflecting surface, an immanent surface where operations unfold – the smooth operational surface of communication.

Something has changed, and the Faustian, Promethean (perhaps Oedipal) period of production and consumption gives way to the 'proteinic' era of networks, to the narcissistic and protean era of connections, contact, contiguity, feedback and general-ised interface that goes with the universe of communication. With the television image – the television being the ultimate and perfect object for this new era – our own body and the whole surrounding universe become a control screen.

If one thinks about it, people no longer project themselves into their objects, with their affects and their representations, their fantasies of possession, loss, mourning, jealousy: the psychological dimension has in a sense vanished, and even if it can always be marked out in detail one feels that it is not really there that things are being played out. Roland Barthes already indicated this some time ago in regard to the automobile: little by little a logic of 'driving' has replaced a very subjective logic of possession and projection.[3] No more fantasies of power, speed and appropriation linked to the object itself, but instead a tactic of potentialities linked to usage: mastery, control and command, an optimalisation of the play of possibilities offered by the car as vector and vehicle, and no longer as object of psychological sanctuary. The subject himself, suddenly transformed, becomes a computer at the wheel, not a drunken demiurge of power. The vehicle now becomes a kind of capsule, its dashboard the brain, the surrounding landscape unfolding like a televised screen (instead of a live-in projectile as it was before).

(But we can conceive of a stage beyond this one, where the car is still a vehicle of performance, a stage where it becomes an information network. The famous Japanese car that talks to you, that 'spontaneously' informs you of its general state and even of your general state, possibly refusing to function if you are not functioning well, the car as deliberating consultant and partner in the general negotiation of a lifestyle, something – or someone: at this point there is no longer any difference – with which you are connected. The fundamental issue becomes the communication with the car itself, a perpetual test of the subject's presence with his own objects, an uninterrupted interface.

It is easy to see that from this point speed and displacement no longer matter. Neither does unconscious projection, nor an individual or social type of competition, nor prestige. Besides, the car began to be de-sacralised in this sense some time ago: it's all over with speed – I drive more and consume less. Now, however, it is an ecological ideal that installs itself at every level. No more expenditure, consumption, performance, but instead regulation, well-tempered functionality, solidarity among all the elements of the same system, control and global management of an ensemble. Each system, including no doubt the domestic universe, forms a sort of ecological niche where the essential thing is to maintain a relational decor, where all the terms must continually communicate among themselves and stay in contact, informed of the respective condition of the others and of the system as a whole, where opacity, resistance or the secrecy of a single term can lead to catastrophe.)[4]

Private 'telematics': each person sees himself at the controls of a hypothetical machine, isolated in a position of perfect and remote sovereignty, at an infinite distance from his universe of origin. Which is to say, in the exact position of an astronaut in his capsule, in a state of weightlessness that necessitates a perpetual orbital flight and a speed sufficient to keep him from crashing back to his planet of origin.

This realisation of a living satellite, *in vivo* in a quotidian space, corresponds to the satellitisation of the real, or what I call the 'hyperrealism of simulation':[5] the elevation of the domestic universe to a spatial power, to a spatial metaphor, with the satellitisation of the two-room-kitchen-and-bath put into orbit in the last lunar module. The very quotidian nature of the terrestrial habitat hypostasised in space means the end of metaphysics. The era of hyperreality now begins. What I mean is this: what was projected psychologically and mentally, what used to be lived out on earth as metaphor, as mental or metaphorical scene, is henceforth projected into reality, without any metaphor at all, into an absolute space which is also that of simulation.

This is only an example, but it signifies as a whole the passage into orbit as orbital and environmental model, of our private sphere itself. It is no longer a scene where the dramatic interiority of the subject, engaged with its objects as with its image, is played out. We are here at the controls of a micro-satellite, in orbit living no longer as an actor or dramaturge but as a terminal of multiple networks. Television is still the most direct prefiguration of this. But today it is the very space of habitation that is conceived as both receiver and distributor, as the space of both reception and operations, the control screen and terminal which as such may be endowed with telematic power – that is, with the capability of regulating everything from a distance, including work in the home and, of course, consumption, play, social relations and leisure. Simulators of leisure or of vacations in the home – like light simulators for aeroplane pilots – become conceivable.

Here we are far from the living-room and close to science fiction. But once more it must be seen that all these changes – the decisive mutations of objects and of the environment in the modern era – have come from an irreversible tendency towards three things: an ever greater formal and operational abstraction of elements and functions and their homogenisation in a single virtual process of functionalisation; the displacement of bodily movements and efforts into electric or electronic commands, and the miniaturisation, in time and space, of processes whose real scene (though it is no longer a scene) is that of infinitesimal memory and the screen with which they are equipped.

There is a problem here, however, to the extent that this electronic 'encephalisation' and miniaturisation of circuits and energy, this transistorisation of the environment, relates to total uselessness, desuetude and almost obscenity all that used to fill the scene of our lives. It is well known how the simple presence of the television changes the rest of the habitat into a kind of archaic envelope, a vestige of human relations whose very survival remains perplexing. As soon as this scene is no longer haunted by its actors and their fantasies, as soon as behaviour is crystallised on certain screens and operational terminals, what's left appears only as a large useless body, deserted and condemned. The real itself appears as a large useless body.

This is the time of miniaturisation, telecommand and the microprocession of time, bodies, pleasures. There is no longer any ideal principle for these things at a higher level, on a human scale. What remains are only concentrated effects, miniaturised and immediately available. This change from human scale to a system of nuclear matrices is visible everywhere: this body, our body, often appears simply superfluous, basically useless in its extension, in the multiplicity and complexity of its organs, its tissues and functions, since today everything is concentrated in the brain and in genetic codes, which alone sum up the operational definition of being. The countryside, the immense geographic countryside, seems to be a deserted body whose expanse and dimensions appear arbitrary (and which is boring to cross even if one leaves the main highways), as soon as all events are epitomised in the towns, themselves undergoing reduction to a few miniaturised highlights. And time: what can be said about this immense free time we are left with, a dimension henceforth useless in its unfolding, as soon as the instantaneity of communication has miniaturised our exchanges into a succession of instants?

Thus the body, landscape, time all progressively disappear as scenes. And the same for public space: the theatre of the social and theatre of politics are both reduced more and more to a large soft body with many heads. Advertising in its new version – which is no longer a more or less baroque, utopian or ecstatic scenario of objects and consumption, but the effect of an omnipresent visibility of enterprises, brands, social interlocuters and the social virtues of communication – advertising in its new dimension invades everything, as public space (the street, monument, market, scene) disappears. It realises, or, if one prefers, it materialises in all its obscenity; it monopolises public life in its exhibition. No longer limited to its traditional language, advertising organises the architecture and realisation of super-objects like Beaubourg and the Forum des Halles, and of future projects (eg Parc de la Villette) which are monuments (or anti-monuments) to advertising, not because they will be geared to consumption but because they are immediately proposed as an anticipated demonstration of the operation of culture, commodities, mass movement and social flux. It is our only architecture today: great screens on which are projected atoms, particles, molecules in motion. Not a public scene or true public space but gigantic spaces of circulation, ventilation and ephemeral connections.

It is the same for private space. In a subtle way, this loss of public space occurs contemporaneously with the loss of private space. The one is no longer a spectacle, the other no longer a secret. Their distinctive opposition, the clear difference of an exterior and an interior exactly described the domestic *scene* of objects, whose rules of play and limits, and the sovereignty of a symbolic space which was also that of the subject. Now this opposition is effaced in a sort of *obscenity* where the most intimate processes of our life become the virtual feeding ground of the media (the Loud family in the United States, the innumerable slices of peasant or patriarchal life on French television). Inversely, the entire universe comes to unfold arbitrarily on your domestic screen (all the useless information that comes to you from the entire world, like a microscopic pornography of the universe, useless, excessive, just like the sexual close-up in a porno film): all this explodes the scene formerly preserved by the minimal separation of public and private, the scene that was played out in a restricted space, according to a secret ritual known only by the actors.

Certainly, this private universe was alienating to the extent that it separated you from others – or from the world, where it was invested as a protective enclosure, an imaginary protector, a defence system. But it also reaped the symbolic benefits of alienation, which is that the Other exists, and that otherness can fool you for the better or the worse. Thus consumer society lived also under the sign of alienation, as a society of the spectacle.[6] But just so: as long as there is alienation, there is spectacle, action, scene. It is not obscenity – the spectacle is never obscene. Obscenity begins precisely when there is no more spectacle, no more scene, when all becomes transparence and immediate visibility, when everything is exposed to the harsh and inexorable light of information and communication.

We are no longer a part of the drama of alienation: we live in the ecstasy of communication. And this ecstasy is obscene. The obscene is what does away with every mirror, every look, every image. The obscene puts an end to every representation. But it is not only the sexual that becomes obscene in pornography; today there is a whole pornography of information and communication, that is to say, of circuits and networks, a pornography of all functions and objects in their readability, their fluidity, their availability, their regulation, in their forced signification, in their performativity, in their branching, in their polyvalence, in their free expression. . . .

It is no longer then the traditional obscenity of what is hidden, repressed, forbidden or obscure; on the contrary, it is the obscenity of the visible, of the all-too-visible, of the more-visible-than-the-visible. It is the obscenity of what no longer has any secret, of what dissolves completely in information and communication.

Marx set forth and denounced the obscenity of the commodity, and this obscenity was linked to its equivalence, to the abject principle of free circulation, beyond all use value of the object. The obscenity of the commodity stems from the fact that it is abstract, formal and light in opposition to the weight, opacity and substance of the object. The commodity is readable: in opposition to the object, which never completely gives up its secret, the commodity always manifests its visible essence, which is its price. It is the formal place of transcription of all possible objects: through it objects communicate. Hence, the commodity form is the first great medium of the modern world. But the message that the objects deliver through it is already extremely simplified, and it is always the same: their exchange value. Thus at bottom the message already no longer exists; it is the medium that imposes itself in its pure circulation. This is what I call (potentially) ecstasy.

One has only to prolong this Marxist analysis, or push it to the second or third power, to grasp the transparence and obscenity of the universe of communication, which leaves far behind it those relative analyses of the universe of the commodity. All functions abolished in a single dimension, that of communication. That's the ecstasy of communication. All secrets, spaces and scenes abolished in a single dimension of information. That's obscenity.

The hot, sexual obscenity of former times is succeeded by the cold and communicational, contactual and motivational obscenity of today. The former clearly implied a type of promiscuity, but it was organic, like the body's viscera, or again like objects piled up and accumulated in a private universe, or like all that is not spoken, teeming in the silence of repression. Unlike this organic, visceral, carnal promiscuity, the promiscuity that reigns over the communication networks is one of superficial saturation, of an incessant solicitation, of an extermination of interstial and protective spaces. I pick up my telephone receiver and it's all there; the whole marginal network catches and harasses me with the insupportable good faith of everything that wants and claims to communicate. Free radio: it speaks, it sings, it expresses itself. Very well, *it* is the sympathetic obscenity of its content. In terms a little different for each medium, this is the result: a space, that of the FM band, is found to be saturated, the stations overlap and mix together (to the point that sometimes it no longer communicates at all. Something that was free by virtue of space is no longer. Speech is free perhaps, but I am less free than before: I no longer succeed in knowing what I want, the space is so saturated, the pressure so great from all who want to make themselves heard.

I fall into the negative ecstasy of the radio.

There is in effect a state of fascination and vertigo linked to this obscene delirium of communication. A singular form of pleasure perhaps, but aleatory and dizzying. If we allow Roger Caillois[7] in his classification of games (it's as good as any other) – games of expression (*mimicry*), games of competition (*agon*) games of chance (*alea*), games of vertigo (*ilynx*) – the whole tendency of our contemporary 'culture' would lead us from a relative disappearance of forms of expression and competition (as we have remarked at the level of objects) to the advantages of forms of risk and vertigo. The latter no longer involves games of scene, mirror, challenge and duality; they are, rather, ecstatic, solitary and narcissistic. The pleasure is no longer one of manifestation, scenic and aesthetic, but rather one of pure fascination, aleatory and psychotropic. This is not necessarily a negative value judgment: here surely there is an original and profound mutation of the very forms of perception and pleasure. We are still measuring the consequences poorly. Wanting to apply our old criteria and the reflexes of a 'scenic' sensibility, we no doubt misapprehend what may be the occurrence, in this sensory sphere, of something new, ecstatic and obscene.

One thing is sure: the scene excites us, the obscene fascinates us. With fascination and ecstasy, passion disappears. Investment, desire, passion, seduction or again, according to Caillois, expression and competition – the hot universe. Ecstasy, obscenity, fascination, communication or again, according to Caillois, hazard, chance and vertigo –

the cold universe (even vertigo is cold, the psychedelic one of drugs in particular).

In any case, we will have to suffer this new state of things, this forced extroversion of all interiority, this forced injection of all exteriority that the categorical imperative of communication literally signifies. There also, one can perhaps make use of the old metaphors of pathology. If hysteria was the pathology of the exacerbated staging of the subject, a pathology of expression, of the body's theatrical and operatic conversion: and if paranoia was the pathology of organisation, of the structuration of a rigid and jealous world; then with communication and information, with the immanent promiscuity of all these networks, with their continual connections, we are now in a new form of schizophrenia. No more hysteria, no more projective paranoia, properly speaking, but this state of terror proper to the schizophrenic: too great a proximity of everything, the unclean promiscuity of everything which touches, invests and penetrates without resistance, with no halo of private protection, not even his own body, to protect him anymore.

The schizo is bereft of every scene, open to everything in spite of himself, living in the greatest confusion. He is himself obscene, the obscene prey of the world's obscenity. What characterises him is less the loss of the real, the light years of estrangement from the real, the pathos of distance and radical separation, as is commonly said: but, very much to the contrary, the absolute proximity, the total instantaneity of things, the feeling of no defence, no retreat. It is the end of interiority and intimacy, the overexposure and transparence of the world which traverses him without obstacle. He can no longer produce the limits of his own being, can no longer play nor stage himself, can no longer produce himself as mirror. He is now only a pure screen, a switching centre for all the networks of influence.

NOTES

1 *Le Système des objets*, Gallimard, Paris, 1968.

2 Baudrillard is alluding here to Marcel Mauss's theory of gift exchange and Georges Bataille's notion of *dépense*. The 'accursed portion' in the latter's theory refers to whatever remains outside of society's rationalised economy of exchanges. See Bataille, *La Part Maudite*, Editions de Minuit, Paris, 1949. Baudrillard's own conception of symbolic exchange, as a form of interaction that lies outside of modern Western society and that therefore 'haunts it like its own death', is developed in his *L'échange symbolique et la mort*, Gallimard, Paris, 1976.

3 See Roland Barthes, 'The New Citroën', *Mythologies*, trans Annette Lavers, Hill & Wang, New York, 1972, pp 88-90.

4 Two observations. First, this is not due alone to the passage, as one wants to call it, from a society of abundance and surplus to a society of crisis and penury (economic reasons have never been worth very much). Just as the effect of consumption was not linked to the use value of things nor to their abundance, but precisely to the passage from use value to sign value, so here there is something new that is not linked to the end of abundance.

Secondly, all this does not mean that the domestic universe – the home, its objects, etc – is not still lived largely in a traditional way – social, psychological, differential, etc. It means rather that the stakes are no longer there, that another arrangement or life-style is virtually in place, even if it is indicated only through a technologistical discourse which is often simply a political gadget. But it is crucial to see that the analysis that one could make of objects and their system in the sixties and seventies essentially began with the language of advertising and the pseudo-conceptual discourse of the expert. 'Consumption', the 'strategy of desire', etc were first only a metadiscourse, the analysis of a projective myth whose actual effect was never really known. How people actually live with their objects – at bottom, one knows no more about this than about the truth of primitive societies. That's why it is often problematic and useless to want to verify (statistically, objectively) these hypotheses, as one ought to be able to do as a good sociologist. As we know, the language of advertising is first for the use of the advertisers themselves. Nothing says that contemporary discourse on computer science and communication is not for the use alone of professionals in these fields. (As for the discourse of intellectuals and sociologists themselves . . .)

5 For an expanded explanation of this idea, see Baudrillard's essay 'La précession des simulacres', *Simulacres et Simulation*, Galilée, Paris, 1981. An English translation appears in *Simulations*, Foreign Agent Series, Semiotext(e) Publications, New York, 1983.

6 A reference to Guy Debord's *La société du spectacle*, Buchet-Chastel, Paris, 1968.

7 Roger Caillois, *Les jeux et les hommes*, Gallimard, Paris, 1958.

From *The Anti-Aesthetic, Essays on Postmodern Culture,* edited by Hal Foster, Bay Press, Port Townsend, Washington, 1983.

Jürgen Habermas
MODERNITY: AN UNFINISHED PROJECT

Now, after the painters and the filmmakers, the architects have also been admitted to the Biennale in Venice. The response to this first architecture Biennale has been disappointment. Those who exhibited in Venice formed an avantgarde with the fronts reversed. Under the slogan 'the presence of the past', they sacrificed the tradition of modernity to a new historicism: 'The fact that the whole Modern Movement drew its sustenance from its confrontation with the past, that Frank Lloyd Wright would not have been thinkable without Japan, Le Corbusier without classical antiquity and Mediterranean architecture, and Mies van der Rohe without Schinkel and Behrens, is passed over in silence.' With this comment the *Frankfurter Allgemeine Zeitung's* critic W Pehnt[1] introduces his thesis, a thesis that goes beyond this event to provide a diagnosis of our times: 'Postmodernity presents itself decisively as Antimodernity.'

This statement refers to an affective current that has penetrated all spheres of intellectual activity and called into being theories of a post-Enlightenment, postmodernity, and posthistory, in short, a new conservatism. Adorno and his work stand in contrast to this current.[2]

Adorno subscribed so wholeheartedly to the spirit of modernity that he sensed the presence of an affective response to the affront of modernity even in the attempt to distinguish an authentic modernity from mere modernism. Hence it may not be inappropriate to express my gratitude for an Adorno Prize by pursuing the question of the current status of the modernist point of view. Is modernity as passé as the postmodernists claim it is? Or is the much-proclaimed postmodernity itself 'phony'? Is *postmodern* a cliché under which all the antagonisms cultural modernity has evoked since the middle of the nineteenth century have been unobtrusively passed on?

The Old and the New

Those who, like Adorno, conceive of 'modernity' as beginning around 1850 look at it through the eyes of Baudelaire and avant-garde art. Let me elucidate this concept of cultural modernity through a brief look at its long prehistory, which has been illuminated by Hans Robert Jauss.[3] The word modern was first used in the late fifth century to delimit the present, which had become officially Christian, from the heathen and Roman past. With varying contents, the term modernity repeatedly expresses the consciousness of an era that relates itself to the past of classical antiquity in order to conceive itself as the result of a transition from the old to the new. This is not true merely of the Renaissance, with which the modern age (*Neuzeit*) begins *for us*; people also thought of themselves as 'modern' at the time of Charlemagne, in the twelfth century, and during the Enlightenment – that is, whenever the consciousness of a new era in Europe developed through a renewed relationship to classical antiquity. In this process, *antiquitas*, antiquity, was considered a normative model to be imitated, up to the famous *querelle des anciens et des modernes*; that is, the dispute with the adherents of classicistic taste in late-seventeenth-century France. Only with the French Enlightenment's ideals of perfection and the notion, inspired by modern science, of the infinite progress of knowledge and an infinite advance toward social and moral betterment was the spell that the classical works of antiquity exerted on the spirit of those *early* moderns at each point gradually broken. Ultimately modernity, opposing the romantic to the classical, sought its past in an idealised Middle Ages. During the course of the nineteenth century this romanticism produced a radicalised consciousness of modernity that detached itself from all historical connections and retained only an abstract opposition to tradition and history as a whole.

At that point, what was considered modern was what helped the spontaneously self-renewing historical contemporaneity of the *Zeitgeist* to achieve objective expression. The signature of such works is the New, which will be surpassed and devalued by the innovation that constitutes the next style. But while the merely modish becomes outmoded when displaced into the past, the modern retains a secret link with the classical. Classical has always meant what survives through the ages. The emphatically modern no longer derives this force from the authority of a past age; it derives it solely from the authenticity of a contemporary relevance that is now in the past. This transformation of present-day relevance into relevance that is now in the past is both destructive and productive; as Jauss observed, it is modernity itself that creates its classicity – these days we speak of 'classical modernity' as though the term were unproblematic. Adorno opposes the distinction between modernity and modernism because 'without the subjective mind-set (*Gesinnung*) inspired by the New no objective modernity can crystallise.'[4]

The Aesthetic Modern Mentality

The aesthetic modern mentality took on clearer contours with Baudelaire and his theory of art, which was influenced by Edgar Allen Poe. It developed in the avantgarde movements and ultimately reached its high point in Surrealism and the Dadaists' Café Voltaire. It is characterised by attitudes crystallised around an altered consciousness of time. This consciousness is expressed in the spatial metaphor of a vanguard – that is, an avant-garde that scouts unknown territory, exposing itself to the risks of sudden and shocking encounters, conquering an as-yet uninhabited future, and orienting itself in an as-yet unsurveyed terrain. But the forward orientation, the anticipation of an undefined, contingent future, and the cult of the New actually mean the glorification of a present that repeatedly gives birth to new, subjectively defined pasts. It is not simply that the new time consciousness, which penetrates into philosophy as well with Bergson, expresses the experience of a society that has been mobilised, a history that has been speeded up, and an everyday life without continuity. What is expressed in the new value accorded the transitory and the ephemeral and in the celebration of dynamism is the longing for an immaculate and unchanging present. Modernism, a self-negating movement, is 'nostalgia for true presence'. This, says Octavio Paz, 'is the secret theme of the best modernist writers'.[5]

This also explains modernism's abstract opposition to history, which is no longer structured as an organised process of transmission that guarantees continuity. Individual epochs lose their distinctive characteristics; instead, the present has a heroic affinity with what is most distant on the one hand and what is closest on the other: Decadence recognises itself immediately in the barbaric, the wild, and the primitive. An anarchistic intention of exploding the continuum of history accounts for the subversive force of an aesthetic consciousness that rebels against the normalising achievements of tradition, that is sustained by the experience of rebelling against everything normative, and that neutralises both the morally good and the practical, a consciousness that continually stages a dialectic of secrecy and scandal, addicted to the fascination of the fright evoked by the act of profanation and at the same time in flight from the trivial results of that profanation. Thus for Adorno 'the stigma of disruption are modernity's seals of authenticity, that through which modernity negates in desperation the closed character of the eternally invariant; explosion is one of modernity's invariants. Antitraditionalist energy becomes a devouring maelstrom. In this sense modernity is myth turned against itself; myth's timelessness becomes the catastrophe of the moment that disrupts temporal continuity.'[6]

The time consciousness articulated in avant-garde art is not simply antihistorical, of course; it is directed only against the false normativity of an understanding of history derived from the imitation of models, an understanding whose traces persist even in Gadamer's philosophical hermeneutics. This time consciousness avails itself of the objectified pasts made available by historicist scholarship but at the same time rebels against the neutralisation of criteria that historicism practices when it locks history up in the museum. in the same spirit, Walter Benjamin construes the relation of modernity to history *posthistoricistically*. He recalls the French Revolution's conception of itself: 'It evoked ancient Rome the way fashion evokes costumes of the past. Fashion has a flair for the topical, no matter where it stirs in the thickets of long ago.'[7] And just as for Robespierre ancient Rome was a past charged with Nowness (*Jetztzeit*), so the historian has to grasp the constellation 'which his own era has formed with a definite earlier one.' This is how Benjamin grounds his concept of 'the present as the "time of the now" (*Jetztzeit*) which is shot through with chips of Messianic time.'[8] Since then this spirit of aesthetic modernity has aged. In the 1960s it was, of course, recited again. But with the 1970s behind us, we must admit that modernism finds almost no resonance today. Even during the 1960s Octavio Paz, a partisan of modernity, noted with melancholy that 'the avant-garde of 1967 repeats the deeds and gestures of the avant-garde of 1917. We are experiencing the end of the idea of modern art.'[9] Following Peter Bürger's work, we now speak of post-avant-garde art, a term that acknowledges the failure of the Surrealist revolt. But what is the significance of this failure? Does it signal the demise of modernity? Does a post-avant-garde mean a transition to postmodernity?

This is in fact how Daniel Bell, a well-known social theorist and the most brilliant of the American neoconservatives, understands the matter. In an interesting book, the *Cultural Contradictions of Capitalism*,[10] Bell develops the thesis that the crisis phenomenon of the developed societies of the West can be traced to a split between culture and society, between cultural modernity and the demands of the economic and administrative systems. Avant-garde art has penetrated the values of daily life and infected the lifeworld with the modernist mentality. Modernism is the great seducer, bringing about the dominance of the principle of unrestricted self-realisation, the demand for authentic experience of the self, and the subjectivism of an overstimulated sensibility, and unleashing hedonistic motives that are incompatible with the discipline of professional life and in general with the moral bases of a purposive-rational mode of life. Hence Bell, like Arnold Gehlen in Germany, puts the blame for the dissolution of the Protestant ethic, something that had disturbed Max Weber earlier, on an 'adversary culture'; that is, a culture whose modernism arouses hostility to the conventions and virtues of a daily life rationalised under economic and administrative imperatives.

On the other hand, on this reading the impulse of modernity is supposed to be definitively exhausted and the avant-garde finished; while still being propagated, it is no longer creative. This poses the question for neoconservatism of how norms can be established that will set limits on libertinage, restore discipline and the work ethic, and oppose the virtues of individual competitiveness to the levelling effects of the welfare state. Bell considers a religious revival the only solution; it would link up with quasi-natural traditions that are immune to criticism, permit clearly defined identities, and provide the individual with existential security.

Cultural Modernity and Social Modernisation

One cannot, of course, simply conjure up authoritative beliefs. Thus the only practical result of analyses like Bell's is an imperative we have seen in Germany as well: intellectual and political confrontation with the intellectual bearers of cultural modernity. To cite Peter Steinfels, a thoughtful observer of the new style the neoconservatives imposed on the intellectual scene in the 1970s:

> The struggle takes the form of exposing every manifestation of what could be considered an oppositionist mentality and tracing its 'logic' so as to link it to various expressions of extremism: drawing the connection between modernism and nihilism ... between government regulation and totalitarianism, between criticism of arms expenditures and subservience to Communism, between women's Liberation or homosexual rights and the destruction of the family ... between the Left generally and terrorism, anti-Semitism, and fascism.[11]

Steinfels is referring only to the United States here, but the parallels are obvious. The personalising and bitterness that characterise the abuse of intellectuals fomented by anti-Enlightenment intellectuals in Germany as well as in the United States cannot be explained in psychological terms; rather, it has its roots in the analytic weaknesses of neoconservative doctrine itself.

For neoconservatism displaces the burdensome consequences of a more or less successful capitalist modernisation of economy and society onto cultural modernity. Because it conceals the connections between the processes of social modernisation it welcomes on the one hand and the crisis of motivation it laments on the other and does not reveal the social-structural causes of altered attitudes towards work, consumer habits, levels of demand, and leisure-time orientation, it can attribute something that looks like hedonism, lack of social identification, incapacity for obedience, narcissism, and a withdrawal from competition for status and achievement directly to a culture that in fact plays only a very mediated role in the process. What is put in place of these unanalysed causes is the intellectuals who continue to consider themselves committed to the project of modernity. To be sure, Daniel Bell sees a further connection between the erosion of bourgeois values and the consumerism of a society that has shifted to mass production. Even Bell, however, unimpressed by his own argument, traces the new permissiveness first and foremost to the spread of a life-style that initially developed in the elite countercultures of bohemian artists. This of course is only a variation on a misunderstanding to which the avant-garde itself has already fallen prey – the idea that the mission of art is to fulfil its indirect promise of happiness through the spread to society as a whole of the artistic life-style that has been defined as its opposite.

Bell remarks of the period in which aesthetic modernity originated that 'radical in economics, the bourgeoisie became conservative in morals and cultural taste.'[12] If that were correct, one could see neoconservatism as a return to a tried-and-true pattern of the bourgeois mentality. But that is too simple. For the mood that feeds neoconservatism today is by no means derived from discontent with the antinomian consequences of a culture that has transgressed its boundaries and broken out of the museums and into life. This discontent is not evoked by modernist intellectuals; it is rooted in more fundamental reactions to a social modernisation that, under pressure from the imperatives of economic growth and state administration, intervenes further and further into the ecology of developed forms of life, into the communicative infrastructure of historical lifeworlds. Thus neopopulist protests are only giving pointed expression to widespread fears of a destruction of urban and natural milieus, the destruction of forms of communal human life. Multiple occasions for discontent and protest arise wherever a one-sided modernisation guided by criteria of economic and administrative rationality penetrates into spheres of life centred around tasks of cultural transmission, social integration, and socialisation, spheres of life that are guided by other criteria, namely those of communicative rationality. But it is precisely from these social processes that neoconservative doctrines divert attention; they project the causes they conceal onto an autonomous subversive culture and its advocates.

To be sure, cultural modernity generates its own aporias as well. And positions that proclaim a postmodernity, recommend return to premodernity, or radically reject modernity, invoke these aporias. Aside from the problematic consequences of *social* modernisation, motives for doubt and despair with the project of modernity arise from the *internal viewpoint* of cultural development.

The Project of Enlightenment

The idea of modernity is intimately tied up with the development of European art, but what I have called the project of modernity comes into focus only when we abandon the usual concentration on art. For Max Weber, what characterised cultural modernity was the separation of the substantive reason expressed in religious and metaphysical worldviews into three moments, the connections between which (through the form of argumentative justification) were now merely formal ones. Since the worldviews in question have disintegrated and their traditional problems have been distributed among the specific perspectives of truth, normative rightness, and authenticity or beauty – that is, can be treated *as* questions of knowledge, justice, or taste – what we have in the modern world is a differentiation of the value spheres of science and scholarship, morality, and art. Scientific discourse, moral and legal inquiry, and art production and criticism are institutionalised in the corresponding cultural systems as matters for experts. The professionalised treatment of cultural transmission in terms of abstract considerations of validity puts the emphasis on the logical structures intrinsic to each of these knowledge-complexes – the cognitive-instrumental, the moral-practical (*Eigengesetzlichkeiten*), and the aesthetic-expressive. From now on there will also be *internal* histories of science and scholarship, moral and legal theory, and art. These are not linear developments, to be sure, but they are learning processes nevertheless. That is one side.

On the other side, the distance between these expert cultures and the general public has increased. The increases in culture produced by specialised treatment and reflection do not *automatically* become the property of everyday practice. Instead, with cultural rationalisation there is a danger that the lifeworld, its traditional substance having been devalued, will become *impoverished*. The project of modernity, formulated in the eighteenth century by the Enlightenment *philosophes*, consists of a relentless development of the objectivating sciences, the universalistic bases of morality and law, and autonomous art in accordance with their internal logic but at the same time a release of the cognitive potentials thus accumulated from their esoteric high forms and their utilisation in praxis; that is, in the rational organisation of living conditions and social relations. Proponents of the Enlightenment like Condorcet still held the extravagant expectation that the arts and sciences would further not only the control of the forces of nature but also the understanding of self and world, moral progress, justice in social institutions, and even human happiness.

The twentieth century has not left us much of this optimism. But the problem has remained, and as before there is a difference of opinion: should we hold to the intentions of the Enlightenment, battered as they may be, or should we abandon the project of modernity? Where cognitive potentials do not result in technical progress, economic growth, and rational administration, should we want to see them checked so that they do not effect a life-praxis dependent on blind traditions?

Even among the philosophers who currently form something like a rearguard of the Enlightenment the project of modernity is strangely splintered. Each places his trust in only one of the moments into which reason has become differentiated. Popper, and I am referring to the theorist of the open society, who has not yet let himself be appropriated by the neoconservatives, holds to the enlightening force of scientific criticism, whose effects extend into the political domain; for this he pays the price of moral scepticism and a general indifference to the aesthetic. Paul Lorenzen is concerned with how a methodically constructed artificial language in which practical reason will be brought to bear can be effective in reforming everyday life. His conception, however, channels science and scholarship into the narrow paths of justifications analogous to moral-practical justifications, and he too neglects the aesthetic. In Adorno, conversely, the emphatic claim to reason has withdrawn into the accusatory gestures of the esoteric work of art, while morality is no longer susceptible of justification, and philosophy is left with the sole task of indicating, through indirect discourse, the critical content concealed in art.

The differentiation of science and scholarship, morality, and art with which Max Weber characterised the rationalism of Western culture, means *both* the specialised treatment of special sectors *and* their detachment from the stream of tradition, which continues in quasi-natural form in the hermeneutics of everyday life. This detachment is the problem to which the autonomous development of the differentiated value spheres gives rise; it has also evoked abortive attempts to 'sublate' the expert cultures. We can see that best in art.

Kant and the Autonomy of the Aesthetic

Simplifying, one can discern a line of progressive antonomisation in the development of modern art. A subject domain categorised exclusively in terms of the beautiful was first constituted in the Renaissance. Then in the course of the eighteenth century, literature, the fine arts, and music were institutionalised as domains of activity separate from ecclesiastical and court life. Finally, around the middle of the nineteenth century an aestheticist conception of art emerged that obliged the artist to produce his works in accordance with the consciousness of *l'art pour l'art*. With this the autonomy of the aesthetic was constituted as a project.

In the first phase of this process, then, the cognitive structures of a new domain, distinct from the complex of science and scholarship and morality, emerged. Later it became the job of philosophical aesthetics to clarify these structures. Kant laboured energetically to specify the distinctive nature of the aesthetic domain. His point of departure was the analysis of the judgment of taste, whose object is something subjective, the free play of the imagination, but which does not indicate mere preference but instead is oriented to intersubjective agreement.

Although aesthetic objects belong neither to the sphere of phenomena known with the help of the categories of the understanding nor to the sphere of free actions subject to the laws of practical reason, works of art (and of natural beauty) are accessible to objective judgment. The beautiful constitutes a further domain of validity alongside those of truth and morality, a domain that forms the basis for the link between art and art criticism. One 'speaks of beauty as if it were a property of things.'[13] Beauty pertains, of course, only to the *representation* of a thing, just as the judgment of taste refers only to the relationship between the mental representation of an object and the feeling of pleasure or displeasure. Only in the medium of semblance (*Medium des Scheins*) can an object be perceived *as* an aesthetic object; only as a fictive object can it affect the sensibility in such a way that it can represent what evades the conceptual character of objectivating thought and moral judgment. Kant characterises the state of mind evoked by the play of the representational capacities, a state set in motion aesthetically, as disinterested pleasure. The quality of a work, then, is defined independently of its connections with practical life.

Whereas the fundamental concepts of classical aesthetics I have mentioned – that is, taste and criticism, beautiful semblance, disinterestedness, and the trandscendance of the work – serve first and foremost to delimit the aesthetic from the other spheres of value and from everyday life, the concept of the *genius* required for the production of a work of art has a positive definition. Kant calls genius 'the exemplary originality of the natural gifts of a subject in the free employment of his cognitive faculties.'[14] When we separate the concept of genius from its romantic origins, we can say, paraphrasing freely: The talented artist can give authentic expression to what he experiences in his concentrated dealings with a decentred subjectivity that is released from the constraints of knowledge and action.

The autonomy of the aesthetic – that is, the objectification of a self-experiencing, decentred subjectivity, the exclusion of the spatio-temporal structures of everyday life, the break with the conventions of perception and purposeful activity, and the dialectic of revelation and shock – could emerge as consciousness of modernity only with the gesture of modernism, and only after two further conditions had been fulfilled. Those conditions were, first, the institutionalisation of art production independent of the market and of a nonpurposeful enjoyment of art mediated by criticism; and second, an aestheticist self-understanding on the part of artists and also critics, who conceive themselves less as advocates of the public than as interpreters who form part of the process of art production itself. At that point, a movement could get under way in painting and literature that some consider to have been anticipated in Baudelaire's art criticism: colours, lines, sounds, and movements stop serving primarily representation; the media of representation and the techniques of production advance to become aesthetic objects in their own right. And Adorno can begin his *Aesthetic Theory* with the statement 'We now take it for granted that nothing concerned with art is taken for granted any more, either in art or in its relation to the whole, not even its right to exist.'[15]

The False Sublation of Culture

Art's right to exist, of course, would not have been called into question by Surrealism if modern art had not contained a promise of happiness that concerned its 'relationship to the whole'. In Schiller the promise that aesthetic contemplation makes but does not fulfil still had the explicit form of a utopia extending beyond art. The line of this aesthetic utopia extends to Marcuse's lament over the affirmative character of culture, a lament he formulated as a critique of ideology. But even in Baudelaire, who repeats the *promesse de bonheur*, the utopia of reconciliation had been turned around to become a critical reflection of the unreconciled character of the social world. The more distant from life art becomes, the more it withdraws into the untouchability of perfect autonomy, the more painfully this lack of reconciliation comes to consciousness. This pain was reflected in the boundless *ennui* of Baudelaire, the outsider who identified with the ragpickers of Paris.

Along such pathways of feeling gather the explosive energies that are finally discharged in rebellion, in the violent attempt to explode the sphere of art, which has only a semblance of autarchy, and to force reconciliation through this sacrifice. Adorno sees very clearly why the Surrealist programme 'renounces art without, however, being able to shake it off.'[16] Attempts to eliminate the discrepancy between art and life, fiction and practice, and illusion and reality; attempts to eliminate the distinction between artifact and object of utility, between something produced and something found, between deliberate shaping and spontaneous impulse; attempts to declare everything art and everyone an artist, to abolish all criteria, to assimilate aesthetic judgments to the expression of subjective experiences – these undertakings, which have been well studied, can now be seen to be nonsense experiments that involuntarily illuminate all the more brightly the very structures of art they were intended to dissolve: the medium of semblance, the transcendance of the work, the concentrated and planful character of artistic production, and the cognitive status of the judgment of taste.[17] Ironically, the radical attempt to sublate art legitimates the categories with which classical aesthetics circumscribed its object domain. In the process, of course, the categories themselves have undergone a change.

The failure of the Surrealist revolt confirms the double error of a false sublation. On the one hand, when the containers of an autonomously developed cultural sphere are shattered, its contents disintegrate. When meaning is desublimated and form destructured, nothing is left; no emancipatory effect is produced. The other error, however, is of more consequence. In the communicative practice of everyday life, cognitive interpretations, moral expectations, expressions, and evaluations must interpenetrate one another. The processes of reaching understanding in the lifeworld require the *whole breadth* of cultural transmission. Hence a rationalised everyday life could not be redeemed from the rigidity of cultural impoverishment through the forcible opening of one cultural domain, in this case art, and the establishment of a link with *one* of the specialised complexes of knowledge. At best, such an attempt merely replaces one form of one-sidedness and one abstraction with another.

There are parallels in the domains of theoretical knowledge and morality to this programme and its unsuccessful practice of false sublation. They are less clearly defined. Like art, science and scholarship on the one hand and moral and legal theory on the other have become autonomous. But the two spheres remain linked to specialised forms of praxis. The one is linked to scientised technology, the other to a legally organised administrative practice dependent on moral justification. And yet, institutionalised science and scholarship and the moral-practical discussions that have been separated off into the legal system have become so distant from everyday life that the programme of the Enlightenment could be transformed into a false sublation in these spheres as well.

There has been talk of the 'sublation of philosophy' since the days of the Young Hegelians, and the question of the relationship of theory and practice has been raised since Marx. Here, the intellectuals, however, have allied themselves with the workers' movement. It is only on the edges of this social movement that sectarian groups have found room to play out their programme of a sublation of philosophy the way the Surrealists played out their sublation of art. The consequences of dogmatism and moral rigorism reveal the same error as in the Surrealist project: when the practice of everyday life that is designed for an unconstrained interplay between the cognitive, the moral-practical, and the aesthetic-expressive, becomes reified, it cannot be cured by being linked with a *single* cultural domain that has been opened by force. Nor should imitation of the life-styles of extraordinary representatives of the value spheres – in other words, generalisation of the subversive forces that Nietzsche, Bakunin, and Baudelaire expressed in their individual lives – be confused with the institutionalisation and the practical utilisation of the knowledge accumulated in science and scholarship, morality, and art.

In specific situations, terrorist activities may be connected with the overextension of one of the cultural moments and thus with the tendency to aestheticise politics, to replace politics by moral rigorism, or to force politics under the dogmatism of a doctrine.

Such relatively impalpable connections, however, should not mislead us into denouncing the intentions of an intransigent Enlightenment as the offspring of a 'terroristic reason'. Those who lump the project of modernity together with the state of mind of individual terrorists and their sensationalistic public actions are just as short-sighted as those who claim that the incomparably more continual and extensive bureaucratic terrorism practiced in darkness, in the cellars of the military and the secret police, in camps and psychiatric institutions, is the *raison d'être* of the modern state (and its positivistically eroded legal domination), simply because this kind of terrorism makes use of the coercive means of the state apparatus.

Alternatives to the False Sublation of Culture

I believe we would do better to learn from the aberrations that have accompanied the project of modernity and the mistakes of these extravagant programmes of sublation than to abandon modernity and its project. Perhaps a way out of the aporias of cultural modernity can be at least suggested, using the example of the reception of art. Since art criticism developed during the Romantic period it has contained countercurrents, which have become more starkly polarised since the emergence of the avant-garde movements. Art criticism claims both the role of a productive supplement to the world of art and the role of an advocate on behalf of the general public's need for interpretation. Bourgeois art addresses *both* of these expectations to its public: on the one hand, the layperson who enjoyed art should educate himself to the level of the expert, and on the other hand, the layperson could act as a connoisseur who relates aesthetic experience to his own life-problems. Perhaps this second, seemingly more harmless mode of reception lost its radical character through its confused relationship to the first mode.

Artistic production, to be sure, of necessity atrophies semantically if it is not carried on as a specialised treatment of autonomous problems, a matter for experts, without regard to exoteric needs. All those involved (including the critic as a technically trained recipient) commit themselves to examining the problems they deal with in terms of an abstract criterion of validity. This concentration on one and only one dimension, however, breaks down as soon as aesthetic experience is brought into the context of an individual life history or a collective form of life. The reception of art by the layperson, or rather the person who is an expert in daily life, takes a different course than the reception of art by a professional critic who is concerned with development in purely artistic terms. Albrecht Wellmer has pointed out to me that an aesthetic experience that is not translated primarily into judgments of taste alters its status. When it is related to life-problems or used on an exploratory basis to illuminate a life-historical situation, it enters into a language game that is no longer that of art criticism. In that case aesthetic experience not only revitalises the need-interpretations in the light of which we perceive the world; it also influences cognitive interpretations and normative expectations and alters the way in which these moments refer to one another.

An example of the exploratory, life-orienting force that can emanate from an encounter with a great painting at a crisis point in the individual's life is depicted by Peter Weiss, who has his hero wander through Paris after a desperate return from the Spanish Civil War and anticipate in his imagination the encounter with Gericault's painting of the shipwrecked men that will shortly take place in the Louvre. A specific variant of the mode of reception I am talking about is captured still better by the heroic process of appropriation the same author depicts in the first volume of his *Aesthetik des Widerstandes*. A group of young people in Berlin in 1937, workers who are politically motivated and eager to learn, are acquiring the means to grasp the history, including the social history, of European painting through evening highschool classes. Out of the hard stone of the objective spirit they are hewing the pieces they assimilate, taking them into the experiential horizon of their milieu, which is as far removed from traditional education as it is from the existing regime, and turning them around until they begin to glow:

> Our conception of a culture only seldom harmonised with what presented itself as a giant reservoir of commodities, stored-up discoveries, and illuminations. As people without property, we approached what had been accumulated at first fearfully, full of awe, until it became clear to us that we had to provide our own evaluation of all this, that the overall concept could be usable only if it said something about our life circumstances as well as the difficulties and peculiarities of our thought processes.[18]

In examples like these, where the expert culture is appropriated from the perspective of the lifeworld, something of the intention of the doomed Surrealist revolt, and even more of Brecht's and even Benjamin's experimental reflections on the reception of nonauratic works of art, has been preserved. One might pursue similar reflections on the spheres of science and scholarship and morality if one considered that the human, social, and behavioural sciences are by no means *fully* divorced from the structures of action-orienting knowledge, and that the focusing of universalist ethics on questions of justice is an abstraction that needs to be linked to the problems of the good life it initially excludes.

Modern culture can be successfully linked back up to a practice of everyday life that is dependent on vital traditions but impoverished by mere traditionalism only if social modernisation *too* can be guided into *other*, noncapitalist directions, and if the lifeworld can develop, on its own, institutions that will lie outside the borders of the inherent dynamics of the economic and administrative systems.

Three Conservatisms

If I am not mistaken, the prospects for this are not good. A climate that promotes tendencies critical of modernism has arisen in virtually the whole of the Western world. In the process, the disillusionment resulting from the failure of programmes for the false sublation of art and philosophy and the aporias of cultural modernity that have become apparent serve as pretexts for the conservative positions. Let me distinguish briefly between the antimodernism of the Young Conservatives, the premodernism of the Old

Conservatives, and the postmodernism of the New Conservatives.

The *Young Conservatives* appropriate the fundamental experience of aesthetic modernity, namely the revelation of a decentred subjectivity emancipated from the constraints of cognition and purposefulness and from the imperatives of labour and utility – and use it to escape from the modern world. They base an implacable antimodernism on a modernist attitude. They transpose the spontaneous forces of the imagination, the experience of the self, and affectivity onto the sphere of the distant and archaic, and they set up a dualistic opposition between instrumental reason and a principle accessible only through evocation, be it sovereignty or the will to power, Being or a Dionysian force of the poetic. In France this line extends from George Bataille through Foucault to Derrida. Over all of them, of course, hovers the spirit of Nietzsche, resurrected in the 1970s.

The *Old Conservatives* do not allow themselves to be contaminated by cultural modernity. They observe the disintegration of substantive reason, the differentiation of science, morality, and art, and the modern understanding of the world and its merely procedural rationality with suspicion and advocate (and here Max Weber discerned a regression to material rationality) a return to positions prior to modernity. Neo-Aristotelianism in particular has enjoyed a certain success. These days the ecological problematic allows it to call for a renewal of cosmological ethics. Along this line, which emanates from Leo Strauss, one finds interesting works by Hans Jonas and Robert Spaemann, for example.

The *New Conservatives* take the most affirmative position on the accomplishments of modernity. They welcome the development of modern science as long as it oversteps its own sphere only to further technical progress, capitalistic growth, and rational administration. For the rest, they advocate a politics of defusing the explosive contents of cultural modernity. One of their theses asserts that science and scholarship, correctly understood, have in any case become meaningless as far as orientation within the lifeworld is concerned. A further thesis is that politics is to be exempted, as far as possible, from the requirements of moral-practical justification. And a third thesis asserts the pure immanence of art, disputes its utopian contents, and appeals to its illusionary character, with the aim of confining aesthetic experience within the private sphere. Here one could adduce the early Wittgenstein, Carl Schmitt in his middle period, and Gottfried Benn in his late period. With science and scholarship, morality, and art definitively confined within autonomous spheres split off from the lifeworld and administered by specialists, all that remains of cultural modernity is what one has left after renouncing the project of modernity. The resulting space is to be filled by traditions which are to be spared demands for justification; it is, of course, difficult to see how these traditions are to survive in the modern world except through governmental backing.

This typology, like any typology, is a simplification, but it may be of some use in analysing current intellectual and political controversies. I fear that antimodernist ideas, with a touch of premodernism added to them, are gaining ground in the circles around the Greens and the alternative groups. In the shift in consciousness within the political parties, on the other hand, we see the result of the ideological shift, namely an alliance of postmodernity with premodernity. None of the parties seems to me to have a monopoly on neoconservatism or abuse of intellectuals. Hence, I have good reason to be grateful for the liberal spirit in which the city of Frankfurt has bestowed on me a prize bearing the name of Adorno, a son of the city who, as a philosopher and a writer, has shaped the image of the intellectual as scarcely anyone else in West Germany has, and who has become a model for intellectuals.

NOTES

1 W Pehnt, 'Die Postmoderne als Lunapark,' *Frankfurter Allgemeine Zeitung*, August 18, 1980, p 17.

2 This text formed the basis of a talk I gave at the Paulskirche in Frankfurt on 11 September 1980, when I was awarded the city's Adorno Prize.

3 Hans Robert Jauss, 'Literarische Tradition und gegenwärtiges Bewusstsein der Moderne', in Jauss, *Literaturgeschichte als Provokation*, Suhrkamp, Frankfurt am Main, 1970, pp 11 ff.

4 Theodor W Adorno, *Aesthetische Theorie*, volume 7 of his *Gesammelte Schriften*, Suhrkamp, Frankfurt am Main, 1970, p 45. The corresponding page in the English translation by Christian Lenhardt, *Aesthetic Theory*, Routledge & Kegan Paul, London and Boston, 1984, is p 38.

5 Octavio Paz, *Essays*, Suhrkamp, Frankfurt am Main, 1979, vol 2, p 159.

6 Adorno, *Aesthetische Theorie*, p 41; *Aesthetic Theory*, p 34.

7 Walter Benjamin, 'Theses on the Philosophy of History', *Illuminations*, trans Harry Zohn, Schocken, New York, 1969, p 261.

8 Benjamin, 'Philosophy of History', p 263.

9 Paz, *Essays*, p 329.

10 Daniel Bell, *Cultural Contradictions of Capitalism*, Basic Books, New York, 1976.

11 Peter Steinfels, *The Neoconservatives*, Simon & Schuster, New York, 1979, p 65.

12 Bell, *The Cultural Contradictions of Capitalism*, p 17.

13 Immanuel Kant, *Kritik der Urteilskraft*, par 7, translated by JH Bernard, *Kant's Critique of Judgment*, Macmillan, London and New York, 1982, p 58.

14 Kant, *Kritik der Urteilskraft*, par 49; Bernard, p 203.

15 Adorno, *Aesthetische Theorie*, p 9; *Aesthetic Theory*, p 1.

16 Adorno, *Aesthetische Theorie*, p 52; *Aesthetic Theory*, p 44.

17 Dieter Wellershoff, *Die Auflösung des Kunstbegriffs*, Suhrkamp, Frankfurt am Main, 1976.

18 Peter Weiss, *Aesthetik des Widerstandes*, Suhrkamp, Frankfurt am Main, 1978, vol 1, p 54.

From *Critical Theory, The Essential Readings*, edited by David Ingram and Julia Simon Ingram, Paragon House, New York, 1991; first published in *Kleine politische Schriften* I-IV © Suhrkamp Verlag, Frankfurt am Main, 1981. All rights reserved.

CHAPTER THREE

LITERATURE, ART, ARCHITECTURE, FILM

David Lynch, *Blue Velvet*, 1986

John Barth
THE LITERATURE OF REPLENISHMENT
POSTMODERNIST FICTION

The word is not yet in our standard dictionaries and encyclopedias, but since the end of World War II, and especially in the United States in the late 1960s and the 1970s, 'postmodernism' has enjoyed a very considerable currency, particularly with regard to our contemporary fiction. There are university courses in the American postmodernist novel; at least one quarterly journal is devoted exclusively to the discussion of postmodernist literature; at the University of Tübingen last June, the annual meeting of the Deutsche Gesellschaft für Amerikastudien took as its theme 'America in the 1970s', with particular emphasis on American postmodernist writing. Three alleged practitioners of that mode – William Gass, John Hawkes, and I – were even there as live exhibits. The December annual convention of the Modern Language Association, just held in San Francisco, likewise scheduled a symposium on 'the self in postmodernist fiction', a subtopic that takes the larger topic for granted.

From all this, one might innocently suppose that such a creature as postmodernism, with defined characteristics, is truly at large in our land. So I myself imagined when, in preparation for the Tübingen Conference, and in response to being frequently labelled a postmodernist writer, I set about to learn what postmodernism is. I had a sense of *déjà vu*: about my very first published fiction, a 1950 undergraduate effort printed in my university's quarterly magazine, a graduate-student critic wrote, 'Mr Barth alters that modernist dictum, "the plain reader be damned": he removes the adjective.' Could that, I wondered now, be postmodernism? What I quickly discovered is that while some of the writers tagged as postmodernist, myself included, may happen to take the tag with some seriousness, a principal activity of postmodernist critics (also called 'metacritics' and 'paracritics'), writing in postmodernist journals or speaking at postmodernist symposia, consists in disagreeing about what postmodernism is or ought to be, and thus about who should be admitted to the club – or clubbed into admission, depending on the critic's view of the phenomenon and of particular writers.

Who are the postmodernists? By my count, the American fictionists most commonly included in the canon, besides the three of us at Tübingen, are Donald Barthelme, Robert Coover, Stanley Elkin, Thomas Pynchon, and Kurt Vonnegut, Jr. Several of the critics I read widen the net to include Saul Bellow and Norman Mailer, different as those two writers would appear to be. Others look beyond the United States to Samuel Beckett, Jorge Luis Borges, and the late Vladimir Nabokov as engendering spirits of the 'movement'; others yet insist upon including the late Raymond Queneau, the French 'new novelists' Michael Butor, Alain Robbe-Grillet, and Claude Mauriac, the even newer French writers of the *Tel Quel* group, the Englishman John Fowles, and the expatriate Argentine Julio Cortázar. Some assert that such filmmakers as Michelangelo Antonioni, Federico Fellini, Jean-Luc Godard, and Alain Resnais are postmodernists. I myself will not join any literary club that doesn't include the expatriate Colombian Gabriel García Márquez and the semi-expatriate Italian Italo Calvino, of both of whom more presently.

Anticipations of the 'postmodernist literary aesthetic' have duly been traced through the great modernists of the first half of the twentieth century – TS Eliot, William Faulkner, André Gide, James Joyce, Franz Kafka, Thomas Mann, Robert Musil, Ezra Pound, Marcel Proust, Gertrude Stein, Miguel Unamuno, Virginia Woolf – through *their* nineteenth-century predecessors – Alfred Jarry, Gustave Flaubert, Charles Baudelaire, Stéphane Mallarmé, and ETA Hoffmann – back to Laurence Sterne's *Tristram Shandy* (1767) and Miguel Cervantes's *Don Quixote* (1615).

On the other hand, among certain commentators the sifting gets exceedingly fine. Professor Jerome Klinkowitz of Northern Iowa, for example, hails Barthelme and Vonnegut as the exemplary 'postcontemporaries' of the American 1970s and consigns Mr Pynchon and me to some 1960-ish outer darkness. I regard the novels of John Hawkes as examples of fine late modernism rather than of postmodernism (and I admire them no less for that). Others might regard most of Bellow, and the Mailer of *The Naked and the Dead*, as comparatively *pre*modernist, along with the works of such more consistently traditionalist American writers as John Cheever, Wallace Stegner, William Styron, and John Updike, for example, or those of most of the leading British writers of this century (as contrasted with the Irish), or those of most of our contemporary American women writers of fiction, whose main literary concern, for better or worse, remains the eloquent issuance of what Richard Locke has called 'secular news reports'.

Even among the productions of a given writer, distinctions can be and often are invoked. Joyce Carol Oates writes all over the aesthetical map. John Gardner's first two published novels I would call distinctly modernist works; his short stories dabble in postmodernism; his polemical nonfiction is aggressively reactionary. Italo Calvino, on the other hand, began as an Italian neo-realist (in *The Path to the Nest of Spiders*, 1947) and matured into an exemplary postmodernist (with *Cosmicomics*, 1965 and *The Castle of Crossed Destinies*, 1974) who on occasion rises, sinks, or merely shifts to modernism (*Invisible Cities*, 1972). My own novels seem to me to have both modernist and postmodernist attributes; my short story series, *Lost in the Funhouse*, strikes me as mainly late-modernist, through some critics have praised or damned it as conspicuously postmodernist. My most recent novel *LETTERS*, is postmodernist by my own definition, not, however, without traces or taints of the modernist mode, even of the premodernist mode.

One certainly does have a sense of having been through this before. Indeed some of us who have been publishing fiction since 1950s have the interesting experience of being praised or damned in that decade as existentialists and in the early 1960s as black humorists. Had our professional careers antedated World War II, we would no doubt have been praised or damned as modernists, in the distinguished company listed above. Now we are praised or damned as postmodernists.

Well, but what *is* postmodernism? When one leaves off the recitation of proper names, and makes due allowance for the differences among any given author's works, do the writers most often called postmodernist share any aesthetic principles or practices as significant as the differences between them? The term itself, like 'postimpressionism', is awkward and faintly epigonic, suggestive less of a vigorous or even interesting new direction in the old art of storytelling than of something anticlimactic, feebly following a very hard act to follow. One is reminded of the early James Joyce's fascination with the word *gnomon* in its negative geometrical sense: the figure that remains when a parallelogram has been removed from a similar but larger parallelogram with which it shares a common corner.

My Johns Hopkins colleague Professor Hugh Kenner, though he does not use the term postmodernist, clearly feels that way in his study of American modernist writers (*A Homemade World*, 1975): after a chapter on William Faulkner entitled 'The Last Novelist', he dismisses Nabokov, Pynchon, and Barth with a sort of sigh. The later John Gardner goes even further in his tract *On Moral Fiction* (1978), an exercise in literary kneecapping that lumps modernists and postmodernists together without distinction and consigns us all to Hell with the indiscriminate fervour characteristic of late converts to the right. Irving Howe (*The Decline of the New*, 1969) and George P Elliott (*Conversions: Literature and the Modernist Deviation*, 1971) would applaud – Professor Howe perhaps less enthusiastically than Professor Elliott. Professor Gerald Graff of Northwestern University, writing in *Tri-Quarterly* in 1975, takes a position somewhat similar to Kenner's, as the titles of two of his admirable essays make clear: 'The Myth of the Postmodernist Breakthrough' (*Tri-Quarterly* 26) and 'Babbitt at the Abyss' (*Tri-Quarterly* 33). Professor Robert Alter of Berkeley, in the same magazine, subtitles *his* essay on postmodernist fiction 'Reflections on the Aftermath of Modernism'. Both critics proceed to a qualified sympathy for what they take to be the postmodernist programme (as does Professor Ihab Hassan of the University of Wisconsin–Milwaukee in his 1971 study *The Dismemberment of Orpheus: Toward a Postmodern Literature*), and both rightly proceed *from* the premise that the programme is in some respects an extension of the programme of modernism, in other respects a reaction against it. The term *postmodernism* clearly suggests both; any discussion of it must therefore either presume that modernism in its turn, at this hour of the world, needs no definition (surely everybody knows what modernism is!) or else must attempt after all to define or redefine that predominant aesthetic of Western literature (and music, painting, sculpture, architecture, and the rest) in the first half of this century.

Professor Alter takes the former course: his aforementioned essay opens with the words 'Over the past two decades, as the high tide of modernism ebbed and its masters died off . . .' and proceeds without further definition to the author's reflections upon the ensuing low tide. Professor Graff, on the other hand, borrowing from Professor Howe, makes a useful quick review of conventions of literary modernism before discussing the mode of fiction which, in his words, 'departs not only from realistic conventions but from modernist ones as well'.

It is good that he does, for it is not only *post*modernism that lacks definition in our standard reference books. My *Oxford English Dictionary* attests *Modernism* to 1737 (Jonathan Swift, in a letter to Alexander Pope) and *Modernist* to 1588, but neither term in the sense we mean. My *American Heritage Dictionary* (1973) gives as its fourth and last definition of lowercase *modernism* 'the theory and practice of modern art', a definition which does not take us very far into our American heritage. My *Columbia Encyclopedia* (1975) discusses modernism only in the theological sense – the reinterpretation of Christian doctrine in the light of modern psychological and scientific discoveries – and follows this with an exemplary entry on *el modernismo*, a nineteenth-century Spanish literary movement which influenced the 'Generation of 98' and inspired the *ultraísmo* of which Jorge Luis Borges was a youthful exponent. Neither my Reader's Encyclopedia (1948) nor my *Reader's Guide to Literary Terms* (1960) enters *modernism* by any definition whatever, much less *postmodernism*.

Now, as a working writer who cut his literary teeth on Eliot, Joyce, Kafka, and the other great modernists, and who is currently branded as a postmodernist, and who in fact has certain notions, no doubt naive, about what the term might conceivably mean if it is to describe anything very good very well, I am grateful to the likes of Professor Graff for not regarding his categories as self-defining. It is quite one thing to compare a line of

Verdi or Tennyson or Tolstoy with a line of Stravinsky of Eliot or Joyce and to recognise that you have put the nineteenth century behind you:

> Happy families are all alike; every unhappy family is unhappy in its own way. (Leo Tolstoy, *Anna Karenina*, trans Constance Garnett)
>
> riverrun, past Eve's and Adam's, from swerve of shore to bend of bay, brings us by a commodius vicus of recirculation back to Howth Castle and Environs. (James Joyce, *Finnegans Wake*)

It is quite another thing to characterise the differences between those two famous opening sentences, to itemise the aesthetic principles – premodernist and modernist – from which each issues, and then to a great *post*modernist opening sentence and show where its aesthetics resemble and differ from those of its parents, so to speak, and those of its grandparents, respectively:

> Many years later, as he faced the firing squad, Colonel Aureliano Buendía was to remember that distant afternoon when his father took him to discover ice. (Gabriel García Márquez, *One Hundred Years of Solitude*, trans Gregory Rabassa)

Professor Graff does not do this, exactly, though no doubt he could if pressed. But I shall borrow his useful checklist of the characteristics of modernist fiction, add a few items to it, summarise as typical his and Professor Alter's differing characterisations of *post*modernist fictions, disagree with them respectfully in some particulars, and then fall silent, except as a storyteller.

The ground motive of modernism, Graff asserts, was criticism of the nineteenth-century bourgeois social order and its world view. Its artistic strategy was the self-conscious overturning of the conventions of bourgeois realism by such tactics and devices as the substitution of a 'mythical' for a 'realistic' method and the 'manipulation of conscious parallels between contemporaneity and antiquity' (Graff is here quoting TS Eliot on James Joyce's *Ulysses*); also the radical disruption of the linear flow of narrative; the frustration of conventional expectations concerning unity and coherence of plot and character and the cause-and-effect 'development' thereof; the deployment of ironic and ambiguous juxtapositions to call into question the moral and philosophical 'meaning' of literary action; the adoption of a tone of epistemological self-mockery aimed at the naive pretensions of bourgeois rationality; the opposition of inward consciousness to rational, public, objective discourse; and an inclination to subjective distortion to point up the evanescence of the objective social world of the nineteenth-century bourgeoisie.

This checklist strikes me as reasonable, if somewhat depressing from our historical perspective. I would add to it the modernists' insistence, borrowed from their romantic forebears, on the special, usually alienated role of the artist in his society, or outside it: James Joyce's priestly, self-exiled artist-hero; Thomas Mann's artist as charlatan, or mountebank; Franz Kafka's artist as anorexic, or bug. I would add, too, what is no doubt implicit in Graff's catalogue, the modernists' foregrounding of language and technique as opposed to straightforward traditional 'content': we remember Thomas Mann's remark (in *Tonio Kröger*, 1903), '. . . what an artist talks *about* is never the main point;' a remark which echoes Gustave Flaubert's to Louise Colet in 1852 – '. . . what I could like to do, is write a book about nothing . . .' – and which anticipates Alain Robbe-Grillet's *obiter dictum* of 1957: '. . . the genuine writer has nothing to say . . . He has only a way of speaking.' Roland Barthes sums up this 'fall from innocence' and ordinary content on the part of modernist literature in *Writing Degree Zero* (1953):

> . . . the whole of literature, from Flaubert to the present day, became the problematics of language.

This is French hyperbole: it is enough to say that one cardinal preoccupation of the modernists was the problematics, not simply of language, but of the medium of literature.

Now, for Professor Alter, Professor Hassan, and others, *post*modernist fiction merely emphasises the 'performing' self-consciousness and self-reflexiveness of modernism, in a spirit of cultural subversiveness and anarchy. With varying results, they maintain, postmodernist writers write a fiction that is more and more about itself and its processes, less and less about objective reality and life in the world. For Gerald Graff, too, postmodern fiction simply carries to its logical and questionable extremes the anti-rationalist, anti-realist, anti-bourgeois programme of modernism, but with neither a solid adversary (the bourgeois having now everywhere co-opted the trappings of modernism and turned its defiant principles into mass-media kitsch) nor solid moorings in the quotidien realism it defines itself against. From this serious charge Graff exempts certain postmodernist satire, in particular the fiction of Donald Barthelme, Saul Bellow, and Stanley Elkin, as managing to be vitalised by the same kitschy society that is its target.

I must say that all this sounds persuasive to me – until I examine more closely what I'm so inclined to nod my head yes to. It goes without saying that critical categories are as more or less fishy as they are less or more useful. I happen to believe that just as an excellent teacher is likely to teach well no matter what pedagogical theory he suffers from, so a gifted writer is likely to rise above what he takes to be his aesthetic principles, not to mention what *others* take to be his aesthetic principles. Indeed, I believe that a truly splendid specimen in whatever aesthetic mode will pull critical ideology along behind it, like an ocean liner trailing seagulls. Actual artists, actual texts, are seldom more than more or less modernist, postmodernist, formalist, symbolist, realist, surrealist, politically committed, aesthetically 'pure', 'experimental', regionalist, internationalist, what have you. The particular work ought always to take primacy over contexts and categories. On the other hand, art lives in human time and history, and general changes in its modes and materials and concerns, even when not obviously related to changes in technology, are doubtless as significant as changes in a culture's general attitudes, which its arts may both inspire and reflect. Some are more or less trendy and superficial, some may be indicative of more or less deep malaises, some are perhaps healthy correctives of or reactions against such malaises. In any case, we can't readily discuss what artists aspire to do and what they end up doing except in terms of aesthetic categories, and so we should look further at this approximately shared impulse called postmodernism.

In my view, if it has no other and larger possibilities than those noted by, for example, Professors Alter, Graff, and Hassan, then postmodernist writing is indeed a kind of pallid, last-ditch decadence, of no more than minor symptomatic interest. There is no want of actual texts illustrative of this view of the 'postmodernist breakthrough'; but that is only to remind us that what Paul Valéry remarked of an earlier generation applies to ours as well: 'Many ape the postures of modernity, without understanding their necessity.' The proper programme for postmodernism is neither a mere extension of the modernist programme as described above, nor a mere intensification of certain aspects of modernism, nor on the contrary a wholesale subversion or repudiation of either modernism or what I'm calling premodernism – 'traditional' bourgeois realism.

To go back a moment to our catalogue of the field-identification marks of modernist writing: two other conspicuous ones are not yet there acknowledged, except by implication. On the one hand, James Joyce & Co set very high standards of artistry, no doubt implicit in their preoccupation with the special remove of the artist from his or her society. On the other hand, we have their famous relative difficulty of access, inherent in their anti-linearity, their aversion to conventional characterisation and cause-and-effect dramaturgy, their celebration of private, subjective experience over public experience, their general inclination to 'metaphoric' as against 'metonymic' means. (But this difficulty is *not* inherent, it is important to note, in their high standards of craftsmanship.)

And from this relative difficulty of access, what Hassan calls their aristocratic cultural spirit, comes of course the relative unpopularity of modernist fiction, outside of intellectual circles and university curricula, by contrast with the fiction of, say, Dickens, Twain, Hugo, Dostoevsky, Tolstoy. From it comes also and notoriously the engenderment of a necessary priestly industry of explicators, annotators, allusion-chasers, to mediate between the text and the reader. If we need a guide, or a guidebook, to steer us through Homer or Aeschylus, it is because the world of the text is so distant from our own, as it presumably was not from Aeschylus's and Homer's original audiences. But with *Finnegans Wake* or Ezra Pound's *Cantos*, we need a guide because of the inherent and immediate difficulty of the text. We are told that Bertold Brecht, out of socialist conviction, kept on his writing desk a toy donkey bearing the sign *Even I must understand it;* the high modernists might aptly have put on their desks a professor of literature doll bearing, unless its speciality happened to be the literature of high modernism, the sign *Not even I can understand it.*

I do not say this in deprecation of these great writers and their sometimes brilliant explicators. If modernist works are often forbidding and require a fair amount of help and training to appreciate, it does not follow that they are not superbly rewarding, as climbing Mount Matterhorn must be, or sailing a small boat around the world. To return to our subject: Let us agree with the commonplace that the rigidities and other limitations of nineteenth-century bourgeois realism, in the light of turn-of-the-century theories and discoveries in physics, psychology, anthropology, and technology, prompted or fuelled the great adversary reaction called modernist art – which came to terms with our new ways of thinking about the world at the frequent expense of democratic access, of immediate or at least ready delight, and often of political responsibility (the politics of Eliot, Joyce, Pound, Nabokov, and Borges, for example, are notoriously inclined either to nonexistence or to the far right). But in North America, in western and northern Europe, in the United Kingdom, and in some of Central and South America, at least, these nineteenth-century rigidities are virtually no more. The modernist aesthetic is in my opinion unquestionably the characteristic aesthetic of the first half of our century – and in my opinion it *belongs* to the first half of our century. The present reaction against it is perfectly understandable and to be sympathised with, both because the modernist coinages are by now more or less debased common currency and because we really don't *need* more *Finnegans Wakes* or *Pisan Cantos*, each with its staff of tenured professors to explain it to us.

But I deplore the artistic and critical cast of mind that repudiates the whole modernist enterprise as an aberration and sets to work as if it hadn't happened; that rushes back into the arms of nineteenth-century middle-class realism as if the first half of the twentieth century hadn't happened. It *did* happen: Freud and Einstein and two world wars and the Russian and sexual revolutions and automobiles and aeroplanes and telephones and radios and movies and urbanisation, and now nuclear weaponry and television and microchip technology and the new feminism and the rest, and there's no going back to Tolstoy and Dickens & Co except on nostalgia trips. As the Russian writer

Yevgeny Zamyatin was already saying in the 1920s (in his essay 'On Literature, Revolution, and Entropy'): 'Euclid's world is very simple, and Einstein's world is very difficult; nevertheless, it is now impossible to return to Euclid's.'

On the other hand, it is no longer necessary, if it ever was, to repudiate *them*, either: the great premodernists. If the modernists, carrying the torch of romanticism, taught us that linearity, rationality, consciousness, cause and effect, naive illusionism, transparent language, innocent anecdote, and middle-class moral conventions are not the whole story, then from the perspective of these closing decades of our century we may appreciate that the contraries of these things are not the whole story either. Disjunction, simultaneity, irrationalism, anti-illusionism, self-reflexiveness, medium-as-message, political olympianism, and a moral pluralism approaching moral entropy – these are not the whole story either.

A worthy programme for postmodernist fiction, I believe, is the synthesis or transcension of these antitheses, which may be summed up as premodernist and modernist modes of writing. My ideal postmodernist author neither merely repudiates nor merely imitates either his twentieth-century modernist parents or his nineteenth-century premodernist grandparents. He has the first half of our century under his belt, but not on his back. Without lapsing into moral or artistic simplism, shoddy craftsmanship, Madison Avenue venality, or either false or real naivety, he nevertheless aspires to a fiction more democratic in its appeal than such late-modernist marvels (by my definition and in my judgment) as Beckett's *Stories and Texts for Nothing* or Nabokov's *Pale Fire*. He may not hope to reach and move the devotees of James Michener and Irving Wallace – not to mention the lobotomised mass-media illiterates. But he *should* hope to reach and delight, at least part of the time, beyond the circle of what Mann used to call the Early Christians: professional devotees of high art.

I feel this in particular for practitioners of the novel, a genre whose historical roots are famously and honourably in middle-class popular culture. The ideal postmodernist novel will somehow rise above the quarrel between realism and irrealism, formalism and 'contentism', pure and committed literature, coterie fiction and junk fiction. Alas for professors of literature, it may not need as much *teaching* as Joyce's or Nabokov's or Pynchon's books, or some of my own. On the other hand, it will not wear its heart on its sleeve, either; at least not its whole heart. (In a recent published exchange between William Gass and John Gardner, Gardner declares that he wants everybody to love his books; Gass replies that he would no more want his books to be loved by everybody than he'd want his daughter to be loved by everybody, and suggests that Gardner is confusing love with promiscuity.) My own analogy would be with good jazz or classical music: one finds much on successive listenings or close examination of the score that one didn't catch the first time through; but the first time through should be so ravishing – and not just to specialists – that one delights in the replay.

Lest this postmodern synthesis sound both sentimental and impossible of attainment, I offer two quite different examples of works that I believe approach it, as perhaps such giants as Dickens and Cervantes may be said to anticipate it. The first and more tentative example (it is not meant to be a blockbuster) is Italo Calvino's *Cosmicomics* (1965): beautifully written, enormously appealing space-age fables – 'perfect dreams', John Updike has called them – whose materials are as modern as the new cosmology and as ancient as folktales, but whose themes are love and loss, change and permanence, illusion and reality, including a good deal of specifically Italian reality. Like all fine fantasists, Calvino grounds his flights in local, palpable detail: along with the nebulae and the black holes and the lyricism, there is a nourishing supply of pasta, bambini, and good-looking women sharply glimpsed and gone forever. A true postmodernist, Calvino keeps one foot always in the narrative past – characteristically the Italian narrative past of Boccaccio, Marco Polo, or Italian fairy tales – and one foot in, one might say, the Parisian structuralist present; one foot in fantasy, one in objective reality. It is appropriate that he has, I understand, been chastised on the left by the Italian Communist critics and on the right by the Italian Catholic critics; it is symptomatic that he has been praised by fellow authors as divergent as John Updike, Gore Vidal, and myself. I urge everyone to read Calvino at once, beginning with *Cosmicomics* and going right on, not only because he exemplifies my postmodernist programme, but because his fiction is both delicious and high in protein.

An even better example is Gabriel García Márquez's *One Hundred Years of Solitude* (1967), as impressive a novel as has been written so far in the second half of our century and one of the splendid specimens of that splendid genre from any century. Here the synthesis of straightforwardness and artifice, realism and magic and myth, political passion and nonpolitical artistry, characterisation and caricature, humour and terror, are so remarkably sustained that one recognises with exhilaration very early on, as with *Don Quixote* and *Great Expectations* and *Huckleberry Finn*, that one is in the presence of a masterpiece not only artistically admirable but humanly wise, loveable, literally marvellous. One had almost forgotten that new fiction could be so *wonderful* as well as so merely important. And the question whether my programme for postmodernism is achievable goes happily out the window, like one of García Márquez's characters on flying carpets. Praise be to the Spanish language and imagination! As Cervantes stands as an exemplar of pre-modernism and a great precursor of much to come, and Jorge Luis Borges as an exemplar of *dernier cri* modernism and at the same time as a bridge between the end of the nineteenth century and the end of the twentieth, so Gabriel García Márquez is in that enviable succession: an exemplary postmodernist and a master of the storyteller's art.

A dozen years ago I published in *The Atlantic* a much-misread essay called 'The Literature of Exhaustion', occasioned by my admiration for the stories of Señor Borges and by my concern, in that somewhat apocalyptic place and time, for the ongoing health of narrative fiction. (The time was the latter 1960s; the place Buffalo, New York, on a university campus embattled by tear-gassing riot police and tear-gassed Vietnam War protesters, while from across the Peace Bridge in Canada came Marshall McLuhan's siren song that we 'print-oriented bastards' were obsolete.) The simple burden of my essay was that the forms and modes of art live in human history and are therefore subject to used-upness, at least in the minds of significant numbers of artists in particular times and places; in other words, that artistic conventions are liable to be retired, subverted, transcended, transformed, or even deployed against themselves to generate new and lively work. I would have thought that point unexceptionable. But a great many people – among them, I fear, Señor Borges himself – mistook me to mean that literature, at least fiction, is *kaput*; that is all been done already; that there is nothing left for contemporary writers but to parody and travesty our great predecessors in our exhausted medium – exactly what some critics deplore as postmodernism.

Leaving aside the celebrated fact that, with *Don Quixote*, the novel may be said to *begin* in self-transcendent parody and has often returned to that mode for its refreshment, let me say at once and plainly that I agree with Borges that literature can never be exhausted, if only because no single literary text can ever exhausted – its 'meaning' residing as it does in its transactions with individual readers over time, space, and language. I like to remind misreaders of my earlier essay that written literature is in fact about 4,500 years old (give or take a few centuries depending on one's definition of literature), but that we have no way of knowing whether 4,500 years constitutes senility, maturity, youth, or mere infancy. The number of splendid sayable things – metaphors for the dawn or the sea, for example – is doubtless finite; it is also doubtless very large, perhaps virtually infinite. In some moods we writers may feel that Homer had it easier than we, getting there early with his rosy-fingered dawn and his wine-dark sea. We should console ourselves that one of the earliest extant literary texts (an Egyptian papyrus of c 2000 BC, cited by Walter Jackson Bate in his 1970 study *The Burden of the Past and the English Poet*) is a complaint by the scribe Khakheperresenb that he has arrived on the scene too late:

Would I had phrases that are not known, utterances that are strange, in new language that has not been used, free from repetition, not an utterance that has gown stale, which men of old have spoken.

What my essay 'The Literature of Exhaustion' was really about, so it seems to me now, was the effective 'exhaustion' not of language or of literature but of the aesthetic of high modernism: that admirable, not-to-be-repudiated, but essentially completed 'programme' of what Hugh Kenner has dubbed 'the Pound era'. In 1966/67 we scarcely had the term *postmodernism* in its current literary-critical usage – at least I hadn't heard it yet – but a number of us, in quite different ways and with varying combinations of intuitive response and conscious deliberation, were already well into the working out, not of the next-best thing after modernism, but of the *best next* thing: what is gropingly now called postmodernist fiction; what I hope might also be thought of one day as a literature of replenishment.

David Lodge
MIMESIS AND DIEGESIS IN MODERN FICTION

How does one begin to map a field as vast, as various as modern fiction? It seems a hopeless endeavour, and, in an absolute sense, it *is* hopeless. Even if one could hold all the relevant data in one's head at one time – which one cannot – and could formulate a typology into which they would all fit, some novelist would soon produce a work that eluded all one's categories, because art lives and develops by deviating unpredictably from aesthetic norms. Nevertheless the effort to generalise, to classify, has to be made; for without some conceptual apparatus for grouping and separating literary fictions criticism could hardly claim to be knowledge, but would be merely the accumulation of opinions about one damn novel after another. This is the justification for literary history, particularly that kind of literary history which has a generic or formal bias, looking for common conventions, strategies, techniques, beneath the infinite variety of subject matter. Such literary history breaks up the endless stream of literary production into manageable blocks or bundles, called 'periods' or 'schools' or 'movements' or 'trends' or 'subgenres'.

We are all familiar with a rough division of the fiction of the last 150 years into three phases, that of classic realism, that of modernism and that of post-modernism (though, it hardly needs saying, these phases overlap both chronologically and formally). And we are familiar with various attempts to break down these large, loose groupings into more delicate and discriminating subcategories. In the case of post-modernist fiction, for instance: transfiction, surfiction, metafiction, new journalism, nonfiction novel, faction, fabulation, *nouveau roman, nouveau nouveau roman*, irrealism, magic realism, and so on. Some of those terms are synonyms, or nearly so. Most of them invoke or imply the idea of the new. British writing rarely figures on such maps of post-modern fiction. Our post-modernism, it is widely believed, has consisted in ignoring, rather than trying to go beyond, the experiments of modernism, reviving and perpetuating the mode of classic realism which Joyce, Woolf and Co thought they had despatched for good.

This kind of map-making usually has an ideological and, in the Popperian sense of the word, historicist motivation. The mode of classic realism, with its concern for coherence and causality in narrative structure, for the autonomy of the individual self in the presentation of character, for a readable homogeneity and urbanity of style, is equated with liberal humanism, with empiricism, common sense and the presentation of bourgeois culture as a kind of nature. The confusions, distortions and disruptions of the post-modernist text, in contrast, reflect a view of the world as not merely subjectively constructed (as modernist fiction implied) but as absurd, meaningless, radically resistant to totalising interpretation.

There is a certain truth in this picture, but it is a half-truth, and therefore a misleading one. The classic realist text was never as homogeneous, as consistent as the model requires; nor do post-modern novelists divide as neatly as it implies into complacent neorealist sheep and dynamic antirealist goats. (It hardly needs to be said that the ideology of the post-modernist avant-garde, reversing proverbial wisdom, prefers goats to sheep, John Barth's *Giles Goat-Boy* being one of its canonical texts.) Perhaps I have a personal interest in this issue, since I write as well as read contemporary fiction. I am dissatisfied with maps of contemporary fiction which take into account only the most deviant and marginal kinds of writing, leaving all the rest white space. But equally unsatisfactory is the bland, middlebrow, market-oriented reviewing of novels in newspapers and magazines which not only shies away from boldly experimental writing, but makes what one might call mainstream fiction seem technically less interesting and innovative than it often is.

Take, for example, the case of the contemporary British novelist, Fay Weldon. She is a successful and highly respected writer, but her work rarely figures in any discussion of post-modernism in the literary quarterlies. Fay Weldon has been pigeonholed as a feminist novelist, and the criticism of her work is almost exclusively thematic. Now there is no doubt that she is a feminist writer, but her handling of narrative is technically very interesting and subtly innovative, and her feminism gets its force precisely from her ability to defamiliarise her material in this way. Typically, her novels follow the fortunes of a heroine, or a group of women, over a longish time span, from childhood in the 1930s and 1940s to the present. The narrator is usually revealed at some point to be the central character, but the narrative discourse mostly uses a third-person reference, typical of traditional authorial narration, often claiming the privileged insight into the interiority of several characters that belongs to that kind of narration, and not to the confessional autobiographical mode. The tense system is similarly unstable, switching erratically between the narrative preterite and the historical present. There is very artful use of condensed duration, that is, the summary narration of events which would have occupied a considerable length of time in reality, and which would be sufficiently important to the people involved to be worth lingering over in a more conventional kind of fiction. This creates a tone of comic despair about the follies and contradictions of human relations, and especially the fate of women. Here is a specimen from Fay Weldon's novel *Female Friends* (1975). Oliver is being promiscuously unfaithful to his wife Chloe and she complains.

'For God's sake,' he says, irritated, 'go out and have a good time yourself. I don't mind.'

He lies in his teeth, but she doesn't know this. She only wants Oliver. It irks him (he says) and cramps his style. He who only wants her to be happy, but whose creativity (he says) demands its nightly dinner of fresh young female flesh.

Gradually the pain abates, or at any rate runs underground. Chloe gets involved in Inigo's school: she helps in the library every Tuesday and escorts learners to the swimming pool on Fridays. She helps at the local birth control clinic and herself attends the fertility sessions, in the hope of increasing her own.

Oh, Oliver! He brings home clap and gives it to Chloe. They are both soon and simply cured. His money buys the most discreet and mirthful doctors; Oliver himself is more shaken than Chloe, and her patience is rewarded: he becomes bored with his nocturnal wanderings and stays home and watches television instead.[1]

The first paragraph of this passage is a familiar kind of combination of direct speech and narrative, deviant only in the use of the present tense for the narrative. The second paragraph exerts the privilege of authorial omniscience somewhat paradoxically, since we know that Chloe is herself narrating the story. It also uses a deviant style of representing speech apparently quoting Oliver in part, and reporting him in part. The effect of direct quotation arises from the congruence of tense between Oliver's speech and the narrator's speech ('it irks . . . he says'); the effect of reported speech arises from the use of the third-person pronoun ('it irks *him*'). This equivocation between quoted and reported speech allows the narrator to slide in a very loaded paraphrase of Oliver's stated need for young women – it is highly unlikely that he himself used that cannibalistic image, the 'nightly dinner of fresh young female flesh'. The penultimate paragraph uses a summary style of narration that seems quite natural because it is describing routine, habitual actions of little narrative interest. But summary is foregrounded in the last paragraph because applied to events which are full of emotional and psychological pain, embarrassment and recrimination – the sort of thing we are used to having presented scenically in fiction.

One way of describing this mode of writing would be to say that it is a mode of telling rather than showing, or, to use a more venerable terminology, of diegesis rather than mimesis. It seems to me a distinctively post-modern phenomenon in that it deviates from the norms of both classic realism and of modernism, as do, more spectacularly, the writers of the post-modernist avant-garde in America. Indeed, if we are looking for a formal, as distinct from an ideological, definition of post-modernism, we could, I believe, look profitably at its foregrounding of diegesis. The simple Platonic distinction between mimesis and diegesis, however, is inadequate to cope with all the varieties and nuances of novelistic discourse. In what follows I want to combine it – or refine it – with the more complex discourse typology of the Russian post-formalists (who may have been one and the same person in some writings) Valentin Volosinov and Mikhail Bakhtin.

In Book III of *The Republic*, Plato distinguishes between diegesis, the representation of actions in the poet's own voice, and mimesis, the representation of action in the imitated voices of the character or characters. Pure diegesis is exemplified by dithyramb, a kind of hymn. (Later poeticians put lyric poetry into this category – a serious mistake according to Gérard Genette,[2] but one which need not concern us here.) Pure mimesis is exemplified by drama. Epic is a mixed form, combining both diegesis and mimesis, that is, combining authorial report, description, summary and commentary on the one hand, with the quoted direct speech of the characters on the other. It is important not to confuse 'mimesis' in this sense with the wider application of the term by Plato (in, for instance, Book X of *The Republic*) and by Aristotle (in *The Poetics*), to mean imitation as opposed to reality. In that sense all art is imitation. In Book III Plato is concerned with two types of discourse by which verbal art imitates reality. To make the distinction clear, Plato (in the person of Socrates) cites the opening scene of *The Iliad*, where the Trojan priest Chryses asks the Greek leaders Menelaus and Agamemnon to release his daughter for a ransom.

> You know then, that as far as the lines
> He prayed the Achaians all,
> But chiefly the two rulers of the people,
> Both sons of Atreus,
> the poet himself speaks, he never tries to turn our thoughts from himself or to
> suggest that anyone else is speaking; but after this he speaks as if he was himself
> Chryses, and tries his best to make us think that the priest, an old man, is speaking
> and not Homer.[3]

In other words, the confrontation is introduced diegetically by the authorial narrator, and then presented mimetically in the speeches of the characters. To make the point even clearer, Plato rewrites the scene diegetically, transposing direct or quoted speech into indirect or reported speech, for example:

> Agamemnon fell into a rage, telling him [Chryses] to go away now and not to come

back, or his staff and the wreathings of the god might not help him; before he would give her up, he said, she should grow old with him in Argos; told him to be off and not to provoke him, if he wanted to get home safe.[4]

The original speech in Homer is translated by Rieu as follows:

'Old man,' he said, 'do not let me catch you loitering by the hollow ships today, nor coming back again, or you may find the god's staff and chaplet a very poor defence. Far from agreeing to set your daughter free, I intend her to grow old in Argos, in my house, a long way from her own country, working at the loom and sharing my bed. Off with you now, and do not provoke me if you want to save your skin.[5]

It is evident that, though there is a clear difference between the two passages, the individuality of Agamemnon's speech is not wholly obliterated by the narrator's speech in the Platonic rewriting, and could be obliterated only by some much more drastic summary, such as Gérard Genette suggests in his discussion of this passage: 'Agamemnon angrily refused Chryses' request.'[6] Plato conceived of the epic as a mixed form in the sense that it simply alternated two distinct kinds of discourse – the poet's speech and the characters' speech – and this is in fact true of Homer; but his own example shows the potential within narrative for a much more complex mixing, more like a fusing, of the two modes, in reported speech. This potential was to be elaborately exploited by the novel, which uses reported speech extensively – not only to represent speech, but to represent thoughts and feelings which are not actually uttered aloud. This is where Volosinov and Bakhtin are useful, because they focus on the way the novelistic treatment of reported speech tends towards an intermingling of authorial speech and characters' speech, of diegesis and mimesis.

In *Marxism and the Philosophy of Language* (1930) Volosinov distinguishes between what he calls (borrowing the terms from Wölfflin's art history) the linear style of reporting, and the pictorial style. The linear style preserves a clear boundary between the reported speech and the reporting context (that is, the author's speech) in terms of information or reference, while suppressing the textual individuality of the reported speech by imposing its own linguistic register, or attributing to the characters exactly the same register as the author's. The linear style is characteristic of prenovelistic narrative, and is associated by Volosinov especially with what he calls authoritarian and rationalistic dogmatism in the medieval and Enlightenment periods. I suggest that *Rasselas* (1759) affords a late example of what Volosinov calls the linear style:

'. . . I sat feasting on intellectual luxury, regardless alike of the examples of the earth and the instructions of the planets. Twenty months are passed. Who shall restore them?' These sorrowful meditations fastened upon his mind; he passed four months in resolving to lose no more time in idle resolves, and was awakened to more vigorous exertion by hearing a maid, who had broken a porcelain cup, remark that what cannot be repaired is not to be regretted.

This was obvious; and Rasselas reproached himself that he had not discovered it – having not known, or not considered, how many useful hints are obtained by chance, and how often the mind, hurried by her own ardour to distant views, neglects the truths that lie open before her. He for a few hours regretted his regret, and from that time bent his whole mind upon the means of escaping from the Valley of Happiness.[7]

In addition to the quoted direct speech of Rasselas at the beginning of the extract, there are two kinds of reported speech here: the reported utterance of the maid, and the reported inner speech, or thoughts, of Rasselas. All are linguistically assimilated to the dominant register of the authorial discourse. The author, Rasselas, and even the maid all seem to speak the same kind of language – balanced, abstract, polite; but the referential contours of the reported speech are very clearly demarcated and judged by the authorial speech. This is typical of Volosinov's linear style and Plato's diegesis: linguistic homogeneity – informational discrimination. It is one of the reasons why we hesitate to describe *Rasselas* as a novel, even though it postdates the development of the English novel. From a novel we expect a more realistic rendering of the individuality and variety of human speech than we get in *Rasselas* – both in direct or quoted speech and in reported speech or thought. (But note that there is a kind of tonal resemblance between the passage from *Rasselas* and the passage from Fay Weldon's *Female Friends* – the cool, confident, detached ironic tone that is generated by the *summary* nature of the narrative discourse – summary being characteristic of diegesis, or what Volosinov calls the linear style.) For Volosinov, naturally influenced by Russian literary history, the rise of the novel virtually coincides with the development of the *pictorial* style of reported speech, in which author's speech and character's speech, diegesis and mimesis interpenetrate. The evolution of the English novel was more gradual.

The rise of the English novel in the eighteenth century began with the discovery of new possibilities of mimesis in prose narrative, through the use of characters as narrators – the pseudo-autobiographers of Defoe, the pseudo-correspondents of Richardson – thus making the narrative discourse a mimesis of an act of diegesis, diegesis at a second remove. These devices brought about a quantum leap in realistic illusion and immediacy, but they tended to confirm Plato's ethical disapproval of mimesis, his fears about the morally debilitating effects of skilful mimesis of imperfect personages. However high-minded were the intentions of Defoe (which is doubtful) or of Richardson (which is not) there is no way in which the reader can be prevented from delighting in and even identifying with Moll Flanders or Lovelace in even their wickedest actions. Fielding, his mind trained in a classical school, restored the diegetic balance in his comic-epic-poem-in-prose: the individuality of characters is represented, and relished, in the reproduction of their distinctive speech – Fielding, unlike Johnson in *Rasselas*, does not make all the characters speak in the same register as himself – but the author's speech (and values) are quite clearly distinguished from the characters' speech and values; mimesis and diegesis are never confused. The same is true of Scott, in whose work there is, notoriously, a stark contrast between the polite literary English of the narrator's discourse, and the richly textured colloquial dialect speech of the Scottish characters – a disparity that becomes particularly striking in the shift from direct to reported speech or thought:

> 'He's a gude creature,' said she, 'and a kind – it's a pity he has sae willyard a powny.' And she immediately turned her thoughts to the important journey which she had commenced, reflecting with pleasure, that, according to her habits of life and of undergoing fatigue, she was now amply or even superfluously provided with the means of encountering the expenses of the road, up and down from London, and all other expenses whatever.[8]

The classic nineteenth-century novel followed the example of Fielding and Scott in maintaining a fairly even balance between mimesis and diegesis, showing and telling, scene and summary; but it also broke down the clear distinction between diegesis and mimesis in the representation of thought and feeling, through what Volosinov called the 'pictorial style' of reported speech. In this, the individuality of the reported speech or thought is retained even as the author's speech 'permeates the reported speech with its own intentions – humour, irony, love or hate, enthusiasm or scorn'.[9] Let me illustrate this with a passage from *Middlemarch* (1871-72):

> She was open, ardent, and not in the least self-admiring; indeed, it was pretty to see how her imagination adorned her sister Celia with attractions altogether superior to her own, and if any gentleman appeared to come to the Grange from some other motive than that of seeing Mr Brooke, she concluded that he must be in love with Celia: Sir James Chettam for example, whom she constantly considered from Celia's point of view, inwardly debating whether it would be good for Celia to accept him. That he should be regarded as a suitor for herself would have seemed to her a ridiculous irrelevance. Dorothea, with all her eagerness to know the truths of life, retained very childlike ideas about marriage. She felt sure that she would have accepted the judicious Hooker, if she had been born in time to save him from that wretched mistake he made in matrimony: or John Milton when his blindness had come on; or any of the other great men whose odd habits it would have been glorious piety to endure; but an amiable handsome baronet, who said 'Exactly' to her remarks even when she expressed uncertainty, – how could he affect her as a lover? The really delightful marriage must be that where your husband was a sort of father, and could teach you even Hebrew, if you wished it.[10]

Up to, and including, the sentence 'Dorothea . . . retained very childlike ideas about marriage', this passage is diegetic: the narrator describes the character of Dorothea authoritatively, in words that Dorothea could not use about herself without contradiction (she cannot, for instance, acknowledge that her ideas are childlike without ceasing to hold them). Then the deixis becomes more problematical. The tag, 'she felt' is an ambiguous signal to the reader, since it can introduce either an objective report by the narrator or subjective reflection by the character. Colloquial phrases in the sequel, such as 'that wretched mistake' and 'when his blindness had come on' seem to be the words in which Dorothea herself would have articulated these ideas, though the equally colloquial 'odd habits' does not. Why does it not? Because, in unexpected collocation with 'great men' ('great men whose odd habits') it seems too rhetorical an irony for Dorothea – it is a kind of oxymoron – and so we attribute it to the narrator. But that is not to imply that Dorothea is incapable of irony. 'Who said "Exactly" to her remarks even when she expressed uncertainty' – do we not infer that Sir James's illogicality has been noted by Dorothea herself in just that crisp, dismissive way? Then what about the immediately succeeding phrase 'how could he affect her as a lover?' If the immediately preceding phrase is attributed to Dorothea, as I suggest, then it would be natural to ascribe this one to her also – but a contradiction then arises. For if Dorothea can formulate the question 'How can Sir James affect me as a lover?', her alleged unconsciousness of her own attractions to visiting gentlemen is compromised. Is the question, then, put by the narrator, appealing directly to the reader, over the heroine's head, to acknowledge the plausibility of her behaviour, meaning, 'You do see, gentle reader, why it never crossed Dorothea's mind that Sir James Chettam was a possible match for her?' There *is* such an implication, but the reason given – that Sir James said 'Exactly' when Dorothea expressed uncertainty – seems too trivial for the narrator to draw the conclusion, 'How could he affect her as a lover?' The fact is that diegesis and mimesis are fused together inextricably here – and for a good reason: for there is a sense in which Dorothea knows what the narrator knows – namely, that Sir James is sexually attracted to her – but is repressing the thought, on account of her determination to marry an intellectual father figure. When Celia finally compels Dorothea to face the truth of the matter, the narrator tells us that 'she was not less angry because certain details asleep in her memory were now awakened to confirm the unwelcome revelation'. One of these details was surely that very habit of Sir James of saying 'Exactly' when she expressed uncertainty – a sign of his admiration, deference and anxiety to please rather than of his stupidity. Here, then, the character's voice and the author's voice are so tightly interwoven that it is impossible at times to disentangle them; and the author's irony, consequently, is affectionate, filled by a warm regard for Dorothea's individuality – very different from Johnson's judicial irony in the passage from *Rasselas*.

In the next stage of the novel's development, Volosinov observes, the reported speech is not merely allowed to retain a certain measure of autonomous life within the authorial context, but actually itself comes to dominate authorial speech in the discourse as a whole. 'The authorial context loses the greater objectivity it normally commands in comparison with reported speech. It begins to be perceived and even recognises itself as if it were subjective.' Volosinov notes that this is often associated with the delegation of the authorial task to a narrator who cannot 'bring to bear against [the] subjective position [of the other characters] a more authoritative and objective world'.[11] In the Russian novel, it seems, Dostoevsky initiated this second phase in the development of the pictorial style. In the English novel I think we would point to the work of James and Conrad at the turn of the century: James's use of unreliable first-person narrators (*The Turn of the Screw*) or sustained focalisation of the narrative through the perspective of characters whose perceptions are narrowly limited, with minimal authorial comment and interpretation ('In the Cage', *The Ambassadors*); Conrad's use of multiple framing via multiple narrators, none of whom is invested with ultimate interpretative authority (*Lord Jim, Nostromo*).

At this point it is useful to switch to Bakhtin's typology of literary discourse. There are three main categories:

1 The direct speech of the author. This corresponds to Plato's diegesis.

2 Represented speech. This includes Plato's mimesis – ie the quoted direct speech of the characters; but also reported speech in the pictorial style.

3 Doubly-oriented speech, that is, speech which not only refers to something in the world but refers to another speech act by another addresser.

Bakhtin subdivides this third type of discourse into four categories, stylisation, parody, *skaz* (the Russian term for oral narration) and what he calls 'dialogue'. Dialogue means here, not the quoted direct speech of the characters, but discourse which alludes to an *absent* speech act. In stylisation, parody and *skaz*, the other speech act is 'reproduced with a new intention'; in 'dialogue' it 'shapes the author's speech while remaining outside its boundaries'. An important type of dialogic discourse in this sense is 'hidden polemic', in which a speaker not only refers to an object in the world but simultaneously replies to, contests, or makes concessions to some other real or anticipated or hypothetical statement about the same object.

These categories all have their subcategories which can be combined and shifted around in the system in a somewhat bewildering way, but the basic distinctions are clear, and I think useful. Let me try and illustrate them with reference to *Ulysses*, a text as encyclopedic in this respect as in all others.

1 The direct speech of the author. This is the narrator who speaks in, for instance, the first lines of the book:

> Stately, plump Buck Mulligan came from the stairhead, bearing a bowl of lather on which a mirror and razor lay crossed.[12]

This is the purely diegetic plane of the text. The sentence describes Mulligan emerging on to the roof of the Martello tower not as Stephen Dedalus sees him (Stephen is below), nor as Mulligan sees himself, but as seen by an objective narrator. Since most narration in *Ulysses* is focalised, and stylistically coloured, by a character's consciousness, or permeated by doubly-oriented speech, such examples are comparatively rare. The author's speech as a distinct medium of communication is scarcely perceptible, in accordance with Joyce's aesthetic of impersonality: 'The artist, like the God of the creation, remains within or behind or beyond or above his handiwork, invisible, refined out of existence, indifferent, paring his fingernails.'[13]

2 Represented speech. This includes all the dialogue in the usual sense of that word – the quoted direct speech of the characters, which Joyce preferred to mark with an introductory dash, rather than the usual inverted commas. This category also includes all the passages of interior monologue – mimesis in Plato's terms, but representing thought instead of uttered speech. Molly Bloom's reverie in the last episode, 'Penelope', is perhaps the purest example:

> Yes because he never did a thing like that before as ask to get his breakfast in bed with a couple of eggs since the City Arms hotel when he used to be pretending to be laid up with a sick voice doing his highness to make himself interesting for that old faggot Mrs Riordan that he thought he had a great leg of . . .

. . . and so on, for twenty thousand uninterrupted words.

The presentation of the thought of Stephen and Leopold Bloom is more varied and complex, combining interior monologue with free indirect speech and focalised narration – in short, a mixture of mimesis and diegesis, in which mimesis dominates. Here, for example, is Bloom in the porkbutcher's shop in 'Calypso':

> A kidney oozed bloodgouts on the willowpatterned dish: the last. He stood by the nextdoor girl at the counter. Would she buy it too, calling the items from a slip in her hand? Chapped: washingsoda. And a pound and a half of Denny's sausages. His eyes rested on her vigorous hips. Woods his name is. Wonder what he does. Wife is oldish. New blood. No followers allowed. Strong pair of arms. Whacking a carpet on the clothesline. She does whack it, by George. The way her crooked skirt swings at each whack.

The various kinds of speech in this passage may be classified as follows:

A kidney oozed bloodgouts on the willowpatterned dish: Narrative (focalised through Bloom).

the last. Interior monologue.

He stood by the nextdoor girl at the counter. Narrative (focalised through Bloom).

Would she buy it too, calling the items from a slip in her hand? Free indirect speech.

Chapped: washingsoda. Interior monologue.

And a pound and a half of Denny's sausages. Free direct speech (ie, the girl's words are quoted but not tagged or marked off typographically from Bloom's).

His eyes rested on her vigorous hips. Narrative (focalised through Bloom).

Woods his name is, etc (to end of paragraph). Interior monologue.

3 Doubly-oriented speech. In the later episodes of *Ulysses*, the authorial narrator who, however self-effacing, was a stable, consistent and reliable voice in the text, disappears; and his place is taken by various manifestations of Bakhtin's doubly-oriented discourse. 'Stylisation' is well exemplified by 'Nausicaa', in which Joyce borrows the discourse of cheap women's magazines and makes it serve his own expressive purpose:

> Gerty was dressed simply but with the instinctive taste of a votary of Dame Fashion for she felt there was just a might that he might be out. A neat blouse of electric blue, self tinted by dolly dyes (because it was expected in the *Lady's Pictorial* that electric blue would be worn) with a smart opening down to the division and

kerchief pocket (in which she always kept a piece of cottonwool scented with her favourite perfume because the handkerchief spoiled the sit) and a navy three quarter skirt cut to the stride showed off her slim graceful figure to perfection.

Who speaks here? Clearly it is not the author – he would not use such debased, cliché-ridden language. But we cannot take it, either, to be the author's report of Gerty's thought in free indirect speech. Free indirect speech can always be transposed into plausible direct speech (first person, present tense) and clearly that would be impossible in this case. It is a written, not a spoken style, and a very debased one. It is neither diegesis nor mimesis, nor a blend of the two, but a kind of pseudodiegesis achieved by the mimesis not of a character's speech but of a discourse, the discourse of cheap women's magazines at the turn of the century. (In fact, the style of today's romantic fiction of the Mills & Boon type displays a remarkable consistency and continuity with Gerty's reading. Compare, for example: 'Her dress was white, made from the Indian cotton. Skimpy little shoulder-straps led to a bodice which was covered with layers of narrow, delicate lace finishing at the waist where it fitted Gina's slender figure to perfection.'[14]) It is essential to the effect of 'Nausicaa' that we should be aware of the style's double reference – to Gerty's experience, and to its own original discursive context. We are not to suppose that Gerty literally thinks in sentences lifted from the *Lady's Pictorial*. But the style of the *Lady's Pictorial* subtly manipulated, heightened, 'objectified' (Bakhtin's word) vividly communicates a sensibility pathetically limited to the concepts and values disseminated by such a medium. The author, like a ventriloquist, is a silent presence in the text, but his very silence is the background against which we appreciate his creative skill.

This is stylisation – not the same thing as parody. Parody, as Bakhtin points out, borrows a style and applies it to expressive purposes that are in some sense the reverse of the original purpose, or at least incongruous with it. For example, one of the headlines in 'Aeolus' parodies the style of American tabloid journalism by applying it to an episode in classical antiquity recalled in more appropriate language by Professor MacHugh:

SOPHIST WALLOPS HAUGHTY HELEN
SQUARE ON PROBOSCIS. SPARTANS GNASH
MOLARS. ITHACANS VOW PEN IS CHAMP

– You remind me of Antisthenes, the professor said, a disciple of Georgias, the sophist. It is said of him that none could tell if he were bitterer against others or against himself. He was the son of a noble and a bondwoman. And he wrote a book in which he took away the palm of beauty from Argive Helen and handed it to poor Penelope.

The anonymous narrator of 'Cyclops' provides an example of Irish *skaz*, the anecdotal chat of pubs and bars:

I was just passing the time of day with old Troy of the DMP at the corner of Arbour Hill there and be damned but a bloody sweep came along and he near drove his gear into my eye. I turned around to let him have the weight of my tongue when who should I see dodging along Stony Batter only Joe Hynes.
– Lo, Joe, says I. How are you blowing? Did you see that bloody chimney-sweep near shove my eye out with his brush?

We never discover who this narrator is, or to whom he is talking, or in what context. But clearly it is oral narration – *skaz*. There is no perceptible difference, either in syntax or type of vocabulary, between the discourse before and after the dash that in *Ulysses* introduces direct or quoted speech.

Of all the many styles in *Ulysses*, perhaps the most baffling to critical analysis and evaluation has been that of 'Eumaeus', a style which Stuart Gilbert classified as 'Narrative: old'. Rambling, elliptical, cliché-ridden, it is, we are told, meant to reflect the nervous and physical exhaustion of the two protagonists. As with 'Nausicaa', we cannot read the discourse either as author's narration or as representation of Bloom's consciousness, though it does seem expressive of Bloom's character in some respects: his friendliness bordering on servility, his fear of rejection, his reliance on proverbial wisdom. Bakhtin's definition of 'hidden polemic' seems to fit it very well: 'Any speech that is servile or overblown, any speech that is determined beforehand not to be itself, any speech replete with reservations, concessions, loopholes and so on. Such speech seems to cringe in the presence, or at the presentiment of, some other person's statement, reply, objection'.[15]

> *En route* to his taciturn, and, not to put too fine a point on it, not yet perfectly sober companion, Mr Bloom who at all events, was in complete possession of his faculties, never more so, in fact, disgustingly sober, spoke a word of caution re the dangers of nighttown, women of ill fame and swell mobsmen, which, barely permissible once in a while though not as a habitual practice, was of the nature of a regular deathtrap for young fellows of his age particularly if they had acquired drinking habits under the influence of liquor unless you knew a little jiujitsu for every contingency as even a fellow on the broad of his back could administer a nasty kick if you didn't look out.

Let me return to the simple tripartite historical scheme with which I began – classic realism, modernism, post-modernism – and see what it looks like in the light of the discourse typology of Plato, Volosinov and Bakhtin. The classic realist text, we may say, was characterised by a balanced and harmonised combination of mimesis and diegesis, reported speech and reporting context, authorial speech and represented speech. The modern novel evolved through an increasing dominance of mimesis over diegesis. Narrative was focalised through character with extensive use of 'pictorial' reported speech or delegated to narrators with mimetically objectified styles. Diegesis, to be sure, does not completely disappear from the modernist novel, but it does become increasingly intractable. One can see the strain in those novelists who could least easily do without it: in Hardy, Forster and Lawrence. Hardy hedges his bets, equivocates, qualifies or contradicts his own authorial dicta, uses tortuous formulae to avoid taking responsibility for authorial description and generalisation. Forster tries to accommodate diegesis by making a joke of it:

> To Margaret – I hope that it will not set the reader against her – the station of King's Cross had always suggested Infinity [. . .] if you think this is ridiculous, remember that it is not Margaret who is telling you about it.[16]

At other times in *Howards End*, with less success, Forster tries to smuggle in his authorial comments as if they were his heroine's.

> Margaret greeted her lord with peculiar tenderness on the morrow. Mature as he was, she might yet be able to help him to the building of the rainbow bridge that should connect the prose in us with the passion. Without it we are meaningless fragments, half monks, half beasts, unconnected arches that have never joined into a man. With it love is born, and alights on the highest curve, glowing against the grey, sober against the fire.[17]

It is not just the rather purple diction, but the slide from narrative preterite to 'gnomic present' in the tenses that gives away the author's voice.

> Lawrence uses the same technique pervasively – for example in the famous passage

where Lady Chatterley drives through Tevershall. She passes the school where a singing lesson is in progress:

> Anything more unlike song, spontaneous song, would be impossible to imagine; a strange bawling yell that followed the outlines of a tune. It was not like savages: savages have subtle rhythms. It was not like animals: animals mean something when they yell. It was like nothing on earth and it was called singing.[18]

The gnomic present tense – 'savages *have*', 'animals *mean*' – indicates that this is not just a transcription of Connie Chatterley's thoughts – that the author is with her, speaking for her, lecturing us over her shoulder.

It has been often enough observed that Lawrence did not always live up to his own prescription that the novelist should keep his thumb out of the pan; but the prescription itself is very much in the spirit of modernism. Impersonality, 'dramatisation', 'showing' rather than 'telling', are the cardinal principles of the modernist fictional aesthetic, as variously formulated and practised by James, Conrad, Ford, Woolf and Joyce. This aesthetic required either the suppression or the displacement of diegesis: suppression by the focalisation of the narrative through the characters; displacement by the use of surrogate narrators, whose own discourse is stylised or objectified – that is, deprived of the author's authority, made itself an object of interpretation. In James, Conrad, Ford, these narrators are naturalised as characters with some role to play in the story, but in *Ulysses* they do not have this validation: as I have tried to show they are conjured out of the air by the author's ventriloquism. This was the most radically experimental aspect of *Ulysses*, the aspect which even sympathetic friends like Pound and Sylvia Beach found hard to accept. They found it difficult to accept, I suggest, because these elaborate exercises in stylisation and parody and dialogic discourse could not be justified, unlike the fragmentary, allusive passages of interior monologue, as a mimesis of character. It is still a common complaint among some readers of *Ulysses* that the introduction of a multiplicity of discourses which have no psychologically mimetic function in such episodes as 'Sirens', 'Cyclops', 'Oxen of the Sun' and 'Ithaca', is mere pedantry and self-indulgence, trivialising the human content of the book. But when we put the enterprise in the perspective of Bakhtin's poetics of fiction we immediately see that in opening up the novel to the play of multiple parodic and stylised discourses Joyce was aiming at a more comprehensive representation of reality than the stylistic decorum of the realist novel allowed; we see how this aim was organically linked to the project of writing a kind of modern epic, or mock epic, a comic inversion of and commentary upon the archetype of Homer. This is Bakhtin in 'Epic and the Novel':

> any and every straightforward genre, any and every direct discourse – epic, tragic, lyric, philosophical – may and indeed must have itself become the object of representation, the object of a parodic, travestying 'mimicry'. It is as if such mimicry rips the word away from its object, disunifies the two, shows that a given straightforward generic word – epic or tragic – is one-sided, bounded, incapable of exhausting the object; the process of parodying forces us to experience those sides of the object that are not otherwise included in a given genre or a given style. Parodic-travestying literature introduces the permanent corrective of laughter, of a critique on the one-sided seriousness of the lofty direct word, the corrective of reality that is always richer, more fundamental and most importantly *too contradictory and heteroglot* to be fitted into a high and straightforward genre.[19]

Bakhtin might have been writing about *Ulysses* in that passage. In fact, he was writing about the fourth play of classical Greek drama, the satyr play, which traditionally followed the tragic trilogy and mocked its grandeur and seriousness. And he notes in passing that 'the figure of the 'comic Odysseus', a parodic travesty of his high epic and tragic image, was one of the most popular figures of satyr plays, of ancient Doric farce and pre-Aristophanic comedy, as well as of a whole series of minor comic epics'.[20] Bloom has an ancient genealogy.

The resistance Joyce's readers often feel when they first encounter the later episodes of *Ulysses* is likely to be even greater in the case of *Finnegans Wake*, a book written entirely in doubly-, or rather trebly-, quadruply-, multiply-oriented discourse. Once again, Bakhtin's theory of the novel, and especially his emphasis on the crucial role of Rabelais in assimilating the folk tradition of carnival into literary narrative, seems very relevant. When Bakhtin writes about *Gargantua and Pantagruel*, he might be writing about *Finnegans Wake:*

> we have the first attempt of any consequence to structure the entire picture of the world around the human conceived as a body. . . . But it is not the individual human body, trapped in an irreversible life sequence that becomes a character – rather it is the impersonal body, the body of the human race as a whole, being born, living, dying the most varied deaths, being born again, an impersonal body that is manifested in its structure, and in all the processes of its life.[21]

The Rabelaisian body and surely, we must say, the body of HCE, is a body defined by the organs of self-transgression, the bowels and the phallus, mouth and anus, a body perpetually in the process of becoming, eating and defecating, copulating, giving birth and dying at the same time through the displacements and condensations of carnival and dream (for what is dream but the carnival of the unconscious? what is carnival but a licensed communal waking dream?). According to Bakhtin, the two crucial ingredients in the Rabelaisian project, which made the novel possible, were *laughter* – the mockery of any and every type of discourse in the folk-carnival tradition, and what he called 'polyglossia', the 'interanimation of languages', such as obtained between Latin and the vernaculars at the Renaissance. Laughter and the interanimation of languages were also the vital ingredients of *Finnegans Wake*.

For most of his contemporaries, Joyce's greatest achievement was his mimetic rendering of the stream of consciousness within individual subjects, and this is what other novelists, like Woolf and Faulkner, tended to learn from him. 'Let us present the atoms as they fall upon the mind in the order in which they fall, let us trace the pattern, however disconnected and incoherent in appearance, which each sight or incident scores upon the consciousness,'[22] exhorted Virginia Woolf in 1919, when the early episodes of *Ulysses* were first appearing in print. In principle, it was through interior monologue – the unvoiced, fragmentary, associative inner speech of the subject – that this programme could be most completely fulfilled. Yet Virginia Woolf herself never used sustained interior monologue, except in *The Waves*, where it is so artificial as to have very little mimetic force. In her most characteristic work an impersonal but eloquent authorial narrator hovers over the characters and links together their streams of consciousness by a fluid blend of authorial report, free indirect speech and fragments of free direct speech and interior monologue. Joyce himself, as I have already remarked, uses undiluted interior monologue only in 'Penelope', and that to a large extent is what Dorrit Cohn calls a memory monologue[23] – that is, Molly is recalling past events rather than recording the atoms of experience in the order in which they fall upon her mind. *The Sound and the Fury* is also made up of memory monologues. The characters are narrating their stories to themselves, and we, as it were, overhear their narrations. The effect is not in essence very different from an old-fashioned epistolary or journal novel though of course much more flexible and interiorised. In this way, mimesis turns back into a second-order diegesis – as it can hardly fail to do in narrative.

In pursuing mimetic methods to their limits, modernist fiction discovered that you cannot abolish the author, you can only suppress or displace him. Post-modernism says, in effect: so why not let him back into the text? The reintroduction of the author's speech, the revival of diegesis, has taken many forms. There is a conservative form – a return to something like the balanced combination of mimesis and diegesis of the nineteenth-century novel. The novels of Mauriac and Greene would be examples. 'The exclusion of the author can go too far,' said Greene in his 1945 essay on Mauriac. 'Even the author, poor devil, has a right to exist, and M Mauriac reaffirms that right.'[24] The note is defensive, however, and Greene's own use of diegesis has been discreet. Very often in this kind of neorealist post-modern fiction the narrator is a character, but with little or no stylisation of his discourse in Bakhtin's sense. The distance between the authorial norms and the character's norms is hardly perceptible. The narrator's perspective is limited, but as far as it goes, reliable. CP Snow's novels might be cited as an example.

More obviously continuous with modernism are those novels in which the discourse of the characterised narrator is doubly-oriented in Bakhtin's sense: for example, stylised *skaz* in *The Catcher in the Rye*, parodic *skaz* in Mailer's *Why Are We in Vietnam?*, hidden polemic in Nabokov's *Pale Fire*. Some post-modernist novels combine a whole spectrum of stylised, parodic and dialogic narrative discourses – eg John Barth's *Letters*, or Gilbert Sorrentino's *Mulligan Stew*.

How, then, does the post-modernist use of narrators differ from the modernist use of narrators? I would suggest that one difference is the emphasis on narration as such in post-modernist fiction. The narrators of modernist novels – eg the teacher of languages in Conrad's *Under Western Eyes*, or Dowell in Ford's *The Good Soldier*, must pretend to be *amateur* narrators, disclaiming any literary skill even while they display the most dazzling command of time shift, symbolism, scenic construction, etc. The narrators of post-modernist fiction are more likely to be explicit about the problems and processes involved in the act of narration, and very often the narrators are themselves writers with a close, sometimes incestuous relationship to the author. I find particularly interesting those post-modernist works in which diegesis is foregrounded by the explicit appearance in the text of the author as maker of his own fiction, the fiction we are reading. There is an instance of this towards the end of Margaret Drabble's recent novel *The Middle Ground* which brings out the distinction between modernist and post-modernist writing by reminding us of one of the great exponents of the former, Virginia Woolf:

> [. . .] how good that it should end so well, and even as she was thinking this, looking round her family circle, feeling as she sat there a sense of immense calm, strength, centrality, as though she were indeed the centre of a circle, in the most old-fashioned of ways, a moving circle – oh, there is no language left to describe such things, we have called it all so much in question, but imagine a circle even so, a circle and moving spheres, for this is her house and there she sits, she has everything and nothing, I give her everything and nothing [. . .].[25]

Here Margaret Drabble evokes a Woolfian epiphany (the allusion to Mrs Ramsay's dinner party in *To the Lighthouse*, whether conscious or not, is inescapable) but at the same time wryly admits the arbitrariness of its construction. In this she shows herself to be not a neorealist (as she is usually categorised, and as her early work certainly encouraged one to think) but a post-modernist.

About three-quarters of the way through Joseph Heller's novel *Good as Gold*, one of its unnumbered chapters begins:

Once again Gold found himself preparing to lunch with someone – Spotty

Weinrock – and the thought arose that he was spending an awful lot of time in this book eating and talking. There was not much else to be done with him. I *was* putting him into bed a lot with Andrea and keeping his wife and children conveniently in the background. For Acapulco, I contemplated fabricating a hectic mix-up which would include a sensual Mexican television actress and a daring attempt to escape in the nude through a stuck second-story bedroom window, while a jealous lover crazed on American drugs was beating down the door with his fists and Belle or packs of wild dogs were waiting below. Certainly he would soon meet a schoolteacher with four children with whom he would fall madly in love, and I would shortly hold out to him the tantalising promise of becoming the country's first Jewish Secretary of State, a promise I did not intend to keep.[26]

Up to this point, Heller's novel, though its satirical comedy about Jewish family life and Washington politics is mannered and stylised, has consistently maintained an illusion of referring to the real world – it has, so to speak, challenged us to deny that the real world is as crazy as Heller represents it. But this passage violates the realistic code in two very obvious, and for the reader disconcerting, ways: firstly, by admitting that Gold is a character, in a book, and not a person, in the world; and secondly by emphasising that this character has no autonomy, but is completely at the disposition of his creator, who is not (or rather once was not) sure what to do with him. Two simple words have a powerful shock effect in this passage, because they have been hitherto suppressed in the narrative discourse in the interests of mimesis: *book* (referring to the novel itself) and *I* (referring to the novelist himself). The same words occur with similar, but even more startling, effect in Kurt Vonnegut's novel *Slaughterhouse Five*.

An American near Billy wailed that he had excreted everything but his brains. Moments later he said, 'There they go, there they go.' He meant his brains.

That was I. That was me. That was the author of this book.[27]

Erving Goffman has designated such gestures 'breaking frame'. The Russian formalists called it 'exposing the device'. A more recent critical term is 'metafiction'. It is not, of course, a new phenomenon in the history of fiction. It is to be found in Cervantes, Fielding, Sterne, Thackeray and Trollope, among others – but not, significantly, in the work of the great modernist writers. At least, I cannot think off-hand of any instance in the work of James, Conrad, Woolf and Joyce (up to and including *Ulysses*) where the fictitiousness of the narrative is exposed as blatantly as in my last few examples. The reason, I believe, is that such exposure foregrounds the existence of the author, the source of the novel's diegesis, in a way which ran counter to the modernist pursuit of impersonality and mimesis of consciousness. Metafictional devices are, however, all-pervasive in post-modernist fiction. I think for example of John Fowles's play with the authorial persona in *The French Lieutenant's Woman*, of Malcolm Bradbury's introduction of himself into *The History Man* as a figure cowed and dispirited by his own character, of BS Johnson's sabotage of his own fictionalising in *Albert Angelo*. I think of the disconcerting authorial footnotes in Beckett's *Watt*, the flaunting of authorial omniscience in Muriel Spark, John Barth's obsessive recycling of his own earlier fictions in *Letters*, and the way the last page of Nabokov's *Ada* spills over on to the book jacket to become its own blurb. Perhaps, to conclude a list which could be much longer, I might mention my own novel *How Far Can You Go?* in which the authorial narrator frequently draws attention to the fictitiousness of the characters and their actions, while at other times presenting them as a kind of history, and inviting the sort of moral and emotional response from the reader that belongs to traditional realistic fiction. For me, and I think for other British novelists, metafiction has been particularly useful as a way of continuing to exploit the resources of realism while acknowledging their conventionality. And need one say that the more nakedly the author appears to reveal himself in such texts, the more inescapable it becomes, paradoxically, that the author as a *voice* is only a function of his own fiction, a rhetorical construct, not a privileged authority but an object of interpretation?

To conclude: what we see happening in post-modernist fiction is a revival of diegesis: not smoothly dovetailed with mimesis as in the classic realist text, and not subordinated to mimesis as in the modernist text, but foregrounded against mimesis. The stream of consciousness has turned into a stream of narration – which would be one way of summarising the difference between the greatest modernist novelist, Joyce, and the greatest post-modernist, Beckett. When the Unnamable says to himself, 'You must go on. I can't go on. I'll go on,' he means, on one level at least, that he must go on narrating.

NOTES

1 Fay Weldon, *Female Friends*, 1977, pp 163-64.
2 Gérard Genette, *Introduction à l'architexte*, Paris, 1979, pp 14-15.
3 *Great Dialogues of Plato*, trans WHD Rouse, New York, 1956, p 190.
4 Ibid, p 191.
5 Homer, *The Iliad*, trans EV Rieu, Harmondsworth, 1950, pp 23-24.
6 Gérard Genette, *Narrative Discourse*, trans Jane E Lewin, Oxford, 1980, p 170.
7 Samuel Johnson, *The History of Rasselas, Prince of Abissinia*, Carlton Classics edn, 1923, p 23.
8 Sir Walter Scott, *The Heart of Midlothian*, Everyman edn, 1909, p 265.
9 Ladislav Matejka and Krystyna Pomovska, ed *Readings in Russian Poetics*, Cambridge, Mass, 1979, p 155.
10 George Eliot, *Middlemarch*, Penguin English Library edn, Harmondsworth, 1965, p 32.
11 Matejka and Pomovska, *Readings in Russian Poetics*, pp 155-56.
12 James Joyce, *Ulysses*, ed Walter Gabler, 1986, p 3. All page references are to this edition.
13 James Joyce, *A Portrait of the Artist as a Young Man*, New York, 1964, p 215.
14 Claudia Jameson, *Lesson in Love*, Mills & Boon, 1982, p 76.
15 Matejka and Pomovska, *Readings in Russian Poetics*, p 188. My account of Bakhtin's discourse typology is based mainly on this extract from Bakhtin's first book, *Problems of Dostoevsky's Art* (1929), later revised and expanded as *Problems of Dostoevsky's Poetics* (1963).
16 EM Forster, *Howards End*, Harmondsworth, 1953, p 139.
17 Ibid, p 54.
18 DH Lawrence, *Lady Chatterley's Lover*, The Hague, 1956, p 139.
19 Mikhail Bakhtin, *The Dialogic Imagination*, ed Michael Holquist, trans C Emerson and Michael Holquist, 1981, p 55.
20 Ibid, p 54.
21 Ibid, pp 171-73.
22 Virginia Woolf, 'Modern Fiction', reprinted in *Twentieth Century Literary Criticism: A Reader*, ed David Lodge, 1972, p 89.
23 Dorrit Cohn, *Transparent Minds, Narrative Modes for Presenting Consciousness*, Princeton, NJ, 1978, pp 247-55.
24 Graham Greene, *Collected Essays*, 1969, p 116.
25 Margaret Drabble, *The Middle Ground*, 1980, pp 246-47.
26 Joseph Heller, *Good as Gold*, 1980, p 321.
27 Kurt Vonnegut, *Slaughterhouse Five*, New York, 1969, p 109.

From *After Bakhtin, Essays on Fiction and Criticism*, Routledge, Chapman and Hall Inc, New York, and Routledge, London, 1990.

Ihab Hassan
PLURALISM IN POSTMODERN PERSPECTIVE

The Eleven 'Definiens' of the term Postmodern

1 Indeterminacy, or rather, indeterminacies. These include all manner of ambiguities, ruptures, and displacements affecting knowledge and society. We think of Werner Karl Heisenberg's principle of uncertainty, Kurt Gödel's proof of incompleteness, Thomas Kuhn's paradigms and Paul Feyerabend's dadaism of science. Or we may think of Harold Rosenberg's anxious art objects, de-defined. And in literary theory? From Mikhail Bakhtin's dialogic imagination, Roland Barthes's *textes scriptibles,* Wolfgang Iser's literary *Unbestimmtheiten,* Harold Bloom's misprisions, Paul de Man's allegorical reading, Stanley Fish's affective stylistics, Norman Holland's transactive analysis, and David Bleich's subjective criticism, to the last fashionable *aporia* of unrecorded time, we undecide, relativise. Indeterminacies pervade our actions, ideas, interpretations; they constitute our world.

2 Fragmentation. Indeterminacy often follows from fragmentation. The postmodernist only disconnects; fragments are all he pretends to trust. His ultimate opprobrium is 'totalisation' – any synthesis whatever, social, epistemic, even poetic. Hence his preference for montage, collage, the found or cut-up literary object, for paratactic over hypnotactic forms, metonymy over metaphor, schizophrenia over paranoia. Hence too, his recourse to paradox, paralogy, parabasis, paracriticism, the openness of brokenness, unjustified margins. Thus Jean-François Lyotard exhorts, 'Let us wage a war on totality; let us be witness to the unpresentable; let us activate the differences and save the honour of the name.'[1] The age demands differences, shifting signifiers, and even atoms dissolve into elusive subparticles, a mere mathematical whisper.

3 Decanonisation. In the largest sense, this applies to all canons, all conventions of authority. We are witnessing, Lyotard argues again, a massive 'delegitimation' of the mastercodes in society, a desuetude of the metanarratives, favouring instead *'les petites histoires'* which preserve the heterogeneity of language games.[2] Thus, from the 'death of god' to the 'death of the author' and 'death of the father', from the derision of authority to revision of the curriculum, we decanonise culture, demystify knowledge, deconstruct the languages of power, desire, deceit. Derision and revision are versions of subversion, of which the most baleful example is the rampant terrorism of our time. But 'subversion' may take other, more benevolent, forms such as minority movements or the feminisation of culture, which also require decanonisation.

4 Self-less-ness. Depth-less-ness. Postmodernism vacates the traditional self, stimulating self-effacement – a fake flatness, without inside/outside – or its opposite, self multiplication, self-reflection. Critics have noted the 'loss of self' in modern literature, but it was originally Nietzsche who declared the 'subject' 'only a fiction': 'the ego of which one speaks when one censures egoism does not exist at all.'[3] Thus postmodernism suppresses or disperses and sometimes tries to recover the 'deep' romantic ego, which remains under dire suspicion in post-structuralist circles as a 'totalising principle'. Losing itself in the play of language, in the differences from which reality is plurally made, the self impersonates its absence even as death stalks its games. It diffuses itself in depthless styles, refusing, eluding, interpretation.[4]

5 *The Unpresentable, Unrepresentable.* Like its predecessor, postmodern art is irrealist, aniconic. Even its 'magic realism' dissolves in ethereal states; its hard, flat surfaces repel mimesis. Postmodern literature, particularly, often seeks its limits, entertains its 'exhaustion', subverts itself in forms of articulate 'silence'. It becomes liminary, contesting the modes of its own representation. Like the Kantian Sublime, which thrives on the formlessness, the emptiness, of the Absolute – 'Thou shalt not make graven images' – 'the postmodern would be,' in Lyotard's analogue, 'that which, in the modern, puts forward the unpresentable in presentation itself'.[5] But the challenge to representation may also lead a writer to other liminal states: the Abject, for instance, rather than the Sublime, or Death itself – more precisely, 'the exchange between signs and death', as Julia Kristeva put it. 'What is unrepresentability?' Kristeva asks. 'That which, through language, is part of no particular language ... That which, through meaning, is intolerable, unthinkable: the horrible, the abject.'[6]

Here, I think we reach a periphery of negations. For with my next 'definien', Irony, we begin to move from the deconstructive to the coexisting reconstructive tendency of postmodernism.

6 *Irony.* This could also be called, after Kenneth Burke, perspectivism. In absence of a cardinal principle or paradigm, we turn to play, interplay, dialogue, polylogue, allegory, self-reflection – in short, to irony. This irony assumes indeterminacy, multivalence; it aspires to clarity, the clarity of demystification, the pure light of absence. We meet variants of it in Bakhtin, Burke, de Man, Jacques Derrida, and Hayden White. And in Alan Wilde we see an effort to discriminate its modes: 'mediate irony', 'disjunctive irony', and 'postmodern' or "suspensive irony' 'with its yet more radical vision of multiplicity, randomness, contingency, and even absurdity'.[7] Irony, perspectivism, reflexiveness: these express the ineluctable recreations of mind in search of a truth that continually eludes it, leaving it with only an ironic access or excess of self-consciousness.

7 *Hybridisation*, or the mutant replication of genres, including parody, travesty, pastiche. The 'de-definition', deformation of cultural genres engenders equivocal modes: 'paracriticism', 'fictual discourse', the 'new journalism', the 'nonfiction novel', and a promiscuous category of 'para-literature' or 'threshold literature', at once young and very old.[8] Cliché and plagiarism ('playgiarism', Raymond Federman punned), parody and pastiche, pop and kitsch enrich *re*-presentation. In this view image or replica may be as valid as its model (the *Quixote* of Borges's Pierre Menard), may even bring an *'augment d'être'*. This makes for a different concept of tradition, one in which continuity and discontinuity, high and low culture, mingle not to imitate but to expand the past in the present. In that plural present all styles are dialectically available in an interplay between the Now and the Not Now, the Same and the Other. Thus in postmodernism, Heidegger's concept of equitemporality, a new relation between historical elements, without any suppression of the past in favour of the present – a point that Fredric Jameson misses when he criticises postmodern literature, film and architecture for their ahistorical character, their 'presentifications'.[9]

8 Carnivalisation. The term, of course, is Bakhtin's, and it riotously embraces indeterminacy, fragmentation, decanonisation, selflessness, irony, hybridisation, all of which I have already adduced. But the term also conveys the comic or absurdist ethos of postmodernism, anticipated in the 'heteroglossia' of Rabelais and Sterne, jocose prepostmodernists. Carnivalisation further means 'polyphony', the centrifugal power of language, the 'gay relativity' of things, perspectivism and performance, participation in the wild disorder of life, the immanence of laughter.[10] Indeed, what Bakhtin calls novel or carnival – that is, antisystem – might stand for postmodernism itself, or at least for its ludic and subversive elements that promise renewal. For in carnival 'the true feast of time, the feast of becoming, change, and renewal', human beings, then as now, discover 'the peculiar logic of the "inside out" (*à l'envers*), of the "turnabout" . . . of numerous parodies and travesties, humiliations, profanations, comic crownings and uncrownings. A second life'.[11]

9 Performance, Participation. Indeterminacy elicits participation; gaps must be filled. The postmodern text, verbal or nonverbal, invites performance: it wants to be written, revised, answered, acted out. Indeed, so much of postmodern art calls itself performance, as it transgresses genres. As performance, art (or theory for that matter) declares its vulnerability to time, to death, to audience, to the Other.[12] 'Theatre' becomes – to the edge of terrorism – the active principle of a paratactic society, decanonised if not really carnivalised. At its best, as Richard Poirier contends, the performing self expresses 'an energy in motion, an energy with its own shape'; yet in its 'self-discovering, self-watching, finally self-pleasuring response to . . . pressures and difficulties', that self may also veer towards solipsism, lapse into narcissism.[13]

10 Constructionism. Since postmodernism is radically tropic, figurative, irrealist – 'what can be thought of must certainly be a fiction,' Nietzsche thought[14] – it 'constructs' reality in post-Kantian, indeed post-Nietzschean, 'fictions'.[15] Scientists seem now more at ease with heuristic fictions than many humanists, last realists of the West. (Some literary critics even kick language, thinking thus to stub their toes on a stone.) Such effective fictions suggest the growing intervention of mind in nature and culture, an aspect of what I have called the 'new gnosticism' evident in science and art, in social relations and high technologies.[16] But constructionism appears also in Burke's 'dramatistic criticism', Pepper's 'world hypothesis', Goodman's 'ways of world making', White's 'prefigurative moves', not to mention current hermeneutic or post-structuralist theory. Thus postmodernism sustains the movement 'from unique truth and a world fixed and found', as Goodman remarked, 'to a diversity of right and even conflicting versions or worlds in the making'.[17]

11 Immanence. This refers, without religious echo, to the growing capacity of mind to generalise itself through symbols. Everywhere now we witness problematic diffusions, dispersals, dissemination; we experience the extension of our senses, as Marshall McLuhan crankily presaged, through new media and technologies. Languages, apt or mendacious, reconstitute the universe – from quasars to quarks and back, from the lettered unconscious to black holes in space – reconstitute it into signs of their own making, turning nature into culture, and culture into an immanent semiotic system. The language animal has emerged, his/her measure the intertextuality of all life. A patina of thought, of signifiers, of 'connections', now lies on everything the mind touches in its gnostic (noö)sphere, which physicists, biologists, and semioticians, no less than mystic theologians like Teilhard de Chardin, explore. The pervasive irony of their explorations is also the reflexive irony of mind meeting itself at every dark turn.[18] Yet in a consuming society such immanences can become more vacuous than fatidic. They become, as Jean Baudrillard says, pervasively 'ob-scene', a 'collective vertigo of neutralisation, a forward escape into the obscenity of pure and empty form'.[19]

These eleven 'definiens' add up to a surd, perhaps absurd. I should be much surprised if they amounted to a definition of postmodernism, which remains, at best, an equivocal concept, a disjunctive category, doubly modified by the impetus of the phenomenon itself and by the shifting perceptions of its critics. (At worst, postmodernism appears to be a mysterious, if ubiquitous, ingredient – like raspberry vinegar, which instantly turns any recipe into *nouvelle cuisine*.)

Nor do I believe that my eleven 'definiens' serve to distinguish postmodernism from modernism; for the latter itself abides as a fierce evasion in our literary histories.[20] But I do suggest that the foregoing points – elliptic, cryptic, partial, provisional – argue twin conclusions: (a) critical pluralism is deeply implicated in the cultural field of postmodernism; and (b) a limited critical pluralism is in some measure a reaction against the radical relativism, the ironic indetermanences, of the postmodern condition; it is an attempt to contain them.

So far, my argument has been prelusive. I must now attend to those efforts that seek to limit – quite rightly, I believe – the potential anarchy of our postmodern condition with cognitive, political, or affective constraints. That is, I must briefly consider criticism as genre, power, and desire – as Kenneth Burke did, long ago, in his vast synoptics of motives.

Is criticism a genre? Critical pluralists often suppose that it may be so.[21] Yet even that most understanding of pluralists, Wayne Booth, is forced finally to admit that a full 'methodological pluralism', which must aspire to a perspective on perspectives, only 'seems to duplicate the problem with which we began'; so he concludes, 'I cannot promise a finally satisfactory encounter with these staggering questions, produced by my simple effort to be a good citizen in the republic of criticism.'[22] Booth's conclusion is modest but also alert. He knows that the epistemic foundations of critical pluralism themselves rest on moral, if not spiritual, grounds. 'Methodological perspectivism' (as he sometimes calls his version of pluralism) depends on 'shared tendencies' which in turn depend on a constitutive act of rational, just, and vitally sympathetic understanding. In the end Booth stands on a kind of Kantian – or is it Christian? – categorical imperative of criticism, with all that it must ethically and metaphysically imply.

Could it have been otherwise? Throughout history, critics have disagreed, pretending to make systems out of their discord and epistemic structures out of their beliefs. The shared tenancies of literary theory may make for 'hermeneutical communities of provisional trust', enclaves of genial critical authority. But can any of these define criticism both as a historical and cognitive genre? That may depend on what we intend by genre. Traditionally, genre assumed recognisable features within a context of both persistence and change; it was a useful assumption of identity upon which critics (somewhat like Stanley and Livingstone) often presumed. But that assumption, in our heteroclitic age seems ever harder to maintain. Even genre theorists invite us, nowadays, to go beyond genre – 'the finest generic classifications of our time,' Paul Hernadi says, 'make us look beyond their immediate concern and focus on the *order of literature*, not on *borders between literary genres*.'[23] Yet the 'order of literature' itself has become moot.

In boundary genres particularly – and certain kinds of criticism may have become precisely that – the ambiguities attain new heights of febrile intensity. For as Gary Saul Morson notes, 'it is not meanings but appropriate procedures for discovering meaning' that become disputable – 'not particular readings, but how to read'.[24] Since genres find their definition, *when* they find any, not only in their formal features but also in labile interpretive conventions, they seldom offer a stable, epistemic norm. This makes for certain paradoxes in the 'law of genre', as Derrida lays it, a 'mad law', though even madness fails to define it. As one might expect from the magus of our deconstructions, Derrida insists on undoing genre, undoing its gender, nature, and potency, on exposing the enigma of its 'exemplarity'. The mad 'law of genre' yields only to the 'law of the law of genre' – 'a principle of contamination, a law of impurity, a parasitical economy.'[25]

One is inclined to believe that even without the de-creations of certain kinds of writing, like my own paracriticism, the configurations we call literature, literary theory, criticism, have now become (quite like postmodernism itself) 'essentially contested concepts', horizons of eristic discourse.[26] Thus, for instance, the latest disconfirmation of critical theory, the latest 'revisionary madness' is Steven Knapp and Walter Benn Michaels's statement against theory.[27] Drawing on the pragmatism of Richard Rorty and the stylistics of Stanley Fish, the authors brilliantly, berserkly contend that 'true belief' and 'knowledge' are epistemologically identical, that critical theory has no methodological consequences whatever. 'If our arguments are true, they can have only one consequence . . . ; theory should stop,' the authors conclude.[28] In fact it is their own conclusion that will have little consequence, as Knapp and Michaels themselves admit. So much, then, for the case of the self-consuming theorist.

My own conclusion about the theory and practice of criticism is securely unoriginal: like all discourse, criticism obeys human imperatives, which continually redefine it. It is a function of language, power, and desire, of history and accident, of purpose and interest, of value. Above all, it is a function of *belief*, which reason articulates and con-sensus, or authority, both enables and constrains.[29] (This statement itself expresses a reasoned belief.) If, then, as Kuhn claims, 'competing schools, *each of which constantly questions the very foundations of the others'* reign in the humanities; if, as Victor Turner thinks, the 'culture of any society at any moment is more like the debris, or "fall out" of past ideological systems, rather than itself a system'; if also, as Jonathan Culler contends, '"interpretive conventions" . . . should be seen as part of . . . [a] boundless context'; again, if as Jeffrey Stout maintains, 'theoretical terms should serve interests and purposes, not the other way around'; and if, as I submit, the principles of literary criticism are historical (that is, at once arbitrary, pragmatic, conventional, and contextual, in any case not axiomatic, apodictic, apophantic), then how can a generic conception of criticism limit critical pluralism or govern the endless deferrals of language, particularly in our indetermanent, our postmodern period?[30]

To exchange a largely cognitive view of our discipline for another that more freely admits politics, desires, beliefs is not necessarily to plunge into Hades or ascend Babel. It is, I think, an act of partial lucidity, responsive to our ideological, our human needs. The act, I stress, remains partial, as I hope will eventually become clear. For the moment, though, I must approach power as a constraint on postmodern relativism and, thus, as a factor in delimiting critical pluralism.

No doubt, the perception that power profoundly engages knowledge reverts to Plato and Aristotle, if not to the *I Ching* and the Egyptian *Book of the Dead*. In the last century, Marx theorised the relation of culture to class; his terms persist in a variety of movements, from totemic Marxism to Marxism with a deconstructionist mask or receptionist face. But it is Foucault, of course, who has given us the most cunning speculations on the topic.[31] The whole burden of his work, since *Folie et déraison* [1961], has been to expose the power of discourse and the discourse of power, to discover the politics of knowledge. More recently, though, his ideology had become antic, to the chagrin of his orthodox critics.

Foucault still maintained that discursive practices 'are embodied in technical processes, in institutions, in patterns for general behaviour, in forms of transmission and diffusion.'[32] But he also accepted the Nietzschean premise that a selfish interest precedes all power and knowledge, shaping them to its own volition, pleasure, excess. Increasingly, Foucault saw power itself as an elusive relation, an immanence of discourse, a conundrum of desire: 'It may be that Marx and Freud cannot satisfy our desire for understanding this enigmatic thing which we call power, which is at once visible and invisible, present and hidden, ubiquitous,' he remarks.[33] That is why, in his late essay 'The Subject and Power', Foucault seemed more concerned with promoting 'new kinds of subjectivity' (based on a refusal of those individual identities which states force upon their citizens than with censuring traditional modes of exploitation.[34]

In a Foucauldian perspective, then, criticism appears as much a discourse of desire as of power, a discourse, anyway, both conative and affective in its personal origins. A neo-Marxist like Jameson, however, would found criticism on collective reality. He would distinguish and 'spell out the priority, within the Marxist tradition, of a "positive hermeneutic" based on social class from those ["negative hermeneutics"] still limited by anarchist categories of the individual subject and individual experience.'[35] Again, a leftist critic like Edward Said would insist that the 'realities of power and authority . . . are the realities that make texts possible, that deliver them to their readers, that solicit the attention of critics'.[36]

Other critics, less partisan and less strenuously political, might concur. Indeed, the 'institutional view' of both literature and criticism now prevails among critics as incongruous in their ideologies as Bleich, Booth, Donald Davie, Fish, ED Hirsch, Frank Kermode, and Richard Ohmann. Here, bravely, is Bleich:

> Literary theory should contribute to the changing of social and professional institutions such as the public lecture, the convention presentation, the classroom, and the processes of tenure and promotion. Theoretical work ought to show how and why no one class of scholars, and no one subject (including theory) is self-justifying, self-explanatory, and self-sustaining.[37]

The ideological concern declares itself everywhere. A bristling issue of *Critical Inquiry* explores the 'politics of interpretation', and the facile correlation of ideology with criticism drives a critic even so disputatious as Gerald Graff to protest the 'pseudo-politics of interpretation' in a subsequent number.[38] At the same time, a critic as exquisitely reticent as Geoffrey Hartman acknowledges the intrusions of politics in his recent work.[39] The activities of GRIP (acronym for the Group for Research on the Institutionalisation and Professionalisation of Literary Study) seem as ubiquitous as those of the KGB or the CIA, though far more benign. And the number of conferences on 'Marxism and Criticism', 'Feminism and Criticism', 'Ethnicity and Criticism', 'Technology and Criticism', 'Mass Culture and Criticism', keeps American airports snarled and air carriers in the black.

All these, of course, refract the shifts in our 'myths of concern' (Northrop Frye's term) since the fifties. But they reflect, too, the changes in our idea of criticism itself, from a Kantian to a Nietzschean, Freudian, or Marxist conception (to name but three), from an ontological to a historical apprehension, from a synchronous or generic discourse to a diachronic or conative activity. The recession of the neo-Kantian idea, which extends through Ernst Cassirer, Suzanne Langer, and the old New Critics, ambiguously to Murray Krieger, implies another loss – that of the imagination as an autochthonous, autotelic, possibly redemptive power of mind. It is also the loss, or at least dilapidation, of the 'imaginary library', a total order of art, analogous to André Malraux's *musée imaginaire*, which triumphs over time and brute destiny.[40] That ideal has now vanished; the library itself may end in rubble. Yet in our eagerness to appropriate art to our own circumstances and exercise our will on texts, we risk denying those capacities – not only literary – which have most richly fulfilled our historical existence.

I confess to some distaste for ideological rage (the worst are now full of passionate intensity *and* lack all conviction) and for the hectoring of both religious and secular dogmatists.[41] I admit to a certain ambivalence toward politics, which can overcrowd our responses to both art and life. For what is politics? Simply, the right action when ripeness calls. But what is politics again? An excuse to bully or shout in public, vengeance vindicating itself as justice and might pretending to be right, a passion for self-avoidance, immanent mendacity, the rule of habit, the place where history rehearses its nightmares, the *dur désir de durer*, a deadly banality of being. Yet we must all heed politics because it structures our theoretical consents, literary evasions, critical recusancies – shapes our ideas of pluralism even as I write here, now.

Politics, we know, becomes tyrannical. It can dominate other modes of discourse, reduce all facts of the human universe – error, epiphany, chance, boredom, pain, dream – to its own terms. Hence the need, as Kristeva says, for a 'psychoanalytic intervention . . . a counterweight, an antidote, to political discourse which, without it, is free to become our modern religion: the final explanation'.[42] Yet the psychoanalytic explanation can also become as reductive as any other, unless desire itself qualifies its knowledge, its words.

I mean desire in the largest sense – personal and collective, biological and ontological, a force that writers from Hesiod and Homer to Nietzsche, William James, and Freud have reckoned with. It includes the Eros of the Universe that Alfred North Whitehead conceived as 'the active entertainment of all ideals, with the urge to their finite realisation, each in its due season'.[43] But I mean desire also in its more particular sense, which Valéry understood when he wryly confessed that every theory is a fragment of an autobiography. (Lately, the fragments have grown larger, as anyone who follows the oedipal *psychomachia* of critics must agree.) And I mean desire, too, as an aspect of the pleasure principle, that principle so freely invoked and seldom evident in criticism.

Here Barthes comes elegantly to mind. For him, the pleasure of the text is perverse, polymorph, created by intermittences of the body even more than of the heart. Rupture, tear, suture, scission enhance that pleasure; so does erotic displacement. 'The text is a fetish object, and *this fetish desires me,*' he confides.[44] Such a text eludes judgment by anterior or exterior norms. In its presence we can only cry, 'That's it for me!' This is the Dionysiac cry par excellence – Dionysiac, that is, in that peculiarly Gallic timbre. Thus, for Barthes, the pleasure of the text derives both from the body's freedom to 'pursue its own ideas' and from 'value shifted to the sumptuous rank of the signifier'.[45]

We need not debate here the celebrated, if dubious, distinctions Barthes makes in that talismanic text; we need only note that pleasure becomes a constitutive critical principle in his later work. Thus in *Leçon*, his inaugural lecture at the Collège de France, Barthes insists on the 'truth of desire' which discovers itself in the multiplicity of discourse: *'autant de langages qu'il y a de désirs.'*[46] The highest role of the professor is to make himself 'fantasmic', to renew his body so that it becomes contemporaneous with his students, to unlearn (*désapprendre*). Perhaps then he can realise true *sapientia:* *'nul pouvoir, un peu de savoir, un peu de sagesse, et le plus saveur possible'.*[47] And in *A Lover's Discourse*, which shows a darker side of desire, Barthes excludes the possibility of explication, of hermeneutics; he would rather stroke language in erotic foreplay: *'Je frotte mon langage contre l'autre. C'est comme si j'avais des mots en guise de doigts.'*[48]

Other versions of this critical suasion come easily to mind.[49] But my point is not only that critical theory is a function of our desires, nor simply that criticism often takes pleasure or desire as its concern, its theme. My point is rather more fundamental: much current criticism conceives language and literature themselves as organs of desire, to which criticism tries to adhere erotically *'se coller'*, Barthes says), stylistically, even epistemically. 'Desire and the desire to know are not strangers to each other,' Kristeva notes; and 'interpretation is infinite because Meaning is made infinite by desire.'[50] Happily, this last remark leads into my inconclusion.

Let me recover, though, the stark lineaments of my argument. Critical pluralism finds itself implicated in our postmodern condition, in its relativisms and indetermenances, which it attempts to restrain. But cognitive, political, and affective restraints remain only partial. They all finally fail to delimit critical pluralism, to create consensual theory or practice – witness the debates of this conference. Is there anything, in our era, that *can* found a wide consensus of discourse?

Clearly, the imagination of postmodern criticism is a disestablished imagination. Yet clearly, too, it is an intellectual imagination of enormous vibrancy and scope. I share in its excitement, my own excitement mixed with unease. That unease touches more than our critical theories; it engages the nature of authority and belief in the world. It is the old Nietzschean cry of nihilism: 'the desert grows!' God, King, Father, Reason, History, Humanism have all come and gone their way, though their power may still flare up in some circles of faith. We have killed our gods – in spite or lucidity, I hardly know – yet we remain ourselves creatures of will, desire, hope, belief. And now we have nothing – nothing that is not partial, provisional, self-created – upon which to found our discourse.

Sometimes I imagine a new Kant, come out of Königsberg, spirited through the Iron Curtain. In his hand he holds the 'fourth critique', which he calls *The Critique of Practical Judgment*. It is a masterwork, resolving all the contradictions of theory and praxis, ethics and aesthetics, metaphysical reason and historical life. I reach for the sublime treatise; the illustrious ghost disappears. Sadly, I turn to my bookshelf and pick out William James's *The Will to Believe*.

Here, it seems, is friendly lucidity, and an imagination that keeps reason on the stretch. James speaks crucially to our condition in a 'pluralistic universe'. I let him speak:

> He who takes for his hypothesis the notion that it [pluralism] is the permanent form of the world is what I call a radical empiricist. For him the crudity of experience remains an eternal element thereof. There is no possible point of view from which the world can appear an absolutely single fact.[51]

This leaves the field open to 'willing nature':

> When I say 'willing nature', I do not mean only such deliberate volitions as may have set up habits of belief that we cannot now escape from, – I mean all such factors of belief as fear and hope, prejudice and passion, imitation and partisanship, the circumpressure of our caste and set. As a matter of fact we find ourselves believing, we hardly know how or why.[52]

This was written nearly a century ago and remains – so I *believe* – impeccable, unimpugnable.

It proposes a different kind of 'authority' [lower case], pragmatic, empirical, permitting pluralist beliefs. Between these beliefs there can be only continual negotiations of reason and interest, mediations of desire, transactions of power or hope. But all these still rest on, rest in, beliefs, which James knew to be the most interesting, most valuable, part of man. In the end our 'passional nature', he says, decides *an option between propositions, whenever it is a genuine option that cannot by its nature be decided on intellectual grounds'.*[53] James even suggests that, biologically considered, 'our minds are as ready to grind out falsehood as veracity, and he who says, "Better go without belief forever than believe a lie!" merely shows his own preponderant private horror of becoming a dupe'.[54]

Contemporary pragmatists, like Rorty, Fish, or Michaels, may not follow James so far. Certainly they would balk, as do most of us now, when James's language turns spiritual:

Is it not sheer dogmatic folly to say that our inner interests can have no real connection with the forces that the hidden world may contain? . . . And if needs of ours outrun the visible universe, why may not that be a sign that an invisible universe is there? . . . God himself, in short, may draw vital strength and increase of very being from our fidelity.[55]

I do not quote this passage to press the claims of metaphysics or religion. I do so only to hint that the ultimate issues of critical pluralism, in our postmodern epoch, point that way. And why, particularly, in our postmodern epoch? Precisely because of its countervailing forces, its indetermanences. Everywhere now we observe societies riven by the double and coeval process of planetisation and retribalisation, totalitarianism and terror, fanatic faith and radical disbelief. Everywhere we meet, in mutant or displaced forms, that conjunctive/disjunctive technological rage which affects postmodern discourse.

It may be that some rough beast will slouch again toward Bethlehem, its haunches bloody, its name echoing in our ears with the din of history. It may be that some natural cataclysm, world calamity, or extra terrestrial intelligence will shock the earth into some sane planetary awareness of its destiny. It may be that we shall simply bungle through, muddle through, wandering in the 'desert' from oasis to oasis, as we have done for decades, perhaps centuries. I have no prophecy in me, only some slight foreboding, which I express now to remind myself that all the evasions of our knowledge and actions thrive on the absence of consensual beliefs, an absence that also energises our tempers, our wills. This is our postmodern condition.

As to things nearer at hand, I openly admit: I do not know how to prevent critical pluralism from slipping into monism or relativism, except to call for pragmatic constituencies of knowledge that would share values, traditions, expectancies, goals. I do not know how to make our 'desert' a little greener, except to invoke enclaves of genial authority where the central task is to restore civil commitments, tolerant beliefs, critical sympathies.[56] I do not know how to give literature or theory or criticism a new hold on the world, except to remythify the imagination, at least locally, and bring back the reign of wonder into our lives. In this, my own elective affinities remain with Emerson: 'Orpheus is no fable: you have only to sing, and the rocks will crystallise; sing, and the plant will organise; sing, and the animal will be born.'[57]

But who nowadays believes it?

NOTES

1 Jean-François Lyotard, 'Answering the Question: What is Postmodernism?' trans Régis Durand, *Innovation/ Renovation*, ed Ihab Hassan and Sally Hassan, Madison, Wis, 1983, p 341 (reproduced in this volume). On the paratactic style in art and society, see also Hayden White, 'The Culture of Criticism', *Liberations: New Essays on the Humanities in Revolution*, ed Ihab Hassan, Middletown, Conn, 1971, pp 66-69; and see William James

on the affinities between parataxis and pluralism: 'It *may* be that some parts of the world are connected so loosely with some other parts as to be strung along by nothing but the copula *and*. . . . This pluralistic view, of a world of *additive* constitution, is one that pragmatism is unable to rule out from serious consideration.' (*'Pragmatism', and Four Essays from 'The Meaning of Truth'*, New York, 1955, p 112.)

2 See Jean-François Lyotard, *La Condition postmoderne: rapport sur le savoir*, Paris, 1979. For other views of decanonisation, see *English Literature: Opening Up the Canon*, ed Leslie Fiedler and Houston A Baker, Jr, Selected Papers from the English Institute, 1979, ns 4, Baltimore, 1981, and *Critical Inquiry* 10, September 1983.

3 Friedrich Nietzsche, *The Will to Power*, ed Walter Kaufmann, trans Walter Kaufmann and RJ Hollingdale, New York, 1967, p 199; see Wylie Sypher, *Loss of Self in Modern Literature and Art*, New York, 1962; see also the discussion of the postmodern self in Charles Caramello, *Silverless Mirrors: Book, Self, and Postmodern American Fiction*, Tallahassee, Fla, 1983.

4 The refusal of depth is, in the widest sense, a refusal of hermeneutics, the 'penetration' of nature or culture. It manifests itself in the white philosophies of post-structuralism as well as in various contemporary arts. See, for instance, Alain Robbe-Grillet, *For a New Novel: Essays on Fiction*, trans Richard Howard, New York, 1965, pp 49-76, and Susan Sontag, *Against Interpretation*, New York, 1963, pp 3-14.

5 Lyotard, 'Answering the Question', p 340. See also the perceptive discussion of the politics of the sublime by Hayden White, 'The Politics of Historical Interpretation: Discipline and De-Sublimation', *Critical Inquiry* 9, September, 1982, pp 124-28.

6 Julia Kristeva, 'Postmodernism?' *Romanticism, Modernism, Postmodernism*, ed Harry R Garvin, Lewisburg, Pa, 1980, p 141. See also her *Powers of Horror: An Essay on Abjection*, trans Leon S Roudiez, New York, 1982, and her most recent discussion of 'the unnameable' in 'Psychoanalysis and the Polis', trans Margaret Waller, *Critical Inquiry* 9, September 1982, p 91.

7 Alan Wilde, *Horizons of Assent: Modernism, Postmodernism, and the Ironic Imagination*, 1981, Baltimore, p 10. Wayne Booth makes a larger claim for the currency of irony in postmodern times, a 'cosmic irony', deflating the claims of man's centrality, and evincing a striking parallel with traditional religious languages. See his 'The Empire of Irony', *Georgia Review* 37, Winter 1983, pp 719-37.

8 The last term is Gary Saul Morson's. Morson provides an excellent discussion of threshold literature, parody, and hybridisation in his *The Boundaries of Genre: Dostoyevsky's 'Diary of a Writer' and the Traditions of Literary Utopia*, Austin, Tex, 1981, esp pp 48-50, 107-8, and 142-43.

9 See Fredric Jameson, 'Postmodernism and Consumer Society', *The Anti-Aesthetic: Essays on Postmodern Culture*, ed Hal Foster, Port Townsend, Wash, 1983. For a counterstatement, see Paolo Portoghesi, *After Modern Architecture*, trans Meg Shore, New York, 1982, p 11, and Matei Calinescu, 'From the One to the Many: Pluralism in Today's Thought', *Innovation/Renovation*, ed Hassan and Hassan, p 286.

10 See MM Bakhtin, *Rabelais and His World*, trans Helena Iswolsky, Cambridge, Mass, 1968, and *The Dialogic Imagination: Four Essays by MM Bakhtin*, ed Michael Holquist, trans Caryl Emerson and Michael Holquist, University of Texas Press Slavic Series, no I, Austin, 1981. See also the forum on Bakhtin, *Critical Inquiry* 10, December 1983.

11 Bakhtin, *Rabelais*, pp 10-11.

12 See Régis Durand's defence, against Michael Fried, of the performing principle in postmodern art ('Theatre/SIGNS/Performance: On Some Transformations of the Theatrical and the Theoretical', in *Innovation/Renovation*, ed Hassan and Hassan, pp 213-17). See also Richard Schechner, 'News, Sex, and Performance Theory', *Innovation/Renovation*, ed Hassan and Hassan, pp 189-210.

13 Richard Poirier, *The Performing Self: Compositions and Decompositions in the Languages of Contemporary Life*, New York, 1971, pp xv, xiii. See also Christopher Lasch, *The Culture of Narcissism: American Life in an Age of Diminishing Expectations*, New York, 1978.

14 Nietzsche, *Will to Power*, p 291.

15 James understood this when he said: 'You can't weed out the human contribution . . . altho the stubborn fact remains that there is a sensible flux, what is *true of it* seems from first to last to be largely a matter of our own creation', *Pragmatism*, p 166.

16 See Ihab Hassan, *Paracriticisms: Seven Speculations of the Times*, Urbana, Ill, 1975, pp 121-50; and Hassan, *The Right Promethean Fire*, pp 139-72. It was Jose Ortega y Gasset, however, who made a prescient, gnostic statement. And before Ortega, James wrote: 'The world is One just so far as its parts hang together by any definite connection. It is many just so far as any definite connection fails to obtain. And finally it is growing more and more unified by those systems of connection at least which human energy keeps framing as time goes on' (*Pragmatism*, p 105). But see also Jean Baudrillard's version of a senseless immanence, 'The Ecstasy of Communication', *Anti-Aesthetic*, ed Foster, pp 126-34.

17 Nelson Goodman, *Ways of Worldmaking*, Indianapolis, 1978, p x.

18 Active, creative, self-reflexive patterns seem also essential to advanced theories of artificial intelligence. See the article on Douglas R Hofstadter's latest work by James Gleick, 'Exploring the Labyrinth of the Mind', *The New York Times Magazine*, 21 August 1983, pp 23-100.

19 Jean Baudrillard, 'What Are You Doing After the Orgy?' *Artforum*, October 1983, p 43.

20 See, for instance, Paul de Man, 'Literary History and Literary Modernity', *Blindness and Insight: Essays in the Rhetoric of Contemporary Criticism*, New York, 1971, and Octavio Paz, *Children of the Mire: Modern Poetry from Romanticism to the Avant-Garde*, Cambridge, Mass, 1974.

21 See, for instance, the persuasive article of Ralph Cohen, 'Literary Theory as Genre', *Centrum* 3, Spring 1975, pp 45-64. Cohen also sees literary change itself as a genre. See his essay, 'A Propadeutic for Literary Change', and the responses of White and Michael Riffaterre to it, in *Critical Exchange* 13, Spring 1983, pp 17, 18-26, 27-38.

22 Wayne Booth, *Critical Understanding: The Powers and Limits of Pluralism*, Chicago, 1979, pp 33-34.

23 Paul Hernadi, *Beyond Genres: New Directions in Literary Classification*, Ithaca, NY, 1972, p 184. See, further, the two issues on convention and genre of *New Literary History* 13, Autumn 1981 and 14, Winter 1983.

24 Morson, *Boundaries of Genre*, p 49.

25 Jacques Derrida, 'La Loi du genre/The Law of Genre', *Glyph* 7, 1980, p 206. This entire issue concerns genre.

26 The term 'essentially contested concept' is developed by WB Gallie in his *Philosophy and the Historical Understanding*, New York, 1968. See also Booth's lucid discussion of it, *Critical Understanding*, pp 211-15 and 366.

27 See Steven Knapp and Walter Benn Michaels, 'Against Theory', *Critical Inquiry* 8, Summer 1982, pp 723-42, and the subsequent responses in *Critical Inquiry* 9, June 1983. 'Revisionary Madness: The Prospects of American Literary Theory at the Present Time' is the title of Daniel T O'Hara's response, pp 726-42.

28 Steven Knapp and Walter Benn Michaels, 'A Reply to Our Critics', *Critical Inquiry* 9, June 1983, p 800.

29 The relevance of belief to knowledge in general and conventions in particular is acknowledged by thinkers of different persuasions, even when they disagree on the nature of truth, realism, and genre. Thus, for instance, Nelson Goodman and Menachem Brinker agree that belief is 'an accepted version' of the world and ED Hirsch concurs with both. See Goodman, 'Realism, Relativism, and Reality', Brinker, 'On Realism's Relativism: A Reply to Nelson Goodman', and Hirsch, 'Beyond Convention?' All appear in *New Literary History* 14, Winter 1983.

30 Thomas S Kuhn, *The Structure of Scientific Revolutions*, 2nd ed, Chicago, 1970, p 163, my emphasis; Victor Turner, *Dramas, Fields, and Metaphors: Symbolic Action in Human Society*, Ithaca, NY, 1974, p 14; Jonathan Culler, 'Convention and Meaning: Derrida and Austin', *New Literary History* 13, Autumn 1981, p 30; Jeffrey Stout, 'What Is the Meaning of a Text?' *New Literary History* 14, Autumn 1982, p 5. I am aware that other thinkers distinguish between 'variety' and 'subjectivity' of understanding in an effort to limit radical perspectivism; see, for instance, Stephen C Pepper, *World Hypotheses: A Study in Evidence*, Berkeley and Los Angeles, 1942; Stephen Toulmin, *Human Understanding: The Collective Use and Evolution of Concepts*, Princeton, NJ, 1972; and George Bealer, *Quality and Concept*, Oxford, 1982. But I wonder why their arguments have failed to eliminate, or at least reduce, their differences with relativists; or why, again, Richard Rorty and Hirsch find it possible to disagree about the 'question of objectivity', which became the theme of a *conference* at the University of Virginia in April 1984.

31 Jürgen Habermas, in *Knowledge and Human Interests*, trans Jeremy J Shapiro, Boston, 1971, and *Technik und Wissenschaft als 'Ideologie'*, Frankfurt am Main, 1968, also offers vigorous neo-Marxist critiques of knowledge and society. Kenneth Burke, in *A Grammar of Motives*, New York, 1945, preceded both Foucault and Habermas in this large political and logological enterprise.

32 Michel Foucault, *Language, Counter-Memory, Practice: Selected Essays and Interviews*, ed Donald F Bouchard, trans Bouchard and Sherry Simon, Ithaca, NY, 1977, p 200.

33 Ibid, p 213.

34 See Michel Foucault, *Beyond Structuralism*, pp 216-20.

35 Fredric Jameson, *The Political Unconscious: Narrative as a Socially Symbolic Act*, Ithaca, NY, 1981, p 286.

36 Edward Said, *The World, the Text, and the Critic*, Cambridge, Mass, 1983, p 5.

37 David Bleich, 'Literary Theory in the University: A Survey', *New Literary History* 14, Winter 1983, p 411. See also *What Is Literature?* ed Hernadi, Bloomington, Ind, 1978, pp 49-112.

38 See *Critical Inquiry* 9, September 1982; and see Gerald Graff, 'The Pseudo-Politics of Interpretation', *Critical Inquiry* 9, March 1983, pp 597-610.

39 See Geoffrey Hartman, 'The New Wilderness: Critics as Connoisseurs of Chaos', *Innovation/Renovation*. ed Hassan and Hassan, pp 87-110.

40 'If social circumstances . . . contradict too powerfully the [Romantic] world-view of literature, then the Imaginary Library, first its enabling beliefs and eventually its institutional manifestations, can no longer

exist,' remarks Alvin B Kernan, *The Imaginary Library: An Essay on Literature and Society*, Princeton, NJ, 1982, p 166.

41 Though 'everything is ideological', as we nowadays like to say, we need still to distinguish between ideologies – fascism, feminism, monetarism, vegetarianism, etc – between their overt claims, their hidden exactions. Even postmodernism, as a political ideology, requires discriminations. Lyotard, for instance, believes that 'the postmodern condition is a stranger to disenchantment as to the blind positivity of delegitimation'. (*La Condition postmoderne*, p 8; my translation); while Foster claims a 'postmodernism of resistance', a 'counterpractice not only to the official culture of modernism but also to the 'false normativity' of a reactionary postmodernism' (*Anti-Aesthetic*, p xii). Interestingly enough, French thinkers of the Left – Foucault, Lyotard, Baudrillard, Gilles Deleuze – seem more subtle in their ideas of 'resistance' than their American counterparts. This is curious, perhaps paradoxical, since the procedures of 'mass', 'consumer', or 'postindustrial' society are more advanced in America than in France. But see also, as a counterstatement, Said's critique of Foucault, 'Travelling Theory', *Raritan* I, Winter 1982, pp 41-67.

42 Kristeva, 'Psychoanalysis and the Polis', p 78. In our therapeutic culture, the language of politics and the discourse of desire constantly seek one another, as if the utopian marriage of Marx and Freud could find consummation, at last, in our words. Hence the political use of such erotic or analytic concepts as 'libidinal economy' (Jean-François Lyotard, *Economie libidinale*, Paris, 1974), 'seduction' (Jean Baudrillard, *De la seduction*, Paris, 1979), 'delirium' or 'abjection' (Julia Kristeva, *Powers of Horror*, 'anti-Oedipus' (Gilles Deleuze and Félix Guattari, *Anti-Oedipus: Capitalism and Schizophrenia*, trans Robert Hurley, Mark Seem, and Helen R Lane, New York, 1977), 'bliss' (Roland Barthes, *The Pleasure of the Text*, trans Richard Miller, New York, 1975), and 'the political unconscious (Jameson, *Political Unconscious*). See also Ihab Hassan, 'Desire and Dissent in the Postmodern Age', *Kenyon Review* ns 5, Winter 1983, p 18.

43 Alfred North Whitehead, *Adventures of Ideas*, New York, 1955, p 276.

44 Barthes, *Pleasure of the Text*, p 27.

45 Ibid, pp 17, 65.

46 Roland Barthes, *Leçon inaugurale faite le vendredi 7 janvier 1977*, Paris, 1978, p 25.

47 Ibid, 46.

48 Roland Barthes, *Fragments d'un discours amoureux*, Paris, 1977, p 87. A few sentences in the paragraph which this sentence concludes have appeared in my earlier essay, 'Parabiography: The Varieties of Critical Experience', *Georgia Review* 34, Fall 1980, p 600.

49 In America, the work of Leo Bersani has addressed such questions as 'Can a psychology of fragmentary and discontinuous desires be reinstated? What are the strategies by which the self might be once again theatricalised? How might desire recover its original capacity for projecting nonstructurable *scenes?'* And it answers them by suggesting that *the* 'desiring self might even disappear as we learn to multiply our discontinuous and partial desiring selves' in language. See *A Future for Astyanax: Character and Desire in Literature*, Boston, 1976, pp 6-7.

50 Kristeva, 'Psychoanalysis and the Polis', pp 82, 86.

51 William James, *'The Will to Believe' and Other Essays in Popular Philosophy*, New York, 1956, p ix.

52 Ibid, p 9.

53 Ibid, p 11.

54 Ibid, p 18.

55 Ibid, pp 55, 56, 61.

56 James once more: 'No one of us ought to issue vetoes to the other, nor should we bandy words of abuse. We ought, on the contrary, delicately and profoundly to respect one another's mental freedom: then only shall we bring about the intellectual republic; then only shall we have that spirit of inner tolerance without which all our outer tolerance is soulless, and which is empiricism's glory; then only shall we live and let live, in speculative as well as in practical things' (ibid, p 30). *How far, beyond this, does any postmodern pluralist go?*

57 *Journals of Ralph Waldo Emerson*, 1820-1872, ed Edward Waldo Emerson and Waldo Emerson Forbes, 10 vols, Boston, 1909-14, 8: p 79.

From *The Postmodern Turn: Essays in Postmodern Theory and Culture*, Ohio State University Press, Columbus, 1987; reprinted by permission. © 1987 by the Ohio State University Press.

Paolo Portoghesi
WHAT IS THE POSTMODERN?

'A spectre is roaming through Europe: the Postmodern.' A columnist from *Le Monde* gave this title to an article on the most passion-stirring event to occur in the world of culture in the past several years. This phenomenon exploded in America at the end of the last decade, but its roots are especially deep in Europe, where it has found the most fertile ground for theoretical debate.

But what exactly is the Postmodern? Is it possible to give a single definition to such a paradoxical and irritating word? I feel that it is indeed possible. But we must first stop thinking of it as a label designating homogeneous and convergent things. Its usefulness lies, rather, in its having allowed us temporarily to put together and compare different things arising from a common dissatisfaction with that group of equally heterogeneous things called modernity. To put it another way, the Postmodern is a refusal, a rupture, a renouncement, much more than a simple change of direction. To define it poetically, we could borrow the celebrated verses of Montale: 'Do not ask us for the key that cannot open . . . Only this we can tell you today, what we are not, and what we do not want.' And exactly what many of us do not want anymore today is the antiquated Modern, that set of formulas which, in the second decade of this century, acquired the rigidity and clarity of a sort of statute in which general laws are collected that must be obeyed. This statute has never come up for discussion again, even though taste has changed more than once since then. Its main article was precisely an annihilation of tradition, the obligation towards renewal, the theology of the new, and difference as an autonomous value.

This perverse guarantee of perpetual renewal has given modernity the appearance of an elusive shadow, difficult to contend with because of its readiness to assume everchanging forms and strategies. But in the end, a sense of uneasiness upset even the certainties of the Modern: the discomfort of men of culture when evaluating its products. Sixty years comprise a man's life, and just as a man of this age looks back (and just as the others tend to judge him), the trial against the Modern has been outlined as a physiological necessity, as an unpostponable goal for the new generations, at least since 1968. Therefore, a trial against the Modern and its consequences, but not only this; the Postmodern is a rebellion originating in the realisation that in the past sixty years everything has changed in the world of social relationships and production; that industry has undergone radical transformations, and the energy crisis has once more uncovered problems that had been thought to be solved for some time.

The statute of modernity had been custom-made for a society in which the revolution of information that has profoundly shaken all the structures of our world had not yet occurred. Before a Postmodern culture, there previously existed a 'postmodern condition', the product of 'post-industrial' society. It was inevitable that sooner or later this creeping, underground revolution would end up changing the direction of artistic research. What was less foreseeable was that instead of developing in the futurist-mechanical sense, in the '2000' style, as many had imagined, art steered its course toward Ithaca. It made its way toward the recovery of certain aspects of tradition, and reopened the discussion, the impassable embankment erected by the avant-garde between present and past, and went back to mix the waters with creative results. This recovery of memory, after the forced amnesia of a half century, is manifest in customs, dress (folk, casual and the various revivals), in the mass diffusion of an interest in history and its products, in the ever vaster need for contemplative experiences and contact with nature that seemed antithetical to the civilisation of machines.

Architecture was one of the first disciplines to go into crisis when faced with the new needs and desires of postmodern society. The reason for this precociousness is simple. Given its direct incidence on daily life, architecture could not elude the practical verification of its users. Modern architecture has thus been judged by its natural product: the modern city, the suburbs without quality, the urban environment devoid of collective values that has become an asphalt jungle and a dormitory; the loss of local character, of the connection with the place: the terrible homologation that has made the outskirts of the cities of the whole world similar to one another, and whose inhabitants have a hard time recognising an identity of their own.

The architects of the new generations have made the city, the mechanisms of the production and reproduction of the city, their preferred field of study. They have discovered that the perpetual invention of and search for the new at all costs, the breaking off of environmental equilibria, perspective decomposition, abstract volumetric play, and all the ingredients of modern architectural cuisine were equally toxic to the physiological regimen of urban growth. They have discovered that the imitation of types is more important than linguistic invention. They also realise that it is once again necessary to learn modesty and the knowledge of rules and canons produced over centuries of experiences and errors, that the character of a place is a patrimony to use and not to mindlessly squander. A kind of new renaissance is thus being outlined which intends to recover certain aspects of the past, not to interrupt history, but to arrest its paralysis. And whoever objects that we are in a time of economic and moral crisis hardly fit for a renaissance should be reminded that Brunelleschi's and Leonardo's times were just as dark.

As always, when change is desired, the Postmoderns have also been the target of the arrows of the new conservatives, of those guardians of modernity at any cost, who refuse to relinquish their privileges and power. Unable to refute the radical criticisms of the tradition of the new, they speak of an incomplete project of modernity that must be continued; they pretend to ignore the fact that in order to really change the essential premises of the modern project, and not its last consequences, must be debated once more. And they refuse to admit that continuity with the great tradition of modern art lies today more in the courage to break with the past (which in this case is precisely what was modern yesterday), than in keeping its surviving traces on ice.

In Italy, the harshest and most subtle attack came from the old exponents of the '63 group, which twenty years ago raised the banner of the neo-avant-garde and experimentalism. Precursors of the Postmodern in many marginal aspects of research (the use of the historical quotation, the new-antique corruption, the semiological and linguistic approach), they refuse the products of this new attitude without even analysing them, making a handy image of these products in order to destroy them with the old weapon of irony. An old system already used once by the enemies of the Modern when it deserved the name. History repeats itself, even if there will always be those who confuse it with a straight line. That postmodern theses have deep roots in the present human condition is confirmed today in the document on architecture issued by the Polish union Solidarity. This text accuses the modern city of being the product of an alliance between bureaucracy and totalitarianism, and singles out the great error of modern architecture in the break of historical continuity. Solidarity's words should be meditated upon, especially by those who have confused a great movement of collective consciousness with a passing fashion.

A New Renaissance

> Zoroaster wants to lose nothing of humanity's past, and wants to throw everything into the crucible. (Nietzsche)

During the last decade, the adjective postmodern has made a journey of varying success through the humanistic disciplines. Used systematically for the first time in 1971 by Ihab Hassan in relation to literature, it then made its way into the social sciences, into semiology and philosophy. In architecture, the adjective postmodern found fertile cultural ground, priming a process which started out from criticism and historiography, and finally became the unifying label of a series of trends, theoretical propositions and concrete experiences.

It is worth our while today to reflect upon the unforeseeable fortune of this word in architecture, in order to try to clear up many misunderstandings, and to establish just how useful it can be in relating parallel phenomena taking place in very different areas. In the field of architecture, the term has been used to designate a plurality of tendencies directed toward an escape from the crisis of the Modern Movement with a radical refusal of its logic of development. In the last several decades, this development had led to a chaotic labyrinth, or to the anachronistic attempt to restore the orthodoxy of the golden age of functionalism; the age, of course, of the Bauhaus and CIAM.

The Postmodern has signalled, therefore, the way out of a movement that had for some time stopped 'moving ahead', that had transformed itself into a gaudy bazaar of inventions motivated only by personal ambition and by the alibi of technological experimentation. The critics who first put into focus the vast and contradictory phenomenon of an exit from orthodoxy tried to control it by putting it into traditional categories. They also tried to simplify it and make it more comprehensible; but in the end, the neutrality of a word like postmodern is tantamount to an absurd definition based on difference more than on identity. With regard to didactic simplification, the same critics finally surrendered to pluralism and complexity. Charles Jencks, the most able of the announcers of this new show, proposed that its specificity can in fact be grasped, since it is the product of architects particularly mindful of the aspects of architecture understood as a language, as a means of communication.

> A Postmodern building is, if a short definition is needed, one which speaks on at least two levels at once: to other architects and a concerned minority who care about specifically architectural meanings, and to the public at large, or the local inhabitants, who care about other issues concerned with comfort, traditional building and a way of life. Thus Postmodern architecture looks hybrid and, if a visual definition is needed, rather like the front of a classical Greek temple. The latter is a geometric architecture of elegantly fluted columns below, and a riotous billboard of struggling giants above, a pediment painted in deep reds and blues. The architects can read the implicit metaphors and subtle meanings of the column drums, whereas the public can respond to the explicit metaphors and messages of the sculptors. Of course everyone responds somewhat to both codes of meaning, as they do in a Postmodern building, but certainly with different intensity and

understanding, and it is this discontinuity in taste cultures which creates both the theoretical base and 'dual-coding' of Postmodernism.[1]

This definition certainly covers the unifying aspect of many of the most significant works realised in the last decade which have overcome the ideological crisis of the Modern Movement. It fails, however, to satisfy the historical need of relating the shift carried out by architectural culture to the profound changes in society, and risks confining the phenomenon to an area completely within the private realm of the architect, therefore remaining more a psychological than an historico-critical definition. It is more correct, in my view, to try to get to the specificity of the phenomenon by revealing the substantial differences with modernity, from which it wishes to distinguish itself, in what are its most typical aspects. And since modernity coincides in Western architectural culture with the progressive rigorous detachment from everything traditional, it should be pointed out that in the field of architecture, the postmodern means that explicit, conscious abolition of the dam carefully built around the pure language elaborated *in vitro* on the basis of the rationalist statute. This language is put into contact again with the universe of the architectural debate, with the entire historical series of its past experiences, with no more distinctions between the periods before or after the first industrial revolution. With the barrier torn down, old and new waters have mixed together. The resulting product is before our eyes, paradoxical and ambiguous but vital, a preparatory moment of something different that can only be imagined: reintegration in architecture of a vast quantity of values, layers, semitones, which the homologation of the International Style had unpardonably dispersed.

The return of architecture to the womb of its history has just begun, but the proportions of this operation are quite different from those which orthodox critics suppose. This reversion to history would always be a laboratory experiment if it were not also the most convincing answer given thus far by architectural culture to the profound transformations of society and culture, to the growth of a 'postmodern condition' following from the development of post-industrial society. To convince ourselves, a synthetic review of the historical symptoms of this condition should suffice.

The Age of Information

No technical revolution has thus far produced such great and lasting transformations as the quantification and elaboration of information, made possible by the new electronic technology. Our age has seen the world of the machine, with its working systems and its rhythms, miss the impact of novelty. It has watched a new artificial universe move ahead, composed of wires and circuits, which resemble more organic material than something really mechanical. Information and communication have therefore become terms of comparison with which to redefine and reinterpret the role of all disciplines. And at that moment when the semiotic aspect of architecture and that of the transmission of information, along with its productive and stylistic aspects, was put into focus, it was inevitable that the constrictive and utopian character of the revolution which took place beginning with the twenties, with the worldwide diffusion of the paradigms of the avant-garde, would be evident. In fact, renouncing the systems of conventions through which it had developed uninterruptedly, since the ancient world (the structural principle of the order, base, column, capital, trabeation, and so on), architecture had lost its specificity and had become, on the one hand, an autonomous figurative art, on the same level as painting, or, on the other hand, had reduced itself to pure material production.

Architecture, instead, seen in the area of the different civilization of man, reveals a much more complex nature and role. It is an instrument of the production and transmission of communicative models, which have for a particular society a value analogous to that of laws and other civil institutions, models whose roots lie in the appropriation and transformation of the places of the earth, and which have for centuries played the part of confirming and developing the identity of places (of cities) and of communities.

The result of the discovery of the sudden impoverishment produced in architecture by the adoption of technologies and morphologies separated from places and traditions has been the reemergence of architectonic archetypes as precious instruments of communication. These archetypes are elementary institutions of the language and practice of architecture that live on in the daily life and collective memory of man. These differ greatly depending on the places where we live and where our spatial experiences were formed. The Postmodern in architecture can therefore be read overall as a reemergence of archetypes, or as a reintegration of architectonic conventions, and thus as a premise to the creation of an *architecture of communication,* an architecture of the image for a civilisation of the image.

The Fall of Centred Systems

Another aspect of the postmodern condition is the progressive dismantling of the bases of the critical theory of bourgeois society. The sharp polarity of social classes, faith in the redeeming capabilities of the socialisation of the means of production, and the analogy of the intricate processes of industrial society in capitalist and socialist countries have placed a profoundly changed reality on guard against the sterility of the dogmatisms and the incapability to explore, with the old tools of consecrated and sclerotic theories.

It should not surprise us that, together with the much more serious and proven ideological scaffolding, even the Modern Movement is in crisis: a variable and undefined container, within which quite different and often divergent phenomena were placed. This was an attempt to construct a linear function of architectural progress, in regard to which it would be possible at all times to distinguish good from evil, decree annexations and impulsions as in a political party. The Modern Movement proposed to change society for the better, avoiding (according to Le Corbusier) the revolution, or carrying it out, as the Russian Constructivists believed. Among its great tasks, the most important was that of teaching man to become modern, to change his way of life according to a model capable of avoiding waste. Today, this undertaking hardly seems valid for a colonialist programme, while the real problem is one of understanding what postmodern man wants, and how he lives. He is not an animal to be programmed in a laboratory, but an already existing species which has almost reached maturity, while architects were still trying to realise their obsolete project of modernity.

The great intellectual work done in the past twenty years on the concept and structures of power has put another drifting mine beneath the fragile and suspect structure of the Modern Movement. Separating the idea of power from the relationships of work and property 'in which,' as Alain Touraine has written, 'it seemed to be totally incarnated', even the role of the architectural avant-gardes has been able to be analysed in different terms, recognising its responsibilities and inadequacies, and putting in crisis the theory that stripped them of responsibility. They attributed all blame to the 'design of capital'.

The history of architecture of the past thirty years could, therefore, be written as the history of a 'way out' of the Modern Movement according to a direction already experimented by the masters in the last years of their lives, at the beginning of the fifties.

The crisis of theoretical legitimation, which Jean-François Lyotard calls the 'scarce credibility of the great *Récits*', and the fact that today we must confront the problem of the meaning 'without having the possibility of responding with the hope of the emancipation of Mankind, as in the school of the Enlightenment, of the Spirit, as in the school of German Idealism, or of the Proletariat, by means of the establishment of a transparent society', has unhinged the fundamental principles of architectural modernity, consisting of a series of equations which have never been verified except through insignificant small samples. These are the equations: useful=beautiful, structural truth=aesthetic prestige, and the dogmatic assertions of the functionalist statute: 'form follows function', 'architecture must coincide with construction', 'ornament is crime', and so on. The truth of architecture as a simple coincidence of appearance and substance contradicts what is greatest and most lasting among the architectural institutions, from the Greek temple to the cathedral; and even what the Modern Movement built under the banner of truth often has its worth in an 'appearance' that has little to do with constructive truth. The great moral tale that hoped to grasp the human aspect of architecture, theorising its function and 'sincerity', by this time has the distant prestige of a fable.

In place of faith in the great centred designs, and the anxious pursuits of salvation, the postmodern condition is gradually substituting the concreteness of small circumstantiated struggles with its precise objectives capable of having a great effect because they change systems of relations.

The Crisis of Resources and the City-Country Relationship
The postmodern condition has put into crisis even that discipline that the Modern Movement had placed beside architecture, as a theoretical guarantee of its socialisation: city planning understood as the science of territorial transformations. From the time when city planning, abandoning the tradition of nineteenth-century urban rhetoric, had become that strange mixture of ineffectual sociological analyses and implacable zoning, the city seemed to have lost the very principle of its reproduction, growing from the addition of fatty or cancerous tissue, lacking essential urban features, as in the great peripheral areas.

The most obvious symptom of the change in direction of architectural research was a return to the study of the city as a complex phenomenon in which building typologies play a role comparable to that of institutions, and profoundly condition the production and change of the urban face. The analytical study of the city has skipped over the functionalist logic of the building block, reproposing instead the theme of the continuity of the urban fabric, and of the fundamental importance of enclosed spaces, actual component cells of the urban environment. The study of collective behaviour divided the criterion of the dismemberment of the urban body into its monofunctioning parts, the standard which informs ideal cities, proposed as models by the matters of modern architecture.

The energy crisis, on the other hand, and the crisis of the governability of the great metropolitan administrations has focused once again on the problem of the alternatives to the indefinite growth of the large cities, and on the necessity of correcting the relationship of exploitation still characterising the city in relation to small centres and the region. The great myth of the double equation, city=progress, development=well-being has given way to the theory of limit and of controlled development. With regard to a postmodern urbanism, an institutional reformism is beginning to be considered that would give new competitive strength to smaller centres through federative initiatives (in Italy, a process of this kind is going on in the Vallo di Diano, under the aegis of Socialist administrators). Ecological problems and the energy crisis have led to the self-criticism of the acritical propensity toward the new technologies that have substituted old ones, often with no advantage whatsoever for the life span of the product, the absorption of manpower and aesthetic quality. A change of direction is inevitable if we do not want to further aggravate economic and social problems. To realise the importance of these programmes, it is sufficient to reflect upon the fact that the energy consumption of a plastic panel is twenty times that needed for the construction of a brick wall of the same area, or that the progressive disappearance of certain trades because of the abandonment of certain techniques would render us, for a lack of skilled workers, unable to restore historic monuments and ancient cities, whose integral preservation seems to have been, at least on paper, one of the great cultural conquests of our time.

The truth is that the postmodern condition has reversed the theoretical scaffolding of so-called modernity. Those who are amazed that, among the most apparent results of the new culture in its infancy, there is also a certain superficial feeling for a 'return to the antique', seem to forget that in every serious mixture, the artificial order of chronology is one of the first structures to be discussed and then dismissed. Just as grandchildren often resemble their grandparents, and certain features of the family reappear after centuries, the world now emerging is searching freely in memory, because it knows how to find its own 'difference' in the removed repetition and utilisation of the entire past. Recently in Japan, sailboats have been built whose sails are manoeuvred not by hundreds of sailors, but by complicated and extremely fast electronic devices. These ships, equipped also with conventional engines, allow for a great saving in fuel. Postmodern architecture, whose naive manifestations of a precocious childhood we see today, will probably resemble these ships that have brought the imaginary even into the world of the machine.

NOTES

1 Charles Jencks, *The Language of Post-Modern Architecture*, Academy, London, 1981.

From *Postmodern, The Architecture of the Postindustrial Society*, Rizzoli, New York, 1983.

Charles Jencks
THE POST-AVANT-GARDE

The avant-garde is a curious term and idea; partly a military metaphor applied to the art and cultural worlds, partly a synonym and substitute for the more anodyne 'Modern' or 'Modern Movement', partly a sociological description of a patronless class of individuals. To some extent it is also a pseudo concept used to confirm the reputations of those who have arrived safely in the Vatican of Modernism, the Museum of Modern Art in New York, that quasi-official institution which turns former acts of invention and destruction into fairly permanent icons to be studied, classified, and, on occasion, worshipped. The contradictions of this last situation have not escaped notice and now artists and critics ask themselves if the avant-garde really staked out new territory in the past so that one of their kind, Vincent van Gogh, should later have his previously unappreciated work exchanged for forty million dollars. 1.6 million dollars for a Rothko, 2.2 million dollars for a Jackson Pollock, three million dollars for a Jasper Johns – the mass media keep us all up on the figures – Old Master Dadaists, Collectible Nihilists. And then another set of statistics – fifty new museums constructed in the United States in one year, 35,000 painters, sculptors and art historians graduating from American schools annually, Modernism accepted as the official culture of our time – can the avant-garde, which has suffered so much disdain and disregard for 160 years, survive all this success and still be 'avant' anything?

Almost all serious critics think the avant-garde is dead as a result of absorption into the establishment and consumer society: if it has joined the centre, if it has made its peace with mass culture, if its ultimate goal is, when all is said and done, to be accepted into the mainstream, into MOMA, MOCA, or LACMA, then the avant-garde is really the Swiss Garde, or Salon Art of our time. This is a verdict with which Robert Hughes, who has been studying Modernism and the marketplace, might agree:

> . . . although the 1970s produced its meed of good art, some of it very interesting indeed, the most striking thing now visible about the decade was an agreement that went on below the art itself: that Modernism, which had been the cultural bedrock of Europe and America for a hundred years, was perhaps over; that we were at the end, as Hilton Kramer put it in a deservedly influential essay in 1972, of 'The Age of the Avant-garde'.[1]

By 1979 the idea of the *avant-garde* had gone. This sudden metamorphosis of one of the popular clichés of art-writing into an un-word took a great many people by surprise. For those who still believed that art had some practical revolutionary functions, it was as baffling as the evaporation of the American radical Left after 1970.

But the question is obviously more complex and subtle than the simple death or life of the avant-garde. The 'death of Modernism' has been proclaimed this century many times and for as long as its Doppelgänger, 'the death of art'. A German book proclaimed its demise in 1907, and this didn't stop its multiple resurrections, nor the museums of the new built on its ashes. Like the Phoenix bird, Modernism seems best off just after it suffers a fatal blow and prepares for its next rebirth. One might even contend that its health depends on these ritual slayings which condition us for the next round of the cycle, the new movement which always promises to be fresh like an unknown future. The person who is tired of the avant-garde and its continual resurrections is, as they say, tired of life, of springtime and fashion, tired of continual change and business cycles: ie almost everybody today. How can we explain this paradox? By looking, briefly, at the four main stages of the avant-garde from the 1820s to the present, we can see how the word and practice have come, through a series of subtle alterations, to change their meaning entirely.

1 The Heroic Avant-Garde

The phrase is of course partly French, but it has been adopted in many countries, notably English-speaking ones, and its primary emphasis is always on the notion of being 'before' – 'avant' other things. Thus the English 'avantalour' meaning 'one who goes before', or 'avant-peach', 'an early variety of peach'. Malory used 'avant-garde' in *Arthur*, 1470 – 'the Lyonses ... had the avantgarde', and this sort of military usage extends up to 1796: 'General Stengel ... commanded the avant-garde of Valence's Army.' All these usages are from the *Oxford English Dictionary*, which, to prove it is aristocratic and *ancien*, actually avoids all the more contemporary meanings of the last 160 years, the only ones that actively concern us. These derive from the French Revolution and Henri de Saint-Simon's notion, formulated in 1825, of a unified avant-garde of artists, scientists and industrialists which would together create the future-positive – soon to be the science of Positivism. Saint-Simon, himself a former soldier, has the artist say to the scientist: 'It is we, artists, who will serve you as avant-garde: the power of the artist is in fact most immediate and most rapid: when we wish to spread new ideas among men, we inscribe them on marble or canvas ... and in that way above all we exert an electric and victorious influence ... if today our role appears nil or at least very secondary, what is lacking to the arts is that which is essential to their energy and to their success, namely, a common drive and a general idea.'[2]

The 'common drive and general idea' was of course social progress; the march towards socialism which gave the avant-garde its direction and purpose. It also gave the artist and architect an important function as the harbingers of change *avant* the main-stream of society. Saint-Simon, as if to underline the Christian aspects of his message (and his own name) gives the avant-garde artists a priestly function: 'What a most beautiful destiny for the arts, that of exercising over society a positive power, a truly priestly function, and of marching forcefully in the van of all the intellectual faculties, in the epoch of their greatest development! This is the duty of artists, this their mission ...'[3]

Karl Marx was later, in the *Communist Manifesto*, to reserve this avant-garde role for the Communist Party, and many radical newspapers in France, after 1848, took on the title *L'Avant-garde* as an emblem of their political positivism. Even those opposed to communism got caught up in the military metaphor. The anarchist Peter Kroptkin, for example, gave the inevitable title to his Swiss magazine – something that was to directly influence the avant-gardism of Le Corbusier. One more quote from this first stage of the avant-garde may be given to underline its heroic and positivist role. It comes from Gabriel-Désiré Laverdant's book, *On the Mission of Art and Role of Artists*, published in France in 1845:

> Art, the expression of society, manifests in its highest soaring the most advanced
> social tendencies: it is the forerunner and the revealer. Therefore, to know whether
> art worthily fulfils its proper mission as initiator, whether the artist is truly of the

avant-garde, one must know where Humanity is going, know what the destiny of the human race is . . .[4]

In other words Laverdant, Saint-Simon and Karl Marx would find today's avant-garde very *arrière*, just as they would find the subsequent split between art and politics into two separate avant-gardes a baneful situation. The split inevitably occurred in the 1880s with a Modernism which focused on each separate art language; the 'art for art's sake' which has remained one of the strongest of the avant-gardes to the present, with the writings of Mallarmé and Clement Greenberg among others.

Nonetheless the 'Heroic' avant-garde was the first and most important version of this changing institution and it gave direction to the efforts of painters such as Gustave Courbet and Utopian planners such as Robert Owen and Charles Fourier. It also led, when it marched on a social and artistic front at the same time – as it did for about ten years – to the 'Heroic' period of Modern architecture in the 1920s: the work of Gropius, Mies and Le Corbusier. The Heroic avant-garde led society, or at least the professions, and the main-garde, or establishment, followed in its wake.

It's worth pausing for a moment to unpack this military metaphor a little further. If the Heroic avant-garde was to be out front annexing territory here and provoking outrageous skirmishes with the enemy there, then it was Serving the Destiny of Humanity, and its job was to be followed up by the main army – perhaps we should call it the *moyen-garde*, or *milieu-garde*, or best of all *centre-garde*, because this last metaphor gives a precise placement in front for the 'avant'. Can there be an avant-garde without a defined *centre* and *arrière,* without a Salon and Establishment, an Academy and Aristocracy? The Heroic avant-garde was itself to be the replacement for the older institution of the elite, with its intelligentsia, professionals and aristocrats. Thus its styles and virtues would be picked up by the rest of society: Le Corbusier and the Bauhaus would set the standards for mass production, the ideal types which would be endlessly repeated and thereby raise the level of mass taste; TS Eliot would 'purify the language of the tribe'; Eisenstein would reform the sensibilities of the film-goer as much as Picasso, Braque and Léger would transform and purify the visual codes of the public. Never mind, for a moment, that this never happened precisely the way they intended: the ideal was strong enough to carry ten generations of Modernists right up to the 1960s. It served to justify their experiments, their will to power, their endless housing estates and attacks on the academies of art.

2 The Purist Avant-Garde

This idea also paved the way for the second type of avant-garde, the Purist stage, because it provided a social pretext for making formal experiments with different art languages, at least on the level of analogy. Where the first ground-breakers could claim a potential social liberation, their successors could claim spiritual freedom: the heavenly city of artistic imagination liberated from previous convention in order to invent new worlds. And this formalist Modernism has proven much stronger and more lasting (though less interesting) than the first avant-garde. From Josef Albers to Frank Stella, from Theo van Doesburg to Peter Eisenman, from Buckminster Fuller to Norman Foster, from Modernist abstraction to Late-Modern formalism and technicism, the Purist avant-garde has dominated art and architectural politics from the twenties to the present and I am tempted to say, with others, that it is the only 'true' avant-garde there can be after the social/artistic one has died – the only one that stakes out new territory, conquers new languages and modes of experience. But I am not fundamentally concerned here with such incessant revolution for its own sake, and so will return to the

LEFT: Le Corbusier, Unité d'habitation, Marseilles, 1947-52 *RIGHT:* V Tatlin, *Monument to the Third International*, 1919-20;

last two types of avant-garde, of which one may deserve the epithet 'so-called', the other 'radical'.

3 The Radical Avant-Garde

The radical avant-garde of the 1910s and 1920s grew out of the attempt to overcome the final boundary, that is the dividing line between art and life. Where the two previous avant-gardes pushed into new social and artistic territories, the radical avant-gardes – the Futurists, Dadaists and Constructivists – sought to do away with all distinctions, all nationalities, all standards and professions (including in a sense themselves) and thus they were not only Radical, but anti-avant-garde as well. Art would go out into the street, and the streets would be turned into art galleries, art would be life and life would become an artwork. Tatlin's machine art, particularly his Monument to the Third International, typifies this radical avant-garde and it's noteworthy that the German Dadaists of the time could interpret it with the slogan 'Art is Dead, Long Live the New Machine Art of the Tatlins'. The Constructivists, after the Russian Revolution, made the most radical assaults on the bourgeois separation of art and life epitomised in the institutional divide between the museum and factory.

The poet Mayakovsky and others proclaimed, 'Down with Museums and Art! We do not need a dead mausoleum of art where dead works are worshipped, but a living factory of the human spirit – in the street, in the tramways, in the factories, workshops and workers' houses'. This attack on the institutionalisation of art within museums and the attendant notion of the autonomous work of art disconnected from society is the *essence* of the avant-garde for those materialists such as Peter Bürger who write on the subject today.[5] It's easy to see why their arguments are persuasive: the art context *does* insulate the work of art, the art market and museum *do* change, however subtly, the meaning of a gesture and style. We can't look at a Julian Schnabel without thinking of the price tag and promotion apparatus surrounding it any more than we can look at Norman Foster's Hongkong Bank without knowing that it is the most expensive Late-Modern building in the world. The mass media and marketplace have made materialists of us all and the only way to transcend this situation is to fully admit its implications and see how the artist and architect deals with this as part of the content of the work.

The extreme examples of this radical avant-gardism occurred first in the early 1920s and then again in the 1960s, with several Pop artists who attempted, in their words, to 'operate in the gap between art and life', close this gap or, like Andy Warhol, act as if it never existed, reducing art to a type of mechanised and stylised life. Warhol's gnomic

LEFT: G Rietveld, *Schroder House*, Utrecht, 1923 *RIGHT:* May Events, Sorbonne Action Committee

utterances, 'I want to be a machine, machines have less problems,' turned the whole positivist and socialist ethos of the avant-garde on its head; his admission that the ultimate content of his art was money showed that the old adversarial position of the avant-garde (as the alternative to mass culture) was dead. With Warhol and the 1960s the period of the classic avant-garde as High Culture came to an end as its critical and revolutionary implications were reabsorbed by Consumer society, and the art market itself started demanding each season a 'new, improved shock of the new', or 'shock of the Neo'. One only has to recall Dwight Macdonald's notion of High Culture as avant-gardism to see how it couldn't work any more. In his 'A Theory Of Mass Culture' written in 1953, he argues:

> The significance of the Avantgarde movement (by which I mean poets such as Rimbaud, novelists such as Joyce, composers such as Stravinsky, and painters such as Picasso) is that it simply refused to compete. Rejecting Academicism – and thus, at a second remove, also Mass Culture – it made a desperate attempt to fence off some area where the serious artist could still function. It created a new compartmentalisation of culture, on the basis of an intellectual rather than a social *élite.* The attempt was remarkably successful: to it we owe almost everything that is living in the art of the last fifty or so years. In fact the High Culture of our times is pretty much identical with Avant-gardism.[6]

With the Pop artists equating High Culture with Low, kitsch with the avant-garde, the old garde could no longer be 'avant' anything: rather it could reflect and play back mass culture on a different, aesthetic level. There was no room here, in Macdonald's phrase, 'to fence off some area where the serious artist could still function' – certainly nowhere safe from the voracious art market.

Just as devastating for the classic avant-garde was the counterculture of the student movements, the protests against the Vietnam War, the activism of feminists and above all 'May 68', the *événements de mai,* which made every Art Gallery Happening, every gesture of anti-art and performance art staged within the museum context look like amateur theatricals, an encounter workshop in a retirement centre located somewhere west of Phoenix, Arizona. The critic Harold Rosenberg saw immediately the damaging implications of the May Events for those who were trying to sustain an anti-art avant-gardism and he wrote about it in *The New Yorker* so that lessons would not be entirely lost on the centre of the art world. He quotes Michel Ragon:

> During the events of May and June, 1968, culture and art no longer seemed to interest anyone. Drawing the unavoidable conclusions, the museum curators

closed their cemeteries of culture. Infected by this example, the private galleries locked their doors ... During the May Revolution, the city once again became a centre of games, it rediscovered its creative quality; there instinctively arose a socialisation of art – the great permanent theatre of the Odéon, the poster studio of the ex-Ecole des Beaux-Arts, the bloody ballets of the CRS [police] and students, the open-air demonstrations and meetings, the public poetry of wall slogans, the dramatic reports by Europe No 1 and Radio Luxembourg, the entire nation in a state of tension, intensive participation, and, in the highest sense of the word, poetry. All this meant dismissal of culture and art.

The death of art has been declared for half a century, but this statement, by the French critic Michel Ragon, forecasts what will replace it. Against art, Ragon poses the political demonstration as a superior form of creation: the public event becomes the model of aesthetic expression. Whatever the merit of this view, its effect is to discredit the anti-art artist, who in demonstrating the death of art has continued to present himself as its heir. From Mondrian to Dubuffet, this has been the century of 'the last painter', whose formulas of negation promised to defy further reduction. Painting divided by zero, however, proved to equal infinity: art might be coming to an end, but there was no end to anti-art. Now the whole game is being put into question not by works of art but by collective action that, in Ragon's phrase, simply 'dismisses' it.[7]

May 1968 produced what was called 'Modernism in the Streets', a twenty-four-hour Art Opening cum Happening which was in some ways more creative and spontaneous – at least while the food and petrol lasted – than what was occurring in the lofts of Soho. But, as we know, this radical avant-gardism of political art didn't last much more than a month, after which the art market and politics returned to their old ways. In retrospect it's obvious that the world's political, cultural and economic systems can overcome most shocks, most business cycles and recessions, accommodate most political and artistic activity directed against them; they are all much stronger than the sixties dissenters had predicted. Indeed these systems thrive on dissent, criticism, cycles of destruction and near collapse; both capitalism and its cultural world need these catalysts as their life blood.

It seems to me, and this is of course more speculation than conventional wisdom, that what is called the 'modern world' depends essentially on production and destruction cycles and that Modernism mirrors quite faithfully this eternal swing of the pendulum, this 'transvaluation of all values' in Nietzsche's terms, this annihilation of the fixed, the valued, the already achieved. The three avant-gardes I have mentioned are like an aggressive multinational out to capture new markets, never content with what it has already done, always intent on the next challenge; 'innovate or die', continually change or dry up, continually destroy in order to create. I'm told that in Foster's Hongkong Bank they changed one third of the layout and organisation last year and envisage such continual cycles of renewal in the future. If that restructuring is the reality of international finance today, it is also reflected directly in the production of art and architecture.

The negative consequences of this have been expressed very poetically by Karl Marx in *The Communist Manifesto*. Before I quote the well-known lines which have implications for the idea of the avant-garde, I should declare a debt to Marshall Berman and his important work on Modernism, called after Marx's words *All That is Solid Melts into Air*, because it is Berman who has shown us how much of a Modernist Marx really was and even, to stretch a point, how much he admired the dynamism and self-realisation of the bourgeoisie. Of course Marx was out to sink capitalism and like the typical son of the bourgeoisie hated his class, but in these attitudes of love/hate he was not unlike the typical avant-gardists of the last 160 years who have sought to overthrow their immediate predecessors, their father's generation, as they realise their own unique style and message. Karl Marx wrote of the continual revolution, or avant-gardism, of the bourgeoisie:

> The bourgeoisie cannot exist without constantly revolutionising the instruments of production, and thereby the relations of production and with them the whole relations of society. Conservation of the old modes of production in unaltered form, was, on the contrary, the first condition of existence for all earlier industrial classes. Constant revolutionising of production, uninterrupted disturbance of all social conditions, everlasting uncertainty and agitation distinguish the bourgeois epoch from all earlier ones. All fixed, fast-frozen relations, with their train of ancient and venerable prejudices and opinions, are swept away, all newly formed ones become antiquated before they can ossify. All that is solid melts into air, all that is holy is profaned and man is at last compelled to face, with sober senses, his real conditions of life, and his relations with his kind.

While this incessant destruction is partly nihilist, as Marx and Nietzsche were to recognise, it also liberates enormous potential for creativity and self-realisation – the development of each individual and society as a whole. It reminds us that Thomas Jefferson, after enjoying the self-realising potential of the American Revolution for his own generation, wanted to guarantee the 'right of revolution' for each future generation, something that hasn't quite occurred in the political world, but does exist in the capitalist economy and the art and architectural markets.

It was the architect and theorist Adolf Loos who at the turn of the century connected the notion of the bourgeoisie with the style of Modernism. Loos, like so many nineteenth-century writers, lamented the absence of an authentic culture comparable with those of the pre-industrial past. Whereas previous ages had their integral style and set of values, the present was lost in eclecticism and copying: while the aristocracy was confident about its traditions, and the peasants naturally followed slow-changing conventions, the bourgeoisie, who were wallowing about at sea, naturally produced and consumed a superior form of kitsch. Therefore, Loos concludes, if the bourgeoisie is to discover its own authentic culture and style it must do so in utility, function, efficiency – in the great, austere monuments that the captains of industry were creating, unselfconsciously, everywhere: bridges, skyscrapers, and engineering works.

This interpretation of Modernism as authentic bourgeois culture is not, as far as I know, formulated as such by Loos, but it is suggested throughout his writings. It's not an interpretation which is likely to find wide assent since the middle class have a dynamic self-image and a conspicuous dislike of the bourgeoisie as a class (one definition of the middle class is that it won't recognise itself). There are different attitudes one can take towards this evasion and loss of self-identity. The Modernist and Late-Modernist attitude is often to adopt a working-class style – a stripped and tough industrial mode that now graces every chic restaurant from Tokyo to Los Angeles. Tom Wolfe, in his amusing caricature of Modernism, *From Bauhaus to Our House*, rests his entire case on this single idea and it's surprising how much juice he can squeeze out of it: the

> ... Bauhaus style proceeded from certain firm assumptions. First, the new architecture was being created for the workers. The holiest of all goals: perfect worker housing. Second, the new architecture was to reject all things bourgeois. Since just about everyone involved, the architects as well as the Social Democratic bureaucrats, was himself 'bourgeois' in the literal, social sense of the word,

R Bofill, Abraxas Spaces, Marne-la-Vallée, 1978-82

'bourgeois' became an epithet that meant whatever you wanted it to mean. It referred to whatever you didn't like in the lives of people above the level of hod carrier. The main thing was not to be caught designing something someone could point to and say of, with a devastating sneer: 'How very bourgeois'.[8]

So we come by way of Karl Marx, Adolf Loos and Tom Wolfe, an unlikely threesome, to the conclusion that Modernism is the natural style of the bourgeoisie (even if disguised in blue jeans and I-beams) and the implication which follows, that the avant-garde which drives Modernism forward directly reflects the dynamism of capitalism, its new waves of destruction and construction, the yearly movements and 'isms' which follow each other as predictably as the seasons.

4 The Post-Avant-Garde

But this situation has changed in the last ten years, not because the bourgeoisie and capitalism have 'melted into air', but because artists, architects, critics and the public have begun to understand these dynamics and have taken up a new position, what I would call, perhaps rather predictably, the 'Post-Avant-Garde'. This new stage of the institution is obviously quite different from the previous three – the Heroic, Purist, and radical avant-gardes – because it doesn't try to conquer new territories: for the old 'shock of the new' of Duchamp, it substitutes the new 'shock of the old' of Mariani.

The territory that 'Post-Avant Garde' discovers is the entire old landscape and it is calculatedly shocking insofar as it's upsetting the taboos of the Modernists – perhaps none so important as the image of the bourgeoisie triumphant and enjoying itself. Ricardo Bofill, for instance, takes the social Utopianism of Fourier and builds those 'heroic *phalanstères*' which were meant to transform the life of the working class as 'palaces for the people': it's incongruous and blatant perhaps, but no more so than Palladio designing Villa Rotondas, and other church/temples, for patricians: or the mansions of the American South which are based on the same appropriations of religious forms.

Most Modernists and even Post-Modernists dislike these works because their classical and bourgeois imagery is so obvious, but ironically the people who live in them often find them preferable to the Modernist solutions offered at the equivalent price. The 'machines for living in' of Le Corbusier, the mass housing based on abstraction and the machine metaphor, have not been embraced by the working class, which was meant to either like them, or improve its taste and learn to love them. Post-Modern architecture, more than Post-Modernism in the other arts, is faced with such clear failures of

Robert Longo, *Master Jazz*, 1982-83

Modernism as the bi-monthly blowing-up of inoperable housing estates, and this is why it has faced the 'death of Modernism' so directly. Modernisation, the destructive/constructive forces of urban renewal and capitalism are nowhere so apparent as in the environment.

The Post-Avant-Garde thus not only acknowledges that it is bourgeois, but in so doing recognises the class-based tastes, and other tastes as well, as valid in themselves. Hence its defining eclectic style, hence its philosophy of pluralism and participation, hence its strategy – articulated by the Venturis and others including myself – of designing partly within the codes of the users

This aspect of current art and architecture is discussed by Howard Fox in the exhibition and catalogue *Avant-Garde in The Eighties* under the category of 'Community, Shared Values and Culture'. Here, as elsewhere, he is a shrewd and wily fox arguing that the present avant-garde is like that of the past because it is concerned with many of the same issues – except in opposite ways. One by one the clever Fox shows that the avant-garde of the 1980s has cancelled all the avant-garde checks of the past 160 years. It leads to the question: 'why then call it the avant-garde?' It reminds me of the definition of a reproduction: 'A reproduction is exactly like the original except in every respect'.

What, then, are the other defining characteristics of this Post-Avant-Garde? It has a new relationship with society, now an expanded audience of different tastes and cultures. Its art is perceived from many differing points of view at once, so it is inevitably ironic and multiply coded, like the work of RB Kitaj and Robert Longo, providing several discontinuous interpretations and based on multiple perspectives, different vanishing points. Narrative, local harmonies and iconology have returned, but they don't, as in the Pre-Modern past, point to a single solution, to a unified world-view or metaphysics.

In this sense Post-Modernism is still partly Modern, acknowledging the discoveries of the famous triad, the Old Testament figures Marx, Freud and Einstein as well as supplementing them with the New Testament prophets – Lévi-Strauss, Chomsky and Foucault. A common figure, or motif, in Post-Modern architecture shows this new metaphysics quite vividly and one can find parallels in art: the return to the absent centre, the centre which could not hold; the return to the circular plaza sited in the heart of the city, which is meant to give the kind of place-centredness – lacking in modern urbanism. Arata Isozaki, Michael Graves, Ricardo Bofill, Charles Moore, James Stirling – virtually every Post Modernist – provide these gathering figures, these enclosing squares, these enveloping rotondas, these centred cities – but then leave the centre blank, an indication of the void at the heart of society, or the lack of a suitable icon to place on the high altar. They provide the necessary social space for the public realm to come into existence, they celebrate and contain this space with a beautiful and permanent masonry, but then leave it up to an agnostic society to provide the final touch; the sculpture, painting, or artefact which will give it precise definition. Much Post-Modern painting shows the search for this missing centre and thereby, as in architecture, the primacy of the rhetorical figure, 'the presence of the absence'.

To conclude I would return to our military metaphor and ask how much can be salvaged. The Post-Avant-Garde comes after the previous three and so this term is quite precise in its description of placement: in fighting terms it is not the front line, but the second echelon, not the *corps d'élite*, but those who come onto the battlefield afterwards, to mop up. The great strength of the Post-Avant-Garde is to recognise what its predecessors couldn't admit to themselves; that it is a small part of the powerful middle class which is indefatigably transforming the world in ways that are simultaneously destructive and constructive. It doesn't seek to hide this self-knowledge, or pretend it can lead the working class or overcome the contradictions between life and art, the programmes and pretensions of the previous avant-gardes, and in this modest self-recognition lies its particular kind of authenticity. It is realistic about the limited role open to any self-elected elite in society: it may set standards, define what is relevant for different professions, but it doesn't march on a wide common front, as the avant-garde did in the 1920s, because there is no enemy to conquer except itself – on a huge scale. And this is the telling joke or revealing paradox of the Post-Avant-Garde: it doesn't exist as an avant-garde because it is everywhere and nowhere, dispersed throughout the world as a series of individuals, and yet still a loosely shared cultural movement of those who come 'after' the previous battles. All the avant-gardes of the past believed that humanity was going somewhere, and it was their joy and duty to discover the new land and see that people arrived there on time; the Post-Avant-Garde believes that humanity is going in several different directions at once, some of them more valid than others, and it is their duty to be guides and critics. No doubt we need a good word for this loose institution, this pressure group and set of groups that now operate in the world village, that communicates quickly and effectively with each other across continents: 'cultural elite', 'intelligentsia', 'interest group', 'leading professionals', 'clerisy' none of these work so I fall back on the partly inadequate label of my title. At least its locational metaphor is extremely accurate.

NOTES

1 Robert Hughes, 'Ten Years That Buried the Avant-Garde', *Sunday Times Magazine*, December 1979-January 1980, p 18.

2 Henri de Saint Simon, *Opinions littéraires, philosophiques et industrielles*, Paris, 1825, quoted in Donald Drew Egbert, *Social Radicalism and the Arts: Western Europe*, Alfred A Knopf, New York, 1970, p 121.

3 Ibid, pp 121-22.

4 Quoted from Renato Poggioli, *The Theory of the Avant-Garde*, Harvard University Press, Cambridge, Mass, p 9.

5 Peter Bürger, *Theory of the Avant Garde*, trans Michael Shaw, University of Minnesota Press, Minneapolis, 1984 (original text 1974, 1980).

6 Dwight Macdonald, 'A Theory of Mass Culture', *Diogenes* No 3, Summer 1953, pp 1-17, reprinted in *Mass Culture and the Popular Arts in America*, ed Bernard Rosenberg and David Manning White, The Free Press, New York, pp 59-73.

7 Harold Rosenberg, 'The Art World: Confrontation', *The New Yorker*, June 6 1970, p 54.

8 Tom Wolfe, *From Bauhaus to Our House*, Pocket Books, New York, 1981, p 17.

Reprinted from *Art & Design* Vol 3, No 7/8, Academy Editions, London, 1987.

Norman K Denzin

BLUE VELVET: POSTMODERN CONTRADICTIONS

It is a strange world, isn't it? (Sandy, in *Blue Velvet*, 1986)

There is no more fiction that life could possibly confront. (Baudrillard)[1]

The Postmodern would be that ... which searches for new presentations ... in order to impart a stronger sense of the unpresentable. (Lyotard)[2]

Introduction

The following thesis organises my argument: contemporary films like David Lynch's *Blue Velvet* (1986) may be read as cultural statements which locate within small-town America (Lumberton, USA), all the terrors and simulated realities that Lyotard and Baudrillard see operating in the late postmodern period.[3] A reading of such films should provide a deeper understanding of the kinds of men, women and biographical experiences the late-postmodern period makes available to its members.[4] Such readings should serve to further clarify the various cultural, aesthetic and sociological meanings of the term postmodern in the late 1980s. They should also contribute to further conceptual and interpretive refinements within postmodern cultural theory.[5] I shall, accordingly, first discuss the narrative structure of this film, and then turn to a reading of it which builds on the interpretive points to be developed below.[6] (This reading will build upon the reviews of the film in the popular culture press.) I will argue, after Grossberg[7] that 'the meaning of a text is always the site of a struggle'. And so it is with this film. Reviewers have been divided over its meanings. Robertson, writing in *The New York Times*, observed:

> The movie – one of the most talked about of the year, seeming to divide audiences into those who love it and find it brilliant and bizarre, and those who hate it and find it sick and disgusting – has been drawing around-the-block lines in New York for the last three weeks.[8]

Interpretive Framework

First, films like *Blue Velvet* simultaneously display the two features of postmodernist texts that Jameson has identified.[9] Namely an effacement of the boundaries between the past and the present (typically given in the forms of pastiche and parody), and a treatment of time which locates the viewing subject in a perpetual present. Second, these films, which I shall call late-postmodern nostalgia, bring the unpresentable (rotting, cut off ears, sexual violence, brutality, insanity, homosexuality, the degradation of women, sado-masochistic rituals, drug and alcohol abuse) in front of the viewer in ways that challenge the boundaries that ordinarily separate private and public life.[10] Third, the wild sexuality and violence that these films represent signify, in the Bataille sense, modes of freedom and self-expression that the late-postmodern period is both fearful of, and drawn to at the same time.[11]

Fourth, *Blue Velvet*, and the other films in this emerging genre, have been read as denigrating women.[12] These are not pro-feminist social texts. Women are treated as traditional sexual objects, and in *Blue Velvet* the recipients of sexual and physical violence. Women are contained within one of two categories: respectable, middle-class marriage, or disrespectable, occupational and sexual categories.[13] These cultural texts maintain images of the gender stratification system that are decidedly pre-postmodern.

Fifth, these films do not just return to the past in a nostalgic sense, and bring the past into the present, as Jameson suggests. They make the past the present, but they locate terror in nostalgia for the past. The signifiers of the past (ie 1950s and 1960s rock and roll music) are signs of destruction. In Lyotard's sense, these films wage a war on nostalgia.

Sixth, in so doing they identify two forms of nostalgia: the safe and the unsafe. By creating the comfortable illusion that adult middle-class life is connected to the past in an unbroken chain, these films argue that the rock and roll music of youth, if carried into adulthood, will lead to self-destruction and violence.

Seventh, by moving two versions of the past (the sacred and the profane) into the present, *Blue Velvet* pushes the boundaries of the present farther into the future where the unreal and the hyperreal[14] are always real, and not just possibilities.

Eighth, in the process, films like *Blue Velvet* expose and bring to the centre of safe society, the margins of the social.[15] These violent margins (dope fiends, sexual perverts), are now placed in small towns, next door to middle- and lower-class Americans who are attempting to live safe, respectable lives. These late-postmodern films locate violence and the simulacrum, not just in Disneyland,[16] MTV or in television commercials. They locate these phenomena within the everyday[17] and give to the simulacram a violent turn that it never had before. It is these arguments that I shall explore in this paper. I turn now to the narrative of the film.

The Narrative

Blue Velvet's narrative is straightforward.[18] It is set in Lumberton, USA. The hero, Jeffrey Beaumont, is the son of a middle-class hardware store owner who suffers a stroke as the film opens. Jeffrey, home from college for the summer, works in the store. Walking across a vacant lot he discovers a severed ear. He takes the ear to a detective and becomes involved in a mystery to discover who the ear belongs to, and how it got in the field. He is aided by the detective's sweet blond daughter, Sandy. Jeffrey and Sandy stake out a disturbed nightclub singer, Dorothy Vallens, who lives on the seventh floor of an apartment building. Jeffrey sneaks into Dorothy's apartment and hides in her closet. He is discovered by Dorothy, who commands him at knife point to strip. She begins to seduce him, but is interrupted by Frank, an obscenity-spouting, drug-inhaling, constantly drinking, local drug dealer. Jeffrey witnesses a bizarre sexual ritual between Frank and Dorothy. Dorothy is the sexual slave of Frank who has kidnapped her son and husband Don. Frank cut off Don's ear. Jeffrey is subsequently drawn into Dorothy's world of wild, sado-masochistic sexuality, and is seduced by her. At her request he beats her. Discovered by Frank, Dorothy and Jeffrey are taken to one of Frank's clubs where Frank's cronies hang out. There they confront Dean Stockwell, a 'suave', mannequin-like nightclub singer who sings 'Sand Man' to Frank and his friends. They leave the club, and go to the edge of town where Jeffrey is beaten up and left. Jeffrey makes his way back to town to Sandy's. They go to a high school party, dance, cheek-to-cheek, like lovers. Driving home they are confronted, on the steps of Sandy's house, by a naked

Dorothy, who proclaims her love to Jeffrey ('Your seed is in me'). Sandy's mother covers up Dorothy, and offers solace to a shocked Sandy. They send Dorothy off to the hospital. Jeffrey leaves for Dorothy's apartment and there he finds two dead men: Don and a corrupt policeman. Sandy's father, the detective comes, takes Jeffrey home. The film closes with Sandy and Jeffrey married, having a barbecue dinner with both sets of family relatives.

The Hegemonic/Realist Reading

How has this film been read at the hegemonic, realist level? In the following section I examine the hegemonic readings that have been given in the 'mainline' American popular culture texts.[19] *Blue Velvet's* morality story is simple. A young man takes on evil in the world. He succumbs to this evil, but is ultimately redeemed, and finds his place back within the safe, sexual confines of married middle-class life, with a beautiful young bride. This simple rite of passage story, however, locates all of the unpresentables in everyday life (cut off ears, murders, wild sexuality, alcohol and drug-related violence, sado-masochistic rituals) within a nostalgia for the past that includes a sound-track full of 1950s and 1960s rock and roll songs ('Mysteries of Love', 'In Dreams', 'Blue Velvet'). These unpresentables are seen as existing next door to and just below the surface of smalltown, homespun American life.

Blue Velvet *as Parable of Sin and Redemption*

Nearly every review read the film as a coming-of-age parable. The following statements are representative. David Ansen of *Newsweek* wrote: '*Blue Velvet* is a guilty parable of sin and redemption and true love in which Betty and Archie and Veronica archetypes are set loose in the hallucinatory world of the id.'[20] Ansen continues: '*Blue Velvet* . . . unfolds like a boys' adventure tale of the forties and fifties, but it's as if a Hardy boy has wandered into a scenario devised by the Marquis de Sade.' Pauline Kael of the *New Yorker* wrote:

> A viewer knows intuitively that this is a coming-of-age picture – that Jeffrey's discovery of this criminal sado-masochistic network has everything to do with his father's becoming an invalid and his own new status as an adult. It's as if David Lynch were saying, 'It's a frightening world out there, and – tapping his head – in here.'[21]

Blue Velvet *as Religious Art Portraying Evil*

The coming-of-age parable, connected with sin and redemption, is further elaborated by those readings which combine the sin elements within a religious text that deals with evil. James M Wall, writing in the *Christian Century*, called it the best film of 1986 because of its sensitive probing of evil as an ugly reality in life.[22] Wall calls the film a contemporary metaphor of one of Paul's letters to the church at Rome. In his letter Paul described sinfulness as a condition of all creatures. The film, Wall argues clearly communicates Paul's point that all of God's creatures are inventors of evil, disobedient to parents, foolish, faithless, heartless, and ruthless' (Romans, 1: 29-30). Still, he states that he can't recommend the film as must-seeing for everyone, because its scenes of brutality and violent sex are so realistic and ugly. Nonetheless, he compares the film to the work of the fifteenth-century artist Hieronymus Bosch. Lynch's film, like Bosch's paintings, goes to the heart of a work of art: it realistically portrays the unpresentable, so as to make its point about ultimate human values. Wall's realist reading is to be contrasted to John Simon's which sees the film as pornography.

Blue Velvet *as Pornographic Cult*
Here is Simon:

> How long has it been since an American movie has garnered a harvest of laurels like the one being heaped on a piece of mindless junk called *Blue Velvet?* . . . True pornography, which does not pretend to be anything else, has at least a shred of honesty to recommend it; *Blue Velvet*, which pretends to be art, and is taken for it by most critics, has dishonesty and stupidity as well as grossness on its conscience.[23]

Simon, contrary to Wall, sees the film's treatment of sado-masochism, voyeurism, latent homosexuality and fetishism as attempt to shock, titillate and sexually arouse the viewer. He sees Lynch's efforts to comment on small-town American mores as pretentious, and suggests that 'this trash' has been raved about because of a decline of intelligence on the part of those critics who write for sophisticated magazines and family newspapers.

Simon goes on to criticise the film's cinematography and acting (poster colours and amateurish).

Bruce Williamson in *Playboy* reads the film, not so much as pornography, but as a text that continues Lynch's reputation as a builder of cult films.[24] Focusing on the film's surreal, bizarre, hypnotic and sex-charged scenes, Williamson suggests that the film 'lapses into gratuitous violence and vulgarity' and that Lynch has gone overboard 'while testing how far a maverick movie-maker can go'.

Locating Blue Velvet *within a Film Genre*
In their attempts to give the film meaning, critics have sought to locate it within a genre. As the foregoing reactions indicate, it has been called both pornographic, and a cult film. Those who call it a cult film, speak of Lynch as a director who has produced earlier cult classics: *The Elephant Man* and *Eraserhead*.

Other critics such as Kael have called it 'gothic', a 'comedy', 'a coming-of-age' film, and 'surrealistic'.[25] Rabkin suggests that it is 1980s *film noir* with its having 'a person getting involved with something over which he has no control'.[26] Corliss locates *Blue Velvet* within the 'small-town' films genre-tradition, and reads it as an extension of the Frank Capra movies of the 1940s.[27]

The inability of critics to agree on what genre the film belongs to, speaks, in part, to its contradictory text and to its arresting sexual and erotic images. By locating a film within a genre, pre-established meanings can be brought to it, and it can be judged by the canons of the genre. Clearly Lynch's film resists classification. Hence it is read in multiple ways. But it is clear that at least some critics lean towards the negative (pornography) in their interpretations.

Lynch on Blue Velvet
What does Lynch say about his film?

> In a way this is still a fantasy film. It's like a dream of strange desires wrapped inside a mystery story. It's what could happen if you ran out of fantasy. [. . .]
> *Blue Velvet* is a trip beneath the surface of a small American town, but it's also a probe into the subconscious or a place where you face things that you don't normally face. [. . .]
> *Blue Velvet* is a very American movie. The look of it was inspired by my childhood in Spokane, Washington. Lumberton is a real name.[28]
> It's like saying that once you've discovered there are heroin addicts in the world and they're murdering people to get money, can you be happy? . . . It's a tricky

question. Real ignorance is bliss. That's what *Blue Velvet* is about.[29]
Asked to locate his film with a genre, Lynch comments: 'It's not a genre film in my mind. It's *Blue Velvet* . . .' On genre, he states, in response to the interviewer, Rabkin, who pushes him to locate the film within a category: 'You're saying it like you find a genre to fit every film into. But you don't have to obey the rules of a genre. There are many things in *Blue Velvet* that are against some sort of rules or this normal set-up'. Asked to discuss the meaning of his film, Lynch remarks:

. . . it doesn't make any difference what I say. It's like digging some guy up after he has been dead for 400 years and asking him about his book. His book is what's there, and what he's going to say about it isn't going to change it . . . I think if you're really allowed to be honest . . . then it could be understood little by little at different levels and still hold true. I think that life is like that, that you can work it down lower and lower and it will always make some kind of fantastic sense.

Lynch, like a reader-response theorist, locates the meaning of his film in the viewer's experiences with its text. For him the film is fantasy, a dream, an exploration of the subconscious, a study of what goes on just below the surface in American small towns.

Viewer Reactions
Viewers, as would be expected, have been divided in their reactions to the film. McGuigan and Huck provide a sampling of these reactions.
– in Chicago two men fainted during the film.
– Outside a Los Angeles movie house, a woman who hated it got into a fight with a stranger who loved it. They settled the dispute by going back in to see it again.
– Elsewhere people have demanded their money back.
– Viewers are shocked by certain images: a severed ear, a scene of sado-masochistic fetishism, a naked woman who's been beaten. Or they're repelled by the outrageously evil bad guy (Dennis Hopper) who violently inhales helium through a face mask.
– I felt like a pervert watching it.
– I wanted to wash as soon as I got out of the movie.
– I was thrilled. I was completely absorbed.
– When people hear I've seen it six times, they say I'm a sick person.
– Wow, I think I might have hated it.
– I don't know what was weirder – the movie or the people watching it.
– It's like Norman Rockwell meets Hieronymus Bosch.[30]

A local film critic (Champaign-Urbana, Illinois) stated: 'I love it. I watched again last night. It's got everything, mystery, film noir, Hitchcock, horror, outstanding sound-track, lighting, atmosphere, the way they changed the melodic structure of the song, "Blue Velvet", how it builds tension.'

These interpretations reflect the same contradictory reactions of the film's critics. As one viewer stated, 'You either love this film or you hate it.' Viewers connect the film's meanings back to the feelings they experienced while viewing it: perverted, dirty, sick person. I will argue below that these opposing, conflictual positions speak to contradictions and tensions in late-postmodern American life. *Blue Velvet* awakens desires and fears that expose the limits of the real and the unreal in contemporary, everyday life.

Interpreting the Hegemonic Realist Readings

The following meanings of *Blue Velvet* can now be enumerated: pornography, parable of sin and redemption, like religious art, a cult film, gothic, coming-of-age film, trash, mindless junk, *film noir*, murder-mystery, small-town film, dream film, comedy, surrealism, the most important film of 1986. The many interpretations of the film speak to and support Grossberg's position that 'the meaning of a text is always the site of a struggle'.

At the hegemonic, realist (and negotiated) levels, two clusters of consensual meanings and interpretations emerge: The film is either high cinematic art or it is trash. It is a coming-of-age film and in its portrayal of evil, violence and wild sexuality it leans towards an expansion of classic 1940s small-town films, or it is perversion and pornography, if not trash.

These two clusters of hegemonic meaning speak, of course, to tensions within the film; but more importantly, they speak to the postmodern desire to see evil, while being repulsed by it. The morally conservative readings thus reify the culture's desire to repress the sexual and violent themes of postmodern life. The morally liberal readings valorise the film's aesthetic qualities, and locate it within the classic film tradition of the 1940s, and earlier religious, symbolic art. As the film evokes these contradictory readings its cult status is elevated. Viewers continue to be drawn to it. This is so because of the opposing emotional meanings that are evoked by its symbolism and by these earlier cultural interpretations. With few exceptions the dominant cultural readings did not dwell on the violent treatment of women in the film's text.

Reading *Blue Velvet* as a Contradictory Postmodern Text

I return now to the eight interpretive points developed above: I will show how this film is pastiche, and parody, an effacement of the boundaries between the past and the present, a presentation of the unpresentable, derogatory of women, an assault on nostalgia, and a threat to safe, middle-class life. The negative and contradictory readings that postmodern texts receive can be explained, in part, by these features.

Pastiche and Parody, Past and Present

From its opening scenes, which begin with a clear blue sky, and bright, blooming red roses waving in front of a white picket fence, to a classic 1940s fire truck with a dalmatian dog on the fender, slowly gliding down a tree-lined street, and the sound track of Bobby Vinton singing 'She wore Blue Velvet' the movie's hyperrealism, signals to the reader that this film is going to be a parody of small-town, 1940s movies. Within four scenes the film shows cars from the 1950s, 1960s and 1980s moving along Lumberton's streets. Sophisticated 1980s computerised medical equipment is shown in a late-1940s hospital room, and a scene from a 1950s movie flashes across a black-and-white TV screen. High school students are shown in dress which spans three decades. This is a film which evokes, mocks, yet lends quasi-reverence for the icons of the past, while it places them in the present. The film has effaced the boundaries between the past and the present. Jeffrey, Sandy, Dorothy and Frank move through the film, as if they were dreaming.

The Unpresentable

Within three minutes Jeffrey has discovered the rotting ear in a vacant lot. The viewer is taken inside the ear. It fills the screen. Strange, roaring sounds are heard. In an even earlier scene Lynch takes the viewer into a front lawn where blades of grass 'as tall as redwood trees'[31] are teeming with big black insects. The film quickly moves from this violence in nature, to the sado-masochistic rituals between Frank and Dorothy and Dorothy and Jeffrey described earlier. Violence, and the unpresentable, Lynch seems to be suggesting, are everywhere, not only in nature, but next door to the middle-class homes in Lumberton, USA.

Women

Dorothy's degradation is used as a vehicle for Jeffrey's sexual education. Sandy's pure sexuality is contrasted to Dorothy's decadence and her sick desire to be abused. By locating women within these opposing identities and by unglamorously photographing Dorothy in her nude scenes, Lynch symbolically and simultaneously makes his film pro- and anti-woman. In so doing he parodies the 'playboy' women of soft pornography, yet sustains a traditional view of the 'pure' woman in American life. His treatment of women contains all the contradictions towards women that the decade of the 1980s has produced.

Nostalgia

Earlier I argued that *Blue Velvet* locates two forms of nostalgia, the safe and the unsafe and that the rock and roll music of the film signifies violence and destruction. Lynch parodies 1950s rock and roll in the character of Dean Stockwell, suggesting that persons risk becoming like Stockwell (and Frank) if they stay too long within this music. Rock and roll loses its youthful innocence in Lynch's film. But by framing the film with rock's sounds he appeals to a 1980s adult generation that still venerates the music of its adolescence. It is as if Lynch were saying this music is not as innocent as it appears to be. But more is involved. By locating the sexual sounds of rock at the centre of his film Lynch is arguing that the central illusions of rock and roll (sexuality, true love) have to be lived out before persons can find their true romantic and sexual identity in life.

Consider the lyrics from the Roy Orbison song 'In Dreams', which is sung in the film's most violent scenes:

A candy-coloured clown they call the sandman.

Tiptoes to my room every night just to sprinkle stardust and whisper

'Go to sleep. Everything is all right.'

In dreams I walk with you

In dreams I talk to you

In dreams you're mine all of the time

Forever in dreams.

Jeffrey lives out his wildest sexual dreams with Dorothy, only to return to Sandy at the end of the film, inside the dreams the sandman sings.

Sandy dreams too. Hers is the dream of a world that was dark 'because there weren't any robins, but then thousands of robins were set free and there was the blinding light of love'. Sandy relates this dream to Jeffrey when they are parked in front of a church, an organ plays in the background. Hearing her dream Jeffrey replies, 'You're a neat girl, Sandy'.

The film ends with a robin flying to the window sill of the family kitchen. Sandy looks up at the robin, it has a worm in its beak. Lynch closes his film, like he opened it, with nature and its violence in front of the viewer.

The Postmodern Terrain

Postmodern cultural texts, like *Blue Velvet* echo and reproduce the tensions and contradictions that define the late 1980s. These texts locate strange, eclectic, violent,

orlds in the present. They make fun of the past as they keep it alive. They
ew ways to present the unpresentable, so as to break down the barriers that
profane out of the everyday. However, they take conservative political
stances, while they valorise, and exploit the radical social margins of society. Nothing
escapes the postmodern eye. But this eye, its visions and its voices, is unrelenting in its
unwillingness to give up the past in the name of the future. The postmodern eye looks
fearfully into the future and it sees technology, uncontrolled sexual violence, universally corrupt political systems. Confronting this vision, it attempts to find safe regions of
escape in the fantasies and nostalgia of the past. Dreams are the postmodern solution to
life in the present.

More than the future is looked into. It is the everyday that has become the subject
matter of these postmodern nostalgia films. Small-town, any-town, USA is no longer
safe. The fantasies of the past have become realities in the present. These realities are
now everywhere. By showing this, these films make the global village even smaller. It is
now called Lumberton. 'The world that dreams are made of. Our town.'[32] Our town is
filled with good people like Jeffrey Beaumount and Sandy. In Lumberton their dreams,
good and bad, come true. And in this fairytale town individuals meet and confront
problems that old-fashioned law and order policemen still help them resolve.

The postmodern landscape and its people are filled with hope. Schizophrenic in their
visions, these people know that in the end everything will turn out all right. And it does.
Villains die, or are reformed. Male heroes transgress moral boundaries but come back
home to mother and father. In the end these films build their stories around individuals
and their fantasies. In so doing they keep alive the middle-class myth of the individual.
The postmodern person still confronts the world through the lens of a nineteenth- and
early twentieth-century political ideology. Perhaps this is the chief function of the 1980s
nostalgia film. As the world political system turns ever more violent and conservative,
the need for cultural texts which sustain the key elements of a conservative political
economy increases. It seems that postmodern individuals want films like *Blue Velvet* for
in them they can have their sex, their myths, their violence and their politics, all at the
same time.

NOTES

1 Jean Baudrillard, *Simulations*, Semiotext(e), Foreign Agent Press, New York, 1983, p 148.

2 Jean-François Lyotard, *The Postmodern Condition: A Report on Knowledge*, University of Minnesota Press, Minneapolis, 1983, p 81.

3 *Blue Velvet* was, according to some critics (eg McGuigan and Huck), the most talked about American film in 1986. Lynch was nominated for an academy award as best director.

4 See C Wright Mills, *The Sociological Imagination*, Oxford University Press, New York, 1959; and Richard Corliss, 'Our Town: George Bailey Meets "True, Blue and Peggy Sue"', *Film Comment* 22, November/December 1986, pp 9-17 for a discussion of this film as well as *True Stories* (1986) and *Peggy Sue Got Married* (1986); *Something Wild* (1986) could also be added to this list.

5 See Norman K Denzin, 'On Semiotics and Symbolic Interactionism', *Symbolic Interaction* 10(1), 1977, pp 1-19; Lyotard, *Postmodern Condition;* Fredric Jameson, 'Post-Modernism and Consumer Society', *The Anti-Aesthetic: Essays on Postmodern Culture*, ed Hal Foster, Bay Press, Port Townsend, Wash; Mike Featherstone, 'Lifestyle and Consumer Culture', *Theory, Culture & Society* 4(1), 1987, pp 55-70, and 'Norbert Elias and Figurational Sociology: Some Prefatory Remarks', *Theory, Culture & Society* 4(4), 1987, pp 197-211; Norbert Elias, 'The Retreat of Sociologists into the Present', *Theory, Culture & Society* 4(4), 1987, pp 223-47; and Stephen Games, 'Postmodern Disagreements', *The Times Literary Supplement* 4,413, 30 October-5 September 1987, p 1194.

6 I will, following Gledhill and Hall, develop hegemonic, negotiated and oppositional readings of this text. Elsewhere, following Gledhill, I have combined these three forms of interpretation into the realist (hegemonic and negotiated) and the subversive (oppositional) categories. I will argue against an intentionist

reading of the text, in favour of a reader-response framework, and thus contrast my readings to Lynch's meanings of his movie, which are themselves open-ended and inconclusive.

7 Lawrence Grossberg, 'Reply to the Critics', *Critical Studies in Mass Communication* 3, 1986, pp 86-95.

8 Nan Robertson, 'The All-American Guy Behind Blue Velvet', *The New York Times*, 11 October 1986, p 11.

9 Jameson, 'Postmodernism and Consumer Society'.

10 Baudrillard, *Simulations*.

11 Georges Bataille, *The Story of the Eye*, Berkeley Books, New York, 1928 and 1982.

12 Cathleen McGuigan and Janet Huck, 'Black and Blue Is Beautiful? Review of *Blue Velvet*', *Newsweek* 108, 27 October 1987, pp 65-67.

13 Christine Gledhill, 'Klute: Part 1: A Contemporary Film Noir and Feminist Criticism', *Women in Film Noir*, British Film Institute, ed Ann Kaplan, London, 1978.

14 Baudrillard, *Simulations*.

15 See Stuart Hall, 'History, Politics and Post-Modernism: Stuart Hall and Cultural Studies', Interview with Lawrence Grossberg, *Journal of Communication Inquiry* 10, Summer 1986, pp 61-77.

16 Baudrillard, *Simulations*.

17 Featherstone, 'Norbert Elias and Figurational Sociology', pp 197-211.

18 David Ansen, 'Stranger Than Paradise', review of *Blue Velvet, Newsweek* 108, September 15, 1986, p 69.

19 These texts include *Newsweek, The New Yorker, The New York Times, New York, Christian Century, Dissent, Fangoria, National Review, Playboy* and the more specialised cinema text, *Film Comment*.

20 Ansen, 'Stranger than Paradise'.

21 Pauline Kael, 'Current Cinema: Out There and In Here: Review of *Blue Velvet*', *The New Yorker* 52, 22 September 1986, pp 99-103.

22 John M Wall, 'The Best Film of 1986: Probing The Depths of Evil', *Christian Century* 60, 7-14 January 1986, pp 7-9.

23 John Simon, 'Neat Trick', *National Review* 38, 7 November 1986, pp 54-6.

24 Bruce Williamson, 'Movies: Review of *Blue Velvet*', *Playboy* 37, December 1986, p 25.

25 Kael, 'Current Cinema'.

26 William Rabkin, 'Deciphering *Blue Velvet*: Interview with David Lynch', *Fangoria* 58, October 1986, p 52-6.

27 Corliss, 'Our Town'.

28 David Lynch in David Chute, 'Out to Lynch', *Film Comment* 22, September/October 1986, pp 32-5.

29 David Lynch in Rabkin, 'Deciphering *Blue Velvet*'.

30 McGuigan and Huck, 'Black and Blue is Beautiful'.

31 Kael, 'Current Cinema'.

32 Corliss, 'Our Town'.

From *Theory, Culture and Society*, Vol 5, Nos 2-3, June 1988, published by Sage Publications Ltd, London, in association with Teesside Polytechnic.

Heinrich Klotz
POSTMODERN ARCHITECTURE

Architecture as a Vehicle of Meaning

Even though the conflict continues and the defenders of modern and postmodern architecture still confront each other as if the final decision is yet to come, history has already decided. A new kind of architecture prevails today, one that differs fundamentally from Das Neue Bauen of the 1920s. Almost every new architectural idea and every creative architectural form developed since the mid 1970s has stood in opposition to the established authority of the Modern Movement.

Nevertheless, as we begin to be surrounded by architecture that seeks validation by modelling itself on the past and revives forms we had disposed of long ago, we ask ourselves what the states of consciousness might be on which such reactions are founded. Postmodernism then appears to us to be a 'premodernism', a return to a state antecedent to the Enlightenment. Hence we find ourselves asking whether we have exchanged progress for regression.

It seems that society, caught as it is in ecological crises, withdraws its trust in progress by drawing back in discouragement from the threshold of the new, seeking instead to recapture the old and to derive security from the past. Doubting the validity of progress seems to correspond to a cultural reversion to historically dated content. Does the assertion of the impossibility of an avant-garde not run parallel to the renunciation of the utopian potential of design? By returning to axial symmetry, are we not seeking an order that ultimately delivers not security but new control and oppression? By endorsing an intimidating neo-monumentalism, do we not surrender the humanness of an environment shaped for ease and transparency; do we not relinquish democratic architecture's openness to experience in favour of new, muscular, boastful posturings of power?

The experiences of the past that are manifest in certain architectural forms are evidently to be permitted to reclaim validity and to distract us from the 'project of modernism',[1] which has held progress to be one of its essential preconditions.

Ever since the concept of postmodernism began to spread, recent historical experience seems to have been divided into a modernism just recently passed and a postmodernism immediately following it – into a progressive past and a reactionary present. The moment when trees are planted in rows like marching soldiers and columns fall in step to make up colonnades, when houses are built embodying hierarchy and symmetrically repeating all their features as if in self-defence, when capitals, cornices, and ornaments extend decoratively over the surfaces and a horror vacui seems to break out where sobriety and economy had reigned – then the great backward fall into the historical furnishings and nostalgic moods of an existence among stage props is complete. Along with the advent of postmodernism comes the demise of truth. All at once everything seems lost – modern architecture, humanity, democracy, and morals. For what is disclosed to us in the projects of today's architecture but the precarious state of a society one ought to fear, because it fears the future? Hence it is fully understandable why the latest developments in architecture are so hotly debated: It is crucial to unmask the defeatists and the reactionaries, because the issue at stake is the defence of progress implied by progressive building technology and modern construction methods and implying the ideologies vested in architecture. The defence of progress in architecture is, by the same token, the defence of the development of society. The existence of building as a vehicle of liberal values is in jeopardy! Isn't it?

At this point, doubts arise in regard to the calamitous conditions of architecture as described above. Could all that have sprung up not in a rebound from the project of modern architecture but as its visionary corrective? Hasn't the time come for drastic measures to halt modern architecture's lapse into rampant functionalism and urban erosion, and to summon back its slipping sense of the responsibility of architecture to its proper niveau? In line with Jürgen Habermas' injunction to 'imperturbably restate and critically continue the tradition of modernism instead of joining the dominant movements of today in their escape from it',[2] one asks whether the critique of modernism has not been accomplished. Isn't postmodernism the critique of modernism; isn't it a continuation of modernism by new but not entirely different means?

The main question implicit in this view is whether in postmodernism the positive qualities of modernism continue to be active (and, conversely, whether postmodern qualities can be judged progressive). One of the possible answers is based on the evaluation of form. Accordingly, we have to inquire whether the essence of modernism and the characteristics of the so-called escape movements have been correctly described in terms of the forms involved. To be precise, we have to discover if the meanings we customarily ascribe to these forms are inexorably fixed to a definite expressive content and to a definite value. Is axiality always an architectural means of coercion by the dictates of power? Is symmetry always a means of order in the service of hierarchy? Does the use of columns always stand for an escape into nostalgia? Do craftsmanship and conventional materials always imply a throwback, in contrast with the progressive stance of the building industry? And, viewed in the opposite way, is the open ground plan always democratic? Are all building procedures that utilise modern materials (such as glass and steel) modern? Do forms have fixed symbolic contents to be associated with them for all time to come?

Clearly, the argument is focused not on the individual forms but on their meaning. In the controversy between modernism and postmodernism, the assumption that a particular form stands for a specific content – that it indicates something beyond its own factual existence – is held to be self-evident.

The very fact that we speak again of the meanings of architecture is the most decisive change in the architectural debate since 1945. For many decades we were indifferent to the meanings of architectural forms, either because we were totally opposed to them or because we could afford to ignore them. The structural aspects of a building and the functional values in terms of cost economisation and optimisation of use were the main objects of interest. The fact that a form could mean one thing or another was not a topic for official discussions, and it remained outside the range of debatable questions for architectural theory. To consciously consider the form of architecture a vehicle of meaning was an exceptional thing to do.[3] In view of the new interest in form, the history of contemporary architecture can be regarded as a history of its decisions in respect to form and its latent or open meanings and its unintended or intended contents and symbolisations.

Whether architects like it or not, a building acts as a vehicle of meaning even if it is supposed to be meaningless. One way or another, it presents a visual aspect. Even the vulgar postwar functionalism that cut the characteristic features of a building to a minimum produced buildings that, as they entered one's visual field, acquired a meaning: an apparently neutral and monotonous uniformity.

In contrast to the kind of architecture that consciously renounced any symbolic effect since by its own definition in terms of functional efficiency any consideration of meaning was too much, the new trends in architecture are predominantly marked by attempts to draw attention to other contents besides the functional qualities of a building – to contents referring to nonarchitectural as well as architectural contexts.

Taking into account the conscious inclusion of new contents into architecture today, one might wish that the criticism directed against so-called postmodernism were to be applied to modernism. If done, this would reveal that the buildings built in observance of orthodox modernism – even those being built today in a kind of brave adherence to enlightenment and progressiveness – suddenly seem empty when they are measured against the new possibilities of architectural symbolisation. Have the formal qualities associated with the International Style – the white walls, the elegant framework of steel and glass, the loosely arranged open ground plan, the transparency of the structure – not become hopelessly exhausted and vapid?

Yet attempts were made to counteract the lingering after-effects of the reductive geometry of modernism by enriching it. The low functionalism was stretched by high formal ambitions. This led first to giant posturings of pure geometry, and then to the solemnisation of buildings as baroque sculptures. These attempts were grounded in the fundamental tenets of modernism, and for this reason interest had to be attracted by other means. The result was interesting forms devoid of meaning, such as Paul Rudolph's mountains of concrete, the restless circular composition of the UN Centre in Vienna, and the Landtag building in Düsseldorf.

Assuming that there exist subliminal connections between the separate arts, we can say that many of today's 'modern' buildings produce a familiar effect equivalent to that of the 'abstract' paintings and sculptures of the late 1950s.

Around 1960 there occurred analogous changes in painting and architecture. In painting, after 'Great Abstraction', after Abstract Expressionism, Tachism, and Informel, an abrupt shift was brought about by Pop Art. Everyday life, consumerism, and so-called subcultures were included among the acceptable contents of art, and it was again legitimate to take into account the reality of the external world. Some architects turned away from geometry as a 'Great Abstraction' and devoted their attention to other contents.

Pop Art, by halting the expansion of abstraction, created a way out of the 'nonobjective' mode and made the appreciation of pure form seem an antiquated cult of aestheticism. All of a sudden the level of art appreciation changed. Gone were the 'disinterested contemplative enjoyment' and the selfsufficient universe of colour as the prevalent concerns of painting; a giant confrontation with the hitherto repressed concreteness of the everyday world took their place. Since then, with the arrival of photographic realism, the recognition of realistic trends in painting, and the New Expressionism of the 'New Wild Painters' and the 'arte cifra', the foreground of the art scene has been occupied by 'representational' trends.

However, buildings are still built on the pretence that the aesthetic of pure form continues to deserve credibility. The nonobjective, pure composition of volumes in the old conservative 'modernism' relies even now on an appreciation in the spirit of and in the terms of abstraction. Yet what we actually see is the 'purely interesting'. The product of the aesthetic of 'purity', of free composition and of the calculations of geometry is: free gesture, empty gesturing!

Thus the efforts in architecture to save modernism on the basis of abstraction have failed.

The Concept of Postmodernism (I)

Long before Charles Jencks named the new tendencies in architecture, a fundamental change had become apparent. The signals came not only from buildings but also from treatises in which architects declared their defection from the dogmas of modernism. Robert Venturi's *Complexity and Contradiction in Architecture* – written in 1962, published by the Museum of Modern Art in 1966, and still making its effects felt today – was the first of these treatises. In the preface, Vincent Scully spoke of something new, something 'hard to see', something 'hard to write about', something 'graceless and inarticulate as only the new can be', and proclaimed Complexity and Contradiction 'the most important writing in the making of architecture since Le Corbusier's *Vers une architecture*.'

Even before the publication of Venturi's book, Christian Norberg-Schulz had tried to establish a broad overview of a new concept of architecture in his *Intentions in Architecture* (Oslo, 1963). 'Only through cultural symbolism', he wrote, 'can architecture show that the everyday has a meaning beyond the immediate situation and a share in the cultural and historical continuum.'

In 1966 – the year in which *Complexity and Contradiction* appeared – Aldo Rossi published his book *L'Architettura della Città*, in which he talked of 'the city as a work of art', introduced his concept of typology, and strove to restore the definitive role of the monumental building.

The year 1968 brought Venturi's 'A Bill Ding' and 'Board Involving Movies, Relics, and Space' (*Architectural Forum*, April, pp 74-76), in which he spoke of his own design for the Football Hall of Fame as 'a shed with ornament on it'.

Meaning in Architecture, edited by Jencks and George Baird and published in London in 1969, was another important contribution to the international architectural discussion. It renewed the discussion of semiology in architecture, and it recalled that as early as 1959 Gillo Dorfles had proposed that architecture be understood as a 'sign system'.

During the first half of the 1970s, the architecture symposia of the International Design Centre in Berlin (organised by the present author) were important events on the European scene. It was at one of these meetings, in 1974, that Venturi, Denise Scott Brown, and Aldo Rossi presented their seminal treatises – 'Functionalism: Yes, but . . .' (Venturi and Scott Brown) and 'Hypotheses of My Work' (Rossi). It was in the course of these symposia that I first attempted to distinguish 'classical modernism' from latter-day 'economic functionalism', and in connection with this I spoke of a 'turn', of the 'sketch of a new environment that would be determined not by an architecture of mere utility but rather by an architecture of metaphor, covering content with fantasy' (*Werk-Archithese* 64, March 1977, p 3). In the article just cited – published in the same year as Jencks' book – I also remarked that the 1974 symposium might well have been titled 'Architecture Before and After Functionalism': today. I believe that the elucidation of the concept of postmodernism would not have been so chaotic and difficult had it been discussed in more restrained terms.

Jencks had the audacity to articulate the criticism at the level of fundamental principles, and thus to set in question the self-understanding of an entire epoch. Nonetheless, he coaxed the philosophers out of their reticence with respect to architecture, and particularly with respect to what Habermas called the 'project of modernism'.

As misleading as the concept of postmodernism may be, at the present we do not have a better one to put in its place. Jencks' idea[4] of borrowing this concept from literary criticism (where it had acquired a negative connotation) and converting it to a positive use in architectural theory was a daring enterprise. In his 1970 treatise on postmodernism, Jost Hermand unmasked all conceivable varieties of modern consumer culture as forces of a reactionary anti-modern (for Hermand, a 'postmodern'[5]) conformism. In accordance with this pejorative tradition, the concept has to be associated in architectural theory with notions of a comfortable escapism to the scene of popular distractions where the garish colours of lollipop culture are joined to the fake patina of the nostalgia products of historicism.

As hopeless as it might seem to give the term *postmodernism* something like pristine innocence and to try to read into it nothing more than the designation of a historical phase as a temporal sequel of modern architecture, there is an argument for keeping the term in use: It has become internationally accepted. In architectural criticism, *postmodern* is used mainly to refer to historicist architecture that does not go beyond a nostalgic replication of the past. The polemical use of the term to censure all kinds of historicist architecture deserves disapproval, for even the most vehement opponent of postmodernism ought to be aware that there are ways of relating to the history of architecture that are more than a nostalgic reprise of the past. The critique of postmodernism becomes more pointed but also more simplistic when turned into a critique of nostalgia. Used polemically, the concept is at its narrowest.

I would like to widen *postmodernism*'s range of meaning in the sense indicated earlier on, and to regard as postmodern buildings that do not slavishly follow the early versions of modernism. Whenever present-day architecture observes other laws in addition to functional aptness and maximum simplicity of basic forms, whenever it moves away from abstraction and tends toward representational objectivisation, I call it postmodern. By this I mean that in such a case architecture does not seek its final end in itself, in pure three-dimensional realisation of volumetric problems, but that it can become a means for the visual realisation of contents of a different, of a manifold nature. Then, architecture becomes a work of the visible emergence of beauty and does not remain merely a means subservient to practical ends.

Hence, I propose to use the word postmodernism in its literal sense: as primarily a designation of a break of continuity, pinpointing the fact that the tradition of the Modern Movement in architecture has ceased to be a continuum. On the other hand, I insist that with the advent of postmodernism architecture was not simply severed from modernism, Charles Jencks has arrived at a similar view, even though he has not realised that with the slogan calling for a sequel to modernism, the end of modernism was proclaimed.

Yet under the present circumstances, and at this stage in the development of architectural theory, one ought to be allowed to stress to a lesser degree the characteristic features of historical continuity and to elaborate all the more the extent of the historical changes taking place. It is important not to succumb any longer to the illusion of still being able to draw from modernism as from a recent and inexhaustible source. Modern architecture has grown old.

Nonetheless, one would be over-reacting if, in the wake of the excesses of functionalism, one were to dismiss modernism altogether. Some of its fundamental insights, as well as some of its methods of building, continue to be valid. Above all, one must keep in mind that the formal vocabulary of modernism can, under certain circumstances, undergo a rejuvenation and be used as unconventionally as the stylistic features made available by historicism.[6] For this reason, I find it an ill-advised move on the part of Jencks, after introducing the problematic concept of postmodernism, to add to it that of 'late modernism',[7] as if it were necessary to subdivide architecture into a postmodernism that has a future and a 'late modernism' that is presumably close to its demise. Doubtless there exist in this analysis mutually exclusive positions between modernism and postmodernism. But there are also correspondences and complementary features, which do not permit us to go on using 'post' and 'late' as parameters delimiting closed worlds that offer us only a choice of different sets of examples. Lately the formal vocabularies are getting detached from their ideological referents and are beginning to be used side by side or to be mixed. For example, James Stirling saturated the historicised building structure of the Stuttgart Staatsgalerie to such a degree with 'high-tech' elements that the total effect of a neoclassical architectural whole does not even have a chance of asserting itself. Then there is Adolfo Natalini, who in his recent office and factory buildings has used the steel framework as a paradigmatic modern building core along with a historicised outer mantle of bricks.[8] As an alternative to high-rise buildings done entirely in the 'high-tech' vocabulary, Helmuth Jahn proposes a historicised version of this building type.

Thus, the possibility of viewing different approaches to contemporary architecture as mutually exclusive 'stylistic attitudes' is decreasing markedly, while 'modern' architecture is seen as equivalent to technically constructivist forms and postmodern architecture as equivalent to historicising forms. In the end, what is decisive is the intentions and the successes of the different vocabularies. Historicising forms can be applied superficially and decoratively (that is, in a nostalgic manner), just as they can be revitalised through a spirited new reinterpretation. The fact that a bad eclectic uses historical material does not suffice to make him a notable architect of postmodernism. On the other hand, if a 'modernist' is capable of employing modern architecture's repertory of forms in a new and significant way and thereby revitalising it – as is Ludwig Leo, for one – then it is nonsensical to ignore him in the name of a merely historicised postmodernism. All that deserves our interest is the high quality of the individual building, which is predicated on the architect's ability to breathe new life into the vocabularies he encounters, be they modernist or historicised. I call the method from which this vitalisation process draws its potential force the *fictionalisation* of architecture.

My primary aim has not been to compile the different stylistic trends present in today's architecture and to give them more or less promising names, but to provide evidence for the dominant principle determining contemporary architecture's positive achievements. This guiding principle can be seen at work where the final shape of a building is consciously tied to the recapturing of content that can become the 'narrative substance' of a building's total form and its subsidiary forms. This does not mean that architecture has to serve the purposes of illustration. The final goal is to liberate architecture from the muteness of 'pure forms' and from the clamour of ostentatious constructions in order that a building might again become an occasion for a creative effort, attuned not only to facts and utilisation programmes but also to poetic ideas and to the handling of subject matter on an epic scale. Then the results will no longer be repositories of function and miracles of construction, but renderings of symbolic contents and pictorial themes – aesthetic fictions which do not remain abstract 'pure forms' but which emerge into view as concrete objectivisations to be multisensorially apperceived.[9]

These reflections on the concept of postmodernism necessarily lead to an equally rigorous examination of the concept of modernism. To see more precisely what contrasts and differences separate modernism and postmodernism, I shall first attempt a brief survey of the history of modern architecture in its several stages. This will also

Robert Venturi, Vanna Venturi House, Chestnut Hill, Pennsylvania, 1962, rear view

reveal how manifold and how partly contradictory is the historical complex labelled 'modern architecture'.

The Concept of Postmodernism (II)

I soon made the mistake of a pure radical abstraction when I developed the conception of a certain work of architecture out of its next trivial purpose alone and out of the construction. What resulted in this case was something dry and rigid that lacked freedom and excluded entirely two essential elements, the historical and the poetical. (Karl Friedrich Schinkel)

There are upheavals in history that take place behind the scenes. It often requires the judgment of the historian to mark the threshold of an epoch – the point at which one thing emerged from another. Only after the event do we become conscious that something has changed, and that there are good reasons for recognising the upheaval as a historical turning point.

The transition from modernism to postmodernism was an almost smooth one, like the transition between the early and the high Renaissance; by no means did all the standards or the priorities change. The protest against modernism is not a determinate and rigid 'No'; rather, it is a 'Yes, but'.[10] This does not diminish the fact that some hard truths were advanced against the guiding notions and the established tradition of modern architecture. Some of the articles of faith of Das Neue Bauen were actually turned upside down. However, Mies and Le Corbusier have not been simply eliminated, even if some 'radical eclecticists' take the liberty of labelling modernism an unfortunate incident of history.

On the other hand, we cannot shut our eyes and, together with the defenders of modernism, take up a sort of radical evocation of modernity. Effective remedies have indeed been advanced against the one-sided dogmaticism of modernism, and these remedies serve as substantial historical evidence of an epochal change. The radical change occurred around 1960. Around 1980, the new reality of postmodern architecture became common knowledge. Here we are faced, as a matter of general principle, with the question whether it is still permissible to extend a concept that covers everything over a historical process whose most characteristic trait is that it is spread out in many directions and is determined by the most divergent tendencies.

At first glance we note two main movements, which have taken on seemingly irreconcilable positions in their programmatic struggle: 'high tech' architecture (which is based predominantly on the expressive qualities of technological procedures and

LEFT: Hans Hollein, Austrian Travel Bureau, Vienna, Austria, 1978. *RIGHT:* Charles Moore, Piazza d'Italia, New Orleans, 1976-79

construction, and which offers the Olympic Stadium in Munich, the Expo Pavilion in Osaka, and the Pompidou Centre in Paris as its best-known examples) and postmodern architecture (which takes into account the history of architecture and refers to the given factors of the whole cultural setting). The latter wants again to be an art, and its most telling renditions are Robert Venturi's 'My Mother's House' and Guild House, Charles Moore's Kresge College and Piazza d'Italia, James Stirling's Staatsgalerie in Stuttgart, Aldo Rossi's cemetery in Modena, and OM Ungers' designs for Enschede and for the Berlin museums.

However, when we look at the different trends of contemporary architecture in terms of the theory of architecture, it becomes obvious that the lines of demarcation run differently than the superficial distinctions in terms of style would have us believe.

Even with a kind of building that forgoes the use of historicising forms, the characteristic objective of postmodernism – to create an architecture of 'narrative contents' – can be achieved. To the bare realisation of the demands of utility are added 'border-violating' contents, which lift architecture out of its primary subservience to function and which use it as a medium extending beyond functionality and serving to represent an 'imaginary world' – that is, as a means of fiction. The contents of postmodernism can refer to a great variety of things. They can indeed create 'a beautiful world of appearances' that distracts one from the bare factuality of architecture as a protective cover and that deflects one's attention to the completely different realms of environment as a narrative representation.

Fiction is not achieved by merely combining successfully some geometric forms. Only after a building is no longer bound up solely with itself, only when the stereometric autonomy of perfect volumetric wholes is destroyed and allusions and associations are permitted that go beyond the building itself, is there a possibility for creating an architectonic fiction. A Palladian villa is a nearly perfect architectural fiction not only because it has perfect dimensions and proportions, but also because it contains an abundance of witty allusions to antiquity that bespeak the sophisticated needs of its users; not only because it does not strive to be only functionally adequate for the routines of daily life, but also because it elevates life to the plane of fiction and provides a background for staging it to the fullest.

Geometry *per se* is, at best, 'interesting'. Only the contents connected to geometry make the fictional a possibility. Bruno Taut's interpretation of Das Neue Bauen as a world of lightness and transparency pitched against the ponderousness of 'seriousism' was such a fiction, containing not only a good dose of social critique but also an equal dose of poetry. As soon as the geometry of modern architecture was deprived of any fictional aspect and only the pure objectivity of functionalism was left, the 'white bodies under the light' revealed the meaninglessness of bare facts. The underlying notion of a modernity connected with simple primary forms withered away with each white block and each rectangular glass building that was added to the city.

To the question of why he wanted to 'get away from the slickness of the International Style', Charles Moore replied that this style was not 'a very useful, interesting, meaningful, worthwhile description of what's going on.'[11] He continued: 'A building itself has the power, by having been built right or wrong or mute or noisy, to be what it wants to be, to say what it wants to say, which starts us looking at buildings for what they're saying rather than just accepting their pure existence in the Corbusian manner. This narrative function that we have been talking about is all of these things together, the building being as descriptive as it can, about what is interesting about it – either the way it's built or the way people use it; the message is either shouting, or being quiet, or hiding, . . . but letting you know what is going on.'[12]

In the realm of architecture, the fictional is always only one aspect of the total whole. A building is not purely a work of art, and it can never come out as independently as a novel or a painting. Architecture is directly connected to the everyday procedures of human life, and it is more subject to the utility and profit considerations of economics than any other art. But under the dominance of functionalism the fictional element was banished from architecture, and the only thing left was the technique of building. A Gothic cathedral, which according to Abbot Suger was an earthly likeness of the City of Heaven and the reflection of God's light on human reality, would never have been built under the conditions of functionalism, which declared the imitative and representational character of architecture – the building as an invented place, an artistic fiction – a fairy tale for children that could not claim any validity among sober adults.

Today we are in the process of liberating architecture from the abstraction of pure utility and restoring to it the potential of making invented places possible again.

Karl Friedrich Schinkel addressed the conflict that still plagues us at the beginning of the nineteenth century. He spoke of 'radical abstraction', which today we recognise as the functionalist formula by which a building is developed 'out of its next trivial purpose along and out of the construction'. In his view, the result of this abstraction was 'something dry, rigid, and lacking freedom'. Today we realise that the architecture of functionalism, which was made from the same recipe, is for the most part equally dry, rigid, and unfree.

The two elements in which Schinkel sought liberation are the answers to 'radical abstraction' in our times: the historical and the poetical. The historical enriches the spectrum of possible references and the wealth of historicising stylistic means, in order that the poetical may emerge. The poetical is the power of the imagination to picture desirable places; it is the generative power of fiction going beyond mere purpose.

Fiction limits abstraction because it confronts the nonobjective directive of mere utility with the contents of the imagination. Schinkel's statement reduces the maxims of a modern architecture limited to functionalism and the injunctions of postmodern architecture to a common denominator. He realised that an architecture that draws its explicit visual character only from trivial purpose and from construction does not attain a satisfactory result. His statement contains a definition of architecture that is also the definition of postmodern architecture. This leads us to the question of how various people have defined postmodernism.

Charles Jencks has emphasised stylistic pluralism as the essential feature of postmodern architecture. From this insight he draws the conclusion that the individual architect must embrace a 'radical eclecticism' – must submit to any change of style that the client desires. What may be valid as a description of a total scene does not have to be an imperative for the individual artist. A certain commitment to one's own idiom should continue to be possible. Nevertheless, it is a fact that no stylistic dogmas are in force any longer. The simultaneous presence of one style next to another, with all their glaring differences, is almost the necessary credential of a highly advanced architectural culture, especially in the United States.

Correspondingly, Achille Bonito Oliva cited the change of style as the most decisive feature of the 'trans-avant-garde':

> The cultural epoch in which the younger generation is living is that of the trans-avant-garde, which views language as a tool of change, as a path of moving from one work to the next, from one style to the next. The avant-garde, in all its variations since the Second World War, developed in the sense of a linguistic Darwinism rooted in the great movements of the early twentieth century. The trans-avant-garde, however, operates outside these limits; it follows a nomadic basic inclination that advocates the interchangeability of all languages of the past. ... The trans-avant-garde overcomes the idea of progress in art, which was aimed entirely at conceptual abstraction. It brings into consideration that the linear development of earlier art can be viewed as one of many different possibilities, and it directs its attention even to languages that had been rejected earlier.[13]

Oliva too speaks of abstraction as the main trend of modernism in the arts. The 'non-objective' in painting has its parallel in the abstraction of the primary forms in architecture, which were supposed to represent nothing but themselves. References to contents other than the stereometry of basic forms, signalled by symbolism or ornamentation, were viewed as blemishes, as antiquated tarnishings of the purity of architectural form.

In contrast, postmodern architecture is characterised by the fact that the previously revoked stylistic means regain their validity, but that these stylistic vocabularies are employed to achieve as a particular goal an architecture which is no longer abstract but which puts its arguments across in a representational manner. The pluralism of styles is not in itself an explanation, but it provides the precondition for the development of architecture's capacity to speak in order to make aesthetic fiction possible. The 'styles' provide the vocabulary needed to substantiate an architectural narrative. They are the repository of forms, the potential raw material of architectonic representation. This is why the pluralism of styles is not the most appropriate formulation of postmodernism. What does adequately define postmodernism is, rather, the insistence of the fictional character of architecture – which is diametrically opposed to the abstractness of modern architecture. Because this key notion exists, and because the fictional concretisation of architecture provides the actual impetus of postmodern building, the variety of the available styles is not at the core of the decisions to be made. Vocabularies can change, and they can adequately serve widely divergent forms of representation and a wide variety of contents, as long as they are used as fictional narrative terms and thus are contributing significance and meanings. I am by no means rehashing here the question asked by Baron Hübsch at the beginning of the nineteenth century: 'In what style should we build?' What is at question is: Which stylistic means are adequate for the visual articulation of a given content? What is at stake is not the choice of what stylistic dogma to restore (say, Gothic or Renaissance) but the decision whether architecture is to remain abstract or whether epic devices will again be recognised as legitimate

...gredients of an architectural statement. If the latter alternative should become a reality, then the wide range of stylistic means forming the material of fiction automatically suggests itself. Again, one is not saying much when one says that stylistic pluralism is the characteristic feature of postmodernism. We need, rather, to see it as a consequence of the new impetus aimed towards representation and directly opposed to abstraction.

Examples: Moore, Hollein, Peichl

The most telling example of postmodern architecture is Charles Moore's Piazza d'Italia in New Orleans, not because the historical forms of the classic orders were used in an almost excessive profusion, but because a fiction was created in a direct way.

The Piazza d'Italia was intended to become the centre of a predominantly Italian section of New Orleans where the Italo-American Institute is located. The immediate area – in fact, the entire part of the city – was in need of renovation and was dominated by large modern edifices. There was nothing alluring or inviting about the area and little to make one linger.

Moore created a totally new site by cutting into the space intended for a projected building (never executed).[14] The site is circular. Groups of columns provide a backdrop for a topographic map of Italy, which juts out from the middle of a large arcade and reaches out into the centre of the concentric circles of the piazza, with a fountain as the Mediterranean. (Sicily has the central position because most of the residents of the neighbourhood are Sicilian.) The piazza wall was supposed to be the purely decorative part of the projected building, against whose modern forms, smooth white facade, and simple square window openings its breathtakingly classical decorum was to contrast sharply.

All the classical orders are present: Doric, Tuscan, Ionian, Corinthian, and Composite. Together they provide the 'boot' of Italy with a complete cultural background and a reminiscence of the heroic columnar orders of Italian architectural facades. However, classical greatness is evoked here with touches of humour and commented on with irony. There are collars of neon-light tubing under the capitals of the central arcade. Other 'columns' are actually curved sheets of steel, with rivulets of water creating the effect of fluting. The Tuscan columns next to these 'Doric columns' are made of stainless steel and are 'cut open' to reveal marble. Their metopes are 'wetopes', with tiny fountains.

On this 'narrative' plane, the classical columnar orders are reinterpreted through the playful divestment of their monumental dignity. Yet, at the same time, the architraves are inscribed with words of dedication and with the title *Fons Sancti Josephi* (Fountain of Saint Joseph), and the architect's face is immortalised in a water-spouting mask in the spandrel.

The Piazza d'Italia was created solely for the purpose of fiction. The collonade fragments of this stage of memory do not want to be serious, perfect architecture. Rather, they want to be the vocabulary of a narrative: architecture between the Old World and the New, between wit and seriousness, between perfection and fragmentation, between historical exactness and humorous alienation. The Piazza risks making the poetical statement 'Here is Italy!' only to add immediately, with a sad smile, 'Italy is not here'.

Hans Hollein's Österreichisches Verkehrsbüro (Austrian Travel Bureau) was built at about the same time as the Piazza d'Italia. Behind the nondescript front of an older building, under a glass roof, Hollein composed an environment that recounts tales of travels in many different ways and even prepares people for travel just as a stage prepares one for a play or an opera. Immediately after entering the travel bureau, one finds oneself before the brass stems of metal palm trees. Against the wall, marble building stones rise in a pyramidal shape that extends beyond the room into infinity. Amid the palms stands the stump of a classical column, in which a shaft of stainless steel is imbedded. This sets one's perceptions oscillating between the longing for classical antiquity and the contemporary myth of technology. Similarly, the white neon tubes on the ceiling above the palms and the column counter the nostalgia for faraway times with the cool objectivity of the present. A plastic Austrian flag appears to be ruffled by a stiff breeze. There is an actual proscenium, with a Serlio stage set – here one buys theatre and opera tickets. On the opposite side, on the same axis, is a pavilion with a golden baldachin roof used in *The Abduction from the Seraglio*. At the far end of the hall, the plot of distant travel thickens. Two eagles soar against a pastel blue sky delicately veiled by whispy clouds: Air travel! In front of the painted sky and behind the counter stands an easel with a piece of canvas representing the same pastel blue sky – a picture within a picture that ironically points out the limits of the larger fiction at work here: the fiction of a narrative environment. The space is the space of the theatre stage, and a visitor moves in it as if playing a part in a play, as if participating in a wider fiction. Architecture blends with images, travel metaphors, and symbols of the theatre. The space is only a frame; it is a plain hall in which a fictional world has been brought into existence that creates an almost irresistible tension between the materialisation and the shattering of an illusion, and that makes architecture the setting of experience. Here the question arises: What would a travel agency built in the manner of the 'Modern Movement', or of functionalism, be like? Surely, it would be like the agencies one sees all over the world: just four walls plastered with travel posters. The difference is what separates postmodern from modern architecture.

Fiction is also at work in Gustav Peichl's water-purification plant at Berlin-Tegel, which brings to life the steamship metaphor – the old favourite of modern architecture. This 'steamship on land' derives from the technomechanical forms of the purification plant the impulse for a highly suggestive symbolism of a steamship taking off into the future. But this fiction, having been developed to the full in the 1920s and having once made a legitimate architectural content out of overconfident promises about the future, no longer has much of an effect. Today the trust in the symbolism of technical forms is well-nigh exhausted. It seems as if the modern continues to seek self-validation in its former success as 'machine-modernism'. But mere repetition is not a sufficient means for the regeneration of an overstrained metaphor. This decay of symbolism[15] is rife in the area of overoptimistic faith in the future, where the fictions were based on an overinflated regard for technology and have become increasingly threadbare. A new symbolic language is emerging which, as the foregoing examples show, refers to the full scope of life and does not limit itself to a faith in progress clad in machine metaphors.

The use of symbolic reference, and especially the recourse to historical material, have shocked some people and have elicited much resistance. But Moore and Hollein made it perfectly clear that their choices of historical forms were not arbitrary, and that the architectural fictions they created were not the product of sheer whimsy, by including special information in the buildings in question. They emphatically used signs calculated to produce certain atmospheres and capable of inducing participatory identification in the users. Hollein's travel bureau attunes the customer to his upcoming travels and creates an atmosphere consonant with the mood of departure. Moore's Piazza d'Italia awakens and localises memories and permits identity to be reformed without forcing anyone to ascribe autonomy to this architecture of signs and references or to declare it a literal surrogate for an Italian city. Moore's system of symbols intentionally retains the character of witty allusion while it points illusionistically to a set of circumstances without claiming to be identical with them. The relativisation of classical forms, neon lights, and steel capitals creates distance, reduces the relationship to the factual reality of Italy to one of mere quotation, and breaks with a modernism marked by a one-sided definition of progress. The Piazza allows one to smile at it and at oneself; it does not seriously tempt one to look in it for a surrogate for Italy. Its main theme is nostalgia, veiled with irony and humour. A pervasive wittiness destroys the bogus 'as if' quality of eclecticism and prevents all this from being accepted as the genuine article. The fiction that has been staged here has qualifying features that keep its illusionistic effect from becoming too strong.

Breakthrough to Postmodernism: Robert Venturi
Complexity and Contradiction
Mies had compressed his reductive architectural theory to one phrase: 'Less is more'. Robert Venturi responded sarcastically: 'Less is a bore'. This exchange presents, in a concentrated paradigmatic form, the turn away from modernism. When Venturi attacked the precept of the Great Simplifier he was fully conscious that he was plunging into the main-stream of the attack on the dogmas of modern architecture. Vincent Scully's remark in his preface to the first edition of *Complexity and Contradiction in Architecture* that Venturi's 1966 treatise was the most significant piece of writing on architecture since Le Corbusier's *Vers une architecture* (1923) has been proved correct by the subsequent developments. Venturi went to the heart of the matter, responding to the vestiges of an architectural theory with a theory of his own – and, indeed, a programmatic one. This was a complete breach of custom; who dared to write anything theoretical on architecture any more! People were offended; they aggressively displayed their hurts and spread their venomous reactions for years afterward. Young Venturi had overstepped the limits of decorum.

The main forum for the ensuing disputes was the architecture department at Yale University. Paul Rudolph felt humiliated and hurt by his young colleague,[16] and Philip Johnson was aghast that someone else had been allowed to be witty. Even Louis Kahn, whose student and assistant Venturi had been, felt compelled in 1969 to call Venturi's buildings bloodless abstractions that illustrated his theories but were inadequate when viewed independently.[17] The reactions to *Complexity and Contradiction* at Yale were to recur for years and decades to come, everywhere in the Western world, whenever Venturi's theories and buildings were to come up: the fundamental rules had been broken; decorum had been disdained; modern architecture appeared in jeopardy.

Venturi had attacked the strongest side of modern architecture, which was also the weakest. Certainly, the reduction of forms and the simplification of functions had been the essential feature of architecture, in Mies' epoch. Venturi attacked with irony the belief that the quality of a building could be heightened by attenuating its form and that the reduction to the lowest common denominator could be the solution of all problems. He spoke out against the omission of contradiction and pleaded in favour of greater complexity. Complexity versus simplification! Venturi began his book with a 'gentle manifesto' in which he declared his fundamental tenets:

> Everywhere, except in architecture, complexity and contradiction have been acknowledged, from Gödel's proof of ultimate inconsistency in mathematics to TS Eliot's analysis of 'difficult' poetry and Joseph Albers' definition of the paradoxical quality of painting.
>
> But architecture is necessarily complex and contradictory in its very inclusion of the traditional Vitruvian elements of commodity, firmness, and delight. And today

the wants of programme, structure, mechanical equipment, and expression, even in single buildings in simple contexts, are diverse and conflicting in ways previously unimaginable. The increasing dimension and scale of architecture in urban and regional planning add to the difficulties. I welcome the problems and exploit the uncertainties. By embracing contradiction as well as complexity, I aim for vitality as well as validity.

Architects can no longer afford to be intimidated by the puritanically moral language of orthodox Modern architecture. I like elements which are hybrid rather than 'pure', compromising rather than 'clean', distorted rather than 'straightforward', ambiguous rather than 'articulated', perverse as well as 'impersonal', boring as well as 'interesting', conventional rather than 'designed', accommodating rather than excluding, redundant rather than simple, vestigial as well as innovating, inconsistent and equivocal rather than direct and clear. I am for messy vitality over obvious unity. I include the non sequitur and proclaim the duality.

I am for richness of meaning rather than clarity of meaning; for the implicit function as well as the explicit function. I prefer 'both-and' to 'either-or', black and white, and sometimes gray, to black or white. A valid architecture evokes many levels of meaning and combinations of focus: its space and its elements become readable and workable in several ways at once.

But an architecture of complexity and contradiction has a special obligation toward the whole: its truth must be in its totality or its implications of totality. It must embody the difficult unity of inclusion rather than the easy unity of exclusion. More is not less.[18]

Venturi's statements caused additional irritation because he buttressed his arguments not only with examples of modern architecture but also with European examples from the Romanesque period up to the nineteenth century. Should it be possible again to claim legitimation of present building practice by referring to historical examples? Venturi showed the Romanesque facade of the Dome of Cremona right next to Le Corbusier's Villa Stein, and the Renaissance palace of François I at Chambord right alongside the Smithsons' plan for Berlin. Thus, it is not surprising that in Venturi's first buildings, in addition to the general principles of 'complexity', historical detail began to play a role (although a marginal one, for the time being).

In his early works Venturi concentrated on finding a formal counter to modern architecture's ideal of simplicity. Here we can hardly speak of symbolisation or of the iconic contents of representational facades. Venturi's critique of modernism was initially formulated as a counterproposal to Mies and to his great simplification historical context did not yet play an important role. Whereas at the Otterlo CIAM the tendency had been to question the main beliefs of modernism by referring to regional influences, Venturi took as his point of departure an explicitly formulated theoretical position, which he set up as a new order of architectural priorities in radical opposition to the established norms of modern architecture. Even though Venturi's first buildings show signs of the first application of the criteria that define postmodern architecture along with the recourse to historical forms, Venturi's argumentation focused not on the consideration of the historical environment but, first and foremost, on the renewal of the principle of manifoldness. For Venturi, complexity means manifold influencing factors being put in action in the form of architecture without the suppression or the smoothing away of contrary or mutually exclusive demands. The driving force of the new architectural aesthetic was not practical response to a given situation but conscious and theoretically formulated reaction against the established norms of architecture.

NOTES

1 See Jürgen Habermas, 'Die Moderne – Ein unvollendetes Projekt', *Die Zeit*, September 19, 1980; Habermas, 'Moderne und postmoderne Architektur', in *Die andere Tradition*, Munich, 1981.

2 Habermas, 'Moderne und postmoderne Architektur', p 10. See also Paolo Portoghesi, 'Die Wiedergeburt der Archätypen', and Heinrich Klotz, 'Aesthetischer Eigensinn', *Arch* + 63/64, 1982, pp 89-93.

3 In art history, on the other hand, the controversy between pure history of form and iconology flared into a heated debate again immediately after the Second World War. In Germany, the works of Hans Sedlmayr and the main work of Günther Bandmann, *Mittelalterliche Architektur als Bedeutungsträger*, Berlin, 1951, served as important directives. In the United States, Rudolf Wittkower's 1949 book *Architectural Principles in the Age of Humanism* had the greatest impact on the discussion of modern architecture; Robert Venturi acknowledged this in his book *Complexity and Contradiction in Architecture*.

4 See Charles Jencks, *The Language of Post-Modern Architecture*, London, 1977.

5 Jost Hermand, 'Pop oder die These vom Ende der Kunst', *Basis, Jahrbuch für deutsche Gegenwartsliteratur* I, 1970, pp 94-115; reprinted in Hermand's *Stile, Ismen, Etiketten*, Wiesbaden, 1978.

6 See, for instance, the work of Rem Koolhaas.

7 See Charles Jencks, *Late-Modern Architecture*, London, 1980.

8 See *Jahrbuch für Architektur*, 1983, pp 180-185.

9 This idea of architecture as a means of plastic elaboration of fictional form is discussed in detail in the chapter 'Architecture as Fiction', in Heinrich Klotz, *The History of Postmodern Architecture*, trans, Radka Donnell, MIT, Cambridge Mass, 1988 (first published Friedr, Vieweg & Sohn, 1984).

10 Robert Venturi and Denise Scott Brown, 'Funktionalismus ja, aber . . .', *Werk-Archithese* 64, March 1977, pp 33-35.

11 See John Cook and Heinrich Klotz, *Conversations with Architects*, New York, 1973, p 242.

12 Ibid, p 243.

13 Achille Bonito Oliva, *Transavantgarde International*, Milan, 1982, p 6.

14 The building was not executed, and thus the surrounding facades are very isolated at the present.

15 See Kähler, *Architektur als Symbolverfall* (note 11 above), pp 182 ff.

16 Venturi had called Rudolph's buildings 'heroic'.

17 Remark made in a conversation with the author in September 1969, in New Haven.

18 Robert Venturi, *Complexity and Contradiction in Architecture*, New York, 1966, pp 22-23.

From *The History of Postmodern Architecture*, Friedr Vieweg & Sohn Verlagsgesellschaft mbH, Braunschweig and Wiesbaden, 1984 and MIT Press, Cambridge, Massachusetts, 1988; translated by Radka Donnell.

CHAPTER FOUR

SOCIOLOGY, POLITICS, GEOGRAPHY

Cesar Pelli, Canary Wharf, Docklands, London, 1988-91

Daniel Bell
THE COMING OF THE POST-INDUSTRIAL SOCIETY

The Dimensions of Post-Industrial Society

Analytically, society can be divided into three parts: the social structure, the polity, and the culture. The social structure comprises the economy, technology, and the occupational system. The polity regulates the distribution of power and adjudicates the conflicting claims and demands of individual and groups. The culture is the realm of expressive symbolism and meanings. It is useful to divide society in this way because each aspect is ruled by a different axial principle. In modern Western society the axial principle of the social structure is *economising* – a way of allocating resources according to principles of least cost, substitutability, optimisation, maximisation, and the like. The axial principle of the modern polity is *participation*, sometimes mobilised or controlled, sometimes demanded from below. The axial principle of the culture is the desire for the *fulfilment and enhancement of the self*. In the past, these three areas were linked by a common value system (and in bourgeois society through a common character structure). But in our times there has been an increasing disjunction of the three and this will widen.

The concept of the post-industrial society deals primarily with changes *in the social structure*, the way in which the economy is being transformed and the occupational system reworked, and with the new relations between theory and empiricism, particularly science and technology. These changes can be charted, as I seek to do in this book. But I do not claim that these changes in social structure *determine* corresponding changes in the polity or the culture. Rather, the changes in social structure pose questions for the rest of society in three ways. First, the social structure – especially the social structure – is a structure of roles, designed to coordinate the actions of individuals to achieve specific ends. Roles segment individuals by defining limited modes of behaviour appropriate to a particular position, but individuals do not always willingly accept the requirements of a role. One aspect of the post-industrial society, for example, is the increasing bureaucratisation of science and the increasing specialisation of intellectual work into minute parts. Yet it is not clear that individuals entering science will accept this segmentation, as did the individuals who entered the factory system 150 years ago.

Second, changes in social structure pose 'management' problems for the political system. In a society which becomes increasingly conscious of its fate, and seeks to control its own fortunes, the political order necessarily becomes paramount since the post-industrial society increases the importance of the technical component of knowledge, it forces the hierophants of the new society – the scientists, engineers, and technocrats – either to compete with politicians or become their allies. The relationship between the social structure and the political order thus becomes one of the chief problems of power in a post-industrial society. And, third, the new modes of life, which depend strongly on the primacy of cognitive and theoretical knowledge, inevitably challenge the tendencies of the culture, which arrives for the enhancement of the self and turns increasingly antinomian and anti-institutional. In this book, I am concerned chiefly with the social structural and political consequences of the post-industrial society. In a later work I shall deal with its relation to culture. But the heart of the endeavour is to trace the societal changes primarily within the social structure.

'Too large a generalisation,' Alfred North Whitehead wrote, 'leads to mere barrenness.' It is the large generalisation, limited by a happy particularity, which is the fruitful conception.'[1] It is easy – and particularly so today – to set forth an extravagant theory which, in its historical sweep, makes a striking claim to originality. But when tested eventually by reality, it turn into a caricature – viz James Burnham's theory of the managerial revolution thirty years ago, or C Wright Mills's conception of the power elite, or WW Rostow's stages of economic growth. I have tried to resist that impulse. Instead, I am dealing here with *tendencies*, and have sought to explore the meaning and consequences of those tendencies if the changes in social structure that I describe were to work themselves to their logical limits. But there is no guarantee that they will. Social tensions and social conflicts may modify a society considerably; wars and recriminations can destroy it; the tendencies may provoke a set of reactions that inhibit change. Thus I am writing what Hans Vahinger called an 'as if', a fiction, a logical construction of what *could* be, against which the future social reality can be compared in order to see what intervened to change society in the direction it did take.

The concept of the post-industrial society is a large generalisation. Its meaning can be more easily understood if one specifies five dimensions, or components, of the term:

1 Economic sector: the change from a goods-producing to a service economy;

2 Occupational distribution: the pre-eminence of the professional and technical class;

3 Axial principle: the centrality of theoretical knowledge as the source of innovation and of policy formulation for the society;

4 Future orientation: the control of technology and technological assessment;

5 Decision-making: the creation of a new 'intellectual technology'.

Creation of a service economy. About thirty years ago, Colin Clark, in his *Conditions of Economic Progress*, analytically divided the economy into three sectors – primary, secondary, and tertiary – the primary being principally agriculture; the secondary, manufacturing or industrial; and the tertiary, services. Any economy is a mixture in different proportions of each. But Clark argued that, as nations became industrialised, there was an inevitable trajectory whereby because of sectorial differences in productivity, a larger proportion of the labour force would pass into manufacturing, and as national incomes rose, there would be a greater demand for services and a corresponding shift in that slope.

By this criterion, the first and simplest characteristic of a post-industrial society is that the majority of the labour force is no longer engaged in agriculture or manufacturing but in services, which are defined residually, as trade, finance, transport, health, recreation, research, education, and government.

Today, the overwhelming number of countries in the world (see Tables 1 and 2) are still dependent on the primary sector: agriculture, mining, fishing, forestry. These economies are based entirely on natural resources. Their productivity is low, and they are subject to wide swings of income because of the fluctuations of raw material and primary-product prices. In Africa and Asia, agrarian economies account for more than seventy per cent of the labour force. In western and northern Europe, Japan, and the Soviet Union, the major portion of the labour force is engaged in industry or the manufacture of goods. The United States today is the only nation in the world in which the service sector accounts for more than half the total employment and more than half the Gross National Product. It is the first service economy, the first nation, in which the major portion of the population is engaged in neither agrarian nor industrial pursuits. Today about sixty per cent of the United States labour force is engaged in services; by 1980, the figure will have risen to seventy per cent.

The term 'services', if used generically, risks being deceptive about the actual trends in the society. Many agrarian societies such as India have a high proportion of persons engaged in services, but of a personal sort (eg household servants) because labour is cheap and usually underemployed. In an industrial society different services tend to increase because of the need for auxiliary help for production, eg transportation and distribution. But in a post-industrial society the emphasis is on a different kind of service. If we group services as personal (retail stores, laundries, garages, beauty shops); business (banking and finance, real estates, insurance); transportation, communication and utilities; and health, education, research, and government; then it is growth of the last category which is decisive for post-industrial society. And this is the category that represents the expansion of a new intelligentsia – in the universities, research organisations, professions, and government.

The pre-eminence of the professional and technical class. The second way of defining a post-industrial society is through the change in occupational distributions; ie not only *where* people work, but the kind of work they do. In large measure, occupation is the most important determinant of class and stratification in the society.

The onset of industrialisation created a new phenomenon, the semi-skilled worker, who could be trained within a few weeks to do the simple routine operations required in machine work. Within industrial societies, the semi-skilled worker has been the single largest category in the labour force. The expansion of the service economy, with its emphasis on office work, education, and government, has naturally brought about a shift to white-collar occupations. In the United States, by 1956, the number of white-collar workers, for the first time in the history of industrial civilisation, outnumbered the blue-collar workers in the occupational structure. Since then the ratio has been widening steadily; by 1970 the white-collar workers outnumbered the blue-collar by more than five to four.

But the most startling change has been the growth of professional and technical employment – jobs that usually require some college education – at a rate twice that of the average. In 1940 there were 3.9 million such persons in the society; by 1964 the number had risen to 8.6 million; and it is estimated that by 1975 there will be 13.2 million professional and technical persons, making it the second-largest of the eight occupational divisions in the country, exceeded only by the semi-skilled workers (see Table 3). One further statistical breakdown will round out the picture – the role of the scientists and engineers, who form the key group in the post-industrial society. While the growth rate of the professional and technical class as a whole has been twice that of the average labour force, the growth rate of the scientists and engineers has been triple that of the working population.

By 1975 the United States may have about 550,000 scientists (natural and social scientists), as against 275,000 in 1960, and almost a million and a half engineers, compared to 800,000 in 1960. Table 4^2 gives the breakdown of the professional and technical occupations – the heart of the post-industrial society.

The primacy of theoretical knowledge. In identifying a new and emerging social system, it is not only in the extrapolated social trends, such as the creation of a service economy or the expansion of the professional and technical class, that one seeks to understand fundamental social change. Rather, it is through some specifically defining

TABLE 1

**The World's Labour Force by Broad Economic Sector
and by Continent and Region, 1960***

REGION	TOTAL LABOUR FORCE (MILLIONS)	PERCENTAGE DISTRIBUTION BY SECTOR		
		AGRICULTURE	INDUSTRY	SERVICES
World	1,296	58	19	23
Africa	112	77	9	14
Western Africa	40	80	8	13
Eastern Africa	30	83	7	10
Middle Africa	14	86	6	8
Northern Africa	22	71	10	19
Southern Africa[a]	6	37	29	34
Northern America[a]	77	8	39	53
Latin America	71	48	20	32
Middle America (mainland)	15	56	18	26
Caribbean	8	53	18	29
Tropical South America	37	52	17	31
Temperate South America[a]	12	25	33	42
Asia	728	71	12	17
East Asia (mainland)	319	75	10	15
Japan[a]	44	33	28	39
Other East Asia	15	62	12	26
Middle South Asia	239	71	14	15
South-East Asia	90	75	8	17
South-West Asia	20	69	14	17
Europe[a]	191	28	38	34
Western Europe[a]	60	14	45	41
Northern Europe[a]	34	10	45	45
Eastern Europe[a]	49	45	31	24
Southern Europe[a]	47	41	32	27
Oceania[b]	6	23	34	43
Australia & New Zealand	5	12	40	49
Melanesia	1	85	5	10
USSR[a]	111	45	28	27

SOURCE: International Labour Review (January-February, 1967); ILO estimates based on national censuses and sample surveys.
NOTE: Owing to independant rounding, the sum of the parts may not add up to group totals.
[a]More developed regions.
[b]Excluding Polynesia and Micronesia.
*An ILO survey for 1970 is due to be published later in the decade. In 1969, however, the OECD in Paris published a breakdown of labor force in West Europe, by sectors, which provides for the comparison in Table 2

TABLE 2
Labour Force and GNP in Western Europe and United States by Sectors, 1969

| COUNTRY | AGRICULTURE | | INDUSTRY | | SERVICES | |
	% of GNP	% of Labour	% of GNP	% of Labour	% of GNP	% of Labour
West Germany	4.1	10.6	49.7	48.0	46.2	41.4
France	7.4	16.6	47.3	40.6	45.3	42.8
Britain	3.3	3.1	45.7	47.2	51.0	49.7
Sweden	5.9	10.1	45.2	41.1	48.9	48.8
Netherlands	7.2	8.3	41.2	41.9	51.6	49.8
Italy	12.4	24.1	40.5	41.1	51.7	45.1
United States	3.0	5.2	36.6	33.7	60.4	61.1

SOURCE: Organisation for Economic Co-operation and Development (Paris, 1969).

TABLE 3
Employment by Major Occupation Group, 1964, and Projected Requirements, 1975[a]

| MAJOR OCCUPATION GROUP | 1964 | | 1975 | | % CHANGE, 1964-1975 |
	Number in millions	%	Number in millions	%	
Total Employment	70.4	100.0	88.7	100.0	26
White-collar workers	31.1	44.2	42.8	48.3	38
Professional, technical, and kindred workers	8.6	12.2	13.2	14.9	54
Managers, officials, and proprietors, except farm	7.5	10.6	9.2	10.4	23
Clerical, and kindred workers	10.7	15.2	14.6	16.5	37
Sales workers	4.5	6.3	5.8	6.5	30
Blue-collar workers	25.5	36.3	29.9	33.7	17
Craftsmen, foremen and kindred workers	9.0	12.8	11.4	12.8	27
Operatives and kindred workers	12.9	18.4	14.8	16.7	15
Laborers, except farm and mine	3.6	5.2	3.7	4.2	b
Service workers	9.3	13.2	12.5	14.1	35
Farmers and farm managers, labourers, and foremen	4.4	6.3	3.5	3.9	-21

SOURCE: *Technology and the American Economy*, Report of the National Commision on Technology, Auto-mation, and Ecconomic Progress, vol 1 (Washington D.C., 1966), p 30; derived from the Bureau of Labour Statistics, *America's Industrial and Occupational Manpower Requirements, 1964-1975*.

NOTE: Because of rounding, sums of individual items may not equal totals.

[a]Projections assume a national unemployment rate of 3% in 1975. The choice of 3% unemployment as a basis for these projections does not indicate an endorsement or even a willingness to accept that level of unemployment.

[b]Less than 3%

TABLE 4
The Make-up of Professional and Technical Occupations, 1960 and 1975 (in thousands)

	1960	1975
Total labour force	66,680	88,660
Total professional and technical	7,475	12,925
Scientific and Egineering	1,092	1,994
Engineers	810	1,450
Natural scientists	236	465
Chemists	91	175
Agricultural scientists	30	53
Geologists and geophysicists	18	29
Mathematicians	21	51
Physicists	24	58
Others	22	35
Social scientists	46	79
Economists	17	31
Statisticians and actuaries	23	36
Others	6	12
Technicians (except medical and dental)	730	1,418
Medical and health	1,321	2,240
Physicians and surgeons	221	374
Nurses, professional	496	860
Dentists	87	125
Pharmacists	114	126
Psychologists	17	40
Technicians (medical and dental)	141	393
Others	245	322
Teachers	1,945	3,063
Elementary	978	1,233
Secondary	603	1,160
College	206	465
Others	158	275
General	2,386	4,210
Accountants	429	660
Clergymen	200	240
Editors and reporters	100	128
Lawyers and judges	225	320
Arts and entertainment	470	774
Architects	30	45
Librarians	80	130
Social workers	105	218
Others (Airline pilots, photographers, personnel relations, etc)	747	1,695

SOURCE: BLS Bulletin 1606, 'Tomorrow's Manpower Needs', vol IV (February 1969), Appendix E, pp 28-29.

characteristic of a social system, which becomes the axial principle, that one establishes a conceptual schema. Industrial society is the coordination of machines and men for the production of goods. Post-industrial society is organised around knowledge, for the purpose of social control and the directing of innovation and change; and this in turn gives rise to new social relationships and new structures which have to be managed politically.

Now, knowledge has of course been necessary in the functioning of any society. What is distinctive about the post-industrial society is the change in the character of knowledge itself. What has become decisive for the organisation of decisions and the direction of change is the centrality of *theoretical* knowledge – the primacy of theory over empiricism and the codification of knowledge into abstract systems of symbols that, as in any axiomatic system, can be used to illuminate many different and varied areas of experience.

The History of An Idea

No idea ever emerges full-blown from the head of Jove, or a secondary muse, and the five dimensions which coalesced in the concept of the post-industrial society have had a long and complicated history. These may be of interest to the reader.

The starting point for me was a theme implicit in my book *The End of Ideology* – the role of technical decision-making in society. Technical decision-making, in fact, can be viewed as the diametric opposite of ideology: the one calculating and instrumental, the other emotional and expressive. The theme of *The End of Ideology* was the exhaustion of old political passions; the theories that developed into 'The Post-Industrial Society' sought to explore technocratic thought in its relation to politics.[3]

The interest in the role of technical decision-making and the nature of the new technical elites was expressed in a section of a paper I wrote in the spring of 1955 for a conference of the Congress for Cultural Freedom, in Milan, 'The Break-up of Family Capitalism'. The argument was, briefly, that capitalism had to be understood not only as an economic system but also as a social system tied through the family enterprise, which provided the system's social cement by creating both a community of interest and a continuity of interest through the family dynasty. The rise of managerial capitalism, therefore, had to be seen not only as part of the professionalisation of the corporation, but as a 'crack' in that social cement. After describing the break-up of family capitalism in America (in part because of the intervention of investment banking), the essay argued that two 'silent revolutions' in the relationship between power and social class were taking place: the decline of inherited power (but not necessarily of wealth) meant that the social upper class of wealthy businessmen and their descendants no longer constituted a ruling class; the rise of the managers meant that there was no continuity of power in the hands of a specific special group. The continuity of power was in the institutional position. Rule was largely in the hands of the technical-intellectual elite, including corporate managers, and the political directorate who occupied the institutional position at the time. Individuals and families pass; the institutional power remains.[4]

A second strand was a series of studies I did in *Fortune* magazine in the early 1950s on the changing composition of the labour force, with particular reference to the decline of the industrial worker relative to the non-production worker in the factory, and the technical and professional employee in the occupational system. Here the influence of Colin Clark's *Conditions of Economic Progress* was apparent. A more direct influence, however, was an article, unjustly neglected, by Paul Hatt and Nelson Foote, in the *American Economic Review* of May 1953, which not only refined Clark's 'tertiary' category (setting forth quaternary and quinary sectors) but linked these sector changes to patterns of social mobility. In relating changes in sector distributions to occupational patterns, Hatt and Foote singled out as the most important development the trend towards professionalisation of work and the crucial importance of the quinary or intellectual sector.

A third influence was Joseph Schumpeter's emphasis on technology as an open sea (ideas which were developed in the various studies by Arthur Cole, Fritz Redlich, and Hugh Aitken at the Harvard Center for Entrepreneurial Studies in the 1950s).[5] Schumpeter's argument, reread in the early 1960s, turned my mind to the question of technological forecasting. Capitalist society had been able to regularise growth when it found the means to institutionalise the mechanisms of savings and credit which could then be transformed into investment. One of the problems of the post-industrial society would be the need to iron out the indeterminacy of the future by some means of 'charting' the open sea. The various efforts at technological forecasting in the 1960s (summed up by Erich Jantsch in *Technological Forecasting in Perspective,* Paris, OECD, 1967) argued the feasibility of the proposition.

And finally, in this inventory of influences, I would single out an essay by the physicist and historian of science, Gerald Holton, in illuminating for me the significance of theoretical knowledge in its changing relation to technology and the codification of theory as the basis for innovation not only in science, which Holton demonstrated, but in technology and economic policy as well. Holton's paper is a masterly exposition of the development of science as a set of codifications and branchings of knowledge.[6]

I first presented many of these ideas, using the term 'post-industrial society', in a series of lectures at the Salzburg Seminar in Austria in the summer of 1959. The emphasis then was largely on the shifts in sectors and the change from a goods-producing to a service society. In the spring of 1962, I wrote a long paper for a forum in Boston entitled, 'The Post-Industrial Society: A Speculative view of the United States in 1985 and Beyond'. Here the theme had shifted to the decisive role of 'intellectual technology' and science in social change and as constituting the significant features of the post-industrial society. Though the paper was not published, it was widely circulated in academic and government circles.[7] A variant of this paper was presented in the winter of 1962-63 before the Seminar on Technology and Social Change at Columbia University, and printed in truncated form a year later in the papers of that seminar edited by Eli Ginzberg. The centrality of the university and of intellectual organisations as institutions of the post-industrial society was a theme I developed in my book, *The Reforming of General Education,* 1966. The emphasis on conceptual schemes arose in connection with my work as chairman of the Commission on the Year 2000, in developing frameworks for the analysis of the future of American society. A number of memoranda I wrote at that time dealt with the concepts of a national society, a communal society, and a post-industrial society as a means of understanding the changes in American society created by the revolutions in transportation and communication, the demand for group rights and the rise of non market public decision-making, and the centrality of theoretical knowledge and research institutions. The idea of axial structures emerged from my efforts to deal more theoretically with problems of social change, and is the basis for a stock-taking of theories of social change that is underway for the Russell Sage Foundation.[8]

The question has been asked why I have called this speculative concept the 'post-industrial' society, rather than the knowledge society, or the information society, or the professional society, all of which are somewhat apt in describing salient aspects of what is emerging. At the time, I was undoubtedly influenced by Ralf Dahrendorf, who in his *Class and Class Conflict in an Industrial Society* (1959) had written of a 'post-capitalist' society, and by WW Rostow, who in his *Stages of Economic Growth* had suggested a 'post-maturity' economy.[9] The sense was present – and still is – that in Western society we are in the midst of a vast historical change in which old social relations (which were property-bound), existing power structures (centred on narrow elites), and bourgeois culture (based on notions of restraint and delayed gratification) are being rapidly eroded. The sources of the upheaval are scientific and technological. But they are also cultural, since culture, I believe, has achieved autonomy in Western society. What these new social forms will be like is not completely clear. Nor is it likely that they will achieve the unity of the economic system and character structure which was character-istic of capitalist civilisation from the mid-eighteenth to the mid-twentieth century. The use of the hyphenated prefix *post-* indicates, thus, that sense of living in interstitial time.

I have been using the idea of the post-industrial society for nearly a decade, and in recent years it has come into more common usage, though with shades of meaning that differ from mine. It may be useful to make note of some of these differences.

Herman Kahn and Anthony J Wiener make the post-industrial society the pivot of their book *The Year 2000*,[10] but they give the term an almost entirely economic meaning (and in their descriptive table it is equated with a post-mass-consumption society). They depict a society so affluent (in which per-capita income is doubled every eighteen years) that work and efficiency have lost their meaning; and increase in the pace of change would produce an 'acculturation' trauma or future shock. Kahn and Wiener almost assume a 'post-economic' society in which there is no scarcity and the only problems are how to use abundance. Yet the concept 'post-economic' has no logical meaning since it implies a social situation in which there are no costs for anything (for economics is the management of costs) or the resources are endless. Some five years ago there was euphoric talk of a triple revolution whereby 'cybernation' would bring about a full cornucopia of goods. Now we hear of a devastated planet and the need for zero economic growth lest we completely pollute or hopelessly deplete all the resources of the world. Both of these apocalyptic visions, I think, are wrong.

Zbigniew Brzezinski thinks he has made an accurate 'fix' on the future through his neologism the 'technetronic' society: 'a society that is shaped culturally, psychologically, socially, and economically by the impact of technology and electronics – particularly in the area of computers and communications.'[11] But the formulation has two drawbacks. First, Brzezinski's neologism shifts the focus of change from theoretical knowledge to the practical applications of technology, yet in his exposition he refers to many kinds of knowledge, pure and applied, from molecular biology to economics, which are of critical importance in the new society. Second, the idea of the 'shaping' nature or primacy of the 'technetronic' factors implies a technological determinism which is belied by the subordination of economics to the political system. I do not believe that the social structure 'determines' other aspects of the society but rather that changes in social structure (which are predictable) pose management problems or policy issues for the political system (whose responses are much less predictable). And as I have indicated, I believe that the present-day autonomy of culture brings about changes in life styles and values which do not derive from changes in the social structure itself.

Another group of writers, such as Kenneth Keniston and Paul Goodman, have used the term post-industrial society to denote a major shift in values for a significant section of youth, among whom, as Keniston writes, there is 'the quest for a world beyond materialism, the rejection of careerism and vocationalism'. Goodman believes there is a turn towards 'a personal subsistence economy independent of the excesses of a machine civilisation'.[12] Whether there is any staying power to these impulses remains to be seen.[13] I think there is a radical disjunction between the social structure and the culture, but its sources lie deep in the anti-bourgeois character of a modernist movement and work themselves out in a much more differentiated way than simply the impulsiveness of a youth movement.[14]

Finally, the theme of the post-industrial society has appeared in the writings of a number of European neo-Marxist theoreticians such as Radovan Richta, Serge Mallet, Andre Gorz, Alain Touraine, and Roger Garaudy, who have emphasised the decisive role of science and technology in transforming the industrial structure and thus calling into question the 'ordained' role of the working class as the historic agent of change in society. Their work has spawned a variety of theories that, in one way or another, emphasise the fusion of science and technical personnel with the 'advanced' working class, or propose the theory of a 'new working class' made up principally of technically skilled personnel. While all these writers have sensed the urgency of the structural changes in the society, they become tediously theological in their debates about the 'old' and 'new' working class, for their aim is not to illuminate actual social changes in the society but to 'save' the Marxist concept of social change and the Leninist idea of the agency of change. For a real ideological crisis does exist. If there is an erosion of the working class in post-industrial society, how can Marx's vision of social change be maintained? And if the working class will not inherit the world (and is in fact shrinking), how does one justify the 'dictatorship of the proletariat' and the role of the Communist Party as the 'vanguard' of the working class? One cannot save the theory by insisting that almost everybody is a member of the 'new working class.'[15]

A post-industrial society is one in which there will necessarily be more conscious decision-making. The chief problem is the stipulation of social choices that accurately reflect the 'ordering' of preferences by individuals. The Condorect paradox, as developed by Kenneth J Arrow, argues that theoretically no such social-welfare choice can be created. What remains therefore is bargaining between groups. But in order to bargain, one has to know social benefits and social costs. At present the society has no such mechanisms to do social accounting and to verify social goals. Finally, the significance of the post-industrial society is that:

1 It strengthens the role of science and cognitive values as a basic institutional necessity of the society;

2 By making decisions more technical, it brings the scientist or economist more directly into the political process;

3 By deepening existing tendencies toward the bureaucratisation of intellectual work, it creates a set of strains for the traditional definitions of intellectual pursuits and values;

4 By creating and extending a technical intelligentsia, it raises crucial questions about the relation of the technical to the literary intellectual

In sum, the emergence of a new kind of society brings into question the distributions of wealth, power, and status that are central to any society. Now wealth, power, and status are *not* dimensions *of* class, but values sought or gained *by* classes. Classes are created in a society by the fundamental axes of stratification. The two major axes of stratification in Western society are property and knowledge. Alongside them is a political system that increasingly manages the two and gives rise to temporary elites (temporary in that there is no necessary continuity of power of a specific social group through office, as there is continuity of a family or class through property and the differential advantage of belonging to a meritocracy).

Our time, too, has not lacked for sociological seers. The habits of the past have been compelling, and even though previous experience warns of caution, the sense of social change is so vivid and the changes in social structure so dramatic that each sociological theorist of any pretension carries a distinctive conceptual map of the social terrain and a set of signposts to the society ahead.

For the new states or underdeveloped countries the prognosis has been standard: they will become industrialised, modernised and westernised, even though it is less clear that they will be communist or socialist, socially transformed by elites (military or political) or revitalised by masses. One sceptic, Clifford Geertz, has remarked that the category 'transitional society' may become a permanent category in the social sciences. Yet for the *tiers monde*, though development may be long and arduous, there is a sense of a turning point in history and the beginning of a new age.

For the advanced industrial societies however the picture is more clouded. Every seer has a sense that an age is ending (how many 'crises', oh Lord, have we experienced), but there is little agreement as to what may be ahead. This common apocalyptic note of a 'sense of an ending' is, as Frank Kermode has noted, the distinctive literary image of the time.

In sociology this sense of marking time, of living in an interregnum, is nowhere symbolised so sharply as in the widespread use of the word *post* – a paradox since it is a prefix denoting posteriority – to define, as a combined form, the age in which we are moving. For Ralf Dahrendorf, we are living in a *post-capitalist society*. What counts in industrial society, he says, is not ownership but authority, and with the diminution in the legal-ownership of the means of production, there is, in consequence, a break between the economic and the political orders. The old industrial conflicts of bourgeoisie and proletariat, he says, are 'institutionally isolated' and there is little carry-over from the job to other areas of life. ('If it is correct that with industry itself industrial conflict has been institutionally isolated in post-capitalist societies, it follows that his occupational role has lost its comprehensive moulding force for the social personality of the industrial worker, and that it determines only a limited sector of his social behaviour.') Authority is autonomous in each realm:

> . . . in post-capitalist society the ruling and the subjected classes of industry and of the political society are no longer identical; that there are, in other words, in principle two independent conflict fronts. Outside the enterprise, the manager may be a mere citizen, the worker a member of parliament; their industrial class position no longer determines their authority position in the political society.

It is post-capitalist society, in short, because relation to the instruments of production no longer decides dominance or power or privilege in society. Economic or property relations, while still generating their own conflicts, no longer carry over or become generalised as the major centre of conflict in society. Who, then, constitutes the ruling class of post-capitalist society? 'We have to look for the ruling class,' writes Dahrendorf, 'in those positions that constitute the head of bureaucratic hierarchies, among those persons who are authorised to give directives to the administrative staff.' But while there may be managerial or capitalist elites, real power is in the hands of the governmental elites. ('It is necessary to think of this elite in the first place, and never to lose sight of its paramount position in the authority structure of the state.') Conflicts occur primarily in the political arena; changes are introduced or prevented by the government elites, and when managerial or capitalist elites seek to exercise outside their domains, they do so by seeking to influence governmental elites.

Who are the governmental elites? The administrative staff of the state, the government ministers in the cabinet, the judges. But since governments represent interests, there are 'groups behind' the elites.

> In abstract, therefore, the ruling political class of post-capitalist societies consists of the administrative staff of the state, the governmental elites at its head and those interested parties which are represented by the governmental elite. This insistence on governmental elites as the core of the ruling class must be truly shocking to anybody thinking in Marxian terms or, more generally, in terms of the traditional concept of class . . .

As Dahrendorf writes, 'if it sounds strange . . . this strangeness is due to the strangeness of reality.'[16]

'The reality is,' according to George Lichtheim, that 'the contemporary industrial society is increasingly 'postbourgeois, the nineteenth-century class structure tending to dissolve along with the institution of private entrepreneurship on which it is pivoted'. Hence the uncertainty that afflicts so much of current political thinking. The reason is, says Lichtheim, that social welfare legislation and income redistribution 'are aspects of a socialisation process' that circumscribe the operation of a market economy, while at the same time the spread of public ownership creates a new balance between the public and private sectors. 'Least of all does it follow that industrial society retains a "bourgeois" complexion. There cannot be a bourgeoisie without a proletariat, and if the one is fading out, so is the other and for the same reason: Modern industrial society does not require either for its operation.'[17]

For Amitai Etzioni, we are in a 'post-modern' era. He opens his book, *The Active Society,* with the portentous pronouncement, 'The modern period ended with the radical transformation of the technologies of communication, knowledge and energy that followed the Second World War.' But unhappily nowhere else, literally in the 670 pages of text, notes, and glossary that follow, is there a discussion of the technologies of communication, knowledge, and energy, or a specification of what, exactly, 'post-modern societies' are like. In the end we have to return to the intention, at the opening lines of the preface:

> A central characteristic of the modern period has been continued increase in the efficacy of the technology of production which poses a growing challenge to the primacy of the values they are supposed to serve. The post-modern period, the onset of which may be set at 1945, will witness either a greater threat to the status of these values by the surging technologies or a reassertion of their normative priority. Which alternative prevails will determine whether society is to be the servant or the master of the instrument it creates.

So, the post-modern, period or society, is not a definition, but only a question.[18]

For Kenneth Boulding, we are at the start of the *post-civilised* era. Since civilisation, as Mr Boulding points out, has had a favourable connotation and post-civilisation may strike one as unfavourable, one might use the word 'technological or the term developed society'. But the distinctive characteristic of this new period for Mr Boulding is the consciousness of using Teilhud's phrase, the *noösphere*, the sphere of knowledge, as the premise for the social direction of society and the achievement of social, as against individual self-consciousness. Thus, the thrust of Boulding's term is to emphasise the possibility of the guidance of society in the new, emerging period of social or mental evolution rather than the adaptive biological or social evolution of the past.[19]

In the epilogue to the 1969 (Vintage) edition of his *British Politics in the Collectivist Age*, Sam Beer talks of a 'post-collectivist' politics. He feels that the collectivist model of British politics which was part-divided, functionalist, and oriented to the welfare state may be coming to a close. The post-collectivist tendency is a 'reaction to the increasing scale and intensity of rationalisation in both government and society'. And even though it would not create a basic rupture in the political mode, it could form a readjustment of the polity in England (p 426).

And so it goes. It used to be that the great literary modifier was the word *beyond:* beyond tragedy, beyond culture, beyond society. But we seem to have exhausted the beyond, and today the sociological modifier is *post:* a theologian, Sydney E Ahlstrom, has described the religious scene in the United States in the 1960s as 'post-Puritan, and post-Christian.'[20] Lewis Feuer has subtitled his book on *Marx and the Intellectuals* as a 'set of post-ideological essays.' John Leonard in *The New York Times* has talked of the 'post-Literature Culture' as being heralded by the McLuhanite age.[21] For SN Eisenstadt, the sociologist, the new states have become 'post-traditional' societies for though they are no longer bound by the norms of the past and they seek consciously to change, they live in a suspended world with little approximation to the modern societies of the West.[22] Earlier, Roderick Seidenberg, foretelling the victory of rationalism, had described a *post-historic man* in which we move from prehistory, in which instinct dominated intelligence, through the transitional period of history into post-history, in which intelligence dominates instinct,[23] just as in *Zarathustra*, man – suspended on the rope above the abyss – is the transition between the animal of the past and the superman to come. And finally in this inventory (only by virtue of humanity) we have the theme of the *post-industrial society.*[24]

The concept of a post-industrial society gains meaning by comparing its attributes with those of an industrial society and pre-industrial society

In pre-industrial societies – still the condition of most of the world today – the labour force is engaged overwhelmingly in the extractive industries: mining, fishing, forestry, agriculture. Life is primarily a game against nature. One works with raw muscle power, inherited ways, and one's sense of the world is conditioned by dependence on the elements – the seasons, the nature of the soil, the amount of water. The rhythm of life is shaped by these contingencies. The sense of time is one of *durée*, of long and short moments, and the pace of work varies with the seasons and the storms. Because it is a game against nature, productivity is low, and the economy is subject to the vicissitudes of tangible nature and to capricious fluctuations of raw-material prices in the world economy. The unit of social life is the extended household. Welfare consists of taking in the extra mouths when necessary – which is almost always. Because of low productivity and large population, there is a high percentage of unemployment, which is usually distributed throughout the agricultural and domestic-service sectors. Thus there is a high service component, but of the personal or household sort. Since individuals often seek only enough to feed themselves, domestic service is cheap and plentiful. (In England, up to the mid-Victorian period, the single largest occupational class in the society was the domestic servant. In *Vanity Fair*, Becky Sharp and Captain Rawdon Crawley are penniless, but they have a servant; Karl Marx and his large family lived in two rooms in Soho in the 1850s and were sometimes evicted for failing to pay rent, but they had a faithful servant, Lenchen, sometimes two.) Pre-industrial societies are agrarian societies structured in traditional ways of routine and authority.

Industrial societies – principally those around the North Atlantic plus the Soviet Union and Japan – are goods-producing societies. Life is a game against fabricated nature. The world has become technical and rationalised. The machine predominates, and the rhythms of life are mechanically paced: time is chronological, methodical, evenly spaced. Energy has replaced raw muscle and provides the power that is the basis of productivity – the art of making more with less – and is responsible for the mass output of goods which characterises industrial society. Energy and machines transform the nature of work. Skills are broken down into simpler components, and the artisan of the past is replaced by two new figures – the engineer, who is responsible for the layout and flow of work, and the semi-skilled worker, the human cog between machines – until the technical ingenuity of the engineer creates a new machine which replaces him as well. It is a world of co-ordination in which men, materials, and markets are dovetailed for the production and distribution of goods. It is a world of scheduling and programming in which the components of goods are brought together at the right time and in the right proportions so as to speed the flow of goods. It is a world of organisation – of hierarchy and bureaucracy – in which men are treated as 'things' because one can more easily co-ordinate things than men. Thus a necessary distinction is introduced between the role and the person, and this is formalised on the organisation chart of the enterprise. Organisations deal with the requirements of roles, not persons. The criterion of *techne* is efficiency, and the mode of life is modelled on economics: how does one extract the greatest amount of energy from a given unit of embedded nature (coal, oil, gas, water power) with the best machine at what comparative price? The watchwords are maximisation and optimisation, in a cosmology derived from utility and the felicific calculus of Jeremy Bentham. The unit of the individual, and the free society is the sum total of individual decisions as aggregated by the demands registered, eventually, in a market. In actual fact, life is never as 'one-dimensional' as those who convert every tendency into an ontological absolute make it out to be. Traditional elements remain. Work groups intervene to impose their own rhythms and 'bogeys' (or output restrictions) when they can. Waste runs high. Particularism and politics abound. These soften the unrelenting quality of industrial life. Yet the essential, technical features remain.

A post-industrial society is based on services. Hence, it is a game between persons. What counts is not raw muscle power, or energy, but information. The central person is the professional, for he is equipped, by his education and training, to provide the kinds of skill which are increasingly demanded in the post-industrial society. If an industrial society is defined by the quantity of goods as marking a standard of living, the post-industrial society is defined by the quality of life as measured by the services and amenities – health, education, recreation, and the arts – which are now deemed desirable and possible for everyone.

The word 'services' disguises different things, and in the transformation of industrial to post-industrial society there are several different stages. First, in the very development of industry there is a necessary expansion of transportation and of public utilities as auxiliary services in the movement of goods and the increasing use of energy, and in increase in the non-manufacturing but still blue-collar force.

Second, in the mass consumption of goods and the growth of populations there is an increase in distribution (wholesale and retail, and finance, real estate, and insurance, the traditional centres of white-collar employment. Third, as national incomes rise, one finds, as in the theorem of Christian Engel, a German statistician of the latter half of the nineteenth century, that the proportion of money devoted to food at home begins to drop, and the marginal increments are used first for durables (clothing, housing, automobiles) and then for luxury items, recreation, and the like. Thus, a third sector, that of personal services, begins to grow: restaurants, hotels, auto services, travel, entertainment, sports, as people's horizons expand and new wants and tastes develop.

But here a new consciousness begins to intervene. The claims to the good life which the society has promised become centred on the two areas that are fundamental to that life – health and education. The elimination of disease and the increasing numbers of people who can live out a full life, make health services a crucial feature of modern society: and the growth of technical requirements and professional skills makes education, and access to higher education, the condition of entry into the post-industrial society itself. So we have here the growth of a new intelligentsia, particularly of teachers. Finally, the claims for more services and the inadequacy of the market in meeting people's needs for a decent environment as well as better health and education lead to the growth of government, particularly at the state and local level, where such needs have to be met.

The post-industrial society, thus is also a 'communal' society in which the social unit is the community rather than the individual, and one has to achieve a 'social decision' as against, simply, the sum total of individual decisions which, when aggregated, end up as nightmares, on the model of the individual automobile and collective traffic congestion. But co-operation between men is more difficult than the management of things. Participation becomes a condition of community, but when many different groups want too many different things and are not prepared for bargaining or trade-off, then increased conflict or deadlocks result. Either there is a politics of consensus or a politics of stymie.

As a game between persons, social life becomes more difficult because political claims and social rights multiply, the rapidity of social change and shifting cultural fashion bewilders the old, and the orientation to the future erodes the traditional guides and moralities of the past. Information becomes a central resource, and within organisations a source of power. Professionalism thus becomes a criterion of position, but it clashes, too, with the populism which is generated by the claims for more rights and greater participation in the society. If the struggle between capitalist and worker, in the locus of the factory, was the hallmark of industrial society, the clash between the professional and the populace, in the organisation and in the community, is the hallmark of conflict in the post-industrial society.

This, then, is the sociological canvas of the scheme of social development leading to the post-industrial society.[25]

NOTES

1 Alfred North Whitehead, *Science and the Modern World*, New York, 1960 (original edition 1925), p 46.

2 In Table 3 the projected figure for the number of professional and technical persons in 1975 is given as 13.2 million and in Table 4 as 12.9 million. The discrepancies are due in part to the fact that the figure in Table 4 was calculated five years later, and also because different assumptions about the unemployment rate were made. I have let the figures stand to indicate the range.

3 It may not be amiss at this point to clear up a misapprehension that derives, perhaps, from those who know a thesis only from the title of a book and never read its argument. In *The End of Ideology* I did not say that all ideological thinking was finished. In fact, I argued that the exhaustion of the old ideologies inevitably led to a hunger for new ones. So I wrote at the time:

> Thus one finds, at the end of the fifties, a disconcerting caesura. In the West, among the intellectuals, the old passions are spent. The new generation, with no meaningful memory of these old debates, and no secure tradition to build upon, finds itself seeking new purposes within a framework of political society that has rejected, intellectually speaking, the old apocalyptic and chiliastic visions. In the search for a 'cause', there is a deep, desperate, almost pathetic anger . . . a restless search for a new intellectual radicalism. . . . The irony . . . for those who seek 'causes' is that the workers, whose grievances were once the driving energy for social change, are more satisfied with society than the intellectuals. . . . The young intellectual is unhappy because the 'middle way' is for the middle-

aged, not for him; it is without passion and is deadening. . . . The emotional energies – and needs – exist, and the question of how one mobilises these energies is a difficult one (*The End of Ideology*, Glencoe, Ill, 1960, pp 374-75).

4 The essay appears as chapter 2 of *The End of Ideology*. The argument is expanded in the next chapter of that book, 'Is there a Ruling Class in America?'

5 See Joseph Schumpeter, *Capitalism, Socialism and Democracy*, New York, 1942, p 118.

6 See Gerald Holton, 'Scientific Research and Scholarship: Notes Toward the Design of Proper Scales', *Daedalus*, Spring 1962.

7 I did not want to publish the paper at that time because I felt that the idea was unfinished. Sections of the paper, which had been circulated at the forum in Boston, were printed without permission by the public-affairs magazine *Current* and by business publication *Dun's Review*, from which, inexplicably, it turned up as a citation in the volume published by the Czechoslovak Academy of Science on the scientific and technological revolutions which were creating a post-industrial society. The degree of circulation of the paper in government circles, particularly by the Office of Science and Technology, was noted in an article in *Science*, 12 June 1964, p 1321.

8 On these earlier versions, see *Technology and Social Change*, ed Eli Ginzberg, New York, 1964, chap 3; *The Reforming of General Education*, New York, 1966, *Toward the Year 2000*, ed Daniel Bell, Boston, 1968. Different aspects of the nature of post-industrial society were presented at Syracuse in 1966, and at the seventy-fifth anniversary celebration of the California Institute of Technology. Those papers were included in the volumes *Scientific Progress and Human Values*, ed Edward and Elizabeth Hutchings, Proceedings of the 75th Anniversary of the California Institute of Technology, New York, 1967; and *A Great Society*, ed Bertram M Gross, the Bentley Lectures at Syracuse University, New York, 1968. The 'Notes on Post-Industrial Society' that appeared in *The Public Interest* 6&7, Winter and Spring 1967, are abridgments of the Cal Tech and Syracuse papers.

9 The question of intellectual priority always takes intriguing turns. In the notes and tables distributed to the Salzburg Seminar participants in 1959, I wrote: 'The term post-industrial society – a term I have coined – denotes a society which has passed from a goods-producing stage to a service society.' I was using 'post-industrial' in contrast to Dahrendorf's 'post-capitalist', since I was dealing with sector changes in the economy, while he was discussing authority relations in the factory. Subsequently, I discovered that David Riesman had used the phrase 'post-industrial society' in an essay entitled 'Leisure and Work in Post-Industrial Society', printed in the compendium *Mass Leisure*, Glencoe, Ill, 1958. Riesman had used 'post-industrial' to connote leisure as opposed to work, but did not in any subsequent essay develop the theme or the phrase. I had quite likely read Riesman's essay at the time and the phrase undoubtedly came from him, though I have used it in a very different way. Ironically, I have recently discovered that the phrase occurs in the title of a book by Arthur J Penty, *Old Worlds for New: A Study of the Post-Industrial State*, London, 1917. Penty, a well-known Guild Socialist of the time and a follower of William Morris and John Ruskin, denounced the 'Leisure State' as collectivist and associated with the Servile State, and called for a return to the decentralised, small workshop artisan society, ennobling work, which he called the 'post-industrialised state'!

10 The major discussion is in chapter IV, 'Post-Industrial Society in the Standard World', esp pp 186-89. See Herman Kahn and Anthony J Wiener, *The Year 2000*, New York, 1967. The work appeared originally as vols II and IIa of the *Working Papers of the Commission on the Year 2000* (privately printed, 1966).

11 Zbigniew Brezezinski, *Between Two Ages: America's Role in the Technetronic Era*, New York, 1970, p 9.

12 See Keniston, *Youth and Dissent*, New York, 1971, esp 'You Have to Grow up in Scarsdale'. For Goodman, see the introduction to Helen and Scott Nearing, *Living the Good Life*, New York, Schocken paper edition, 1971. Goodman is close to Penty's view of the artisan guild society. Recently a group of young political scientists have argued that 'important groups among the populations of Western societies have passed beyond [subsistence] stages', and they use the concept of post-industrial society to denote a situation in which groups of persons 'no longer have a direct relationship to the imperatives of economic security'. See, for example, Ronald Inglehart, 'The Silent Revolution in Europe: Intergenerational Change in Post-Industrial Societies', *American Political Science Review*, December 1971, pp 991-1017.

13 For evidence of the growing conservation of each radical generation as the cohort gets older, see SM Lipset and EC Ladd, Jr, 'College Generations – from the 1930s to the 1960s', *The Public Interest* 25, Fall 1971.

14 This is a theme implicit in Lionel Trilling's conception of the 'adversary culture'. See Trilling, *Beyond Culture*, New York, 1965.

15 It is surely too simple-minded to insist that since there are fewer and fewer independent entrepreneurs or self-employed professionals, *all* wage and salaried workers are members of the working class. And since the

majority of workers are now on salary, rather than piece- or time-work, how can one call for a 'dictatorship of the salariat'? And over whom?

16 Ralf Dahrendorf, *Class and Class Conflict in an Industrial Society*, Stanford, 1959. See chapters VII and VIII, 'Classes in Post-Capitalist Society (I) Industrial Conflict, (II) Political Conflict'. Quotations above are from pp 272, 275-76, 301-03.

17 George Lichtheim, *The New Europe: Today and Tomorrow*, New York, 1965, p 194.

18 Amitai Etzioni, *The Active Society*, New York, 1968, p vii.

19 Kenneth Boulding, *The Meaning of the Twentieth Century: The Great Transition*, New York, 1964.

20 Sydney Ahlstrom, 'The Radical Turn in Theology and Ethics', *The Annals*, January 1970.

21 *The New York Times*, November 26, 1970.

22 This was the theme of a Daedalus-sponsored seminar in Paris, 9-10 June 1970. Eric Hobsbawm has written of 'post-tribal societies', arguing that social classes only begin at such stages of social development. See his essay, 'Social History and the History of Society', in *Daedalus* issue entitled *Historical Studies Today*, Winter 1971, p 36.

23 Roderick Seidenberg, *Post-Historic Man*, Chapel Hill, NC, 1950.

24 Tom Burns, of Edinburgh, though scoffing at the phrase 'post-industrial' society, talks of the 'post-market society and post-organisation society phase of industrialism' in 'The Rationale of the Corporate System' (p 50), unpublished ms for the Harvard Program on Technology and Society, 1970. To this litany we should add 'post-economic', a possibility envisaged by Herman Kahn of a time when incomes will be so high that cost would be of little practical matter in any decision. (See his briefing paper, 'Forces for Change in the Final Third of the Twentieth Century', Hudson Institute, 1970). In the logic of the situation, some radicals (vide the discussions in *Social Policy* I, 1&4) have talked of a 'post-scarcity' society, while Gideon Sjoberg and his collaborators have written of a 'post-welfare' society. And in his new book *Freedom in a Rocking Boat*, Sir Geoffrey Vickers talks of a 'post-liberal era'. In all, this is a catalogue of twenty different uses of the word *post* to denote some new phase in our society.

Robin Murray
FORDISM AND POST-FORDISM

During the first two centuries of the industrial revolution, the focus of employment shifted from the farm to the factory. It is now shifting once more, from the factory to the office and the shop. A third of Britain's paid labour force now works in offices. A third of the value of national output is in the distribution sector. Meanwhile 2.5 million jobs have been lost in British manufacturing since 1960. If the Ford plants at Halewood and Dagenham represented late industrialism, Centrepoint and Habitat are the symbols of a new age.

The Right portrayed the growth of services as a portent of a post-industrial society with growing individualism, a weakened state and a multiplicity of markets. I want to argue that it reflects a deeper change in the production process. It is one that affects manufacturing and agriculture as well as services, and has implications for the way in which we think about socialist alternatives. I see this as a shift from the dominant form of twentieth-century production, known as Fordism, to a new form, post-Fordism.

Fordism is an industrial era whose secret is to be found in the mass production systems pioneered by Henry Ford. These systems were based on four principles from which all else followed:

a) products were standardised; this meant that each part and each task could also be standardised. Unlike craft production – where each part had to be specially designed, made and fitted – for a run of mass-produced cars, the same headlight could be fitted to the same model in the same way.

b) if tasks are the same, then some can be mechanised; thus mass production plants developed special-purpose machinery for each model, much of which could not be switched from product to product.

c) those tasks which remained were subject to scientific management or Taylorism, whereby any task was broken down into its component parts, redesigned by work-study specialists on time-and-motion principles, who then instructed manual workers on how the job should be done.

d) flowline replaced nodal assembly, so that instead of workers moving to and from the product (the node), the product flowed past the workers.

Ford did not invent these principles. What he did was to combine them in the production of a complex commodity, which undercut craft-made cars as decisively as the handloom weavers had been undercut in the 1830s. Ford's Model T sold for less than a tenth of the price of a craft-built car in the US in 1916, and he took fifty per cent of the market.

This revolutionary production system was to transform sector after sector during the twentieth century, from processed food to furniture, clothes, cookers, and even ships after the Second World War. The economies came from the scale of production, for although mass production might be more costly to set up because of the purpose-built machinery, once in place the cost of an extra unit was discontinuously cheap.

Many of the structures of Fordism followed from this tension between high fixed costs and low variable ones, and the consequent drive for volume. First, as Ford himself emphasised, mass production presupposes mass consumption. Consumers must be willing to buy standardised products. Mass advertising played a central part in establishing a mass consumption norm. So did the provision of the infrastructure of consumption – housing and roads. To ensure that the road system dominated over rail, General Motors, Standard Oil and Firestone Tyres bought up and then dismantled the electric trolley and transit systems in forty-four urban areas.

Second, Fordism was linked to a system of protected national markets, which allowed the mass producers to recoup their fixed costs at home and compete on the basis of marginal costs on the world market, or through the replication of existing models via foreign investment.

Third, mass producers were particularly vulnerable to sudden falls in demand. Ford unsuccessfully tried to offset the effect of the 1930s depression by raising wages. Instalment credit, Keynesian demand and monetary management, and new wage and welfare systems were all more effective in stabilising the markets for mass producers in the postwar period. HP and the dole cheque became as much the symbols of the Fordist age as the tower block and the motorway.

The mass producers not only faced the hazard of changes in consumption. With production concentrated in large factories, they were also vulnerable to the new 'mass worker' they had created. Like Taylorism, mass production had taken the skill out of work, it fragmented tasks into a set of repetitive movements, and erected a rigid division between mental and manual labour. It treated human beings as interchangeable parts of a machine, paid according to the job they did rather than who they were.

The result was high labour turnover, shopfloor resistance, and strikes. The mass producers in turn sought constant new reservoirs of labour, particularly from groups facing discrimination, from rural areas and from less developed regions abroad. The contractual core of Taylorism – higher wages in return for managerial control of production – still applied, and a system of industrial unions grew up to bargain over these wage levels. In the USA, and to an extent the UK, a national system of wage bargaining developed in the postwar period, centred on high-profile car industry negotiations, that linked wage rises to productivity growth, and then set wage standards for other large-scale producers and the state. It was a system of collective bargaining that has been described as implementing a Keynesian incomes policy without a Keynesian state. As long as the new labour reservoirs could be tapped, it was a system that held together the distinct wage relation of Fordism.

Taylorism was also characteristic of the structure of management and supplier relations. Fordist bureaucracies are fiercely hierarchical with links between the divisions and departments being made through the centre rather than at the base. Planning is done by specialists; rulebooks and guide-lines are issued for lower management to carry out. If you enter a Ford factory in any part of the world, you will find its layout, materials, even the position of its Coca Cola machines, all similar, set up as they are on the basis of a massive construction manual drawn up in Detroit. Managers themselves complain of deskilling and the lack of room for initiative, as do suppliers who are confined to producing blueprints at a low margin price.

These threads – of production and consumption, of the semi-skilled worker and collective bargaining, of a managed national market and centralised organisation – together make up the fabric of Fordism. They have given rise to an economic culture which extends beyond the complex assembly industries, to agriculture, the service industries and parts of the state. It is marked by its commitment to scale and the standard product (whether it is a Mars bar or an episode of *Dallas*); by a competitive strategy based on cost reduction; by authoritarian relations, centralised planning, and a rigid organisation built round exclusive job descriptions.

These structures and their culture are often equated with industrialism, and regarded as an inevitable part of the modern age. I am suggesting that they are linked to a particular form of industrialism, one that developed in the late nineteenth century and reached its most dynamic expression in the postwar boom. Its impact can be felt not just in the economy, but in politics (in the mass party) and in much broader cultural fields – whether American football, or classical ballet (Diaghilev was a Taylorist in dance), industrial design or modern architecture. The technological *hubris* of this outlook, its Faustian bargain of dictatorship in production in exchange for mass consumption, and above all its destructiveness in the name of progress and the economy of time, all this places Fordism at the centre of modernism.

Why we need to understand these deep structures of Fordism is that they are embedded, too, in traditional socialist economies. Soviet-type planning is the apogee of Fordism. Lenin embraced Taylor and the stopwatch. Soviet industrialisation was centred on the construction of giant plants, the majority of them based on western mass-production technology. So deep is the idea of scale burnt into Soviet economies that there is a hairdresser's in Moscow with 120 barbers' chairs. The focus of Soviet production is on volume and because of its lack of consumer discipline it has caricatured certain features of western mass production, notably a hoarding of stocks, and inadequate quality control.

In social-democratic thinking, state planning has a more modest place. But in the writings of Fabian economists in the 1930s, as in the Morrisonian model of the public corporation, and Labour's postwar policies, we see the same emphasis on centralist planning, scale, Taylorist technology, and hierarchical organisation. The image of planning was the railway timetable, the goal of planning was stable demand and cost-reduction. In the welfare state, the idea of the standard product was given a democratic interpretation as the universal service to meet basic needs, and although in Thatcher's Britain this formulation is still important, it effectively forecloses the issue of varied public services and user choice. The shadow of Fordism haunts us even in the terms in which we oppose it.

The Break-Up of Fordism

Fordism as a vision – both left and right – had always been challenged, on the shopfloor, in the political party, the seminar room and the studio. In 1968 this challenge exploded in Europe and the USA. It was a cultural as much as an industrial revolt, attacking the central principles of Fordism, its definitions of work and consumption, its shaping of towns and its overriding of nature.

From that time we can see a fracturing of the foundations of predictability on which Fordism was based. Demand became more volatile and fragmented. Productivity growth fell as the result of workplace resistance. The decline in profit drove down investment. Exchange rates were fluctuating, oil prices rose and in 1974 came the greatest slump the West had had since the 1930s.

The consensus response was a Keynesian one, to restore profitability through a managed increase in demand and an incomes policy. For monetarism the route to profitability went through the weakening of labour, a cut in state spending and a reclaiming of the public sector for private accumulation. Economists and politicians were re-fighting the battles of the last slump. Private capital on the other hand was dealing with the present one. It was using new technology and new production principles to make Fordism flexible, and in doing so stood much of the old culture on its head.

In Britain, the groundwork for the new system was laid not in manufacturing but in retailing. Since the 1950s, retailers had been using computers to transform the distribution system. All mass producers have the problem of forecasting demand. If they produce too little they lose market share. If they produce too much, they are left with stocks, which are costly to hold, or have to be sold at a discount. Retailers face this problem not just for a few products, but for thousands. Their answer has been to develop information and supply systems which allow them to order supplies to coincide with demand. Every evening Sainsbury's receives details of the sales of all 12,000 lines from each of its shops; these are turned into orders for warehouse deliveries for the coming night, and replacement production for the following day. With computerised control of stocks in the shop, transport networks, automatic loading and unloading, Sainsbury's flow-line make-to-order system has conquered the Fordist problem of stocks.

They have also overcome the limits of the mass product. For, in contrast to the discount stores which are confined to a few, fast-selling items, Sainsbury's, like the new wave of high street shops, can handle ranges of products geared to segments of the market. Market niching has become the slogan of the high street. Market researches break down market by age (youth, young adults, 'grey power'), by household types (dinkies, single-gender couples, one-parent families), by income, occupation, housing and increasingly, by locality. They analyse 'lifestyles', correlating consumption patterns across commodities, from food to clothing, and health to holidays.

The point of this new anthropology of consumption is to target both product and shops to particular segments. Burton's – once a mass producer with generalised retail outlets – has changed in the 1980s to being a niche market retailer with a team of anthropologists, a group of segmented stores – Top Shop, Top Man, Dorothy Perkins, Principles and Burton's itself – and now has no manufacturing plants of its own. Conran's Storehouse group – Habitat, Heals, Mothercare, Richards and BHS – all geared to different groups, offers not only clothes, but furniture and furnishings, in other words entire lifestyles. At the heart of Conran's organisation in London is what amounts to a factory of 150 designers, with collages of different lifestyles on the wall, Bold Primary, Orchid, mid-Atlantic and the Cottage Garden.

In all these shops the emphasis has shifted from the manufacturer's economies of scale to the retailer's economies of scope. The economies come from offering an integrated range from which customers choose their own basket of products. There is also an economy of innovation, for the modern retail systems allow new product ideas to be tested in practice, through shop sales, and the successful ones then to be ordered for wider distribution. Innovation has become a leading edge of the new competition. Product life has become shorter, for fashion goods and consumer durables.

A centre-piece of this new retailing is design. Designers produce the innovations. They shape the lifestyles. They design the shops, which are described as 'stages' for the act of shopping. There are now 29,000 people working in design consultancies in the UK, which have sales of £1,600 million per annum. They are the engineers of designer capitalism. With market researchers they have steered the high street from being retailers of goods to retailers of style.

These changes are a response to, and a means of shaping, the shift from mass consumption. Instead of keeping up with the Joneses there has been a move to be different from the Joneses. Many of these differences are vertical, intended to confirm status and class. But some are horizontal centred and round group identities, linked to age, or region or ethnicity. In spite of the fact that basic needs are still unmet, the high street does offer a new variety and creativity in consumption which the Left's puritan tradition should also address. Whatever our responses, the revolution in retailing reflects new principles of production, a new pluralism of products and a new importance for innovation. As such it marks a shift to a post-Fordist age.

There have been parallel shifts in manufacturing, not least in response to the retailers' just-in-time system of ordering. In some sectors where the manufacturers are a little more than subcontractors to the retailers, their flexibility has been achieved at the expense of labour. In others, capital itself has suffered, as furniture retailers like MFI squeeze their suppliers, driving down prices, limiting design, and thereby destroying much of the mass-production furniture industry during the downturns.

But the most successful manufacturing regions have been ones which have linked flexible manufacturing systems, with innovative organisation and an emphasis on 'customisation' design and quality. Part of the flexibility has been achieved through new technology, and the introduction of programmable machines which can switch from product to product with little manual resetting and downtime. Benetton's automatic dyeing plant, for example, allows it to change its colours in time with demand. In the car industry, whereas General Motors took nine hours to change the dyes on its presses in the early 1980s, Toyota have lowered the time to two minutes, and have cut the average lot size of body parts from 5,000 to 500 in the process. The line, in short, has become flexible. Instead of using purpose-built machines to make standard products, flexible automation uses general-purpose machines to produce a variety of products.

Japanisation

Manufacturers have also been adopting the retailers' answer to stocks. The pioneer is Toyota which stands to the new era as Ford did to the old. Toyota, the founder of Toyota, inspired by a visit to an American supermarket, applied the just-in-time system to his component suppliers, ordering on the basis of his daily production plans, and getting the components delivered right beside the line. Most of Toyota's components are still produced on the same day as they are assembled.

Toyota's prime principle of the elimination of wasteful practices meant going beyond the problem of stocks. His firm has used design and materials technology to simplify complex elements, cutting down the number of parts and operations. It adopted a zero-defect policy, developing machines which stopped automatically, when a fault occurred, as well as statistical quality control techniques. As in retailing, the complex web of processes, inside and outside the plant, were co-ordinated through computers, a process that economists have called systemation (in contrast to automation). The result of these practices is a discontinuous speed-up in what Marx called the circulation of capital. Toyota turns over its materials and products ten times more quickly than western car producers, saving material and energy in the process.

The key point about the Toyota system, however, is not so much that it speeds up the making of a car. It is in order to make these changes that it has adopted quite different methods of labour control and organisation. Toyota saw that traditional Taylorism did not work. Central management had no access to all the information needed for continuous innovation. Quality could not be achieved with deskilled manual workers. Taylorism wasted what they called 'the gold in workers' heads'.

Toyota, and the Japanese more generally, having broken the industrial unions in the

1950s, have developed a core of multi-skilled workers whose tasks include not only manufacture and maintenance, but the improvement of the products and processes under their control. Each breakdown is seen as a chance for improvement. Even hourly-paid workers are trained in statistical techniques and monitoring, and register and interpret statistics to identify deviations from a norm – tasks customarily reserved for management in Fordism. Quality circles are a further way of tapping the ideas of the workforce. In post-Fordism, the worker is designed to act as a computer as well as a machine.

As a consequence the Taylorist contract changes. Workers are no longer interchangeable. They gather experience. The Japanese job-for-life and corporate welfare system provides security. For the firm it secures an asset. Continuous training, payment by seniority, a breakdown of job demarcations, are all part of the Japanese core wage relation. The EETPU's lead in embracing private pension schemes, BUPA, internal flexibility, union-organised training and single-company unions are all consistent with this path of post-Fordist industrial relations.

Not the least of the dangers of this path is that it further hardens the divisions between the core and the peripheral workforce. The cost of employing lifetime workers means an incentive to subcontract all jobs not essential to the core. The other side of the Japanese jobs-for-life is a majority of low-paid, fragmented peripheral workers, facing an underfunded and inadequate welfare state. The duality in the labour market, and in the welfare economy, could be taken as a description of Thatcherism. The point is that neither the EETPU's policy nor that of Mrs Thatcher should read as purely political. There is a material basis to both, rooted in changes in production.

There are parallel changes in corporate organisation. With the revision of Taylorism, a layer of management has been stripped away. Greater central control has allowed the decentralisation of work. Day-to-day autonomy has been given to work groups and plant managers. Teams linking departments horizontally have replaced the rigid verticality of Fordist bureaucracies.

It is only a short step from here to sub-contracting and franchising. This is often simply a means of labour control. But in engineering and light consumer industries networks and semi-independent firms have often proved more innovative than vertically integrated producers. A mark of post-Fordism is close two-way relations between customer and supplier, and between specialised producers in the same industry. Co-operative competition replaces the competition of the jungle. These new relationships within and between enterprises and on the shopfloor have made least headway in the countries in which Fordism took fullest root, the USA and the UK. Here firms have tried to match continental and Japanese flexibility through automation while retaining Fordist shopfloor, managerial and competitive relations.

Yet in spite of this we can see in this country a culture of post-Fordist capitalism emerging. Consumption has a new place. As for production the keyword is flexibility – of plant and machinery, as of products and labour. Emphasis shifts from scale to scope, and from cost to quality. Organisations are geared to respond to rather than regulate markets. They are seen as frameworks for learning as much as instruments of control. Their hierarchies are flatter and their structures more open. The guerrilla force takes over from the standing army. All this has liberated the centre from the tyranny of the immediate. Its task shifts from planning to strategy, and to the promotion of the instruments of post-Fordist control – systems, software, corporate culture and cash.

On the bookshelf, Peters and Waterman replace FW Taylor. In the theatre the audience is served lentils by the actors. At home Channel 4 takes its place beside ITV.

Majorities are transformed into minorities, as we enter the age of proportional representation. And under the shadow of Chernobyl even Fordism's scientific modernism is being brought to book, as we realise there is more than one way up the technological mountain.

Not all these can be read off from the new production systems. Some are rooted in the popular opposition to Fordism. They represent an alternative version of post-Fordism, which flowered after 1968 in the community movements and the new craft trade unionism of alternative plans. Their organisational forms – networks, work-place democracy, co-operatives, the dissolving of the platform speaker into meetings in the round have echoes in the new textbooks of management, indeed capital has been quick to take up progressive innovations for its own purposes. There are then many sources and contested versions of post-Fordist culture. What they share is a break with the era of Ford.

Post-Fordism is being introduced under the sway of the market and in accordance with the requirements of capital accumulation. It validates only what can command a place in the market; it cuts the labour force in two, and leaves large numbers without any work at all. Its prodigious productivity gains are ploughed back into yet further accumulation and the quickening consumption of symbols in the Post-Modern market place. In the UK, Thatcherism has strengthened the prevailing wind of the commodity economy, liberating the power of private purses and so fragmenting the social sphere.

To judge from Kamata's celebrated account, working for Toyota is hardly a step forward from working for Ford. As one British worker in a Japanese factory in the North-East of England put it, 'they want us to live for work, where we want to work to live'. Japanisation has no place in any modern *News From Nowhere*.

Yet post-Fordism has shaken the kaleidoscope of the economy, and exposed an old politics. We have to respond to its challenges and draw lessons from its systems.

Political Consequences of Post-Fordism

Firstly there is the question of consumption. How reluctant the Left has been to take this on, in spite of the fact that it is a sphere of unpaid production, and, as Gorz insists, one of creative activity. Which local council pays as much attention to its users, as does the market research industry on behalf of commodities? Which bus or railway service cuts queues and speeds the traveller with as much care as retailers show to their just-in-time stocks? The perspective of consumption – so central to the early socialist movement – is emerging from under the tarpaulin of production: the effects of food additives and low-level radiation, of the air we breathe and surroundings we live in, the availability of childcare and community centres, or access to privatised city centres and transport geared to particular needs. These are issues of consumption, where the social and the human have been threatened by the market. In each case the market solutions have been contested by popular movements. Yet their causes and the relations of consumption have been given only walk-on parts in party programmes. They should now come to the centre of the stage.

Secondly, there is labour. Post-Fordism sees labour as the key asset of modern production. Rank Xerox is trying to change its accounting system so that machinery becomes a cost, and labour its fixed asset. The Japanese emphasise labour and learning. The Left should widen this reversal of Taylorism, and promote a discontinuous expansion of adult education inside and outside the workplace.

They should also provide an alternative to the new management of time. The conservative sociologist Daniel Bell sees the management of time as the key issue of post-industrial society. Post-Fordist capital is restructuring working time for its own convenience: with new shifts, split shifts, rostering, weekend working, and the regulation of labour, through part-time and casual contracts, to the daily and weekly cycles of work. Computer systems allow Tesco to manage more than 130 different types of labour contract in its large stores. These systems of employment and welfare legislation should be moulded for the benefit not the detriment of labour. The length of the working day, of the working week, and year, and lifetime, should be shaped to accommodate the many responsibilities and needs away from work.

The most pressing danger from post-Fordism, however, is the way it is widening the split between core and periphery in the labour market and the welfare system. The EETPU's building a fortress round the core is as divisive as Thatcherism itself. We need bridges across the divide, with trade unions representing core workers using their power to extend benefits to all, as IG Metall have been doing in Germany. A priority for any Labour government would be to put a floor under the labour market, and remove the discriminations faced by the low paid. The Liberals pursued such a policy in late nineteenth-century London. Labour should reintroduce it in late twentieth-century Britain.

Underlying this split is the post-Fordist bargain which offers security in return for flexibility. Because of its cost, Japanese capital restricts this bargain to the core; in the peripheral workforce, flexibility is achieved through insecurity. Sweden has tried to widen the core bargain to the whole population with a policy of full employment, minimum incomes, extensive retraining programmes, and egalitarian income distribution. These are the two options, and Thatcherism favours the first.

Could Labour deliver the second? How real is a policy of full employment when the speed of technical change destroys jobs as rapidly as growth creates them? The question – as Sweden has shown – is one of distribution. There is the distribution of working time: the campaign for the thirty-five hour week and the redistribution of overtime should be at the centre of Labour policy in the 1990s. There is also the distribution of income and the incidence of tax. Lafontaine's idea of shifting tax from labour to energy is an interesting one. Equally important is the need to tax heavily the speculative gains from property, the rent from oil, and unearned and inherited income. Finally taxes will need to be raised on higher incomes, and should be argued for not only in terms of full employment, but in terms of the improvements to the caring services, the environment, and the social economy which the market of the 1980s has done so much to destroy. Full employment is possible. It should be based on detailed local plans, decentralised public services and full employment centres. It cannot be delivered from Westminster alone.

Thirdly, we need to learn from post-Fordism's organisational innovations, and apply them within our own public and political structures. Representative democracy within Fordist bureaucracies is not enough. What matters is the structure of the bureaucracy and its external relations. In the state this means redefining its role as strategist, as innovator, co-ordinator, and supporter of producers. In some cases the span of co-ordination needs to be extended (notably in integrating public transport and the movement of freight): in others production should be decentralised and the drive for scale reversed (the electricity industry, education and health have all suffered from over-centralised operations). Public services should move beyond the universal to the differentiated service. Nothing has been more outrageous than the attack on local government as loony leftist, when councils have sought to shape policies to the needs of groups facing discrimination. Capitalist retailers and market researchers make these distinctions in the pursuit of sales, and socialists should match them in pursuit of service. If greater user control and internal democracy were added to this, then we would be some way towards the dismantling of mass-produced administration, and the creation of a progressive and flexible state.

Lastly, there is private industry. In many sectors both industry and public policy are frozen in Fordism, even as the leading edge of competition has shifted from scale to product, and from costs to strategy. In spite of the restructuring that has taken place in the 1980s, largely at the expense of labour, manufacturing competitiveness continues to decline. By 1984 only five out of thirty-four major manufacturing sectors did not have a negative trade balance.

The Left's response to this decline has been couched largely in terms of macro policy: devaluing the pound, controlling wage levels and expanding investment. Industrial policy has taken second place, and centred on amalgamations and scale and the encouragement of new technology. This has been Labour's version of modernisation.

The fact remains that size has not secured competitiveness. Neither has a declining exchange rate with the yen, nor wage levels which have made the UK one of the cheap labour havens of Europe. The changes are much deeper than this.

An alternative needs to start not from plans but from strategies. Strategic capacity within British industry is thin and even thinner in the state and the labour movement. Sector and enterprise strategies need to take on board the nature of the new competition, the centrality of skilled labour, the need for specialisation and quality, and for continuous innovation.

What public policy should do is to find ways of ensuring that the resultant restructuring takes account of social priorities: labour and educational reform is one part of this; industrial democracy another; environmental and energy saving a third; user concerns about quality and variety a fourth. Some of these will require new laws; others incentive schemes; others collective bargaining. They all need to be a part of strategic restructuring.

In each sector there will be giants barring the path towards such a programme. One will be the stock-market. A priority for a Labour government will be to reduce the stock-market's power to undermine long-term strategic investment (in this we need to follow the example of the Japanese). Another will be multinationals which dominate so many industrial and service sectors in the economy. The urgent task here is to form coalitions of states, unions and municipalities across the European Community to press for common strategic alternatives at the European level. A third will be the retailers. In some cases retailers will be important allies in restructuring industry progressively (the co-op has a role here); in others the conduct of retailers is destructive, and a Labour government should take direct measures against them.

At the same time, Labour needs to develop a network of social industrial institutions, decentralised, innovative and entrepreneurial. For each sector and area there should be established one or more enterprise boards. They would be channels for long-term funds for new technology, for strategic support across a sector, for common services, and for initiatives and advice on the social priorities.

Public purchasing should be co-ordinated and used not just to provide protection in the old manner, but as supporters of the sectoral programme, as contributors to the improvement of quality, and as sources of ideas. New technology networks should also be set up, linking universities and polytechnics with the sectors and unions (this is an effective part of Dukakis's Massachusetts programme).

In short we need a new model of the public economy made up of a honeycomb of decentralised, yet synthetic institutions, integrated by a common strategy, and intervening in the economy at the level of production rather than trying vainly to plan all from on high. The success of the Italian consortia, and the German industrial regions has been centrally dependent on such a network of municipal and regional government support.

A key role in taking forward this industrial programme should be played by the unions. Restructuring has put them on the defensive. They have found their power weakened and their position isolated. Few have had the resources to develop alternative strategies and build coalitions of communities and users around them. Yet this is now a priority if unions are to reclaim their position as spokespeople of an alternative economy rather than defenders of a sectional interest. Research departments should be expanded, and commissions given to external researchers. There should be joint commissions of members, and users and other related groups, as well as supportive local authorities. The production of the policy would itself be a form of democratic politics.

Mrs Thatcher has led an attack on the key institutions of Fordism: on manufacturing, on the centralised state, on industrial unions and on the national economy. She has opened up Britain to one version of post-Fordism, one that has strengthened the control of finance and international capital, has increased inequality and destroyed whole areas of collective life.

There is an alternative. It has grown up in the new movements, in the trade unions, and in local government over the past twenty years. It has broken through the bounds of the Left's Fordist inheritance, in culture, structure and economics. From it can develop – as is already happening in Europe – an alternative socialism adequate to the post-Fordist age.

From *New Times: The Changing Face of Politics in the 1990s*, edited by Stuart Hall and Martin Jacques, Lawrence and Wishart, London, 1989.

Edward W Soja
TAKING LOS ANGELES APART
TOWARDS A POSTMODERN GEOGRAPHY

Urban and Regional Restructuring

1 One prevailing trend has been the increasing centralisation and concentration of capital ownership, typified by the formation of huge corporate conglomerates combining diversified industrial production, finance, real estate, information processing, entertainment and other service activities. This conglomeration process goes several steps further than the horizontal mergers of the late nineteenth century and the later vertical mergers and state-managed monopolies that were so central to the rise of Fordism. Formal management structures are often less centrally controlled and more flexible, while the core production processes have increasingly been broken into separate segments operating, unlike the integrated Fordist assembly line, at many different locations. The multiplication of branches adds further flexibility through parallel production, while more extensive subcontracting expands the vital transactions of the conglomerate even further beyond the bounds of ownership.

2 Added to the corporate conglomeration of ownership has been a more technologically-based integration of diversified industrial, research, and service activities that similarly reallocates capital and labour into sprawling spatial systems of production linking centres of administrative power over capital investment to a constellation of parallel branches, subsidiaries, subcontracting firms, and specialised public and private services. More than ever before, the spatial scope of these production systems has become global, but they also have a powerful urbanisation effect through the local agglomeration of new territorial industrial complexes (usually located outside the old centres of Fordist industry). Here again there seems to be a paradoxical pairing of deconcentration and reconcentration in the geographical landscape.

3 Linked to increased capital concentration and oligopoly has been a more pronounced internationalisation and global involvement of productive and finance capital, sustained by new arrangements for credit and liquidity organised on a world scale. This transnational or global capital is able to explore and exploit commodity, financial, consumer, and labour markets all over the world with fewer territorial constraints (especially from direct state control) than ever before. As a result, purely domestic capital has been playing a decreasing role in the local and national economies of the advanced industrial countries as these economies increasingly internationalise.

4 The weakening of local controls and state regulation over an increasingly 'footloose' and mobile capital has contributed to an extraordinary global restructuring of industrial production. Large-scale capitalist industrialisation has been occurring in a series of peripheral countries and regions for the first time, while many core countries have been experiencing an extensive regional industrial decline. This combination of deindustrialisation

and reindustrialisation has shattered long-standing global definitions of core and periphery, First-Second-Third Worlds, and created the tentative outlines of a different, if not an entirely new, international division of labour.

5 In the USA and elsewhere, the accelerated geographical mobility of industrial and industry-related capital has triggered and intensified territorial competition among government units for new investments (and for maintaining existing firms in place). These 'regional wars for jobs and dollars' absorb increasing amounts of public funds and often dominate the urban and regional planning process (at the expense of local social services and welfare). As capital increasingly co-operates, communities increasingly compete, another old paradox that is becoming particularly intensified in the present period.

6 Paralleling what has been happening at the global scale, the regional division of labour within countries has been changing more dramatically than it has over the past hundred years. Regions containing the manufacturing sectors that led the Fordist postwar boom (motor cars, steel, construction, civilian aircraft, consumer durables) are being disciplined and 'rationalised' through a varying mix of capital flight and plant closures, the introduction of new labour-saving technology, and more direct attacks on organised labour (deunionisation, labour givebacks, constraints on collective bargaining). A selective reindustrialisation based primarily on advanced technologies of production and centred on less-unionised sectors is simultaneously either arresting the decline in a few of the more successfully rationalised regions (for example, New England) or focusing industrial expansion on new territorial industrial complexes (typically on the periphery of major metropolitan areas).

7 Accompanying these processes are major changes in the structure of urban labour markets. Deeper segmentation and fragmentation is occurring, with a more pronounced polarisation of occupations between high pay/high skill and low pay/low skill workers, and an increasingly specialised residential segregation based on occupation, race, ethnicity, immigrant status, income, lifestyle, and other employment related variables. An overall decrease in the relative proportion of manufacturing employment (due mainly to declining employment in the older, more unionised heavy industries), accompanied by a rapid increase in lower wage tertiary employment, tends to produce significantly reduced (if not negative) rates of growth in wage levels and real income for workers and curtailed increases in productivity levels in the national economy wherever this shifting sectoral structure is most pronounced.

8 Job growth tends to be concentrated in those sectors which can most easily avail themselves of comparatively cheap, weakly organised, and easily manipulable labour pools and which are thus better able to compete within an international market (or obtain significant protection against international competition from the local or national state). The leading job growth sectors are thus both high and low technology based, and draw upon a mix of skilled technicians, part-time workers, immigrants and women. This creates a squeeze in the middle of the labour market, with a small bulging at the top and an even greater bulging at the bottom (especially if one includes the burgeoning informal economy as well). Only in the United States, however, among all the advanced industrial countries at least, has this dramatic employment restructuring been associated with substantial aggregate job growth.[2]

These and other prevailing restructuring processes have injected a peculiar equivo-calness into the changing geographical landscape, a combination of opposites that defies simple categorical generalisation. Never before has the spatiality of the industrial capitalist city or the mosaic of uneven regional development become so kaleidoscopic, so loosened from its nineteenth-century moorings, so filled with unsettling contrariety. On the one hand, there is significant urban deindustrialisation emptying the old nodal concentrations not only to the suburban rings, a pattern which began as far back as the late nineteenth century, but much further afield – into small non-metropolitan towns and 'greenfield' sites or beyond, to the NICs and NIRs. On the other hand, a new kind of industrial base is being established in the major metropolitan regions, with an 'urbanisation effect' that is almost oblivious to the locational advantages embedded in the former urban-industrial landscape.[3] To speak of the 'post-industrial' city is thus, at best, a half-truth and at worst a baffling misinterpretation of contemporary urban and regional dynamics, for industrialisation remains the primary propulsive force in development everywhere in the contemporary world.

Growing, in large part, out of this combination of deindustrialisation and reindustrialisation is an equally paradoxical internal restructuring of metropolitan regions, marked by both a decentring and recentring of urban nodalities. Sprawling suburbanisation/metropolitanisation continues but it no longer seems as unambigu-ously associated with the decline of the downtown centres. Carefully orchestrated downtown 'renaissance' is occurring in both booming and declining metropolitan regions. At the same time, what some have called 'outer cities', rather amorphous agglomerations that defy conventional definitions of urban-suburban-exurban, are forming new concentrations within the metropolitan fabric and provoking a spray of neologisms which try to capture their distinctiveness: technopolis, technoburb, 'urban village', metroplex, silicon landscape.

The internationalisation process has created another set of paradoxes, for it involves both a reaching out from the urban to the global and a reaching in from the global to the urban locale. This has given new meaning to the notion of the 'world city' as an urban condensation of the restructured international division of labour.[4] More than ever be-fore, the macro-political economy of the world is becoming contextualised and reproduced in the city. First World cities are being filled with Third World populations that, in some cases, are now the majority. While these combinatorial world cities increasingly stretch out to shape the international economy in a form of global spatial planning, they also increasingly incorporate internally the political and economic tensions and battlegrounds of international relations.

Neither conventional urban theory nor the Marxist urban political economy that consolidated in the 1970s has been able to make theoretical and political sense of this enigmatic contemporary urban restructuring. Whereas the former tends to overspecify the urban, making the assertion of urbanism take the place of explanation, the latter has tended, for the most part, to underspecify the urban, passing abstractly over its causal power and its integral positioning within the historical geography of capitalism. Both have tended to overemphasise consumption issues and neglect the urbanisation effects of industrial production, a narrowing which may have been politically appropriate to the 1960s but is now too short-sighted to contend effectively with contemporary restructuring processes.

In many ways, the same can be said for the neo-Marxist international political economy that evolved in tandem with the urban. It, too, tended to oversimplify the complexities of capitalist production and labour processes, or to assume that historical materialism had already solved all its riddles. Much was accomplished in exploring the multiple circuits of capital shaping the world system and in retracing their historical origins and geographical development. But the prevailing perspectives were caught short by the dramatic shifts in the international division of labour brought about by an essentially unexpected and world-wide industrial restructuring.

At present, the relatively new field of regional political economy and a reinvigorated and reoriented regional industrial geography seem to be the most insightful and innovative arenas for analysing the macro-, meso-, and micro-political economies of restructuring. Both can be called flexible specialisations, for they are less concerned with old boundaries and disciplinary constraints and are thus more open to timely adaptation to meet new demands and challenges. The regional perspective facilitates the synthesis of the urban and the global while remaining cognisant of the powerful mediating role of the national state even as this role dwindles somewhat in the current era. The mutually responsive interplay of regionalisation and regionalism provides a particularly insightful window onto the dynamics of spatialisation and geographically uneven development, gives greater depth and political meaning to the notion of spatial divisions of labour, and abounds with useful connections to the revamped social ontologies discussed earlier. Just as important, its openness and flexibility, its inclination to try new combinations of ideas rather than fall back to old categorical dualities, makes critical regional studies the most likely point of confluence for the three streams of contemporary restructuring. Here is where our understanding of postfordism, postmodernism, and a post-historicist critical social theory may most bountifully take place.

Taking Los Angeles Apart: Towards A Postmodern Geography

'The Aleph?' I repeated.

'Yes, the only place on earth where all places are – seen from every angle, each standing clear, without any confusion or blending.'

. . . Then I saw the Aleph . . . And here begins my despair as a writer. All language is a set of symbols whose use among its speakers assumes a shared past. How, then, can I translate into words the limitless Aleph, which my floundering mind can scarcely encompass?' (Jorge Luis Borges, *The Aleph*)

Los Angeles, like Borges's Aleph, is exceedingly tough-to-track, peculiarly resistant to conventional description. It is difficult to grasp persuasively in a temporal narrative for it generates too many conflicting images, confounding historicisation, always seeming to stretch laterally instead of unfolding sequentially. At the same time, its spatiality challenges orthodox analysis and interpretation, for it too seems limitless and constantly in motion, never still enough to encompass, too filled with 'other spaces' to be informatively described. Looking at Los Angeles from the inside, introspectively, one tends to see only fragments and immediacies, fixed sites of myopic understanding impulsively generalised to represent the whole. To the more far-sighted outsider, the visible aggregate of the whole of Los Angeles churns so confusingly that it induces little more than illusionary stereotypes or self-serving caricatures – if its reality is ever seen at all.

What is this place? Even knowing where to focus, to find a starting point, is not easy, for, perhaps more than any other place, Los Angeles is everywhere. It is global in the fullest sense of the word. Nowhere is this more evident than in its cultural projection and ideological reach, its almost ubiquitous screening of itself as a rectangular dream machine for the world. Los Angeles broadcasts its self-imagery so widely that probably more people have seen this place – or at least fragments of it than any other on the planet. As a result, the seers of Los Angeles have become countless, even more so as the progressive globalisation of its urban political economy flows along similar channels, making Los Angeles perhaps the epitomising world-city, *une ville devenue monde*.

Everywhere seems also to be in Los Angeles. To it flows the bulk of the transpacific trade of the United States, a cargo which currently surpasses that of the smaller ocean to the east. Global currents of people, information and ideas accompany the trade. It was once dubbed Iowa's seaport, but today Los Angeles has become an entrepot to the world, a true pivot of the four quarters, a congeries of east and west, north and south. And from every quarter's teeming shores have poured a pool of cultures so diverse that contemporary Los Angeles represents the world in connected urban microcosms, reproducing *in situ* the customary colours and confrontations of a hundred different homelands. Extraordinary heterogeneity can be exemplified endlessly in this fulsome urban landscape. The only place on earth where all places are? Again I appeal to Borges and the Aleph for appropriate insight:

> Really, what I want to do is impossible, for any listing of an endless series is doomed to be infinitesimal. In that single gigantic instant I saw millions of acts both delightful and awful; not one of them amazed me more than the fact that all of them occupied the same point in space, without overlapping or transparency. What my eyes beheld was simultaneous, but what I shall now write down will be successive, because language is successive. Nonetheless, I will try to recollect what I can.

I too will try to recollect what I can, knowing well that any totalising description of the LA-leph is impossible. What follows then is a succession of fragmentary glimpses, a freed association of reflective and interpretive field notes which aim to construct a critical human geography of the Los Angeles urban region. My observations are necessarily and contingently incomplete and ambiguous, but the target I hope will remain clear: to appreciate the specificity and uniqueness of a particularly restless geographical landscape while simultaneously seeking to extract insights at higher levels of abstraction, to explore through Los Angeles glimmers of the fundamental spatiality of social life, the adhesive relations between society and space, history and geography, the splendidly idiographic and the enticingly generalisable features of a postmodern urban geography.

A Round Around Los Angeles

> I saw a small iridescent sphere of almost unbearable brilliance. At first I thought it was revolving; then I realised that this movement was an illusion created by the dizzying world it bounded . . . (*The Aleph*, 13)

We must have a place to start, to begin reading the context. However much the formative space of Los Angeles may be global (or perhaps Mandelbrotian, constructed in zig-zagging nests of fractals), it must be reduced to a more familiar and localised geometry to be seen. Appropriately enough, just such a reductionist mapping has popularly presented itself. It is defined by an embracing circle drawn sixty miles (about a hundred kilometres) out from a central point located in the downtown core of the City of Los Angeles. Whether the precise central point is City Hall or perhaps one of the more recently erected corporate towers, I do not know. But I prefer the monumental twenty-eight storey City Hall, up to the 1920s the only erection in the entire region allowed to surpass the allegedly earthquake-proofing 150-foot height limitation. It is an impressive punctuation point, capped by an interpretation of the Mausoleum of Halicarnassus, wrapped around a Byzantine rotunda, and etched with this infatuating inscription: 'THE CITY CAME INTO BEING TO PRESERVE LIFE, IT EXISTS FOR THE GOOD LIFE'. Significantly, City Hall sits at the corner of Temple and Spring Streets.

The Sixty-Mile Circle, so inscribed, covers the thinly sprawling 'built-up' area of five counties, a population of more than twelve million individuals, at least 132 incorporated cities and, it is claimed, the greatest concentration of technocratic expertise and militaristic imagination in the USA. Its workers produce, when last estimated, a gross annual output worth nearly $250 billion, more than the 800 million people of India produce each year. This is certainly Greater Los Angeles, a dizzying world.

The determination of the Sixty-Mile Circle is the product of the largest bank headquartered within its bounds, a bank potently named by connecting together two definitive pillars of the circumscribed economy: 'security' and 'pacific'.[5] How ironic, indeed oxymoronic, is the combination of these two words, security and pacific. The first is redolent of the lethal arsenal emanating from the Sixty-Mile Circle's technicians and scientists, surely today the most powerful assemblage of weapon-making expertise ever grounded into one place. In contrast, the second signals peacefulness, tranquillity, moderation, amity, concord. Holocaust attached to halcyon, another of the many simultaneous contraries, interposed opposites, which epitomise Los Angeles and help to explain why conventional categorical logic can never hope to capture its historical and geographic signification. One must return again and again to these simultaneous contraries to depict Los Angeles.

Circumspection

Securing the Pacific rim has been the manifest destiny of Los Angeles, a theme which defines its sprawling urbanisation perhaps more than any other analytical construct. Efforts to secure the Pacific signpost the history of Los Angeles from its smoky inception as El Pueblo de Nuestra Señora la Reina de Los Angeles de Porciuncula in 1781, through its heated competition for commercial and financial hegemony with San Francisco, to the unfolding sequence of Pacific wars that has marked the past forty-five years of the American century. It is not always easy to see the imprint of this imperial history on the material landscape, but an imaginative cruise directly above the contemporary circumference of the Sixty-Mile Circle can be unusually revealing.

The Circle cuts the south coast at the border between Orange and San Diego Counties, near one of the key checkpoints regularly set up to intercept the northward flow of undocumented migrants, and not far from the San Clemente 'White House' of Richard Nixon and the fitful SONGS of the San Onofre Nuclear Generating Station. The first rampart to watch, however, is Camp Pendleton Marine Corps Base, the largest military base in California in terms of personnel, the freed spouses of whom have helped to build a growing high-technology complex in northern San Diego County. After cruising over the moors of Camp Pendleton, the Cleveland National Forest, and the vital Colorado River Aqueduct draining in from the east[6] we can land directly in Rampart #2, March Air Force Base, adjacent to the city of Riverside. The insides of March are a ready outpost for the roaming Strategic Air Command.

Another quick hop over Sunnymead, the Box Spring Mountains, and Redlands takes us to Rampart #3, Norton Air Force Base, next to the city of San Bernardino and just south of the almost empty San Manuel Indian Reservation. The guide books tell us that the primary mission of Norton is military airlifts, just in case. To move on we must rise still higher to pass over the ski-sloped peaks of the San Bernardino Mountains and National Forest, through Cajon Pass and passing the old Santa Fe Trail, into the picturesque Mojave Desert. Near Victorville is Rampart #4, George Air Force Base, specialising in air defence and interception. Almost the same distance away – our stops seem remarkably evenly spaced thus far – takes us by dry Mirage Lake to the giant Edwards Air Force Base, Rampart #5, site of NASA and USAF research and development activities and a primary landing field for unexploded Space Shuttles. Stretching off to the south is an important aerospace corridor through Lancaster, to Palmdale Airport and Air Force Plant 42, which serves Edwards's key historical function as testing ground for advanced fighters and bombers. People who live around here call it Canyon Country and many want it broken off from the County of Los Angeles down below.

The next leg is longer and more serene: over the Antelope Valley and the Los Angeles Aqueduct (tapping the Los Angeles-owned segments of the life-giving but rapidly dying Owens River Valley two hundred miles further away); across Interstate 5 (the main freeway corridor to the north), a long stretch of Los Padres National Forest and the Wild Condor Refuge,[7] to the idyll-ised town of Ojai (site for the filming of 'Lost Horizon'), and then to the Pacific again at the Mission of San Buenaventura, in Ventura County. A few miles away (the Sixty-Mile Circle actually cut right through the others) is Rampart #6, a complex consisting of a now inactive Air Force Base at Oxnard, the Naval Construction Battalion Centre of Port Hueneme, and, far above all, the longsighted Naval Air Missile Centre at Point Mugu. If we wished, we could complete the full circle of coincidence over the Pacific, picking up almost directly below us the US Naval Facilities on San Nicolas and San Clemente Islands. These islands rarely appear on maps of Los Angeles and they remain invisible on ours.

It is startling how much of the circumference is owned and preserved by the Federal Government in one way or another. Premeditation may be impossible to ascribe, but post-meditation on the circumscriptive federal presence is certainly in order.

Enclosures
What in the world lies behind this Herculean wall? What appears to need such formidable protection? In essence, we return to the same question with which we began: What is this place? There is, of course, that far-reaching Dream Machine and its launching pads, transmitting visual images and evocative sounds of that 'good life' announced on the facade of City Hall. But the 'entertainment' industry is itself a facade and, significant though it may be, there is much more being screened behind it, much more that has developed within the Sixty-Mile Circle that demands to be protected and preserved.

If there has emerged a compelling focus to the recent academic literature on Los Angeles, it is the discovery of extraordinary industrial production, a eureka so contrary to popular perceptions of Los Angeles that its explorers are often compelled to exaggerate to keep their lines of vision sufficiently open and clear against external obfuscations. Yet it is no exaggeration to claim that the Sixty-Mile Circle contains the premier industrial growth pole of the twentieth century, at least within the advanced capitalist countries. Oil, orange groves, films and flying set the scene at the beginning of the century and tend to remain fixed in many contemporary images of industrious, but not industrial, Los Angeles. Since 1930, however, Los Angeles has probably led all other major metropolitan areas in the USA, decade by decade, in the accumulation of new manufacturing employment.

For many, industrial Los Angeles nevertheless remains a contradiction in terms. When a colleague at UCLA (University of California, Los Angeles) began his explorations of the industrial geography of Los Angeles, his appeal to a prominent national scientific

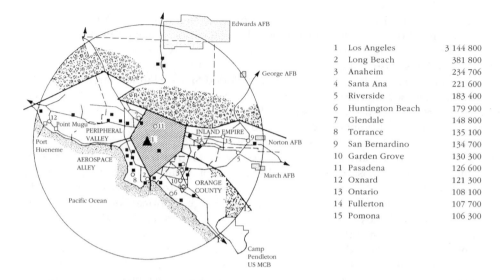

1	Los Angeles	3 144 800
2	Long Beach	381 800
3	Anaheim	234 706
4	Santa Ana	221 600
5	Riverside	183 400
6	Huntington Beach	179 900
7	Glendale	148 800
8	Torrance	135 100
9	San Bernardino	134 700
10	Garden Grove	130 300
11	Pasadena	126 600
12	Oxnard	121 300
13	Ontario	108 100
14	Fullerton	107 700
15	Pomona	106 300

Figure 11 A view of the outer spaces of Los Angeles. The urban core is outlined in the shape of a pentagon, with the Central City denoted by the black triangle. The major military bases on the perimeter of the Sixty-Mile Circle are identified and the black squares are the sites of the largest defence contractors in the region. Also shown are county boundaries, the freeway system outside the central pentagon, and the location of all cities with more than 100,000 inhabitants (small open circles)

funding agency brought back a confidential referee's report (an economist, it appeared) proclaiming the absurdity of studying such a fanciful subject, something akin to examining wheat farming in Long Island. Fortunately sounder minds prevailed and the research progressed in exemplary fashion. Further evidence of the apparent invisibility of industrial production in Los Angeles came at about the same time from *Forbes* magazine, that self-proclaimed sourcebook for knowing capitalists (who should know better). In 1984, *Forbes* published a map identifying the major centres of high technology development in the USA. Cartographic attention was properly drawn to the Silicon Valley and the Route 128 axis around Boston, but all of Southern California was left conspicuously blank! Apparently invisible, hidden from view, was not only one of the historical source-regions for advanced technology in aerospace and electronics, but also what may well be the largest concentration of high technology industry and employment in the country (if not the world), the foremost silicon landscape, a region that has added over the past fifteen years a high-technology employment pool roughly equivalent to that of the whole image-fixing Silicon Valley of Santa Clara County to the north.

Still partially hidden behind this revelation are the primary generative agencies and the intricate processes producing this pre-eminent production complex. One key link, however, is abundantly clear. In the past half century, no other area has been so pumped with federal money as Los Angeles, via the Department of Defense to be sure, but also through numerous federal programmes subsidising suburban consumption (suburbsidising?) and the development of housing, transportation and water delivery systems. From the last Great Depression to the present, Los Angeles has been the prototypical Keynesian state-city, a federalised metro-sea of state-rescued capitalism enjoying its place in the sunbelt, demonstrating decade by decade its redoubtable ability to go first and multiply the public seed money invested in its promising economic landscape.[8] No wonder it remains so protected. In it are embedded many of the crown jewels of advanced industrial capitalism.

If anything, the federal flow is accelerating under the aegis of the military Keynesianism of the Reagan administration and the permanent arms economy of the Warfare State. At Hughes Aircraft Company in El Segundo, engineers have already used some of its sixty million dollars in prime 'Star Wars' contracts to mock up a giant infra-red sensor so acute that it can pick up the warmth of a human body at a distance of a thousand miles in space, part of their experimentation with 'kinetic' weapons systems. Nearby, TRW Inc (eighty-four million dollars) and Rockwell International's Rocketdyne division (thirty-two million dollars) competitively search for more powerful space lasers, capable, it seems, of incinerating whole cities if necessary, under such project code-names as Miracl, Alpha and Rachel. Research houses such as the Rand Corporation, just to the north in Santa Monica, jockey for more strategic positions, eager to claim part of what could potentially reach a total of 1.5 trillion dollars if not stopped in time.[9] Today, it is not only the space of the Pacific that is being secured and watched over from inside the Sixty-Mile Circle.

Outer Spaces
The effulgent Star Wars colony currently booming around Los Angeles International Airport (LAX) is part of a much larger outer city which has taken shape along the Pacific slope of Los Angeles County. In the context of this landscape, through the story-line of the aerospace industry, can be read the explosive history and geography of the National Security State and what Mike Davis has called the 'Californianisation of Late-Imperial America'.[10]

If there is a single birthplace for this Californianisation, it can be found at old Douglas Field in Santa Monica, today close by an important transit-point for President Reagan's frequent West Coast trips. From this spot fifty years ago, the first DC-3 took off to begin a career of military accomplishment in war after war after war. Spinning off in its tracks has been an intricate tracery of links, from defence- and space-related expenditures on research and development and the associated formation of the aerospace industry upon the base of civilian aircraft manufacturing; to the piggy-backed instigation of computerised electronics and modern information-processing technology, meshing with an ancillary network of suppliers and demanders of goods and services that stretches out to virtually every sector of the contemporary economy and society.[11] Over half a million people now live in this 'Aerospace Alley', as it has come to be called. During working hours, perhaps 800,000 are present to sustain its global pre-eminence. Untold millions more lie within its extended orbit.

Attached around the axes of production are the representative locales of the industrialised outer city: the busy international airport; corridors filled with new office buildings, hotels, and global shopping malls; neatly packaged playgrounds and leisure villages; specialised and masterplanned residential communities for the high technocracy; armed and guarded housing estates for top professionals and executives; residual communities of low-pay service workers living in overpriced homes; and the accessible enclaves and ghettoes which provide dependable flows of the cheapest labour power to the bottom bulge of the bimodal local labour market. The LAX – City compage reproduces the segmentation and segregation of the inner city based on race, class, and ethnicity, but manages to break it down still further to fragment residential communities according to specific occupational categories, household composition, and a broad range of individual attributes, affinities, desired lifestyles and moods.

This extraordinary differentiation, fragmentation, and social control over specialised pools of labour is expensive. Housing prices and rental costs in the outer city are easily among the highest in the country and the provision of appropriate housing increasingly absorbs the energy not only of the army of real estate agents but of local corporate and community planners as well, often at the expense of long-time residents fighting to maintain their foothold in 'preferred' locations. From the give and take of this competition have emerged peculiarly intensified urban landscapes. Along the shores of the South Bay, for example, part of what Rayner Banham once called 'Surfurbia',[12] there has developed the largest and most homogenous residential enclave of scientists and engineers in the world. Coincidentally, this beach-head of the high technocracy is also one of the most formidable racial redoubts in the region. Although just a few miles away, across the fortifying boundary of the San Diego freeway, is the edge of the largest and most tightly segregated concentration of Blacks west of Chicago, the sun-belted beach communities stretching south from the airport have remained almost 100 per cent white.[13]

The Sixty-Mile Circle is ringed with a series of these outer cities at varying stages of development, each a laboratory for exploring the contemporaneity of capitalist urbanisation. At least two are combined in Orange County, seamlessly webbed together into the largest and probably fastest growing outer city complex in the country (world?). The key nucleus here is the industrial complex embedded in the land empire of the Irvine Company, which owns one sixth of the entire county. Arrayed around it is a remarkable accretion of masterplanned new towns which paradigmatically evince the global cultural aspirations of the outer city imposed atop local visions of the experimental community of tomorrow.

Illustratively, the new town of Mission Viejo (never mind the bilingual pun) is partially blocked out to recreate the places and people of Cervantes's Spain and other quixotic intimations of the Mediterranean. Simultaneously, its ordered environment specifically appeals to Olympian dreams. Stacked with the most modern facilities and trainers, Mission Viejo has attracted an elite of sport-minded parents and accommodating children. The prowess of determined local athletes was sufficient for Mission Viejo to have finished ahead of 133 of the 140 countries competing in the 1984 Olympic Games in the number of medals received. Advertised as 'The California Promise' by its developer, currently the Philip Morris Company, Mission Viejo coughs up enticing portions of the American Dream to the chosen few. As one compromising resident described it, 'You must be happy, you must be well rounded and you must have children who do a lot of things. If you don't jog or walk or bike, people wonder if you have diabetes or some other disabling disease'.[14]

The Orange County complex has also been the focus for detailed research into the high technology industrial agglomerations that have been recentralising the urban fabric of the Los Angeles region and inducing the fluorescence of masterplanned new towns. This pioneering work has helped us see more clearly the transactional web of industrial linkages that draws out and geographically clusters specialised networks of firms, feeds off the flow of federal contracts, and spills over to precipitate a supportive local space economy.[15] What has been provided is a revealing glimpse into the generative processes behind the urbanisation of Orange County and, through this window, into the deeper historical interplay between industrialisation and urbanisation that has defined the development of the capitalist city wherever it is found.

There are other outer cities fringing the older pentagonal urban core. One has taken shape in the Ventura Corridor through the west San Fernando Valley into Ventura County (now being called the 'Peripheral Valley', with its primary cores in 'Gallium

Gulch' and the Chatsworth area).[16] Another is being promoted (although not yet in place) in the 'Inland Empire' stretching eastwards from Pomona (General Dynamics is there) through Ontario (with Lockheed and a growing International Airport and Free Trade Zone) to the county seats of San Bernardino and Riverside, hard by their military ramparts. The inland empire, however, is still more of an anticipatory outer city, cruelly packed with new housing estates that automaniacally lure families ever further away from their places of work in Los Angeles and Orange counties, a truly transitory landscape.

Inland empirics aside, these new territorial complexes seem to be turning the industrial city inside-out, recentring the urban to transform the metropolitan periphery into the core region of advanced industrial production. Decentralisation from the inner city has been taking place selectively for at least a century all over the world, but only recently has the peripheral condensation become sufficiently dense to challenge the older urban cores as centres of industrial production, employment nodality, and urbanism. This restructuring process is far from being completed but it is beginning to have some profound repercussions on the way we think about the city, on the words we use to describe urban forms and functions, and on the language of urban theory and analysis.

Back to the Centre

> I saw the teeming sea; I saw daybreak and nightfall; I saw the multitudes of America; I saw a silvery cobweb in the centre of a black pyramid; I saw a splintered labyrinth . . . I saw, close up, unending eyes watching themselves in me as in a mirror. (*The Aleph*)

To see more of Los Angeles, it is necessary to move away from the riveting periphery and return, literally and figuratively, to the centre of things to the still adhesive core of the urbanised landscape. In Los Angeles as in every city, the nodality of the centre defines and gives substance to the specificity of the urban, its distinctive social and spatial meaning. Urbanisation and the spatial divisions of labour associated with it revolve around a socially constructed pattern of nodality and the power of the occupied centres both to cluster and disperse, to centralise and decentralise, to structure spatially all that is social and socially produced. Nodality situates and contextualises urban society by giving material form to essential social relations. Only with a persistent centrality can there be outer cities and peripheral urbanisation. Otherwise, there is no urban at all.

It is easy to overlook the tendential processes of urban structuration that emanate from the centre, especially in the postmodern capitalist landscape. Indeed, in contemporary societies the authoritative and allocative power of the urban centre is purposefully obscured or, alternatively, detached from place, ripped out of context, and given the stretched-out appearance of democratic ubiquity. In addition, as we have seen, the historical development of urbanisation over the past century has been marked by a selective dispersal and decentralisation, emptying the centre of many of the activities and populations which once aggregated densely around it. For some, this has signalled a negation of nodality, a submergence of the power of central places, perhaps even a Derridean deconstruction of all differences between the 'central' and the 'marginal'.

Yet the centres hold. Even as some things fall apart, dissipate, new nodalities form and old ones are reinforced. The specifying centrifuge is always spinning but the centripetal force of nodality never disappears. And it is the persistent residual of political power which continues to precipitate, specify, and contextualise the urban, making it all stick together. The first cities appeared with the simultaneous concentration of commanding symbolic forms, civic centres designed to announce, ceremonialise, administer, acculturate, discipline, and control. In and around the institutionalised locale of the citadel adhered people and their node-ordered social relations, creating a civil society and an accordingly built environment which were urbanised and regionalised through the interplay between two interactive processes, surveillance and adherence, looking out from and in towards a centre through the panoptic eye of power. To be urbanised still means to adhere, to be made an adherent, a believer in a specified collective ideology rooted in extensions of *polis* (politics, policy, polity, police) and *civitas* (civil, civic, citizen, civilian, civilisation). In contrast, the population beyond the reach of the urban is comprised of *idiotes*, from the Greek root *idios*, meaning 'one's own, a private person', unlearned in the ways of the *polis* (a root akin to the Latin *sui*, 'of its own kind', with *generis*, 'constituting a class alone'). Thus to speak of the 'idiocy' of rural life or the urbanity of its opposition is primarily a statement of relative political socialisation and spatialisation, of the degree of adherence/separation in the collective social order, a social order hingeing on urban nodality.

To maintain adhesiveness, the civic centre has always served as a key surveillant node of the state, supervising locales of production, consumption and exchange. It still continues to do so, even after centuries of urban recomposition and restructuring, after waves of reagglomerative industrialisation. It is not production or consumption or exchange in themselves that specifies the urban, but rather their collective surveillance, supervision and anticipated control within the power-filled context of nodality. In Foucauldian terms, cities are the convergent sites of (social) space, knowledge, and power, the headquarters of societal modes of regulation (from *regula* and *regere*, to rule; the root of our keyword: region).

This does not mean that a mechanical determinism is assigned to nodality in the specification of the urban. Adherence is a sticky notion and is not automatically enacted by location in an urbanised landscape; nor is it always awarely expressed in practical consciousness. Surveillance too is problematic, for it can exist without being embracingly effective – and can be embracingly effective without appearing to exist! There is thus always room for resistance, rejection, and redirection in the nonetheless structured field of urban locales, creating an active politics of spatiality, struggles for place, space, and position within the regionalised and nodal urban landscape. As a result, adherence and surveillance are unevenly developed in their geographical manifestation, their regionalisation, their reactive regionalisms. Simultaneously, this patterned differentiation, this immediate superstructure of the urban spatial division of labour, becomes a critical arena in which the human geography of the city is shaped, in which spatialisation takes place. It maps out an urban cartography of power and political praxis that is often hidden in idiographic (from *idios* again) histories and geographies.

Signifying Downtown
The downtown core of the City of Los Angeles, which the signs call 'Central City' is the agglomerative and symbolic nucleus of the Sixty-Mile Circle, certainly the oldest but also the newest major node in the region. Given what is contained within the Circle, the physical size and appearance of downtown Los Angeles seem almost modest, even today after a period of enormous expansion. As usual, however, appearances can be deceptive.

Perhaps more than ever before, downtown serves in ways no other place can as a strategic vantage point, an urban panopticon counter-posed to the encirclement of watchful military ramparts and defensive outer cities. Like the central well in Bentham's eminently utilitarian design for a circular prison, the original panopticon, downtown can be seen (when visibility permits) by each separate individual, from each territorial cell, within its orbit. Only from the advantageous outlook of the centre, however, can the surveillant eye see everyone collectively, disembedded but interconnected. Not surprisingly, from its origin, the central city has been an aggregation of overseers, a primary locale for social control, political administration, cultural codification, ideological surveillance, and the incumbent regionalisation of its adherent hinterland.

Looking down and out from City Hall, the site is especially impressive to the observer. Immediately below and around is the largest concentration of government offices and bureaucracy in the country outside the federal capital district. To the east, over a pedestrian skyway, are City Hall East and City Hall South, relatively new civic additions enclosing a shopping mall, some murals, a children's museum, and the Triforium, a splashy sixty-foot fountain of water, light, and music entertaining the lunchtime masses. Just beyond is the imposing police administration building, Parker Center, hallowing the name of a former police chief of note. Looking further, outside the central well of downtown but within its eastern salient, one can see an area which houses twenty-five per cent of California's prison population, at least 12,000 inmates held in four jails designed to hold half that number. Included within this carceral wedge are the largest women's prison in the country (Sybil Brand) and the seventh largest men's prison (Men's Central). More enclosures are being insistently planned by the state to meet the rising demand.

On the south, along First Street, are the State Department of Transportation (CALTRANS) with its electronic wall maps monitoring the arterial freeways of the region, the California State Office Building, and the headquarters of the fourth estate, the monumental Times-Mirror building complex, which many have claimed houses the unofficial governing power of Los Angeles, the source of many stories that mirror the times and spaces of the city. Near the spatial sanctum of the *Los Angeles Times* is also St Vibiana's Cathedral, mother church to one of the largest Catholic archdioceses in the world (nearly four million strong) and controller of another estate of significant proportions. The Pope slept here, across the street from Skid Row missions temporarily closed so that he could not see all his adherents.

Looking westward now, towards the Pacific and the smog-hued sunsets which brilliantly paint the nightfalls of Los Angeles, is first the Criminal Courts Building, then the Hall of Records and Law Library, and next the huge Los Angeles County Courthouse and Hall of Administration, major seats of power for what is by far the country's largest county in total population (now over eight million). Standing across Grand Avenue is the most prominent cultural centre of Los Angeles, described by Unique Media Incorporated in their pictorial booster maps of downtown as 'the cultural crown of Southern California, reigning over orchestral music, vocal performance, opera, theatre and dance'. They add that the Music Center 'tops Bunker Hill like a contemporary Acropolis, one which has dominated civil cultural life since it was inaugurated in 1964'.[17] Just beyond this cultural crown is the Department of Water and Power (surrounded by usually waterless fountains) and a multi-level extravaganza of freeway interchanges connecting with every corner of the Sixty-Mile Circle, a peak point of accessibility within the regional transportation network. On its edge, one of Japan's greatest architects has designed a Gateway Building to punctuate the teeming sea.

Along the northern flank is the Hall of Justice, the US Federal Courthouse, and the Federal Building, completing the ring of local, city, state and federal government authority which comprises the potent civic centre. Sitting more tranquilly just beyond, cut off by a swathe of freeway, is the preserved remains of the old civic centre, now part of El Pueblo de Los Angeles State Historical Park, additional testimony to the lasting power of the central place. Since the origins of Los Angeles the sites described have served as the political citadel, designed with other citadels to command, protect, socialise and dominate the surrounding urban population.

There is still another segment of the citadel – panopticon which cannot be overlooked. Its form and function may be more specific to the contemporary capitalist city but its mercantile roots entwine historically with the citadels of all urbanised societies. Today, it has become the acknowledged symbol of the urbanity of Los Angeles, the visual evidence of the successful search for a city by the surrounding sea of suburbs. This skylined sight contains the bunched castles and cathedrals of corporate power, the gleaming new 'central business district' of the 'central city', pinned next to its ageing predecessor just to the east. Here too the LA-leph's unending eyes are kept open and reflective, reaching out to and mirroring global spheres of influence, localising the world that is within its reach.

Nearly all the landmarks of the new LA CBD have been built over the past fifteen years and flashily signify the consolidation of Los Angeles as a world city. Now more than half the major properties are in part or wholly foreign owned, although much of this landed presence is shielded from view. The most visible wardens are the banks which light up their logos atop the highest towers: Security Pacific (there again), First Interstate, Bank of America (co-owner of the sleek-black Arco Towers before their recent purchase by the Japanese), Crocker, Union, Wells Fargo, Citicorp (billing itself as 'the newest city in town'). Reading the skyline one sees the usual corporate panorama: large insurance companies (Manulife, Transamerica, Prudential), IBM and major oil companies, the real estate giant Coldwell Banker, the new offices of the Pacific Stock Exchange, all serving as attachment points for silvery webs of financial and commercial transactions extending practically everywhere on earth.

The two poles of the citadel, political and economic, connect physically through the condominium towers of renewed Bunker Hill but 'interface' less overtly in the planning apparatus of the local state. Contrary to popular opinion, Los Angeles is a tightly planned and plotted urban environment, especially with regard to the social and spatial divisions of labour necessary to sustain its pre-eminent industrialisation and consumerism. Planning choreographs Los Angeles through the fungible movements of the zoning game and the flexible staging of supportive community participation (when there are communities to be found), a dance filled with honourable intent, dedicated expertise, and selective beneficence. It has excelled, however, as an ambivalent but nonetheless enriching pipeline and place-maker to the domestic and foreign developers of Los Angeles, using its influential reach to prepare the groundwork and facilitate the selling of specialised locations and populations to suit the needs of the most powerful organisers of the urban space-economy.[18]

Although conspiracy and corruption can be easily found, the planned and packaged selling of Los Angeles usually follows a more mundane rhythm played to the legitimising beat of dull and thumping market forces. In the created spaces which surround the twin citadels of Los Angeles, the beat has drummed with a particularly insistent and mesmerising effect. Through a historic act of preservation and renewal, there now exists around downtown a deceptively harmonised showcase of ethni-cities and specialised economic enclaves which play key roles, albeit somewhat noisily at times, in the contemporary redevelopment and internationalisation of Los Angeles.

Primarily responsible for this packaged and planned production of the inner city is the Community Redevelopment Agency, probably the leading public entrepreneur of the Sixty-Mile Circle.[16]

There is a dazzling array of sites in this compartmentalised corona of the inner city: the Vietnamese shops and Hong Kong housing of a redeveloping Chinatown; the Big Tokyo financed modernisation of old Little Tokyo's still resisting remains; the induced pseudo-SoHo of artists' lofts and galleries hovering near the exhibitions of the 'Temporary Contemporary' art warehouse; the protected remains of El Pueblo along Calmexified Olvera Street and in the renewed Old Plaza; the strangely anachronistic wholesale markets for produce and flowers and jewellery growing bigger while other downtowns displace their equivalents; the foetid sweatshops and bustling merchandise marts of the booming garment district; the Latino retail festival along pedestrian-packed Broadway (another preserved zone and inch-for-inch probably the most profitable shopping street in the region); the capital site of urban homelessness in the CRA-gilded skid row district; the enormous muralled *barrio* stretching eastward to the still unincorporated East Los Angeles; the de-industrialising and virtually resident-less wholesaling City of Vernon to the south filled with chickens and pigs awaiting their slaughter; the Central American and Mexican communities of Pico-Union and Alvarado abutting the high-rises on the west; the obtrusive oil wells and aggressive graffiti in the backyards of predominantly immigrant Temple-Beaudry progressively being eaten away by the spread of Central City West (now being called 'The Left Bank' of downtown); the intentionally yuppifying South Park redevelopment zone hard by the slightly seedy Convention Center; the revenue-milked towers and fortresses of Bunker Hill; the resplendently gentrified pocket of 'Victorian' homes in old Angelino Heights overlooking the citadel; the massive new Koreatown pushing out west and south against the edge of Black Los Angeles; the Filipino pockets to the north-west still uncoalesced into a 'town' of their own; and so much more: a constellation of Foucauldian heterotopias 'capable of juxtaposing in a single real place several spaces, several sites that are in themselves incompatible' but 'function in relation to all the space that remains'.

What stands out from a hard look at the inner city seems almost like an obverse (and perverse) reflection of the outer city, an agglomerative complex of dilapidated and overcrowded housing, low technology workshops, relics and residuals of an older urbanisation, a sprinkling of niches for recentred professionals and supervisors, and, above all, the largest concentration of cheap, culturally-splintered/occupationally-manipulable Third World immigrant labour to be found so tangibly available in any First World urban region. Here in this colonial corona is another of the crown jewels of Los Angeles, carefully watched over, artfully maintained and reproduced to service the continued development of the manufactured region.

The extent and persistence of agglomerated power and ever-watchful eyes in downtown Los Angeles cannot be ignored by either captive participants or outside observers. The industrialisation of the urban periphery may be turning the space economy of the region inside-out, but the old centre is more than holding its own as the pre-eminent political and economic citadel. Peripheral visions are thus not enough when looking at Los Angeles. To conclude this spiralling tour around the power-filled central city, it may be useful to turn back to Giddens's observations on the structured and structuring landscapes of modern capitalism.

The distinctive structural principle of the class societies of modern capitalism is to be found in the disembedding, yet interconnecting, of state and economic institutions. The tremendous economic power generated by the harnessing of allocative resources to a generic tendency towards technical improvement is matched by an enormous expansion in the administrative 'reach' of the state. Surveillance – the coding of information relevant to the administration of subject populations, plus the direct supervision by officials and administrators of all sorts – becomes a key mechanism furthering a breaking away of system from social integration. Traditional practices are dispersed (without, of course, disappearing altogether) under the impact of the penetration of day-to-day life by codified administrative procedures. The locales which provide the settings for interaction in situations of co-presence [the basis for social integration] undergo a major set of transmutations. The old city-countryside relation is replaced by a sprawling expansion of a manufactured or 'created environment'.

Here we have another definition of spatial planning, another indication of the instrumentality of space and power, another example of spatialisation.

Lateral Extensions

Radiating from the specifying nodality of the central city are the hypothesised pathways of traditional urban theory, the transects of eagerly anticipated symmetries and salience which have absorbed so much of the attention of older generations of urban theoreticians and empiricists. Formal models of urban morphology have conventionally begun with the assumption of a structuring central place organising an adherent landscape into discoverable patterns of hinterland development and regionalisation. The deeper sources of this structuring process are usually glossed over and its problematic historical geography is almost universally simplified, but the resultant surfaces of social geometry continue to be visible as geographical expressions of the crude orderliness induced by the effects of nodality. They too are part of the spatialisation of social life, the extended specificity of the urban.

The most primitive urban geometry arises from the radial attenuation of land use 'intensity' around the centre to an outer edge, a reflection of the Thunian landscape that has become codified most figuratively in the irrepressible Two-Parameter Negative Exponential Population Density Gradient. The TPNEPDG, in part because of its nearly universal and monotonous exemplification, has obsessed urban theorists with its projectable objectivity and apparent explanatory powers. From the Urban Ecologists of the old Chicago School to the New Urban Economists, and including all those who are convinced that geographical analysis naturally begins with the primal explanation of variegated population densities (the most bourgeois of analytical assumptions Marx claimed), the TPNEPDG has been the lodestar for a monocentric understanding of urbanism. And within its own limited bands of confidence, it works efficiently.

Population densities do mound up around the centres of cities, even in the polycentric archipelago of Los Angeles (where there may be several dozen such mounds, although the most pronounced still falls off from the central city). There is also an accompanying concentric residential rhythm associated with the family life cycle and the relative premiums placed on access to the dense peaks versus the availability of living space in the sparseness of the valleys (at least for those who can afford such freedoms of choice). Land values (when they can be accurately calculated) and some job densities also tend to follow in diminishing peaks outwards from the centre, bringing back to mind those tented webs of the urban geography textbooks.

Adding direction to the decadence of distance reduces the Euclidian elegance of concentric gradations, and many of the most mathematical of urban geometricians have accordingly refused to follow this slightly unsettling path. But direction does indeed induce another fit by pointing out the emanation of fortuitous wedges or sectors starting from the centre. The sectoral wedges of Los Angeles are especially pronounced once you leave the inner circle around downtown.

The Wilshire Corridor, for example, extends the citadels of the central city almost twenty miles westwards to the Pacific, picking up several other prominent but smaller downtowns en route (the Miracle Mile that initiated this extension, Beverly Hills, Century City, Westwood, Brentwood, Santa Monica). Watching above it is an even lengthier wedge of the wealthiest residences, running with almost staggering homogeneities to the Pacific Palisades and the privatised beaches of Malibu, sprinkled with announcements of armed responsiveness and signs which say that 'trespassers will be shot'. Here are the hearths of the most vocal home-owners movements, arms raised to slow growth and preserve their putative neighbourhoods in the face of the encroaching, view-blocking, street-clogging, and *declassé* downtowns.

As if in counterbalance, on the other side of the tracks east of downtown is the salient containing the largest Latino *barrio* in Anglo-America, where many of those who might be shot are carefully barricaded in poverty. And there is at least one more prominent wedge, stretching southward from downtown to the twin ports of Los Angeles-Long Beach, still reputed to be one of the largest consistently industrial urban sectors in the world. This is the primary axis of Ruhral Los Angeles.

A third ecological order perturbs the geometrical neatness still further, punching holes into the monocentric gradients and wedges as a result of the territorial segregation of races and ethnicities. Segregation is so noisy that it overloads the conventional statistical methods of urban factorial ecology with scores of tiny but 'significant' eco-components. In Los Angeles, arguably the most segregated city in the country, these components are so numerous they operate statistically to obscure the spatiality of social class relations deeply embedded in the zones and wedges of the urban landscape, as if they needed to be obscured any further.[21]

These broad social geometries provide an attractive model of the urban geography of Los Angeles, but like most of the inherited overviews of formal urban theory they are seriously diverting and illusory. They mislead not because there is disagreement over their degree of fit – such regular empiricist arguments merely induce a temporary insensibility by forcing debate onto the usually sterile grounds of technical discourse. Instead, they deceive by involuting explanation, by the legerdemain of making the nodality of the urban explain itself through its mere existence, one outcome explaining another. Geographical covariance in the form of empirico-statistical regularity is elevated to causation and frozen into place without a history – and without a human geography which recognises that the organisation of space is a social product filled with politics and ideology, contradiction and struggle, comparable to the making of history. Empirical regularities are there to be found in the surface geometry of any city, including Los Angeles, but they are not explained in the discovery, as is so often assumed. Different routes and different roots must be explored to achieve a practical understanding and critical reading of urban landscapes. The illusions of empirical opaqueness must be shattered, along with the other disciplining effects of Modern Geography.

Deconstruction

Back in the centre, shining from its circular turrets of bronzed glass, stands the Bonaventure Hotel, an amazingly storeyed architectural symbol of the splintered labyrinth that stretches sixty miles around it.[22] Like many other Portman-teaus which dot the eyes of urban citadels in New York and San Francisco, Atlanta and Detroit, the Bonaventure has become a concentrated representation of the restructured spatiality of the late capitalist city: fragmented and fragmenting, homogeneous and homogenising, divertingly packaged yet curiously incomprehensible, seemingly open in presenting itself to view but constantly pressing to enclose, to compartmentalise, to circumscribe, to incarcerate. Everything imaginable appears to be available in this micro-urb but real places are difficult to find, its spaces confuse an effective cognitive mapping, its pastiche of superficial reflections bewilder co-ordination and encourage submission instead. Entry by land is forbidding to those who carelessly walk but entrance is nevertheless encouraged at many different levels, from the truly pedestrian skyways above to the bunkered inlets below. Once inside, however, it becomes daunting to get out again without bureaucratic assistance. In so many ways, its architecture recapitulates and reflects the sprawling manufactured spaces of Los Angeles.

There has been no conspiracy of design behind the building of the Bonaventure or the socially constructed spatiality of the New World Cities. Both designs have been conjunctural reflecting the specifications and exigencies of time and place, of period and region. The Bonaventure both simulates the restructured landscape of Los Angeles and is simultaneously simulated by it. From this interpretive interplay of micro- and macro-simulations there emerges an alternative way of looking critically at the human geography of contemporary Los Angeles, of seeing it as a mesocosm of postmodernity.

From the centre to the periphery, in both inner and outer cities, the Sixty-Mile Circle today encloses a shattered metro-sea of fragmented yet homogenised communities, cultures, and economies confusingly arranged into a contingently ordered spatial division of labour and power. As is true for so much of the patterning of twentieth-century urbanisation, Los Angeles both sets the historical pace and most vividly epitomises the extremes of contemporary expression. Municipal boundary making and territorial incorporation, to take one illustrative example, has produced the most extraordinary crazy quilt of opportunism to be found in any metropolitan area. Tiny enclaves of county land and whole cities such as Beverly Hills, West Hollywood, Culver City, and Santa Monica pock-mark the 'Westside' bulk of the incorporated City of Los Angeles, while thin slivers of city land reach out like tentacles to grab on to the key seaside outlets of the port at San Pedro and Los Angeles International Airport.[23] Nearly half the population of the city, however, lives in the quintessentially suburban San Fernando Valley, one and a half million people who statistically are counted as a part of the central city of the Los Angeles-Long Beach Standard Metropolitan Statistical Area. Few other places make such a definitive mockery of the standard classifications of urban, suburban, and exurban.

Over 130 other municipalities and scores of county-administered areas adhere loosely around the irregular City of Los Angeles in a dazzling, sprawling patchwork mosaic. Some have names which are startlingly self-explanatory. Where else can there be a City of Industry and a City of Commerce, so flagrantly commemorating the fractions of capital which guaranteed their incorporation. In other places, names casually try to recapture a romanticised history (as in the many new communities called Rancho something-or-other) or to ensconce the memory of alternative geographies (as in Venice, Naples, Hawaiian Gardens, Ontario, Manhattan Beach, Westminster). In naming, as in so many other contemporary urban processes, time and space, the 'once' and the 'there', are being increasingly played with and packaged to serve the needs of the here and the now, making the lived experience of the urban increasingly vicarious, screened through *simulacra*, those exact copies for which the real originals have been lost.

A recent clipping from the *Los Angeles Times*[24] tells of the 433 signs which bestow identity within the hyperspace of the City of Los Angeles, described as 'A City Divided and Proud of It'. Hollywood, Wilshire Boulevard's Miracle Mile, and the Central City were among the first to get these community signs as part of a 'city identification programme' organised by the Transportation Department. One of the newest signs, for what was proclaimed 'the city's newest community', recognises the formation of 'Harbor Gateway' in the thin eight-mile long Blue-collar area threading south to the harbour, the old Shoestring Strip where many of the 32,000 residents often forgot their ties to the city. One of the founders of the programme pondered its development: 'At first, in the early 1960s, the Traffic Department took the position that all the communities were part of Los Angeles and we didn't want cities within cities . . . but we finally gave in. Philosophically it made sense. Los Angeles is huge. The city had to recognise that there were communities that needed identification. . . . What we tried to avoid was putting up signs at every intersection that had stores.' Ultimately, the city signs are described as 'A Reflection of Pride in the Suburbs'. Where are we then in this nominal and noumenal fantasyland?

For at least fifty years, Los Angeles has been defying conventional categorical description of the urban, of what is city and what is suburb, of what can be identified as community or neighbourhood, of what co-presence means in the elastic urban context. It has in effect been deconstructing the urban into a confusing collage of signs which advertise what are often little more than imaginary communities and outlandish representations of urban locality. I do not mean to say that there are no genuine neighbourhoods to be found in Los Angeles. Indeed, finding them through car-voyages of exploration has become a popular local pastime, especially for those who have become so isolated from propinquitous community in the repetitive sprawl of truly ordinary-looking landscapes that make up most of the region. But again the urban experience becomes increasingly vicarious, adding more layers of opaqueness to *l'espace vecu*.

Underneath this semiotic blanket[25] there remains an economic order, an instrumental nodal structure, an essentially exploitative spatial division of labour, and this spatially organised urban system has for the past half century been more continuously productive than almost any other in the world. But it has also been increasingly obscured from view, imaginatively mystified in an environment more specialised in the production of encompassing mystifications than practically any other you can name. As has so often been the case in the United States, this conservative deconstruction is accompanied by a numbing depoliticisation of fundamental class and gender relations and conflicts. When all that is seen is so fragmented and filled with whimsy and pastiche, the hard edges of the capitalist, racist and patriarchal landscape seem to disappear, melt into air.

With exquisite irony, contemporary Los Angeles has come to resemble more than ever before a gigantic agglomeration of theme parks, a lifespace comprised of Disneyworlds. It is a realm divided into showcases of global village cultures and mimetic American landscapes, all-embracing shopping malls and crafty Main Streets, corporation-sponsored magic kingdoms, high-technology-based experimental prototype communities of tomorrow, attractively packaged places for rest and recreation all cleverly hiding the buzzing workstations and labour processes which help to keep it together. Like the original 'Happiest Place on Earth', the enclosed spaces are subtly but tightly controlled by invisible overseers despite the open appearance of fantastic freedoms of choice. The experience of living here can be extremely diverting and exceptionally enjoyable, especially for those who can afford to remain inside long enough to establish their own modes of transit and places to rest. And, of course, the enterprise has been enormously profitable over the years. After all, it was built on what began as relatively cheap land, has been sustained by a constantly replenishing army of even cheaper imported labour, is filled with the most modern technological gadgetry, enjoys extraordinary levels of protection and surveillance, and runs under the smooth aggression of the most efficient management systems, almost always capable of delivering what is promised just in time to be useful.

Afterwords

O God! I could be bounded in a nutshell, and count myself a King of infinite space . . . (*Hamlet*, 11, 2; first prescript to *The Aleph*)

But they will teach us that Eternity is the Standing still of the Present Time, a *Nunc-stans* (as the Schools call it); which neither they, nor any else understand, no more than they would a *Hic-stans* for an infinite greatness of place. (*Leviathan*, IV, 46; second prescript to *The Aleph*)

I have been looking at Los Angeles from many different points of view and each way of seeing assists in sorting out the interjacent medley of the subject landscape. The perspectives explored are purposeful, eclectic, fragmentary, incomplete, and frequently contradictory, but so too is Los Angeles and, indeed, the experienced historical geography of every urban landscape. Totalising visions, attractive though they may be, can never capture all the meanings and significations of the urban when the landscape is critically read and envisioned as a fulsome geographical text. There are too many *auteurs* to identify, the *literalité* (materiality?) of the manufactured environment is too multilayered to be allowed to speak for itself, and the countervailing metaphors and metonyms frequently clash, like discordant symbols drowning out the underlying themes. More seriously, we still know too little about the descriptive grammar and syntax of human geographies, the phonemes and epistemes of spatial interpretation. We are constrained by language much more than we know, as Borges so knowingly admits: what we can see in Los Angeles and in the spatiality of social life is stubbornly simultaneous, but what we write down is successive, because language is successive. The task of comprehensive, holistic regional description may therefore be impossible, as may be the construction of a complete historico-geographical materialism.

There is hope nonetheless. The critical and theoretical interpretation of geographical landscapes has recently expanded into realms that functionally had been spatially illiterate for most of the twentieth century. New and avid readers abound as never before, many are directly attuned to the specificity of the urban, and several have significantly turned their eyes to Los Angeles. Moreover, many practised readers of surface geographies have begun to see through the alternatively myopic and hypermetropic distortions of past perspectives to bring new insight to spatial analysis and social theory. Here too Los Angeles has attracted observant readers after a history of neglect and misapprehension, for it insistently presents itself as one of the most informative palimpsests and paradigms of twentieth-century urban-industrial development and popular consciousness.

As I have seen and said in various ways, everything seems to come together in Los Angeles, the totalising Aleph. Its representations of spatiality and historicity are archetypes of vividness, simultaneity, and interconnection. They beckon inquiry at once into their telling uniqueness and, at the same time, into their assertive but cautionary generalisability. Not all can be understood, appearances as well as essences persistently deceive, and what is real cannot always be captured even in extraordinary language. But this makes the challenge more compelling, especially if once in a while one has the opportunity to take it all apart and reconstruct the context. The reassertion of space in critical social theory and in critical political praxis – will depend upon a continued deconstruction of a still occlusive historicism and many additional voyages of exploration into the heterotopias of contemporary postmodern geographies.

NOTES

1 R Goodman, *The Last Entrepreneurs: America's Regional Wars for Jobs and Dollars*, Simon and Schuster, New York, 1979.

2 The nature of this 'Great American Job Machine' has some have begun to call it, is still difficult to grasp. Suggestive, however, are two recent lists of the ten fastest growing occupations, published by the Institute for Research on Educational Finance and Governance at Stanford University. In terms of absolute numbers, the top ten occupations are building custodian, cashier, secretary, general office clerk, sales clerk, professional nurse, waiter/waitress, kindergarten/elementary school teacher, truck driver, and nurse's aide/orderly. The largest percentage increase expected over the next decade (reflecting the past decade) are for computer service technician, legal assistant, computer systems analyst, computer programmer, office machine repairer, physical therapy assistant, electrical engineer, civil engineering technician, personal computer equipment operator, and computer operator.

3 A Scott, 'Industrial Organization and the Logic of Intrametropolitan Location III: A Case Study of the Printed Circuit Industry in the Greater Los Angeles Region', Economic Geography 59, 1983, pp 343-67; idem, 'High Technology Industry and Territorial Development: the Rise of the Orange County Complex, 1955-1984', Urban Geography 60, 1986, pp 3-27.

4 J Friedmann and G Wolff, 'World City Formation: an Agenda for Research and Action', *International Journal of Urban and Regional Research* 6, 1982, pp 309-44.

5 At least eight editions of a pamphlet on 'The Sixty-Mile Circle' have been published by the Economics Department of the Security Pacific National Bank, the first broadsheet version appearing nearly twenty years ago. The 1981 edition aimed to celebrate the Los Angeles Bicentennial. The edition I refer to, for 1984, advertises Security Pacific's support of the Olympic Games.

6 The imperial history of the watering of Los Angeles is a key part of the growth of Southern California, but it cannot be treated here.

7 The last remaining condors were recently removed to zoos after lead-poisoning threatened their extinction in the 'wild'.

8 The federalisation of the Sixty-Mile Circle still remains poorly studied but in this process are the forceful clues necessary for understanding the uneven regional development of the entire United States, Sunbelt and Frostbelt included.

9 D Sanger, 'Star Wars Industry Rises', *New York Times*, 19 November, Business Day, 1985, pp 25, 32.

10 Mike Davies, 'The Political Economy of Later Imperial America', *New Left Review* 164, 1984, pp 6-38.

11 In 1965, it was estimated in a Bank of America study that nearly forty-three per cent of total manufacturing employment in Los Angeles and Orange counties was linked to defence and space expenditures. Some percentages by sector included paperboard containers and boxes (twelve per cent), fabricated rubber (thirty-six per cent), computing machines (fifty-four per cent), photographic equipment (sixty-nine per cent), screw-machines (seventy per cent) and machine shop jobbing and repairs (seventy-eight per cent). By 1983, almost half the manufacturing jobs in Los Angeles County were related directly or indirectly to the aerospace industry and nearly half of these aerospace workers were employed on military projects (R Scheer, 'California Wedden to Military Economy but Bliss is Shaky', *Los Angeles Times*, 10 July, part VI, pp 13, 14). There is no reason to believe these figures have changed significantly since 1983.

12 R Banham, *Los Angeles: The Architecture of the Four Ecologies*, Harper and Row, New York, 1971.

13 K Mate, "For Whites Only": The South Bay Perfects Racism for the '80s', LA Weekly 6-12, August 1982, pp 11 ff.

14 Landsbaum and Evans, 1984.

15 A Scott, 'High Technology Industry'.

16 Gallium arsenide chips operate at higher frequencies and allegedly compute faster than silicon chips.

Developed primarily for military use, they are expected by some to take an increasing share of the world semiconductor market in the future. 'Gallium Gulch' contains a cluster of recently formed companies experimenting with the new technology, all of which are headed by alumni of Rockwell International (A Goldstein, 'Southland Firms Race for Lead in High-tech Material', *Los Angeles Times*, 6 August 1985, part IV, pp 2, 6).

17 Colourful pictorial maps, so convenient for the exaggerated representation of presences and absences, seem to be multiplying at an unusually rapid pace all over Los Angeles, quietly erasing the unsightly, distorting spatial relations for effect and calling attention to the fantastic and the most merchandisable.

18 Investigative reports of the political corruptibility of the planning process surface repeatedly in Los Angeles with relatively little effect, for what is exposed is characteristically accepted as normal (if not normative) by the prominent practitioners. Two particularly thorough analyses appeared in 1985: Tony Castro, 'LA Inc', a three-part series in the *Herald Examiner* ('How politics built downtown', 10 March; 'Exercising political clout atop Bunker Hill', 11 March; and 'Critics claim CRA bulldozes over wishes of poor and powerless', 12 March); and Ron Curran and Lewis MacAdams, 'The selling of LA County', *LA Weekly*, 22-28 November. Nothing comparable appeared in the *Los Angeles Times*.

19 The CRA is a California state-legislated agency directly responsible to the Los Angeles City Council. It functions publicly in downtown Los Angeles in facilitative ways which resemble the masterplanning operations of the Irvine company in its private domains of Orange County.

20 A Giddens, *The Constitution of Society: Outline of the Theory of Structuration*, Polity Press, Cambridge; University of California Press, Berkeley and Los Angeles, 1981, pp 183-84.

21 Compacted Black Los Angeles has been particularly perplexing. For many statistical years, it contained both some of the lowest and the highest median family income census tracts in the county. And before 1970, the highest density of Black residents in any census tract was found not in the demarcable ghetto but in south Santa Monica. Blacks were among the original founders of Los Angeles in 1781, but there are virtually no major studies of the historical geography of Black Los Angeles currently available.

22 The Westin Bonaventure, financed and owned by the Japanese, figures prominently (if not with the correct spelling) in Jameson's perceptive analysis of postmodernism (1985). See also the rejoinder by Davis ('Urban Renaissance and the Spirit of Postmodernism', *New Left Review* 143, pp 106-13) and an essay on postmodern planning by Michael Dear ('Postmodernism and Planning', *Environment and Planning D: Society and Space* 4 pp 367-84). These writings form part of the first round of a continuing debate on postmodernism in Los Angeles.

23 Another outlet reached near LAX is the Hyperion Sewage Treatment Plant, expectorating from the City of Los Angeles a volume of waste equivalent to the fifth or sixth largest river to reach the ocean in California; and creating an increasingly poisoned food-chain reaching back into the population of its drainage basin. Over the past several years, there have been claims that Santa Monica Bay may have the highest levels of toxic chemicals along the West coast. Signs were posted to warn of the hazards of locally caught fish (especially the so aptly named croaker) and doctors warned many of their patients not to swim off certain beaches. The fault-lines in the garbage-chains of the region may ultimately prove more threatening than those better known cracks in the earth's surface.

24 Herbert, 1985.

25 The root of semiotic and semiology is the Greek *semeion*, which means sign, mark, spot or *point in space*. You arrange to meet someone at a *semeion*, a particular place. The significance of this connection between semiotics and spatiality is too often forgotten.

From *Postmodern Geographies: The Reassertion of Space in Critical Social Theories*, Verso, London, 1990.

David Harvey
THE CONDITION OF POSTMODERNITY

The Argument

There has been a sea-change in cultural as well as in political-economic practices since around 1972.

This sea-change is bound up with the emergence of new dominant ways in which we experience space and time.

While simultaneity in the shifting dimensions of time and space is no proof of necessary or causal connection, strong a priori grounds can be adduced for the proposition that there is some kind of necessary relation between the rise of postmodernist cultural forms, the emergence of more flexible modes of capital accumulation, and a new round of 'time-space compression' in the organisation of capitalism. But these changes, when set against the basic rules of capitalistic accumulation, appear more as shifts in surface appearance rather than as signs of the emergence of some entirely new postcapitalist or even post-industrial society . . .

Introduction

I was recently reminded of Raban's evocative descriptions while visiting an exhibition of Cindy Sherman's photographs. The photographs depict seemingly different women drawn from many walks of life. It takes a little while to realise, with a certain shock, that these are portraits of the same woman in different guises. Only the catalogue tells you that it is the artist herself who is that woman. The parallel with Raban's insistence upon the plasticity of human personality through the malleability of appearances and surfaces is striking, as is the self-referential positioning of the authors to themselves as subject. Cindy Sherman is considered a major figure in the postmodern movement.

So what is the postmodern of which many now speak? Has social life so changed since the early 1970s that we can reasonably talk about living in a postmodern culture, a postmodern age? Or is it simply that trends in high culture have taken, as is their wont, yet another twist, and that academic fashions have also changed with scarcely a ripple of effect or an echo of correspondence in the daily life of ordinary citizens? Raban's book suggests that there is more to matters than the latest intellectual fad imported from Paris or the latest twirl in the New York art market. There is more to it, too, than the shift in architectural style that Jencks records,[1] though here we approach a realm that has the potential to bring high cultural concerns closer to daily life through the production of built form. Major changes have indeed occurred in the qualities of urban life since 1970 or so. But whether such drifts deserve the apellation of 'postmodern' is another question. The answer depends rather directly, of course, on exactly what we might mean by that term. And here we do have to grapple with the latest intellectual fads imported from Paris and twists in the New York art market, because it is out of those ferments that the concept of the 'postmodern' has emerged. No one exactly agrees as to what is meant by the term, except, perhaps, that 'postmodernism' represents some kind of reaction to, or departure from, 'modernism'. Since the meaning of modernism is also very confused, the reaction or departure known as 'postmodernism' is doubly so. The literary critic Terry Eagleton tries to define the term as follows:

> There is perhaps, a degree of consensus that the typical postmodernist artefact is playful, self-ironising and even schizoid; and that it reacts to the austere autonomy of high modernism by impudently embracing the language of commerce and the commodity. Its stance towards cultural tradition is one of irreverent pastiche, and its contrived depthlessness undermines all metaphysical solemnities, sometimes by a brutal aesthetics of squalor and shock.[2]

In more positive vein, the editors of architectural journal *PRECIS* see postmodernism as a legitimate reaction to the 'monotony' of universal modernism's vision of the world. 'Generally perceived as positivistic, technocentric, and rationalistic, universal modernism has been identified with the belief in linear progress, absolute truths, the rational planning of ideal social orders and the standardisation of knowledge and production.'[3] Postmodernism by way of contrast, privileges 'heterogeneity and difference as liberative forces in the redefinition of cultural discourse'. Fragmentation, indeterminacy, and intense distrust of all universal or 'totalising' discourses (to use the favoured phrase) are the hallmark of postmodernist thought. The rediscovery of pragmatism in philosophy,[4] the shift of ideas about the philosophy of science wrought by Kuhn and Feyerabend,[5] Foucault's emphasis upon discontinuity and difference in history and his privileging of 'polymorphous correlations in place of simple or complex causality', new developments in mathematics emphasising indeterminacy (catastrophe and chaos theory, fractal geometry). The re-emergence of concern in ethics, politics, and anthropology for the validity and dignity of 'the other', all indicate a widespread and profound shift in 'the structure of feeling'. What all these examples have in common is a rejection of 'meta-narratives' (large scale theoretical interpretations purportedly of universal application), which leads Eagleton to complete his description of postmodernism thus:

> Post-modernism signals the death of such 'meta-narratives' whose secretly terroristic function was to ground and legitimate the illusion of a 'universal' human history. We are now in the process of wakening from the nightmare of modernity, with its manipulative reason and fetish of the totality, into the laid-back pluralism of the post-modern, that heterogeneous range of life-styles and language games which has renounced the nostalgic urge to totalise and legitimate itself . . . Science and philosophy must jettison their grandiose metaphysical claims and view themselves more modestly as just another set of narratives.

If these depictions are correct, then it would certainly seem as if Raban's *Soft City* is suffused with postmodernist sentiment. But the real import of that has still to be established. Since the only agreed point of departure for understanding the postmodern is in its purported relation to the modern, it is to the meaning of the latter term that I shall first attend . . .

Postmodernism

Over the last two decades 'postmodernism' has become a concept to be wrestled with, and such a battleground of conflicting opinions and political forces that it can no longer be ignored. 'The culture of the advanced capitalist societiet,' announce the editors of *PRECIS*, 'has undergone a profound shift in the structure of feeling.' Most, I think, would now agree with Huyssen's more cautious statement:

> What appears on one level as the latest fad, advertising pitch and hollow spectacle is part of a slowly emerging cultural transformation in Western societies, a change

in sensibility for which the term 'post-modern' is actually, at least for now, wholly adequate. The nature and depth of that transformation are debatable, but transformation it is. I don't want to be misunderstood as claiming that there is a wholesale paradigm shift of the cultural, social, and economic orders; any such claim clearly would be overblown. But in an important sector of our culture there is a noticeable shift in sensibility, practices and discourse formations which distinguishes a post-modern set of assumptions, experiences and proportions from that of a preceding period.[6]

With respect to architecture, for example, Charles Jencks dates the symbolic end of modernism and the passage to the postmodern as 3.32 pm on 15 July 1972, when the Pruitt-Igoe housing development in St Louis (a prize-winning version of Le Corbusier's 'machine for modern living') was dynamited as an uninhabitable environment for the low-income people it housed. Thereafter, the ideas of the CIAM, Le Corbusier, and the other apostles of 'high modernism' increasingly gave way before an onslaught of diverse possibilities, of which those set forth in the influential *Learning from Las Vegas* by Venturi, Scott Brown, and Izenour (also published in 1972) proved to be but one powerful cutting edge. The point of that work, as its title implies, was to insist that architects had more to learn from the study of popular and vernacular landscapes (such as those of suburbs and commercial strips) than from the pursuit of some abstract, theoretical, and doctrinaire ideals. It was time, they said, to build for people rather than for Man. The glass towers, concrete blocks, and steel slabs that seemed set fair to steamroller over every urban landscape from Paris to Tokyo and from Rio to Montreal, denouncing all ornament as crime, all individualism as sentimentality, all romanticism as kitsch, have progressively given way to ornamented tower blocks, imitation mediaeval squares and fishing villages, custom-designed or vernacular housing, renovated factories and warehouses, and rehabilitated landscapes of all kinds, all in the name of procuring some more 'satisfying' urban environment. So popular has this quest become that no less a figure than Prince Charles has weighed in with vigorous denunciations of the errors of postwar urban redevelopment and the developer destruction that has done more to wreck London, he claims, then the Luftwaffe's attacks in World War II.

In planning circles we can track a similar evolution. Douglas Lee's influential article 'Requiem for large-scale planning models' appeared in a 1973 issue of the *Journal of the American Institute of Planners* and correctly predicted the demise of what he saw as the futile efforts of the 1960s to develop large-scale, comprehensive, and integrated planning models (many of them specified with all the rigour that computerised mathematical modelling could then command) for metropolitan regions. Shortly thereafter, *The New York Times* (13 June 1976) described as 'mainstream' the radical planners (inspired by Jane Jacobs) who had mounted such a violent attack upon the soulless sins of modernist urban planning in the 1960s. It is nowadays the norm to seek out 'pluralistic' and 'organic' strategies for approaching urban development as a 'collage' of highly differentiated spaces and mixtures, rather than pursuing grandiose plans based on functional zoning of different activities. 'Collage city' is now the theme and 'urban revitalisation' has replaced the vilified 'urban renewal' as the key buzz-word in the planners' lexicon. 'Make no little plans,' Daniel Burnham wrote in the first wave of modernist planning euphoria at the end of the nineteenth century, to which a postmodernist like Aldo Rossi can now more modestly reply: 'To what, then, could I have aspired in my craft? Certainly to small things, having seen that the possibility of great ones was historically precluded.'

Shifts of this sort can be documented across a whole range of diverse fields. The postmodern novel, McHale argues, is characterised by a shift from an 'epistemological' to an 'ontological' dominant.[7] By this he means a shift from the kind of perspectivism that allowed the modernist to get a better bearing on the meaning of a complex but nevertheless singular reality, to the foregrounding of questions as to how radically different realities may coexist, collide, and interpenetrate. The boundary between fiction and science fiction has, as a consequence, effectively dissolved, while postmodernist characters often seem confused as to which world they are in, and how they should act with respect to it. Even to reduce the problem of perspective to autobiography, says one of Borges's characters, is to enter the labyrinth: 'Who was I? Today's self, bewildered, yesterday's, forgotten; tomorrow's, unpredictable?' The question marks tell it all.

In philosophy, the intermingling of a revived American pragmatism with the post-Marxist and poststructuralist wave that struck Paris after 1968 produced what Bernstein calls 'a rage against humanism and the Enlightenment legacy.'[8] This spilled over into vigorous denunciation of abstract reason and a deep aversion to any project that sought universal human emancipation through mobilisation of the powers of technology, science, and reason. Here, also, no less a person than Pope John Paul II has entered the fray on the side of the postmodern. The Pope 'does not attack Marxism or liberal secularism because they are the wave of the future,' says Rocco Buttiglione, a theologian close to the Pope, but because the 'philosophies of the twentieth century have lost their appeal, their time has already passed.' The moral crisis of our time is a crisis of Enlightenment thought. For while the latter may indeed have allowed man to emancipate himself 'from community and tradition of the Middle Ages in which his individual freedom was submerged,' the Enlightenment affirmation of 'self without God' in the end negated itself because reason, a means, was left, in the absence of God's truth, without any spiritual or moral goal. If lust and power are 'the only values that don't need the light of reason to be discovered', then reason had to become a mere instrument to subjugate others.[9] The postmodern theological project is to reaffirm God's truth without abandoning the powers of reason.

With such illustrious (and centrist) figures as the Prince of Wales and Pope John Paul II resorting to postmodernist rhetoric and argumentation, there can be little doubt as to the breadth of change that has occurred in 'the structure of feeling' in the 1980s. Yet there is still abundant confusion as to what the new 'structure of feeling' might entail. Modernist sentiments may have been undermined, deconstructed, surpassed, or bypassed, but there is little certitude as to the coherence or meaning of the systems of thought that may have replaced them. Such uncertainty makes it peculiarly difficult to evaluate, interpret, and explain the shift that everyone agrees has occurred.

Does postmodernism, for example, represent a radical break with modernism, or is it simply a revolt within modernism against a certain form of 'high modernism' as represented, say, in the architecture of Mies van der Rohe and the blank surfaces of minimalist abstract expressionist painting? Is postmodernism a style (in which case we can reasonably trace its precursors back to Dada, Nietzsche, or even, as Kroker and Cook prefer,[10] to St Augustine's *Confessions* in the fourth century) or should we view it strictly as a periodising concept (in which case we debate whether it originated in the 1950s, 1960s, or 1970s)? Does it have a revolutionary potential by virtue of its opposition to all forms of meta-narratives (including Marxism, Freudianism, and all forms of Enlightenment reason) and its close attention to 'other worlds' and to 'other voices' that have for too long been silenced (women, gays, blacks, colonised peoples with their own histories)? Or is it simply the commercialisation and domestication of modernism, and a reduction of the latter's already tarnished aspirations to a *laissez-faire*, 'anything goes' market eclecticism? Does it, therefore, undermine or integrate with neo-conserva-tive politics? And do we attach its rise to some radical restructuring of capitalism, the emergence of some 'postindustrial' society, view it, even, as the 'art of an inflationary era or as the 'cultural logic of late capitalism' (as Newman and Jameson have proposed)?

We can, I think, begin to get a grip on these difficult questions by casting an eye over the schematic differences between modernism and postmodernism as laid out by Hassan; see Table). Hassan sets up a series of stylistic oppositions in order to capture the ways in which postmodernism might be portrayed as a reaction to the modern. I say 'might' because I think it dangerous (as does Hassan) to depict complex relations as simple polarisations, when almost certainly the true state of sensibility, the real 'structure of feeling' in both the modern and postmodern periods, lies in the manner in which these stylistic oppositions are synthesised. Nevertheless, I think Hassan's tabular schema provides a useful starting point.

There is much to contemplate in this schema, drawing as it does on fields as diverse as linguistics, anthropology, philosophy, rhetoric, political science, and theology. Hassan is quick to point out how the dichotomies are themselves insecure, equivocal. Yet there is much here that captures a sense of what the differences might be. 'Modernist' town planners, for example, do tend to look for 'mastery' of the metropolis as a 'totality' by deliberately designing a 'closed form', whereas postmodernists tend to view the urban process as uncontrollable and 'chaotic', one in which 'anarchy' and 'change' can 'play' in entirely 'open' situations. 'Modernist' literary critics do tend to look at works as examples of a 'genre' and to judge them by the 'master code' that prevails within the 'boundary' of the genre, whereas the 'postmodern' style is simply to view a work as a 'text' with its own particular 'rhetoric' and 'idiolect', but which can in principle be compared with any other text of no matter what sort. Hassan's oppositions may be caricatures, but there is scarcely an arena of present intellectual practice where we cannot spot some of them at work. In what follows I shall try and take up a few of them in the richer detail they deserve.

I begin with what appears to be the most startling fact about postmodernism: its total acceptance of the ephemerality, fragmentation, discontinuity, and the chaotic that formed the one half of Baudelaire's conception of modernity. But postmodernism responds to the fact of that in a very particular way. It does not try to transcend it, counteract it, or even to define the 'eternal and immutable' elements that might lie within it. Postmodernism swims, even wallows, in the fragmentary and the chaotic currents of change as if that is all there is. Foucault instructs us, for example, to 'develop action, thought, and desires by proliferation, juxtaposition, and disjunction', and 'to prefer what is positive and multiple, difference over uniformity, flows over unities, mobile arrangements over systems. Believe that what is productive is not sedentary but nomadic.' To the degree that it does try to legitimate itself by reference to the past, therefore, postmodernism typically harks back to that wing of thought, Nietzsche in particular, that emphasises the deep chaos of modern life and its intractability before rational thought. This does not imply, however, that postmodernism is simply a version of modernism; real revolutions in sensibility can occur when latent and dominated ideas in one period become explicit and dominant in another. Nevertheless, the continuity of the condition of fragmentation, ephemerality, discontinuity, and chaotic change in both modernist and postmodernist thought is important. I shall make much of it in what follows.

Embracing the fragmentation and ephemerality in an affirmative fashion implies a whole host of consequences that bear directly on Hassan's oppositions. To begin with, we find writers like Foucault and Lyotard explicitly attacking any notion that there

TABLE
Schematic Differences Between Modernism and Postmodernism

modernism	postmodernism
romanticism/Symbolism	paraphysics/Dadaism
form (conjunctive, closed)	antiform (disjunctive, open)
purpose	play
design	chance
hierarchy	anarchy
mastery/logos	exhaustion/silence
art object/finished work	process/performance/happening
distance	participation
creation/totalisation/synthesis	decreation/deconstruction/antithesis
presence	absence
centring	dispersal
genre/boundary	text/intertext
semantics	rhetoric
paradigm	syntagm
hypotaxis	parataxis
metaphor	metonymy
selection	combination
root/depth	rhizome/surface
interpretation/reading	against interpretation/misreading
signified	signifier
lisible (readerly)	scriptible (writable)
narrative/*grande histoire*	anti-narrative/*petite histoire*
mastercode	idiolect
symptom	desire
type	mutant
genital/phallic	polymorphous/androgynous
paranoia	schizophrenia
origin/cause	difference-difference/trace
God the Father	The Holy Ghost
metaphysics	irony
determinacy	indeterminacy
transcendence	immanence

SOURCE: Ihab Hassan, *Paracriticisms: Seven Speculations of the Times,* Urbana, Ill, 1985, pp 123-24

might be a meta-language, meta-narrative, or meta-theory through which all things can be connected or represented. Universal and eternal truths, if they exist at all, cannot be specified. Condemning meta-narratives (broad interpretative schemes like those deployed by Marx or Freud) as 'totalising', they insist upon the plurality of 'power-discourse' formations (Foucault), or of 'language games' (Lyotard). Lyotard in fact defines the postmodern simply as 'incredulity towards meta-narratives'.

Foucault's ideas – particularly as developed in his early works – deserve attention since they have been a fecund source for postmodernist argument. The relation between power and knowledge is there a central theme. But Foucault breaks with the notion that power is ultimately located within the state, and abjures us to 'conduct an *ascending* analysis of power, starting that is from its infinitesimal mechanisms, which each have their own history, their own trajectory, their own techniques and tactics, and then see how these mechanisms of power have been – and continue to be – invested, colonised, utilised, involuted, transformed, displaced, extended, etc by ever more general mechanisms and by forms of global domination.'[11] Close scrutiny of the micro-politics of power relations in different localities, contexts, and social situations leads him to conclude that there is an intimate relation between the systems of knowledge ('discourses') which codify techniques and practices for the exercise of social control and domination within particular localised contexts. The prison, the asylum, the hospital, the university, the school, the psychiatrist's office, are all examples of sites where a dispersed and piecemeal organisation of power is built up independently of any systematic strategy of class domination. What happens at each site cannot be understood by appeal to some overarching general theory. Indeed the only irreducible in Foucault's scheme of things is the human body, for that is the 'site' at which all forms of repression are ultimately registered. So while there are, in Foucault's celebrated dictum, 'no relations of power without resistances' he equally insists that no utopian scheme can ever hope to escape the power-knowledge relation in non-repressive ways. He here echoes Max Weber's pessimism as to our ability to avoid the 'iron cage' of repressive bureaucratic-technical rationality. More particularly, he interprets Soviet repression as the inevitable outcome of a utopian revolutionary theory (Marxism) which appealed to the same techniques and knowledge systems as those embedded in the capitalist system it sought to replace. The only way open to 'eliminate the fascism in our heads' is to explore and build upon the open qualities of human discourse, and thereby intervene in the way knowledge is produced and constituted at the particular sites where a localised power-discourse prevails. Foucault's work with homosexuals and prisoners was not aimed at producing reforms in state practices, but dedicated to the cultivation and enhancement of localised resistance to the institutions, techniques, and discourses of organised repression.

Foucault evidently believed that it was only through such a multi-faceted and pluralistic attack upon localised practices of repression that any global challenge to capitalism might be mounted without replicating all the multiple repressions of capitalism in a new form. His ideas appeal to the various social movements that sprang into existence during the 1960s (feminists, gays, ethnic and religious groupings, regional autonomists, etc) as well as to those disillusioned with the practices of communism and the politics of communist parties. Yet it leaves open, particularly so in the deliberate rejection of any holistic theory of capitalism, the question of the path whereby such localised struggles might add up to a progressive, rather than regressive, attack upon the central forms of capitalist exploitation and repression. Localised struggles of the sort that Foucault appears to encourage have not generally had the effect of challenging capitalism, though Foucault might reasonably respond that only struggles fought in such a way as to challenge all forms of power-discourse might have such a result.

Lyotard, for his part, puts a similar argument, though on a rather different basis. He takes the modernist preoccupation with language and pushes it to extremes of dispersal. While 'the social bond is linguistic,' he argues, it 'is not woven with a single thread' but by an 'indeterminate number' of 'language games.' Each of us lives 'at the intersection of many of these' and we do not necessarily establish 'stable language combinations and the properties of the ones we do establish are not necessarily communicable.' As a consequence, 'the social subject itself seems to dissolve in this dissemination of language games.' Interestingly, Lyotard here employs a lengthy metaphor of Wittgenstein's (the pioneer of the theory of language games), to illuminate the condition of postmodern knowledge: 'Our language can be seen as an ancient city: a maze of little streets and squares, of old and new houses, and of houses with additions from different periods; and this surrounded by a multitude of new boroughs with straight regular streets and uniform houses.'

The 'atomisation of the social into flexible networks of language games' suggests that each of us may resort to a quite different set of codes depending upon the situation in which we find ourselves (at home, at work, at church, in the street or pub, at a memorial service, etc). To the degree that Lyotard (like Foucault) accepts that 'knowledge is the principal force of production' these days, so the problem is to define the locus of that power when it is evidently 'dispersed in clouds of narrative elements' within a heterogeneity of language games. Lyotard (again like Foucault) accepts the potential open qualities of ordinary conversations in which rules can bend and shift so as 'to encourage the greatest flexibility of utterance'. He makes much of the seeming contradiction between this openness and the rigidities with which institutions (Foucault's 'non-discursive domains') circumscribe what is or is not admissible within their boundaries. The realms of law, of the academy, of science and bureaucratic government, of military and political control, of electoral politics, and corporate power, all circumscribe what can be said and how it can be said in important ways. But the 'limits the institution imposes on potential language "moves" are never established once and for all,' they are 'themselves the stakes and provisional results of language strategies, within the institution and without.' We ought not, therefore, to reify institutions prematurely, but to recognise how the differentiated performance of language games creates institutional languages and powers in the first place. If 'there are many different language games – a heterogeneity of elements' we have then also to recognise that they can 'only give rise to institutions in patches – local determinism'.

Such 'local determinisms' have been understood by others[12] as 'interpretative communities', made up of both producers and consumers of particular kinds of knowledge, of texts, often operating within a particular institutional context (such as the university, the legal system, religious groupings), within particular divisions of cultural labour (such as architecture, painting, theatre, dance), or within particular places (neighbourhoods, nations, etc). Individuals and groups are held to control mutually within these domains what they consider to be valid knowledge.

To the degree that multiple sources of oppression in society and multiple foci of resistance to domination can be identified, so this kind of thinking has been taken up in radical politics, even imported into the heart of Marxism itself. We thus find Aronowitz arguing in *The Crisis of Historical Materialism* that 'the multiple, local, autonomous struggles for liberation occurring throughout the postmodern world make all incarnations of master discourses absolutely illegitimate'.[13] Aronowitz is here seduced, I sus-pect, by the most liberative and therefore most appealing aspect of postmodern thought – its concern with 'otherness'. Huyssen (1984) particularly castigates the imperialism of an enlightened modernity that presumed to speak for others (colonised peoples, blacks and minorities, religious groups, women, the working class) with a unified voice. The very title of Carol Gilligan's *In a Different Voice* – a feminist work which challenges the male bias in setting out fixed stages in the moral development of personality – illustrates a process of counterattack upon such universalising presumptions.[14] The idea that all groups have a right to speak for themselves, in their own voice, and have that voice accepted as authentic and legitimate is essential to the pluralistic stance of postmodernism. Foucault's work with marginal and interstitial groups has influenced a whole host of researchers, in fields as diverse as criminology and anthropology, into new ways to reconstruct and represent the voices and experiences of their subjects. Huyssen, for his part, emphasises the opening given in postmodernism to understanding difference and otherness, as well as the liberatory potential it offers for a whole host of new social movements (women, gays, blacks, ecologists, regional autonomists, etc). Curiously, most movements of this sort, though they have definitely helped change 'the structure of feeling', pay scant attention to postmodernist arguments, and some feminists are hostile for reasons that we will later consider.[15]

Interestingly, we can detect this same preoccupation with 'otherness' and 'other worlds' in postmodernist fiction. McHale, in emphasising the pluralism of worlds that coexist within postmodernist fiction, finds Foucault's concept of a heterotopia a perfectly appropriate image to capture what that fiction is striving to depict. By heterotopia, Foucault means the coexistence in 'an impossible space' of a 'large number of fragmentary possible words' or, more simply, juxtaposed or superimposed upon each other. Characters no longer contemplate how they can unravel or unmask a central mystery, but are forced to ask, 'Which world is this? What is to be done in it? Which of myselves is to do it?' instead. The same shift can be detected in the cinema. In a modernist classic like *Citizen Kane* a reporter seeks to unravel the mystery of Kane's life and character by collecting multiple reminiscences and perspectives from those who had known him. In a more postmodernist format of the contemporary cinema we find, in a film like *Blue Velvet*, the central character revolving between two quite incongruous worlds – that of a conventional 1950s small-town America with its high school, drugstore culture, and a bizarre, violent, sex-crazed underworld of drugs, dementia, and sexual perversion. It seems impossible that these two worlds should exist in the same space, and the central character moves between them, unsure which is the true reality, until the two worlds collide in a terrible denouement. A postmodernist painter like David Salle likewise tends to 'collage together incompatible source materials as an alternative to choosing between them'.[16] Pfeil even goes so far as to depict the total field of postmodernism as 'a distilled representation of the whole antagonistic, voracious world of otherness.'[17]

But to accept the fragmentation, the pluralism, and the authenticity of other voices and other worlds poses the acute problem of communication and the means of exercising power through command thereof. Most postmodernist thinkers are fascinated by the new possibilities for information and knowledge production, analysis, and transfer. Lyotard for example, firmly locates his arguments in the context of new technologies of communication and, drawing upon Bell's and Touraine's theses of the passage to a 'postindustrial' information-based society, situates the rise of postmodern thought in the heart of what he sees as a dramatic social and political transition in the languages of communication in advanced capitalist societies.[18] He looks closely at the new technologies for the production, dissemination and use of that knowledge as a 'principal force of production'. The problem, however, is that knowledge can now be coded in all kinds of ways, some of which are more accessible than others. There is more than a hint in Lyotard's work, therefore, that modernism has changed because the technical and social conditions of communication have changed.

Postmodernists tend to accept, also, a rather different theory as to what language and communication are all about. Whereas modernists had presupposed that there was a tight and identifiable relation between what was being said (the signified or 'message') and how it was being said (the signifier or 'medium'), poststructuralist thinking sees these as 'continually breaking apart and re-attaching in new combinations'. 'Deconstructionism' (a movement initiated by Derrida's reading of Martin Heidegger in the late 1960s) here enters the picture as a powerful stimulus to postmodernist ways of thought. Deconstructionism is less a philosophical position than a way of thinking about and 'reading' texts. Writers who create texts or use words do so on the basis of other texts and words they have encountered, while readers deal with them in the same way. Cultural life is then viewed as a series of texts intersecting with other texts, producing more texts (including that of the literary critic, who aims to produce another piece of literature in which texts under consideration are intersecting freely with other texts that happen to have affected his or her thinking). This intertextual weaving has a life of its own. Whatever we write conveys meanings we do not or could not possibly intend, and our words cannot say what we mean. It is vain to try and master a text because the perpetual interweaving of texts and meanings is beyond our control. Language works through us. Recognising that, the deconstructionist impulse is to look inside one text for another, dissolve one text into another, or build one text into another.

Derrida considers, therefore, collage/montage as the primary form of postmodern discourse. The inherent heterogeneity of that (be it in painting, writing, architecture) stimulates us, the receivers of the text or image, 'to produce a signification which could be neither univocal nor stable'. Both producers and consumers of 'texts' (cultural artefacts) participate in the production of significations and meanings (hence Hassan's emphasis upon 'process', 'performance', 'happening', and 'participation' in the postmodernist style). Minimising the authority of the cultural producer creates the opportunity for popular participation and democratic determinations of cultural values, but at the price of a certain incoherence or, more problematic, vulnerability to mass-market manipulation. However this may be, the cultural producer merely creates raw materials (fragments and elements), leaving it open to consumers to recombine those elements in any way they wish. The effect is to break (deconstruct) the power of the author to impose meanings or offer a continuous narrative. Each cited element says Derrida, 'breaks the continuity or the linearity of discourse and leads necessarily to a double reading: that of the fragment perceived in relation to its text of origin; that of the fragment as incorporated into a new whole, a different totality'. Continuity is given only in 'the trace' of the fragment as it moves from production to consumption. The effect is to call into question all the illusions of fixed systems of representation.[19]

There is more than a hint of this sort of thinking within the modernist tradition (directly from surrealism, for example) and there is a danger here of thinking of the meta-narratives in the Enlightenment tradition as more fixed and stable than they truly were. Marx, as Ollman observes,[20] deployed his concepts relationally, so that terms like value, labour, capital, are 'continually breaking apart and re-attaching in new combinations' in an open-ended struggle to come to terms with the totalising processes of capitalism. Benjamin, a complex thinker in the Marxist tradition, worked the idea of collage/montage to perfection, in order to try and capture the many-layered and fragmented relations between economy, politics, and culture without ever abandoning the standpoint of a totality of practices that constitute capitalism. Taylor likewise concludes, after reviewing the historical evidence of its use (particularly by Picasso), that collage is a far from adequate indicator of difference between modernist and postmodernist painting.[21]

But if, as the postmodernists insist, we cannot aspire to any unified representation of the world, or picture it as a totality full of connections and differentiations rather than as perpetually shifting fragments, then how can we possible aspire to act coherently with respect to the world? The simple postmodernist answer is that since coherent representation and action are either repressive or illusionary (and therefore doomed to be self-dissolving and self-defeating), we should not even try to engage in some global project, Pragmatism (of the Dewey sort) then becomes the only possible philosophy of action. We thus find Rorty, one of the major US philosophers in the postmodern movement, dismissing 'the canonical sequence of philosophers from Descartes to Nietzsche as a distraction from the history of concrete social engineering which made the contemporary North American culture what it is now, with all its glories and all its dangers'.[22] Action can be conceived of and decided only within the confines of some local determinism, some interpretative community, and its purported meanings and anticipated effects are bound to break down when taken out of these isolated domains, even when coherent within them. We similarly find Lyotard arguing that 'consensus has become an outmoded and suspect value' but then adding, rather surprisingly, that since 'justice as a value is neither outmoded nor suspect' (how it could remain such a universal, untouched by the diversity of language games, he does not tell us), we 'must arrive at an idea and practice of justice that is not linked to that of consensus'.[23]

It is precisely this kind of relativism and defeatism that Habermas seeks to combat in his defence of the Enlightenment project. While Habermas is more than willing to admit what he calls 'the deformed realisation of reason in history' and the dangers that attach to the simplified imposition of some meta-narrative on complex relations and events, he also insists that 'theory can locate a gentle, but obstinate, a never silent although seldom redeemed claim to reason, a claim that must be recognised de facto whenever and wherever there is to be consensual action.' He, too, turns to the question of language, and in *The Theory of Communicative Action* insists upon the dialogical qualities of human communication in which speaker and hearer are necessarily oriented to the task of reciprocal understanding. Out of this, Habermas argues, consensual and normative statements do arise, thus grounding the role of universalising reason in daily life. It is this that allows 'communication reason' to operate 'in history as an avenging force'. Habermas's critics are, however, more numerous than his defenders.

The portrait of postmodernism I have so far sketched in seems to depend for its validity upon a particular way of experiencing, interpreting, and being in the world. This brings us to what is, perhaps, the most problematic facet of postmodernism, its psychological pre-suppositions with respect to personality, motivation, and behaviour. Preoccupation with the fragmentation and instability of language and discourses carries over directly, for example, into a certain conception of personality. Encapsulated, this conception focuses on schizophrenia (not, it should be emphasised, in its narrow clinical sense), rather than on alienation and paranoia (see Hassan's schema). Jameson explores this theme to very telling effect. He uses Lacan's description of schizophrenia as a linguistic disorder, as a breakdown in the signifying chain of meaning that creates a simple sentence. When the signifying chain snaps, then 'we have schizophrenia in the form of a rubble of distinct and unrelated signifiers.' If personal identity is forged through 'a certain temporal unification of the past and future with the present before me', and if sentences move through the same trajectory, then an inability to unify past, present, and future in the sentence betokens a similar inability to 'unify the past, present, and future of our own biographical experience or psychic life'. This fits, of course, with postmodernism's preoccupation with the signifier rather than the signified, with participation, performance, and happening rather than with an authoritative and finished art object, with surface appearances rather than roots (again, see Hassan's schema). The effect of such a breakdown in the signifying chain is to reduce experience to 'a series of pure and unrelated presents in time'. Offering no counterweight, Derrida's conception of language colludes in the production of a certain schizophrenic effect, thus, perhaps, explaining Eagleton's and Hassan's characterisation of the typical postmodernist artefact as schizoid. Deleuze and Guattari,[24] in their supposedly playful exposition *Anti-Oedipus*, Hypothesise a relationship between schizophrenia and capitalism that prevails 'at the deepest level of one and the same economy, one and the same production process', concluding that 'our society produces schizos the same way it produces Prell shampoo or Ford cars, the only difference being that the schizos are not saleable.'

A number of consequences follow from the domination of this motif in postmodernist thought. We can no longer conceive of the individual as alienated in the classical Marxist sense, because to be alienated presupposes a coherent rather than a fragmented sense of self from which to be alienated. It is only in terms of such a centred sense of personal identity that individuals can pursue projects over time, or think cogently about the production of a future significantly better than time present and time past Modernism was very much about the pursuit of better futures, even if perpetual frustration of that aim was conducive to paranoia. But postmodernism typically strips away that possibility by concentrating upon the schizophrenic circumstances induced by fragmentation and all those instabilities (including those of language) that prevent us even picturing coherently, let alone devising strategies to produce some radically different future. Modernism, of course, was not without its schizoid moments – particularly when it sought to combine myth with heroic modernity – and there has been a sufficient history of the 'deformation of reason' and of 'reactionary modernisms' to suggest that the schizophrenic circumstance, though for the most part dominated, was always latent within the modernist movement. Nevertheless, there is good reason to believe that 'alienation of the subject is displaced by fragmentation of the subject' in postmodern aesthetics.[25] If, as Marx insisted, it takes the alienated individual to pursue the Enlightenment project with a tenacity and coherence sufficient to bring us to some better future, then loss of the alienated subject would seen to preclude the conscious construction of alternative social futures.

The reduction of experience to 'a pure and unrelated presents' further implies that the 'experience of the present becomes powerfully, overwhelmingly vivid and 'material': the world comes before the schizophrenic with heightened intensity, bearing the mysterious and oppressive charge of affect, glowing with hallucinatory energy'.[26] The image, the appearance, the spectacle can all be experienced with an intensity (joy or terror) made possible only by their appreciation as pure and unrelated presents in time. So what does it matter 'if the world thereby momentarily loses its depth and threatens to become a glossy skin, a stereoscopic illusion, a rush of filmic images without density?'[27] The immediacy of events, the sensationalism of the spectacle (political, scientific, military, as well as those of entertainment), become the stuff of which consciousness is forged.

Such a breakdown of the temporal order of things also gives rise to a peculiar treatment of the past. Eschewing the idea of progress, postmodernism abandons all sense of historical continuity and memory, while simultaneously developing an incredible ability to plunder history and absorb whatever it finds there as some aspect of the present. Postmodernist architecture, for example, takes bits and pieces from the past quite eclectically and mixes them together at will. Another example, taken from painting, is given by Crimp.[28] Manet's *Olympia*, one of the seminal paintings of the early modernist movement, was modelled on Titian's *Venus*. But the manner of its modelling signalled a self-conscious break between modernity and tradition, and the active intervention of the artist in that transition.[29] Rauschenberg, one of the pioneers of the postmodernist movement, deployed images of Velazquez's *Rokeby Venus* and Rubens's *Venus at her Toilet* in a series of paintings in the 1960s. But he uses these images in a very different way, simply silk-screening a photographic original onto a surface that contains all kinds of other features (trucks, helicopters, car keys). Rauschenberg simply *reproduces*, whereas Manet *produces*, and it is this move, says Crimp, 'that requires us to think of Rauschenberg as a post-modernist'. The modernist 'aura' of the artist as producer is dispensed with. 'The fiction of the creating subject gives way to frank confiscation, quotation, excerption, accumulation and repetition of already existing images.'

This sort of shift carries over into all other fields with powerful implications. Given the evaporation of any sense of historical continuity and memory, and the rejection of meta-narratives, the only role left for the historian, for example, is to become, as Foucault insisted, an archaeologist of the past, digging up its remnants as Borges does in his fiction, and assembling them, side by side, in the museum of modern knowledge. Rorty, in attacking the idea that philosophy can ever hope to define some permanent epistemological framework for enquiry, likewise ends up insisting that the only role of the philosopher, in the midst of the cacophony of cross-cutting conversations that comprise a culture, is to 'decry the notion of having a view while avoiding having a view about having views'.[30] 'The essential trope of fiction,' we are told by the post-modernist writers of it, is a 'technique that requires suspension of belief as well as of disbelief'.[31] There is in postmodernism, little overt attempt to sustain continuity of values, beliefs, or even disbeliefs.

This loss of historical continuity in values and beliefs, taken together with the reduction of the work of art to a text stressing discontinuity and allegory, poses all kinds of problems for aesthetic and critical judgment. Refusing (and actively 'deconstructing') all authoritative or supposedly immutable standards of aesthetic judgment, postmodernism can judge the spectacle only in terms of how spectacular it is, Barthes proposes a particularly sophisticated version of that strategy. He distinguishes between *pleasure* and *'jouissance'* (perhaps best translated as 'sublime physical and mental bliss') and suggests we strive to realise the second, more orgasmic effect (note the connection to Jameson's description of schizophrenia) through a particular mode of encounter with the otherwise lifeless cultural artefacts that litter our social landscape. Since most of us are not schizoid in the clinical sense, Barthes defines a kind of 'mandarin practice' that allows us to achieve 'jouissance' and to use that experience as a basis for aesthetic and critical judgments. This means identification with the act of writing (creation) rather than reading (reception). Huyssen reserves his sharpest irony for Barthes, however, arguing that he reinstitutes one of the tiredest modernist and bourgeois distinctions: that 'there are lower pleasures for the rabble, ie mass culture, and then there is *nouvelle cuisine* of the pleasure of the text, *jouissance*.'[32] This reintroduction of the highbrow/

low-brow disjunction avoids the whole problem of the potential debasement of modern cultural forms by their assimilation to pop culture through pop art. 'The euphoric American appropriation of Barthes's *jouissance* is predicated on ignoring such problems and on enjoying, not unlike the 1984 yuppies, the pleasures of writerly connoisseurism and textual gentrification. Huyssen's image, as Raban's descriptions in *Soft City* suggest, may be more than a little appropriate.

The other side to the loss of temporality and the search for instantaneous impact is a parallel loss of depth. Jameson has been particularly emphatic as to the 'depthlessness' of much of contemporary cultural production, its fixation with appearances, surfaces, and instant impacts that have no sustaining power over time.[33] The image sequences of Sherman's photographs are of exactly that quality, and as Charles Newman remarked in a *New York Times* review on the state of the American novel (17 July 1987):

> The fact of the matter is that a sense of diminishing control, loss of individual autonomy and generalised helplessness has never been so instantaneously recognisable in our literature – the flattest possible characters in the flattest possible landscapes rendered in the flattest possible diction. The presumption seems to be that American is a vast fibrous desert in which a few laconic weeds nevertheless manage to sprout in the cracks.

'Contrived depthlessness' is how Jameson describes postmodern architecture, and it is hard not to give credence to this sensibility as *the* overwhelming motif in postmodernism, offset only by Barthes's attempts to help us to the moment of *jouissance*. Attention to surfaces has, of course, always been important to modernist thought and practice (particularly since the cubists), but it has always been paralleled by the kind of question that Raban posed about urban life: how can we build, represent, and attend to these surfaces with the requisite sympathy and seriousness in order to get behind them and identify essential meanings? Postmodernism, with its resignation to bottomless fragmentation and ephemerality, generally refuses to contemplate that question.

The collapse of time horizons and the preoccupation with instantaneity have in part arisen through the contemporary emphasis in cultural production on events, spectacles, happenings, and media images. Cultural producers have learned to explore and use new technologies, the media, and ultimately multi-media possibilities. The effect, however, has been to re-emphasise the fleeting qualities of modern life and even to celebrate them. But it has also permitted a *rapprochement*, in spite of Barthes's inter-ventions, between popular culture and what once remained isolated as 'high culture'. Such a *rapprochement* has been sought before, though nearly always in a more revolutionary mode, as movements like Dada and early surrealism, constructivism, and expressionism tried to bring their art to the people as part and parcel of a modernist project of social transformation. Such avant-gardist movements possessed a strong faith in their own aims as well as immense faith in new technologies. The closing of the gap between popular culture and cultural production in the contemporary period, while strongly dependent on new technologies of communication, seems to lack any avant-gardist or revolutionary impulse, leading many to accuse postmodernism of a simple and direct surrender to commodification, commercialisation, and the market.[34] However this may be, much of postmodernism is consciously anti-auratic and anti-avant-garde and seeks to explore media and cultural arenas open to all. It is no accident that Sherman, for example, use photography and evokes pop images as if from film stills in the poses she assumes.

This raises the most difficult of all questions about the postmodern movement, namely its relationship with, and integration into, the culture of daily life. Although much of the discussion of it proceeds in the abstract, and therefore in the not very accessible terms that I have been forced to use here, there are innumerable points of contact between producers of cultural artefacts and the public: architecture, advertising, fashion, films, staging of multi-media events, grand spectacles, political campaigns, as well as the ubiquitous television. It is not always clear who is influencing whom in this process.

Venturi et al recommend that we learn our architectural aesthetics from the Las Vegas strip or from much-maligned suburbs like Levittown, simply because people evidently like such environments.[35] 'One does not have to agree with hard hat politics,' they go on to say, 'to support the rights of the middle-middle class to their own architectural aesthetics, and we have found that Levittown-type aesthetics are shared by most members of the middle-middle class, black as well as white, liberal as well as conservative.' There is absolutely nothing wrong, they insist, with giving people what they want, and Venturi himself was even quoted in *The New York Times* (22 October 1972), in an article fittingly entitled 'Mickey Mouse Teaches the Architects', saying 'Disney World is nearer to what people want than what architects have over given them.' Disneyland, he asserts, is 'the symbolic American utopia'.

There are those, however, who see such a concession of high culture to Disneyland aesthetics as a matter of necessity rather than choice. Daniel Bell, for example, depicts postmodernism as the exhaustion of modernism through the institutionalisation of creative and rebellious impulses by what he calls 'the cultural mass' (the millions of people working in broadcast media, films, theatre, universities, publishing houses, advertising and communications industries, etc who process and influence the reception of serious cultural products and produce the popular materials for the wider mass-culture audience).[36] The degeneration of high-brow authority over cultural taste in the 1960s, and its replacement by pop art, pop culture, ephemeral fashion, and mass taste is seen as a sign of the mindless hedonism of capitalist consumerism.

Iain Chambers interprets a similar process rather differently.[37] Working-class youth in Britain found enough money in their pockets during the postwar boom to participate in the capitalist consumer culture, and actively used fashion to construct a sense of their own public identities, even defined their own pop-art forms, in the face of a fashion industry that sought to impose taste through advertising and media pressures. The consequent democratisation of taste across a variety of sub-cultures (from inner-city macho male to college campuses) is interpreted as the outcome of a vital struggle that pitched the rights of even the relatively underprivileged to shape their own identities in the face of a powerfully organised commercialism. The urban based cultural ferments that began in the early 1960s and continue to this very day lie, in Chambers's view at the root of the postmodern turn:

> Post modernism, whatever form its intellectualising might take, has been funda-
> mentally anticipated in the metropolitan cultures of the last twenty years: among
> the electronic signifiers of cinema, television and video, in recording studios and
> record players, in fashion and youth styles, in all those sounds, images and diverse
> histories that are daily mixed, recycled and 'scratched' together on that giant
> screen which is the contemporary city.

It is hard, also, not to attribute some kind of shaping role to the proliferation of television use. After all, the average American is now reputed to watch television for more than seven hours a day, and television and video ownership (the latter now covering at least half all US households) is now so widespread throughout the capitalist world that some effects must surely be registered. Postmodernist concerns with surface, for example, can be traced to the necessary format of television images. Television is also, as Taylor points out, 'the first cultural medium in the whole of history to present the artistic achievements of the past as a stitched-together collage of equi-important and simultaneously existing phenomena, largely divorced from geography and material history and transported to the living rooms and studios of the West in a more or less uninterrupted flow.'[38] It posits a viewer, furthermore, 'who shares the medium's own perception of history as an endless reserve of equal events.' It is hardly surprising that the artist's relation to history (the peculiar historicism we have already noted) has shifted, that in the era of mass television there has emerged an attachment to surfaces rather than roots, to collage rather than in-depth work, to super-imposed quoted images rather than worked surfaces, to a collapsed sense of time and space rather than solidly achieved cultural artefact. And these are all vital aspects of artistic practice in the post-modern condition.

To point to the potency of such a force in shaping culture as a total way of life is not necessarily to lapse, however, into a simple-minded technological determinism of the 'television causes post-modernism' variety. For television is itself a product of late capitalism and, as such, has to be seen in the context of the promotion of a culture of consumerism. This directs our attention to the production of needs and wants, the mobilisation of desire and fantasy, of the politics of distraction as part and parcel of the push to sustain sufficient buoyancy of demand in consumer markets to keep capitalist production profitable. Charles Newman sees much of the postmodernist aesthetic as a response to the inflationary surge of late capitalism.[39] 'Inflation,' he argues, 'affects the ideas exchange just as surely as it does commercial markets.' Thus 'we are witness to continual internecine warfare and spasmodic change in fashion, the simultaneous display of all past styles in their infinite mutations, and the continuous circulation of diverse and contradictory intellectual elites, which signal the reign of the cult of creativity in all areas of behaviour, an unprecedented non-judgmental receptivity to Art, a tolerance which finally amounts to indifference.' From this standpoint, Newman concludes, 'the vaunted fragmentation of art is no longer an aesthetic choice: it is simply a cultural aspect of the economic and social fabric.'

This would certainly go some way to explain the postmodernist thrust to integrate into popular culture through the kind of frank, even crass, commercialisation that modernists tended to eschew by their deep resistance to the idea (though never quite the fact) of commodification of their production. There are those however, who attribute the exhaustion of high modernism precisely to its absorption as the formal aesthetics of corporate capitalism and the bureaucratic state. Postmodernism then signals nothing more than a logical extension of the power of the market over the whole range of cultural production. Crimp waxes quite acerbic on this point:

> What we have seen in the last several years is the virtual takeover of art by big corporate interests. For whatever role capital played in the art of modernism, the current phenomenon is new precisely because of its scope. Corporations have become the major patrons of art in every respect. They form huge collections. They fund every major museum exhibition. . . . Auction houses have become lending institutions, giving a completely new value to art as collateral. And all of this affects not only the inflation of value of old masters but art production itself. . . . [The corporations] are buying cheap and in quantity, counting on the escalation of the value of young artists. . . . The return to painting and sculpture of a traditional cast is the return to commodity production, and I would suggest that, whereas traditionally art had an ambiguous commodity status, it now has a thoroughly unambiguous one.[40]

The growth of a museum culture (in Britain a museum opens every three weeks, and in Japan over 500 have opened up in the last fifteen years) and a burgeoning 'heritage industry' that took off in the early 1970s, add another populist (though this time very middle-class) twist to the commercialisation of history and cultural forms. 'Post-modernism and the heritage industry are linked,' says Hewison, since 'both conspire to create a shallow screen that intervenes between our present lives and our history.'[41] History becomes a 'contemporary creation, more costume drama and re-enactment than critical discourse.' We are, he concludes, quoting Jameson, condemned to seek History by way of our own pop images and simulacra of that history which itself remains for ever out of reach. 'The house is viewed no longer as a machine but as an antique for living in.'

The invocation of Jameson brings us, finally, to his daring thesis that postmodernism is nothing more than the cultural logic of late capitalism. Following Mandel, he argues that we have moved into a new era since the early 1960s in which the production of culture 'has become integrated into commodity production generally: the frantic urgency of producing fresh waves of ever more novel seeming goods (from clothes to airplanes), at ever greater rates of turnover, now assigns an increasingly essential structural function to aesthetic innovation and experimentation.' The struggles that were once exclusively waged in the arena of production have, as a consequence, now spilled outwards to make of cultural production an arena of fierce social conflict. Such a shift entails a definite change in consumer habits and attitudes as well as a new role for aesthetic definitions and interventions. While some would argue that the counter-cultural movements of the 1960s created an environment of unfulfilled needs and repressed desires that postmodernist popular cultural production has merely set out to satisfy as best it can in commodity form, others would suggest that capitalism, in order to sustain its markets, has been forced to produce desire and so titillate individual sensibilities as to create a new aesthetic over and against traditional forms of high culture in either case, I think it important to accept the proposition that the cultural evolution which has taken place since the early 1960s, and which asserted itself as hegemonic in the early 1970s, has not occurred in a social, economic, or political vacuum. The deployment of advertising as 'the official art of capitalism' brings advertising strategies into art, and art into advertising strategies. It is interesting, therefore, to ruminate upon the stylistic shift that Hassan sets up in relation to the forces that emanate from mass-consumer culture: the mobilisation of fashion, pop art, television and other forms of media image, and the variety of urban life styles that have become part and parcel of daily life under capitalism. Whatever else we do with the concept, we should not read postmodernism as some autonomous artistic current. Its rootedness in daily life is one of its most patently transparent features.

The portrait of postmodernism I have here constructed, with the help of Hassan's schema, is certainly incomplete. It is equally certainly rendered fragmentary and ephemeral by the sheer plurality and elusiveness of cultural forms wrapped in the mysteries of rapid flux and change. But I think I have said enough as to what constitutes the general frame of that 'profound shift in the structure of feeling' that separates modernity from postmodernity to begin upon the task of unravelling its origins and speculatively constructing an interpretation of what it might betoken for our future.

NOTES

1 C Jencks, *The Language of Post-Modern Architecture*, London, 1984.

2 T Eagleton, 'Awakening from Modernity', *Times Literary Supplement*, 20 February 1987.

3 *PRECIS* 6, *The Culture of Fragments*, Columbia University Graduate School of Architecture, New York, 1987.

4 Eg Richard Rorty, *Philosophy and the Mirror of Nature*, Princeton, NJ, 1979.

5 T Kuhn, *The Structure of Scientific Revolutions*, Chicago, Ill, 1962; P Feyerabend, *Against Method*, London, 1975.

6 A Huyssen, 'Mapping the Post-Modern', *New German Critique* 33, pp 5-52.

7 B McHale, *Postmodernist Fiction*, London, 1987.

8 R Bernstein, ed *Habermas and Modernity*, Oxford, 1985.

9 *Baltimore Sun* 9, September 1987.

10 A Kroker and D Cook, *The Postmodern Scene: Excremental Culture and Hyper-Aesthetics*, New York, 1986.

11 M Foucault, Power/Knowledge, New York, 1972.

12 Eg S Fish, *Is there a Text in this Class? The Authority of Interpretive Communities*, Cambridge, Mass, 1980.

13 P Bove, 'The Ineluctability of Difference: Scientific Pluralism and the Critical Intelligence', *Postmodernism and Politics*, ed J Arac, Manchester, 1986, p 18.

14 C Gilligan, *In a Different Voice: Psychological Theory and Women's Development*, Cambridge, Mass, 1982.

15 Eg N Hartsock, 'Rethinking Modernism: Minority Versus Majority Theories', *Cultural Critique* 7, 1987, pp 187-206.

16 B Taylor, *Modernism, Postmodernism, Realism: A Critical Perspective for Art*, Winchester, 1987.

17 F Pfeil, 'Postmodernism as a "Structure of Feeling"', *Marxism and the Interpretation of Culture*, ed C Nelson and L Grossberg, Urbana, Ill, 1988.

18 J-F Lyotard, *The Postmodern Condition*, Manchester, 1984.

19 H Foster, ed *The Anti-Aesthetic: Essays on Postmodern Culture*, Port Townsend, Wash, 1983.

20 B Ollman, *Alienation*, Cambridge, 1971.

21 Taylor, *Modernism, Postmodernism, Reality*, pp 53-65.

22 R Rorty, 'Habermas and Lyotard on Postmodernity', *Habermas and Modernity*, ed Bernstein, p 173.

23 Lyotard, *Postmodern Condition*, p 66.

24 G Deleuze and F Guattari, *Anti-Oedipus: Capitalism and Schizophrenia*, London, 1984.

25 F Jameson, 'The Politics of Theory: Ideological Positions in the Post-Modernism Debate', *New German Critique* 33, p 120.

26 F Jameson, 'Postmodernism and the Cultural Logic of Late Capitalism', *New Left Review* 146, 1984, p 120.

27 Ibid.

28 D Crimp, 'On the Museum's Ruins', *Anti-Aesthetic*, ed H Foster, pp 44-45.

29 TJ Clark, *The Painting of Modern Life: Paris in the Art of Manet and his Followers*, New York, 1983.

30 R Rorty, *Philosophy and the Mirror of Nature*, Princeton, NJ, 1979, p 371.

31 McHale, *Postmodernist Fiction*, pp 27-33.

32 Huyssen, 'Mapping the Post-Modern', pp 38-45.

33 Jameson, 'Politics of Theory'; idem, 'Cultural Logic'.

34 H Foster, *Recodings: Art, Spectacle, Cultural Politics*, Port Townsend, Wash, 1985.

35 R Venturi, D Scott Brown and S Izenour, *Learning from Las Vegas*, Cambridge, Mass, 1972.

36 D Bell, *The Cultural Contradictions of Capitalism*, New York, 1978.

37 I Chambers, *Popular Culture: The Metropolitan Experience*, London, 1986; idem, 'Maps for the Metropolis: A Possible Guide to the Present', *Cultural Studies* 1, 1987, pp 1-22.

38 Taylor, *Modernism, Post-Modernism, Realism*, pp 103-05.

39 C Newman, 'The Postmodern Aura: The Act of Fiction in an Age of Inflation', *Salmagundi* 63-64, 1984, pp 3-199.

40 D Crimp, 'Art in the 80s: The Myth of Autonomy', *PRECIS* 6, p 85.

41 R Hewison, *The Heritage Industry*, London, 1987, p 135.

From *The Condition of Postmodernity*, Basil Blackwell Inc, Cambridge, Massachusetts and Basil Blackwell, Oxford, 1989.

CHAPTER FIVE

FEMINISM

Barbara Kruger, *Untitled (You are not yourself)*, 1983, gelatin silver print 18.2 x 121.9 cm

Susan Rubin Suleiman

FEMINISM AND POSTMODERNISM
A QUESTION OF POLITICS

> . . . and to this day young authors sally forth in fiction like majestic – indeed, divinely ordained! – picaros to discover, again and again, their manhood. (Robert Coover)

> To write a quality cliché you have to come up with something new. (Jenny Holzer)

Contrary to what some recent commentators on postmodernism seem to think, there was life before Jean-François Lyotard.[1] The term 'postmodernism', designating a cultural sequel and/or challenge to modernism (however one defined that term) existed well before the publication of *La condition postmoderne* (1979).[2] It is ironic that Lyotard's book, or rather its English translation, *The Postmodern Condition* (1981), should have become the required starting point for all current discussions of postmodernism by American and English critics, when Lyotard himself, in what I have called elsewhere a 'rare instance of "reverse importation" in the French-American theoretical marketplace', credited his use of the term to American critics, notably to Ihab Hassan.[3]

One would not be altogether wrong to see in this displacement, whereby the French philosopher 'takes the place of' all his American predecessors, a sign of what Fredric Jameson diagnosed as the absence of historical consciousness in postmodern culture – as if the memory of those who discuss postmodernism in the 1980s did not extend beyond the confines of the decade itself; or perhaps, more ironically, to see in it a sign of the snob appeal of 'genuine French imports' (or what are mistakenly thought to be such) in a certain sector of American intellectual life. But if this view would not be altogether wrong it would not be altogether right either, for although Lyotard's book did not initiate the discourse on postmodernism, it did place it on a new theoretical and philosophical footing. Most notably, it articulated the links between French poststructuralist philosophy and postmodern cultural practices ('culture' being understood to include science and everyday life as well as the arts), so that the latter could be seen – at least in the ideal sketched by Lyotard – as an instantiation of the former.

All of the concepts Lyotard invoked to define the innovative aspects of postmodern knowledge – the crisis of legitimation and the refusal of 'grand narratives', the choice of models of dissent and heterogeneity over models of consensus and systemic totality, the view of cultural practices as overlapping language games with constantly shifting rules and players – are concepts grounded in poststructuralist thought, as the latter was elaborated in France in the 1960s and 1970s by Lyotard, Derrida, Foucault and others. *The Postmodern Condition* can thus be read as a poststructuralist manifesto or 'manifesto of decentred subjectivities', expressing the optimism for the future that the manifesto genre requires. Although Lyotard is aware of the nightmarish possibilities offered by the 'computerisation of society' (his model of postmodern knowledge invokes and seeks to generalise the new technologies and conceptualisations – such as Mandelbrot's fractals

– made possible by the computer), he emphasises instead its potentialities as a positive dream. The dream is of a society in which knowledge would consist of language games that would be 'non-zero-sum games', where there would be no losers or winners, only players in a constantly evolving process; where openness would be the rule, with information and data banks available to all; where instability and 'temporary contracts' would lead neither to alienation nor to anarchy, but to 'a politics that would respect both the desire for justice and the desire for the unknown'.[4]

In short, a utopian – or cautiously utopian, if such a thing is possible – version of Babel, a positive counterargument to the pessimistic views being elaborated, during the same post-1968 decade, by Jean Baudrillard. Lyotard was seeing the same things as Baudrillard, but interpreting them differently: what to Baudrillard appeared as the increasingly horrifying world of simulacra evacuating the real, indeed evacuating the very concept of a difference between the simulacrum and the real, appeared to Lyotard – at least potentially – as a world of increasing possibilities for innovation, brought about precisely by the breakdown of stable categories like 'the real'. Where Baudrillard saw the 'postmodern condition' (a term he did not use) as the end of all possibility for (real) action, community, resistance, or change, Lyotard saw it as potentially a whole new game, whose possibilities remained open.[5]

That difference marked one of the stakes in what was soon to become, with the entry of Jürgen Habermas into the fray, the best-known version of the 'modernism-postmodernism debate.'[6] Since then, the debate has shifted again: What is now in question is not so much whether postmodernism constitutes a totally new development or 'break' in relation to modernism (most people, it seems to me, have now accepted that as a given, even if they don't agree on all the details of why and how), but rather the current significance and future direction of the new development as such. What does all this have to do with women or feminism? And with earlier American discourses about postmodernism, which I accused other recent commentators of ignoring and then proceeded to ignore myself? Obviously, this is not the place to undertake a full-scale history of discourses on the postmodern.[7] Suffice it to say that, like a number of other important 'isms', (romanticism, modernism, classicism), postmodernism has functioned as both a formal/stylistic category and a broadly cultural category. From the start, the most provocative discussions have been those that linked the formal or stylistic to the broadly cultural. Irving Howe's 1959 essay, for example, 'Mass Society and Postmodern Fiction', which is generally credited with first use of the term 'postmodern' in its current sense, saw in the emergence of a new kind of American fiction (roughly, that of the Beat generation) both a stylistic sequel to modernism – exemplified by Joyce, Mann, and Kafka as well as Hemingway and Fitzgerald – and a cultural symptom of the transformations that had occurred in Western countries after the Second World War.[8] A similar argument, although adopting a different, more positive judgment on these transformations and on the literature that accompanied them, was made by Leslie Fiedler a few years later; it was also suggested, again in positive terms, by Robert Venturi and Denise Scott Brown around the same time regarding architecture, in the essay that was to become the basis for their famous (or infamous) manifesto of postmodern architecture, *Learning from Las Vegas*.[9]

A few years ago, I argued that as far as literature was concerned, it made no sense to try and establish clear-cut formal differences between the 'modernist' and the 'postmodernist', for such an attempt invariably involved oversimplification and flattening out of both categories.[10] Although I would now want to change some of the premises of that earlier argument, I still believe that the effort to define postmodernism chiefly as a formal (or even as a formal and thematic) category and to oppose it as such to modernism is, even when successful, of limited interest.[11] If postmodernist practice in the arts has provoked controversy and debate, it is because of what it 'does' (or does not do), not because of what it 'is'. In other words, it is as an object 'to be read', an intervention in the sense of an action or a statement requiring a response, rather than as an object of descriptive poetics, that postmodernism, whether in literature or in the other arts, strikes me as significant today.

This position, whether explicitly stated or not, seems to me to be shared by all those who are currently involved in the 'postmodernism debate'. Where is postmodernist practice going? Can it be political? – should it be? Does it offer possibilities for opposition, critique, resistance to dominant ideologies? Or is it irremediably compromised by its complicity with the market, with mass culture, capitalism, commercialism? Familiar questions, questions that have been asked in one form or another, at one time or another, about every avant-garde movement and experimental practice since Impressionism. Which does not make them less significant when asked about postmodernism, though it suggests that no definitive answers may be forthcoming.

And women? And feminism?

Discourses on the Postmodern and the Emergence of Feminist Postmodernism

It should come as no surprise, knowing what we know about earlier avant-garde movements and their historians, to learn that the first writings about postmodernism made absolutely no mention of the work of women. One could argue that if early commentators like Irving Howe and Leslie Fiedler, whose prime examples of the postmodern were the Beats (Fiedler also mentioned Pop Art in the visual arts), did not mention women's work, it was because there was little or no such work around to be mentioned at the time. This would mean that the Beats and the Pop Artists were male avant-gardes similar to certain earlier movements like Surrealism, excluding women during their most dynamic period.[12] In fact, there were some women, active in both movements, if not at the very beginning, then close enough to it (Diane Di Prima among the writers, Marisol among the painters). Still, as in the case of Surrealism, one can ascribe the early critics' silence not only to ordinary sexism ('not seeing' women who are there), but also to a real scarcity of women's work in those movements.

Critics who started to write about postmodernism in the 1970s or 1980 had less of an excuse for excluding the work of women; for in what I take to be a genuinely *new (inédit,* as they say on bookcovers in Paris) historical development, women's participation in experimental literary and visual work during those two decades reached a level, both in terms of quantity and quality, that could no longer be ignored. Some critics, of course, even among the most brilliant, managed to ignore it, as late as the mid 1980s others, less brilliant, went so far as to theorise its absence. (A few years ago, I received a letter from a European doctoral student who asked whether I agreed with her professor that 'women have not produced any postmodernist fiction', and if so, to what I attributed that lack. I replied that the lack may have been in the beholder rather than in the object.)

In the 1980s women's work began to be mentioned, and even featured, in academic discussions of postmodernism, especially in the visual arts. Rosalind Krauss's important 1981 article, 'The Originality of the Avant-Garde: A Postmodernist Repetition', which made a strong, polemically 'pro-postmodernist' case for the difference between postmodernism and its modernist or historical avant-garde predecessors (the difference residing, according to Krauss, in postmodernism's 'radical questioning of the concept of origin . . . and originality'), cited as exemplary postmodernist works the photographs of Sherrie Levine; two years earlier, in the pages of the same journal, Douglas Crimp had argued for the innovativeness (originality?) of postmodernist 'pictures' and cited, among other examples, the photographs of Levine and Cindy Sherman.[13]

To discuss the work of women as part of a new movement, trend, or cultural paradigm one is defending is undoubtedly a desirable thing. As Renato Poggioli showed, every avant-garde has its critical defenders and explicators;[14] their work, in turn, becomes a basis on which the movement, once it goes beyond its 'scandalous' phase, is integrated into the standard literary and cultural histories. It is quite another thing, however, to take into account not only the existence of women's work, but also its (possibly) feminine or feminist specificity; and to raise, furthermore, the question of how the specificity, whether sexual or political, of women's work within a larger movement affects one's understanding of the movement itself.

In his 1983 essay, 'The Discourse of Others: Feminists and Postmodernism', Craig Owens made one of those conceptual leaps that later turn out to have initiated a whole new train of thought. Simply, what Owens did was to theorise the political implications of the intersection between the 'feminist critique of patriarchy and the postmodernist critique of representation.'[15] He was not the first to suggest the political potential of poststructuralism (which, in the preceding sentence and in Owens's argument, is virtually interchangeable with postmodernism); the ideological critique of the unified bourgeois subject' and of classical representation had been a continuing theme in French poststructuralist writing from the late 1960s on, and had been part of the political platform of *Tel Quel* in its most revolutionary period.[16] Nor was the linking of the feminist critique of patriarchy with poststructuralism surprising, since French feminist theory had from the beginning acknowledged its linking to deconstruction, and even proclaimed it in its famous portmanteau word, 'phallogocentrism'. The novelty, indeed the pathbreaking quality of Owens's essay was that it placed the feminist issue at the centre of the debate on postmodernism (which was also, if one wishes, a debate on poststructuralism), as that debate was unfolding in the United States (and, with a bit of delay, in England) after the publication of Lyotard's *The Postmodern Condition*.[17]

On the one hand, Owens quite rightly criticised the major players in the debate for ignoring both the 'insistent feminist voice' in postmodern culture and the whole issue of sexual difference in their discussions of postmodernist practices: thus even those critics who, like Crimp, Krauss, and Hal Foster (and Owens himself, in an earlier essay), discussed women's work an important part of postmodernist art, could be faulted for ignoring the specifically feminist – or even 'feminine' – meanings of that work.[18] On the other hand, Owens suggested that if the feminist/critical aspect of postmodernist work was taken into account, there would result a new and more politically sharpened view of postmodernism itself – for feminism, after all, is not only a theory or an aesthetics, it is also a politics.

By linking feminist politics with postmodernist artistic practice, Owens provided the pro-postmodernists in the debate with a precious argument, whose advantages they were quick to grasp. Feminism provided for postmodernism a concrete political edge, or wedge, that could be used to counter the accusatory pessimism of a Baudrillard or a Jameson: for if there existed a genuinely feminist postmodernist practice, then postmodernism could no longer be seen only as the expression of a fragmented, exhausted culture steeped in nostalgia for a lost centre. Indeed, such a view of postmodernism, with its sense of irremediable decline and loss, could now itself be shown to be implicated in the Western, patriarchal logic of the 'grand narratives' – the very logic that feminism, and feminist postmodernism, contested. As Hal Foster, in a 1984 essay that I read as a response to and development of Owens's argument, eloquently noted:

> Here, then we begin to see what is at stake in [the] so-called dispersal of the subject. For what is this subject that, threatened by loss, is so bemoaned? For some, for many, this may indeed be a great loss, a loss which leads to narcissistic laments and hysterical disavowals of the end of art, of culture, of the west. But for others, precisely for Others, it is no great loss at all.[19]

Andreas Huyssen, around the same time, was arguing that feminism and the women's movement, together with anti-imperialism, the ecology movement, and the growing awareness of 'other cultures, non-European, non-Western cultures,' had created a new 'postmodernism of resistance' that would 'satisfy the needs of the political and those of the aesthetic.'[20] Most recently, following up on these arguments, Linda Hutcheon has spoken of the overlapping agendas between postmodernism and 'ex-centrics': blacks, women, and other traditionally marginalised groups.[21]

In short, feminism brings to postmodernism the political guarantee postmodernism needs in order to feel respectable as an avant-garde practice. Postmodernism, in turn, brings feminism into a certain kind of 'high theoretical' discourse on the frontiers of culture, traditionally an exclusively male domain.[22]

If this summary sounds cynical, the effect is only partly intended. There is, I believe, an element of mutual opportunism in the alliance of feminists and postmodernists, but it is not necessarily a bad thing. The opportunism operates not so much, or perhaps not at all, in the actual practice of feminist postmodernist artists, but rather in the public discourse about that practice: influential critics who write about the work of feminist postmodernists, especially in the realm of the visual arts, are both advancing their own reputations as 'high theorists' and contributing to – or even creating – the market value of those artists' work, while other, less fashionable feminist work may go unnoticed. And once it becomes valuable on the market, the feminist postmodernist work may lose its critical edge.

This is not a new problem, as I have already suggested and will suggest again. In a world in which everything, even the discourse of high postmodernist theory, has an exchange value, should one reject the advantages of the feminist-postmodernist alliance for the sake of an ideal of aesthetic or intellectual purity? If every avant-garde has its public defenders and promoters, why not feminist postmodernism?

Oh dear oh dear, now I do sound excessively cynical. Let me therefore quickly affirm that I take the theoretical arguments advanced by Owens, Foster, Huyssen, and Hutcheon in favour of the feminism/postmodernism alliance extremely seriously, and indeed subscribe to them (mostly); that I believe it is important to look for the critical and political possibilities of avant-garde practices in general, and of postmodernism in particular; and that I think women and feminists rightfully belong in the centre of such discussions and practices – in the middle of the margin, as it were.[23] As I said earlier, with postmodernism we have arrived at a totally new situation for women artists: for the first time in the history of avant-gardes (or in history *tout court*), there exists a critical mass of outstanding, innovative work by women, both in the visual arts and in literature.[24] Simone de Beauvoir's complaint, in *The Second Sex*, that women artists lacked genius – that is, the audacity to take real risks and to carry 'the weight of the world on their shoulders' – is no longer true, if it ever was. Today, thanks in part to the existence of predecessors like Beauvoir, there are women artists who possess genius in her sense – and who are aware at the same time that 'genius', like every other abstract universal category, is determined by particulars: race, sex, nationality, religion, history. As Christine Brooke-Rose has recently noted, 'genius' has the same Indo-European root as gender, genre, and genesis.[25]

Still, it would be unwise to celebrate postmodernism, even more so feminist postmodernism, without keeping one's ears open to dissenting voices, or without acknowledging things that don't 'fit.' Feminist postmodernism, like postmodernism in general, must confront anew some of the dilemmas that have plagued every successful avant-garde for the past century or more: the dilemma of political effectiveness versus stylistic indirection and innovation, numbingly familiar to students of the 1930s; or the dilemma of the market and the avant-garde's relation to mass culture, which dominated, as Andreas Huyssen has shown, the 'Greenberg and Adorno decades' after the Second World War. In addition, feminist postmodernism must confront the specific questions and challenges posed to it from within the feminist movement, notably as concerns the political status of the 'de-centred subject.'

Not a short order, in sum. Enough to fill a whole book, in fact. But I shall fill only a few more pages, with thoughts and notes for future reflection and work, whether by me or others.

Opposition in Babel? The Political Status of (Postmodern, Ironic) Intertextuality

Then I shall enter with my hypotheses and sweep the detritus of civilisation.
(Christine Brooke-Rose, *Amalgamemnon*)
The vital thing is to have an alternative so that people will realise that there's no
such thing as a true story. (Jeanette Winterson, *Boating for Beginners*)
The appropriation, misappropriation, montage, collage, hybridisation, and general mixing up of visual and verbal texts and discourses, from all periods of the past as well as from the multiple social and linguistic fields of the present, is probably the most characteristic feature of what can be called the 'postmodern style'. The question, as it has emerged in the debate on postmodernism, is: Does this style have a critical political meaning or effect, or is it – in Fredric Jameson's words – merely 'blank parody', a 'neutral practice' devoid of any critical impulse or historical consciousness?[26]

There is not much point in looking for a single 'right' answer to that question, since it is precisely the object of the debate. One can, however, try to refine and clarify the question; and one must, sooner or later, state one's own position on it. What, then, does it mean to talk about the political effect of a novel or painting or photograph? If one means that in a particular historical circumstance an art work can be used for political ends, well and good: Picasso's *Guernica*, exhibited in major European and American capitals between 1937 and 1939, earned a lot of sympathy as well as material support for the Spanish Republic before coming to rest for a few decades in the Museum of Modern Art. If one means that the work elicits a political response, whether in the form of public commentaries or private reactions, including the production of other art works that build on it (*Guernica* is again a good example), that is also well and good.[27] What seems to me wrongheaded, or at the very least problematic, is to talk about the political effect or meaning of a work – especially of a self-conscious, insistently intertextual, often multiply ironic work – as if that meaning were clear, immutable, and immanent to the 'text,' rather than determined by its interpretive context.

Political readings – indeed, all interpretations – tend to speak of works as if their meanings and effects were immanent; in order to convince someone else of the validity of one's reading, one has to claim, or at least imply, that it is the best reading, the reading most closely corresponding to the 'work itself'. When Jameson made his often-quoted claim that postmodern pastiche 'is a neutral practice of . . . mimicry, without any of parody's ulterior motives, amputated of the 'satiric impulse, devoid of laughter and of any conviction that . . . some healthy linguistic normality still exists,' implicit in the claim (which was used to support his general argument that postmodernism lacked authentic historical awareness) was the assumption that works of art determine their own meaning and reading. Linda Hutcheon, who strongly criticises Jameson for not citing any examples, and offers many examples of her own to show that postmodern parody does not lack the satiric impulse' and is not apolitical or ahistorical, is no doubt justified in her critique; but as the very act of citing counterexamples shows, she shares Jameson's assumption that political meanings reside in works, not in their readings.

As the by now familiar theories of 'reader-oriented criticism' have shown, however, this assumption is extremely problematic, and probably downright wrong. Stanley Fish and others have argued that every reading of a text, no matter how personal or 'quirky', can be shown to be part of a collective discourse and analysed historically and ideologically as characteristic of a group, or what Fish has called an interpretive community.[28] It is a matter of having learned, in the classroom or through scholarly exchange, or through more informal modes of communication, certain shared ways of approaching a text: asking certain questions of it, and elaborating a language and an interpretive 'strategy' for answering those questions.

Displacing the political effect from the work to its reading has the advantage of moving the debate from the question of what postmodernism 'is' to the question of what it does – in a particular place, for a particular public (which can be a public of one, but as I have just suggested, every individual is part of a larger interpretive community) at a particular time. That displacement does not, however, alter the basic questions about the politics of intertextuality or of irony, or more generally about the relation between symbolic action and 'real' action in the world. It merely . . . displaces them, from the work to its readings and readers.

Jameson, reading postmodernist intertextuality as an expression of advanced capitalism, 'a field of stylistic and discursive heterogeneity without a norm,' calls it 'blank parody, a statue with blind eyeballs'.[29] But postmodernist intertextuality (is it the 'same' one?) can also be thought of, for example in the British artist Mary Kelly's terms, as a sign of critical commitment to the contemporary world. According to Kelly, this commitment distinguished British postmodernist art of the 1970s and early 1980s from its American counterpart: whereas the Americans merely 'purloined' previous images and 'pilfered' the contemporary world's 'cultural estate', the British were 'exploring its boundaries, deconstructing its centre, proposing the decolonisation of its visual codes and of language itself.'[30]

It is not clear from Kelly's comparison how one can distinguish, objectively, 'mere pilfering' from political deconstruction and decolonisation. Similarly, Jameson's recent attempt to distinguish the 'ahistorical' postmodernism he deplores from its 'homeopathic critique' in the works of EL Doctorow, works he admires and finds salutary, strikes me as dubitable at best.[31] So, for that matter, do all the other attempts that have been made to distinguish a 'good' postmodernism (of resistance) from a 'bad' postmodernism (what Lyotard calls the 'anything goes' variety).[32]

It seems a good bet that almost any given work can be shown to belong to either of those categories, depending on how one reads it. Cindy Sherman's early work, the series of *Untitled Film Stills* from nonexistent Hollywood films, which the artist interprets as being 'about the fakeness of role playing as well as contempt for the domineering "male" audience who would read the images as sexy',[33] and which some critics have read in those terms as a form of feminist ironic critique, have been read by other critics as works that play up to the 'male gaze' for the usual profit: 'the work seems a slicked-up version of the original, a new commodity. In fact, much of this work has proved quite salable, easy to show, easy to write about, easy to sell.'[34] Even the 'Third World' and 'women of colour', those brave new banners under which (together with feminism) the postmodernism of resistance has sought its political credentials, can be shown, if one is so inclined, to be caught up in the logic of the simulacrum and in the economics of multinational capitalism. In today's world, one can argue, there are no more places outside; the Third World too is part of the society of the spectacle.

Perhaps it all comes down, in the end, to how one understands Christine Brooke-Rose's evocative phrase about 'sweeping the detritus of civilisation'. Does (can?) the sweeper hope to clear the detritus, or is she merely making new patterns with it and thus adding to the heap? And if the latter, should the sweeper put away her broom?

Yet another twist: If postmodernist intertextuality can be read both ways, that fact itself is open to interpretation. For Linda Hutcheon, it proves that postmodernist works are ambivalent and contradictory, 'doubly encoded', and that they therefore constitute not a 'break' but a 'challenge to culture from within.'[35] For Craig Owens, it proves that postmodernism is the true art of deconstruction, for it recognises the 'unavoidable necessity of participating in the very activity that is being denounced precisely in order to denounce it.'[36] On the other hand, one could call this apology for postmodernism itself part of a strategy of 'anything goes', with the added proviso: 'as long as I recognise that I am not innocent.' This was already, in an ethical and existential perspective, the strategy of Camus's 'penitent judge' in *La Chute* (1956). Clamence is more than willing to admit his own guilt, as long as it allows him to denounce everyone else. But Clamence is not exactly an admirable character. . . .

And so it goes – the twists may be unending.

Does that mean we should no longer play?

Martha Rosler, who calls her work 'didactic' but not 'hortatory', and whom critics consider a political postmodernist, worries that if the ironic work is not 'derived from a process of politicisation, although it claims a politics', it will simply end up in the art-critical establishment, where even feminist work – which has been affiliated with a politics – may become no more than 'just a competing style of the sixties and seventies . . . outdated by fashion.'[37] I recognise in Rosler's worry the outlines of two old but apparently inexhaustible arguments: can art which claims an oppositional edge take the risk of entering a museum? Can it afford to be negative and individualistic, rather than offering a positive, collective 'alternative vision' of 'how things might be different'?[38]

Related to these arguments is the question of the symbolic versus the real. Meaghan Morris recently criticised the facile uses that apologists for postmodernism have made of the verb 'appropriate':

> it outrages humanist commitments, adds a little frisson of impropriety and risk by romanticising as violation the intertextual *sine qua non* of all cultural activity, and semantically guarantees a politics to practitioners by installing predation as the universal rule of cultural exchange. . . . All energies become seizures and we all get a piece of the action.[39]

Morris's critique is both humorous and apt: it is too easy to endow metaphorical appropriation with the power of real takeovers, and one *should* look for connections between 'the politics of culture and the politics of politics'.[40] One should also, however, not belittle the value of symbolic interventions in the field of the real. Is it necessary to belabour the fact that language is part of the world (the 'real world') and plays a non-negligible part in shaping both our perceptions of it and our actions in it?

And then there are those who believe only a certain kind of 'real' can be political. Laura Kipnis, who identifies herself as a video artist and critic, dismisses all 'first-world' writing that is not concerned with immediate political action – for example, French feminist theory – as an elitist luxury: 'real shifts in world power and economic distribution have little to do with jouissance, the pre-Oedipal, or 'fluids,' she notes sarcastically.[41] (Sarcasm, as we know, is not to be confused, with 'blank' postmodern pastiche.) For Kipnis, if I read her right, the true postmodernist critique is an act of international terrorism in which 'retaliation is taken, as has been announced, for "American arrogance"' and a truly new form of political struggle, which the West in its blindness has not recognised, is one 'in which civilian tourists are held responsible for the actions of their governments'.[42]

This position, for all its hard-nosed charm, strikes me as too close for comfort to the murderous anti-intellectualism of commissars and other ayatollahs – or, since Kipnis is neither, to the traditional self-hatred of intellectuals who dream of getting their hands dirty.

Jeanette Winterson's *Boating for Beginners* is an outrageously blasphemous rewriting of the Flood story from Genesis. It is also very funny. Has it escaped the censorious eyes of those who picket Scorsese's *Last Temptation of Christ* because it is 'only a novel', by an author who is not a household name? Or because it is not 'serious'? And yet, what could be more serious than the realisation (if indeed it is true) that 'there is no such thing as a true story'?

Postmodernism for postmodernism, politics for politics, I'd rather be an ironist than a terrorist.

To Market, to Market: Oppositional Art in Mass Culture

The whole world is constrained to pass through the filter of the culture industry.

(Max Horkheimer and Theodor Adorno, *Dialectic of Enlightenment*)

Horkheimer and Adorno's pessimistic analysis of the power of the culture industry has become so much a part of contemporary intellectual discourse (to the point that it is almost itself a cliché, part of an anonymous 'general wisdom') that one may wonder whether there is any new way to conceptualise the relation between authentic art and degraded entertainment, or between genuine thought and the manipulated thought-control of advertising and the mass media.[43] It is not that their argument hasn't been criticised for its elitism – it has been, most recently by Andreas Huyssen. Furthermore, it can be criticised as a 'grand narrative', explaining all of contemporary culture in terms of a single paradigm: the culture industry, in their analysis, appears to be a monolithic mechanism whose effects are omnipresent and inescapable.

Yet, the argument still has power; it is hard to get around. One possible conclusion to which their analysis leads has been stated by Thomas Crow, concerning the deep logic of innovative art since the mid-nineteenth century: 'the avant-garde serves as a kind of research and development arm of the culture industry.'[44] According to Crow (whose rich and complex argument would be worth following in detail), there exists a predictable pattern from Impressionism on, in which the avant-garde 'appropriates' certain dynamic oppositional practices from 'below,' from marginal groups or subcultures (here Crow differs significantly from Horkheimer and Adorno); these practices, transformed into avant-garde invention, become, after a moment of productive tension between the 'high' and the 'low' (or between the oppositional and the institutional), simply a part of 'high' art, but are eventually recuperated by the culture industry and returned to the lower zone of mass culture – in a form, however, where the avant-garde invention is 'drained of its original force and integrity'.[45] This cycle, alternating between 'moments of negation and an ultimately overwhelming recuperative inertia',[46] accounts for the chronically problematic status of avant-garde art movements, which claim to want to have a real effect in the world but are always, in the end, 'domesticated.'

What hope is there for postmodernism, and specifically for feminist postmodernism, as an oppositional avant-garde practice? Quite possibly, not much – or not more than for previous avant-gardes. But that does not mean that the attempt is not worth making. Rozsika Parker and Griselda Pollock suggest that 'feminism explores the pleasures of resistance, of deconstruction, of discovery, of defining, of fragmenting, of redefining'.[47] Is it possible that such pleasures can be experienced by more than a privileged few and still maintain their critical charge? I think it is significant that a number of politically motivated experimental women artists working today have found some unexpected ways to use technologies associated with the culture industry.[48] Jenny Holzer's use of electronic signs in airports and other public places – such as the Spectacolor Board in Times Square, which flashed her message in huge letters (part of a series titled *Truisms*): PRIVATE PROPERTY CREATED CRIME – is one well-known example; Barbara Kruger, who has used billboards to display some of her photomontages has also used the Spectacolor Board, to display the message: I AM NOT TRYING TO SELL YOU ANYTHING.

In an interview in 1985, Holzer explained: 'My work has been designed to be stumbled across in the course of a person's daily life. I think it has the most impact when someone is just walking along, not thinking about anything in particular, and then finds these unusual statements either on a poster or on a sign.'[49] In the same interview, Holzer mentioned her discovery that 'television is not prohibitively expensive. . . . You can buy thirty seconds in the middle of "Laverne & Shirley" for about seventy-five dollars, or you can enhance the CBS Morning News for a few hundred dollars. The audience is all of Connecticut and a little bit of New York and Massachusetts, which is enough people'.[50] Barbara Kruger has expressed a similar view. While harbouring no illusions about the alienating effects of television ('TV is an industry that manufactures blind eyes'), Kruger, like Holzer, seeks new ways to use it: for Kruger it is in the very 'site of the stereotype', characteristic of TV representations, that 'the rules of the game can be changed and subtle reformations can be enacted'.[51]

The hope expressed in such statements is that it is possible to find openings even in the monolithic mechanism of the culture industry; that it is possible for innovative, critical work to reach a large audience without passing through the 'upward and downward' cycle analysed by Crow, where what reaches the mass public is always already 'evacuated cultural goods,' deprived of force and integrity. I am sure there must exist arguments to deflate this hope. But I will not look for them here.

Of Cyborgs and (Other) 'Women': The Political Status of Decentred Subjects

What kind of politics could embrace partial, contradictory, permanently unclosed constructions of personal and collective selves and still be faithful, effective – and, ironically, socialist feminist? (Donna Haraway, 'A Manifesto for Cyborgs')

The question asked by Donna Haraway sums up, as well as any could, what is at stake in the feminist embrace, but also in the feminist suspicion, of postmodernism.[52] Haraway, proposing the technological cyborg as an ' ironic political myth' to take the place of earlier, naturalistic myths of the goddess, celebrates the postmodernist model of 'identity out of otherness and difference'; she proclaims herself antiessentialist, antinaturalist, antidualist, antimaternal, utopically 'for a monstrous world without gender'.[53] All of this ironically, and politically to boot.

Next to such inventiveness, those feminists who want to hang on to a notion of feminine specificity may look (in Naomi Schor's ironic selfcharacterisation) like 'wallflowers at the carnival of plural sexualities.'[54] But the differences between worshippers of the goddess and celebrants of the cyborg may themselves need to be put into question.

'If authenticity is relational, there can be no essence except as a political, cultural invention, a local tactic,' writes James Clifford.[55] Which makes me think that sometimes it is politic to 'be' a goddess, at other times a cyborg – and at still other times, a laughing mother[56] or an 'alone-standing woman'[57] who sweeps the detritus of civilisation.

Julia Kristeva's recent book, an exploration of what it means to be 'foreign', reached the best-seller list in France – a country, Kristeva writes, which is both the best and the worst place to be an *étranger*. It is the worst, because the French consider everything that is not French 'an unpardonable offence to universal taste';[58] it is the best, because (as Kristeva, being herself one, knows) in France a foreigner is a constant object of fascination, loved or hated, never ignored.

Of course it makes a difference (nor would Kristeva suggest otherwise) whether one feels loved or hated. It also makes a difference if one is actively persecuted for being 'different'. Still, for yet another ironic myth, I feel much drawn to her evocation of the 'happy cosmopolitan,' foreign not to others but to him or herself, harbouring not an essence but a 'pulverised origin.' Such a person 'transmutes into games what for some is a misfortune and for others an untouchable void'.[59] Which may not be a bad description of a feminist postmodernist.

As for politics, I don't hesitate to make my own ('appropriate' is the word) a message I recently found on a card sold at the Centre Georges Pompidou. The card is by Jamie Reid, the British artist whose work appeared on posters and jacket covers for the short-lived punk rock group the Sex Pistols. I bought it at the Paris opening (February 1989) of the exhibition on Situationism, a revolutionary movement of the 1960s that spurned museums (their chief spokesman was Guy Debord – he was not at the opening). Some of Reid's other work, ironic and anti-Thatcher, is shown in the exhibit.

The card is quite expensive, as cards go, and comes wrapped in cellophane; it is sold only in the museum. The picture on the cover shows Delacroix's *Liberty Leading the People*, against a background formed by four tilted modernist skyscrapers. The message reads (not exactly in this order): 'Live in the Present. Learn from the Past. Look to the Future.'

NOTES

1 This essay is a shortened version of the last chapter of my book, *Subversive Intent: Gender, Politics, and the Avant-Garde*, Harvard University Press, Cambridge, 1990. Besides the people I mention in specific notes, I wish to thank Ingeborg Hoesterey and Mary Russo for their careful reading and very useful suggestions regarding this essay.

2 Jean-François Lyotard, *La condition postmoderne: rapport sur le savoir*, Editions de Minuit, Paris, 1979. English translation: *The Postmodern Condition: A Report on Knowledge*, trans Geoff Bennington and Brian Massumi, University of Minnesota Press, Minneapolis, 1981.

3 Susan Suleiman, 'Naming and Difference: Reflections on "Modernism versus Postmodernism" in Literature', *Approaching Postmodernism*, ed Douwe Fokkema and Hans Bertens, John Benjamins, Amsterdam and Philadelphia, 1986, p 255. As I note in that essay, the first footnote in Lyotard's book cites Hassan, *The Dismemberment of Orpheus: Toward a Postmodern Literature*, Oxford University Press, New York, 1971, as a source for his use of the term 'postmodern'; in the introduction to his book, Lyotard justifies his choice of

'postmodern' to characterise 'the condition of knowledge in the most highly developed societies', by noting that 'the word is in current use on the American continent among sociologists and critics' (*The Postmodern Condition*, p xxiii).

Recent works on postmodernism that use Lyotard as an obligatory reference and make virtually no mention of any work before his on the subject include: *Universal Abandon? The Politics of Postmodernism*, ed Andrew Ross, University of Minnesota Press, Minneapolis, 1988; *Postmodernism and Its Discontents*, ed E Ann Kaplan, Verso, London, 1988; 'Modernity and Modernism, Postmodernity and Postmodernism', special issue of *Cultural Critique* 5, Winter 1986-87; 'Postmodernism', special issue of *Social Text* 18, Winter 1987-88. This may be a specifically American, or Anglo-American phenomenon, I should add; Richard Martin informs me that in Germany, where he teaches, Lyotard's book is known but Hassan's work remains the starting reference. I wish to thank Richard Martin for his careful reading and very useful criticisms of this essay.

4 Lyotard, *Postmodern Condition*, p 67.

5 Lyotard situates himself explicitly in opposition to Baudrillard early on in *The Postmodern Condition*, when he notes that the 'breaking up of the grand Narratives . . . leads to what some authors analyse in terms of the dissolution of the social bond and the disintegration of social aggregates into a mass of individual atoms thrown into the absurdity of Brownian motion. Nothing of the kind is happening: this point of view, it seems to me, is haunted by the paradisiac representation of a lost 'organic' society' (p 15). Although he does not name Baudrillard in the text, Lyotard footnotes Baudrillard's 1978 book, *A l'ombre des majorités silencieuses*, as the one example of the analyses he is contesting here. Baudrillard's theory of the simulacrum, to which I referred, dates from 1975: *L'échange symbolique et la mort*, Gallimard, Paris. This theory is much indebted to Debord's theory of the 'society of the spectacle', which dates from just before 1968. (Guy Debord, *La société du spectacle*, Buchet-Chastel, Paris, 1967). In 1988, Debord published a short commentary on his earlier book, which reiterates and reinforces his earlier pessimistic analyses. See his *Commentaires sur la société du spectacle*, Gerard Lebovici, Paris, 1988.

6 Habermas's contribution to the debate was the now famous essay, 'Modernity – An Incomplete Project' (1981), reprinted in *The Anti-Aesthetic: Essays on Postmodern Culture*, ed Hal Foster, Bay Press, Wash, 1986, pp 3-15. Habermas criticised all those, including the French poststructuralists (whom he called 'anti-modernist young conservatives'), who argued for a 'break' with the 'modernist' project of the Enlightenment. Habermas does not seem to have been responding here to Lyotard's book (the essay does not mention Lyotard), and he did not link postmodernism to poststructuralism. Lyotard, however, responded to Habermas in his 1982 essay, 'Réponse à la question: qu'est-ce que le postmoderne?' which appears in English as an appendix to *The Postmodern Condition*. It was after that essay that the version of the 'modernism-postmodernism' debate associated with the names of Lyotard and Habermas reached full swing. There are other versions of the debate as well. For an American response specifically to this debate, see Richard Rorty, 'Habermas and Lyotard on Postmodernity', reprinted in *Zeitgeist in Babel*, ed Ingeborg Hoesterey, Indiana University Press, Bloomington, 1991.

7 For a somewhat useful historical overview (as of about 1985), see Hans Bertens, 'The Postmodern *Weltanschauung* and Its Relation with Modernism: An Introductory Survey', *Approaching Postmodernism*, pp 9-51. My essay in the same volume, 'Naming and Difference', distinguishes various discourses on the postmodern in terms of their founding impulse: ideological, diagnostic, or classificatory.

8 Irving Howe, 'Mass Society and Postmodern Fiction', *The Decline of the New*, Harcourt, Brace and World, New York, 1970; first published in *Partisan Review* in 1959. The term *postmodernismo* was, it appears, already used in Spain by Federico de Onis in 1934; however, its meaning was quite different. See John Barth, 'Postmodernism Revisited', *The Review of Contemporary Fiction* 8, no 3, Fall 1988, pp 8.

9 Leslie Fiedler, 'The New Mutants' (1965), reprinted in *Collected Essays*, vol 2, Stein and Day, New York, 1971, pp 379-400; Robert Venturi, Denise Scott Brown, and Steven Izenour, *Learning from Las Vegas: The Forgotten Symbolism of Architectural Form*, revised edition, MIT Press, Cambridge, 1988 (original ed 1977). In the preface to the first edition, Brown and Venturi cite their 1968 article, 'A Significance for A&P Parking Lots, or, Learning from Las Vegas', as the basis for the book.

10 Suleiman, 'Naming and Difference'.

11 The most successful effort of this kind so far, I believe, is Brian McHale's *Postmodernist Fiction*, Methuen, New York and London, 1987. Describing his work as an example of 'descriptive poetics', McHale makes no attempt to link postmodernist fiction to any contemporary or cultural issues – indeed, he concludes that postmodernist fiction, like all scientific literature, treats the eternal themes of love and death. Within its self-imposed formalist parameters, I find McHale's criterion for distinguishing modernist from postmodernist fiction (the former being dominated by epistemological issues, the latter by ontological ones) extremely

interesting, and his detailed readings of postmodernist works in terms of the ontological criterion suggestive and persuasive.

12 I develop the argument about Surrealism and analyse the place of women in that movement's history (which, I suggest, differs in significant ways from the place of women in the history of Anglo-American modernism) in chapter 1 of my book, *Subversive Intent*.

13 Rosalind Krauss, 'The Originality of the Avant-Garde: A Postmodernist Repetition' (1981), reprinted in *Zeitgeist in Babel*, ed Hoesterey; Douglas Crimp, 'Pictures', *October* 8, Spring 1979, pp 75-88, both reprinted in *Art after Modernism: Rethinking Representation*, ed Brian Wallis, The New Museum of Contemporary Art, New York and David R Godine, Boston, 1984. Among literary critics, Brian McHale has included some discussion of the work of women, notably Angela Carter and Christine Brooke-Rose, in his *Postmodernist Fiction*, without, however, raising the question of sexual difference. Ihab Hassan, in the new postface to the second edition of *The Dismemberment of Orpheus*, cites Brooke-Rose's name in some of his postmodernist lists (she was not cited in the first edition, 1971). The only general study of postmodernist writing to date which discusses women's work (along with that of other marginal groups) and also makes some attempt to take into account its political specificity is Linda Hutcheon, *A Poetics of Postmodernism; History, Theory, Fiction*, Routledge, New York and London, 1988.

14 Renato Poggioli, *The Theory of the Avant-Garde*, Harvard University Press, Cambridge, 1968, chaps 5, 8.

15 Craig Owens, 'The Discourse of Others: Feminists and Postmodernism', *Anti-Aesthetic*, ed Foster, p 59.

16 I discuss the politics of *Tel Quel* as an avant-garde movement in my essay, 'As Is', *A New History of French Literature*, ed Denis Hollier et al, Harvard University Press, Cambridge, 1989.

17 See note 6 above. The most explicit linking of postmodernism and poststructuralism in the debate was made by Terry Eagleton, in his highly negative Marxist critique, 'Capitalism, Modernism and Postmodernism', *New Left Review* 152, 1985, pp 60-73.

18 Owens, 'Discourse of Others', pp 73-77.

19 Hal Foster, '(Post)Modern Polemics', *Recodings: Art, Spectacle, Cultural Politics*, Bay Press, Seattle, Wash, 1985, p 136.

20 Andreas Huyssen, 'Mapping the Postmodern', *After the Great Divide: Modernism, Mass Culture, Postmodernism*, Indiana University Press, Bloomington, 1986, pp 219-21.

21 Hutcheon, *A Poetics of Postmodernism*, chap 4.

22 It is true, as Richard Martin reminds me, that some feminists are critical of this 'high theoretical' discourse (or of any theoretical discourse closely associated with a male tradition) and would just as soon not participate in it. That raises a whole number of other questions regarding alliances and dialogue between men and women, which I will not attempt to develop here. My own favouring of dialogue and 'complication' over separatist and binarist positions is explicitly argued in chaps 4, 6, and 7 of *Subversive Intent*.

23 The same argument can be made (as Linda Hutcheon's grouping together of 'ex-centrics' and Huyssen's and Foster's use of the concept 'Others' shows) for the alliance between postmodernism and Third World minorities or Afro-American writers, male and female. Many black American critics (Henry Louis Gates comes especially to mind) have recognised the similarity of concerns and of analytic concepts between feminist criticism and Afro-American criticism. The links between Afro-American writing and postmodernism have also been recognised, notably in the novels of Ishmael Reed. Black women writers, however, have rarely been called postmodernists, and even less feminist postmodernists. A case can be made for considering Toni Morrison and Ntozake Shange (among others) 'black women feminist postmodernists'. But the question of priorities (race or gender?) remains.

24 To be sure, there were a number of important women writers and artists associated with Anglo-American modernism and other earlier movements who were ignored or belittled by male critics, as recent feminist scholarship has shown. (See, for example, Sandra Gilbert and Susan Gubar, *No Man's Land*, vol 1, *The War of the Words*, Yale University Press, New Haven, 1987. And as I have argued elsewhere, there are significant historical and national differences that must be taken into account when discussing the participation of women in avant-garde movements. My sense is, however, that none of the early movements had the *critical mass of outstanding, innovative work by women, both in the visual arts and in literature* (the phrase is worth restating and underlining) that exists today.

Is naming names necessary? Here, for the doubtful, is a partial list of outstanding English and American women artists working today, who can be (and at some time or other have been) called feminist postmodernists: In performance, Joanne Akalaitis, Laurie Anderson, Karen Finley, Suzanne Lacy, Meredith Monk, Carolee Schneemann; in film and video, Lizzie Borden, Cecilia Condit, Laura Mulvey, Sally Potter, Yvonne Rainer, Martha Rosler; in photography and visual arts, Jenny Holzer, Mary Kelly, Barbara Kruger,

Sherrie Levine, Cindy Sherman, Nancy Spero; in fiction, Kathy Acker, Christine Brooke-Rose, Angela Carter, Rikki Ducornet, Emily Prager, Jeanette Winterson. (See also note 23.) I thank Elinor Fuchs and Judith Piper for sharing their expertise with me about women in postmodern performance. For more on contemporary women performers and visual artists, see the exhibition catalogue (which bears out my point about critical mass), *Making Their Mark: Women Artists Move into the Mainstream, 1970-1985*, Abbeville Press, New York, 1989.

25 Christine Brooke-Rose, 'Illiterations', *Breaking the Sequence: Women's Experimental Fiction*, ed Ellen G Friedman and Miriam Fuchs, Princeton University Press, 1989, p 59.

26 Fredric Jameson, 'Postmodernism, or the Cultural Logic of Late Capitalism', *New Left Review* 146, July-August 1984, pp 53-92.

27 For an excellent collection of responses to *Guernica* and a clear exposition of its history as a 'political' painting, see Picasso's *Guernica: Illustrations, Introductory Essay, Documents, Poetry, Criticism, Analysis*, ed Ellen C Oppler, Norton, New York, 1988.

28 Stanley Fish, *Is There a Text in This Class?* Harvard University Press, Cambridge, 1980. For an overview of theories of reading, see my introductory essay, 'Varieties of Reader-Oriented Criticism', *The Reader in the Text: Essays on Audience and Interpretation*, ed Susan R Suleiman and Inge K Crosman, Princeton University Press, 1980, pp 3-45.

29 Jameson, 'Cultural Logic', p 65.

30 Mary Kelly, 'Beyond the Purloined Image' (essay on a 1983 London exhibition with the same title, curated by Kelly), quoted in Rozsika Parker and Griselda Pollock, 'Fifteen Years of Feminist Action: From Practical Strategies to Strategic Practices', *Framing Feminism: Art and the Women's Movement 1970-85*, Pandora Press, London and New York, 1987, p 53. Aside from the excellent introductory essays by Parker and Pollock, this book offers a rich selection of written and visual work by women involved in various British feminist avant-garde art movements of the seventies and early eighties.

31 See Anders Stephanson, 'Regarding Postmodernism – A Conversation with Fredric Jameson', *Universal Abandon? The Politics of Postmodernism*, pp 3-30. Jameson suggests that Doctorow's works offer the possibility 'to undo postmodernism homeopathically by the methods of postmodernism to work at dissolving the pastiche by using all the instruments of pastiche itself, to reconquer some genuine historical sense by using the instruments of what I have called substitutes for history' (p 17). The question Jameson does not answer (or raise) is: How does one tell the 'fake' (homeopathic) postmodernist pastiche from the 'real' one – which is itself a 'fake', a substitute for history? The play of mirrors here may strike one as quite postmodernist.

32 Lyotard, 'Answering the Question: What is Postmodernism?' trans Regis Durand, *The Postmodern Condition*, p 77. Huyssen picks up the distinction in *Mapping the Postmodern*, p 220. See also Foster, '(Post)Modern Polemics', *Recodings*.

33 See Sherman's interview with Jeanne Siegel, *Artworks 2: Discourse on the Early 80's*, ed Jeanne Siegel, Ann Arbor and UMI Research Press, London, 1988, p 272.

34 Martha Rosler, 'Notes on Quotes', *Wedge* 2, Fall 1982, p 71. Rosler does not refer to anyone by name, but her critique here appears clearly to be directed at the work of Kruger, Levine, and Sherman.

35 Hutcheon, *Poetics of Postmodernism*, p xiii and passim.

36 Craig Owens, 'The Allegorical Impulse: Toward a Theory of Postmodernism', *Art After Modernism*, ed Wallis, p 235.

37 Rosler, 'Notes on Quotes', pp 72, 73. Rosler's characterisation of her work as didactic but not hortatory is in an interview with Jane Weinstock, *October* 17, Summer 1981, p 78.

38 Ibid, p 72.

39 Meaghan Morris, 'Tooth and Claw: Tales of Survival and *Crocodile Dundee*', *Universal Abandon?* p 123.

40 Ibid, p 125.

41 Laura Kipnis, 'Feminism: The Political Conscience of Postmodernism?' *Universal Abandon?* p 162.

42 Ibid, p 13.

43 Max Horkheimer and Theodor W Adorno, 'The Culture Industry: Enlightenment As Mass Deception', *Dialectic of Enlightenment*, trans John Cumming, Continuum, New York, 1982, pp 120-67.

44 Thomas Crow, 'Modernism and Mass Culture in the Visual Arts', *Pollock and After*, p 257. I wish to thank Bernard Gendron for bringing Crow's essay, in particular the remark I have quoted about the avant-garde and the culture industry, to my attention; and for his thoughtful reading and criticism of my own essay.

45 Ibid, p 258.

46 Ibid, p 259.

47 Rozsika Parker and Griselda Pollock, 'Fifteen years of feminist action: from practical strategies to strategic practices', *Framing Feminism*, p 54.

48 Women postmodernists are not the only ones to have practised a kind of public intervention, of course; among men doing comparable things, Hans Haacke and Daniel Buren come to mind (though Buren's work questions more the politics of museums than the 'politics of politics'). Nor is all of the political work by women exclusively feminist. These considerations do not invalidate my general point; rather, they enlarge it.

49 Interview with Jeanne Siegel, 'Jenny Holzer's Language Games', *Artwords* 2, p 286. See also, in the same volume, the interview with Barbara Kruger, where Kruger refers to her use of billboards and of the Times Square Spectacolor Board, pp 299-311.

50 Ibid, p 297.

51 Barbara Kruger, interview with Jeanne Siegel, *Artwords* 2, p 304.

52 Donna Haraway, 'A Manifesto for Cyborgs: Science, Technology, and Socialist Feminism in the 1980s', *Socialist Review* 50, 1984, p 75.

53 Ibid, p 100.

54 Naomi Schor, 'Dreaming Dissymetry', *Men in Feminism*, ed Alice Jardine and Paul Smith, Methuen, New York and London, 1987, p 109.

55 James Clifford, *The Predicament of Culture*, Harvard University Press, Cambridge, 1988, p 12.

56 On the figure of the 'laughing mother', see Suleiman, *Subversive Intent*.

57 On the figure of the 'alone-standing woman' – a fictional creation of Christine Brooke-Rose – as an emblem of postmodernity, see my essay on Brooke-Rose's novel, *Between:* 'Living Between, or the Lone(love)liness of the alleinstehende Frau', *The Review of Contemporary Fiction*, Fall 1989, pp 124-27.

58 Julia Kristeva, *Etrangers à nous-mêmes*, Fayard, Paris, 1988, p 58, my translation.

59 Ibid, p 57.

Craig Owens
THE DISCOURSE OF OTHERS: FEMINISTS AND POSTMODERNISM

Postmodern knowledge (*le savoir postmoderne*) is not simply an instrument of power. It refines our sensitivity to differences and increases our tolerance of incommensurability. (J-F Lyotard, *La Condition postmoderne*)

Decentred, allegorical, schizophrenic . . . however we choose to diagnose its symptoms, postmodernism is usually treated, by its protagonists and antagonists alike, as a crisis of cultural authority, specifically of the authority vested in Western European culture and its institutions. That the hegemony of European civilisation is drawing to a close is hardly a new perception; since the mid-1950s, at least, we have recognised the necessity of encountering different cultures by means other than the shock of domination and conquest. Among the relevant texts are Arnold Toynbee's discussion, in the eighth volume of his monumental *A Study of History*, of the end of the modern age (an age that began, Toynbee contends, in the late fifteenth century when Europe began to exert its influence over vast land areas and populations not its own) and the beginning of a new, properly postmodern age characterised by the coexistence of different cultures. Claude Lévi-Strauss's critique of Western ethnocentrism could also be cited in this context, as well as Jacques Derrida's critique of this critique in *Of Grammatology*. But perhaps the most eloquent testimony to the end of Western sovereignty has been that of Paul Ricoeur, who wrote in 1962 that 'the discovery of the plurality of cultures is never a harmless experience'.

> When we discover that there are several cultures instead of just one and consequently at the time when we acknowledge the end of a sort of cultural monopoly, be it illusory or real, we are threatened with the destruction of our own discovery. Suddenly it becomes possible that there are just *others*, that we ourselves are an 'other' among others. All meaning and every goal having disappeared, it becomes possible to wander through civilisations as if through vestiges and ruins. The whole of mankind becomes an imaginary museum: where shall we go this weekend – visit the Angkor ruins or take a stroll in the Tivoli of Copenhagen? We can very easily imagine a time close at hand when any fairly well-to-do person will be able to leave his country indefinitely in order to taste his own national death in an interminable, aimless voyage.[1]

Lately, we have come to regard this condition as postmodern. Indeed, Ricoeur's account of the more dispiriting effects of our culture's recent loss of mastery anticipates both the melancholia and the eclecticism that pervade current cultural production – not to mention its much-touted pluralism. Pluralism, however, reduces us to being an other among others; it is not a recognition, but a reduction to difference to absolute indifference, equivalence, interchangeability (what Jean Baudrillard calls 'implosion'). What is at stake, then, is not only the hegemony of Western culture, but also (our sense of) our identity as a culture. These two stakes, however, are so inextricably intertwined

t has taught us, the positing of an Other is a necessary moment in the
n, the incorporation of any cultural body) that it is possible to speculate that
pled our claims to sovereignty is actually the realisation that our culture is
neither as homogeneous nor as monolithic as we once believed it to be. In other words,
the causes of modernity's demise – at least as Ricoeur describes its effects – lie as much
within as without. Ricoeur, however, deals only with the difference without. What about
the difference within?

In the modern period the authority of the work of art, its claim to represent some
authentic vision of the world, did not reside in its uniqueness or singularity, as is often
said; rather, that authority was based on the universality modern aesthetics attributed to
the *forms* utilised for the representation of vision, over and above differences in content
due to the production of works in concrete historical circumstances.[2] (For example, Kant's
demand that the judgment of taste be universal – ie, universally communicable – that it
derive from 'grounds deep-seated and shared alike by all men, underlying their
agreement in estimating the forms under which objects are given to them'.) Not only
does the postmodernist work claim no such authority, it also actively seeks to
undermine all such claims; hence, its generally deconstructive thrust. As recent analyses
of the 'enunciative apparatus' of visual representation – its poles of emission and
reception – confirm, the representational systems of the West admit only one vision –
that of the constitutive male subject – or, rather, they posit the subject of representation
as absolutely centred, unitary, masculine.[3]

The postmodernist work attempts to upset the reassuring stability of that mastering
position. This same project has, of course, been attributed by writers like Julia Kristeva
and Roland Barthes to the *modernist* avant-garde, which through the introduction of
heterogeneity, discontinuity, glossolalia, etc, supposedly put the subject of representation in crisis. But the avant-garde sought to transcend representation in favour of
presence and immediacy; it proclaimed the autonomy of the signifier, its liberation from
the 'tyranny of the signified'; postmodernists instead expose the tyranny of the *signifier*,
the violence of its law.[4] (Lacan spoke of the necessity of submitting to the 'defiles' of the
signifier; should we not ask rather who in our culture is defiled by the signifier?)
Recently, Derrida has cautioned against a wholesale condemnation of representation,
not only because such a condemnation may appear to advocate a rehabilitation of
presence and immediacy and thereby serve the interests of the most reactionary
political tendencies, but more importantly, perhaps, because that which exceeds,
'transgresses the figure of all possible representation', may ultimately be none other
than ... the law. Which obliges us, Derrida concludes, 'to thinking altogether
differently'.[5]

It is precisely at the legislative frontier between what can be represented and what
cannot that the postmodernist operation is being staged – not in order to transcend
representation, but in order to expose that system of power that authorises certain
representations while blocking, prohibiting or invalidating others. Among those
prohibited from Western representation, whose representations are denied all legitimacy,
are women. Excluded from representation by its very structure, they return within it as a
figure for – a representation of – the unrepresentable (Nature, Truth, the Sublime, etc).
This prohibition bears primarily on woman as the subject, and rarely as the object of
representation, for there is certainly no shortage of images of women. Yet in being
represented by, women have been rendered an absence within the dominant culture as
Michèle Montrelay proposes when she asks 'whether psychoanalysis was not articulated
precisely in order to repress femininity (in the sense of producing its symbolic

representation)'.[6] In order to speak, to represent herself, a woman assumes a masculine position; perhaps this is why femininity is frequently associated with masquerade, with false representation with simulation and seduction. Montrelay, in fact, identifies women as the 'ruin of representation': not only have they nothing to lose; their exteriority to Western representation exposes its limits.

Here, we arrive at an apparent crossing of the feminist critique of patriarchy and the postmodernist critique of representation; this essay is a provisional attempt to explore the implications of that intersection. My intention is not to posit identity between these two critiques; nor is it to place them in a relation of antagonism or opposition. Rather, if I have chosen to negotiate the treacherous course between postmodernism and feminism, it is in order to introduce the issue of sexual difference into the modernism/postmodernism debate – a debate which has until now been scandalously in-different.[7]

'A Remarkable Oversight'[8]

Several years ago I began the second of two essays devoted to an allegorical impulse in contemporary art – an impulse that I identified as postmodernist – with a discussion of Laurie Anderson's multi-media performance *Americans on the Move*.[9] Addressed to transportation as a metaphor for communication – the transfer of meaning from one place to another – *Americans on the Move* proceeded primarily as verbal commentary on visual images projected on a screen behind the performers. Near the beginning Anderson introduced the schematic image of a nude man and woman, the former's right arm raised in greeting, that had been emblazoned on the Pioneer spacecraft. Here is what she had to say about this picture; significantly, it was spoken by a distinctly male voice (Anderson's own processed through a harmoniser, which dropped it an octave – a kind of electronic vocal transvestism):

> In our country, we send pictures of our sign language into outer space. They are speaking our sign language in these pictures. Do you think they will think his hand is permanently attached that way? Or do you think they will read our signs? In our country, good-bye looks just like hello.

Here is my commentary on this passage:

> Two alternatives: either the extraterrestrial recipient of this message will assume that it is simply a picture, that is, an analogical likeness of the human figure, in which case he might logically conclude that male inhabitants of Earth walk around with their right arms permanently raised. Or he will somehow divine that this gesture is addressed to him and attempt to read it, in which case he will be stymied, since a single gesture signifies both greeting and farewell, and any reading of it must oscillate between these two extremes. The same gesture could also mean 'Halt!' or represent the taking of an oath, but if Anderson's text does not consider these two alternatives that is because it is not concerned with ambiguity, with multiple meanings engendered by a single sign; rather, two *clearly defined but mutually incompatible* readings are engaged in blind confrontation in such a way that it is impossible to choose between them.

This analysis strikes me as a case of gross critical negligence. For in my eagerness to rewrite Anderson's text in terms of the debate over determinate versus indeterminate meaning, I had overlooked something – something that is so obvious, so 'natural' that it may at the time have seemed unworthy of comment. It does not seem that way to me today. For this is, of course, an image of sexual difference or, rather, of sexual differentiation according to the distribution of the phallus – as it is marked and then re-marked by the man's right arm, which appears less to have been raised than erected in

ng. I was, however, close to the 'truth' of the image when I suggested that men on
might walk around with something permanently raised – close perhaps, but no
r. (Would my reading have been different – or less in-different – had I known then
that, earlier in her career, Anderson had executed a work which consisted of
photographs of men who had accosted her in the street?)[10] Like all representations of
sexual difference that our culture produces, this is an image not simply of anatomical
difference, but of the values assigned to it. Here, the phallus is a signifier (that is, it
represents the subject for another signifier); it is, in fact, the privileged signifier, the
signifier of privilege, of the power and prestige that accrue to the male in our society. As
such, it designates the effects of signification in general. For in this (Lacanian) image,
chosen to represent the inhabitants of Earth for the extraterrestrial Other, it is the man
who speaks, who represents mankind. The woman is only represented; she is (as
always) already spoken for.

If I return to this passage here, it is not simply to correct my own remarkable
oversight, but more importantly to indicate a blind spot in our discussions of
postmodernism in general: our failure to address the issue of sexual difference – not
only in the objects we discuss, but in our own enunciation as well.[11] However restricted
its field of inquiry may be, every discourse on postmodernism – at least insofar as it
seeks to account for certain recent mutations within that field – aspires to the status of a
general theory of contemporary culture. Among the most significant developments of
the past decade – it may well turn out to have been *the* most significant – has been the
emergence, in nearly every area of cultural activity, of a specifically feminist practice. A
great deal of effort has been devoted to the recovery and revaluation of previously
marginalised or underestimated work; everywhere this project has been accompanied
by energetic new production. As one engaged in these activities – Martha Rosler –
observes, they have contributed significantly to debunking the privileged status
modernism claimed for the work of art: 'The interpretation of the meaning and social
origin and rootedness of those (earlier) forms helped undermine the modernist tenet of
the separateness of the aesthetic from the rest of human life, and an analysis of the
oppressiveness of the seemingly unmotivated forms of high culture was companion to
this work.'[12]

Still, if one of the most salient aspects of our postmodern culture is the presence of an
insistent feminist voice (and I use the terms *presence* and *voice* advisedly), theories of
postmodernism have tended either to neglect or to repress that voice. The absence of
discussions of sexual difference in writings about postmodernism, as well as the fact
that few women have engaged in the modernism/postmodernism debate, suggest that
postmodernism may be another masculine invention engineered to exclude women. I
would like to propose, however, that women's insistence on difference and incommensurability may not only be compatible with, but also an instance of postmodern
thought. Postmodern thought is no longer binary thought (as Lyotard observes when he
writes, 'Thinking by means of oppositions does not correspond to the liveliest modes of
postmodern knowledge [*le savoir postmoderne*]').[13] The critique of binarism is sometimes dismissed as intellectual fashion; it is, however an intellectual imperative, since
the hierarchical opposition of marked and unmarked terms (the decisive/divisive
presence/absence of the phallus) is the dominant form both of representing difference
and justifying its subordination in our society. What we must learn, then, is how to
conceive difference without opposition.

Although sympathetic male critics respect feminism (an old theme: respect for
women)[14] and wish it well, they have in general declined the dialogue in which their

female colleagues are trying to engage them. Sometimes feminists are accused of going too far, at others, not far enough.[15] The feminist voice is usually regarded as one among many, its insistence on difference as testimony to the pluralism of the times. Thus, feminism is rapidly assimilated to a whole string of liberation or self-determination movements. Here is one recent list, by a prominent male critic: 'ethnic groups, neighbourhood movements, feminism, various "counter-cultural" or alternative life-style groups, rank-and-file labour dissidence, student movements, single-issue movements.' Not only does this forced coalition treat feminism itself as monolithic, thereby suppressing its multiple internal differences (essentialist, culturalist, linguistic, Freudian, anti-Freudian . . .); it also posits a vast, undifferentiated category, 'Difference', to which all marginalised or oppressed groups can be assimilated, and for which women can then stand as an emblem, a *pars totalis* (another old theme: woman is incomplete, not whole). But the specificity of the feminist critique of patriarchy is thereby denied, along with that of all other forms of opposition to sexual, racial and class discrimination. (Rosler warns against using woman as 'a token for all markers of difference', observing that 'appreciation of the work of women whose subject is oppression exhausts consideration of all oppressions'.)

Moreover, men appear unwilling to address the issues placed on the critical agenda by women unless those issues have first been neut(e)ralised – although this, too, is a problem of assimilation: to the already known, the already written. In *The Political Unconscious*, to take but one example, Fredric Jameson calls for the 'reaudition of the oppositional voices of black and ethnic cultures, women's or gay literature, "naive" or marginalised folk art *and the like'* (thus, women's cultural production is anachronistically identified as folk art), but he immediately modifies this petition: The affirmation of such non hegemonic cultural voices remains ineffective,' he argues, if they are not first *rewritten* in terms of their proper place in 'the dialogical system of the social classes.'[16] Certainly, the class determinants of sexuality – and of sexual oppression – are too often overlooked. But sexual inequality cannot be reduced to an instance of economic exploitation – the exchange of women among men – and explained in terms of class struggle alone; to invert Rosler's statement, exclusive attention to economic oppression can exhaust consideration of other forms of oppression.

To claim that the division of the sexes is irreducible to the division of labour is to risk polarising feminism and Marxism; this danger is real, given the latter's fundamentally patriarchal bias. Marxism privileges the characteristically masculine activity of production as the *definitively human* activity (Marx: men begin to distinguish themselves from animals as soon as they begin to produce their means of subsistence');[17] women historically consigned to the spheres of nonproductive or reproductive labour, are thereby situated outside the society of male producers, in a state of nature. (As Lyotard has written, 'The frontier passing between the sexes does not separate two parts of the same social entity.')[18] What is at issue, however, is not simply the oppressiveness of Marxist discourse, but its totalising ambitions, its claim to account for every form of social experience. But this claim is characteristic of all theoretical discourse, which is one reason women frequently condemn it as phallocratic.[19] It is not always theory per se that women repudiate, nor simply, as Lyotard has suggested, the priority men have granted to it, its rigid opposition to practical experience. Rather, what they challenge is the distance it maintains between itself and its objects – a distance which objectifies and masters.

Because of the tremendous effort of reconceptualisation necessary to prevent a phallologic relapse in their own discourse, many feminist artists have, in fact, forged a new (or renewed) alliance with theory – most profitably, perhaps, with the writing of women influenced by Lacanian psychoanalysis (Luce Irigaray, Hélène Cixous, Montrelay . . .). Many of these artists have themselves made major theoretical contributions: film-maker Laura Mulvey's 1975 essay on 'Visual Pleasure and Narrative Cinema', for example, has generated a great deal of critical discussion on the masculinity of the cinematic gaze.[20] Whether influenced by psycho-analysis or not, feminist artists often regard critical or theoretical writing as an important arena of strategic intervention: Martha Rosler's critical texts on the documentary tradition in photography – among the best in the field – are a crucial part of her activity *as an artist.* Many modernist artists, of course, produced texts about their own production, but writing was almost always considered supplementary to their primary work as painters, sculptors, photographers, etc,[21] whereas the kind of simultaneous activity on multiple fronts that characterises many feminist practices is a postmodern phenomenon. And one of the things it challenges is modernism's rigid opposition of artistic practice and theory.

At the same time, postmodern feminist practice may question theory – and not only *aesthetic* theory. Consider Mary Kelly's *Post-Partum Document* (1973-79), a six-part, 165-piece art work (plus footnotes) that utilises multiple representational modes (literary, scientific, psychoanalytic, linguistic, archeological and so forth) to chronicle the first six years of her son's life. Part archive, part exhibition, part case history, the *Post-Partum Document* is also a contribution to as well as a critique of Lacanian theory. Beginning as it does with a series of diagrams taken from *Ecrits* (diagrams which Kelly presents as *pictures*), the work might be (mis)read as a straightforward application or illustration of psychoanalysis. It is, rather, a mother's interrogation of Lacan, an interrogation that ultimately reveals a remarkable oversight within the Lacanian narrative of the child's relation to the mother – the construction of the mother's fantasies vis-à-vis the child. Thus, the *Post-Partum Document* has proven to be a controversial work, for it appears to offer evidence of *female* fetishism (the various substitutes the mother invests in order to disavow separation from the child); Kelly thereby exposes a lack within the theory of fetishism, a perversion heretofore reserved for the male. Kelly's work is not anti-theory; rather, as her use of multiple representational systems testifies, it demonstrates that no one narrative can possibly account for all aspects of human experience. Or as the artist herself has said, 'There's no single theoretical discourse which is going to offer an explanation for all forms of social relations or for every mode of political practice.'[22]

A la Recherche du Récit Perdu

'No single theoretical discourse . . .' this feminist position is also a postmodern condition. In fact, Lyotard diagnoses *the* postmodern condition as one in which the *grands récits* of modernity – the dialectic of Spirit, the emancipation of the worker, the accumulation of wealth, the classless society – have all lost credibility. Lyotard defines a discourse as modern when it appeals to one or another of these *grands récits* for its le-gitimacy; the advent of postmodernity, then, signals a crisis in narrative's legitimising function, its ability to compel consensus. Narrative, he argues, is out of its element(s) – 'the great dangers, the great journeys, the great goal'. Instead, 'it is dispersed into clouds of linguistic particles – narrative ones, but also denotative, prescriptive, descriptive, etc – each with its own pragmatic valence. Today, each of us lives in the vicinity of many of these. We do not necessarily form stable linguistic communities, and the properties of those we do form are not necessarily communicable.'[23.]

Lyotard does not, however, mourn modernity's passing, even though his own activity as a philosopher is at stake. 'For most people,' he writes, 'nostalgia for the lost narrative (*le récit perdu*) is a thing of the past.'[24] 'Most people' does not include Fredric Jameson, although he diagnoses the postmodern condition in similar terms (as a loss of narrative's social function) and distinguishes between modernist and postmodernist works according to their different relations to the '"truth-content" of art, its claim to possess some truth or epistemological value'. His description of a crisis in modernist literature stands metonymically for the crisis in modernity itself:

> At its most vital, the experience of modernism was not one of a single historical movement or process, but of a 'shock of discovery, a commitment and an adherence to its individual forms through a series of religious conversions'. One did not simply read DH Lawrence or Rilke, see Jean Renoir or Hitchcock, or listen to Stravinsky as distinct manifestations of what we now term modernism. Rather one read all the works of a particular writer, learned a style and a phenomenological world, to which one converted. . . . This meant, however, that the experience of one form of modernism was incompatible with another, so that one entered one world only at the price of abandoning another. . . . The crisis of modernism came, then, when it suddenly became clear that 'DH Lawrence' was not an absolute after all, not the final achieved figuration of the truth of the world, but only one art-language among others, only one shelf of works in a whole dizzying library.[25]

Although a reader of Foucault might locate this realisation at the origin of modernism (Flaubert, Manet) rather than at its conclusion,[26] Jameson's account of the crisis of modernity strikes me as both persuasive and problematic – problematic because persuasive. Like Lyotard, he plunges us into a radical Nietzschean perspectivism: each oeuvre represents not simply a different view of the same world, but corresponds to an entirely different world. Unlike Lyotard, however, he does so only in order to extricate us from it. For Jameson, the loss of narrative is equivalent to the loss of our ability to locate ourselves historically; hence, his diagnosis of postmodernism as 'schizophrenic', meaning that it is characterised by a collapsed sense of temporality.[27] Thus, in *The Political Unconscious* he urges the resurrection not simply of narrative – as a 'socially symbolic act' – but specifically of what he identifies as the Marxist 'master narrative' – the story of mankind's 'collective struggle to wrest a realm of Freedom from a realm of Necessity'.[28]

Master narrative – how else to translate Lyotard's *grand récit*? And in this translation we glimpse the terms of another analysis of modernity's demise, one that speaks not of the incompatibility of the various modern narratives, but instead of their fundamental solidarity. For what made the *grands récits* of modernity master narratives if not the fact that they were all narratives of mastery, of man seeking his telos in the conquest of nature? What function did these narratives play other than to legitimise Western man's self-appointed mission of transforming the entire planet in his own image And what form did this mission take if not that of man's placing of his stamp on everything that exists – that is, the transformation of the world into a representation, with man as its subject? In this respect, however, the phrase *master narrative* seems tautologous, since all narrative, by virtue of 'its power to master the dispiriting effects of the corrosive force of the temporal process',[29] may be narrative of mastery.[30]

What is at stake, then, is not only the status of narrative, but of representation itself. For the modern age was not only the age of the master narrative, it was also the age of representation – at least this is what Martin Heidegger proposed in a 1938 lecture delivered in Freiburg im Breisgau, but not published until 1952 as 'The Age of the World Picture' (*Die Zeit die Weltbildes*).[31] According to Heidegger, the transition to modernity was not accomplished by the replacement of a medieval by a modern world picture, 'but rather the fact that the world becomes a picture at all is what distinguishes the essence of the modern age'. For modern man, everything that exists does so only in and through representation. To claim this is also to claim that the world exists only in and through a *subject* who believes that he is producing the world in producing its representation:

> The fundamental event of the modern age is the conquest of the world as picture. The word 'picture' (*Bild*) now means the structured image (*Gebild*) that is the creature of man's producing which represents and sets before. In such producing, man contends for the position in which he can be that particular being who gives the measure and draws up the guidelines for everything that is.

Thus, with the 'interweaving of these two events' – the transformation of the world into a picture and man into a subject – 'there begins that way of being human which mans the realm of human capability given over to measuring and executing, for the purpose of gaining mastery of that which is as a whole.' For what is representation if not a 'laying hold and grasping' (appropriation), a 'making-stand-over-against, an objectifying that goes forward and masters'?[32] Thus, when in a recent interview Jameson calls for 'the *reconquest* of certain forms of representation' (which he equates with narrative: '"Narrative",' he argues, 'is, I think, generally what people have in mind when they rehearse the usual post-structuralist "critique of representation"'),[33] he is in fact calling for the rehabilitation of the entire social project of modernity itself. Since the Marxist master narrative is only one version among many of the modern narrative of mastery (for what is the 'collective struggle to wrest a realm of Freedom from a realm of Necessity' if not mankind's progressive exploitation of the Earth?), Jameson's desire to resurrect (this) narrative is a modern desire, a desire *for* modernity. It is one symptom of our postmodern condition, which is experienced everywhere today as a tremendous loss of mastery and thereby gives rise to therapeutic programmes, from both the Left and the Right, for recuperating that loss. Although Lyotard warns – correctly, I believe – against explaining transformations in modern/postmodern culture primarily as effects of social transformations (the hypothetical advent of a postindustrial society, for example),[34] it is clear that what has been lost is not primarily a cultural mastery, but an economic, technical and political one. For what if not the emergence of Third-World nations, the 'revolt of nature' and the women's movement – that is, the voices of the conquered – has challenged the West's desire for ever-greater domination and control?

Symptoms of our recent loss of mastery are everywhere apparent in cultural activity today – nowhere more so than in the visual arts. The modernist project of joining forces with science and technology for the transformation of the environment after rational principles of function and utility (Productivism, the Bauhaus) has long since been abandoned; what we witness in its place is a desperate, often hysterical attempt to recover some sense of mastery via the resurrection of heroic large-scale easel painting and monumental cast-bronze sculpture – mediums themselves identified with the cultural hegemony of Western Europe. Yet contemporary artists are able at best to *simulate* mastery, to manipulate its signs; since in the modern period mastery was invariably associated with human labour, aesthetic production has degenerated today into a massive deployment of the signs of artistic labour – violent, 'impassioned' brushwork, for example. Such simulacra of mastery testify, however, only to its loss; in fact, contemporary artists seem engaged in a collective act of disavowal – and disavowal always pertains to a loss . . . of virility, masculinity, potency.[35]

This contingent of artists is accompanied by another which refuses the simulation of mastery in favour of melancholic contemplation of its loss. One such artist speaks of 'the impossibility of passion in a culture that has institutionalised self-expression'; another, of 'the aesthetic as something which is really about longing and loss rather than completion'. A painter unearths the discarded genre of landscape painting only to borrow for his own canvases, through an implicit equation between their ravaged surfaces and the barren fields he depicts, something of the exhaustion of the earth itself (which is thereby glamorised); another dramatises his anxieties through the most conventional figure men have conceived for the threat of castration – Woman . . . aloof, remote, unapproachable. Whether they disavow or advertise their own powerlessness, pose as heroes or as victims, these artists have, needless to say, been warmly received by a society unwilling to admit that it has been driven from its position of centrality; theirs is an 'official' art which, like the culture that produced it, has yet to come to terms with its own impoverishment.

Postmodernist artists speak of impoverishment – but in a very different way. Sometimes the postmodernist work testifies to a deliberate refusal of mastery, for example, Martha Rosler's *The Bowery in Two Inadequate Descriptive Systems* (1974-75), in which photographs of Bowery storefronts alternate with clusters of typewritten words signifying inebriety. Although her photographs are intentionally flat-footed, Rosler's refusal of mastery in this work is more than technical. On the one hand, she denies the caption/text its conventional function of supplying the image with something it lacks; instead, her juxtaposition of two representational systems, visual and verbal, is calculated (as the title suggests) to 'undermine' rather than 'underline' the truth value of each.[36] More importantly Rosler has refused to photograph the inhabitants of Skid Row, to speak on their behalf, to illuminate them from a safe distance (photography as social work in the tradition of Jacob Riis). For 'concerned' or what Rosler calls 'victim' photography overlooks the constitutive role of its own activity, which is held to be merely representative (the 'myth' of photographic transparency and objectivity). Despite his or her benevolence in representing those who have been denied access to the means of representation, the photographer inevitably functions as an agent of the system of power that silenced these people in the first place. Thus, they are twice victimised: first by society, and then by the photographer who presumes the right to speak on their behalf. In fact, in such photography it is the photographer rather than the 'subject' who poses – as the subject's consciousness, indeed, as conscience itself. Although Rosler may not, in this work, have initiated a counter-discourse of drunkenness – which would consist of the drunks' own theories about their conditions of existence – she has nevertheless pointed negatively to the crucial issue of a politically motivated art practice today: 'the indignity of speaking for others'.[37]

Rosler's position poses a challenge to criticism as well, specifically, to the critic's substitution of his own discourse for the work of art. At this point in my text, then, my own voice must yield to the artist's; in the essay 'in, around and afterthoughts (on documentary photography)' which accompanies *The Bowery . . .*, Rosler writes:

> If impoverishment is a subject here, it is more certainly the impoverishment of representational strategies tottering abut alone than that of a mode of surviving. The photographs are powerless to *deal with* the reality that is yet totally compre-hended-in-advance by ideology, and they are as diversionary as the word formations – which at least are closer to being located within the culture of drunkenness rather than being framed on it from without.[38]

The Visible and the Invisible
A work like *The Bowery in Two Inadequate Descriptive Systems* not only exposes the

'myths' of photographic objectivity and transparency; it also upsets the (modern) belief in vision as a privileged means of access to certainty and truth ('Seeing is believing'). Modern aesthetics claimed that vision was superior to the other senses because of its detachment from its objects: 'Vision', Hegel tells us in his *Lectures on Aesthetics*, 'finds itself in a purely theoretical relationship with objects, through the intermediary of light, that immaterial matter which truly leaves objects their freedom, lighting and illuminating them without consuming them.' [39] Postmodernist artists do not deny this detachment, but neither do they celebrate it. Rather, they investigate the particular interests it serves. For vision is hardly disinterested; nor is it indifferent, as Luce Irigaray has observed: 'Investment in the look is not privileged in women as in men. More than the other senses, the eye objectifies and masters. It sets at a distance, maintains the distance. In our culture, the predominance of the look over smell, taste, touch, hearing, has brought about an impoverishment of bodily relations. . . . The moment the look dominates, the body loses its materiality.' [40] That is, it is transformed into an image.

That the priority our culture grants to vision is a sensory impoverishment is hardly a new perception; the feminist critique, however, links the privileging of vision with sexual privilege. Freud identified the transition from a matriarchal to a patriarchal society with the simultaneous devaluation of an olfactory sexuality and promotion of a more mediated, sublimated visual sexuality. [41] What is more, in the Freudian scenario it is by looking that the child discovers sexual difference, the presence or absence of the phallus according to which the child's sexual identity will be assumed. As Jane Gallop reminds us in her recent book *Feminism and Psychoanalysis: The Daughter's Seduction*, 'Freud articulated the "discovery of castration" around a sight: sight of a phallic presence in the boy, sight of a phallic absence in the girl, ultimately sight of a phallic absence in the mother. *Sexual difference takes its decisive significance from a sighting.*' [42] Is it not because the phallus is the most visible sign of sexual difference that it has become the 'privileged signifier'? However, it is not only the discovery of difference, but also its denial that hinges upon vision (although the reduction of difference to a common measure – woman judged according to the man's standard and found lacking – is already a denial). As Freud proposed in his 1926 paper on 'Fetishism', the male child often takes the last visual impression prior to the 'traumatic' sighting as a substitute for the mother's 'missing' penis:

> Thus the foot or the shoe owes its attraction as a fetish, or part of it, to the circumstance that the inquisitive boy used to peer up at the woman's legs towards her genitals. Velvet and fur reproduce – as has long been suspected – the sight of the pubic hair which ought to have revealed the longed-for penis; the underlinen so often adopted as a fetish reproduces the scene of undressing, the last moment in which the woman could still be regarded as phallic. [43]

What can be said about the visual arts in a patriarchal order that privileges vision over the other senses? Can we not expect them to be a domain of masculine privilege – as their histories indeed prove them to be – a means, perhaps, of mastering through representation the 'threat' posed by the female? In recent years there has emerged a visual arts practice informed by feminist theory and addressed, more or less explicitly, to the issue of representation and sexuality – both masculine and feminine. Male artists have tended to investigate the social construction of masculinity (Mike Glier, Eric Bogosian, the early work of Richard Prince); women have begun the long-overdue process of deconstructing femininity. Few have produced new, 'positive' images of a revised femininity; to do so would simply supply and thereby prolong the life of the existing representational apparatus. Some refuse to represent women at all, believing that no representation of the female body in our culture can be free from phallic prejudice. Most of these artists, however, work with the existing repertory of cultural imagery – not because they either lack originality or criticise it – but because their subject, feminine sexuality, is always constituted in and as representation, a representation of difference. It must be emphasised that these artists are not primarily interested in what representations say about women; rather, they investigate what representation *does* to women (for example, the way it invariably positions them as objects of the male gaze). For, as Lacan wrote, 'Images and symbols *for* the woman cannot be isolated from images and symbols *of* the woman. . . . It is representation, the representation of feminine sexuality whether repressed or not, which conditions how it comes into play.'[44]

Critical discussions of this work have, however, assiduously avoided – skirted – the issue of gender. Because of its generally deconstructive ambition, this practice is sometimes assimilated to the modernist tradition of demystification. (Thus, the critique of representation is this work is collapsed into ideological critique.) In an essay devoted (again) to allegorical procedures in contemporary art, Benjamin Buchloh discusses the work of six women artists – Dara Birnbaum, Jenny Holzer, Barbara Kruger, Louise Lawler, Sherrie Levine, Martha Rosler – claiming them for the model of 'secondary mythification' elaborated in Roland Barthes's 1957 *Mythologies*. Buchloh does not acknowledge the fact that Barthes later repudiated this methodology – a repudiation that must be seen as part of his increasing refusal of mastery from *The Pleasure of the Text* on.[45] Nor does Buchloh grant any particular significance to the fact that all these artists are women; instead, he provides them with a distinctly male genealogy in the dada tradition of collage and montage. Thus, all six artists are said to manipulate the languages of popular culture – television, advertising, photography – in such a way that 'their ideological functions and effects become *transparent*'; or again, in their work, 'the minute and seemingly inextricable interaction of behaviour and ideology' supposedly becomes an '*observable* pattern'.[46]

But what does it mean to claim that these artists render the invisible visible, especially in a culture in which visibility is always on the side of the male, invisibility on the side of the female? And what is the critic really saying when he states that these artists reveal, expose, 'unveil' (this last word is used throughout Buchloh's text) hidden ideological agendas in mass-cultural imagery? Consider, for the moment, Buchloh's discussion of the work of Dara Birnbaum, a video artist who re-edits footage taped directly from broadcast television. Of Birnbaum's *Technology/Transformation: Wonder Woman* (1978-79), based on the popular television series of the same name, Buchloh writes that it 'unveils the puberty fantasy of Wonder Woman'. Yet, like all of Birnbaum's work, this tape is dealing not simply with mass-cultural imagery, but with mass-cultural *images of women*. Are not the activities of unveiling, stripping, laying bare in relation to a female body unmistakably male prerogatives?[47] Moreover, the women Birnbaum represents are usually athletes and performers absorbed in the display of their own physical perfection. They are without defect, without lack, and therefore with neither history nor desire. (Wonder Woman is the perfect embodiment of the phallic mother.) What we recognise in her work is the Freudian trope of the narcissistic woman, or the Lacanian 'theme' of femininity as contained spectacle, which exists only as a representation of masculine desire.[48]

The deconstructive impulse that animates this work has also suggested affinities with poststructuralist textual strategies, and much of the critical writing about these artists – including my own – has tended simply to translate their work into French. Certainly, Foucault's discussion of the West's strategies of marginalisation and exclusion, Derrida's charges of 'phallocentrism', Deleuze and Guattari's 'body without organs' would all seem to be congenial to a feminist perspective. (As Irigaray has observed, is not the 'body without organs' the historical condition of woman?)[49] Still, the affinities between poststructuralist theories and postmodernist practice can blind a critic to the fact that, when women are concerned, similar techniques have very different meanings. Thus, when Sherrie Levine appropriates – literally takes – Walker Evans's photographs of the rural poor or, perhaps more pertinently, Edward Weston's photographs of his *son* Neil posed as a classical Greek torso, is she simply dramatising the diminished possibilities for creativity in an image-saturated culture, as is often repeated? Or is her refusal of authorship not in fact a refusal of the role of creator as 'father' of his work, of the paternal rights assigned to the Author by law?[50] (This reading of Levine's strategies is supported by the fact that the images she appropriates are invariably images of the Other: women, nature, children, the poor, the insane . . .)[51] Levine's disrespect for paternal authority suggests that her activity is less one of appropriation – a laying hold and grasping – and more one of expropriation: she expropriates the appropriators.

Sometimes Levine collaborates with Louise Lawler under the collective title 'A Picture is No Substitute for Anything' – an unequivocal critique of representation as traditionally defined. (EH Gombrich: 'All art is image-making, and all image-making is the creation of substitutes.') Does not their collaboration move us to ask what the picture is supposedly a substitute for, what it replaces, what absence it conceals? And when Lawler shows 'A Movie without the Picture', as she did in 1979 in Los Angeles and again in 1983 in New York, is she simply soliciting the spectator as a collaborator in the production of the image? Or is she not also denying the viewer the kind of visual pleasure which cinema customarily provides – a pleasure that has been linked with the masculine perversions voyeurism and scopophilia?[52] It seems fitting, then, that in Los Angeles she screened (or didn't screen) *The Misfits* – Marilyn Monroe's last completed film. So that what Lawler withdrew was not simply a picture, but the archetypal image of feminine desirability.

When Cindy Sherman, in her untitled black-and-white studies for film stills (made in the late seventies and early eighties), first costumed herself to resemble heroines of grade-B Hollywood films of the late fifties and early sixties and then photographed herself in situations suggesting some immanent danger lurking just beyond the frame, was she simply attacking the rhetoric of 'auteurism by equating the known artifice of the actress in front of the camera with the supposed authenticity of the director behind it'?[53] Or was her play-acting not also an acting out of the psychoanalytic notion of femininity as masquerade, that is, as a representation of male desire? As Hélène Cixous has written, 'One is always in representation, and when a woman is asked to take place in this representation, she is, of course, asked to represent man's desire.'[54] Indeed, Sherman's photographs themselves function as mirror-masks that reflect back at the viewer his own desire (and the spectator posited by this work is invariably male) – specifically, the masculine desire to fix the woman in a stable and stabilising identity. But this is precisely what Sherman's work denies: for while her photographs are always self-portraits, in them the artist never appears to be the same, indeed, not even the same model; while we can presume to recognise the same person, we are forced at the same time to recognise a trembling around the edges of that identity.[55] In a subsequent series of works, Sherman abandoned the film-still format for that of the magazine centrefold, opening herself to charges that she was an accomplice in her own objectification, reinforcing the image of the woman bound by the frame.[56] This may be true; but while Sherman may pose as a pin-up, she still cannot be pinned down.

Finally, when Barbara Kruger collages the words 'Your gaze hits the side of my face' over an image culled from a fifties photo-annual of a female bust, is she simply 'making an equation . . . between aesthetic reflection and the alienation of the gaze: both reify'?[57] Or is she not speaking instead of the *masculinity* of the look; the ways in which it objectifies and masters? Or when the words 'You invest in the divinity of the masterpiece' appear over a blown-up detail of the creation scene from the Sistine ceiling, is she simply parodying our reverence for works of art, or is this not a commentary on artistic production as a contract between fathers and sons? The address of Kruger's work is always gender-specific; her point, however, is not that masculinity and femininity are fixed positions assigned in advance by the representational apparatus. Rather, Kruger uses a term with no fixed content, the linguistic shifter ('I/ you'), in order to demonstrate that masculine and feminine themselves are not stable identities, but subject to ex-change.

There is irony in the fact that all these practices, as well as the theoretical work that sustains them, have emerged in a historical situation supposedly characterised by its complete indifference. In the visual arts we have witnessed the gradual dissolution of once fundamental distinctions – original/copy, authentic/inauthentic, function/ornament. Each term now seems to contain its opposite, and this indeterminacy brings with it an impossibility of choice or, rather, the absolute equivalence and hence interchangeabil- ity of choices. Or so it is said.[58] The existence of feminism, with its insistence on difference, forces us to reconsider. For in our country good-bye may look just like hello, but only from a masculine position. Women have learned – perhaps they have always known – how to recognise the difference.

NOTES

1 Paul Ricoeur, 'Civilization and National Cultures', *History and Truth*, trans Chas A Kelbley, Northwestern University Press, Evanston, 1965, p 278.

2 Hayden White, 'Getting Out of History', *diacritics* 12, 3, Fall 1982, p 3. Nowhere does White acknowledge that it is precisely this universality that is in question today.

3 See, for example, Louis Marin, 'Toward A Theory of Reading in the Visual Arts: Poussin's *The Arcadian Shepherds'*, *The Reader in the Text*, ed S Suleiman and I Crosman, Princeton University Press, 1980, pp 293- 324. This essay reiterates the main points of the first section of Marin's *Détruire le peinture*, Galilée, Paris, 1977. See also Christian Metz's discussion of the enunciative apparatus of cinematic representation in his 'History Discourse: A Note on Two Voyeurisms', *The Imaginary Signifier*, trans Britton, Williams, Brewster and Guzzetti, Indiana University Press, Bloomington, 1982. And for a general survey of these analyses, see my 'Representation, Appropriation & Power', *Art in America* 70, 5, May 1982, pp 9-21.

4 Hence Kristeva's problematic identification of avant-garde practice as feminine – problematic because it appears to act in complicity with all those discourses which exclude women from the order of representation, associating them instead with the presymbolic (Nature, the Unconscious, the body, etc).

5 Jacques Derrida, 'Sending: On Representation', trans P and MA Caws, *Social Research* 49, 2, Summer 1982, pp 325, 326, italics added. (In this essay Derrida is discussing Heidegger's 'The Age of the World Picture', a text to which I will return.) 'Today there is a great deal of thought against representation,' Derrida writes. 'In a more or less articulated or rigorous way, this judgment is easily arrived at: representation is bad . . . And yet, whatever the strength and the obscurity of this dominant current, the authority of representation constrains us, imposing itself on our thought through a whole dense, enigmatic, and heavily stratified history. It programmes us and precedes us and warns us too severely for us to make a mere object of it, a representation, an object of representation confronting us, before us like a theme' (p 304). Thus, Derrida concludes that 'the essence of representation is not a representation, it is not representable, *there is no rep- resentation of representation*' (p 314, italics added).

6 Michèle Montrelay, 'Recherches sur la femininité', *Critique* 278, July 1970; trans Parveen Adams as 'Inquiry into Femininity', *m/f* 1, 1978; repr in *Semiotext(e)* 10, 1981, p 232.

7 Many of the issues treated in the following pages – the critique of binary thought, for example, or the privileging of vision over the other senses – have had long careers in the history of philosophy. I am interested, however, in the ways in which feminist theory articulates them onto the issue of sexual privilege.

Thus, issues frequently condemned as merely epistemological turn out to be political as well. (For an example of this kind of condemnation, see Andreas Huyssen, 'Critical Theory and Modernity', *New German Critique* 26, Spring/Summer 1982, pp 3-11.) In fact, feminism demonstrates the impossibility of maintaining the split between the two.

8 'What is unquestionably involved here is a conceptual foregrounding of the sexuality of the woman, which brings to our attention a remarkable oversight.' Jacques Lacan, 'Guiding Remarks for a Congress on Feminine Sexuality', *Feminine Sexuality*, ed J Mitchell and J Rose, Norton and Pantheon, New York, 1982, p 87.

9 See my 'The Allegorical Impulse: Toward a Theory of Postmodernism' (part 2), *October* 13, Summer 1980, pp 59-80. *Americans on the Move* was first performed at The Kitchen Centre for Video, Music, and Dance in New York City in April 1979; it has since been revised and incorporated into Anderson's two-evening work *United States, Parts I-IV*, first seen in its entirety in February 1983 at the Brooklyn Academy of Music.

10 This project was brought to my attention by Rosalyn Deutsche.

11 As Stephen Heath writes, 'Any discourse which fails to take account of the problem of sexual difference in its own enunciation and address will be, within a patriarchal order, precisely indifferent, a reflection of male domination.' 'Difference', *Screen* 19, 4, Winter 1978-79, p 53.

12 Martha Rosler, 'Notes on Quotes', *Wedge* 2, Fall 1982, p 69.

13 Jean-François Lyotard, *La Condition postmoderne*, Minuit, Paris, 1979, p 29.

14 See Sarah Kofman, *Le Respect des femmes*, Galilée, Paris, 1982. A partial English translation appears as 'The Economy of Respect: Kant and Respect for Women', trans N Fisher, *Social Research* 49, 2, Summer, 1982, pp 383-404.

15 Why is it always a question of *distance*? For example, Edward Said writes, 'Nearly everyone producing literary or cultural studies makes no allowance for the truth that all intellectual or cultural work occurs somewhere, at some times, on some very precisely mapped-out and permissible terrain, which is ultimately contained by the State. Feminist critics have opened this question part of the way, but *they have not gone the whole distance*.' 'American "Left" Literary Criticism', *The World, the Text, and the Critic*, Harvard University Press, Cambridge, 1983, p 169. Italics added.

16 Fredric Jameson, *The Political Unconscious*, Cornell University Press, Ithaca, 1981, p 84.

17 Marx and Engels, *The German Ideology*, International Publishers, New York, 1970, p 42. One of the things that feminism has exposed is Marxism's scandalous blindness to sexual inequality. Both Marx and Engels viewed patriarchy as part of a precapitalist mode of production, claiming that the transition from a feudal to a capitalist mode of production was a transition from male domination to domination by capital. Thus, in the *Communist Manifesto* they write, 'The bourgeoisie, wherever it has got the upper hand, has put an end to all feudal, patriarchal ... relations.' The revisionist attempt (such as Jameson proposes in *The Political Unconscious*) to explain the persistence of patriarchy as survival of a previous mode of production is an inadequate response to the challenge posed by feminism to Marxism. Marxism's difficulty with feminism is not part of an ideological bias inherited from outside; rather, it is a structural effect of its privileging of production as the definitively human activity. On these problems, see Isaac D Balbus, *Marxism and Domination*, Princeton University Press, 1982, esp chap 2, 'Marxist Theories of Patriarchy', and chap 5, 'Neo-Marxist Theories of Patriarchy'. See also Stanley Aronowitz, *The Crisis in Historical Materialism*, JF Bergin, Booklyn, 1981, esp chap 4, 'The Question of Class'.

18 Lyotard, 'One of the Things at Stake in Women's Struggles', *Substance* 20, 1978, p 15.

19 Perhaps the most vociferous feminist antitheoretical statement is Marguerite Duras's: 'The criterion on which men judge intelligence is still the capacity to theorise and in all the movements that one sees now, in whatever area it may be, cinema, theatre, literature, the theoretical sphere is losing influence. It has been under attack for centuries. It ought to be crushed by now, it should lose itself in a reawakening of the senses, blind itself, and be still'. In E Marks and I de Courtivron, ed *New French Feminisms*, Schocken, New York, 1981, p 111. The implicit connection here between the privilege men grant to theory and that which they grant to vision over the other senses recalls the etymology of *theoria*; see below.

Perhaps it is more accurate to say that most feminists are ambivalent about theory. For example, in Sally Potter's film *Thriller* (1979) – which addresses the question 'Who is responsible for Mimi's death?' in *La Bohème* – the heroine breaks out laughing while reading aloud from Kristeva's introduction to *Théorie d'ensemble*. As a result, Potter's film has been interpreted as an antitheoretical statement. What seems to be at issue, however, is the inadequacy of currently existing theoretical constructs to account for the specificity of a woman's experience. For as we are told, the heroine of the film is 'searching for a theory that would explain her life and her death'. On *Thriller*, see Jane Weinstock, 'She Who Laughs First Laughs Last', *Camera Obscura* 5, 1980.

20 Published in *Screen* 16, 3, Autumn 1975.

21 See my 'Earthwords', *October* 10, Fall 1979, pp 120-132.

22 'No Essential Femininity: A Conversation between Mary Kelly and Paul Smith', *Parachute* 26, Spring 1982, p 33.

23 Lyotard, *La Condition postmoderne*, p 8.

24 Ibid, p 68.

25 Fredric Jameson, '"In the constructive Element Immerse": Hans-Jürgen Syberberg and Cultural Revolution', *October* 17, Summer 1981, p 113.

26 See, for example, 'Fantasia of the Library', *Language, counter-memory, practice*, ed DF Bouchard, Cornell University Press, Ithaca, 1977, pp 87-109. See also Douglas Crimp, 'On the Museum's Ruins', *The Anti-Aesthetic*, ed Hal Foster, Bay Press, Seattle, Wash, 1983.

27 See Jameson, 'Postmodernism and Consumer Society', *Anti-Aesthetic*, ed Foster.

28 Jameson, *Political Unconscious*, p 19.

29 White, 'Getting Out of History', p 3.

30 Thus, the antithesis to narrative may well be allegory, which Angus Fletcher identifies as the 'epitome of counter-narrative'. Condemned by modern aesthetics because it speaks of the inevitable reclamation of the works of man by nature, allegory is also the epitome of the antimodern, for it views history as an irreversible process of dissolution and decay. The melancholic, contemplative gaze of the allegorist need not, however, be a sign of defeat; it may represent the superior wisdom of one who has relinquished all claims to mastery.

31 Translated by William Lovitt and published in *The Question Concerning Technology*, Harper and Row, New York 1977, pp 115-54. I have, of course, oversimplified Heidegger's complex and, I believe, extremely important argument.

32 Ibid, p 149, 50). Heidegger's definition of the modern age – as the age of representation for the purpose of mastery – coincides with Theodor Adorno and Max Horkheimer's treatment of modernity in their *Dialectic of Enlightenment* (written in exile in 1944, but without real impact until its republication in 1969). 'What men want to learn from nature,' Adorno and Horkheimer write, 'is how to use it in order wholly to dominate it and other men.' And the primary means of realising this desire is (what Heidegger, at least, would recognise as) representation – the suppression of 'the multitudinous affinities between existents' in favour of 'the single relation between the subject who bestows meaning and the meaningless object.' What seems even more significant, in the context of this essay, is that Adorno and Horkheimer repeatedly identify this operation as 'patriarchal'.

33 Fredric Jameson, 'Interview', *diacritics* 12, 3, Fall 1982, p 87.

34 Lyotard, *La Condition postmoderne*, p 63. Here, Lyotard argues that the *grands récits* of modernity contain the seeds of their own delegitimation.

35 For more on this group of painters, see my 'Honour, Power and the Love of Women', *Art in America* 71, 1, January 1983, pp 7-13.

36 Martha Rosler interviewed by Martha Gever in *Afterimage*, October 1981, p 15. *The Bowery in Two Inadequate Descriptive Systems* has been published in Rosler's book *3 Works*, The Press of The Nova Scotia College of Art and Design, Halifax, 1981.

37 'Intellectuals and Power: A conversation between Michel Foucault and Gilles Deleuze', *Language, counter-memory, practice*, p 209. Deleuze to Foucault: 'In my opinion, you were the first – in your books and in the practical sphere – to teach us something absolutely fundamental: the indignity of speaking for others.'

The idea of a counter-discourse also derives from this conversation, specifically from Foucault's work with the 'Groupe d'information de prisons'. Thus, Foucault: 'When the prisoners began to speak, they possessed an individual theory of prisons, the penal system, and justice. It is this form of discourse which ultimately matters, a discourse against power, the counter-discourse of prisoners and those we call delinquents – and not a theory *about* delinquency.'

38 Martha Rosler, 'in, around, and afterthoughts (on documentary photography)', *3 Works*, p 79.

39 Quoted in Heath, 'Difference', p 84.

40 Interview with Luce Irigaray in M-F Hans and G Lapouge, ed *Les femmes, la pornographie, l'erotisme*, Paris, 1978, p 50.

41 *Civilization and Its Discontents*, trans J Strachey, Norton, New York, 1962, pp 46-7.

42 Jane Gallop, *Feminism and Psychoanalysis: The Daughter's Seduction*, Cornell University Press, Ithaca, 1982, p 27.

43 'On Fetishism', repr in Philip Rieff, ed *Sexuality and the Psychology of Love*, Collier, New York, 1963, p 217.

44 Lacan, p 90.

45 On Barthes's refusal of mastery, see Paul Smith, 'We Always Fail – Barthes' Last Writings', *Substance* 36, 1982, pp 34-39. Smith is one of the few male critics to have directly engaged the feminist critique of patriarchy without attempting to rewrite it.

46 Benjamin Buchloh, 'Allegorical Procedures: Appropriation and Montage in Contemporary Art', *Artforum* XXI, 1, September 1982, pp 43-56.

47 Lacan's suggestion that 'the phallus can play its role only when veiled' suggests a different inflection of the term 'unveil' – one that is not, however, Buchloh's.

48 On Birnbaum's work, see my 'Phantasmagoria of the Media', *Art in America* 70, 5, May 1982, pp 98-100.

49 See Alice A Jardine, 'Theories of the Feminine: Kristeva', *enclitic* 4, 2, Fall 1980, pp 5-15.

50 'The author is reputed the father and owner of his work: literary science therefore teaches respect for the manuscript and the author's declared intentions, while society asserts the legality of the relation of author to work (the *'droit d'auteur'* or 'copyright', in fact of recent date since it was only really legalised at the time of the French Revolution). As for the Text, it reads without the inscription of the Father. Roland Barthes, 'From Work to Text', *Image/Music/Text*, trans S Heath, Hill and Wang, New York, 1977, pp 160-61.

51 Levine's first appropriations were images of maternity (women in their natural role) from ladies' magazines. She then took landscape photographs by Eliot Porter and Andreas Feininger, then Weston's portraits of Neil, then Walker Evans's FSA photographs. Her recent work is concerned with Expressionist painting, but the involvement with images of alterity remains: she has exhibited reproductions of Franz Marc's pastoral depictions of animals, and Egon Schiele's self-portraits (madness). On the thematic consistency of Levine's 'work', see my review, 'Sherrie Levine at A&M Artworks', *Art in America* 70, 6, Summer 1982, p 148.

52 See Metz, 'The Imaginary Signifier'.

53 Douglas Crimp, 'Appropriating Appropriation', *Image Scavengers: Photography*, ed Paula Marincola, Institute of Contemporary Art, Philadelphia, 1982, p 34.

54 Hélène Cixous, 'Entretien avec Françoise van Rossum-Guyon', quoted in Heath, 'Difference', p 6.

55 Sherman's shifting identity is reminiscent of the authorial strategies of Eugenie Lemoine-Luccioni as discussed by Jane Gallop; see *Feminism and Psychoanalysis*, p 105: 'Like children, the various productions of an author date from different moments, and cannot strictly be considered to have the same origin, the same author. At least we must avoid the fiction that a person is the same, unchanging throughout time. Lemoine-Luccioni makes the difficulty patent by signing each text with a different name, all of which are "hers".'

56 See, for example, Martha Rosler's criticisms in 'Notes on Quotes', p 73: 'Repeating the images of woman bound in the frame will, like Pop, soon be seen as a *confirmation* by the "post-feminist" society.'

From *The Anti-Aesthetic: Essays on Postmodern Culture*, edited by Hal Foster, Bay Press, Port Townsend, Washington, 1983.

CHAPTER SIX

SCIENCE AND RELIGION

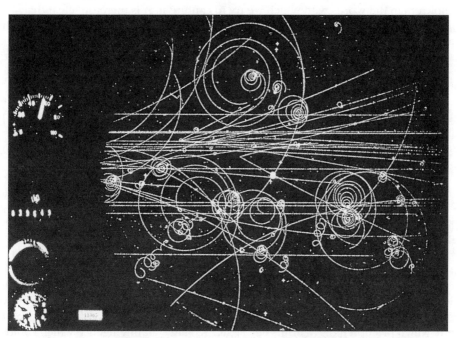

Production of particle jets by 16 GeV negative pions (p- mesons) in the first CERN liquid hydrogen
bubble chamber; it was only 30 cm in diameter.

Tito Arecchi

CHAOS AND COMPLEXITY

People now speak of a third revolution in physics, to follow the first one sparked off by Galileo and Newton, and the second, which took place during the first decades of this century and laid the foundations of relativity and quantum mechanics. This third wave may be called the physics of complexity.

The Galilean revolution consisted of choosing one single point of view from which to interpret the world: a quantitative one. We easily agree that reality is much more complex than the words with which we try to capture it. It is therefore clear that – even with the best will in the world – it is possible to talk about the same thing without managing to reach agreement; simply because it is being looked at from different points of view. The essence of the Galilean method is quite simple: using appropriate apparatus, numbers are extrapolated from things. It is possible to reach agreement on the type of measurement to be carried out excluding all possible ambiguity. The numbers are related mathematically, being organised into equations, and the solutions are used to predict the future. Thus, lack of ambiguity and predictability are the two characteristics of this new language. This approach to knowledge imposes limits on itself from the very start and excludes the possibility of answering questions which do not fall within the scope of the point of view selected.

The success of this approach has given rise to the mistaken belief that it is the only way to knowledge. This misunderstanding, which has become an ideology with practical implications, has been called *scientism*. It has permeated our language, influencing all other sciences from biology to anthropology, and has affected our whole culture and even our ethics.

Leaving aside this ideological aspect, the physical sciences developed with the introduction of suggestive suppositions which, at the time, simplified our view of the world, but which subsequently turned out to be superfluous elements, of little relevance to physics. Of this kind were Newton's absolute space and time, which were criticised by Einstein from 1905 onwards. A similar view was taken of the deterministic 'faith' which prompted the Marquis de Laplace to state: 'an intelligence which could at a given moment have knowledge of the position and velocity of all the particles in the universe would be able to predict with certainty the entire future of the universe.' At the level of the microscopic objects studied by microphysics this belief was discredited by Heisenberg's principle of indeterminacy, which established the impossibility of measuring simultaneously and precisely the position and velocity of a particle. Nevertheless, determinism seemed to retain its validity at the level of macroscopic objects – those which we can observe normally, using our senses.

The end of this belief in macroscopic determinism came with the idea of so-called 'deterministic chaos'. This seems to be a contradiction in terms. What it means, in essence, is that chaos, or the impossibility of long-term prediction, is not a prerogative of highly complex systems, but is rather to be found even in the physics of a small number of objects: it is enough to go from two (Newton's earth-sun system) up to three (earth-sun and any third body in the solar system). The first person to become aware of this was Poincaré in 1890, but the idea of deterministic chaos has only borne experimental fruit in the past few years, now that physics has reached the end of the long period of symmetries and regularity which seemed compatible with Laplace's belief. In other words, in going from a problem involving the trajectory of two heavenly bodies to one involving three, it emerges that, although a trajectory may be unique in starting from certain initial conditions, it is enough for it to have a minimal uncertainty to lose the predictability of its future path. Now these minimal uncertainties are intrinsic to the method of measurement itself. In translating objects into numbers, all we can establish with any accuracy are the rational numbers (relationships between two whole numbers), but by far the majority are irrational numbers (such as the square root of 2), which consist of an infinite number of figures. As infinity can neither be encompassed using our systems of measurement nor recorded in our memory, the truncated version of an infinite number introduces a tiny initial uncertainty, the effects of which become enormous when we try to extend our prediction beyond a certain time. We can express in a diagram (Fig 1) how it is possible to deviate from the 'unique' path. Let us compare two equal paths but with different surrounding 'landscapes': the first with a valley floor, the second with the ridge of a hill. The initial 'exact' position A gives the required path; a slightly wrong position B gives a path which in the first case converges with the correct one (time rectifies our error), but in the second diverges (passage of time increases the initial error). Even simple physical systems like Poincaré's problem of three bodies have critical paths which run along a ridge and can give rise to deterministic chaos. This lack of predictability in the long term was rediscovered by the meteorologist E Lorenz in 1963. Similar effects can be observed nowadays in various different situations: chemical reactions, the motion of fluids, lasers, cardiac rhythms, the movements of asteroids, economic and social trends etc.

The fact is – as René Thom has put it – that the only physical problem with an exact solution is Newton's earth-sun problem. For all others, physicists have limited themselves to looking for situations of stable equilibrium and have only then examined tiny movements around these. Now these tiny movements obey *linear* dynamics – that is, with a return force towards the point of equilibrium which is proportional to the displacement: 'ut tensio sic vis', as Hooke put it in the seventeenth century; and these dynamics always produce trajectories with valley floors, that is, ensure future predictability.

Thus it is not the case that nature was more benign prior to Poincaré but rather that the simplified models used to study nature excluded certain pathologies. Non-linear dynamics – those to which proportionality does not apply – are, however, the way in which nature normally behaves. To enter this domain is to open a Pandora's box – to discover the world of complexity. The fact that one's starting-point is never a geometric point from which there emerges a single line into the future (as Laplace believed), but in general a small blob from which there fan out lines in all directions, can be seen as a case of dynamic complexity, that is, as an infringement of the simplicity requirement which forms the basis of the Galilean method. Complexity has indeed 'exploded' in the hands of physicists as a new paradigm which is undermining the very foundations of that method for providing unambiguous knowledge of the world.

But even his belief in the existence of a privileged viewpoint from which to measure the world, on which all physicists could agree, has failed as well. In effect, if problems of this kind did not exist there would be no need to reward scientific creativity. For

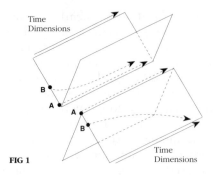

FIG 1

I *random sequence*
a o e e a a a o a e

II *regular sequence*
a e o a e o a e o

III *sequence from the first*
Canto of the Divine Comedy
e e o e a o a a
o a e a e a o a
e a a a e a a a

FIG 2

example, the helical symmetry of proteins and the double helix of DNA would be an obvious consequence of the links between atoms in a molecule, and it would not have been necessary to award the Nobel Prize for discovering the former to Linus Pauling and for the latter to Watson and Crick. The problem is that deductive reasoning, based on what is known about the constituent elements, would require a length of time and intellectual effort beyond the capacity of a human being in order to reconstruct from among a range of possible worlds the one which actually exists. The physicist Phil Anderson, in a stimulating article entitled 'More is Different' (which appeared in the journal *Science* in 1972), criticised 'constructionism', or the presumption that one can construct the behaviour of a complex object conceptually on the basis of one's knowledge of its component parts:

> The constructionist hypothesis fails when it is faced with the double problem of scale and complexity. The behaviour of large and complex aggregates of elementary particles cannot be encompassed in terms of a simple extrapolation of the properties of a few small particles. At every level of complexity there appear new properties, and to understand the new behaviour one requires research which in my opinion is just as basic in its nature as that of elementary particles.

Thus, in addition to the dynamic complexity of deterministic chaos, we can see the emergence of a structural complexity which consists of the impossibility of satisfactorily describing a complex object by reducing it to an interplay of its component parts with their elementary laws. In respecting the various, irreducible levels of the description of reality, physics is on the one hand respecting the scientific organisation of other areas of science (from biology to sociology without trying any longer to reduce these to 'applied physics'; on the other hand it is rehabilitating certain aspects of the Aristotelian 'organicism' for which 'a house is not the sum of its bricks and beams inasmuch as the architect's plan is an integral part of it'.

The two problem areas sketched above, that of deterministic chaos and that of complexity, are beginning to be translated into quantitative parameters. It is precisely the limits on predictability which impose a continual introduction of information if we are to be able to continue to make predictions about the future. The speed with which information is used up is indicated by a parameter K (after the mathematician Kolmogorov, who made an important contribution to this field). Moreover, tentative attempts are being made to portray structural complexity with a parameter C, which indicates the cost of a computer programme capable of realising a predefined complex objective. Figure 2 shows three sequences of the letters a, e and o; the first one is random, the second is regular and the third one is derived from the first three lines of the first Canto of Dante's *Divine Comedy*.

Let us agree to define as complexity the cost of the computer programme (length of

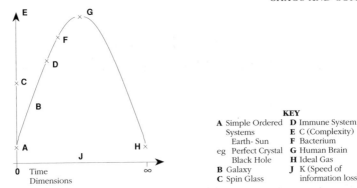

KEY

A Simple Ordered	**D** Immune System
Systems	**E** C (Complexity)
Earth- Sun	**F** Bacterium
eg Perfect Crystal	**G** Human Brain
Black Hole	**H** Ideal Gas
B Galaxy	**J** K (Speed of
C Spin Glass	information loss)

FIG 3 — Time / Dimensions — 0 ... ∞

the instructions multiplied by processing time) which enables us to realise one of the three sequences. In the case of sequence I the programme is simple: 'write at random a, or e, or o.' For II the instruction is very short; in III there exists no programme which would be shorter than the *Divine Comedy* itself. Sequence III we may call complex, the other two simple.

In conclusion, we can classify the limits which physics imposes on itself at present with a diagram C-K (Fig 3). Note the significance of the diagram. Let us start with the horizontal axis: K = O means predictable, highly ordered systems (for two reasons: either because they are static and do not change over time, or because they develop according to deterministic laws). A very high K means that the information disappears very rapidly as in the systems with maximum entropy from a thermodynamic point of view (a typical example would be Boltzmann's gas).

In the centre, with intermediate amounts of K, there are various dynamic systems affected to greater or lesser degree by deterministic chaos. While the horizontal axis tells us how things develop in time, it tells us nothing about the structure of the object being studied. The structure is represented by the complexity C. Objects in traditional physics, from the Newtonian system to Black Holes, are relatively simple. But contrast the 'non-ergodic' systems – a technical term meaning that they allow many possible states of equilibrium – are the objects of more recent study (from the 1970s onwards). These can be regarded like those systems in which the objectives to be achieved are in mutual conflict so that if one is achieved, the others have to be relinquished. We can say, in anthropomorphic terms, that complex systems are those in which choice operates. Obviously all the physics of living organisms finds its natural description in terms of these complex models. Maximum complexity is represented by the human brain. We are very far from being able to measure C or K, not just for the brain, but even for a bacterium. All we know is that they are objects which are much richer (high C) and less predictable (high K) than a galaxy or other objects in conventional physics.

In conclusion, the move from a single viewpoint to a multiplicity of legitimate viewpoints is like the Copernican revolution as compared with the monocentrism of the Ptolemaic system; it rectifies the long-standing disagreements between the 'two cultures', reopening a fertile area of interdisciplinary debate. Before Galileo, Leonardo had tried to investigate complex aspects of nature (clouds, vortices in rivers, the anatomy of animals and plants) in a way which went beyond pure classification. Now his dream is coming true; the physics of complexity is beginning to put forward answers to even these problems – problems which are far more complex than the pendulum or the celestial earth-sun system.

From *Liber* 1, *Times Literary Supplement*, 6 October 1989, trans RG Harrison.

David Ray Griffin
THE REENCHANTMENT OF SCIENCE

Recent Developments in Science

The move away from the mechanistic, deterministic, reductionistic worldview associated with modern science has been based not only on formal reflections upon the nature of modern science[1] but also on substantive developments within science itself.

Many discussions of this topic focus primarily, if not exclusively, upon quantum physics, seeing it as not only destroying the Cartesian-Newtonian worldview but as also suggesting a new worldview – or a return to an old one, usually a mystical worldview, perhaps Taoist or Buddhist. However, the dominant interpretation of quantum physics, the Copenhagen interpretation, is limited to rules of calculation to predict the content of observations.[2] In other words, it is a nonrealist, phenomenalist interpretation, in which the attempt to describe what is really going on in the world of subatomic entities, independently of human measurement, is eschewed. Most popular accounts of the implications of quantum physics for our worldview neglect this fundamental point. The phenomenalist descriptions are presented as if they tell us something deep about the nature of reality.

A recent interpretation of the significance of quantum physics for the worldview of the founders of quantum theory themselves presents a more sophisticated account. Rejecting the notion that a direct connection exists between quantum theory and mysticism, Ken Wilber argues that quantum theory did nevertheless promote mysticism, but only indirectly. That is, as these physicists became aware that physical theory gave them only shadows and symbols of reality, rather than reality itself, they became freed from the materialistic worldview and hence open to taking their own conscious experience as real and revelatory.[3]

But, regardless of the way the dominant interpretation of quantum physics did in fact loosen the grip of the mechanistic worldview, it does not provide us with the basis for a new worldview. The question remains whether quantum physics, under a different interpretation, might say something more directly helpful about the nature of reality.

There are some physicists, such as David Bohm and Henry Stapp, who have sought to develop a realistic (nonphenomenalist) account of the quantum realm. Bohm has thereby been led to distinguish between the 'explicate' order, upon which physics thus far has focused, and the 'implicate' order, which a more complete physics would describe.[4] In this implicate order, enduring things are not separate from each other, as they appear to be in the explicate order, but are mutually enfolded in each other. Each electron, for example, in some sense enfolds in itself the universe as a whole and hence all its other parts. Accordingly, internal relatedness to other things which we directly experience in our conscious experience is generalised analogically all the way down to the simplest individuals. As Bohm points out, in overcoming the dualism between mind and matter this view implies the transcendence of the modern separation between facts and values, truth and virtue. Henry Stapp likewise regards each event as a process of enfoldment: each event enfolds previous events within itself.[5]

This view, that the events of nature are internally constituted by their appropriations from other things, is the central theme of those who are suggesting that the mechanistic paradigm in science be replaced by an ecological one – such as Charles Birch, John Cobb, and Frederick Ferré.[6] The term *ecological* most readily suggests biology. But it is important to all of these thinkers that internal relations are characteristic not only of living beings but also of the most elementary physical units. For one thing, only when this view prevails will the current drive to make mechanistic explanations ultimate even in the science of ecology be overcome.

Because internal relatedness is a necessary feature of subjects, the attribution of internal relations to individuals at all levels is one condition for overcoming an ultimate dualism between subjects and objects; *completely* overcoming dualism would involve the attribution of other essential features of subjects, such as feeling, memory, and aim or decision, at least in embryonic form, all the way down. Birch refers to Donald Griffin, who is one of several scientists calling for the scientific study of animals to go beyond behaviourism by speaking of subjective experience. Although 'thinking' may occur only in the higher animals, Griffin suggests, the notions of memory and internal imaging seem necessary to understand the behaviour of bats and even bees.[7] Whereas bats and bees are very complex, highly evolved organisms, bacteria are unicellular microorganisms, the simplest form of life, which evidently emerged about four billion years ago, according to the most recent discoveries. Daniel Koshland and his colleagues have provided evidence of rudimentary forms of both 'memory' and 'decision' in bacteria.[8] Going even further down, there is reason now to believe that DNA and RNA macromolecules are not simply passive entities which change as their parts are changed, but that they are active organisms which actively transpose their parts.[9] Going even further, it has been suggested that the Pauli Principle provides reason to think of an atom as a self-regulating whole.[10]

Against the ontological reductionism of the materialistic worldview, according to which all causation runs sideways and upward, from parts to parts and from parts to the whole (with all apparent wholes really being aggregates), there are now developments in science stressing 'downward causation', from the whole to the parts. One of the most striking developments is evidence that the genes, which neo-Darwinism considers necessarily impervious to influence from the organism as a purposive whole, are in fact influenced by the organism.[11]

This recognition of downward causation from mind to body is aided if materialism and dualism are transcended. Those positions made it inconceivable that subjective purposes, feelings, decisions, and the like could influence the body. But if bodily cells and their components themselves have subjective experience, then downward causation from mind to body is no longer counterintuitive and the recognition of downward as well as upward causation between other levels will be easier.

More inclusive forms of downward causation would be involved in assertions of the influence of the planet as a living organism, and of the universe as a whole, on their parts. Something like the former could be suggested by the 'Gaia hypotheses' of JE Lovelock and Lynn Margulis.[12] The latter is involved in David Bohm's view that every natural unit, as an act of enfoldment, in some sense enfolds the activity of the universe as a whole within it. Because the universe as an active whole can be regarded as divine,[13] Bohm in effect is suggesting that postmodern science, in speaking of the implicate order, would include reference to divine activity. He is thus reversing the dedivinisation of nature bemoaned by Schiller.

The organismic view also overcomes the modern (and premodern) view that, for the world at its most fundamental level, temporality, in the sense of an irreversible distinction between past and future, is unreal. The notion that each electronic or protonic event enfolds past events within itself makes reversibility no more conceivable at the subatomic than at the human level.[14] According to Brian Swimme, we should, instead of regarding the historical evolution of the cosmos as an epiphenomenal development on the surface of the immutable laws of physics, see these laws themselves as products of a temporal development. Accordingly, physics no longer disenchants our stories; physics itself provides us with a new story which can become a common, unifying story underneath our more particular stories. Rupert Sheldrake, agreeing with Swimme that the laws of physics should not be considered changeless,[15] suggests further that they be conceived as habits that have evolved and that continue to evolve. The laws of nature hence become sociological laws, an idea that reduces further the modern dualism between humanity and nature. Rather than seeing mechanisms as fundamental and organisms as derivative phenomena to be explained mechanistically, Sheldrake suggests the opposite: mechanistic phenomena represent the extreme possibility of habit formation on the part of organisms. Sheldrake here restates a major theme of organismic scientists, that while a mechanistic starting point cannot account for genuine organisms, an organismic starting point can account for all the mechanistic phenomena evident in the world.

Sheldrake's original contribution is his hypothesis about the way such habits could be formed. This hypothesis of morphic resonance, which attributes a cumulative power to the repetition of a similar form, depends not only upon the irreversibility of time, but also upon influence at a distance, that is, over both temporal and spatial gaps. He is thereby bringing back, in a postmodern form, one of the notions that early modern thought most vigorously opposed.[16] That Sheldrake's proposal was condemned by a representative of the modern scientific establishment even prior to its testing is no surprise.[17]

The issue of action at a distance is, of course, central to the controversies about parapsychology. Numerous treatments show that the main difficulty with parapsychological claims, probably even more fundamental than the problem of repeatability, is the fact that 'paranormal claims seem to clash with our twentieth-century presuppositions about reality'.[18] And, as concluded by a recent reexamination of CD Broad's 'basic limiting principles' which paranormal claims seem to violate, the crucial principle is that 'any event that is said to cause another event (the second event being referred to as an "effect") must be related to the effect through some causal chain.'[19] This principle is violated by telepathy, clairvoyance, and psychokinesis (and precognition, which also violates the principle that the cause must precede the effect temporally). The author concluded that 'the absence of a specifiable and recognisably causal chain seems to constitute a difficult, if not insurmountable, objection to our giving a coherent account of what it means to make such a claim.'[20] CD Broad himself had suggested that, if there are any well-established facts that are exceptions to these principles, the good thinker 'will want to revise his fundamental concepts and basic limiting principles in such a way as to include the old and new facts in a single coherent system.'[21] The notion that a 'causal chain' of contiguous events or things must exist between a cause and an effect at a distance is part and parcel of the mechanistic worldview and is based on the assumption that the constituents of the world are bits of matter, analogous to billiard balls or parts of a machine, which can only affect each other by contact.[22] But if the basic units of the world are less like cogs or billiard balls than like moments of experience, which enfold influences from previous moments of experience into themselves, that all influence must come from contiguous events is no longer intuitively self-evident. Hence, in line with their nonmechanistic, organismic views of nature, Bohm and Stapp in physics and Sheldrake in biology point to evidence of nonlocal effects.[23] In this context, the claims of parapsychologists need not be rejected *a priori*, on the grounds that they clash with the rest of our worldview. In fact, Bohm, Sheldrake, and Stapp (as did Whitehead before them) all suggest that events exert two forms of influence on the future, one form on contiguous events, another on noncontiguous ones.[24] They use this nonlocal causation, in which what is normally called *physical energy* is not involved, to explain phenomena that seem inexplicable in terms of causation through chains of contiguous events alone.

These recent developments in the scientific community are reversing the disenchantment of science and its worldview. They are carrying forward what Floyd Matson described in 1964 as 'the affirmative countermovement in postmodern science'.[25]

Reflections on the Relation between Mind and Matter

The main philosophical reason for rejecting the mechanistic, nonanimistic view of nature is that that view makes the relation between mind and matter problematic. Four aspects of this problem can be distinguished: the traditional mind-body problem, the problem of mind as the Great Exception, the problem of emergence, and the problem of where to draw the line.

This mind-body problem is due to the conjunction of a directly known fact, an apparent fact, and an inference. The *directly known fact* is that we have, or are, a mind, in the sense of a stream of experiences. As Descartes stressed, if there is one thing I cannot doubt, it is that I am experiencing. The *apparent fact* is that the mind and the body seem to interact; that is, the mind seems to be affected by the body and seems to affect it in return. The *inference* is that the human body is composed of things that are devoid of experience. The resulting problem is: How is it understandable that these two totally unlike things appear to interact? The problem is intensified once we realise that the dualism between nonexperiencing and experiencing things entails a *set* of absolute contrasts, so that the question becomes: How can the impenetrably spatial relate to the nonspatial, the nontemporal to the temporal, the mechanistically caused to the purposively acting, the idea-less to the idea-filled, the purely factual to the value-laden, the externally locomotive to the internally becoming?

Because the founders and early defenders of the dualistic[26] worldview were supernaturalistic theists, they did not find the problem insurmountable. Although they differed in details (with Descartes speaking of an ethereal pineal gland, Malebranche of occasionalism, Leibniz of preestablished harmony or parallelism), they all agreed in essence with Thomas Reid, who simply said that God, being omnipotent, can cause mind and matter to interact, even if such interaction is inconceivable to us.[27] These thinkers thereby illustrated Whitehead's complaint about supernaturalists: having a God who can rise superior to metaphysical difficulties, they did not rethink their metaphysical principles but simply invoked God to prevent those principles from collapsing.[28]

However, as this appeal to God has become unacceptable, dualists are left with no answer. They either ignore the problem or regard it as a mystery we simply must accept. For example, at one time Karl Popper said: 'What we want is to understand how such nonphysical things as *purposes, deliberations, plans, decisions, theories, tensions,* and *values* can play a part in bringing about physical changes in the physical world.'[29] At a later time, however, he evidently decided that no such understanding was possible. He still confessed to belief in a 'ghost in a machine', but dismissed the question of their interacting with the lame comment that 'complete understanding, like complete knowledge, is unlikely to be achieved'.[30] Materialists use this admitted unintelligibility of dualistic interaction as the basis for equating mind and brain.

The second problem raised against dualism by some materialists is the implausibility of the idea that everything in the universe except human experience can be understood in physicalistic terms. This is the problem of the human mind as the Great Exception. JCC Smart says: 'That everything should be explicable in terms of physics . . . except the occurrence of sensations seems to me to be frankly unbelievable.'[31] This problem is lessened somewhat when dualists extend experience to all animals having central nervous systems, as do many dualists; it is lessened even more if experience is attributed all the way down to the lowest forms of life.

However, this solution simply raises the problem of interaction in a new form, resulting in a third problem, the problem of emergence. Whether the ontological gap is located between the human mind and its body or between an experiencing cell and its insentient atoms, the communication across the gap is equally unintelligible. As Smart states: 'How could a nonphysical property or entity suddenly arise in the course of animal evolution? . . . What sort of chemical process could lead to the springing into existence of something nonphysical? No enzyme can catalyse the production of a spook!'[32]

A fourth problem for dualists, if they try to solve the first two by extending experience below the human mind, is just *where* to draw the absolute line between sentient and insentient things. Drawing the line with Descartes between the human soul and the rest of nature, so that dogs are simply barking machines, was never very plausible, and it became less so with the theory of evolution. But drawing an absolute line anywhere else seems arbitrary, especially in an evolutionary context. Some vitalists have drawn an absolute line between living and nonliving matter, but the once-clear line between living and nonliving has become vague. Is the cell living and sentient, while its remarkable DNA and RNA macromolecules are insentient mechanisms? Is the bacterium a sentient organism, while the virus is not? Any such line seems arbitrary. For example, while agreeing that crystals and DNA molecules show signs of memory, and that even atoms and elementary particles have 'propensities', Karl Popper refuses to attribute experience any further down than to single-celled animals.[33] The reason Popper cannot attribute experience to atoms and electrons is clear; it is that he, being a modern man, shares 'with old-fashioned materialists the view that . . . solid material bodies are the paradigms of reality'.[34]

Given that modern starting point, the only way to avoid the insoluble problems of dualism is to affirm total materialism. Materialists avoid the problem of mind-body dualism by affirming identism, the doctrine that mind and brain are identical. JCC Smart, not being able to believe that experience is 'made of ghost stuff' says that it is 'composed of brain stuff'. In other words: 'Sensations are nothing over and above brain processes.'[35] In DM Armstrong's words, 'mental states are in fact nothing but physical states of the central nervous system.'[36]

Materialism has even more problems than does dualism, because it shares most of the problems of dualism and then adds some of its own. To begin with the problems it shares with dualism: First, it has not really escaped the problem of emergence which it levels against dualism. The identist's claim is that conscious experience is a quality that has 'emerged' in the evolutionary process analogously to the way in which other properties have emerged, such as saltiness, wetness, and furriness. Just as saltiness emerged out of a particular configuration of things none of which were by themselves salty, so experience has arisen out of a particular configuration of things (neurons) none of which by themselves had experience. In spite of the initial analogical plausibility of this argument, it hinges on a 'category mistake'. All the other emergent properties (saltiness, etc) are properties of things *as they appear* to us from without, ie, to our conscious sensory perception. *But conscious experience itself is not a property of things as they appear to us from without; it is what we are in and for ourselves.* The suggestion that an analogy exists between the other examples of emergent properties and the alleged emergence of sentience out of insentient things confuses two entirely different matters under a single category.[37] All the other examples involve the emergence of one more characteristic of things as they appear to others; *only* in the case of experience is the alleged new property a feature of what the thing is for itself. Surely the question of whether an individual is something for itself is categorically different from the question of what it is for others. Once this is seen, that materialism has the same problem of unintelligibility as does dualism is evident. It equally involves the claim that a thing that is something for itself emerged out of things that are mere objects for others. The fact that the thing in question is called a distinct mind by dualists and a brain by materialists is a secondary matter; an absolutely unique type of causal relation is still being posited. Things that are nothing for themselves are said to causally produce a thing (a brain) that is metaphysically unique in being not only an object for others, but a subject for itself.

Most materialistic identists also share with dualists the implausible idea that experiencing things constitute a Great Exception. For example, after suggesting that mind is strictly identical with matter, so that there is 'only one reality which is represented in two different conceptual systems', ie, physics and phenomenological psychology, Herbert Feigl makes clear that he does not intend panpsychism: 'nothing in the least like a psyche is ascribed to lifeless matter.' Rather, whereas the language of physics applies everywhere, the language of psychology is applicable 'only to an extremely small part of the world'.[38]

The materialist identist also shares the dualist's problem of where to draw the line between things that can be described in physical terms alone, and those to which psychological terms are appropriate. Drawing a line is equally arbitrary whether or not the things with experience are thought to be distinct actualities.

Some identists seek to overcome these problems by denying that psychological language need be used at all, even for our own experience. All language about pains, colours, intentions, emotions and the like would be eliminated. One would talk entirely in physicalistic terms, for example, by talking in terms of certain neuron firings instead of anger, in terms of other neuron firings instead of pain, etc.[39] This so-called eliminative materialism shows the desperate straights to which the mechanistic view of nature can lead.

Besides the problems that identism shares with dualism, it has several of its own. One is that, while claiming to be empirical, it denies the full reality of the directly known in the name of the inferred. That is, the one thing we know from inside, so that we know what it is *in itself*, is our own conscious experience. As almost all modern philosophers have insisted, we do not directly know what objects of sensory perception are in themselves, but only how they appear to us. The idea that these objects are *mere* objects, mere matter, can only be the result of metaphysical speculation. And yet materialists, on the basis of the speculative inference that the human body is composed of 'matter' which is *in itself devoid of experience*, deny that our directly known conscious experience can be a distinct actual thing on the grounds that that hypothesis requires interaction between experiencing and nonexperiencing things.

A second problem unique to materialism is that, in denying the distinction between the mind and the brain, it gives up the hypothesis that had provided the materialistic or mechanistic view of nature its *prima facie* plausibility in the first place. That is, the mechanistic view entailed a distinction between so-called *primary* qualities, which were really attributes of physical things, and *secondary* and *tertiary* qualities, which were only in the mind, although they might falsely appear to be in nature. Hence, nature consisted solely of quantitative factors, locomotion, and mechanistic causation; all colour and smells, all pain and pleasure, all good and evil, and all purposes and self-motion, resided solely in the mind. By having two types of actual things, dualism could deny that these nonphysical qualities exist in nature without making the counterintuitive assertion that they are wholly unreal. But in materialistic identism the modern worldview has lost its mind and must thereby deny that most of the qualities that are immediately experienced are real. They are illusions created by an illusion.

The materialistic denial that experience plays a causal role in the world also creates a problem of understanding how experience, and then conscious experience, ever emerged. Within an evolutionary framework, especially the neo-Darwinian one presupposed by materialists, the emergence and stabilisation of a new property only can be explained in terms of its enhancement of the chances for survival. But the point of materialistic identism is to deny that experience exerts causal power on the physical world; experience is a concomitant of some physical processes that would by hypothesis interact with the rest of the world in the same way if they were devoid of experience.[40] Hence, by this view, experience cannot enhance an organism's chances of survival. The materialist therefore has no evolutionary explanation as to why any of the things in the world should have experience of any sort, let alone conscious and self-conscious experience.

Adding further to the difficulties of materialistic identism is the fact that, in rejecting the dualism between mind and body, it necessitates a dualism between theory and practice. Whereas dualism said that the mind was the one thing with the power of self-motion, a large part of the motivation for the materialistic denial of nonmaterial mind is to deny that there is any part of the world that is not subject to the deterministic, reductionistic method of modern science. But we all, including the avowed materialists among us, live in practice as if we and other people were partly free from total determination from beyond ourselves. The resulting dualism between theory and practice is at least as vicious as that between mind and matter.

In summary, both dualism and materialism are unintelligible. But if the modern premise that the elementary units of nature are insentient is accepted, dualism and materialism are the only options. This fact suggests that the premise that lies behind the modern disenchantment of the world is false.

Accordingly, a strong philosophical argument converges with recent developments in the philosophy, sociology, and history of science, and in science itself, to undermine the basis for the modern disenchantment of the world.

Postmodern Organicism and the Unity of Science

The postmodern organicism has been inspired primarily by the scientist-turned-philosopher Alfred North Whitehead. Without trying to summarise the whole position, I will indicate briefly how it relates to the question of the unity of science, with a focus on the question of causation. I will do this in terms of a contrast of 'paradigms' understood as the basic worldviews presupposed by communities of scientists.

This postmodern organicism can be considered a synthesis of the Aristotelian, Galilean (both forms), and Hermetic paradigms. Aristotelian organicism had a unified science by attributing purposive or final causation to everything, most notoriously saying that a falling stone seeks a state of rest. The Galilean paradigm, in its first form, distinguished absolutely between two types of primary beings: (1) those that exercised purposive or final causation; and (2) those that did not and could consequently be understood completely in terms of receiving and transmitting efficient causation. At first, limiting the beings in the first category to human minds was customary, but that limitation is neither necessary to the dualistic paradigm nor very credible. Many Galilean dualists have accordingly, as mentioned in the previous section, extended final causation further down the animal kingdom: those who are termed *vitalists* see it as arising with the first form of life. Wherever the line was drawn, the drawing of a line between two ontologically different types of primary beings split science into two parts. One science spoke only of efficient causes; the other science (psychology) spoke in terms of final causes or purposes. The second form of the Galilean paradigm tried to restore unity to science by abolishing an internalistic psychology of final causes. Psychology, under the name of *behaviourism*, was transformed into an attempt to describe and explain human and other animal behaviour solely in terms of efficient causes and other externalistic terms. *Eliminative materialism*, mentioned earlier, is the extreme version of this way to achieve unity.

Postmodern organicism holds that all primary individuals are organisms who exercise at least some iota of purposive causation. But it does not hold that all visible objects, such as stones and planets, are primary individuals or even analogous to primary individuals. Rather, it distinguishes between two ways in which primary organisms can be organised: (1) as a compound individual,[41] in which an all-inclusive subject emerges; and (2) as a nonindividuated object, in which no unifying subjectivity is found. Animals belong to the first class; stones to the second. In other words, there is no ontological dualism, but there *is* an organisational duality which takes account of the important and obvious distinction that the dualists rightly refused to relinquish. Hence, there are (1) things whose behaviour can only be understood in terms of both efficient causes and their own purposive response to these causes, and (2) things whose behaviour can be understood, for most purposes, without any reference to purposive or final causation. In this sense, there is a duality within science.

However, the qualification *for most purposes* is important. Whereas the Galilean paradigm maintained that a nonteleological explanation of material things could be adequate for all purposes, including a complete understanding, at least in principle, the postmodern paradigm contends that any explanation devoid of purposive causation will necessarily abstract from concrete facts. *Fully* to understand even the interaction between two billiard balls requires reference to purposive reactions – not indeed of the balls as aggregates, but of their constituents. Because the study of nonindividual objects as well as that of primary individuals and compound individuals requires, at least ultimately, reference to final as well as efficient causes, there is a unity of science.

The relation between final and efficient causation in Whiteheadian postmodern organicism is different from their relation in any previous form of thought, even from other forms of panexperientialism (often called panpsychism), although it was anticipated in Buddhist thought. Other forms of thought that have attributed experience to all individuals, such as that of Gottfried Leibniz and Teilhard de Chardin, have assumed the ultimate constituents of the world to be enduring individuals. An individual was physical from without to others, but was conscious or mental from within, for itself. From without, it interacted with other enduring individuals in terms of efficient causation; from within, it lived in terms of purposes or final causation. Given this picture, relating efficient and final causation to each other was difficult. The common view has been that they do not relate, but simply run along parallel to each other. However, as discussed above in relation to materialistic identism, this parallelism raises serious problems. If experience or mentality makes no difference to an individual's interactions with its environment, how can we explain why the higher forms of experience have evolved? And without appeal to a supernatural coordinator, how can we explain the parallelism between inner and outer; eg, why should my brain's signal to my hand to lift a glass follow right after my mental decision to have a drink, if my decision in no way *causes* the appropriate neurons in the brain to fire?

However, if the ultimate individuals of the world are momentary events, rather than enduring individuals, a positive relation can exist between efficient and final causation. Efficient causation still applies to the exterior of an individual and final causation to the interior. But because an enduring individual, such as a proton, neuron, or human psyche, is a temporal *society* of momentary events, exterior and interior oscillate and feed into each other rather than running parallel. Each momentary event in an enduring individual originates through the inrush of efficient causation from the past world, ie from previous events, including the previous events that were members of the same enduring individual. The momentary subject then makes a self-determining response to the causal influences; this is the moment of final causation; it is a purposive response to the efficient causes on the event. When this moment of subjective final causation is over, the event becomes an object which exerts efficient causation on future events. Exactly what efficient causation it exerts is a function both of the efficient causes upon it *and* of its own final causation. Hence, the efficient causes of the world do not run along as if there were no mentality with its final causation. An event does not necessarily simply transmit to others what it received; it may do this, but it may also deflect and transform the energy it receives to some degree or other, before passing it on. (*We* do this to the greatest degree when we return good for evil.)

To say that the categories of both final and efficient causation must be employed for the study of all actual beings does *not* imply that the two categories will be *equally* relevant for all beings. Indeed, as already indicated, an appeal to final causation is irrelevant for almost all purposes when studying nonindividuated objects, such as rocks, stars, and computers.[42] Even with regard to individuals, the importance of final or purposive causation will vary enormously. In primary individuals, such as photons and electrons (or quarks, if such there be), final causation is minimal. For the most part, the behaviour of these individuals is understandable in terms of efficient causes alone. They mainly just conform to what they have received and pass it on to the future in a predictable way. But not completely: behind the epistemic 'indeterminacy' of quantum physics lies a germ of ontic self-determinacy. The importance of self-determination or final causation increases in compound individuals, especially in those normally called *living*. It becomes increasingly important as the study focuses upon more complex, highly evolved animals; all the evidence suggests that final causation is the most important, on our planet, in determining the experience and behaviour of human beings. The importance of efficient causes, ie of influence from the past, does not diminish as one moves towards the higher individuals; indeed, in a sense higher beings are influenced by *more* past events than are lower ones. But the totality of efficient causes from the past becomes less and less explanatory of experience and behaviour, and the individual's own present self-determination in terms of desired ends becomes more explanatory.

From this perspective we can understand why a mechanistic, reductionist approach has been so spectacularly successful in certain areas and so unsuccessful in others. The modern Galilean paradigm was based on the study of nonindividuated objects, such as stellar masses and steel balls, which exercise *no final causation* either in determining their own behaviour or that of their elementary parts. Absolute predictability and reduction is possible in principle. This paradigm was next applied to very low-grade individuals, in which the final causation is *negligible* for most purposes except to the most refined observation. With this refinement, the absolute predictability of behaviour broke down with the most elementary individuals; the ideal of predictability could be salvaged only by making it statistical and applying it to large numbers of individuals. With low-grade forms of life, and in particular with their inherited characteristics and certain abstract features of their behaviour, Galilean science has still been very successful, but not completely. Certain features of even low-grade life seemed intractable to this approach, just those features which led to the rise of vitalism. This paradigm has been even less successful with rats than with bacteria. At this level, various problems are virtually ignored, because little chance of success is apparent, and scientists are interested in applying their method where the chances for success are most promising. Finally, the method has been less successful yet with humans than with rats. The record of success at this level is so miserable that many scientists and philosophers of science refuse to think of the so-called social or human sciences, such as psychology, sociology, economics, and political science, as sciences at all. This pattern of success and failure of the Galilean paradigm fits exactly what the postmodern paradigm predicts. As one leaves nonindividuated objects for individuals, and as one deals with increasingly higher individuals, final causation becomes increasingly important, and regularity and hence predictability become increasingly less possible. Hence, nothing but confusion and unrealistic expectations can result from continuing to regard physics as the paradigmatic science.[43]

This framework can explain why it has been even less possible to discover regularities and attain repeatability in parapsychology than in certain aspects of ordinary psychology. Although every event (by hypothesis) exerts influence directly upon remote as well as spatially and temporally contiguous events, its influence on contiguous events is much more powerful. Hence, the effects of the kind of influence that is exerted upon remote events indirectly via a chain of contiguous events will be much more regular and hence predictable than the effects of the kind of influence that is exerted on remote events directly, without the intervening chain. Accordingly, because sensory perception arises from a chain of contiguous events (photons and neuron firings in vision) connecting the remote object with the psyche, the sensory perception of external objects is much more regular and reliable, hence predictable, than any extrasensory perception of them. Likewise, because effects produced in the external world by the psyche by means of the body are mediated by a chain of contiguous causes, whose reliability, like that of the sensory system, has been perfected over billions of years of evolution, such effects are much more reliable than any psychokinetic effects produced by the direct influence of the psyche upon outer objects without the body's mediation. Additionally, although *unconscious* extrasensory perception and *subtle* and *diffused* psychokinetic action occur continually (by hypothesis), the power to produce *conscious* extrasensory perception and *conspicuous* psychokinetic effects *on specific objects* is – at least for the majority of human beings most of the time – evidently lodged in an unconscious level of experience, which by definition is not under conscious control. Given these assumptions, the fact that parapsychology has attained little repeatability with conspicuous psychokinetic effects and conscious extrasensory perception is what should be expected.[44] In this way, the element of truth in the Hermetic paradigm is coordinated with the elements of truth from the Aristotelian and Galilean paradigms.

What then is science – what constitutes its unity? The anarchistic or relativistic view that 'anything goes', that there is no such thing as a scientific method, is surely too strong. But it serves a useful function, as indeed it was intended,[45] to shake us free from parochial limitations on what counts as science. A description of science for a postmodern world must be much looser than the modern descriptions (which were really prescriptions).

Any activity properly called *science* and any conclusions properly called *scientific* must, first, be based on an overriding concern to discover truth.[46] Other concerns will of course play a role, but the concern for truth must be overriding, or the activity and its results would be better called by another name, such as *ideology*, or *propaganda*, or *politics*.[47] Second, science involves demonstration. More particularly, it involves testing hypotheses through data or experiences that are in some sense repeatable and hence open to confirmation or refutation by peers. In sum, science involves the attempt to establish truth through demonstrations open to experiential replication. What is left out of this account of science are (1) limitations to any particular domain, (2) any particular type of repeatability and demonstration, or (3) any particular contingent beliefs.

(1) Science is not restricted to the domain of things assumed to be wholly physical, operating in terms of efficient causes alone, or even to the physical aspects of things, understood as the aspects knowable to sensory perception or instruments designed to magnify the senses.[48] As the impossibility of behaviourism in human and even animal psychology has shown, science must refer to experience and purposes to comprehend (and even to predict) animal behaviour. Although we cannot *see* the purposes motivating our fellow humans or other animals, assuming that such purposes play a causal role is not unscientific, if this hypothesis can be publically demonstrated to account for the observable behaviour better than the opposite hypothesis. And, once it is explicitly recognised that science *can* deal with subjectivity, there is no reason in principle for it to limit itself to the objective or physical side of other things, if there is good reason to suspect that an experiencing side exercising final causation exists. At the very least, even if we cannot imagine very concretely what the experience of a bacterium or a DNA molecule would be like, we need not try to account for its observable behaviour on the metaphysical assumption that it has no experience and hence no purposes.

Just as the need for experiential replication by peers does not limit science to the physical or objective side of actual things, it does not even limit it to the realm of actuality. Mathematics deals with relationships among ideal entities, and is able to achieve great consensus; geometry was for Descartes of course the paradigmatic science. Therefore, the fact that logic, aesthetics, and ethics deal with ideal entities does not, in itself, exclude them from the realm of science.

Furthermore, the domain of scientific study should not be thought to be limited to regularities, or law-like behaviour. There is no reason why the discussion of the origin of laws should not belong to science. If the laws of nature are reconceived as habits, the question of how the habits originated should not be declared off-limits.[49] In fact, we should follow Bohm in replacing the language of 'laws' with the more inclusive notion of 'orders', for the reasons Evelyn Fox Keller has suggested: the notion of 'laws of nature' retains the connotation of theological imposition, which is no longer appropriate but continues to sanction unidirectional, hierarchical explanations; it makes the simplicity of classical physics the ideal, so that the study of more complex orders is regarded as 'softer' and less fully scientific; and it implies that nature is dead and 'obedient' rather than generative and resourceful.[50]

(2) While science requires repeatable experiential demonstration, it does not require one particular type of demonstration, such as the laboratory experiment. As Patrick Grim says:

> Field studies, expeditions, and the appearances of comets have played a major role in the history of science. Contemporary reliance on mathematics reflects a willingness to accept a priori deductive as well as inductive demonstration. And there are times when the course of science quite properly shifts on the basis of what appear to be almost purely philosophical arguments.[51]

In regard to Grim's last example, I have suggested above that the philosophical difficulties with both dualism and materialistic identism provide a good reason for the scientific community to reconsider the metaphysical-scientific hypothesis that the ultimate constituents of nature are entirely devoid of experience and purpose. More generally, the bias toward the laboratory experiment in the philosophy of science has philosophically reflected the materialistic, nonecological assumption that things are essentially independent of their environments, so that the scientist abstracts from nothing essential in (say) removing cells from the human body or animals from a jungle to study them in a laboratory; it reflects the reductionistic assumption that all complex things are really no more self-determining than the elementary parts in isolation, so that they should be subject to the same kind of strong laboratory repeatability;[52] it reflects the assumption that the main purpose of science is to predict and control repeatable phenomena; and it reflects the assumption that the domain of science is limited to the actual, especially the physical. Recognising the wide domain of science means recognising the necessity and hence appropriateness of diverse types of demonstrations, and the artificiality of holding up one type as the ideal.

(3) Besides not being limited to one domain or one type of demonstration, the scientific pursuit of truth is not tied to any set of contingent beliefs, meaning beliefs that are not inevitably presupposed by human practice, including thought, itself. Science is, therefore, not limited to any particular type of explanation.[53] For example, science is not tied to the belief that the elementary units of nature are devoid of sentience, intrinsic value, and internal relations, that time does not exist for these units, that the laws of nature for these units are eternal, that all natural phenomena result from the (currently four) forces rooted in these elementary units, that accordingly all causation is upward and that freedom and purposive or teleological causation are illusory,[54] that ideal entities other than mathematical forms play no role in nature, that there is no influence at a distance,[55] that the universe as a whole is not an organism which influences its parts, or that the universe and its evolution have no inherent meaning.

However, the fact that science as such is not permanently wedded to these contingent beliefs that reigned during the modern period does not mean that there are *no* beliefs that science as such must presuppose. If beliefs exist that are presupposed by human practice, including human thought, as such, then scientific practice and thought must presuppose them. Any theories that verbally deny them should therefore be eschewed on this ground alone. Although any such beliefs would transcend perspectivalism, because they by hypothesis would be common to all people, regardless of their worldview, the questions of whether there are any such beliefs, and if so what they are, are matters not for pontification from some supposedly neutral point of view, because no human point of view is neutral, but for proposals to be subjected to ongoing public discussion among those with diverse worldviews.[56]

To illustrate the types of beliefs intended and to show that they are not limited to innocuous, noncontroversial issues, I propose five principles as candidates. The first three principles relate to the crucial issue of causality. First, every event is causally influenced by other events. This principle rules out, for example, the idea that the universe arose out of absolute nothingness or out of pure possibility![57] Second, neither human experience nor anything analogous to it is wholly determined by external events; rather, every genuine individual is partially self-determining. Incidentally, these first two principles, taken together, provide the basis for a scientific understanding of the activity of scientists themselves in terms of a combination of external and internal causes, which is increasingly seen to be necessary.[58]

Third, every event that exerts causal influence upon another event precedes that event temporally. (Self-determination or self-causation does not fall under this principle, because in it the same event is both cause and effect.) This principle rules out the notion of particles 'going backwards in time' the notion of 'backward causation', and any notion of 'precognition' interpreted to mean that an event affected the knower before it happened or to mean that temporal relations are ultimately unreal.[59]

The final two principles proffered deal with science's concern for truth. These are the traditional principles of correspondence and noncontradiction, which are recovered in a postmodern context.

The idea that truth is a correspondence between statements and objective reality has been subject to a great deal of criticism. Much of this criticism is based upon confusion, inasmuch as the critics, often while verbally rejecting positivism, still presuppose the positivistic equation of the meaning of a statement with the means of its verification. The correspondence notion of truth properly refers only to the *meaning* of 'truth', which is not even identical with the question of knowledge, let alone with the question of the justification of knowledge-claims. Much of the rejection of the relevance of the correspondence notion of truth has conflated truth with knowledge and then assumed that there could be no knowledge, in the sense of justified true belief, in the absence of adequate evidence to defend the knowledge-claim.[60]

However, much of the criticism of the notion of truth as correspondence is valid, especially in relation to naively realistic ideas of a one-to-one correspondence between statements and objective facts. For one thing, our ideas about physical objects, insofar as they are based primarily upon visual and tactile perception, surely involve enormous simplifications, constructions, and distortions of the realities existing independently of our perception. For another, language is inherently vague and, in any case, cannot as such 'correspond' in the sense of being similar to nonlinguistic entities. Language aside, the way in which an idea can correspond to a physical object is not self-evident, because an idea can only be similar to another idea. Even many conceptions of truth as the correspondence between one's ideas and the ideas in another mind are held in falsely naive ways, insofar as it is assumed that achieving truth, in the sense of absolute correspondence, is possible. Many critics go on from these valid starting points to argue that the meaning of a statement is exhausted by its relation to other statements, so that language constitutes a closed system, or in some other way argue that our statements can in no meaningful sense correspond to any nonlinguistic entities. Science, in this extreme view, is a linguistic system disconnected from any larger world.

Postmodern organicism rejects this view of language. While language as such does not correspond to anything other than language, it expresses and evokes modes of apprehending nonlinguistic reality that can more or less accurately correspond to features of that reality.[61] Hence, science can lead to ways of thinking about the world that can increasingly approximate to patterns and structures genuinely characteristic of nature.

The other traditional principle involved in science's concern for truth is the principle of noncontradiction. It says that if two statements contradict each other, both cannot be true. This principle has also been subject to much valid criticism. Certainly two statements that appear to contradict each other may not in reality when one or both are more deeply understood. This can be because language is vague and elusive, because various levels of meaning exist, and/or because seemingly contradictory assertions may apply to diverse features of the referent or to different stages of its development. There are yet other objections to simple-minded applications of the principle of noncontradiction. But after all necessary subtleties and qualifications have been added, the principle remains valid and is necessarily presupposed even in attempts to refute it. Accordingly, science must aim for coherence between all its propositions and between its propositions and all those that are inevitably presupposed in human practice and thought in general. (Obtaining such coherence is indeed the primary method of checking for correspondence.)

All of these principles are in harmony with postmodern organicism. Indeed, they are not epistemically neutral principles but ones that are, especially in regard to their exact formulation, suggested by postmodern organicism. However, the claim is made that they are, in fact, implicit in human practice, including human thought (although not, of course, in the content of all the theories produced by human thought). If this claim is sustained through widespread conversation, then this set of beliefs (along with any others that could prove their universality in the same way) should be considered to belong to science as such.[62]

To summarise: Whereas modern science has led to the disenchantment of the world and itself, a number of factors today are converging toward a postmodern organicism in which science and the world are reenchanted. Besides providing a basis for overcoming the distinctive problems of modernity that are due primarily to disenchantment, this postmodern organicism gives science a better basis than it has heretofore had for understanding its own unity.

NOTES

1 The prior sections in the essay from which this segment was abstracted dealt with the ways in which modern science led to the disenchantment of the world, then suggested that several converging reasons were reversing this disenchantment. The first of those reasons were a new view of the nature of science, and a new view of the origin of modern science.

2 Henry P Stapp, 'Einstein Time and Process Time', *Physics and the Ultimate Significance of Time: Bohm, Prigogine, and Process Philosophy*, ed David Ray Griffin, State University of New York Press, Albany, 1986, pp 264-70, esp 264.

3 'Introduction: Of Shadows and Symbols', *Quantum Questions: Mystical Writings of the World's Great Physicists*, ed Ken Wilber, Shambhala, Boston, 1984, pp 3-29.

4 David Bohm, 'The Implicate Order: A New Order for Physics', *Process Studies* 8/2, ed Dean Fowler, Summer 1978, pp 73-102; *Wholeness and the Implicate Order*, Routledge & Kegan Paul, London, 1980; 'Hidden Variables and the Implicate Order', *Zygon* 20/2, June 1985, pp 111-24; 'Time, the Implicate Order and Pre-Space', *Physics and the Ultimate Significance of Time*, ed David Ray Griffin, pp 177-208.

5 David Bohm, 'Postmodern Science and a Postmodern World', *The Reenchantment of Science: Postmodern Proposals*, ed David R Griffin, State University of New York Press, Albany, 1988, pp 57-68; Stapp, 'Einstein Time and Process Time'; 'Whiteheadian Approach to Quantum Theory and the Generalised Bell's Theorem', *Foundations of Physics* 9/1-2, 1979, pp 1-25.

6 See their essays in *The Reenchantment of Science*, ed David R Griffin, State University of New York Press, Albany, 1988.

7 Donald R Griffin, *The Question of Animal Awareness: Evolutionary Continuity of Mental Experience*, Rockefeller University Press, New York, pp 14, 23.

8 A Goldbeter and DE Koshland, Jr, 'Simple Molecular Model for Sensing and Adaptation Based on Receptor Modification with Application to Bacterial Chemotaxis', *Journal of Molecular Biology* 161/3, 1982, pp 395-416; Jess Stock, Greg Kersulis, and Daniel E Koshland, Jr, 'Neither Methylating nor Demethylating Enzymes are Required for Bacterial Chemotaxis', *Cell* 42/2, 1985, pp 683-90.

9 John H Campbell, 'Autonomy in Evolution', *Perspectives on Evolution*, ed R Milkman, Sinauer Assoc, Sunderland, Mass, 1982, pp 190-200, and 'An Organisational Interpretation of Evolution', *Evolution at a Crossroads: The New Biology and the New Philosophy of Science*, ed David J Depew and Bruce H Weber, MIT Press, Cambridge, 1985, pp 133-68; see also the discussion by Depew and Weber, pp xiv, 248. The lonely pioneer in the study of 'transposons' was Barbara McClintock; see Evelyn Fox Keller, *A Feeling for the Organism: The Life and Work of Barbara McClintock*, Freeman, New York, 1983.

10 Ian Barbour, *Issues in Science and Religion*, Prentice-Hall, Englewood Cliffs, 1966, pp 295-99, 333.

11 Campbell, 'Organisational Interpretation of Evolution', pp 134-35.

12 JE Lovelock and Lynn Margulis, 'Atmospheric Homeostasis by and for the Biosphere: The Gaia Hypothesis', *Tellus* 26/2, 1973; JE Lovelock, *Gaia: A New Look at Life on Earth*, Oxford University Press, 1979; Lynn Margulis and Dorion Sagan, *Micro-Cosmos: Four Billion Years of Microbial Evolution*, Summit Books, New York, 1986. Neither Lovelock nor Margulis draws organismic conclusions from their hypothesis. Lovelock has distanced himself from the view that the planet as a whole is sentient and teleological, suggesting that all the phenomena can be interpreted cybernetically (*Gaia*, pp ix-x, 61-63), and Margulis has endorsed a fully mechanistic, reductionistic philosophy (*Micro-Cosmos*, pp 229, 256-75).

13 Bohm is reluctant to use the term *God* because of its supernaturalistic connotations. But he does think of the holomovement as holy, and as embodying intelligence and compassion; 'Hidden Variables', p 124; Renee Weber, 'The Enfolding-Unfolding Universe: A Conversation with David Bohm', *The Holographic Paradigm and Other Paradoxes*, ed Ken Wilber, Shambhala, Boulder, Colo, 1982, pp 187-214, esp 60-70.

14 I have dealt with this issue in the 'Introduction', *Physics and the Ultimate Significance of Time*, pp 10-15.

15 See the essays by Swimme and Sheldrake in *The Reenchantment of Science*, ed David R Griffin.

16 See note 22 below.

17 An editorial in a British journal (*Nature* 293, 24 September 1981, pp 245-46) condemned Sheldrake's book, *A New Science as Life: The Hypothesis of Formative Causation*, Blond & Briggs, London, 1981, as an 'infuriating tract' and 'the best candidate for burning there has been for a long time'. The editorial complained that the book was being hailed as an answer to materialistic science and was becoming 'a point of reference for the motley crew of creationists, anti-reductionists, neoLamarckians and the rest'. Calling the book 'pseudo-science', it dismissed Sheldrake's claim that the hypothesis is testable, adding that 'no self-respecting grantmaking agency will take the proposals seriously'. Of particular interest for the present discussion was the editor's statement that 'finding a place for magic within scientific discussion . . . may have been part of the [author's] objective' and his apparent view that anti-reductionists and neo-Lamarckians are as far from the true faith as creationists. This editorial evoked a number of critical responses from scientists, including Nobel prizewinning physicist Brian Josephson (*Nature* 293, 29 October, p 594). In response to the editor's complaint that Sheldrake had not described the nature or origin of morphogenetic fields, Josephson said that the properties of heat, light, sound, electricity, and magnetism were investigated long before their natures were understood. The editor's stipulation that *all* aspects of a theory must be testable if it is to be called scientific would, Josephson added, bar general relativity, black holes, and many other concepts of modern science from the status of legitimate scientific ideas. Josephson closed by saying: 'The fundamental weakness is failure to admit even the possibility that genuine physical facts may exist which lie outside the scope of current scientific descriptions. Indeed, a new kind of understanding of nature is now emerging, with concepts like implicate order and subject-dependent reality (and now maybe formative causation). These developments have not yet penetrated to the leading journals. One can only hope that editors will soon cease to obstruct this avenue of progress. . . .'

18 Jane Duran, 'Philosophical Difficulties with Paranormal Knowledge Claims', *Philosophy of Science and the Occult*, ed Patrick Grim, State University of New York Press, Albany, 1982, pp 196-206, esp 196. Paul Kurtz says that parapsychology's findings 'contradict the general conceptual framework of scientific knowledge' (*A Skeptic's Handbook of Parapsychology*, ed Paul Kurtz, Prometheus, Buffalo, NY, 1985 p 504). James Alcott, another critic, says that its constructs involve 'drastic violations of the currently accepted laws of nature' (ibid, p 540). On this ground they insist that the evidence for parapsychological interactions would have to be more repeatable and undeniable than the evidence demanded by some other sciences (pp 510, 540).

19 Duran, 'Philosophical Difficulties', p 196; these limiting principles are taken from 'The Relevance of Physical Research to Philosophy', CD Broad, *Religion, Philosophy and Psychical Research*, Humanities Press, New York, 1969, pp 7-26. Paul Kurtz, in referring to these principles, expresses the conventional, empiricist view that they 'have been built up from a mass of observations' (*A Skeptic's Handbook*, ed Kurtz, p 504.) But we have learned that the denial of influence at a distance was based instead on *a priori*, originally theological, considerations. See Brian Easlea's book in note 22.

20 Duran, 'Philosophical Difficulties', p 202.

21 Broad, 'Relevence of Physical Research', p 9, cited by Duran, 'Philosophical Difficulties', p 197.

22 Mary Hesse points out that the rejection of action-at-a-distance in favour of action-by-contact explanations was based on the replacement of all organismic and psychological explanations by mechanical ones (*Forces and Fields: The Concept of Action at a Distance in the History of Physics*, Adams & Co, Littlefield, 1965, pp 98, 291). Richard Westfall makes clear how central was the change:

> the mechanical philosophy also banished . . . attractions of any kind. No scorn was too great to heap upon such a notion. From one end of the century to another, the idea of attractions, the action of one

body upon another with which it is not in contact, was anathema. . . . An attraction was an occult virtue, and 'occult virtue' was the mechanical philosophy's term of opprobrium.

Westfall reports that Christiaan Huygens wrote that he did not care for whether Newton was a Cartesian 'as long as he doesn't serve us up conjectures such as attractions' ('The Influence of Alchemy on Newton', *Science, Pseudo-Science and Society*, ed Marsha P Hanen, Margaret J Osler and Robert G Weynant, Wilfrid Laurier University Press, Waterloo, Ontario, 1989, pp 145-70, esp 147, 150). Brian Easlea has provided convincing evidence that the desire to rule out the possibility of attraction at a distance was, in fact, the main motivation behind the mechanical philosophy and its denial of all hidden qualities within matter; see his *Witch Hunting, Magic and the New Philosophy: An Introduction to the Debates of the Scientific Revolution 1450-1750*, Humanities Press, Atlantic Highlands, NJ, 1980, esp pp 93-95, 108-15, 121, 132, 135, where he discusses the theological and sociological motives behind the rejection of action-at-a-distance. Another supporter of the view that the mechanistic worldview was adopted primarily for extra-scientific reasons is Jerome Ravetz, who says:

> The 'scientific revolution' itself becomes comprehensible if we see it as a campaign for a reform of ideas *about* science, introduced quite suddenly, injected into a continuous process of technical progress *within* science . . . [S]cientific revolution was primarily and essentially about metaphysics; and the various technical studies were largely conceived and received as corroborating statements of a challenging world-view. This consisted essentially of two Great Denials: the restriction of ordinary faculties such as sympathy and intelligence to humans and to a remote Deity; and the relegation of extra-ordinary faculties to the realms of the nonexistent or insignificant. . . . The great historical myth of this philosophy is that it was the necessary and sufficient cause of the great scientific progress of the seventeeth century. This was a central point in its propaganda, for itself at the time and in histories ever since. Yet the results of historical enquiry, some old and some new, contradict this claim. ('The Varieties of Scientific Experience', *The Sciences and Theology in the Twentieth Century*, ed Arthur Peacocke, Notre Dame University Press, Ind, 1981, pp 197-206, at 200-01).

23 Bohm, 'The Implicate Order', pp 87-93; Stapp, 'Whiteheadian Approach to Quantum Theory'; Sheldrake, *A New Science of Life*, pp 93-96.

24 Bohm, 'Wholeness and the Implicate Order', pp 129, 186; Renée Weber, 'Conversations between Rupert Sheldrake, Renée Weber, David Bohm', *ReVISION* 5/2, Fall 1982, esp pp 39, 44 (reprinted in *Dialogues with Scientists and Sages: The Search for Unity*, ed Renée Weber, Routledge & Kegan Paul, London, 1986); Sheldrake, *A New Science of Life*, pp 95-96; Henry P Stapp, 'Bell's Theorem and the Foundations of Quantum Physics', *American Journal of Physics* 53, 1985, pp 306-17; Alfred North Whitehead, *Process and Reality*, corrected edition, ed David Ray Griffin and Donald W Sherburne, Free Press, New York, 1978, p 308, and *Adventures of Ideas*, Free Press, New York, 1978, p 248. For a comparison of Sheldrake and Whitehead on this point, see my review of Sheldrake's book in *Process Studies* 12/1, Spring 1982, pp 38-40.

25 Floyd W Matson, *The Broken Image: Man, Science and Society*, 1964; Doubleday & Co, Garden City, NY, 1966, p vi. In the light of Stephen Toulmin's crediting Frederick Ferré with having coined the term 'postmodern science' (*The Return to Cosmology: Postmodern Science and the Theology of Nature*, University of California Press, Berkeley, 1982, p 210), surely with reference to Ferré's 1976 book, *Shaping the Future: Resources for the Postmodern World*, it is of pedantic historical interest to note that Matson had, unbeknownst to Ferré and Toulmin, spoken of postmodern science in 1964.

26 The term *dualism* is perhaps the most ambiguous, multivalent term in our language. It can refer, among other things, to a distinction between any of the following: (1) a natural and a supernatural world; (2) an actual and an ideal world; (3) time and eternity; (4) good and evil; (5) good and evil cosmic agents; (6) sentient and insentient things; (7) living and nonliving things; or (8) mind and body. Discussions about dualism often become unnecessarily charged because dualism in one sense is assumed to entail dualism in one or more of the other senses when it does not. In this discussion, dualism is always used, unless stated otherwise, to mean either (7) or (8) *in conjunction with* (6). The term *dualism* should not be used for (8) alone, ie, for the assertion that mind and body (or brain) are numerically distinct, rather than numerically identical, because this doctrine does not necessarily imply (6), ie, the assertion that the mind is sentient while the brain and its components are insentient. Because the term *dualism* in this context inevitably connotes *Cartesian* dualism, with its problem of interaction, the term should not be used unless meaning (6) is also involved.

27 Thomas Reid, *Essays on the Intellectual Powers of Man*, MIT Press, Cambridge, 1969, pp 96-97, 99, 110, 118, 123, 220, 240, 318.

28 Whitehead, *Science and the Modern World*, Free Press, New York, 1967, p 156; *Process and Reality*, p 343.

29 Karl R Popper, *Of Clouds and Clocks*, Washington University Press, St Louis, 1966, p 15; emphasis his.

30 Karl R Popper and John C Eccles, *The Self and its Brain: An Argument for Interaction*, Springer-Verlag, Heidelberg, 1977, pp 16, 37, 105.

31 JCC Smart, 'Sensations and Brain Processes', *The Mind-Brain Identity Theory*, ed CV Borst, Macmillan, London, 1979, pp 52-66, esp 53-54.

32 JCC Smart, 'Materialism', ibid, pp 159-70, esp 165, 168-69.

33 Popper and Eccles, *The Self and its Brain*, pp 29-30.

34 Ibid, p 10.

35 Smart, 'Sensations and Brain Processes', pp 63, 56.

36 DM Armstrong, 'The Nature of Mind', *Mind-Brain Identity Theory*, ed Borst, pp 67-79, esp 75.

37 As Thomas Nagel says, 'much obscurity has been shed on the [mind-body] problem by faulty analogies between the mental-physical relation and relations between the physical and other objective aspects of reality' (*Mortal Questions*, Cambridge University Press, 1979, p 202). He argues that it is unintelligible to speak of the emergence of experience, which is something for itself, out of things that are purely physical: 'One cannot derive a *pour soi* from an *en soi*. . . . This gap is logically unbridgeable. If a bodiless god wanted to create a conscious being, he could not expect to do it by combining together in organic form a lot of particles with none but physical properties' (p 189; see also pp 166, 172, 182, 188).

38 Herbert Feigl, 'Mind-Body, *Not* a Pseudoproblem', *Dimensions of Mind*, ed Sydney Hook, New York University Press, NY, 1960, pp 24-36, esp 32, 33.

39 Richard Rorty, 'Mind-Body Identity, Privacy and Categories', *Review of Metaphysics* 19, 1965, pp 25-54; *Philosophy and the Mirror of Nature*, Princeton University Press, Princeton, NJ, 1979, pp 70-127. Rorty claims in his later 'pragmatic' position no longer to espouse eliminative materialism, but it seems still to be presupposed.

40 DE Wooldridge, in *The Machinery of the Brain*, McGrawHill, New York, 1963, p 240 says:

No useful purpose has yet been established for the sense of awareness that illumines a small fraction of the mental activities of a few species of higher animals. It is not clear that the behaviour of any individual or the course of world history would have been affected in any way if awareness were nonexistent p 240.

41 See Charles Hartshorne, 'The Compound Individual', *Philosophical Essays for Alfred North Whitehead*, ed Otis H Lee, Longmans Green, New York, 1936, pp 193-220.

42 Of course, to understand a computer one must take into account final causation in the sense of the purpose for which it was made. But throughout this discussion the subject is internal, immanent final causation, not external, imposed final causation .

43 Sandra Harding supports this change, pointing out that physics, among other restrictions, 'looks at either simple systems or simple aspects of complex systems' so that it need not deal with the difficult question of intentional causality (*The Science Question in Feminism*, Cornell University Press, Ithaca, New York, 1986, pp 44, 46).

44 For a development of the ideas in these two sentences, see the writings of psychiatrist Jule Eisenbud, whom philosopher Stephen Braude has called 'parapsychology's premier living theoretician'. Many of Eisenbud's essays have been collected in *Parapsychology and the Unconscious*, North Atlantic Books, Berkeley, Calif, 1983, the 'Preface' of which contains the accolade by Braude (p 7). For the various ideas, see pp 21, 22, 40, 72, 125, 167, 173, 183. On the resultant unlikelihood of obtaining repeatable experiments in the ordinary sense, see pp 156-61. These points are also supported in Braude's own *The Limits of Influence: Psychokinesis and the Philosophy of Science*, Routledge & Kegan Paul, London, 1986, esp pp 7-10, 23, 70, 278.

45 Feyerabend's reputation as an extremist is due in large part to his advocacy of an 'anarchistic' theory of knowledge; but he clearly says that he intends his anarchism only as a medicine, not as an epistemology and philosophy of science (*Science in a Free Society*, NLB, London, 1978, p 127). What he has consistently opposed is the notion that the (modern) scientific method, as the successor to the One True Religion, gives us 'the one true method' (*Against Method: Outline of An Anarchist Theory of Knowledge*, Verso, London, 1975, pp 216-18).

46 My discussion in this and the following paragraph is dependent upon Grim, ed *Philosophy of Science and the Occult*, pp 314-15; Wilber, *Quantum Questions*, pp 13-14; and Nicholas Rescher, 'The Unpredictability of Future Science', *Physics, Philosophy and Psychoanalysis: Essays in Honor of Adolf Grünbaum*, ed Robert S Cohen and Larry Lauden, D Reidel, Dordrecht, 1983, pp 153-68.

47 It is often said that power and knowledge (or truth) have been the twin aims of modern science (eg Evelyn Fox Keller, *Reflections on Gender and Science*, Yale University Press, New Haven, 1985, p 71). Of these twin aims, traditional descriptions spoke mainly of the quest for truth, while recent appraisals, whether condem-

natory or positivistic, have seen the drive for power as the central aim. My position is that, while much of modern science has sought those truths that would provide power over nature (and sometimes thereby over other humans), it is not the quest for power that makes modern science 'science' but the quest for truth (in the way specified in the second criterion), regardless of how limited these truths are and of the ulterior purposes for which they are sought.

48 Rescher ('The Unpredictability of Future Science', p 165) says: 'Domain limitations purport to put entire sectors of fact wholly outside the effective range of scientific explanation, maintaining that an entire range of phenomena in nature defies scientific rationalisation.' See also Wilber, *Quantum Questions*, p 14.

49 This is one topic on which I disagree with Rupert Sheldrake, who wishes to exclude the topic of the origin of laws from science, assigning it instead to theology or metaphysics; see the final chapter of his *A New Science of Life*.

50 Fox Keller, *Reflections on Gender and Science*, pp 131-36.

51 Grim, *Philosophy of Science and the Occult*, p 315.

52 Jule Eisenbud (*Psi and Psychoanalysis*, Grune & Stratton, New York, 1970, p 96) says that one particular kind of repeatability has given parts of physics such reliability that 'few people (strangely) question its right to provide a model of "reality"'. But, as he says, this kind of repeatability is only one of many considerations in authentication, not relevant for many questions in geology, meteorology, astronomy, biology, and much of psychology. Both Kurtz and Alcott (see notes 18 and 19 above) have claimed that parapsychological experiments, to be acceptable, would have to exemplify 'strong' repeatability, meaning that, in Alcott's words, 'any competent researcher following the prescribed procedure can obtain the reported effect' p 540). But if the kind of phenomenon with which parapsychology is concerned is held to be an inherently elusive, not consciously controllable one, as Eisenbud and Stephen Braude hold (see note 44 above), this requirement for strong replicability amounts to a 'Catch-22': parapsychologists could only prove that it exists by proving that it does not!

53 Nicholas Rescher ('The Unpredictability of Future Science', p 163) says: 'The contention that this or that explanatory resource is inherently unscientific should always be met with instant scorn. For the unscientific can only lie on the side of process and not that of product – on the side of *modes* of explanation and not its *mechanism*; of arguments rather than phenomena.'

54 Rescher (ibid, p 166) says that 'there is no reason why, in human affairs any more than in quantum theory, the boundaries of science should be so drawn as to exclude the unpredictable'. Long ago, William James said: 'The spirit and principles of science are mere affairs of method; there is nothing in them that need hinder science from dealing successfully with a world in which personal forces are the starting-point of new effects' (*William James on Psychical Research*, ed Gardner Murphy and Robert Ballou, Viking, New York, 1960, p 47).

55 Rescher (ibid, p 169) says:

> Not only can we never claim with confidence that the science of tomorrow will not resolve the issues that the science of today sees as intractable, but one can never be sure that the science of tomorrow will not endorse what the science of today rejects. This is why it is infinitely risky to speak of this or that explanatory resource (action at a distance, stochastic processes, mesmerism, etc) as inherently unscientific. Even if X lies outside the range of science as we nowadays construe it, it by no means follows that X lies outside science as such.

56 If there are such common beliefs, their recognition by members of diverse linguistic communities is, while difficult, not impossible. Even though a given worldview will predispose its adherents to recognise some such beliefs while ignoring, distorting, or even verbally denying other such beliefs that are noticed by adherents of other worldviews, it is possible, when the search for truth through public demonstration is sincere, to recognise such beliefs through conversation and self-observation.

57 In spite of my agreement, expressed in prior notes, with Nicholas Rescher's formal ideas, I cannot accept his substantive idea that actualities could have emerged out of a realm of mere possibility. I do not see how we can abandon the notion that agency requires actuality, and hence the 'hoary dogma', as Rescher calls it, that *ex nihilo nihilfit*. I have reviewed Rescher's *The Riddle of Existence: An Essay in Idealistic Metaphysics*, University of America Press, Lanham, Md, 1985, in *Canadian Philosophical Reviews*, December 1986, pp 531-32.

58 Sandra Harding points out that the one-sided attempts to explain science either from a purely externalist or a purely internalist approach lead to paradox. The externalist approach, which understands the development of science in terms of external causes alone, leads to a self-refuting relativism. 'Why should changes in economic, technological, and political arrangements make the new ideas reflecting these arrangements bet-

ter ideas? Why shouldn't we regard the externalist programme itself as simply an epiphenomenon of nine-teenth- and twentieth-century social relations destined to be replaced as history moves along?' (*Science Question in Feminism*, p 215). The internalist or intentionalist approach praises natural science for showing that all natural and social phenomena are to be explained in externalistic terms, then supports the truth of this idea by 'defending an intentionalist approach to explaining the development of science alone' (p 212). What we need is an approach that recognises the two-way causal influences between ideas and social relations, and which thereby allow us both to understand how 'social arrangements shape human consciousness' and 'to retain the internalist assumption that not all beliefs are equally good' (pp 209, 231, 214).

59 I have dealt with these issues in 'Introduction: Time and the Fallacy of Misplaced Concreteness', *Physics and the Ultimate Significance of Time*; there is a brief discussion of apparent precognition on pp 30-31. See also Eisenbud, *Parapsychology and the Unconscious*, p 45. Although Stephen Braude has not changed his earlier opinion that arguments against the very intelligibility of backward causation are unconvincing, perhaps be-cause he has not developed a general theory of causation (*Limits of Influence*, p 261), he has concluded that the idea is very problematic, and that ostensible precognition can be explained without resort to this idea (pp 261-77). I have dealt much more extensively with this issue in 'Parapsychology and Philosophy: A Whiteheadian Postmodern Perspective', forthcoming in the *Journal of the American Society for Psychical Research*.

60 Frederick Suppe has pointed out that most discussions of the idea of knowledge as 'justified true belief' have assumed that 'knowing that X is true' entails 'knowing that one knows that X is true', ie having adequate evidence to defend the claim to know that it is true (*The Structure of Scientific Theories*, pp 717-28). This unjustified requirement, which leads to a vicious infinite regress, lies behind Hume's skeptical attacks on the possibility of knowledge and most recent rejections, by Kuhn, Feyerabend, and others, of the relevance of the corre-spondence notion of truth to scientific beliefs (pp 718, 719, 723). Suppe argues rightly for 'a separation of the role of evidence in the rational evaluation and defense of knowledge claims from the role evidence plays in obtaining knowledge' (p 725). With that separation, we can maintain the traditional definitions of knowledge as justified true belief and of truth as correspondence of belief to reality. None of this entails, I would insist perhaps more strongly than Suppe, that the modern scientific worldview is true, or that any of the current scientific theories gives us anything approaching the whole truth about their referents. Indeed, it is only if we hold to these traditional definitions of truth and knowledge that we have a rational standard in terms of which to criticise the dominant contemporary knowledge-claims.

61 For the way in which panexperiential philosophy can make sense of a notion of correspondence, see my discussion in *Varieties of Postmodern Theology*, David Ray Griffin, William A Beardslee and Joe Holland, State University of New York Press, Albany, 1989, pp 133-41.

62 These principles, especially the latter four, have all, in fact, been denied by modern science-related thought. However, their explicit denial has been accompanied by implicit affirmation, producing massive incoher-ence. The reason for their explicit denial is *not* that they conflict with the implications of any other equally universal principles but that they conflict with the implications of contingent beliefs of modernity, which have been discussed above.

From *The Reenchantment of Science, Postmodern Proposals*, edited by David Ray Griffin, State University of New York Press, Albany, 1988.

David Ray Griffin
CREATIVITY AND POSTMODERN RELIGION

In the transition to the postmodern view, according to which all things are embodiments of creativity, Henri Bergson is of overwhelming importance. He spoke of evolution as 'creative', to mean bringing forth something new, something that was not already implicit in the past. At first he was dualistic, limiting creativity to minds. But he later overcame this dualism, viewing even inanimate matter as creative. Creativity was not in a being transcendent to nature, but was the very stuff of nature itself.[1]

One thinker influenced by Bergson was Nicolas Berdyaev, who put creativity at the heart of his thought and used it to reinterpret Christian theology. Berdyaev completely rejected the attribution of omnipotence to God and the notion of creation out of nothing. Rather, he saw 'uncaused freedom'[2] as the fundamental reality out of which the world is formed. God should not be understood in terms of 'power and might'. Our relation to God should not be understood in terms of servile categories such as 'dependence' (Schleiermacher) or 'obedience' (Barth).[3] That kind of theology is guilty of sociomorphism, transferring to God categories from a particular form of human society. 'What God expects from man is not servile submission, not obedience, not the fear of condemnation, but free creative acts. . . . Sin does not lie in disobedience to the commandments and prohibitions of God, but in slavery, in the loss of freedom. . . .' God finds expression in the world in freedom, not in domination. God is not a diminution of human freedom and activity but their very condition.[4] The Christian ethic should be an 'ethic of creativeness'.

Berdyaev's theology of creativity is rich, exciting, and suggestive. But it is limited. He limits creativity or uncaused freedom to human existence, not seeing it as fundamental to all levels of creation. Perhaps his commitment to a Kantian dualism prevented the generalisation of creativity to nature. He gives no explanation of the relation between creativity and causal determination, simply stating that 'events which take place in the existential sphere lie outside any causal sequence.' And, after rejecting traditional notions of God's all-controlling providence, he provides no positive way to understand the God-world relation: 'The inconsistency and the paradoxical nature of the relation between the divine and the human is resolved only in the divine mystery about which no human words can express anything at all.'[5]

Berdyaev's position also makes the goodness of God problematic. The problem arises because he, as Bergson at least appeared to do in his early writings, equated God with creativity. His position is thereby similar, as he himself pointed out,[6] to the Advaita Vedantist form of Hinduism, according to which our deepest self, or Atman, is identical with Brahman, the divine reality. If this is taken to mean that our own power of self-determination – our freedom or creativity – is simply divine, a serious problem results from the fact that we often exercise our creativity in evil ways. If the word *God* means the freedom or creativity exercised in the world, we cannot speak of God as unambiguously good, thereby worthy of worship without qualification. Creativity as such is, to be sure, the source of all good – of all life, all truth, all beauty, all moral goodness. But it is also the source of all evil – of all killing, all lies, all ugliness, all depravity. Creativity is both creator and destroyer; it is 'beyond good and evil'. Some forms of Hinduism and some other traditions have indeed used this language for the divine reality. But the religions arising out of the biblical tradition have usually insisted that the divine reality is perfectly good. The straightforward identification of God with creativity made it difficult for Berdyaev to articulate that intuition.

Another thinker heavily influenced by Bergson was Alfred North Whitehead. His position, along with the closely related position of Charles Hartshorne, does not restrict creativity to human life but makes it, as did Bergson, the central category for interpreting reality as a whole. Unlike Berdyaev, and perhaps the early Bergson, however, Whitehead and Hartshorne do not simply equate God with creativity but regard creativity as the ultimate reality which is embodied by both God and all worldly individuals. For Whitehead, creativity is the ultimate reality of which all things are instances. This means that the basic things or entities are events, spatiotemporal processes of becoming. Whitehead's view not only generalised the Einsteinian notion of the convertibility of matter and energy, but also employed another basic Einsteinian notion, which is that space and time are inseparable. One cannot speak of space and time as separate, but only of space-time, or time-space.[7] Whitehead's way of explaining this idea is that the things comprising the world are not essentially nontemporal things that just happen to be in time. They are essentially spatio-temporal events. They take – or make – time, as well as space, to occur. There is no 'nature at an instant' – taking *instant* in the technical sense as having no duration or temporal extension. There are also no actualities devoid of spatial extension. All actualities are temporal-spatial events. Whitehead therefore says that all actual entities are 'actual occasions'. No actual things simply endure passively. Each real thing is a spatio-temporal happening.

These actual occasions or events can be extremely brief, with hundreds, thousands, millions, or even billions within a second. Things that endure, such as electrons, atoms, molecules, cells, and minds, are each comprised of a series of brief events.

Moments in the life-history of an electron, a cell, and a human being obviously differ immensely in duration and in terms of the forms they embody. But they all have one thing in common: each is an instance of creativity. Creativity is in this sense the ultimate reality, that which all actualities embody. All actual entities are thereby creative events.

The creativity of an event has two sides. On one side, the event creates itself out of its predecessors. This self-creative side has two moments. The first moment is the event as receptive, taking in influences from the past and repeating them. This is the event's *physical pole*. The second moment of the event's self-creative activity is its response to possibilities. The event thereby creates itself out of potentiality as well as actuality. This moment of the event is called its *mental pole*, because it responds to ideality, not to physicality. Because of this response to ideal possibilities, the event is not totally determined by its past, although it is heavily conditioned by it.

The other side of the event's creativity is its creative influence upon the future. Once the event has completed its self-creative activity, it begins its career as an influence upon subsequent events. Just as it had used previous events as its own food, it now becomes food for later events. Much of an electronic event's immediate influence is received by the next event in that enduring society we call the electron. Much of my influence in this moment is taken up by the next moment of my experience, as I embody much the same character as did the previous moment and carry out its intentions. But obviously not all of the influence is limited to the next event in the enduring society.

Much of the influence from my present experience is exerted upon the cells in my body in the next millisecond. The electron influences the other electrons in its atom, the events comprising the nucleons, the atom as a whole, neighbouring atoms, and more remote ones (for example, by gravitational attraction).

I have already implied that various levels of creative events exist. All the creativity in the universe is *not* embodied in subatomic particles, with the creativity of the more complex things being reducible to the creativity of their constituents. The world instead contains various types of *compound individuals*, to use Hartshorne's term for organisms that have both complexity and individuality. The creativity of the atom is not simply the creativity of its subatomic parts added together. The atom as a whole has its own creativity. It responds to its environment – neighbouring atomic events, the events of its own constituents, and the events of any larger society of which it is a part, such as a living cell; and it, in turn, influences subsequent events which find it in their environments. Likewise, the molecule as a whole can be thought to have its own level of creative activity, as can the cell as a whole. And the psyche of the multi-celled animal, especially one with a central nervous system, has its own level of creativity with which to create itself and then to influence others.

Whitehead and Hartshorne have generalised the Einsteinian notion of energy. The physicist's energy is an abstraction from the full-fledged creativity which is the ultimate reality of the universe, of which all individual things are instances. Saying that the reality pointed to by this larger notion is the 'what' of all things implies that individuals at all levels are equally real. Against the reductionism of modern thought, this view says that living cells are not less real than their atoms and that souls are not less real than the brain cells with which they are associated.

Even to describe the ultimate reality as creativity is an abstraction. Creativity is always *creative experience;* that is, besides exercising creativity to some degree, every individual event enjoys experience of some sort. With this point brought out explicitly, all the elements needed for a solution of modernity's mind-body problem are provided. Because the soul or mind is not different in kind from the cells comprising the brain, interaction between mind and body is not unintelligible, as it was for modern dualism. Because dualism is overcome not by denying the reality of the mind or soul but by attributing creativity and experience to cells and their constituents, the freedom or creativity of the person is not denied, as it was by modern materialism.

Creative Experience and the God-World Relation

The idea that creativity is the ultimate reality also forms the basis for postmodern solutions to the problems that resulted in early modernity because of its portrayal of the God-world relation, and those that resulted in late modernity from its complete denial of a divine reality. These solutions all follow from a new understanding of the relation between creativity and divinity.

The idea that creativity is the ultimate reality in everything, combined with a positive view of the relation between creativity and the divine, could lead to their complete identification. The divine reality would therefore be not a distinct being but that creative energy surging through all things. As we saw in relation to Berdyaev, this view makes it impossible to insist that the divine reality is perfectly good, the source of good but not evil. Whitehead, while giving a highly positive evaluation of creativity, provides a way to hold to this insistence.

Whitehead at first followed the early Bergson's apparent position in the equation of creativity (then called *substantial activity*) and the divine. But he soon distinguished between creativity and God, defining the latter as the principle of limitation and of rightness, which divides good from evil.[8] At this point, God was not an instance of creativity, but only an abstract principle qualifying it. Before long, however, Whitehead portrayed God as *embodying* creativity.[9] God not only exerts a creative influence on all other actual entities (God's 'primordial nature'); God also exemplifies the receptive creativity characteristic of all other actual entities (God's 'consequent nature'). God is said to be not the exception to the metaphysical principles applying to other actual entities, but their 'chief exemplification'.[10] Creativity is not God, but creativity is the ultimate reality, which God and the most trivial puff of existence in far-off space both exemplify.

John Cobb has suggested that we should think in terms of two ultimates.[11] The *ultimate reality*, which is called creativity by Whitehead, is similar to that which is called *Being* by Heidegger, *Emptiness* by Buddhists, and *Nirguna Brahman* by Vedantists. God, who is the source of all physical, aesthetic, and ethical principles, is the *ultimate actuality*. Whitehead differs from Advaita Vedantists and most Buddhists by not making this source of forms or principles subordinate to the ultimate reality. The ultimate reality and the ultimate actuality are equally primordial. God does not create creativity, but neither does creativity generate God. Each equally presupposes the other. Creativity that is uninfluenced by God's persuasion towards ordered beauty therefore never occurs. Nor could God exist alone as the only embodiment of creativity, the sole possessor of power.

This last point, which is crucial for the solution to the problem of evil, requires explanation. Given the notion of the ultimacy of creativity, a multiplicity of creative individuals must always exist. Why? Because it belongs to the very meaning of creativity that 'the many become one, and are increased by one'.[12] To be actual is to be an instance of creativity, which is to create oneself out of the many actualities which are given, and then to be added to that many as a creative influence out of which the next acts of creative synthesis will arise. To be a unity, an individual, is to be a creative synthesis out of a multiplicity. It would therefore be impossible by definition to be a one without a multiplicity, a one alone with itself.

The essential point is that creativity does not belong to God any more than it does to the world. As Hartshorne puts it, creativity must be embodied in both divine and nondivine instances of it.[13] That the finite embodiments exist is as essential as that the all-inclusive embodiment exists.

Given this notion of what it means to be an individual, the notion of creation *ex nihilo* is self-contradictory, if it means that once upon a time (or before time, whatever that might mean) God existed all alone, without any other actualities. Our world was created, to be sure. It is contingent. It arose historically. But it arose, according to this view, out of chaos, or, to use Berdyaev's term, out of *relative* nothingness, not out of absolute nothingness. It arose as the gradual development of order among actual occasions. Perhaps at one time all actual occasions occurred randomly, without even being ordered into very primitive enduring objects such as protons, electrons, or quarks. So-called empty space is perhaps comprised of such random events. The rise of quarks, protons, atoms, molecules, macromolecules, cells, and so on was the gradual rise of increasingly complex forms of order.

Because each actual occasion is affected by the creative influence of all previous occasions and also has its own inherent power of self-creation, God can never be the total cause of any event. God is a creative influence on all events, but never the sole creator of any, because each is partially created by its past world and by itself. God is uniquely the creator of our world, in that God is the one embodiment of creativity who is both everlasting and omnipresent. As such, God is the only enduring being who has influenced every event in the world directly. It is through the steady divine persuasion that order has been coaxed out of chaos and that the higher forms of existence, which make possible the higher forms of value, have come into being. But God is not and could not have been totally responsible for the details of the world.

The creative power of the creatures, their freedom in relation to God, is not a contingent matter. It is not that God could have created a world of actualities devoid of creativity but chose instead to make a world with self-creative creatures in it. Creativity does not belong essentially to God and only voluntarily, by gift, to the creatures. The embodiment of creativity in a plurality of individuals is the ultimate metaphysical truth (according to this hypothesis): any actual world would necessarily be composed of events with the twofold power of self-creation and creative influence on others. God's stimulation of the world to bring forth higher forms of creatures with greater embodiments of creativity, however, *can* be considered a voluntary matter. In *this* sense the creation of our world is due to divine volition. Our *high degree* of freedom is a gift of God. But that the worldly creatures have some degree of freedom is not due to divine choice.

Nor was it due to divine choice that higher creatures, with capacities for the higher forms of value experience, also have more power to create themselves and to affect other creatures. A world with more valuable creatures is therefore *necessarily* a more dangerous world, both because higher creatures can more radically deviate from the divine persuasion for them and because this deviation can create more havoc than the deviations of lesser creatures. A theology of universal creativity can in this way portray God as perfectly good while being consistent with the fact not only that the world has some evil in it but that it has *horrific* evils due to the presence of human beings.[14]

From the point of view of a theology of universal creativity, the existence of chaos and evil is no surprise. They are to be expected, given a multiplicity of centres of creative power. The surprise is the existence of order and goodness. They beg for explanation in terms of an all-inclusive creative influence. Whereas starting with the concentration of all creativity in one divine being finally led to the denial of God, starting with many centres of creativity leads to the affirmation of God.

The postmodern God who is thereby affirmed is, of course, not the God that late modernity denied. With this new idea of God, we can explain the order reflected throughout nature, and the teleological order reflected in the directionality of the evolutionary process, without having our hypothesis contradicted by the vast disorder of the world. The compatibility between evolution and this idea of God is discussed elsewhere.[15]

Finally, this postmodern position allows for an idea of 'inspiration' that overcomes the modern dichotomy between infallible inspiration and a complete denial of divine inspiration. Had the idea that all beings embody inherent creativity been presupposed, biblical criticism would not have played the negative, shocking role it has played in modern religion. The Bible would have been approached, like other books, with the expectation that the authors would express their own individualities, their own limited ideas, and their sin (for example, by projecting their desire for vengeance onto God), and that one author would often contradict another. With all of this expected, attention might have been focused on the amazing extent to which some of these writers, in some passages, transcend what we would normally expect from 'all-too-human' writers. Without the preconception of infallibility, we might have marvelled more at the signs of genuine inspiration. We would have seen that this inspiration differs only in degree, not in kind, from the inspiration toward truth, beauty, and goodness that characterises all human experience to some degree. Given this realistic account of divine inspiration, we would not have gone to the opposite extreme of denying divine inspiration altogether, which made late modernity unable to explain its own commitment to truth and the limited but real unanimity found in all cultures on aesthetic and moral values. By taking the universality of both creativity and divine inspiration seriously, we can be adequate to both the diversity and the commonality found in ideas of truth, beauty, and goodness.

Having shown how this postmodern theism can overcome the various conflicts between theory and fact that modernity created for itself by denying creativity to nature, I turn now to the topic of spirituality.

Whiteheadian Postmodern Spirituality

Spiritual discipline will again become a pervasive feature of life, not just the practice of a minority dissenting from the prevailing culture, only if the antispiritual worldview of modernity is replaced by another dominant outlook.[16] A new worldview does seem to be emerging in our time. This worldview can be called *postmodern*, in that it preserves many modern beliefs, values, and practices but places them in a larger framework, in which many premodern truths and values can be recovered. Closely connected with this emergence is the rise of a renewed interest in spiritual discipline. While this movement is very diverse, I believe that the best framework for articulating the new worldview and supporting the related postmodern spirituality is that of Alfred North Whitehead, although this position needs supplementation and modification from other sources.

I will here discuss this worldview in terms of its theological support for spiritual discipline, with particular attention to the issues central to Augustinian theology and the modern worldview.

Whitehead agrees with Augustine in several ways. First, just as Augustine defended cosmological freedom[17] against the Manicheans, Whitehead defends it against modern thought. Augustine's concern was to portray the human soul not as an impotent, passive thing, hedged in by and on the defensive against the material world, but as a reality with power to shape itself and its environment. Whitehead rejects the claim of the modern worldview according to which only the most elementary physical entities or forces, such as electrons and atoms, have causal influence. He portrays instead a hierarchy of creative cosmological powers, with living cells above molecules, and psyches above cells. There is now increasing evidence for this view. The facts of psychosomatic studies and psychical research can be added to our own common experience to support the notion that the human soul, far from being an impotent spectator, is the most powerful of the earthly actors in the cosmic drama.

Whitehead provides a new basis for Augustine's concerns in a second way. Against the Pelagians, who affirmed God's grace only in the establishment of the basic conditions of human life, Augustine insisted that divine grace was present and effective in every moment. Modern thought, insofar as it has retained a transcendent deity at all, has been deistic, affirming divine influence with the Pelagians only 'once upon a time'. Whiteheadian postmodern theology affirms God's gracious influence in every moment of the world process, therefore in every moment of human experience. This theology can with Augustine summarise the position of Christian faith with the cry 'Emmanuel!' – God is with us! When we come to the question of the *relation* between this divine activity and our own freedom, however, Whitehead parts company with Augustine, and precisely at the point at which Augustine's view of divine grace undermined the concern for spiritual discipline. Whitehead denies that our relation to God is unilaterally determined by God. A positive relation is instead due to our cooperating, our working together.[18]

While the idea of 'cooperation' or 'synergism' has always been anathema to Augustinians because of their denial of theological freedom, many other Christian thinkers have also been uncomfortable with it. The problem seems to arise from the fact that most theologies have portrayed divine and human power as competitive. On this model, the more efficacy God exerts in our lives, the less freedom we have; the more freedom we affirm for ourselves, the less we are influenced by God. Augustinian theology, fearing that the affirmation of genuine human freedom in relation to God would demean the sovereignty of God, denies theological freedom. In reaction, atheists usually assume that the affirmation of genuine human freedom requires the denial of divine efficacy in our lives. Doctrines called *synergistic* have usually been compromise positions within the competitive model. They limit the divine influence to make room for some human freedom. The reluctance to speak of divine-human cooperation in Western (as opposed to Eastern) Christianity, manifest even in Christian thinkers who affirm theological freedom, is due, I suspect, not only to Augustinian prohibitions but also to the belief that cooperation implies a diminution of divine efficacy.

But should the intuition of the radical otherness of God not lead us to consider a noncompetitive relation between God and the creatures, in which the *greater* efficacy of God in our lives might mean *more* rather than less freedom? This was surely Augustine's own deepest intuition: True freedom, he said, comes only through bondage to God; divine determinism does not conflict with human freedom. And yet his way of formulating this intuition did deny our freedom.

Some modern theologies have tried to overcome the competition between God and the creatures. Paul Tillich says that we must transcend the theistic God to the 'God beyond God', which is Being Itself, if the affirmation of God is not to conflict with belief in human freedom. In Tillich's theology, however, this transcendence of the competitive model is achieved at the cost of denying individuality, hence personhood, hence causal influence, hence prevenient grace, to the divine reality. God is equated with what has been called in Aristotelian language the 'material cause' of all things – the basic stuff (the 'being itself') which all beings embody. Theologians have usually recognised that this idea of the holy reality is profoundly alien to the biblical vision.

Whiteheadian theology provides a noncompetitive understanding of the divine-human relation that does not deny personhood and hence causal influence to the divine reality. Prevenient grace consists in the provision of possibilities that free us from being simply determined by the past. Accordingly, it is precisely God's causal influence that provides us with both cosmological freedom and the possibility of axiological freedom. And yet this divine causal influence works in such a way that we also have theological freedom – freedom in relation to God.

I will try to explain this difficult idea briefly. According to Whitehead, our soul is not an enduring substance that is what it is, and has the powers it has, prior to its relations with other things. That notion of the soul as an independent substance is what leads to the competitive model: we must become less of ourselves if God is to become more in us. Whitehead has suggested that we think of our soul instead as a *series of momentary experiences*. Each experience is a synthesis of its relations to other things; each experience includes, in some sense, those other things into itself, making itself out of them. Given this understanding, I am not in competition with my environment; I need not shield it out to be authentically myself. Rather, the more of my environment I can take into myself, making it my own, the richer my experience is.

If our environment, however, were limited to everything we normally call our 'environment' – our bodies, the things we experience through our physical senses, the ideas given to us thereby through books and other people – we would not be free, no matter how rich our experience might be. We would be condemned simply to take into ourselves the data that came our way according to the strength with which they forced themselves upon us. We would have no cosmological freedom. This would be the situation if our environment were limited to *actualities*.

But our environment includes something else: we find that *possibilities* as well as actualities are given. The given actualities can always be synthesised in various possible ways; possibilities must therefore also be given. This synthesis can thereby be a creative synthesis, rather than one that was determined by forces external to it. And we sometimes experience as given rather *novel* possibilities that allow us to transcend the actual past quite dramatically.

But how are possibilities given? As mere possibilities, they can hardly take the initiative to give themselves. Whiteheadian theology reformulates the medieval view that they are given by God. Our freedom is due to the fact that our environment includes God and thereby includes possibilities. God constantly calls us with these possibilities, calling us not simply to accept actuality but to respond creatively to it. God especially calls us to respond to our actual environment in terms of those possibilities through which truth, beauty, goodness, adventure, and peace will be embodied and promoted .

This divine lure to embody spiritual values is prevenient grace. It is always there, prior to every move on our part. But this grace is not wholly irresistible. We resist it to some degree in most moments of experience. Whiteheadian theology, while not being Pelagian, does agree with the protest of the Pelagians – and of countless persons through the ages – against the view that divine grace is incompatible with theological freedom. We are partly free, not only in relation to the stars above and the molecules below, but also in relation to the ubiquitous divine reality around us.

From the point of view of postmodern theology, therefore, St Paul's paradox – we are to work out our own salvation, for it is God who works in us – does not involve a contradiction. God is working in us every moment, but this does not mean that we need not work. Although it is God who offers us freedom, we decide how and to what degree to respond to this offer. And how we respond to God's grace in one moment determines the nature of the gracious invitation that can be extended to us in the next moment. To the degree that we develop a habit of responding positively to the divine initiatives, higher divine possibilities can be presented in the future. Spiritual growth is possible.

Postmodern theology, in agreeing with Augustine against Pelagius that God is directly present to us, thereby transcends modern theology insofar as the latter has been deistic. Much modern theology, for example, in speaking of how we 'encounter' God, has said that we do so only indirectly, through the neighbour. This approach, which is geared to foster an ethical as opposed to mystical form of faith, is ultimately self-defeating. If I never encounter God directly, the same must be true of my neighbour. But if my neighbour does not encounter God directly, then how do I encounter God through him or her? Presumably because he or she encountered God through someone else, but this answer leads to an infinite regress. Without a direct experience of God, which is at the heart of mysticism, the roots of the ethical side of spirituality will shrivel up. Postmodern theology provides a new basis for the Augustinian vision of a direct relation between the soul and God, but without the denial of theological freedom against which the Pelagians, and modern deists, protested.

I turn now from the issue between Augustine and the Pelagians to that between him and the Donatists.[19] While the Pelagian controversy involved the issue of God's *direct* influence on us, the Donatist controversy involved God's *indirect* influence. From the postmodern viewpoint, the denial that God is only present to us indirectly does not mean that the indirect presence of God is unimportant.

Just as the indirect presence of God presupposes God's direct presence to us, so does the direct presence of the divine depend upon its indirect presence. God, in this postmodern vision, directly presents to us the best possibilities, including the highest spiritual values, that we are capable of incorporating. What is genuinely possible for us at any moment depends upon the kind of person we have become prior to that moment. And this depends, to a great extent, upon the nature of the traditions and institutions into which we are born and spend our formative years. What beliefs and values are incarnate in those traditions and institutions, and therefore in the people in which they are embodied, such as our parents, peer group, teachers, and cultural heroes? In theological terms: To what degree do these traditions, institutions, and people embody the divine spirit, and to what degree an antispiritual spirit? The kind of persons we become is determined to a great extent by these given realities which, to the degree that they are positive, can be regarded as indirectly mediating divine grace to us.

Not everything, however, is settled by these large-scale, long-term processes over which most of us have little control. Although the culture generally determines the average kind of persons it will produce, it does not determine the heights or the depths to which any particular individual may rise or fall. And we are shaped in our formative years not only by the general features of the culture, which are widely embodied, but also by the particularities of the crucial people in our lives. A parent, a friend, a teacher, a pastor, a priest, or a rabbi may exert a decisive influence, opening up possibilities that would have otherwise remained closed. In other words, the possibilities toward which we are *directly* called by the divine reality may be decisively influenced by an *indirect* encounter with divine grace through a fellow human being, due to some unique feature of that person which reflected his or her own spiritual development.

The theological point that distinguishes the Whiteheadian from the Augustinian position on this Donatist issue is finally the same as that distinguishing the two theologies on the Pelagian issue: (divine) grace does not destroy (human) nature. In the Pelagian issue, the point was that divine power does not override our power of self-determination. In this Donatist issue, the point is that divine power does not cancel the power of others to influence us, for good or ill. Augustinian supernaturalism held that the divine power to bring about effects in us could not be limited by the decisions of other persons. Whiteheadian naturalistic theism, while holding that the divine reality is distinct from the world and can present novel possibilities which transcend the options provided to us by the world, also holds that these novel possibilities through which God calls us beyond the past must be closely related to the possibilities that have already been achieved in that past. Einstein could not have been produced in the thirteenth century, Jesus in India, nor Gautama in Israel. What the divine grace can accomplish in the present moment is largely determined by the ways in which divine grace has been effective in the events prior to that moment.

To personalise this issue: The kind of person you are, as a minister (whether professional or not) of God's grace to others, does make a difference to their relation to God. The Donatists were right insofar as they were making this point. The way God's grace can affect your neighbour is not independent of your relation to God. In fact, evidence from psychical research suggests that your soul affects others for good or ill not only through what you say and do bodily, but also directly, one soul to another. If this is true, it undermines the modern notion that our inner state is unimportant as long as our outer actions are proper. What we are will come through, in spite of our best efforts at hypocrisy. In any case, through the way we in our small way either raise or lower the general level of the culture, and through the dramatic effects we can have, for good or ill, on the lives of other individuals, our present responses to divine grace partly determine what divine grace will be able to achieve in the future.

NOTES

1 On Bergson's views, see Andrew G Bjelland, 'Evolutionary Epistemology, Durational Metaphysics, and Theoretical Physics: Capek and the Bergsonian Tradition', *Physics and the Ultimate Significance of Time: Bohm, Prigogine, and Process Philosophy*, ed David Ray Griffin, State University of New York Press, Albany, 1986, pp 51-80; PAY Gunter, 'Introduction', *Henri Bergson: A Bibliography*, Philosophy Documentation Centre, Bowling Green, Ohio, 1974; or in Peter AY Gunter, ed *Bergson and the Evolution of Physics*, University of Tennessee Press, Knoxville, 1969; Milic Capek, *Bergson and Modern Physics*, Vol 7 of Boston Studies in the Philosophy of Science, D Reidel, Dordrecht; Humanities Press, New York, 1971; and *The New Aspects of Time*, Kluwer, Dordrecht and Boston, 1991.

5 Nicolas Berdyaev, *The Destiny of Man*, Harper & Row, New York, 1960, pp 22-35; idem, *Truth and Revelation*, Collier Books, New York, 1962, pp 124.

3 Berdyaev, *Truth and Revelation*, pp 59, 65.

4 Ibid, pp 122, 114.

5 Ibid, pp 15, 56.

6 Ibid, pp 16, 17, 112, 120.

7 See Milic Capek, 'Time Space Rather than Space-Time', *New Aspects of Time*, pp 324-43

8 The difference occurs between Whitehead's Lowell Lectures in 1924 and their revision and expansion into *Science and the Modern World*, Macmillan, New York, 1925.

9 Perhaps in *Religion in the Making*, Macmillan, New York, 1926, and definitely in *Process and Reality*, which was first published in 1929.

10 Alfred North Whitehead, *Process and Reality*, corrected edition, ed David Ray Griffin and Donald W Sherbourne, Free Press, New York, 1978, pp 343.

11 John B Cobb, Jr, 'Buddhist Emptiness and the Christian God', *Journal of the American Academy of Religion* XLV/I, March 1979, pp 11-26; *Beyond Dialogue: Toward a Mutual Transformation of Christianity and Buddhism* , Fortress Press, Philadelphia, 1982, esp pp 42-43, 86-90, 110-14.

12 Whitehead, *Process and Reality*, pp 21.

13 Charles Hartshorne, *Creative Synthesis and Philosophic Method*, Open Court, La Salle, Ill, 1970; University Press of America, Lanham, Md, 1983, chap VIII.

14 For a fuller treatment, see my *God, Power, and Evil: A Process Theodicy*, 1976, University of America, Lanham, Md, 1991, and *Evil Revisited: Responses and Reconsiderations*, State University of New York Press, Albany, 1991.

15 See 'Evolution and Postmodern Theism' in my *God and Religion in the Postmodern World*, State University of New York Press, Albany, 1989.

16 The earlier sections of the essay from which this concluding section was extracted had described how spiritual discipline was supported, but only unstably, by medieval Augustinian theology and then by the early modern worldview, and how the late modern worldview has completely undermined it.

17 Earlier in the essay from which this section was extracted, three types of freedom had been distinguished. *Cosmological freedom* is the freedom of the mind or soul in relation to other things within the created cosmos, such as the stars above and the molecules within one's body. *Theological freedom* is the power of the mind or soul *vis-à-vis* God. *Axiological freedom* is the power of the soul to do what it sees to be good. Pelagians affirmed all three types of freedom; Augustine affirmed only cosmological freedom, rejecting both theological and axiological freedom.

18 Here I refer only to divine grace in the sense of liberating, transforming, sanctifying grace, which Reinhold Niebuhr called 'grace in us'. The effectiveness of grace in this sense depends upon our response. The situation is quite otherwise with forgiving grace, or 'grace over us', meaning God's unconditional forgiveness, compassion, and everlasting cherishing of us. In this sense our relation to God is determined by God alone. Many of the problems in Christian theology have resulted from speaking about grace in us in terms that are appropriate only to grace over us.

19 The Donatists said that a priest's lack of virtue affected the validity of the sacraments he administered, so that sacraments served by a wicked priest might not be efficacious for salvation. Augustine rejected this belief on the basis of divine omnipotence: nothing a human being did could prevent God's grace from being efficacious.

From *God and Religion in the Postmodern World: Essays in Postmodern Theology*, State University of New York Press, Albany, 1989.

David Bohm
POSTMODERN SCIENCE
AND A POSTMODERN WORLD

Modern Physics and the Modern World

With the coming of the modern era, human beings' view of their world and themselves underwent a fundamental change. The earlier, basically religious approach to life was replaced by a secular approach. This approach has assumed that nature could be thoroughly understood and eventually brought under control by means of the systematic development of scientific knowledge through observation, experiment, and rational thought. This idea became powerful in the seventeenth and eighteenth centuries. In fact, the great seal of the United States has as part of its motto 'the new secular order', showing the way the founders of the country were thinking. The main focus of attention was on discerning the order of the universe as it manifests itself in the laws of nature. The principle path to human happiness was to be in the discovery of these laws, in complying with them, in utilising them wherever possible for the benefit of humankind.

So great is the change in the whole context of thought thereby brought about that Huston Smith and some others have described it as the onset of the modern mind.[1] This mind is in contrast with the mind of the medieval period, in which it was generally supposed that the order of nature was beyond human comprehension and in which human happiness consisted in being aware of the revealed knowledge of God and carrying out the divine commandments. A total revolution occurred in the way people were aiming to live.

The modern mind went from one triumph to another for several centuries through science, technology, industry, and it seemed to be solidly based for all time. But in the early twentieth century, it began to have its foundations questioned. The challenge coming from physics was especially serious because it was in this science that the modern mind was thought to have its firmest foundation. In particular, relativity theory, to a certain extent, and quantum theory, to a much greater extent, led to questioning the assumption of an intuitively imaginable and knowable order in the universe. The nature of the world began to fade out into something almost indescribable. For the most part, physicists began to give up the attempt to grasp the world as an intuitively comprehensible whole; they instead restricted their work mostly to developing a mathematical formalism with rules to apply in the laboratory and eventually in technology. Of course, a great deal of unity has emerged in this work, but it is almost entirely in the mathematical formalism. It has little or no imaginative or intuitive expression (whereas Newton's ideas were quite easily understandable by any reasonably educated person).

A similar current of thought has been developing at the same time in other fields. In philosophy, the trend has been to relinquish any notion that the general nature of reality could be known through some kind of metaphysics or worldview. Existentialists like Kierkegaard and Nietzsche and others following this line have emphasised instead what is personal and peculiar to each human being. Other philosophers have emphasised language as the main point, and positivists have said that the role of science is nothing more than a systematic and rationally ordered way of organising our observational data. In art, as in literature and other fields, universal values have also generally been dropped, replaced for the most part by a focus on personal reactions or on some kind of formal structure.

Clearly, during the twentieth century the basis of the modern mind has been dissolving, even in the midst of its greatest technological triumphs. The whole foundation is dissolving while the thing is flowering, as it were. The dissolution is characterised by a general sense of loss of a common meaning of life as a whole. This loss of meaning is very serious, as meaning in the sense intended here is the basis of *value*. Without that, what is left to move people to work together towards great common aims sensed as having high value? Merely to operate at the level of solving problems in science and technology, or even of extending them into new domains, is a very narrow and limited goal which cannot really captivate the majority of the people. It cannot liberate humanity's highest and most comprehensive creative energies. Without such liberation, humanity is sinking into a vast mass of petty and transitory concerns. This leads, in the short run, to meaningless activity that is often counter-productive; in the long run, it is bringing humankind ever closer to the brink of self-destruction.

Needless to say, the development described above will have serious consequences for the individual human being, for society as a whole, and for the overall quality of relationships among human beings and between human beings and the rest of nature. Our entire world order has, in fact, been dissolving away for well over a century. This dissolution has tended further to erode all our basic values on which the stability of the world order must depend. Hence, we are now confronted with a world-wide breakdown which is self-evident not only at the political level but also in smaller groups and in the consciousness of the individual. The resort to mindless violence is growing and behind it all is the even more mindless threat of mutual annihilation, which is implicit in our current international situation and which could make everything we are doing quite pointless. I suggest that if we are to survive in a meaningful way in the face of this disintegration of the overall world order, a truly creative movement to a new kind of wholeness is needed, a movement that must ultimately give rise to a new order, in the consciousness of both the individual and society. This order will have to be as different from the modern order as was the modern from the medieval order. We cannot go back to a premodern order. A postmodern world must come into being before the modern world destroys itself so thoroughly that little can be done for a long time to come.

Even though physics is by now a rather specialised profession and even though the question of metaphysics or worldview is discussed seriously by only a few people within this profession, the worldview that physics provides is clearly still playing a crucial role as a foundation for the general mode of thinking which prevails throughout society. That is the worldview that physics provided from the sixteenth through the nineteenth centuries. It is therefore important to ask whether twentieth-century physics actually implies a universe that is beyond intuitive and imaginative comprehension, as well as whether this universe is without any deep meaning, being only something to be computed mathematically and manipulated technically. For example, one of the leading physicists at this time, Steven Weinberg, has said that the more he looks at the universe the less it seems to have any meaning, that we have to invent our own meaning if any is to exist. But, if we find that that is the wrong conclusion to be drawn from recent physics, this discovery may help open the way to the truly original and creative step that is now required of humankind. We *cannot* go on as we are; we must have something really new and creative. This step cannot be merely a reaction to the breakdown of the modern world order, but it must arise out of a fresh insight that would make it possible to move out of this morass into which we have been sinking.

The possibility of a postmodern physics, extended also to postmodern science in general, may be of crucial significance for this sort of insight. A postmodern science should not separate matter and consciousness and should therefore not separate facts, meaning, and value. Science would then be inseparable from a kind of intrinsic morality, and truth and virtue would not be kept apart as they currently are in science. This separation is part of the reason we are in our present desperate situation.

Of course, this proposal runs entirely contrary to the prevailing view of what science should be, which is a morally neutral way of manipulating nature, either for good or for evil, according to the choices of the people who apply it. I hope in this essay to indicate how a very different approach to science is possible, one that it is consistent and plausible and that fits better the actual development of modern physics than does the current approach.

Mechanistic Physics

I begin by outlining briefly the mechanistic view in physics, which was characteristic of the modern view and which reached its highest point toward the end of the nineteenth century. This view remains the basis of the approach of most physicists and other scientists today. Although the more recent physics has dissolved the mechanistic view, not very many scientists and even fewer members of the general public are aware of this fact; therefore, the mechanistic view is still the dominant view as far as effectiveness is concerned. In discussing this mechanistic view, I start by listing the principal characteristics of mechanism in physics. To clarify this view, I contrast it with that of ancient times, which was organic rather than mechanistic.

The first point about mechanism is that the world is reduced as far as possible to a set of basic elements. Typically, these elements take the form of particles. They can be called atoms or sometimes these are broken into electrons, protons, and neutrons; now the most elementary particles are called quarks, maybe there will be subquarks. Whatever they may be called, the assumption is that a basic element exists which we either have or hope to have. To these elementary particles, various continuous fields, such as electromagnetic and gravitational fields, must be added.

Second, these elements are basically external to each other; not only are they separate in space, but even more important, the fundamental nature of each is independent of that of the other. Each particle just has its own nature; it may be somewhat affected by being pushed around by the others, but that is all. The elements do not grow organically as parts of a whole, but are rather more like parts of a machine whose forms are determined externally to the structure of the machine in which they are working. By contrast, organic parts, the parts of an organism, all grow together with the organism.

Third, because the elements only interact mechanically by sort of pushing each other around, the forces of interaction do not affect their inner natures. In an organism or a society, by contrast, the very nature of each part is profoundly affected by changes in the other parts, so that the parts are internally related. If a man comes into a group, the consciousness of the whole group may change, depending on what he does. He does not push people's consciousnesses around as if they were parts of a machine. In the mechanistic view, this sort of organismic behaviour is admitted, but it is explained eventually by analysing everything into still smaller particles out of which the organs of the body are made, such as DNA molecules, ordinary molecules, atoms, and so on. This view says that eventually everything is reducible to something mechanical.

The mechanistic programme has been very successful and is still successful in certain areas, for example, in genetic engineering to control heredity by treating the molecules on which heredity depends. Advocates do admit that the programme still has much to achieve, but this mechanistic reductionistic programme assumes that there is nothing that cannot eventually be treated in this way – that if we just keep on going this way we will deal with anything that may arise.

The adherence to this programme has been so successful as to threaten our very existence as well as to produce all sorts of other dangers, but, of course, such success does not prove its truth. To a certain extent the reductionistic picture is still an article of faith, and faith in the mechanistic reductionistic programme still provides the motivation of most of the scientific enterprise, the faith that this approach can deal with everything. This is a counterpart of the religious faith that people had earlier which allowed them to do great things.

How far can this faith in mechanism be justified? People try endlessly to justify faith in their religions through theology, and much similar work has gone into justifying faith in mechanism through the philosophy of science. Of course, that the mechanism works in a very important domain is given, thereby bringing about a revolution in our life.

During the nineteenth century, the Newtonian worldview seemed so certain and complete that no serious scientist was able to doubt it. In fact, we may refer to Lord Kelvin, one of the leading theoretical physicists at the time. He expressed the opinion that physics was more or less finished, advising young people not to go into the field because further work was only a matter of minor refinements. He did point, however, to two small clouds on the horizon. One was the negative results of the Michelson-Morley experiment and the other was the difficulty in understanding black-body radiation. Now he certainly chose his clouds well: the first one led to the theory of relativity and the second to quantum theory. Those little clouds became tremendous storms; but the sky is not even as clear today as it was then – plenty of clouds are still around. The fact that relativity and quantum together overturned the Newtonian physics shows the danger of complacency about worldview. It shows that we constantly must look at our worldviews as provisional, as exploratory, and to inquire. We must have a worldview but we must not make it an absolute thing that leaves no room for inquiry and change. We must avoid dogmatism.

The Beginning of Nonmechanistic Physics: Relativity Theory

Relativity theory was the first important step away from the mechanistic vision. It introduced new concepts of space, time, and matter. Instead of having separate little particles as the constituents of matter, Einstein thought of a field spread through all space, which would have strong and weak regions. Some strong regions, which are stable, represent particles. If you watch a whirlpool or a vortex, you see the water going around and you see that the movement gets weaker the farther away it is from the centre, but it never ends. Now the vortex does not actually exist; there is only the moving water. The vortex is a pattern and a form your mind abstracts from the sensations you have of moving water. If two vortices are put together, they will affect each other; a changing pattern will exist where they modify each other, but it will still be only one pattern. You can say that two exist but this is only a convenient way of thinking. As they become even closer together, they may merge. When you have flowing water with patterns in them, none of those patterns actually has a separate existence. They are appearances or forms in the flowing movement, which the mind abstracts momentarily for the sake of convenience. The flowing pattern is the ultimate reality, at least at that level. Of course, all the nineteenth-century physicists knew this perfectly well, but they said that *really* water is made of little atoms that neither the vortices nor the water are the reality: the reality is the little atoms out of which it is all made. So the problem did not bother them.

But with the theory of relativity, Einstein gave arguments showing that thinking of these separate atoms as existent would not be consistent. His solution was to think of a field not so different from the flowing water, a field that spreads through all space and time and in which every particle is a stable form of movement, just as the vortex or whirlpool is a temporarily stable form that can be thought of as an entity which can be given a name. We speak of a whirlpool, but one does not exist. In the same way, we can speak of a particle, but one does not exist: *particle* is a name for a certain form in the field of movement. If you bring two particles together, they will gradually modify each other and eventually become one. Consequently, this approach contradicted the assumption of separate, elementary, mechanical constituents of the universe. In doing so, it brought in a view which I call *unbroken wholeness* or *flowing wholeness:* it has also been called *seamless wholeness.* The universe is one seamless, unbroken whole, and all the forms we see in it are abstracted by our way of looking and thinking, which is convenient at times, helping us with our technology, for example.

Nonetheless, relativity theory retains certain essential features of mechanism, in that the fields at different points in space were thought to exist separately and not to be internally related. The separate existence of these basic elements was emphasised by the idea that they were only locally connected, that the field at one point could affect a field only infinitesimally nearby. There was no direct effect of a field here on something far away. This notion is now being called *locality* by physicists; it is the notion of no long-distance connection. This notion is essential to the kind of mechanistic materialism developing throughout the science of the modern era, the notion of separate elements not internally related and not connected to things far away. The animistic view of earlier times was that spirits were behind everything and that these spirits were not located anywhere. Therefore, things far away would tend to be related. This view was taken to be most natural by astrologers and alchemists. But that view had been turned completely around in the modern period, and the modern view seemed so fruitful and so powerful that there arose the utter conviction of its truth.

More Fully Nonmechanistic Physics: Quantum Theory

With quantum theory, a much bigger change occurred. The main point is that all action or all motion is found in a discrete indivisible unit called a *quantum*. In the early form of the theory, electrons had to jump from one orbit to the other without passing in between. The whole idea of the continuous motion of particles, an idea at the heart of mechanism, was thereby being questioned. The ordinary visible movement, like my hand moving, was thought to comprise a vast number of quantum movements, just as, if enough fine grains of sand are in the hourglass, the flow seems continuous. All movements were said to comprise very tiny, discrete movements that do not, as it were, go from one place to another by passing through the space in between. This was a very mysterious idea.

Second, matter and energy had a dual nature; they manifest either like a wave or like a particle according to how they were treated in an experiment. An electron is ordinarily a particle, but it can also behave like waves, and light which ordinarily behaves like waves can also behave like particles; their behaviour depends on the context in which they are treated. That is, the quality of the thing depends on the context. This idea is utterly opposed to mechanism, because in mechanism the particle is just what it is no matter what the context. Of course, with complex things, this is a familiar fact; it is clear, for example, that organs depend very much on context, that the brain depends on the context, that the mind functions differently in a different context. The new suggestion of quantum theory is that this context-dependence is true of the ultimate units of nature. They hence begin to look more like something organic than like something mechanical.

A third point of quantum theory was the property of non-local connection. In certain areas, things could apparently be connected with other things any distance away without any apparent force to carry the connection. This 'non-locality' was very opposed to what Einstein wanted and very opposed to mechanism.

A fourth new feature of quantum physics, which was against mechanism, was that the whole organises the parts, even in ordinary matter. One can see it doing so in living matter, in organisms, where the state of the whole organises the various parts in the organism. But something a bit similar happens in electrons, too, in various phenomena such as super-conductivity. The whole of chemistry, in fact, depends on this idea.

In summary, according to quantum physics, ultimately no continuous motion exists; an internal relationship between the parts and the whole, among the various parts, and a context-dependence, which is very much a part of the same thing, all do exist. An indivisible connection between elements also exists which cannot be further analysed. All of that adds up to the notion that the world is one unbroken whole. Quantum physics thereby says what relativity theory said, but in a very different way.

These phenomena are evident only with highly refined modes of observation. At the ordinary order of refinement, which was available during the nineteenth century, there was no evidence that any of this was occurring. People formed the mechanistic philosophy on the basis of fairly crude observations, which demonstrates the danger of deciding a final philosophy on the basis of any particular observations; even our present observations may be too crude for something still deeper.

Now one may ask: if there has been such a disproof of mechanism why is it that most scientists are still mechanistic? The first reason is that this disproof takes place only in a very esoteric part of modern physics, called *quantum mechanical field theories*, which only a few people understand, and most of those only deal with it mathematically, being committed to the idea they could never understand it beyond that level. Second, most other physicists have only the vaguest idea of what quantum mechanical field theorists are doing, and scientists in other fields have still less knowledge about it. Science has become so specialised that people in one branch can apply another branch without really understanding what it means. In a way this is humorous, but it has some very serious consequences.

Unbroken Wholeness and Postmechanistic Physics

I propose a view that I have called *unbroken wholeness*. Relativity and quantum physics agree in suggesting unbroken wholeness, although they disagree on everything else. That is, relativity requires strict continuity, strict determinism, and strict locality, while quantum mechanics requires just the opposite – discontinuity, indeterminism, and non-locality. The two basic theories of physics have entirely contradictory concepts which have not been brought together; this is one of the problems that remains. They both agree, however, on the unbroken wholeness of the universe, although in different ways. So it has seemed to me that we could use this unbroken wholeness as our starting point for understanding the new situation.

The question is then how to understand this wholeness. The entire language of physics is now analytic. If we use this language, we are committed to analysing into parts, even though our intention may be quite the opposite. Therefore, the task is quite difficult.

What I want to suggest is that one of the most important problems is that of *order*. Worldviews have always had views of order. The ancient Greeks had the view of the earth as the centre of the universe and of various spheres in order of increasing perfection. In Newtonian physics, the order is that of the particles and the way they move. That is a mechanical order, and coordinates are used mathematically to express that order. What kind of order will enable us to consider unbroken wholeness?

What *is* order? That is a very deep question, because everything we say presupposes order. A few examples: There is the order of the numbers, the order of the words here, the order of the walls, the order in which the body works, the order in which thought works, the order in which language works. We cannot really define order, but we nevertheless understand order somewhat, because we cannot think, talk, or do anything without beginning from some kind of order.

The order physics has been using is the order of separation. Here the lens is the basic idea. If one takes a photograph, one point on the object corresponds to one point on the image. This fact has affected us very greatly, suggesting that everything is made of points. The camera was thereby a very important instrument for helping to strengthen the mechanistic philosophy. It gives an experience that allows everybody to see what is meant by the idea that the universe is nothing but separate parts.

Another instrument, the *holograph*, can also illustrate this point. The Greek word *holo* means *whole*, and *graph* means to write; consequently, a holograph writes the whole. With the aid of a laser, which produces highly ordered light, the waves of light from everywhere can be brought to one spot, and just the waves, rather than the image of the object, can be photographed. What is remarkable is that in the resulting picture, each part of it can produce an image of the whole object. Unlike the picture produced by a camera, no point-to-point correspondence with the object obtains. Information about each object is enfolded in each part; an image is produced when this enfolded information is unfolded. The holograph hence suggests a new kind of knowledge and a new understanding of the universe in which information about the whole is enfolded in each part and in which the various objects of the world result from the unfolding of this information.

In my proposal of unbroken wholeness, I turn the mechanistic picture upside down. Whereas the mechanistic picture regarded discrete objects as the primary reality, and the enfolding and unfolding of organisms including minds, as secondary phenomena, I suggest that the unbroken movements of enfolding and unfolding, which I call the *holomovement* is primary while the apparently discrete objects are secondary phenomena. They are related to the holomovement somewhat as the vortex, in the above example, is related to the unbroken flow of water. An essential part of this proposal is that the whole universe is *actively* enfolded to some degree in each of the parts. Because the whole is enfolded in each part, so are all other parts, in some way and to some degree. Hence, the mechanistic picture, according to which the parts are only externally related to each other is denied. That is, it is denied to be the primary truth; external relatedness is a secondary, derivative truth, applicable only to the secondary order of things, which I call the explicate or unfolded order. This is, of course, the order on which modern science has focused. The more fundamental truth is the truth of internal relatedness, because it is true of the more fundamental order, which I call the implicate order, because in this order the whole and hence all the other parts are enfolded in each part.

In my technical writings,[2] I have sought to show that the mathematical laws of quantum theory can be understood as describing the holomovement in which the whole is enfolded in each region, and the region is unfolded into the whole. Whereas modern physics has tried to understand the whole reductively by beginning with the most elementary parts, I am proposing a postmodern physics which begins with the whole.

Postmodern Science and Questions of Meaning and Value

We have seen that fragmentary thinking is giving rise to a reality that is constantly breaking up into disorderly, disharmonious, and destructive partial activities. Therefore, seriously exploring a mode of thinking that starts from the most encompassing possible whole and goes down to the parts (sub-wholes) in a way appropriate to the actual nature of things seems reasonable. This approach tends to bring about a different reality, one that is orderly, harmonious, and creative. For this actually to happen, however, a thoroughgoing end to fragmentation is necessary.

One source of fragmentation – perhaps the *major* one – is the belief that our thinking processes and what we are thinking about are fundamentally distinct. In this essay, I have stressed that everything is internally related to everything through mutual enfoldment. And evidently the whole world, both society and nature, is internally related to our thinking processes through enfoldment in our consciousness. For the content of our thought is just the world as we perceive it and know it (which includes ourselves). This content is not just a superficial part of us. Rather, in its totality, it provides us with the ground of all meaning in our lives, out of which arise our intentions, wishes, motivations, and actions. Indeed, even imagining what life could mean to us without the world of nature and society enfolded within us is impossible.

The general way we think of this world will thus be a crucially important factor of our consciousness, and thus of our whole being. If we think of the world as separate from us, and constituted of disjoint parts to be manipulated with the aid of calculations, we will tend to try to become separate people, whose main motivation with regard to each other and to nature is also manipulation and calculation. But if we can obtain an intuitive and imaginative feeling of the whole world as constituting an implicate order that is also enfolded in us, we will sense ourselves to be one with this world. We will no longer be satisfied merely to manipulate it technically to our supposed advantage, but we will feel genuine love for it. We will want to care for it, as we would for anyone who is close to us and therefore enfolded in us as an inseparable part.

Vice versa, however, the idea of implicate order means that we are enfolded in the world – not only in other people, but in nature as a whole. We have already seen an indication of this fact in that, when we approach the world in a fragmentary way, its response is correspondingly fragmentary. Indeed, it can be said that, as we are not complete without the world which is enfolded in us, so the world is not complete without us who are enfolded in it. It is a mistake to think that the world has a totally defined existence separate from our own and that there is merely an external 'interaction' between us and the world. It follows that if we approach the world through enfolding its wholeness in our consciousness and thus act with love, the world, which enfolds our own being within itself, will respond in a corresponding way. This can obviously happen in the world of society. But even the world of nature will cease to respond with degeneration, due to pollution, destruction of forests, and so on, and will begin to act in a more orderly and favourable way.

I want to emphasise this point. Because we are enfolded inseparably in the world, with no ultimate division between matter and consciousness, *meaning and value are as much integral aspects of the world as they are of us*. If science is carried out with an amoral attitude, the world will, ultimately respond to science in a destructive way. Postmodern science must therefore overcome the separation between truth and virtue, value and fact, ethics and practical necessity. To call for this non-separation is, of course, to ask for a tremendous revolution in our whole attitude to knowledge. But such a change is now necessary and indeed long overdue. Can humanity meet in time the challenge of what is required? The coming years will be crucial in revealing the answer to this question.

NOTES

1 See Huston Smith, *Beyond the Post-Modern Mind*, Crossroad, New York, 1982, esp chap 8, 'Beyond the Modern Western Mind-set'.

2 See David Bohm, *Wholeness and the Implicate Order*, Routledge & Kegan Paul, London, 1980 and other references given therein.

From *The Reenchantment of Science, Postmodern Proposals*, edited by David Ray Griffin, State University of New York Press, Albany, 1988.

Charles Birch
THE POSTMODERN CHALLENGE TO BIOLOGY

The dominant model of life in biology today is strictly mechanistic (substantialist) and reductionist. But it is not the model of life of the founders of modern biology in the sixteenth and seventeenth centuries. Vesalius, Harvey, and others had a more organic view of life. What they discovered was later set in a mechanistic framework by their successors, particularly René Descartes. The methodology of mechanistic biology is to investigate the living organism as if it were a machine. Many biologists, probably most of them since Descartes, take the next step, a metaphysical one, and conclude that the living organism *is* a machine.

To be critical of the mechanistic model in biology is not to deny that it has been highly successful. The triumphs of molecular biology in describing and manipulating genes are triumphs of the mechanistic and reductionist approach. There are mechanical aspects of living entities. Limbs operate as levers. The heart operates as a pump. As Levins and Lewontin say:

> The great success of Cartesian method and the Cartesian view of nature is in part a result of a historical path of least resistance. Those problems that yield to the attack are pursued most vigorously, precisely because the method works there. Other problems and other phenomena are left behind, walled off from understanding by the commitment to Cartesianism.[1]

To be critical of the mechanistic model is not to deny a role to this way of thinking. It is to recognise that there are some problems in biology that have been singularly unresponsive to the mechanistic approach. These are developmental biology, the function of the central nervous system, aspects of animal behaviour, and the evolution of mind and consciousness.

Contrast Between the Mechanistic and the Ecological Models

The mechanistic model of life recognises only one set of causes as operative in a living organism. These are external relations – those components of the organism's environment that push it or pull it. Descartes wanted to reduce the laws of biology to the laws of matter in motion. 'Give me matter and motion,' he said in effect, 'and I shall construct a universe.' Mind was recognised to exist only in human beings. The rest of the created things on our planet, including the human body, were understood in strictly mechanistic terms.

The postmodern challenge to biology is to recognise a second set of causes in addition to external relations. This second set is internal relations. We recognise internal relations in ourselves when our lives are profoundly influenced by a compelling purpose. Human lives are changed by such influences. I am what I am partly as a consequence of all the external relations that have impinged on me since conception. But I am also what I am by virtue of internal relations – the ways I have chosen to respond to those external conditions. An internal relation determines the nature of the entity, indeed even its very existence.

The notion of internal relation as causal strikes at the heart of the strictly mechanistic and reductionistic model. The ideal of this model is to divide the world into next to nothing as possible – call those entities 'atoms' or what you will – and then try to build the world up again from those building blocks. When you do that, of course, you get a machine. In the mechanistic model the building blocks are substances. They have no internal relations. The definition of a substance is something that exists independently of anything else. In substance thinking, an atom of hydrogen is the same atom of hydrogen whether it be in the heart of the sun or in the molecules of my brain. It is what it is independently of its environment. That is the substance notion of a hydrogen atom. The idea of internal relations is that a human being, let us say, is not the same person independent of his or her environment. The human being is a subject and not simply an object pushed around by external relations. To be a subject is to be responsive, to constitute oneself purposefully in response to one's environment.

The postmodern view that makes most sense to me is the one that takes human experience as a high-level exemplification of entities in general, be they cells or atoms or electrons. All are subjects. All have internal relations. Consequently, in biology a distinction is made between a biology that is *compositional* (substantialist) and one that is *relational* (ecological).

As one moves up levels of organisation – electrons, atoms, molecules, cells, etc – the properties of each larger whole are given not merely by the units of which it is composed but also by the new relations between these units. It is not simply that the whole is more than the sum of its parts. The parts are themselves redefined and recreated in the process of evolution from one level to another. This means that the properties of matter relevant at, say, the atomic level do not begin to predict the properties of matter at the cellular level, let alone at the level of complex organisms. That is why, already fifty years ago, the Danish physicist Niels Bohr advised his students that the new laws of physics were most likely to be discovered in biology. This introduces a principle unrecognised by the mechanistic model, that as well as interpreting the higher levels in terms of the lower, we also interpret the lower levels in terms of the higher.

I have drawn a contrast between an organism or natural entity and a machine. The parts of a machine are subject only to the laws of mechanics, with its external forces acting on these parts. In some modern machines, such as computers, nuts and bolts are replaced by transistors and microchips. There is no evolution of computers in any real sense, but only change in design brought about by the designer outside the machine. There is of course also natural selection – in the market place! Likewise, in the mechanical model of life, no real evolution occurs, merely rearrangements of parts and natural selection among the different arrangements. Nuts and bolts cannot evolve! They can only be rearranged. This means that a completely mechanistic account of evolution is a gross abstraction from nature. Whitehead perceived this critical distinction when he wrote:

A thoroughgoing evolutionary philosophy is inconsistent with materialism. The aboriginal stuff, or material, from which a materialistic philosophy starts, is incapable of evolution. This material is in itself the ultimate substance. Evolution, on the materialistic theory, is reduced to the role of being another word for the description of the changes of the external relations between portions of matter. There is nothing to evolve, because one set of external relations is as good as any other set of external relations. There can be merely change, purposeless and unprogressive. . . . The doctrine thus cries aloud for a conception of organism as fundamental to nature.[2]

Evolution, according to the ecological or organic model, is the evolution not of substances but of subjects. The critical thing that happens in evolution is change in internal relations of subjects.

Putting the Ecological Model into Practice

It is one thing, says Lewontin,[3] to call for a biology that is relational rather than compositional. It is quite another to put it into practice. Lewontin makes some attempt to do this in relation to his model of dialectical materialism. I want to do this in relation to the ecological model which I find more illuminating than dialectical materialism. What follows are some examples.

A mechanistic brain physiologist analyses my sitting at a word processor in terms of light waves impinging on my retina from the keyboard and the screen which set in train chemical processes in my nerves and brain. Messages from the brain to my muscles cause them to contract in ways that result in very complex movements of my fingers as I sit at the machine. This interpretation is fine as far as it goes – but it does not go very far. It does not account for the fact that I have some thoughts in mind that I purpose to put into writing. My thoughts initiate the complex sequence of events the physiologist studies. What the physiologist describes are external relations. The influence of my thoughts are internal relations. The distinction between these two sorts of causes in human behaviour was clearly made by Socrates as reported in Plato's dialogue the *Phaedo*. There are some, he tells us, who argue that the cause of his actions as he sits in prison awaiting death are the mechanical forces on his bones and muscles and sinews. But the real cause of his sitting in prison was that he made a *choice* to bow to the Athenians' sentence. In the mechanistic analysis, an immense gap exists between what the scientist describes and what I experience. This is recognised by some brain physiologists, notably Sperry,[4] who considers that a thought itself can initiate chemical and electrical impulses in cells in the brain. His attempt to bring the mental and the physical together provides a richer understanding than the view that regards the physical account as exclusive and sufficient.

Some activities, such as the movement of fingers, appear to be represented in the brain in particular groups of cells. But in the case of visual memory, the brain does not seem to store information locally but widely. Karl Pribram and his colleagues[5] produced a holographic model of the brain in which the image is not represented in the brain as a point-to-point image from an object to a photographic plate. Rather, it is represented such that if some cells of the brain are removed, this removal does not destroy just one part of the image but reduces the clarity of the image as a whole. Dissecting the visual image down to particular cells is not possible. The image is a consequence of the interrelation of many cells as a whole. This is a far more ecological model of the brain than the strictly mechanistic model provided by most brain physiologists.

A mechanistic student of animal behaviour seeks to interpret all behaviour in terms of stimulus and response, analogously to the way in which a photoelectric cell receives a message from our approach to a door and responds with a message to a motor to open the door. These sorts of relationships can be made quite complex by incorporating negative feedback (cybernetic) mechanisms. We can then construct complex robots that perform quite complex activities. Such models add something to our understanding of animal behaviour. But the environment of these robots is extremely simple compared to the environment of any animal in the wild. The non-mechanistic student of animal behaviour tries to study animals in their complex relations with a complex world, as Jane Goodall has done with chimpanzees in Gombe Reserve.[6] Her success was dependent upon her establishing a rapport with the chimpanzee and, presumably, vice versa. She tried to think like a chimpanzee and to imagine what it was like to be one. She was, in fact, taking into account what she perceived to be critically important internal relations in their lives.

Hartshorne provided evidence that supports his view that birds have some musical feeling and that their song is not simply a matter of attracting the attention of mates.[7] In more general terms, Donald R Griffin argues that the needed step in research in animal behaviour is to attempt to understand the mind of the animal and he suggests ways to approach this.[8] I cannot really know what it is to be a chimpanzee, let alone a bee, unless I am one. Nor can I know what it is to be you instead of me. But in this latter case, we struggle imaginatively to enter one another's lives. Why should we not seek to do the same with other living organisms? Is not our neighbour all that participates in life? If so, the implication for ethics is revolutionary. If the needs of neighbours stretch beyond human need, so does the reach of love.

A mechanistic sociobiologist argues that individual human limitations imposed by genes place constraints on society. The non-mechanistic student of societies argues that social organisations are able to negate individual limitations. Lewontin makes the analogy of human beings and flight.[9] Human beings cannot fly by flapping their arms and legs. Yet we do fly because of the existence of aircraft, pilots, fuel production, radios – all products of social organisation. Moreover, it is not society that flies, but the individuals who have acquired this property as a consequence of socialisation. The individual can be understood only in terms of the total environment. In different environments we have different properties. We are indeed different.

The naively mechanistic geneticist says that genes are particles located on chromosomes, that genes make proteins, proteins make us, and that genes replicate themselves. The non-mechanistic geneticist says genes are not like particles at all. What a gene is depends upon neighbouring genes on the same and on different chromosomes and upon other aspects of its environment in the cell. The gene (DNA) makes nothing by itself. It does not even make more DNA. It depends on enzymes in the cell to do all these things. Geneticists no longer teach 'particulate genetics'. And molecular biology is properly called *molecular ecology*. We know that a particular DNA molecule can express itself in a great variety of ways – *which* way depends upon the environment of the cell and therefore of the molecule at the time.

The molecule and its chemical environment are in a state of perpetual dynamic equilibrium depending upon the magnitude of the physical forces and the concentrations of chemicals inside the cell. Which chemical pathway is *chosen is* a matter of probability rather than absolute determinism. The difference between 100 per cent determinism and even 99.99 per cent determinism is all the difference in the world. It is the difference between being completely determined by the environment and having a degree of self-determination. A thoroughgoing mechanist might argue that the difference between 100 per cent and 99.99 per cent may be due to defective functioning of a deterministic system, which is precisely the point. If accident can happen in the system, determinism by the environment is not complete. Self-determinism or choice is therefore possible. The substance or billiard-ball concept of the gene is no longer credible. The classical notion that genes were pellets of matter that remained in all respects self-identical, whatever the environment, has to be abandoned in the light of modern knowledge.

The challenge of postmodern thought to molecular biology is to pursue further this avenue of thought. I would claim that to exhibit self-determination is to exhibit mind. It is to have some degree of freedom, no doubt minute at the molecular level. I am not saying that, having investigated the life of the cell, biologists have found mind. I am saying that what they have found is *more consistent with* the proposition that the cells and their DNA molecules are mind-like in the sense of having internal relations than with the proposition that they are machine-like. They take account of their environment in the deep sense of taking account: They are constituted by their relations. Molecular genetics was the last into mechanistic biology. Maybe it will be the first out.

Mechanistic developmental biologists thought that an organism developed in complexity from a single fertilised egg into a complex living organism in the way a motor car is built up from individual bits and pieces. But we now know that if you cut out the limb bud of a developing frog embryo at a very early stage, shake the cells loose and put them back at random in a lump, a normal leg develops. It is not as though each cell in its particular place was initially destined to become a particular part. Each cell could become any part of the leg (but not of the eye) depending upon its total environment. Unlike a machine, which can be pulled to pieces and reassembled, the bits and pieces of the embryo seem to come into existence as a consequence of their spatial relationships at critical moments in the development of the embryo. Says Lewontin:

> If development is really, in an important sense, a consequence of the relations between things, how are we to reduce the incredible complexity of relationships to a manageable set of regularities? And how are we to do this using an experimental method that is itself so wedded to Cartesian analysis?[10]

An example of how developmental biology was misled along the Cartesian path was the hunt for the so-called organiser in development. For sixty years biochemists hunted for a single molecule or group of molecules that might be responsible for 'organising' the development of the parts of the embryo, such as a leg or an eye. But they found no 'organiser'. This reductionist programme was a colossal distraction.[11] Development evidently cannot be reduced to the action of single chemicals.

The mechanistic evolutionist seeks to interpret all in terms of chance and necessity. 'Chance alone,' said Monod, 'is at the source of every innovation, of all creation in the biosphere.'[12] He contrasts his position with those who sought to find in every detail of nature evidence of deterministic design. The choice he gives us is complete chance or complete determinism.

Darwinism was a shattering blow to those who conceived of nature as completely determined, be it by an outside designer or some inbuilt principle in nature. To take chance seriously is the first step in moving away from the concept of deterministic design. This was a problem for Darwin. It seems he could not admit the reality of chance, despite the role he attributed to it. In this respect, he was like Einstein who could not believe that God plays dice. 'I cannot think,' said Darwin, 'that the world . . . is the result of chance; yet I cannot look at each separate thing as the result of Design . . . I am, and shall ever remain, in a hopeless muddle.' So wrote Darwin in a letter to the Harvard botanist Asa Gray. Again and again Darwin's letters reiterate this refrain – is it all determined or is it all a result of chance? But are these the only possibilities?

Hartshorne hits the nail on the head when he says: 'Neither pure chance nor the pure absence of chance can explain the world.'[13] He goes on to say: 'There must be something positive limiting chance and something more than mere matter in matter, or Darwinism fails to explain life.'

The *something positive* that limits chance and the *something more* than mere matter in matter is the degree of self-determination exercised by natural entities in response to possibilities of their future. In other words, a causal role in evolution is played by internal relations as well as the external relation of natural selection about which Darwin wrote. Chance (plus natural selection) alone cannot explain the evolution of life. Chance and purpose together provide a more substantial base for thinking about evolution.

This thought is not as revolutionary as it might at first appear. Evolutionary biologists have accepted an important role for purpose in human evolution in what is called *cultural evolution*. Cultural choices have determined the direction of genetical evolution. Cultural evolution and genetical evolution go hand in hand. But we can also recognise a role that choice and purpose play in the lives of other animals. For them, too, cultural evolution is a reality. How far down the line are we prepared to go with this argument? Logically there is no need to draw a line anywhere in the total evolutionary sequence from atoms to humans. This is a challenge of postmodern thought to evolutionary biology today – to propose a role for purpose together with chance in evolution all down the line. This is to propose that, in addition to external relations as causal, internal relations are causal also in determining the direction of evolution.

Evolution raises a profound question: Why did atoms evolve into cells and into plants and animals? Why didn't creativity stop with the first DNA molecule? Mechanism provides no answer. The ecological model opens up ways to explore it in terms of lure and response, or purposive influence and self-determination. Self-determination is minimal at the atomic level. It is greatest in the higher organisms. Because natural entities are always, with their own particular degree of freedom, in process of relating to the lure to fulfilment, a constant tension between chaos and order occurs in nature.

Implicit in what I have said is that the scientists' methodology and the way in which they interpret the data depend upon their metaphysical stance. Scientists always take sides. I have given one alternative to Cartesian mechanistic biology. There are others and we need to see the parallels and differences between them.

In addition to the biologists I have already mentioned, others provide a challenge to mechanistic reductionistic biology, including Sewall Wright[14] in evolutionary biology, CH Waddington[15] in developmental biology, Ilya Prigogine and Isabelle Stengers[16] in molecular biology, and, in the broad field of all biology, JZ Young,[17] Rupert Sheldrake,[18] and John Cobb and me.[19]

The contrast between a bits-and-pieces view of nature and an holistic one is captured by Henry Reed in his poem, 'Naming of Parts' which begins:

Today we have naming of parts, Yesterday
we had daily cleaning. And tomorrow morning
we shall have what to do after firing. But today,
Today we have naming of parts. Japonica
Glistens like coral in all of the neighbouring gardens,
And today we have naming of parts.

NOTES

1 Richard Levins and Richard Lewontin, *The Dialectical Biologist*, Harvard University Press, 1985, pp 2-3.

2 AN Whitehead, *Science and the Modern World*, Cambridge University Press, 1933, pp 134-35.

3 Richard Lewontin, 'The Corpse in the Elevator', *New York Review of Books* 30, 1983, pp 14-37, esp 36.

4 Roger Sperry, *Science and Moral Priority: Merging Mind, Brain and Human Values*, Blackwell, Oxford, 1983; 'Interview with Roger Sperry', *Omni* 5/ii, 1983, pp 69-100.

5 Karl H Pribram, 'Holonomy and Structure in the Organization of Perception', *Images, Perception and Knowledge*, ed John M Nicholas, Reidel, Dordrecht, 1977, pp 155-85; KH Pribram, M Nuwer, and R Baron,

'The Holographic Hypothesis of Memory Structure in Brain Function and Structure, *Contemporary Developments in Mathematical Psychology*, vol 2, ed R Atkinson, O Krantz, R Luce and P Suppes, Freeman, San Francisco, 1974, pp 416-57.

6 Jane van Lawick Goodall, *In the Shadow of Man*, Houghton Miflin Co, Boston, 1971; *The Chimpanzees of Gombe: Patterns of Behavior*, Harvard University Press, 1986.

7 Charles Hartshorne, *Born to Sing: An Interpretation and World Survey of Bird Song*, Indiana University Press, Bloomington, 1973; *Omnipotence and Other Theological Mistakes*, State University of New York Press, Albany, 1984.

8 Donald R Griffin, *The Question of Animal Awareness: Evolutionary Continuity of Mental Experience*, Rockefeller University Press, New York, 1976; *Animal Thinking*, Harvard University Press, 1984.

9 Lewontin, 'The Corpse in the Elevator', p 37.

10 Ibid, p 36.

11 Mae-Wah Ho and PT Saunders, *Beyond Neo-Darwinism: An Introduction to the New Evolutionary Paradigm*, Harcourt Brace Janovich, New York, 1984, pp 10, 267-90; Jam Witowski, 'The Hunting of the Organiser: An Episode in Biochemical Embryology', *Trends in Biochemical Science* 10, 1985, pp 379-81.

12 Jacques Monod, *Chance and Necessity: An Essay on the Natural Philosophy of Modern Biology*, Fontana/Collins, London, 1974, p 110.

13 Charles Hartshorne, *Omnipotence and Other Theological Mistakes*, p 69.

14 Sewall Wright, 'Biology and the Philosophy of Science', *Process and Divinity*, ed WL Reese and E Freeman, Open Court, La Salle, Ill, 1964, pp 101-25.

15 CH Waddington, ed *Toward A Theoretical Biology*, Vol 2, *Sketches*, Edinburgh University Press, 1969, pp 72-81.

16 Ilya Prigogine and Isabelle Stengers, *Order out of Chaos. Man's New Dialogue with Nature*, Bantam Books, New York, 1984.

17 JZ Young, *Programmes of the Brain*, Oxford University Press, 1978.

18 Rupert Sheldrake, *A New Science of Life: The Hypothesis of Formative Causation*, Blond and Briggs, London, 1981.

19 Charles Birch and John B Cobb, Jr, *The Liberation of Life: From the Cell to the Community*, Cambridge University Press, 1981.

From *The Reenchantment of Science, Postmodern Proposals*, edited by David Ray Griffin, State University of New York Press, Albany, 1988.

Edward Goldsmith
GAIA AND EVOLUTION

The 'survival of the fittest' maxim of Darwinism is widely used to justify the disastrous process of unrestrained technological progress and economic development. However, if the world is seen as a single self-regulating system, then progress through competition becomes fundamentally anti-evolutionary. Cooperation is the true evolutionary strategy.

Neither Darwinism, nor the neo-Darwinism of Bateson and Weissman, nor its latest version, the Synthetic Theory, provides an evolutionary theory that is reconcilable with our knowledge of the structure and function of the world of living things. This is particularly so if the biosphere is seen as a single living system, whose constituent parts co-operate in achieving a specific strategy – the maintenance of its basic features or organisation in the face of internal or external challenges, that is to say its stability or homeostasis.

Little attempt has been made to provide any serious evidence for the Darwinist theory. This has been noted by a number of critics, for example Karl Popper, who considered that 'neither Darwin nor any Darwinian has so far given an actual causal explanation of the adaptive evolution of any single organism or any single organ. All that has been shown – and this is very much a hypothesis – is that such explanations might exist (that is to say, they are not logically impossible).' Popper does not, for that reason, consider Darwinism a scientific theory – though he does not necessarily reject it.

Michael Polanyi accepts that though 'neo-Darwinism is firmly accredited and highly regarded by Science . . . there is little direct evidence for it.' Ludwig von Bertalanffy makes the same point. In the debate on evolution, he writes, there has been no more concern with proof 'than in the operation of a Tibetan prayer wheel'.

These criticisms apply equally to the role that random variations or random mutations, or indeed randomness itself, are supposed to play in the evolutionary process, and to the role which is supposed to be played in that process by natural selection.

Randomness

The notion that the biosphere is the production of random variations could not be stated more unequivocally – and indeed more dogmatically – than by Jacques Monod:

> Chance alone was the source of every innovation, of all creation in the biosphere. Pure chance, absolutely free but blind is at the very root of the stupendous edifices of evolution. This central concept of modern biology is no longer one among other conceivable hypotheses. It is the only conceivable hypothesis, the only one that squares with observed and tested fact. And nothing warrants the supposition – or the hope – that on this score our position is likely ever to be revised.

In the same way non-human animals are seen as learning by random trial and error, and humans by 'induction', which involves making naive correlations between random observations. Human history is seen as composed of random events, and historians such as H.A.L. Fisher pour scorn upon historicists such as Arnold Toynbee and Spengler, who sought to introduce a pattern into our historical experience.

To tell us, as Monod does, that the thesis of randomness is the only conceivable thesis 'that squares with observed and tested fact' is untenable. There is no possible way of determining empirically whether an event is random. All that we can say of an event that appears to be random is that we do not know the circumstances that brought it about.

Lamarck noted this: '*Le mot hazard n'exprime que notre ignorance des causes.*' Poincaré said the same thing in slightly different words: '*Le Hazard n'est que la mesure de notre ignorance.*' Waddington also intimated that gene mutations may only appear to be random because of our present lack of knowledge. 'A gene mutation which consists of some alteration in the sequence of nucleotides in the DNA is from a chemical point of view presumably not wholly at random. There may well be quite considerable regularities in the processes by which the alterations come about: however, we know very little about them as yet.'

The important role attributed to random mutations appeared more credible in the days when the genome was seen as a random assortment of genes. It makes far less sense, however, now that the genome is known to be a highly sophisticated and elaborately regulated organisation, capable, among other things, as Lerner has shown, of maintaining its own homoeostasis.

In response to such criticisms, neo-Darwinists have modified their position, cosmetically at least. Mutations may well be caused by factors that we ignore, they tell us, but as Julian Huxley wrote: 'in all cases they are random in relation to evolution. Their effects are not related to the needs of the organism or to the condition in which it is placed. They occur without reference to their biological uses.' Dobzhansky and Waddington stated the same principle in slightly different words.

But this concession changes very little. Randomness necessarily means randomness vis-à-vis a specific process. An event cannot be random to all processes, as this would mean that it had occurred spontaneously, which would violate the principle of causality that is critical to the paradigm of reductionist science. Indeed, if an event is seen as the product of a 'cause', it cannot be random to the causal process of which it is the effect. The official position is thus still very close to Jacques Monod's and it is an untenable one – one that is in complete conflict with our knowledge of life processes in the world we live in.

Randomness: Fact or Fiction?

Indeed, even ordinary cultural phenomena with which we are all acquainted, and which, in terms of the paradigm of reductionist science, are interpreted as random, are not, in reality, random at all. For instance, art styles do not develop at random, but closely reflect the cultures in which they developed. The clothes people wear are indicative of the image of themselves they wish to communicate to others. The way people walk, eat, light cigarettes, blow their noses, do up their shoelaces, all convey some information as to the personality of the individuals concerned.

In fact, behaviour exhibits so little 'randomness' that it is questionable whether living things are in fact capable of behaving in a random way, even if they make a determined attempt to do so. This appears to be confirmed by various experiments such as those described by WR Ramsay and Anne Broadhurst, who experimented with a panel of seventy-two people by asking them to repeat in time to a metronome a series of numbers between 1 and 9, in as random a manner as possible. They found that '. . . in accordance with other studies on randomness and response in human subjects, the result of this experiment shows that even when subjects try to be random, there is a high degree of stereotype.'

In the world of living things, randomness is so rare that to achieve a state which even approximates it, it has to be 'manufactured' artificially. Stafford Beer points out the absurdity of such a situation:

> It really is ludicrous that we should have gone so far with Epicurius as to manufacture chaos where none exists, in order to provide ourselves with the properly certificated raw materials for system building. Take my own case. There are a random number of tables on my bookshelf; there are computer tapes for producing pseudo-random numbers next door; there is a large electronic machine for generating noise upstairs; down the road there is a room full of equipment designed to hurl thousands of little metal balls about in a random way; and I use ten-sided dice as paper-weights. The upkeep of this armoury is considerable. Think of all the time we spend trying to ensure that these artefacts produce results which are 'genuinely random' – whatever that may mean. This tremendous practical problem of guaranteeing disorderliness ought to be enough to satisfy any systems man that nothing is more unnatural than chaos.

Indeed, living things actively seek to eliminate randomness. We know, for instance, that mutant genes tend to be eliminated. Lerner has shown us how a genome tends to maintain its structure, thereby countering random changes. We know that random bodies within a biological organism are eliminated with the aid of the immune system; and that in all known vernacular societies, people whose behaviour is socially random, in that it diverts from the traditional norm, are ostracised or eliminated. We know too that the ability of natural systems to eliminate randomness increases as they develop or evolve, and that climax ecosystems are very much better at doing this than pioneer ecosystems. Natural systems are, in fact, committed to the elimination of randomness by virtue of the fact that they function cybernetically to maintain the basic features of their order – and hence their stability or homoeostasis. Life, in fact, develops and indeed evolves at the expense of randomness.

Natural Selection: The Motor of Evolution?

Randomness is essential to the Darwinian notion of natural selection. Yet, it is hard enough to demonstrate that natural selection from random variations is even *one* of the mechanisms of evolution, as Darwin maintained, since the term 'natural selection' is a very vague one, indeed Darwin actually admitted that he used it metaphorically. To demonstrate that natural selection is the *only* mechanism of evolution, as is maintained by the neo-Darwinists, is still more difficult.

How do neo-Darwinists know that no other factors are involved? In particular, how do they know that no 'internal factors' are operative, that living things, in fact, do not evolve as a result of their own behavioural efforts and ontogenetic adaptations?

There is no epistemological justification for maintaining such a thesis. Neo-Darwinists simply assume that living things do not evolve in that way.

That natural selection is operated by the 'environment' is a further unjustified assumption. Why should the environment behave in that way? What motivates it to do so? How is it capable of displaying such highly discriminatory and indeed highly teleological behaviour? These questions have never been answered, nor can they be since the term 'environment' is never defined, it is simply taken to be that which is 'out there' – some strange mystical entity to which all the dynamic, creative, intelligent features of life have somehow been delegated.

Selection as God

If natural selection from random mutations is indeed the only mechanism of evolution, then the most sophisticated achievements must be attributed to it – and indeed they are. Thus, according to Ruse, natural selection can act not only to cause evolutionary change 'in the sense that it can cause change in gene ratios', it can also act 'as a conservative force preventing change, that is keeping gene ratios stable'.

Merrell tells us that natural selection 'will tend to operate in such a way as to minimise interspecific competition.' It is also capable of deciding, if we are to believe MacArthur and Wilson, whether to favour 'increased reproductive rates' (K selection) or 'greater efficiency of conversion of food and other resources into offspring' (R selection).

Selection can also decide, if we are to believe Lerner, whether it should be 'intensive' or 'less intensive'. It has the ability to eliminate deviants and thereby favour stability, hence Waddington's 'stabilising selection'. According to Dobzhansky, it is responsible 'for directedness of the general as well as for the grouping of particular evolution'.

Alistair Hardy notes too that 'moral and aesthetic qualities in man are not infrequently said to be explained by the operation of natural selection.' This is true of the sociobiologists who even see natural selection as giving rise to altruism (kinship selection). Similarly, Waddington, when it was suggested to him by Piaget that it might be difficult for such a crude mechanistic device to create complexity, answered that Piaget greatly underestimated the capacity of natural selection.

Selection is thus invoked to explain everything, (which indeed it must be, if we are to accept the neo-Darwinist thesis). Julian Huxley explicitly states:

> The hoary objection of the improbability of an eye or a hand or a brain being evolved by 'blind chance' has lost its force because natural selection, operating over stretches of geological time, *explains everything*.

Lewontin claims to have established this principle experimentally. 'There appears to be no character – morphogenetic, behavioural, physiological or cytological,' he writes, 'that cannot be selected in *Drosophila.*'

Selection, like God, is thus omnipotent. Neo-Darwinists may laugh at Lamarck's idea that if an animal needs some organ, that need will somehow call the organ into existence. Dawkins regards this notion as 'so obviously mystical to the modern mind that it is fairer to Lamarck for us to concentrate on those parts of his theory that at least seem to have some chance of explaining evolution.' But the neo-Darwinists entertain an almost identical notion, the only difference being that it is the environment's 'need' that 'will call the organ into existence', which seems just as mystical.

The question that needs to be asked is how does 'natural selection' – supposedly a purely mechanical process, like a sorting machine in a post office, that does no more than sort the 'fit' from the 'unfit' – achieve this omnipotence? How can this mechanical sorting machine create complex living things?

One can understand that by selecting the most viable living things, and allowing them to reproduce themselves, their characteristics will be transmitted to the next generation, which will become correspondingly more viable, but this is only possible if living things can transmit such characteristics to the next generation. Billiard balls cannot, and it is difficult to see how they might be made to evolve by natural selection however much variability they might exhibit.

Whitehead noted this: 'A thorough going evolutionary philosophy is inconsistent with materialism. The aboriginal stuff, or material, from which a materialistic philoso-phy starts, is *incapable of evolution.*'

Woodger made the same point. The Darwinian doctrine, he noted, 'is committed to ascribe to "bits of matter" properties which they do not exhibit today, instead of searching for an adequate conception of organism.'

Popper also pointed out that 'only an organism which exhibits in its behaviour a strong tendency or disposition or propensity to struggle for its survival will in fact be likely to survive.' But to compete *is to exhibit goal-directedness.* Indeed, as Popper notes, goal-directedness is one of the conditions for evolution. But there are many other such conditions. Indeed, one can draw up a whole catalogue of conditions which must obtain before a sorting machine could conceivably be used to bring about constructive changes in the structure and function of living things, however great the diversity of random or non-random variations which it may have the privilege to select from. Von Bertalanffy notes this:

Selection *presupposes* self-maintenance, adaptability, reproduction, etc of the living system. These therefore cannot be the effect of selection. This is the oft-discussed circularity of the selectionist argument. Proto-organisms would arise, and organisms further evolve by chance mutations and subsequent selection. But, in order to do so, *they must already have had the essential attributes to life.*

For Woodger, the neo-Darwinist thesis is unacceptable on this count alone: 'An explanation of this kind can only make out a case for itself by begging the fundamental question at issue – the essential characteristics of an organism *have to be surreptitiously introduced in vague general language.*'

They are so introduced largely by attributing to natural selection – the mechanical sorting machine – qualities which no machine can possibly display, and that are, in effect, little more than the very 'internal factors' whose role in determining the evolutionary process, neo-Darwinists are at such pains to deny.

The following passage makes clear how Darwin 'surreptitiously introduced' the highly sophisticated features of life processes into what he made out to be a purely mechanical process. In it, Darwin tries to explain how so phenomenally complex an organ as the eye could have been produced by natural selection:

We must suppose that there is a power, represented by natural selection or the survival of the fittest, always intently watching each slight alteration in the transparent layers; and carefully preserving each which, under varied circum-stances, in any way or in any degree, tends to produce a distincter image. We must suppose each new state of the instrument to be multiplied by the million; each to be preserved until a better one is produced, and then the old ones to be all destroyed. In living bodies, variation will cause the slight alterations, generation will multiply them almost infinitely, and natural selection will pick out with unerring skill each improvement. Let this process go on for millions of years; and during each year on millions of individuals of many kinds; and may we not believe that a living optical instrument might thus be formed as superior to one of glass, as the works of the creator are to those of man?

Note that selection is referred to as a 'power', that it is 'intently watching' each slight alteration, that it picks out each improvement 'with unerring skill'. Is Darwin really talking about a mechanical sorting machine? Indeed, it is difficult to avoid the feeling that there is some living being endowed with such non mechanistic qualities as purpose, reason, knowledge and intelligence lurking in the background and secretly manipulating the sorting machine.

This is not altogether surprising, since a machine needs a living designer and operator. That is in itself sufficient reason why a mechanistic theory of evolution can only superficially replace a theistic, a vitalistic or an ecological theory.

Equating Selection with Adaptation

The subterfuge of disguising complex life processes as crude mechanistic processes by the use of the appropriate words and imagery is probably most discernible in the attempt by neo-Darwinists to prove, how, in specific instances, natural selection has actually occurred.

The subterfuge consists in noting that adaptation has occurred and then *quite brazenly taking such adaptation as constituting evidence of natural selection at work.* Instead of demonstrating that natural selection leads to adaptive change, *it is simply assumed to do so by the expedient of equating natural selection with adaptation.* It thereby suffices to show that adaptation has occurred in order to prove, in the eyes of neo-Darwinists at least, that the corresponding adaptive characteristics have been elected.

Thus on the subject of the finches of the Galapagos that so impressed Darwin, Ruse writes, 'we find that all the different species show the effects of selection.' What are these effects we might ask?

> Peculiar characteristic after peculiar characteristic *has some special adaptive function.* Some finches have evolved in such a way that they are ideally suited to the consumption of plant food; some mainly for the consumption of animal food; some solely for animal food. Then there are beaks for cactus eating, beaks for insect eating on the wing, beaks for general scavenging. One species has even developed the ability to probe with twigs for insects in hollow parts of trees.

In this passage, Ruse's identification of selection with adaptation is quite explicit. The fact that he is assuming what he set out to prove could not be more evident.

That evolution and natural selection are synonymous, so that to prove that the former has occurred provides proof of the effectiveness of the latter, is also assumed by Charlesworth:

> Probably the most general relevant prediction of the theory of natural selection is that episodes of rapid evolution should coincide with periods when the direction of selection is changing; this seems to be borne out at many different levels of evolution. Insecticide resistance evolves in populations exposed to a new insecticide. The molluscs of Lake Turkhana changed when the level of the lake altered. The drosophila of Hawaii evolved an array of diverse species as they colonised an archipelago with numerous vacant ecological niches. And modern mammals underwent their period of most rapid evolution and diversification after the dominant land reptiles of the Cretaceous era went extinct.

But how do we know that these instances of rapid adaptation to new conditions are the result of natural selection? We do not, *unless that is we have already assumed, as does Charlesworth, that natural selection and adaptation are one and the same – unless in fact we start out by assuming what we set off to prove.* Von Bertalanffy was fully aware of this subterfuge:

> The principle of selection is a tautology in the sense that the selectionist explanation is always a construction *a posteriori.* Every surviving form, structure or behaviour – however bizarre, unnecessarily complex or outright crazy it may appear – must, *ipso facto* have been viable or of some selective advantage, for otherwise it would not have survived. *But this is no proof that it was a product of selection.*

Neo-Darwinism: The Dogma of Reductionist Science

Since there is absolutely no evidence for the neo-Darwinist thesis, and since it fits in so very poorly with our knowledge of the world of living things, the only reason why it should prove so durable seems to be that it fits in so well with the paradigm of reductionist science and hence with the worldview of modernism that the latter so faithfully reflects.

This was the view of Michael Polanyi. 'Neo-Darwinism', he wrote 'is firmly accredited and highly regarded by science though there is little direct evidence for it *because it fits in beautifully* with the mechanistic system of the universe and bears on the subject – the origin of man – which is of the utmost intrinsic interest.' This was also the view of Ludwig von Bertalanffy, who considered:

> that a theory so vague, so insufficiently verifiable and so far from the criteria otherwise applied in 'hard' science, has become a dogma, can only be explained *on sociological grounds*. Society and science have been so steeped in the ideas of mechanism, utilitarianism and the economic concept of free competition that instead of God, selection was enthroned as ultimate reality.

Many biologists are now involved in developing a new post-Darwinian evolutionary theory. Such a theory, if it is to be a realistic one, is likely to clash with, rather than conform to, the paradigm of reductionist science, for which reason it is unlikely to be accepted until such time as that paradigm itself undergoes considerable change – and indeed itself becomes more realistic. This process is already under way. The paradigm of reductionist science is under assault across a broad front. Its transformation is indeed necessary because, among other things, it faithfully reflects the worldview of modernism which serves above all to rationalise and hence to validate the Promethean enterprise to which modern society is committed, a path that is leading to the systematic annihilation of the world of living things.

Indeed, if humans are to survive for very long, one of the requirements of their survival will be the replacement of the paradigm of reductionist science by a new ecological paradigm. This new paradigm would also reflect a very different worldview, one that would serve to rationalise and hence validate a society committed to systematically reducing the impact of our economic activities on the ecosphere and, thereby, to the extent that this is still possible, of restoring the proper functioning of the Gaian process that can alone assure that our planet remain habitable.

A Post-Darwinian Evolutionary Theory

According to the Gaia thesis, the biosphere, together with its atmospheric environment, forms a single entity or natural system. This system is the product of organic forces that are highly coordinated by the system itself. Gaia has, in effect, created herself, not in a random manner but in a goal-directed manner since the system is highly stable and is capable of maintaining its stability in the face of internal and external challenges. It is, in fact, a cybernetic system, and for this to be possible, Gaia must display considerable order, indeed, she must be seen as a vast cooperative enterprise, very much as nature was seen by the Natural Theologists of the nineteenth century.

Such a view of the world of living things is, needless to say, totally incompatible with neo-Darwinism. Indeed, an evolutionary theory that would be consistent with this view of the world would be the very *negation of neo-Darwinism*. I shall suggest what some of its features might be:

Gaia as the Unit of Evolution: If Gaia is a single natural system that has created herself in a coordinated and goal-directed way, *then Gaia is clearly the unit of evolution*, not the individual living thing as neo-Darwinists insist.

Gaia is Evolution: Gaia is not just a contemporaneous organisation of living things. She is a *spatio-temporal system.* It is difficult for us to grasp the notion of a spatio-temporal system, as our language makes a clear distinction between things and processes and our thinking is clearly influenced by our language. It is nevertheless essential that we realise that all living things have a *temporal* as well as a *spatial* component. They exist in time just as much as in space. This means that Gaia is not only an entity but also a process, and what is that process *if it is not evolution?*

If this is so, *then the Gaian process – or evolution – must display the same fundamental structure as Gaia does when seen as a spatial entity.* If the latter is a biological, social and ecological structure, then the Gaian process cannot possibly be merely physical and mechanical as the neo-Darwinists tell us; it *must clearly also be seen in biological, social and ecological terms.*

Gaia as a Total Spatio-Temporal System: But what part of the temporal process must be seen as evolving? We assume that it must be the contemporaneous process, the one occurring before our eyes. But how do we justify this assumption? I suggest that the total process is involved, stretching back into the mists of time. The reason for suggesting this is that the information passed on from generation to generation of living things must reflect the experience of *the total spatio-temporal system involved and not just of part of it.*

This information appears to be organised hierarchically, the most general information, that which reflects the longest experience, being particularly non-plastic, the more particular information, that which reflects the more recent experience, being very much more plastic and hence more easily adaptable to short-term environmental contingencies. This arrangement is clearly that which best assures the continuity or the stability of the total spatio-temporal Gaian system. If this is so, this means, among other things, that *evolution is a long-term strategy not just a set of ad hoc adaptations.*

Evolution as a Living Process: If Gaia creates herself, then the living world must be seen as dynamic and creative, not as passive and robot-like. The qualities that are tacitly attributed to the vague undefined 'environment' must be ascribed as well to the living things which it is seen as managing. Evolution is thereby no longer the mere product of natural selection from random variations or genetic mutations, but of living things exhibiting all those features whose involvement in the evolutionary process neo-Darwinists have been at such pains to deny.

Evolution as a Cybernetic Process: If Gaia is evolution, then evolution must also be a cybernetic process. Lovelock's 'Daisy World' model is a cybernetic process but a very rudimentary one. One must suppose that the cybernetic process that led to the development of a system as complex as Gaia herself must be very much more sophisticated.

Now we are beginning to understand how living cybernetic processes operate. Human behaviour, as Kenneth Craik was the first to show, is mediated on the basis of a mental model of an individual's relationship with his environment, in the light of which diversions from the appropriate pattern of behaviour are corrected.

Gerardo Reichel Dolmatoff and others have shown how the behaviour of tribal groups in Amazonia is controlled in similar fashion, the model of the tribe's relationship with its environment being formulated in the language of its mythology. I do not think that it is too outlandish to ask whether Gaia herself is not endowed with a similar model?

What is certain is that a cybernetic system must be capable of monitoring its responses otherwise it could not correct diversions from its optimum course, and hence maintain its *homeorhesos* and thereby its stability. How then is evolution monitored? There can only be one answer and that is ontogenetically and behaviourally. That such feedback must occur has been clear to serious students of evolution for a long time. Baldwin, Lloyd Morgan, Goldschmidt, Waddington and Schmallhausen have all proposed mechanisms that might achieve this. The case for such feedback is put very forcefully by Piaget in his excellent book. *Le Comportement Moteur de l'Evolution*. The whole issue becomes much clearer, of course, once it is realised that the information that serves to mediate evolution is not just genetic but is formulated in different informational media including the cultural medium.

Evolution is a Goal-Directed Process: If evolution is a cybernetic process, then it must be goal-directed. The reason should be clear. To say that a process is under control means that it is maintaining itself on its optimum course or 'chreod' as Waddington referred to it, that which will enable it to achieve its optimum end-state or goal – a baby in the case of the embryological process, the climax ecosystem in the case of an ecological one. This implies that there is an optimum course and also that there is an end-state or goal. If there is not, then the very notion of control becomes meaningless.

Once a system has achieved its end-state, then to say that it is under control is to say that it is capable of maintaining itself at that end-state or thereabouts, that it is in fact homoeostatic. Again this implies that there is an end-state. If there was not, then clearly it could not maintain itself there. It seems to me that one has to overcome the scientist's irrational attitude towards goal-directedness or purposiveness. Teleology is a fact of life, a fundamental feature of life-processes, including evolution.

Stability is the Goal: To say that a cybernetic system maintains its homoeostasis, and that its constituent parts co-operate with it in this enterprise, is to say that its goal is the maintenance of its homoeostasis or stability – in effect the same thing. This implies that Gaia does not seek to evolve, and that the changes that it undergoes are simply those that it must undergo in order to avoid bigger and more disruptive changes. They are but part of a dynamic and creative strategy for maintaining the stability of the total spatio-temporal system that constitutes Gaia. Indeed, it is only by adapting the particularities of its structure to environmental contingencies, that a dynamic system such as Gaia can best maintain the generalities of its structure and hence its stability or homoeostasis.

Order and Cooperation: If Gaia is to be capable of acting as a cybernetic system and maintaining its homoeostasis, then it must display that specific structure that enables it to do so. It quite clearly cannot be but random assortment of competitive individuals all frantically striving to achieve their own egotistic ends as the neo-Darwinists maintain. Instead, Gaia must be seen, as Lovelock sees her, as a vast co-operative enterprise geared to the maintenance of its overall structure in the face of change. Clearly competition occurs: but it is not the most fundamental relationship between living things. It is a secondary relationship. So too, there is selection, but such selection is operated by the various natural systems that make up the Gaian hierarchy, acting their constituent parts, rather than by the vague, undefined 'environment' of neo-Darwinists. Its role, what is more, is not to assure the 'survival of the fittest' (in the sense of the most individualistic, and the most competitive), but on the contrary to eliminate such undesirable individuals, since they do not fit into Gaia's co-operative structure, assuring in this way the survival of those who do fit into Gaia and thereby contribute to the achievement of her strategy.

Evolution and Anti-Evolution: It must be noted that to attribute the above characteristics to the evolutionary process is simply to bring it into line with other life-processes such as ontogeny, behaviour and indeed the Gaian life process itself as depicted by Lovelock.

It is quite clear that these are living processes rather than mechanical ones, that they are dynamic rather than passive, and orderly and goal-directed rather than random. It is equally clear that they are cybernetic processes – each sub-process being monitored so that diversions from their proper goal are corrected by the overall life process. For this to be possible they must be seen as co-operative and well co-ordinated, rather than competitive and individualistic. Why should evolution be different?

Finally, such life processes can go wrong. Nature is neither omniscient nor omnipotent. When life processes go wrong they are no longer under control. They cease to be properly co-ordinated, they become atomised and individualistic, order gives rise to disorder, and to further atomisation, co-ordination ceases, competition and aggression take over. This atomisation process gives rise to undifferentiated or random Gaian tissue that rapidly replaces Gaia's critical structure – that which she must display if she is to be capable of maintaining her homoeostasis or stability.

When they occur at the level of the individual biological organism, these destructive processes are seen as pathological. For neo-Darwinists, however, they are the normal features of the evolutionary process. How can they be? Why should the overall life process behave in a diametrically opposite manner from all other life processes? Is it not apparent that they have got it completely wrong, that they have failed to distinguish between pathology and physiology, between the growth of a malignant tumour and the development of a differentiated tissue – between anti-evolution and evolution?

BIBLIOGRAPHY

Krishna Chaitanya, *The Biology of Freedom*, Somaiya Publications, 1975.
Pierre P Grasse, *L'Evolution du Vivant*, Albin Michel, 1973.
Julian Huxley, *Evolution, the Modern Synthesis*, George Allen and Unwin, London, third impression, 1942.
Erich Jantsch and Conrad C Waddington, ed *Evolution and Consciousness, Human Systems in Transition*, Addiston Wesley Publishing Co, Reading, Mass, 1976.
Koestler and Smythies, ed *Beyond Reductionism, The Alpbach Symposium*, Hutchinson, 1969.
IM Lerner, *Genetic Homeostasis*, Oliver and Boyd, 1954.
Peter and JS Medawar, *The Life Science, Current Ideas of Biology*, Wildwood House, London, 1977.
Peter Medawar, *The Hope of Progress*, Wildwood House, London, 1974.
Peter Medawar, *Pluto's Republic*, Oxford University Press, 1982.
Jean Piaget, *Le Comportement moteur de l'Evolution*, Gallimard, 1976.
Ilya Prigogine and Isabelle Stengers, *La Nouvelle Alliance*, Editions Gallimard, 1979.
Michael Polanyi, *Personal Knowledge, Towards a Post-Critical Philosophy*, Routledge & Kegan Paul, 1958.
Karl R Popper, *Objective Knowledge, An Evolutionary Approach*, Clarendon Press, Oxford, 1972.
Michael Ruse, *Darwinism Defended, A Guide to the Evolution Controversies*, Addison Wesley, Reading, Mass, 1982.
CH Waddington, *The Ethical Animal*, University of Chicago Press, George Allen & Unwin, London, 1960.
JH Woodger, *Biological Principles*, Routledge & Kegan Paul, 1976.

From *The Ecologist*, Vol 19, No 4, 1989. Also published in *Ecology and Moral Choice*, the Centre for Human Ecology, University of Edinburgh.

Hans Küng
WHY WE NEED A GLOBAL ETHIC

Limit Experiences and Breakthroughs in Innovation
The need for a prophylactic for crises

The following situation cannot be ignored: the pace of technological progress has increased so terrifically that it constantly threatens to overtake political forms. Legislation pursues technological developments with its tongue hanging out, like a hound pursuing its prey. This situation is unsatisfactory, indeed intolerable. Many enthusiastic technological expectations are proving deceptive, and many results ambivalent. So what seems necessary is a forward-looking estimation of the consequences of scientific and technological research, an estimation with a scientific basis which can be translated into practical politics.

Previously, ethics has usually come too late, in so far as it is reflection on the morality of human behaviour. Too often people have asked what we may do only after we have been able to do it. But for the future the decisive thing is that we should know what we may do before we can do it and do indeed do it.[1] Ethics, although it is always conditioned by a particular period and society, should therefore not just be reflection on crises; those who constantly look in the mirror at the way along which they have come will miss the way forward. By means of prognoses of crises which take worst cases into account (as H Jonas argues), ethics should be a prophylactic for crises. Leading ethicists now agree that we need a preventive ethics. And this should not just begin with industrial production, but already at the stage of experimentation (which has extremely serious consequences in both atomic technology and gene technology), indeed even at the stage of scientific and theoretical reflection, with its priorities and preferences.

Experiences of the limits to what can be done

For it is all too evident that the new millennium will be characterised by extremely dangerous technological limit experiences. New limit experiences, which equally indicate a shift in epochs, can be seen in:

1 The use of atomic power, which can be for peaceful or military ends and which would result in the self-destruction of humankind by a geostrategic blow and counterblow;

2 The development of communication technologies (information technology + telecommunication = telematics), which lead to a gigantic impetus towards excessive information that individuals can no longer cope with because they are completely disorientated;

3 The development of a world stock market, a world money market and a virtually simultaneous world stock exchange which even now can let loose global turbulence in the structure of the currencies and economies of whole continents because it is beyond the control of any authority;

4 The development of gene technology which through scientific ambition (the 3 billion dollar 'genome project') and unscientific profit motives threatens to lead to

monstrous manipulations of human beings and their heredity;

5 The development of medical technology, which raises questions about the implantation and treatment of embryos in accord with human dignity, and also about dying and actively helping people to die in accord with human dignity;

6 The north-south division of the earth: the impoverishment and indebtedness of the Third and Fourth Worlds, which in the 1980s rose from 400 to 1,300 billion dollars; we hear that almost eight million children, mostly in Africa and Latin America, will die in 1990 because of a lack of basic foodstuffs and inoculations.

And yet, precisely as a theologian, my intention here is not to develop a terrifying apocalyptic scenario demonstrating our arrogance about our capabilities and then go on where possible to bring in the Christian religion or even the Christian churches as saviours from all ills. For it is impossible to overlook the positive elements contained specifically in those three modern revolutions which are abiding presuppositions for the breakthroughs into postmodernity.

The post-industrial society

The scientific and technological revolution of the seventeenth century and the socio-political revolution of the eighteenth century (the American and French Revolutions) were followed in the nineteenth century by the industrial revolution. Starting from Great Britain, it embraced all the European and North American states, and also Japan, and everywhere produced modern industrial society instead of static agricultural economy. But following this first industrial revolution, which replaced muscle-power with machines and mechanisation (steam power, electricity and chemicals), after the Second World War there was a second industrial revolution,[2] which strengthened or replaced human brainpower by machines (through computers and telecommunications). With such innovative technological developments (electronics, miniaturisation, digitalisation, software), which permeate not only particular areas but the whole of social life, human utopias that once looked fantastic now seem to be being fulfilled.

A post-industrial society is coming into being in postmodernity. By this is to be understood not just a 'leisure society' (to use a term which the American sociologist David Riesman coined as early as the 1950s[3]) but a change in the whole social structure. According to Daniel Bell,[4] it could include the following dimensions, primarily for developed societies:

– In the economy: an increasing predominance of services (the tertiary sector: trade, transport and health, education and training, research and administration) as opposed to productive businesses (primary and secondary sector: agriculture and industry).

– In technology: the central position of theoretical knowledge and the new intellectual technology.

– In social structures: the rise of new technological elites and the transition from a producer society to an information and knowledge society.

Certainly, hitherto all excessively optimistic expectations that a more humane period will come into being automatically have been disappointed: human beings continue to have murderous aggressive and destructive drives, and the dismantling of old antagonisms can and will be followed by the construction of new ones. But pessimistic utopians like O Spengler, who expected the 'decline of the West' any day, have also been disappointed. Granted, further and great ecological catastrophes are possible and even probable, but at the same time there are also signs of breakthroughs in innovation which would make survival easier for humanity.[5] The following key innovations should be noted:

The conversion of armaments: the redeployment of personnel and technology to civil tasks instead of the production of armaments;

2 Eco-technology: recycling and waste management which respects the environment instead of mountains of waste;

3 Energy-saving technology: solar technology instead of the squandering of fossil fuels;

4 Nuclear fusion: atomic fusion instead of atomic fission;

5 The invention of new materials: environment-friendly instead of environment-hostile materials.

And with innovations in products, social innovations could become established: structures of partnership, new forms of the active integration say of older people into education, business and politics. All in all, given the acceleration in the dynamics of the world economy, a breakthrough seems possible to an ecological, economy which is more orientated on peace. Or are all these only illusions?

The postmodern break-through
1989, the very year of the Great European Revolution, gave encouragement and hope to many people. For the first time since the Second World War, there seem to be concrete possibilities of a world which is not only without war, but also peaceful and cooperative. Despite all the old tensions and new ethnic and religious antagonisms, despite all the possible conflicts and setbacks, the possibility of global collaboration in the interest of progress for all no longer seems to be an unrealistic vision. For,

– Militarism seems to be fading into the background; the period of the Cold War between East and West and with it also the intermediate phase of the domination of two superpowers seems to be over; politically, the East-West situation is more favourable than at any time since the Second World War;

– Billions of dollars, roubles, marks, francs and pounds which are now becoming free as a result of the radical reduction of military establishments could be diverted to the civil sector;[6]

– For the first time since the end of the Second World War the lands of the Eastern bloc are getting the opportunity to link up with the development of the West and slowly raise their own economic level, with the aim of mass prosperity;

– The West – America and the Europe that is growing together – is getting the opportunity finally to implement *perestroika* in its own sphere, above all in connection with agriculture, social policy and homebuilding, protectionist trade policies and national deficits;

– Powers being released from the East-West crisis could finally be diverted to overcome not only the social and economic north-south crisis but also the global ecological crisis.

There is no trace of an 'end of history' – as constantly conjectured in Hegel's 'philosophy of art', in Alexandre Kojève's Hegel studies or in the political speculation of the American Francis Fukuyama! That makes all the more urgent the question: what aims are meaningful, what values capable of achieving a consensus, what convictions justifiable? This is a question not only for social scientists, philosophers and theologians but for anyone, man or woman, old or young, who takes an active part in the course of this world. Here it is not just a question of individual goals, values and convictions, nor even simply of 'Megatrends 2000', superficially extrapolated and optimistically added together, which are to culminate in the 'end of the welfare state' (Thatcherism) and in the 'triumph of the individual'.[7] Here – particularly in view of the change in civilisation which is accelerating as steadily as ever – it is a question of a fundamental and long-term change in the world order which has to be assessed realistically: a new basic orientation, a new macroparadigm, a new overall postmodern constellation.[8] I shall now attempt to give a summary description of it.

The Rising World Constellation of Postmodernity
Dimensions of the overall constellation of postmodernity
We saw that already since the two world wars humankind has been caught up in an epoch-making paradigm-shift from modernity to postmodernity, in a change of overall constellation which has now also broken through into mass consciousness. At present we still do not even know what our new age will be called, what names (like 'Reformation', 'Enlightenment') or nicknames ('baroque', 'rococo') will be given to it. However, the substitute term 'postmodern' can already be replaced by some positive definitions. Increasingly more clearly – despite all counter-movements, deviant trends and crises that are to be expected – the postmodern world constellation, to put it briefly, shows the following dimensions:

– Geopolitically, we have a post-Eurocentric constellation: the domination of the world by five rival European national states (England, France, Austria, Prussia/Germany and Russia) is over. Today we are confronted with a polycentric constellation of different regions of the world, with North America, Soviet Russia, the European community in the lead, and later probably also China and India.
– Foreign policy has to reckon with a post-colonial and post-imperialist world society. Specifically (in the ideal case) this means nations which cooperate internationally and are truly united.
– Economic policy has to reckon with the development of a post-capitalist, post-socialist economy. With some justification it can be called an eco-social market economy.
– Social policy has to recognise the increasing formation of a post-capitalist, post-socialist society. In the developed countries it will be increasingly a society dominated by service industries and communication.
– Those concerned with sexual equality see the appearance of a post-patriarchal society. In family, professional, and public life a relationship is clearly developing between men and women which is more a partnership.
– Culturally, we are moving in the direction of a post-ideological culture. In future it will be a culture more orientated on an overall plurality.
– In religious terms, a post-confessional and inter-religious world is coming into being. In other words, slowly and laboriously a multiconfessional ecumenical world society is coming into being.

This epoch-making paradigm shift which covers the world in which we live, our working world, the cultural world, and the world of the state, is concerned not least with new values. But precisely at this point an approach which is pessimistic about culture can easily miss the essentials.

Not a destruction of values but a change of values
The paradigm shift does not necessary include a destruction of values, but rather a fundamental shift in values:[9]
– From an ethic-free society to an ethically responsible society;
– From a technocracy which dominates people to a technology which serves the humanity of men and women;
 m an industry which destroys the environment to an industry which furthers the terests and needs of men and women in accord with nature;
 the legal form of a democracy to a democracy which is lived out and in which

freedom and justice are reconciled.

It also follows that this is a social shift not against, averse to, science, technology, industry and democracy, but a shift with, in alliance with, these social powers which formerly were absolutised but have now been relativised. The specific values of industrial modernity – diligence (*industrial*), rationality, order, thoroughness, punctuality, sobriety, achievement, efficiency – are not just to be done away with but to be reinterpreted in a new constellation and combined with the new values of postmodernity: with imagination, sensitivity, emotion, warmth, tenderness, humanity. So it is not a matter of repudiations and condemnations, but of counterbalances, counter-plans, counter directions and counter-movements.

A holistic view

From the changes in physics through the alternative methods of homeopathic medicine to humanistic psychology and the new awareness of the environment, nowadays an intensified holistic way of thinking can be seen which could also make possible a balance between the European-American and the Asiatic way of thinking.[10] At any rate, what is required today – and here there may be agreement between the most rationalistic systematic theoreticians (like N Luhmann) and hermeneutical philosophers (like G Gadamer), through serious researchers into the future (like R Jungk, E Laszlo) to the pioneers of the New Age (like F Capra) – is an equilibrium between the rational tendencies and the emotional and aesthetic tendencies of human beings, indeed a holistic view of the world and human beings in their different dimensions. For along with the economic, social and political dimension there is also the aesthetic, ethical and religious dimension of human beings and humanity.

Human society is also multi-dimensional, and nowadays we must adjust to complex, interwoven and dynamic inter-relationships. And if in view of all the trends and tendencies towards 'globalisation' or 'homologisation' (world-wide standardisation, from eating and drinking habits through fashions and media to concrete structures), counter-trends and counter-tendencies in the direction of cultural, linguistic and religious self-assertion manifest themselves, these may not be dismissed *a priori* as cultural nationalism, linguistic chauvinism and religious traditionalism.

What should become clear from these remarks is that it is not my concern to opt for a new unitary ideology, to present the new global outline of a social utopia. What is important, rather, is soberly and modestly to seek a way into the future from the needs and distresses of the modern age: a postmodern way. I think that I have already set the markers clearly enough to right and left and can sum them up here.

Not contra-modernity, not ultra-modernity, but taking modernity up into what transcends and replaces it

Postmodernity in the sense that I have described cannot be content with a radical pluralism or relativism ('truth, justice, humanity in the plural', to refer to J-F Lyotard[11] and W Welsch[12]), which in fact are characteristics of the disintegration of late modernity. Randomness, colourfulness, the mixing-up of all and everything, the anarchy of trends of thought and styles, the methodological 'anything goes', the moral 'all is permissible': this and similar phenomena cannot be the signature of the postmodern period. To this degree conservative criticism of modernity (like that of R Spaemann)[13] is quite justified.

However, postmodernity cannot aim at a uniform interpretation of the world in which we live. Nor can wholeness in the sense of totality and integrity and some premodern church integralism, or a 'postmodern classicism in architecture', or an 'essentialism or "Neoaristotelianism" in philosophy',[14] be hallmarks of the postmodern period either. Even within the new paradigm there will be a multiplicity of heterogeneous options for living, patterns of action, language games, forms of life, scientific conceptions, economic systems, social models and communities of faith, but these do not rule out a fundamental social consensus.

Postmodernity as developed here means neither just romanticising cosmetic operations in architecture or society nor a theory which is a panacea for social, economic, political, cultural or religious organisation. Postmodernity in the sense developed above strives for a new basic consensus of integrative, humane convictions in a new world constellation towards which democratic pluralistic society is inexorably directed if it is to survive. In principle, this means:

1 Postmodernity does not mean anti-modernity! A sweeping anti-modernism in the religions, orientated on the past, is no contribution to overcoming our epoch-making crisis. Here is no conservative prejudice for the old. Any form of programmatic anti-Enlightenment and church conservatism is to be rejected. A 'renewed Christian Europe' in the premodern sense in which those who believe otherwise or do not believe at all are in fact excluded is a clerical delusion. And much as a spiritual renewal of Europe is necessary, one form of it may be doomed to failure from the start. That is the backward-looking utopia of a 'spiritual unity of Europe' in which the confessional walls between Catholics, Protestants and Orthodox are retained, leading to the restoration programme of a 're-evangelisation of Europe' in a Roman Catholic direction which John Paul II proclaimed in 1982 in the mediaeval pilgrimage centre of Santiago di Compostela and again in 1990 in Prague (at the same time insisting on the need for obedience to the church). For such a programme is accompanied by a constant denunciation of Western democracy as consumerism, hedonism and materialism, not by an unambiguous affirmation of the modern values of freedom, pluralism and tolerance – right into the sphere of the Pope's own church (questions of birth control and sexual morality!).[15] And are Christians self-righteously going to criticise Islam (for a theocratic conception of the state, the exclusion of women from public life, rigorous sexual morality and xenophobia)? To put it bluntly: no regressive or repressive religion – whether Christian, Islamic, Jewish or of whatever provenance – has a long-term future.[16]

2 But postmodern does not mean ultra-modern either! An apologetic modernism with a fixation on the present is likewise no contribution towards the solution of the epoch-making crisis. There can be no progressive prejudice for the new. A simple heightening, potentiation and modernisation of modernity – postmodernity as a philosophical development and consummation of modernity – does not take the break in epochs seriously. Modernism too can become traditionalism. So here, too, the mere reproduction and continuation of the Enlightenment can fail. Reason cannot simply be rehabilitated by reason, nor can the basic defects of science and the great damage done by technology simply be removed by yet more science and yet more technology, as many people of action in economics and politics think, in a remarkable coalition with the 'intractable supporters of the Enlightenment'.

Natural science and technology can displace a past ethic, but they cannot themselves produce a new ethic or even provide the justification for it.

3 If the epoch-making paradigm shift can be compressed into one term, the modern paradigm must be 'sublated' into modernity in Hegel's threefold term. Modernity is:
– to be affirmed in its humane content,
– to be denied in its inhuman limits, and
– to be transcended in a new, differentiated, pluralistic and holistic synthesis.[17]

NOTES

1 Cf D Mieth, 'Moral der Zukunft – Zukunft der Moral?', in *Kirche in der Zeit. Walter Kasper zur Bischofsweihe*, ed HJ Vogt, Munich, 1990, pp 198-223.

2 N Weiner, *The Human Use of Human Beings. Cybernetics and Society*, New York, 1950.

3 Cf D Riesman, 'Leisure and Work in Post-Industrial Society', *Mass Leisure*, ed E Larrabee and R Meyersohn, Glencoe, 1958, pp 363-85.

4 Cf D Bell, *The Coming of Post-Industrial Society. A Venture in Social Forecasting*, New York, 1973, esp pp 29-56, 374-6; A Touraine, *La société post-industrielle*, Paris, 1969 (a 1968 analysis of the contradiction between business mechanisms and social organisation in the light of the student movement, in connection with a 'programmed society').

5 Cf P Oertli-Cajacob, ed *Innovation statt Resignation. 35 Perspektiven für eine neue Zeit*, Berne, 1989, Part V: 'Einblick, Überblick, Ausblick', pp 351-72.

6 A proposal made in the American Senate to save just one per cent of the defence budget (which in 1989 was 125 billion dollars) for the reconstruction of Eastern Europe represented 1,250 million dollars in immediately available resources.

7 Cf J Naisbitt and P Aburdene, *Megatrends 2000. Ten New Directions for the 1990s*, New York, 1990. In chapter 8, 'The Age of Biology' – before the chapter on 'The Revival of the Religions' which brings together a great variety of data and curiosities (all from the USA) – one reads with amusement a thesis like this, printed in bold type: 'Philosophers and theologians – for centuries chronically underemployed – are now as sought-after and desired as information theorists' (p 339). For *Megatrends 2000* see the justified criticism by L Niethammer, 'Erdbeertunke des Optimismus', *Der Spiegel* 16, 1990, pp 237-41.

8 For the concept of the paradigm cf Hans Küng, *Does God Exist? An Answer for Today*, (1978!), London and New York, 1980, AIII.1; *Theologie im Aufbruch. Eine ökumenische*, Munich, 1987, BII-IV. 'Paradigm shift' comes from the American historican of science Thomas S Kuhn, *The Structure of Scientific Revolutions*, Chicago, 1962; it was first investigated systematically and theoretically for the discovery of truth in the sphere of the natural sciences. It does not mean the alteration of a method or a theory but the change of an 'entire constellation of beliefs, values, techniques, and so on shared by the members of a given community' (p 175). In the context of religion, paradigm shift means a change in the whole constellation, the basic model, basic framework by which human beings perceive themselves, society, the world and God.

When transferred from the history of science to history generally and the history of Christianity in particular, the term 'paradigm shift' does not just denote some swing of the pendulum or wave, nor just a change of mood or a particular political change. Rather, it means a change in the view of things generally which is both fundamental and long-term, and finally is perceived widely: a shift in the macroparadigm, which always includes many meso- and microparadigms. What is decisive for the replacement of a paradigm is the breakthrough of many individual innovative signals of the past (in pioneering thinkers, critical groups of all kinds which are before their time, for example postmoderns 'avant la lettre'), so that it becomes an overall trend which is perceived by the broader masses. The decisive factor is not that individual indicators of the crisis and the shift were 'already there' but what has really 'made history'.

9 On this see K-H Hillmann, *Wertwandel. Zur Frage soziokultureller Voraussetzungen alternativer Lebensformen*, Darmstadt, 1989. The thematic volume of the international journal *Concilium* 191, 1987, *Changing Values and Virtues*, ed D Mieth and J Pohier, is concerned throughout with contemporary ethical problems.

10 Cf O Weggel, *Die Asiaten*, Munich, 1989, pp 38-53: the real difference from the West is totality or harmony (in accord with the human environment, nature, what lies beyond the senses).

11 In his final conclusions J-F Lyotard writes polemically – it seems to me wrongly – against the discursive ethics of Jürgen Habermas, who would like to solve the problem of legitimation by a universal consensus: 'Consensus has become an obsolete and suspect value, but not justice. So we must arrive at an idea and a praxis of justice which is not tied to that of justice' (*La Condition postmoderne,* Paris, 1979, p 190). On this cf M Frank, *Die Grenzen der Verständigung. Ein Geistergespräch zwischen Lyotard und Habermas*, Frankfurt, 1988.

12 W Welsch, *Unsere postmoderne Moderne*, Weinheim, 1988, p 4f; cf p 5, 'pluralism in principle'. At the second Bertelsmann Colloquium on 17/18 February 1989, 'The Future of Basic Values', the Swiss ethicist Walther C Zimmerli (Bamberg) similarly marked the opposite point of view to the thesis of Welsch, which were also presented there:

> One of the category errors which contributes to the rise of the present defeatism over ethics is the 'confusion of the levels of unity and multiplicity'. This consists in the assumption that unity and multiplicity exclude each other, in that the plurality of value systems does not allow the unity of a consensus. However, precisely the opposite is the case . . . The plurality of first-order conceptions of

value not only allows a consensus at a second level (that plurality may be allowed), but virtually presupposes it. A further category error which is connected with this, and can be found no less frequently, is the confusion of relativity and ethical relativism: it indeed follows from the fact that in a pluralistic society a variety of notions of value evidently coexist synchronously and replace one another diachronically that all notions of value have validity only relative to the system in which they belong. But that means that they must have absolute validity within this value system. Ethical relativism (which would be a contradiction in itself) does not follow from ethical relativity (which is a fact).

13 Cf R Spaemann, 'Ende der Modernität?', *Moderne oder Postmoderne? Zur Signatur des gegenwärtigen Zeitalters*, ed P Koslowski, R Spaemann and R Löw, Weinheim, 1986, pp 19-40.

14 Cf P Koslowski, 'Die Baustellen der Postmoderne – Wider den Vollendungszwang der Moderne', ibid, pp 1-16. Koslowski's not unjustified criticism of modernity suffers from a vague historical definition of the concept of modernity, which should already include the Reformation, the Counter Reformation and baroque. His clearly premodern 'essentialism in art and philosophy' (p 11), taking 'the legacy of antiquity and the Middle Ages' as an example, does not become 'postmodern' as a result of his desire to avoid academism and elitism.

15 In a clear-sighted analysis in the American *National Catholic Reporter* of 13 April 1990, the British theologian and Vaticanologist P Hebblethwaite has analysed the anxieties of the Pope over a secularisation of Europe and even Poland and stressed that the premodern vision of this Pope will soon no longer have any visual model, because culturally Western Europe is not looking to Eastern Europe, but Eastern Europe to Western Europe: 'So while John Paul might broadly welcome the political consequences of the events, their religious consequences are less encouraging. If Poland, because of the changed circumstances, can no longer provide a model for the church, then what country can?' For the messianic sense of mission which in all probability is the greatest strength of the Polish Pope, but perhaps also his greatest weakness (a lack of self-criticism), see R Modras, 'Ein Mann der Widersprüche? Die frühen Schriften des Karel Wojtyla', in N Greinacher and H Küng, *Katholische Kirche – Wohin? Wider den Verrat am Konzil*, Munich, 1986, pp 225-39.

16 On this see T Meyer, *Fundamentalismus. Aufstand gegen die Moderne*, Hamburg, 1989; idem, ed *Fundamentalismus in der modernen Welt. Die Internationale der Unvernunft*, Frankfurt, 1989; J Niewiandomski, ed *Eindeutige Antworten? Fundamentalistische Versuchung in Religion und Gesellschaft*, Thaur, 1988. In a model example of historical writing orientated on the social sciences, U Altermatt, a historian at the University of Fribourg, Switzerland, in his *Katholizismus und Moderne. Zur Sozial- und Mentalitätsgeschichte der Schweizer Katholiken im 19 und 20 Jahrhundert*, Zurich, 1989, gives an account of the problems of resistance and adaptation to modernity which still shape the behaviour of Catholics to the present day.

In the face of reactionary trends and growing criticism of the Roman course from the Catholic centre, I have documented and systematically summarised my own position in the church, which has been attacked over the past three decades, in *Reforming the Church Today*, Edinburgh and New York, 1990.

17 I feel endorsed in this definition of postmodernity by the recent book of DR Griffin, *God and Religion in the Postmodern World. Essays in Postmodern Theology*, Albany, NY, 1989. Griffin speaks of 'constructive postmodernism' to distinguish it from antimodernism and ultramodernism. 'This postmodernity seeks to overcome the modern worldview not through the elimination of the possibility of worldviews generally, but through the construction of a postmodern worldview by means of the revision of modern presuppositions and traditional concepts. This constructive or renewed postmodernism implies a new unity of scientific, ethical, aesthetic and traditional concepts. It does not reject science as such, but just that scientism in which only the data of modern science is allowed to contribute to the construction of our worldview' (p x). With all this Griffin is aiming at 'postmodern persons' with a 'postmodern spirituality' with a view to a 'postmodern society' and a 'postmodern world order'. Most recently of all, D Solle, *Thinking about God. An Introduction to Theology*, London and Philadelphia, 1990, has taken over elements of my analysis of theological paradigms, though without, it seems, having herself mastered the necessary basic literature in the theory of science. Thus for her (p 7) the definition of paradigm does not come directly from Kuhn's work, as I have indicated, but from my article. On p 21 she reprints my schema on Reformation theology as her own without giving any sources (cf Küng, *Theologie im Aufbruch*, p 230). All this would not be so bad if she did not seek to press the whole of the theology of the second millennium into a scheme which looks suspiciously ideological: orthodox (including K Barth?), liberal (including R Bultmann and P Tillich?) and 'radical' ('only liberation theological minorities'?). She hardly does justice to the complex postmodern situation with this historically inaccurate schema which systematises superficially.